At last we have a t ... *examples.*
Tony Dawson, Liverpool John M...

The pedagogical fe ... *concepts to real-lif* ... *learn the concepts* ...
Olof Brunninge, Jonkoping International B...

The authors raise international issues and in doing s ... *and international students. I particularly like the way* ... *appropriate theory.*
Derek Watson, University of Sunderland, UK

This text takes a contemporary perspective and looks at the key issues and trends in OB. The cases are current and well chosen; a lot of useful discussion and work could emerge from them.
Vivienne Byers, Dublin Institute of Technology

Organizational Behaviour

Organizational Behaviour

Ray French · Charlotte Rayner · Gary Rees · Sally Rumbles

John Schermerhorn Jr
James Hunt
Richard Osborn

John Wiley & Sons, Ltd

Authorized adaptation of the ninth edition by John R. Schermerhorn, James G. Hunt
and Richard N. Osborn, *Organizational Behaviour*, (ISBN 0-471-68170-9),
published by John Wiley & Sons, New York, USA. Copyright © 2005 in the United
States of America by John Wiley & Sons, Inc. All rights reserved. Reproduced by permission.

Material taken from the first Australasian edition by Jack Wood, Rachid Zeffane, Michele
Fromholtz, Janna Fitzgerald, *Organizational Behaviour: Core Concepts and Applications*, (ISBN 0-470-80951-
5), published by John Wiley & Sons Australia, Ltd, Queensland, Australia. Copyright © 2006 by John
Wiley & Sons Australia, Ltd. All rights reserved. Reproduced by permission.

US edition © 2005   John Wiley & Sons, Inc.
Australasian edition © 2006   John Wiley & Sons Australia, Ltd.

This edition © 2008   John Wiley & Sons, Ltd
                                      The Atrium, Southern Gate, Chichester,
                                      West Sussex PO19 8SQ, England
                                      Telephone +44 (0) 1243 779777

Email (for orders and customer service enquiries): cs-books@wiley.co.uk
Visit our Home Page on www.wiley.com

Other Wiley Editorial Offices

John Wiley & Sons Inc., 111 River Street, Hoboken, NJ 07030, USA

Jossey-Bass, 989 Market Street, San Francisco, CA 94103-1741, USA

Wiley-VCH Verlag GmbH, Boschstr. 12, D-69469 Weinheim, Germany

John Wiley & Sons Australia Ltd, 42 McDougall Street, Milton, Queensland 4064, Australia

John Wiley & Sons (Asia) Pte Ltd, 2 Clementi Loop #02-01, Jin Xing Distripark, Singapore 129809

John Wiley & Sons Canada Ltd, 6045 Freemont Blvd, Mississauga, ONT, L5R 4J3

Wiley also publishes its books in a variety of electronic formats. Some content that appears in print may not be
available in electronic books.

Library of Congress Cataloging-in-Publication Data

Organizational behaviour / Ray French ... [et al.].
       p. cm.
"Authorised adaptation of the ninth edition by John R. Schermerhorn, James
G. Hunt"–P.

A catalogue record for this book is available from the British Library

ISBN: 978-0-470-51106-0

Typeset by Aptara Inc., New Delhi, India
Printed and bound in Spain by Grafos SA, Barcelona

This book is printed on acid-free paper responsibly manufactured from sustainable forestry in which at least
two trees are planted for each one used for paper production.

BRIEF CONTENTS

CONTENTS

PART 3 MANAGING GROUP DYNAMICS AND TEAM PERFORMANCE 261

PART 4 MANAGING ORGANIZATIONAL PROCESSES AND PERFORMANCE 325

PART 5   CASE STUDIES   601

ABOUT THE AUTHORS

The authors all work in the Department of Human Resource and Marketing Management in the University of Portsmouth, UK.

(From left to right...)

- **Ray French** is a Principal Lecturer in Organizational Behaviour. He has a particular interest in crosscultural aspects of work, organization and managing people. He is the author of *Cross-Cultural Management in Work Organisations* (2007), CIPD: London. His other publications include two chapters on recruitment and selection and job design in Rayner, C. & Adam-Smith, D. (eds) (2005), *Managing and Leading People*, CIPD: London. Ray has extensive experience of managing business degree courses taught across Europe and in Asia.

- **Charlotte Rayner** is Professor of Human Resource Management. She has a particular interest in the topic of bullying at work and has been involved in research in this area since the mid-1990s when she completed the first major UK survey for the BBC. Charlotte has recently published a book, *Workplace Bullying: What We Know, Who is to Blame and What Can We Do?* with Cary Cooper and Helge Hoel. Charlotte is particularly interested in strategies to prevent bullying and other forms of negative behaviour.

- **Gary Rees** is a Principal Lecturer and Director of Postgraduate Human Resource Management Programmes at Portsmouth Business School. His recent publications include two chapters on performance management and learning training and development in Rayner, C. & Adam-Smith, D. (eds) (2005), *Managing and Leading People*, CIPD: London. Gary has consultancy experience in the private and public sectors and is an active member of the Portsmouth Chartered Institute of Personnel Development (CIPD). He is also a member of the British Psychological Society.

- **Sally Rumbles** is a Senior Lecturer in Human Resource Management. She co-authored a chapter on recruitment and selection in Rayner, C. & Adam-Smith, D. (eds) (2005), *Managing and Leading People*, CIPD: London. Sally is also a contributor to a new human resource management textbook edited by Dr Steve Williams, scheduled for publication in 2009. She has worked as a human resource manager in both the private and public sectors and is a member of the Chartered Institute of Personnel and Development (CIPD). Her main research interests are in the areas of flexibility and work–life balance. Sally teaches OB and HR on a range of undergraduate and graduate programmes.

HOW TO USE THIS BOOK

The book is divided into five **Parts,** each with a chapter list and part introduction to help navigate the text.

PART 2

INDIVIDUAL DIFFERENCES AND WORK PERFORMANCE

2 Individual attributes and their effects on job performance

3 Learning, reinforcement and self-management

4 Motivation and empowerment

5 Job design, goal setting and flexible work arrangements

Journal article: Makin, P.J. & Sutherland, V.J. (1994), Reducing accidents using a behavioural approach. *Leadership and Organization Development Journal,* **15** (5), 5–10.

In this section of the book we explore a range of topics comprising the psychological perspective on organizational behaviour, in which the essential focus is on the individual person. An important tradition within OB has identified links between individual attributes and behaviour at work. Some writers stress individual uniqueness based on our own life experiences but others have sought to group people by personality type or preferred styles of learning. This latter perspective has led to a preponderance of psychometric testing enabling organizations to identify and choose the 'right person', from their point of view. We will examine the validity of such psychometric predictions and also consider the important ethical considerations involved.

In the following chapters, we will highlight the importance of individual attributes within the performance equation. We will also delve into the specific topic areas of *perception* – the process by which we select, interpret and respond to information from the world around us – *personality, learning* and *motivation.* While we will show how individual attributes can impact on the way we work, this relationship is two-sided and in the chapter on job design, we indicate how the ways in which work is designed and organized will, in turn, impact on the individual worker and their attitudes.

Journal Article

REDUCING ACCIDENTS USING A BEHAVIOURAL APPROACH

Peter J. Makin and Valerie J. Sutherland

Despite the evident success of behavioural approaches to various organizational problems (see Luthans and Martinko, 1987), in a number of different contexts (Walsh *et al.*, 1993), it remains, in the authors' opinion, under-utilized. One reason for this possible under-utilization is suggested by attribution theory. This theory describes the way people assign causality for events, whether they be safety-related or more general. In particular, it is concerned with explanations for peoples' behaviour, and how people attribute the causes for such behaviour.

ATTRIBUTION THEORY

When we seek to understand why individuals behave the way they do, there are two major types of explanation that people use. Behaviour can be perceived as being caused by factors that are either *internal* or *external* to the individual. Internal factors are those that can be seen as being "within" the individual. Examples include things such as personality traits, attitudes, and moods. In fact, the original title for these factors was "dispositional". An explanation of a person's behaviour using an internal attribution would see the behaviour as being caused by, for example, their negligence, or them being foolhardy, or even "accident-prone". External factors, on the other hand, are those that are part of the external "situation". Behaviour that is perceived as being caused "externally" would place emphasis on the individual reacting to events in the environment, rather than being driven by their personality or attitudes. For example, many people explain any mistakes they make while driving, on the situation – "the road signs were inadequate", rather than their own carelessness – "I wasn't paying attention".

How people make such attributions, and the factors that influence the attributions they make, is a complex process (see Hewstone, 1989). However, there do appear to be certain "biases" which predispose people towards the making of certain attributions. The example given above concerning the attributions for driving errors, highlights a very common "bias". When asked to describe the causes for their own behaviour people are more likely to provide an explanation in terms of them reacting to the situation. As evidence for the validity of this explanation, individuals will often point out that other people, as well as themselves, regularly undertake this pattern of behaviour. The reason for using the behaviour of others as evidence for an external cause is simple. If most people, despite their differing personalities and attitudes, behave the same way in the same situation, then the cause is likely to be external.

The "actors" in a situation are likely to attribute external factors as influencing their behaviour, especially when that behaviour is seen as being undesirable. Outside observers,

Reproduced with permission from the Journal of Leadership & Organizational Development, 15(5), 5–10 (1994).

Each part ends with a full length **journal article** with associated questions.

CHAPTER 2

Individual attributes and their effects on job performance

LEARNING OBJECTIVES

After studying this chapter you should be able to:

- explain the individual performance equation
- comprehend the perceptual process and its importance in determining workplace attitudes and behaviour
- locate competency characteristics that distinguish individuals
- discuss personality characteristics that distinguish individuals
- identify competencies arising from values and attitudes, which enable managers to capitalize on workforce diversity in their organizations
- define and understand the nature of values and attitudes and their importance within organizational behaviour.

SLAYING THE DRAGONS

Dragons' Den is a popular television programme in which potential entrepreneurs present their ideas to a panel of business experts – the self-styled 'dragons'. If the dragons are sufficiently impressed by the presentation they can offer a contestant investment finance in return for a percentage of the new company. Contestants have approximately two hours to promote their ideas, although only a 5-minute extract is screened on air. The viewer sees this condensed version of the proposal followed by questioning by the dragons and negotiation on the value of the company and the dragons' potential stake. The programme originated in Japan and by 2007 versions were screened in a number of countries including the UK, Israel and the Netherlands. It is possible that it may be rolled out to still more countries in future.

The judgements made on individual business ideas by the dragons are essentially based on *perception.* As such, although the dragons are comprised of experienced and successful figures from the world of business, their record in identifying good ideas, even when they are right in front of them, is less than perfect. One example of where quick perceptions did not predict future success can be seen in the case of Rachel Lowe and her board game *Destination,* screened in the British version of the show. This board game is based around the 'rules' of taxi journeys (collecting fares, obeying traffic rules and completing a working shift before fuel runs out). Based on Rachel's own experience as a taxi driver in Portsmouth, the game expanded to include versions set in other UK cities including London, Cardiff and Sheffield. The global nature of this venture has seen versions set in cities such as Dublin, Paris, Delhi and New York. In 2007 Rachel signed deals for a *Destination Hogwarts,* based on the Harry Potter books as well as a tie-up with Disney Pixar, so we can anticipate future editions such as *Destination Finding Nemo* and *Monsters Inc.*

Although *Destination* was the best-selling product at London's Hamleys toy store at Christmas 2004, Rachel's appearance on Dragons' Den, screened in January 2005 was, on her own admission, a less than happy experience. Three of the dragons questioned her awareness of the proposed market for the game and cast doubt on her financial forecasts. All of the dragons claimed that Rachel was unaware of the difference between gross and net profit. On the basis of their conclusions, they declined to take a stake in her company in exchange for investment finance. Yet, as we have seen, Rachel's idea was already taking off at the time of the programme and has continued to thrive. What lessons can we learn from the *Destination* story and its implications for the study of organizational behaviour?

First, as already noted, the dragons' view of Rachel and her business scheme was essentially based on perception. Their need for a quick assessment is typical of many business situations such as selection interviewing where decisions have to be made swiftly, in an artificial setting and on the basis of incomplete

Source: www.rtlgames.co.uk/enterthedragon.html, accessed 22 May 2007.

Each chapter begins with an engaging **short vignette** that offers a snapshot of OB issues and trends in contemporary real-life situations.

The key **learning objectives** to be achieved are stated at the beginning of each chapter.

OB in Action boxes provide thought-provoking examples drawn from wide-ranging work settings and international research.

Key terms

All the key terms are defined in the margin of the text for easy reference.
A **Glossary** collects them all together at the end of the book.

Counterpoint boxes

encourage critical discussion of OB theories through consideration of negative work situations and alternative perspectives.

Effective Manager boxes include practical tips on managing in the real world.

Research in OB boxes link to a full length journal article either in the text (at the end of each Part) or on the book companion Web site at **www. wileyeurope. com/college/ french**

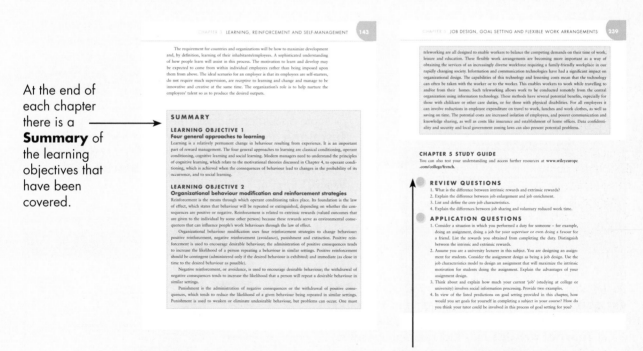

Case Studies at the end of each chapter and in Part 5 illustrate innovative and revealing aspects of OB from companies worldwide.

At the end of each chapter there is a **Summary** of the learning objectives that have been covered.

The Study Guide at the end of each chapter offers a wealth of questions including **Review Questions** (an overview of the chapter concepts), **Application Questions** (applying theory to real-life situations) and **Research Questions** (more in-depth questions requiring some research.)

The **Running Project** asks you to choose a company and apply ideas and theories to this company as you work through the book.

2. Search the Internet for an organization in any of the transport, health, hospitality, banking or retail industries and notice the values that it espouses in its mission or goal statement and related materials. Do you think that these values are the most appropriate for this organization? Can you find any evidence that this organization is putting its values into practice? Does the organization monitor the values and attitudes of its staff to ensure alignment with corporate objectives and, if so, how?

RUNNING PROJECT

Using the information you have available about your organization, perform the following activities:

1. What does management look for in potential employees to ensure a good fit between employees and job requirements?
2. Assess the validity of selection methods chosen by the organization including any psychometric tests it uses.
3. How diverse is the workforce of your organization? Assess the strategies your organization has in place to encourage and benefit from workforce diversity.
4. Ascertain the importance the organization attaches to core values.

INDIVIDUAL ACTIVITY

Personal values
For the following 16 items, rate how important each one is to you. Write a number between 0 and 100 on the line to the left of each item.
Not important   Important   Very important
0 10 20 30 40 50 60 70 80 90 100
1. An enjoyable, satisfying job
2. A high-paying job
3. A strong intimate relationship
4. Meeting new people; social events.
5. Involvement in community activities
6. Religion and spirituality
7. Exercising, playing sports
8. Intellectual development

9. A career with challenging opportunities
10. Nice cars, clothes, home etc.
11. Spending time with family
12. Having several close friends
13. Volunteer work for not-for-profit organizations, like a medical charity
14. Meditation, quiet time to think and contemplate.
15. A healthy balanced diet
16. Educational reading, and/or self-improvement programmes.

Below, transfer the numbers beside each of the 16 items to the appropriate column, then add the two numbers in each column.

Professional	Financial	Family	Social
1.	2.	3.	4.
9.	10.	11.	12.
Totals			

Community	Spiritual	Physical	Intellectual
5.	6.	7.	8.
13.	14.	15.	16.
Totals			

The higher the total in any area, the higher the value you place on that particular area. The closer the numbers are in all eight areas, the more well rounded you are – that is your values encompass a number of areas.

Think about the time and effort you put into your top three values. Is it sufficient to allow you to achieve the level of success you want in each area? If not, what can you do to change the situation? Is there any area in which you feel you should have a higher value total? If yes, which area? What can you do to realize this wish?

GROUP ACTIVITY

Building a more positive self-concept
Objective
To develop a more positive self-concept.

Total time: 5–15 minutes.

Preparation
The objective of this activity is to develop a more positive self-concept. According to humanistic theory, the self-concept is important in the development of personality –

In the **Individual Project**, students are questioned about their values and opinions, and a **Group Project** facilitates classroom exercises and discussion.

Lecturer and student companion web sites accompany this book at www.wileyeurope.com/college/french

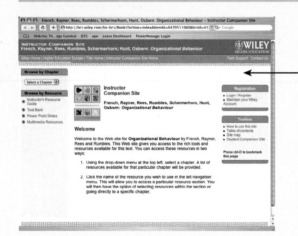

The Instructor companion Website provides you with all the resources you need to teach OB: a comprehensive **Instructor's Resource Guide** with visual overviews, discussion topics, class activities and suggested answers to all of the questions in the text. There are **Video and audio clips** that you can use to illustrate concepts and promote discussion in class. There is also a comprehensive **Test Bank** and a set of **PowerPoint lecture slides** that you can edit to use in your teaching. In addition all the materials are available to lecturers in **Blackboard** and **WebCT** format.

On the Student companion Web site you will find **Self-test quizzes** to test your understanding as you progress through the book. Also, you can access additional full length **Journal articles** here that are highlighted in the text. There are **Interactive exercises** you can complete as well as an online version of the **Glossary**.

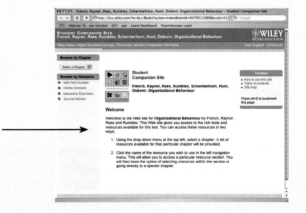

PREFACE

This first edition of *Organizational Behaviour* is based on several previous editions published in different parts of the world. It draws on ten best-selling US editions written by Professors John Schermerhorn, James Hunt and Richard Osborn. We have also adapted material from the first Australasian edition authored by Professor Jack Wood, Dr Rachid Zeffane, Michele Fromholz and Dr Janna Fitzgerald. The Australasian edition was the first to present subject content in a format that allowed for coverage within both one-semester and year-long teaching and learning patterns. We have continued this approach in our new book, while including more examples and cases from Europe and Asia. Previous versions of this book have been designed to introduce readers to new realities of work and knowledge-based organizations in the early twenty-first century. In particular, *Organizational Behaviour* has stressed the importance of a thorough understanding of organizational behaviour (OB) frameworks and practices for existing and aspiring managers – and indeed all other workers – to help them to meet increasingly challenging performance targets. In highlighting challenges associated with the emergence of knowledge-based organizations and an increasingly 'globalized' business environment, previous editions of *Organizational Behaviour* have brought out the inherently relevant and topical nature of OB. The American and Australian authors have developed the themes of relevance and topicality most successfully, due in part to the lucidity of their writing style, considered use of case studies and other examples and by including an extensive and diverse range of learning resources, thereby encouraging readers to reflect on how OB models and concepts touch their own lives. We trust that these major strengths of the previous editions will also be apparent in this new version.

What are the distinctive features of our new contribution to the extensive body of OB literature? In preparing this edition, we have set out to marry academic rigour with relevance within a perspective that stresses organizational success. We realize from talking to our own students that value for money will also guide readers in their choice of book. The following points summarize some of the themes underlying this book, which we hope you will find useful as you approach the study of OB.

Organizational behaviour is a relatively new subject area but has already developed some central and enduring tenets. Equally some theories and concepts have proven to be transitory, possessing a limited 'shelf life', whereas other seemingly radical departures from existing thought can, on closer examination, be revealed to be more akin to 'old wine in new bottles'. The challenging task for students is to appreciate what is changing and what is enduring within OB. Despite the undoubtedly rapid and profound changes affecting work organizations, are some underlying themes in OB still valid? We will highlight the extent of deep and profound change, as opposed to more cosmetic modifications in the subject area, throughout this book. A historical perspective, outlining the developmental nature of much OB material can greatly help us in this regard.

A related theme centres on the *applicability* of knowledge derived from OB. We take the view that effective interventions, based on OB models and theories, can lead both to employees' needs and expectations being met and also to enhanced organizational performance in 'bottom-line' terms. But equally a quizzical view of the relevance of some concepts is advisable, together with the need to maintain a balanced perspective on topics. This is, in any case, necessary as mutually exclusive theories on aspects of people at work are a characteristic of organizational behaviour. A rounded approach, which we aim to provide in subsequent chapters, should result in a deeper awareness of both the overall subject and individual topic areas. Our *counterpoint* feature, included in all chapters, will alert you to negative occurrences within workplaces and alternative political perspectives. This should also help promote a balanced view.

All too often the study of OB can move swiftly from one topic to another, focusing on surface summaries of theories and models. Sometimes little attention is given to the actual research from which such views emerge. In this book we seek to rectify this deficiency by including a number of research articles. Four are distributed throughout the text (one at the end of each of the first four parts of the book) and another eight can be found on our Web site at **www.wileyeurope.com/college/french**. You might wish to look at these articles in order to gain an in-depth view of how OB knowledge is generated. Note, for example, the research methods used in the studies referred to – are they valid in your view? Questions regarding how 'scientific' the study of OB is and what we can, in any case, infer from that term when seeking to understand human attitudes and behaviour, are also addressed in Chapter 1.

We have sought to apply OB concepts squarely within a twenty-first century work and organizational context. Organizations have been subject to very significant changes since the late 1980s and, in some cases, working arrangements bear scant resemblance to those experienced by previous generations. For example, remote or teleworking patterns mean that many of us spend as much, or more, time working from home – or on trains and in planes – than we do in a conventional office. How do we apply theories of motivation and leadership (to take just two topics) in such a situation? Many organizations have also sought to outsource their operations, developing so-called network structures, far removed from the classical twentieth-century bureaucratic form. How do we understand these new organizational arrangements in terms of their structure and culture? We will address these contemporary issues consistently in relevant chapters.

A focus on contemporary trends may lead us to question the value of existing prescriptive models of human behaviour in the workplace and instead highlight *contingency* approaches – the conclusion being that no academic theory or practical method can always work well and that it will all depend on specific circumstances. Such approaches are not new – they emerged in the field of leadership in the 1950s, for example. However, they may be judged to be especially applicable in such a rapidly changing context. One important area in this regard is national culture. We no longer need to migrate to encounter people from different cultural backgrounds at work. The multicultural makeup of workforces in cities such as London, Amsterdam and Berlin testifies to this fact. But most OB knowledge emerges from an Anglo-American context. There is, of course, nothing wrong with this *per se*. However, we might legitimately question whether motivation theories developed in the US can be applied to Chinese, Indian or Spanish workers. At the very least we should consider applying contingency (flexible) models in new situations. We will argue, for example, that workers have increasingly changed *psychological contracts* – see Chapters 1 and 2 – meaning that they will need to be managed in new and imaginative ways at work. A flexible contingency approach is adopted throughout this book.

We have sought, finally, to put together a book that can be used in a one-semester course but, equally, one in which the content can be stretched to encompass a longer period of study. As such, we trust that this book will not be too unwieldy. Please also refer to our Web site **www.wileyeurope.com/college/french**, which contains additional exercises and articles. Most importantly, please do not regard this book as the sum resource for your study of organizational behaviour. We hope that it will be the springboard to a lifetime's interest in a fascinating area which affects us all.

Dr Ray French

ACKNOWLEDGEMENTS

The author team would like to acknowledge the contributions of the academics who have compiled the US and Australasian editions of this book: Professor John R. Schermerhorn, Professor James G. (Jerry) Hunt, Professor Richard N. Osborn, Professor Jack Wood, Dr Rachid Zeffane, Michele Fromholz and Dr Janna (Anneke) Fitzgerald. We would also like to thank the academics who have contributed to the case studies contained in Part 5 of this book: Val Morrison of Southern Cross University, Tony Dawson of Liverpool John Moores University, Dr Henner Hentze of the Fachochschule Munster, and we are grateful to the compilers of the Jossey-Bass/Pfeiffer classroom collection for permission to include the Motorola case study. We would also like to acknowledge the work of the late Professor Iain Mangham who devised the scenario that formed the basis of our Channel 6 TV case study.

We have benefited from an excellent working relationship with the editorial, development and production team at John Wiley & Sons in Chichester. We would like to thank Sarah Booth who first envisaged a European edition of the book and encouraged its development. More recently, Deborah Egleton, Anneli Mockett and Emma Cooper have greatly helped in steering the book towards completion. We are also grateful for the particularly constructive feedback from reviewers of the draft book and trust that we have responded to points made in the final version.

PART 1

INTRODUCTION

1 What is organizational behaviour?

Journal article: Challiol, H. & Mignonac, K. (2005), Relocation decision-making and couple relation-ships: a quantitative and qualitative study of dual-earner couples. *Journal of Organizational Behaviour,* **26**, 247–274.

Managing people in work organizations is frequently identified as a critically important element in terms of achieving an organization's aims and working towards its ultimate success. However, people can behave in unpredictable and seemingly contrary ways, so the management of people at work, while both interesting and rewarding, is also a challenging area. Organizational behaviour (OB) focuses on the behaviour of individuals and groups at work and seeks to provide explanations for such behaviour through a wide range of topics – which we will go on to explore in this book.

In this first part of our book we aim to underpin the subject matter set out in subsequent chapters by highlighting some broader issues relating to OB. We will explore the nature of this subject area by identifying differing definitions of OB and will also examine some of its underlying traditions and perspectives. In this context, one important issue is the extent to which findings from OB research can be regarded as valid in academic terms – how far can and/or should OB be regarded as 'scientific'? We furthermore aim to signal some key trends and issues affecting contemporary organizations and, in so doing, show how an understanding of OB can illuminate the reality of work organizations, to the benefit of everyone connected with them.

CHAPTER

1

What is organizational behaviour?

LEARNING OBJECTIVES

After studying this chapter you should be able to:

- recognize a range of definitions of organizational behaviour (OB)
- comprehend some of the theoretical traditions and political perspectives which inhabit the OB subject area
- discuss the role of people management in fostering effective performance within organizations
- identify some of the key issues affecting organizations today
- explain why organizations' members, including managers, can benefit from a thorough understanding of OB principles and insights.

A GREAT PLACE TO WORK?

Since 2001 the London-based *Sunday Times* has produced a list of the '100 best companies to work for'. The newspaper publishes the results of a large-scale annual survey highlighting examples of organizational policies and practices that, it is claimed, contribute to high levels of satisfaction among employees. The underlying question posed in the survey is what makes organizations great to work for? The survey has separate categories for 'small', 'mid-sized' and 'large' companies. Organizations are nominated for participation in the survey and data are mainly obtained via employee opinion questionnaires, although there is also input from the company itself. In 2007, 148 000 employees contributed to the survey.

THE SUNDAY TIMES

100

BEST COMPANIES TO WORK FOR | 2007

The key premise that underlies the survey and resulting list of 'best companies' is that employee satisfaction (at least in their working lives) is linked to specific areas. These are listed below and are, we propose, central to the academic field of OB. Another critically important proposal that we will discuss – and in some cases question – throughout this book is that worker satisfaction is an important factor influencing organizations' performance.

The *Sunday Times* survey methodology seeks to unravel workers' perceptions of eight factors (or key areas). Work organizations score strongly, and hence feature in the upper echelons of the list of best companies if employees 'exhibit strength'[1] in the following broad topic areas:

- *leadership* – under this heading workers are asked to give their views on the company head, senior managers and the quality of leadership provided by these individuals
- *wellbeing* – this factor encompasses perceived stress levels and in particular work/home life balance
- *my manager* – recognizing that senior managers may have little or no day-to-day contact with workers, this category records peoples' feelings about their 'immediate' supervisor(s) or manager(s)
- *my team* – this aspect explores employees' feelings concerning close work colleagues at a similar level in terms of role and seniority
- *fair deal* – here workers express their feelings on their pay and other benefits within the broad area of remuneration and reward
- *giving something back* – workers are asked to comment on how much they believe their company 'puts back' into society and more specifically the local community in which they are based
- *my company* – the questioning in this case centres on feelings towards the employing organization, as opposed to co-workers
- *personal growth* – employees record their views on the extent to which they feel challenged by their own job, whether their skills and other attributes are fully used and on their perceived scope for advancement.

Source: Unbeatable Gore marches fourth into top spot again, *Sunday Times*, 11 March 2007.

The eight elements making up the *Sunday Times* survey and subsequent findings are intrinsic to the subject of OB. Questions on the nature of effective supervision (or empowerment), team working and what really motivates people at work lie at the very heart of much research in OB – although, as we will show in this book, OB is a broad area of study that often extends far beyond the workplace. Issues addressed within OB should be of personal interest to all of us in our possible roles as managers or other workers *within* organizations or as external stakeholders; for example shareholders, customers, clients or neighbours of organizations. We are all affected by organizations throughout our lives: health providers play an important role in our birth, most of us are educated within institutions such as schools and universities, we can spend large parts of our lives as employees and our friends and relatives will be concerned with the service provided by funeral directors when we die. It would be implausible to claim that OB has no relevance to our lives.

We also frequently encounter the view that the study of OB is important in business terms; namely that insights deriving from the academic field can be applied within organizations with a view to *enhancing performance.* In this sense OB can form part of management studies, with theories and research data being applied to the task of effective management of people. This *managerial focus* will be analysed along with other perspectives on OB later in this chapter. The overall winner of the *Sunday Times* 'best company' survey in 2007 was W.L. Gore & Associates, which is involved in diverse activities and is perhaps best known for its fabric, Gore-Tex, used extensively in outdoor clothing. W.L. Gore has been awarded the title of best overall company for four consecutive years. The company has a highly distinctive organizational culture (this term is covered fully in Chapter 8). There are no job titles and no formally designated managers – rather, everyone is an associate. Gore, in attaining first place in the *Sunday Times* listings, scored particularly highly in the categories of team spirit and identification both with co-workers and the company and its ethos. This resulted overall in a strong sense of personal growth amongst employees. The company certainly sees advantages in its approach, both in ethical and pragmatic terms. John Housego manufacturing plant leader, when accepting Gore's award, claimed that:

> Workplace engagement, we strongly believe, is a competitive advantage. Competitive advantage when used correctly not only creates income and profit, which we are great at doing, but also comes with a responsibility to society as a whole. We are successful because of the ability of our associates to grow, explore and learn in an environment of freedom and trust.[2]

The picture of work organizations as essentially integrated and harmonious entities (as exemplified by the Gore example) should be viewed with some caution. Within the *Sunday Times* survey there is evidence of negative indicators, even amongst the '20 best big companies'. For example, there was a significant fall in employee perceptions of wellbeing across the six-year period covered by the survey, with increasing levels of workplace stress evident, together with difficulty expressed in reconciling work, social and domestic commitments, in part due to a long-hours culture. The British psychologist Oliver James[3] has counselled against the negative effects of this phenomenon, which he interestingly characterizes as an Anglo-American problem. One commentator on the *Sunday Times* survey noted furthermore that: 'the data did not reveal any information covering some very important workplace issues such as race, bullying and harassment, sickness policies, absenteeism rates, average salaries or trade union involvement.'[4] However a preoccupation with fostering a sense of belonging does seem to work for W.L. Gore and it reflects many of the fundamental ingredients of a successful organization: its members are engaged and happy with their task; ideas are shared; workers are supported; the organization is delivering a product that satisfies its customers and the customers make the company profitable.

Throughout this book you will learn about the complex field of OB – what people and groups do in organizations, and why. We will place a particular emphasis on identifying those management skills that extend beyond task-related competencies. Technical ability will not be sufficient if you wish to be a successful manager in the twenty-first century. The attributes needed to be at least a *potentially* effective manager in the organizations of today and tomorrow instead reflect the need to ensure that the work experiences of others are both productive and satisfying. According to Clegg *et al.*[5] 'managers today are expected to have some of the skills of a workplace psychologist, therapist, and counsellor and, as such, need a basic understanding of psychological principles and theories to help them in the complex task of managing people'. Existing or aspiring managers also need to be aware of the profound changes taking place in the business environment. Bratton *et al.*[6] identify the following significant influences on organizations since 1985:

- political/economic changes, for example the implosion of Eastern European communist regimes, the expansion of the EU and NAFTA and the emergence of new major economic players such as China and India
- technological advances in microelectronics and the rapid spread of the Internet
- the advent of flexible and 'virtual' organizational arrangements
- structural economic change resulting (at least in the European context) in increasing prevalence of knowledge-based organizations

We might add the emergence of increasingly diverse workforces – in part a consequence of globalization – and some significant shifts in how employers and employees view each other. These types of changes require managers and other organizational members who are committed to learning about both classical and emerging themes in OB and who can then put them into effect. We hope this book will help you along that path.

Questions
1. Look again at the eight factors or key areas listed in the *Sunday Times* survey. Which are the three most important to you and why? Rank them.
2. Identify organizations that in your experience are not 'great places to work'. Give reasons for your conclusions.

WHAT IS OB?

Although there is broad agreement on the subject matter covered by OB there are some illuminating differences in actual definitions or conceptions of the term. Consider, for example, the varying nuances of meaning contained in two remarks taken from leading OB textbooks. The first is this: 'Organizational behaviour is concerned with the study of people within an organizational setting. It involves the understanding, prediction and control of human behaviour.'[7] Contrast this with the statement that organizational behaviour should be viewed: 'first and foremost as practices of organizing and meaning-making, involving thinking, feeling and acting, that are not so dissimilar to everyday life.'[8] The differences can be related to the philosophical stances taken by the authors. The first statement is explicitly managerial; the second seems to point to shifting and constructed notions of reality, while focusing on the subjective experience of organizational actors.

For our purposes organizational behaviour is defined as *the study of individuals and groups in organizations*. This is a stripped-down definition that identifies the core elements of the subject while allowing readers to take insights and evidence from the OB 'knowledge bank' and to use these in a variety of contexts and from eclectic perspectives. While the overall tone of this book is moderately managerial (we welcome situations where the goals of employers and employees coincide and happy workers contribute to legitimate organizational success), we also acknowledge alternative critical perspectives. The experiences of many workers are in reality often repugnant and we will refer to negative occurrences, possibly caused by unethical business conduct, within our 'counter-point' features.

Organizational behaviour is a composite subject – often regarded as multidisciplinary – which draws on individual subject disciplines such as **psychology**, **sociology** and **anthropology**. There are also links to other social sciences such as economics and political science. Often the subjects are interrelated and it is necessary to draw on this variety of scholarly vantage points to build concepts, theories and understandings about human behaviour in organizations.

Organizational behaviour *is the study of individuals and groups in organizations.*

Psychology *is the study of mental life with a particular focus on the individual's thought processes and behaviour.*

Sociology *is the study of social structures and patterns, both in whole societies and subgroups.*

Anthropology *is the comparative study of different societies or tribes.*

OB IN ACTION

Immigrants have boosted UK growth

A report in the British newspaper, the *Independent*, in August 2006,[9] cast doubt on some popularly received 'common-sense' perceptions of the migration of Eastern European workers into the UK and the effects of this phenomenon. The author

concluded that, according to research from the Ernst & Young Item Club, 'the stereotypical image of Polish builders and plumbers has been blown apart by research showing that one in three immigrants from eastern Europe are taking up office managerial posts. The stereotype of the Polish plumber is well wide of the mark.' The research indicated that nearly one-third of Eastern European entrants to the UK labour market in 2005 took up positions in administration, business and management services compared with 4% joining the construction industry. This research showed that approximately 300 000 citizens of the 10 countries that joined the European Union in 2004 have since taken new jobs in the UK. Item noted several positive aspects and consequences of the migration pattern, concluding that in 2006 interest rates were half a per cent lower than they would otherwise have been without the influx of new workers, suggesting also that this immigrant workforce would boost growth by 0.2% in 2006 and 0.4% in 2007.

The phenomenon of Eastern European migration into the UK can be approached and understood from a variety of vantage points within OB, thereby supporting our conception of its eclectic and multidisciplinary nature. First, the issue is amenable to analysis from a *psychological perspective*, focusing, for example, on the perceptions of hosts and incoming workers and possible feelings of culture shock experienced by migrating Eastern European workers. However one could also approach the topic from a *sociological* viewpoint. Sociology takes as its focus for study societies and wider social groupings. Elements of the new migration pattern that could be studied from this viewpoint include cultural differences made real via globalization, power issues both at micro-organizational and macrosocial level (see Chapter 10) and change issues (covered in Chapter 12). In all cases it would be entirely inadequate (and wrong) to focus on any one society by adopting an ethnocentric stance. For example, if significant migration has occurred from Poland to the UK it is felt appropriate to focus on the impact in *both* societies.

Organizational behaviour is unique in its focus on applying diverse insights to create better understanding and management of human behaviour in organizations. Among the special characteristics of OB are its:

- *Applied focus.* The ultimate goals of the field are to help people and organizations achieve high performance levels and to help ensure that all members of organizations achieve satisfaction from their task contributions and work experiences. A concern to locate OB material within a practical orientation pervades this book. Nonetheless the effects of using OB with management interventions are by no means easy to quantify. Grey (2005) goes further in claiming that managerial analyses of organizations: 'for all their desire to speak effectively to the world of practice have consistently failed to come up with anything of much use to managers and others, a fact for which they are consistently criticized by others and over which they themselves persistently agonize.'[10] We hope that material presented in this book will not lend itself to this degree of suspicion, although we recognize some issues of credibility in this respect. Note, for example, the reaction of a manager who had commissioned a knowledge transfer project from the authors' own university. In acknowledging the success of the project in 'bottom-line' terms, he recorded that he 'imagined they'd be a bunch of theorists who couldn't run a hamburger stall, but the work they've done for us has given a major boost to our productivity.' The authors are academics – although one of us has run a candyfloss stall – however we are concerned to show the potential of OB in business terms and in some cases demonstrable actual benefits.

- *Contingency orientation.* Rather than assume that there is a universal way in which to manage people and organizations, OB scholars have from the 1960s onwards tended to adopt a contingency approach.[11] That is, they recognize that behaviour may vary systematically depending on the circumstances and the people involved. For example, writers in the OB field increasingly recognize that 'cultural differences' among people may affect the way theories and concepts of management apply in different countries.[12] Management practices cannot simply be transferred from one part of the world to another without considering the cultural implications of the different settings in which they are to be applied.

- *Emphasis on rigorous study.* Organizational behaviour is highly relevant to all of us and is an accessible subject in that we have our own preformed views – not necessarily based on experience – on such questions as how workers can be effectively motivated or how to assess other people's personalities. This very relevance, which enhances many students' enjoyment of the subject, contains certain dangers. There is, for example, a tendency to regard the study of people in work organizations as akin to commonsense. The implication here is that knowledge in this area of study is obvious and unambiguous. Academics studying and researching in OB areas have felt a particular responsibility therefore to conduct their work in a rigorous and systematic way. So-called commonsense thinking is, of course, frequently flawed and based on misperceptions or even disinformation. Research on leadership and human resource management more generally in Germany,[13] has revealed that the system of co-determination (or joint decision making) endemic within that country has led to a typically consultative style being adopted when managing people. This may be far removed from the preconceptions that many people may have concerning preferred German leadership styles, particularly if these views have been influenced by hostile and prejudiced media reporting – this is especially true in the UK. At any rate it is incumbent on researchers in OB to conduct open-minded studies that capture the *reality* of working life as opposed to relying on possibly inaccurate, stereotypical and outdated viewpoints as drivers of their work. As students of OB you are entitled to expect that knowledge in the field has been obtained via sound methods resulting from fair-minded enquiry.

A **contingency approach** in OB identifies how situations can be understood and managed in ways that appropriately respond to their unique characteristics or circumstances.

Commonsense thinking is apparently obvious or assumed analysis of OB topics, without reference to rigorous study or evidence, which can result in false conclusions.

Positivism is the view that social sciences such as OB can and should be studied in the same way as natural sciences like physics using similar methods with a view to predicting and controlling behaviour and performance.

There is a tradition within OB which uses – and believes one can legitimately use – natural scientific methods (as found in physics or chemistry) to develop and empirically test generalizations about behaviour in organizations. This idea is often referred to as positivism. The three key characteristics of positivist OB research and study are: the controlled and systematic process of data collection; careful testing of the proposed explanations; and acceptance of only explanations that can be scientifically verified.

One example of how this philosophical approach can work in reality is found in the work of Hendrick.[14] Hendrick conducted experimental-style research that compared samples of experienced and inexperienced aircraft pilots when normal control stick conditions were reversed. In other words when pilots would normally move the stick forward to ascend and back to descend, these controls were reversed from the norm and a similar change was made to the left/right turn instruments. The experiment was (prudently) carried out in a flight simulator and revealed clear statistically relevant differences in performance. More experienced pilots made significantly more errors than their inexperienced counterparts. This finding was the result of entrenched learning and habit formation, which made experienced pilots less able on average to adapt to new conditions. The experiment can be firmly located within the positivist tradition. The research was predicated on a *hypothesis* – itself based on actual events (in this case air crashes). The hypothesis was tested using experimental conditions and the researchers were mindful of other variables (such as age of the pilots) confounding the results. Results were tested and verified through replication of the study. There is also a clear practical benefit to the study, for example in the design of training programmes when new aircraft types are introduced. The data also contribute to knowledge in OB – here in the topic of learning, which we address in Chapter 3.

It should be acknowledged though that positivist style research such as that illustrated above is comparatively rare in OB. More common are qualitative methods that do not seek to lead to general theories or even laws, but instead attempt to capture the meanings that individuals give to their actions and experiences. This approach is known as the interpretivist school of thought. It has a long tradition within the social sciences and is particularly associated with the work of Max Weber (1864–1920). Weber used the term *verstehen* – translated from the German as intrinsic understanding – and believed that research into people's behaviour should address the subjects' understanding of their own behaviour and that of other people and should also address the meaning(s) that they attach to actions. This tradition necessarily promotes methods of study that do not attempt to emulate the natural sciences. Instead we find observation, participant observation and, most recently, focus groups. Proponents of these methods claim that they are well placed to capture a deep understanding of behaviour and indeed people's inner lives – those thoughts and feelings that do not demonstrably result in particular patterns of behaviour or indeed actions *per se*.

In 2006, Ward and Winstanley conducted a study exploring the experiences of sexual minorities in a unit and specific shifts or *watches* within the UK fire service.[15] The chief method employed in the study involved presenting stories and experiences from sexual minorities to focus groups within the organization for discussion. In this way the study identified habitual ways of working in the fire service and highlighted the everyday vocabulary, signs and symbols – what social scientists term discourse – used in those workplaces, which determined or *framed* reality there. Such language and symbols impacted on the experiences of gay men and lesbians within the fire service. As sexual orientation is seen as invisible, unlike other areas of diversity, some gay workers experienced feelings of isolation

---

The interpretivist tradition within OB believes that research into human behaviour should incorporate the subject's understanding of their own and other people's behaviour and the meanings attached to actions. Research within this tradition typically uses qualitative methods specific to social sciences.

Participant observation is a method of study that involves researchers becoming members of the groups that they are studying, either overtly or via 'undercover' involvement.

Focus groups are a form of qualitative research method in which groups of people are asked about their attitudes towards particular items or issues.

Discourse involves ways of presenting and understanding any facet of the world via ideas, assumptions, vocabulary and actions. In this way reality is framed, thereby informing people's understanding and behaviour.

in a work setting that stressed and promoted a strong subculture at workplace or watch level. It is unlikely that the insightful and illuminating data that emerged from this study – which could plausibly inform management actions in future – would have been obtained via more quantitative or impersonal methods; the insights here are inherently bound up with the methods used.

RESEARCH IN

Throughout this book we will stress that insights from OB can inform our understanding of work organizations and that concepts, theories and models deriving from the subject are superior to commonsense thinking. One reason for this conclusion lies in the rich tradition of research study in OB. At the end of each part of the book we have presented one research-based journal article in full, to give you a sense of the type of work carried out by academics working in this area. There are also additional journal articles on our Web site at **www.wileyeurope.com/college/french** that we will point you to throughout the text. At this point, you may wish to look at the article by Challiol and Mignonac on the reasons why dual-earner couples make work relocation decisions (at the end of Part 1, on pages 52–70) and the specific questions we have added to the article. Note in particular, the combination of quantitative (survey) and qualitative (in-depth interviews) methods that these authors found necessary in order to research their chosen topic.

THE RELEVANCE OF OB

Organizational behaviour is not a static discipline. Managers are constantly seeking new insights and ideas to improve their effectiveness. Maybe you have already heard of some of these concepts – the learning organization, the virtual workplace and knowledge management, to name just a few. The study of OB is improving our understanding of old and new concepts alike including such issues as stress, emotional intelligence and instinctive drive. You will learn about these as you progress through this book.

Organizational behaviour should help managers both deal with and learn from their workplace experiences. Managers who understand organizational behaviour are better prepared to know what to look for in work situations, to understand what they find and to take (or help others to take) the required action.

Performance equation: *job performance = attributes × work effort × organizational support.*

Effective managers need to understand the people they rely on for the performance of their unit. Each person, team/group and organization is complex and unique but the performance of an individual, team, group or organization depends on their capacity to work, willingness to work and opportunity to work. This concept can be summarized by the **performance equation** (Figure 1.1). The performance equation views performance as a combination of personal and/or group attributes, the work effort people make and the organizational support they receive.

| Job performance | = | attributes | × | work effort | × | organizational support |

Figure 1.1: The performance equation.

This equation can be applied to the three different units of analysis that form the structure of this book: individual, group/team and organization. The multiplication signs indicate that all three factors must be present for high performance to be achieved. This means that each factor should be maximized for each of the three units of analysis in work settings if the maximum level of accomplishment is to be realized. Every manager should be capable of understanding how these three factors, acting either alone or in combination, affect performance. We will use this equation as the theoretical guide for much of the material presented in this book. Part 2 looks at individual behaviour and performance. In Chapter 2 we will address individual attributes required to generate performance capacity; Chapters 3 and 4 deal with learning and motivation respectively to generate a willingness to perform and Chapter 5 points to how organizations can provide individuals with the best opportunity to perform through innovative job design. Part 3 of the book (Chapter 6) approaches the issue of organizational performance from a group/team and organizational perspective. Part 4 combines individual performance, group performance and organizational processes in the context of OB via an examination of the diverse topics of structure, culture, leadership, power, communication and change. Even though these concepts are presented in different parts and chapters of this book, they are highly related. Remember that the multiplication sign in the performance equation indicates that all three factors (attributes, work effort and organizational support) must be present to gain a high level of performance.

For practitioners, the performance equation raises the question of whether performance is predictable. It is suggested that cognitive ability, or intelligence, is a reasonable predictor of job performance.[16] However, many human resource managers would argue that additional testing is required to ensure a good fit between capability and expected performance. Over the past few years the concept of **emotional intelligence** (EI or EQ) has surfaced, sparking hopes for creating another way to predict performance. Emotional intelligence is defined as a form of social intelligence that allows us to monitor and shape our emotions and those of others. Daniel Goleman, closely associated with the concept, suggests that *emotional competence* is a learned capability, based on emotional intelligence, which is associated with outstanding work performance. In these domains EI is considered to be a competency for performance. For example, people with a high level of emotional intelligence would be competent in recognizing their own strengths and weaknesses.

Reuven Bar-On developed a self-assessment instrument (emotional quotient inventory, or EQi)[17] measuring traits and abilities related to social knowledge. The EQi is a measure of psychological wellbeing and adaptation and can be a measure related to performance. Jack Meyer and Peter Salovey claim that EI is composed of mental abilities and skills.[18] They see EI as a form of intelligence that processes and benefits from emotions. They believe that other measures of intelligence fail to take into account individual differences in the

Emotional intelligence *is a form of social intelligence that allows us to monitor and shape our emotions and those of others.*

ability to perceive, process and manage emotions. In Chapter 2 we expand on the notion of emotional intelligence as one of the individual attributes predicting capacity to perform at a high level.

BUT WE'RE NOT ALL MANAGERS!

The performance equation may be a useful model for managers to appreciate the intricacies of employee performance and ways to improve it and an awareness of emotional competencies, as outlined earlier, can help managers to monitor and shape emotions with a view to enhancing performance. There are many other OB concepts – see for example Chapter 4 on motivation – which can aid managers in carrying out their varied jobs effectively through an understanding of peoples' attitudes and behaviour. Organizational Behaviour is also of interest however, to the bulk of the population who are not currently in managerial roles and may not necessarily aspire to occupy such positions. It provides us with an opportunity to reflect on our own experiences of work organizations and can lead to us becoming more self-aware. We can also gain a fuller understanding of events affecting us. For example, theories on sources of power within organizations (covered in Chapter 10) could help us become reconciled to losing out on a promotion if we can see clearly the games a successful rival colleague has played to manoeuvre into a winning position. It may even be the case that OB awareness is of benefit to those whose sympathies are not with managers and other members of an organization's dominant coalition but rather with so-called underdogs. For example, it is illuminating to read qualitative research documenting service sector workers' attempts to 'manage' difficult customers.[19] In an important sense OB can illuminate the realities of working life focusing on what *does*, as well as what *should*, routinely happen. A critical tradition within OB questions whether the subject should take as its primary focus managing people for performance and often adopts a stance which questions the dominant role of managers, both in actual and philosophical terms. Nonetheless as many of our readers are studying OB as part of business and management courses, we will adopt a largely managerial approach throughout this book – albeit a quizzical one in places.

WHY DO ORGANIZATIONS EXIST?

Simply stated, organizations exist because individuals are limited in their physical and mental capabilities. Organizations are mechanisms through which many people combine their efforts and work together to accomplish more than any one person could alone. The trend in Europe, North America and parts of Asia has been for increasingly large organizations following the 'industrialization' of societies in these regions. Increasing size of organizations has been accompanied by greater *formality* and *complexity* – see Chapter 7 for a full treatment of the topic of organization structure. As successful organizations cannot be static and must evolve and adapt to external trends and pressures, so the pattern of organizations is continually changing. In the early twenty-first century for example, we can discern a trend for organizations to minimize their core activities and to outsource work or otherwise enter interorganizational networking arrangements. Consider, for instance, the Ford Motor Company, which for much of the twentieth century, sought to bring its operations in-house, at one point buying up railway companies and forests in order to control supply and distribution infrastructure. In the twenty-first century, Ford contrastingly operates an elaborate system of outsourcing and supplier-production-dealer networks. Interorganizational networking encompasses cooperative ventures including sharing of resources with a view to maintaining independence, while *collaboration* involves sharing of aspects of organizations' competence, including intellectual property. The proliferation of such arrangements has led to a renewed interest in trust and a concern among senior managers to avoid betrayal through opportunistic behaviour by prospective or actual partners. It should be recognized however, that despite the undoubted impact of outsourcing and widespread job reduction, resulting in many smaller 'core workforces', many people still routinely come into contact with, and have their lives shaped by, large organizations.

Outsourcing *involves organizations obtaining aspects of their work, for example production systems, from external suppliers for reasons of cost and/or quality rather than carrying out the work themselves.*

A primary purpose of any organization is to produce a product or provide a service. Large and small businesses produce a diverse array of consumer products and services such as motor vehicles, appliances, telecommunications and accommodation. Not-for-profit organizations organize services with public benefits, such as health care and rehabilitation, public education and environmental management.

A clear statement of purpose, or 'goal statement', is seen as important in guiding the activities of an organization and its members. To illustrate, the following are goals of some prominent organizations:

- 'to be the world's mobile communications leader – enriching customers' lives, helping individuals, businesses and communities be more connected in a mobile world' (Vodafone Group)[20]
- 'to enhance our businesses and strengthen our position as a premier integrated communications services provider in the Asia Pacific region' (SingTel)[21]
- 'to become the most admired company in our industry as seen by our stakeholders' (Philips).[22]

In stressing the purposive nature of work organizations, one should not fall into the trap of thinking that there is likely to be unanimous ongoing agreement and compliance with organizational goals. Humans are thinking beings capable of taking a self-interested strategic view of their current situation and future intentions. It may also be that people within an organization are not always aware of its goals or may lose sight of them. In short managers cannot automatically assume that individuals, specifically workers, will commit to stated goals and may need to expend time and effort in re-emphasizing or promoting them.

A **dominant coalition** denotes the people who are in a strong position of power and influence within organizations at any one time. Dominant coalitions are shifting and can be replaced by others.

Division of labour is the process of breaking the work to be done into specialized tasks that individuals or groups can perform.

Synergy is the creation of a whole that is greater than the sum of its parts.

Deskilling refers to a diminution of the attributes and proficiency required to perform work tasks. In Braverman's view deskilling is a deliberate strategy by owners and managers of organizations in order to reassert control over work.

Empowerment is the process by which managers delegate power to employees who therefore have an enhanced view of their work and role within the organization.

The preceding analysis stressing the importance of *organizational goals* follows many other OB textbooks in using that term. However to say that organizations have goals is not literally true; organizations are not living entities, except in the metaphorical sense. The goals and purposes referred to are those of particular actors, typically the owners and senior managers of that organization. The term dominant coalition has been used to denote the people who are in a position of power and influence and who will in all likelihood have formulated or reformulated its goals. As new coalitions can emerge – in some cases replacing others – it follows that the stated goals of organizations are potentially transitory.

To achieve its purpose, any organization depends on human effort. The division of labour is the process of breaking the work to be done into specialized tasks that individuals or groups can perform: it is a way of organizing the efforts of many people to the best advantage of that employing organization and ideally the workers themselves.

The division of labour and task specialization will be quite clear in a typical fast-food restaurant; McDonald's with outlets across large parts of the planet, will provide an evocative example for many readers. Certain people take your order and your money, others cook the food, and still others clean after everyone else has gone home for the night. By dividing the labour and training of employees; orienting them to perform highly specialized tasks, such an organization strives for excellence in task accomplishment. In the fast-food sector, excellence is partly denoted by standardization.

The aim of effective division of labour is to help managers of organizations to mobilize the work of many people to achieve its purpose.

A well-functioning organization with a clear purpose and appropriate division of labour, like those of fast-food restaurants, achieves synergy, which is the creation of a whole that is greater than the sum of its parts. Synergy in organizations occurs when people work well together while using available resources to pursue a common purpose. In psychology this is called a 'gestalt'.[23] Within an effective organization, this 'gestalt' is created by the organization's division of labour, task specialization and hierarchy of authority, as well as by effective managerial behaviour.

The aforementioned summary of organizational design involving coordination of the efforts of others is an essentially managerial analysis. Other writers taking a critical stance, most influentially Braverman, have stressed the *deskilling* of work and its negative impact on workers.[24] The examples of fast-food restaurants and the contemporary phenomenon of call centres with their routinized work and scripted customer encounters, lend themselves relatively easily to explanations within a critical deskilling perspective... should one wish to. It is also the case that the experience of work will vary enormously in different organizational settings, with some employees working within a framework of multiskilling whereby they have to use a wide range of skills to fulfil their work roles. Other organizations employ terms like empowerment, and put structures and working practices in place that enable employees who are low down in the hierarchy to feel a sense of freedom or autonomy in their day-to-day working lives.

OB IN ACTION

Cité de l'Image

France needs more entrepreneurs like Stephane Ledoux, a fast-talking salesman in his early 30s who started work straight after leaving school at 18. Today he owns a specialist photo-processing company, Cité de l'Image, which employs 67 people at its labs on the south-western fringes of Paris. M. Ledoux borrowed money and bought the business from a larger group for which he had been working. He considered moving the labs to low-wage Poland or Romania but quickly realised that would be counter-productive.

Cité de l'Image is a photo-processing and pre-press production house for an international clientele that runs from Guerlain and Yves Rocher to Xerox, Henkel and Air France. The work requires expensive, sophisticated equipment and highly skilled staff. Some simple work has been passed to Poland and Romania for over-night processing, but the core of the business has stayed in Paris. To cut costs, M. Ledoux has outsourced functions such as IT and payroll processing. Last month a private-equity group, Green Recovery, recruited him to run a much bigger business: the collection of photo agencies and image-processing firms (including famous names such as Gamma, Keystone and Jacana) that it had bought from the Hachette Filipacchi publishing group.[25]

This extract from a 2007 article from *The Economist* deals with a number of issues facing twenty-first century mangers. Note how it is possible that differential skill levels will be linked to specific countries in future. Consider too the outsourcing of parts of the business – a trend referred to earlier.

ORGANIZATIONS AS OPEN SYSTEMS

Organizations ultimately depend for their success on the activities and collective efforts of many people. People are the essential human resources of an organization – the individuals and groups whose performance contributions enable the organization to serve particular purposes. But organizations need more than people if they are to survive and prosper. They also need material resources, which are the technology, information, physical equipment and facilities, raw materials and money necessary for an organization to produce some useful product or service.

Human resources *are the individuals and groups whose contributions enable the organization to serve a particular purpose.*

Many OB scholars believe that organizations can be best understood as open systems that transform human and material resource 'inputs' received from their environment, into product 'outputs' in the form of finished goods and/or services. The outputs are then offered to the environment for consumption. If everything works, measured via feedback, the environment accepts these outputs and allows the organization to obtain the resource inputs it needs to continue operating in the future (Figure 1.2)

Material resources *are the technology, information, physical equipment and facilities, raw material and money that are necessary for an organization to produce some product or service.*

Open systems *transform human and physical resources received from their environment into goods and services that are then returned to the environment.*

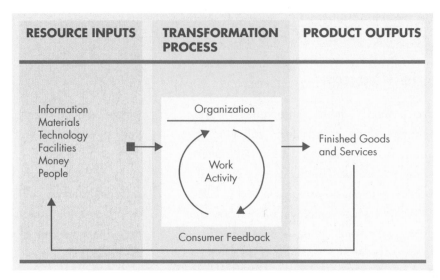

Figure 1.2: Organization and environment relationships.

Of course, things can go wrong. An organization's survival depends on satisfying environmental demands. When the organization's goods and/or services are not well received by the environment, it will sooner or later have difficulty obtaining the resource inputs it needs to operate.

OB IN ACTION

Just as business outcomes have an impact on the business environment and society as a whole, world events can also influence business survival. The tourism industry was greatly affected by the 2004 Boxing Day tsunami and the October 2002 and 2005 terrorism attacks in Bali. Although initially the tourism industry in Indonesia and Malaysia slumped as a result of these events, the industry responded by applying survival strategies and some improved their performance as a direct result of refocusing the market. For example, after the 2002 bombings, the Indonesian tourism authorities and commercial providers actively promoted Bali to markets that, unlike Australia, did not have an emotional association with the Bali bombings. This resulted in a boost for Bali, where visitors from Singapore to Bali lifted from 17 666 in 2002 to 26 881 in 2003.[26]

Other tourism businesses in the Asia-Pacific region responded to the change in business environment. After the Bali bombings, Australia promoted its destinations as 'safe' and the Philippines promoted its resorts as unaffected by the Boxing Day tsunami. Both countries seized upon the opportunity to attract tourists who might otherwise have travelled to Bali or the Malaysian coast.[27] Time will tell if these tourism businesses are able to sustain growth by attracting returning tourists in the future, or if loyal Bali and Malaysian coast patrons return to their previous preferred destinations.

MANAGERS IN ORGANIZATIONS

Now that we have examined some fundamental features of organizations, we can speak more precisely about what it means to be a manager. A **manager** is a person in an organization who is responsible for work that is accomplished through the performance contributions of one or more other people.

Today, the focus of both management research and practice is not so much on the manager as on the work team or unit. A **work team** or unit is a task-oriented group that includes a manager and his or her direct subordinates. Such groups are found in organizations of all types; whether small or large. Examples include departments in a retail store, divisions of a corporation, branches of a bank, wards in a hospital and teams in a manufacturing plant. Even university classes can be considered a work team; lecturers are their managers (they may prefer to use the term 'facilitators') and the students are team members. The study of such work teams has become a key area of OB research.

WHAT IS AN EFFECTIVE MANAGER?

It is not easy to define what makes a manager an effective manager within a business context. The list of managerial competencies identified over the past few decades helps us understand more clearly the competencies required for effective management. However, such research also illustrates the difficulties in defining effective management because it is still hard to achieve expert consensus on what constitutes a basic core of competencies. It is even more difficult to find agreement on prioritized rankings of such competencies.[28] Many of the best known writers in the management literature typically emphasize one managerial competence at the expense of all others. Fayol and Urwick have portrayed good managers as controllers.[29] This is a typical conclusion from the *classical school* of management in its assumption that managers should direct the work of others, in this case through formal mechanisms of control. The manager remains clearly in control while designing and monitoring structures within which employees carry out tasks and systems of work which are operated by workers. Later approaches to management (although the *human relations school* dates back as far as the 1930s), emphasize the important role of managing relationships.

Mintzberg[30] has drawn up a multifaceted concept of managers' work, identifying *interpersonal, informational* and *decisional* roles within the overall 'umbrella heading' of the term manager. Note that *all 10 roles* set out by Mintzberg, involve dealing with other people, even those that are not designated as interpersonal roles.

Fundamentally, any manager should seek two key results for a work unit or work team: **task performance**, which is defined by the quality and quantity of the work produced, or the services provided by the work unit and **human resource performance**, which involves the attraction and continuation of a capable workforce over time. This latter notion, while too often neglected, is extremely important. It is not enough for a work unit to achieve high performance on any given day; it must be able to achieve this level of input

A **Manager** is responsible for work that is accomplished through the performance contributions of others. A manager concerned with making things happen and keeping work on schedule, engaging in routine interactions to fulfil planned actions.

Work teams or units are task-oriented groups that include a manager and his or her direct subordinates.

Task performance is the quality and quantity of work produced.

Human resource performance. This must be sustained if it is to have meaning; high performance should be sustainable. High levels of performance are affected by a manager's attention to a range of matters under the people management heading.

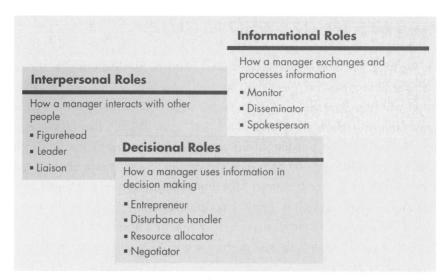

Figure 1.3: Ten roles of effective managers.

Source: Mintzberg, H. (1990), The Design School: reconsidering the basic premises of strategic management, *Strategic Management Journal*, **11**, pp176–195. © 1990 Reproduced by permission of John Wiley & Sons, Ltd.

and outcome every day, both now and into the future. Good human resource performance is a major concern of OB. It directs a manager's attention to matters such as job satisfaction, job involvement, organizational commitment, absenteeism and turnover, as well as performance. Wendy Lenton, Vodafone director of people and brand, points out that 'The theory is that if you care for your people, your people will care for you, but if people feel unappreciated or unhappy at work, the anxiety manifests into ill health, low motivation, low productivity and absenteeism.'[31]

This book treats high task and human resource performance as results that any manager should seek. Indeed, the two results can be seen as twin criteria for an effective manager – that is, a manager whose work unit achieves high levels of task accomplishment and maintains itself as a capable workforce over time. This concept of the 'effective manager' offers an important framework for understanding OB and developing personal managerial skills. A special text feature, the 'effective manager' is used in this and later chapters to help remind us of these applications.

MANAGING TASK PERFORMANCE

Productivity *is a summary measure of the quantity and quality of work performance that also accounts for resource use.*

Recall that task performance is determined by the quality and quantity of the work produced or the services provided. An effective manager must be concerned with the 'productivity' of work units and their members, although this can sometimes be difficult to evaluate. Formally defined, productivity is a summary measure of the quantity and quality of work performance achieved (task performance) that also accounts for resource use. It is not acceptable simply to 'get a job done'; any job must be done with the best use of available resources – human and material. Productivity is a benchmark of managerial and organizational success.

The best organizations want – and actively seek out – value-added managers whose efforts clearly enable their work units to achieve high productivity and improve 'bottom-line' performance. Value-added managers create high-performance systems in which individuals and groups work well together to the benefit of the entire organization and its clients or customers. In many ways this book is about identifying the knowledge and attributes needed by value-added managers. You can thus evaluate the contribution that you could make in this regard. To reinforce a point made earlier, not all readers will aspire to management positions and material presented in this book should aid all of us when we come into contact with work organizations.

Today's managers are confronted with a considerable dilemma. They are asked to secure ever increasing added value from their stock of human capital but measures to improve worker productivity also have the potential to increase worker stress, burnout and absenteeism and ultimately to result in a decline in worker productivity. To maximize the potential benefits of new initiatives, we must balance their effect on productivity alongside a careful consideration of quality of work–life issues. The next section provides more detail on the broader issue of human resource performance.

HUMAN RESOURCE PERFORMANCE

The need to ensure long-term and sustainable high performance helps to focus a manager's attention on the need to *maintain* all of a work unit's resources (human and material resources alike). Just as managers should not allow a valuable machine to break down for lack of proper maintenance, they should never allow a valuable human contribution to be lost for lack of proper care.

Through their daily actions, the best managers in twenty-first century workplaces will be able to create conditions in which people achieve their highest performance potential while experiencing a high quality of work–life. The concept of quality of work–life (QWL) gained deserved prominence in OB study as an indicator of the overall quality of human experience in the workplace. It expresses a special way of thinking about people, their work and the organizations in which their careers are fulfilled. It establishes a clear objective that high productivity should be achieved along with job satisfaction for the people who do the required work. To take one example, Vodafone says it takes 'a holistic approach to work and lifestyle.'[32]

Quality of work–life *refers to the overall quality of human experience in the workplace.*

Quality of work–life activities represent special applications of the many OB concepts and theories discussed throughout this book. In particular, the following benchmarks of managerial excellence highlight true commitments to quality of work–life:[33]

- participation – involving people from all levels of responsibility in decision making
- trust – redesigning jobs, systems and structures to give people more freedom at work
- reinforcement – creating reward systems that are fair, relevant and contingent on work performance
- responsiveness – making the work setting more pleasant and able to serve individual needs.

It is important to remember that a broader social value associated with work makes any manager's responsibilities more complex. Quality of work–life is an important component in the quality of life: negative work experiences can affect a person's nonworking life. Some common social problems – for example drug abuse – may be linked with the adjustment problems of people who are unable to find meaning and self-respect in their work.[34] The social importance of managers as major influences on the quality of work–life experienced by other people is well established. The study of OB recognizes that poor management can decrease overall quality of life, not just the quality of work–life. It also recognizes that good management can increase both.

THE PSYCHOLOGICAL CONTRACT

The **psychological contract** *specifies what an individual expects to give to and receive from an organization.*

You are probably familiar with the word 'contract' as it pertains to formal, written agreements such as a workplace agreement or an agreement between a union and an employer. Another, less formal contract deals with the 'relationship' between employees and their organization. We call this the psychological contract – specifically, what the individual and the organization expect to give to and receive from each other in the course of their working relationship. This contract represents the expected exchange of values that encourages the individual to work for the organization and motivates the organization to employ that person. When the individual is being recruited by the organization, this exchange is an anticipated one; later, during actual employment, expectations are either confirmed or denied. Part of the manager's job is to ensure that both the individual and the organization continue to receive a fair exchange of values under the psychological contract.

Contributions *are individual work efforts of value to the organization.*

Figure 1.4 depicts an exchange of values between the individual and the organization, as expressed in the psychological contract. The individual offers contributions, or work inputs of value, to the organization. These contributions – such as effort, skills, surrender of autonomy, loyalty and creativity – are extremely significant within the life of the individual worker, while one important measure of any organization's success is its ability to attract and maintain a high-quality workforce. The psychological contract is therefore a truly reciprocal exchange. In return for the worker's perceived inputs the organization gives the individual inducements – such as pay, benefits, status and job security – to encourage participation. These inducements are of value to the individual as ways of satisfying one or more important needs or expectations – see Chapter 4 for more detail on motivation theories.

Inducements *are what the organization gives to the individual on behalf of the group.*

When the exchange of values in the psychological contract is felt to be fair, a balance exists between inducements and contributions. This ideal condition creates a healthy psychological contract – one that fosters job satisfaction by allowing individuals to feel good about their work and relationship with the organization. When the exchange of values is perceived to be unfair, the psychological contract is unhealthy. Consequently, the individual may develop negative attitudes and lose the desire to work hard. These feelings correlate with absenteeism and job turnover rates, as otherwise good workers seek jobs elsewhere. As we will see in later chapters, the work of Adams is also relevant in his belief

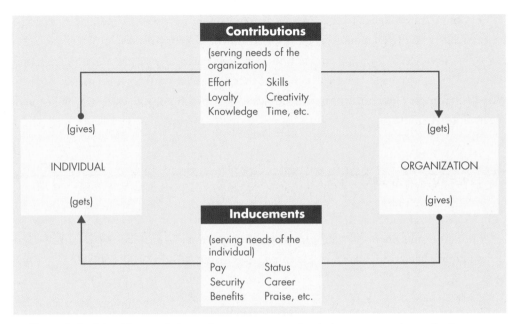

Figure 1.4: A healthy psychological contract means that inducements and contributions are in balance.

that our perceived inputs and outcomes are compared with those of others. Feelings of *equity* or inequity with others therefore also inform our psychological contract.

Some pressures in today's economic and business environment can make the management of psychological contracts a difficult task. Think about the sense of betrayed loyalty experienced by people who lose their jobs or who see others lose their jobs when an organization is 'downsized' or restructured to increase productivity.

REALIGNING THE PSYCHOLOGICAL CONTRACT

Most employees feel that their psychological contracts have been violated in some way by their employer at some time. Misunderstandings are often ignored. However, when a violation takes a serious form, such as a breach of promise and trust, feelings of betrayal can surface. According to Denise Rousseau[35] there are four main courses of action an individual may take in response to a perceived violation of psychological contract:

- *Voice* is a constructive effort to change and focus on restoring trust by discussing issues of concern with a manager or other appropriate colleague/supervisor.
- *Silence* reflects a willingness to accept unfavourable circumstances in the hope that they may improve.
- *Destruction/neglect* is most common when voice channels do not exist or if there is a history of conflict. This often causes counterproductive behaviours including theft, slowing or stopping work and intentions to destroy relationships.
- *Exit* is often the last resort when dealing with contract violations and refers to voluntary termination of the relationship.

One of the challenges faced by many managers is how to keep aligning psychological contracts in a rapidly changing business environment. Change is almost always accompanied by increasingly complex systems and increased performance pressures on individual staff members. Managers need to be aware that increased performance pressures in formerly less complex organizations can be seen as a psychological contract violation for longer tenured employees.

THE MANAGEMENT PROCESS

Managers use four functions in seeking to deploy organizational resources to achieve high performance results in both task performance and human resource performance. These four functions of management are planning, organizing, leading and controlling (see also Figure 1.5)

- Planning is the process of setting performance objectives and identifying the actions needed to accomplish these objectives.
- Organizing is the process of dividing up the work to be done and coordinating the results to achieve a desired purpose.
- Leading is the process of directing the work efforts of other people to help them to accomplish their assigned tasks.
- Controlling is the process of monitoring performance, comparing the results with the objectives and taking corrective action as necessary.

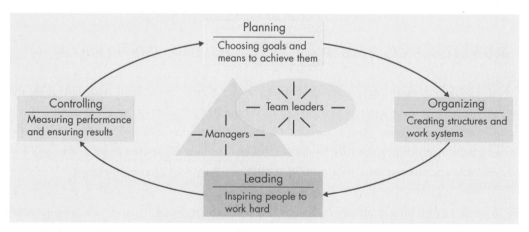

Figure 1.5: The management process of planning, organizing, leading and controlling.

There is no doubt that the task of managing both efficiently and effectively is becoming more complex. So far we have briefly discussed core and established OB themes. In addition to these well-established OB principles, today's business environment requires managers – and, of course, all other workers – to deal with emerging and fast-evolving challenges. The next part of this chapter will place the key concepts of OB into the real-world environment in which we are likely to work in future.

CONTEMPORARY THEMES IN OB

Among the biggest challenges that managers must deal with are globalization, the changing nature of work, the changing nature of the workforce, and the changing nature of the relationships between employers and employees. These in turn create another challenge: that of managing change itself. One approach is process re-engineering – defined as 'the fundamental rethinking and radical redesign of business processes to achieve dramatic improvements in critical contemporary measures of performance such as cost, quality, service and speed'.[36] The result can involve a substantial shift in values, as shown in Effective Manager 1.1 below.

Process re-engineering *is the fundamental rethinking and radical redesign of business processes to achieve improvements in performance.*

EFFECTIVE MANAGER 1.1

Moving from traditional to re-engineered values

Traditional work values:

* the boss pays our salaries; keep the boss happy
* to keep your job, stay quiet and don't make waves
* when things go wrong, pass problems to others
* the more direct subordinates you control the better; a good manager builds an empire
* the future is predictable; past success means future success.

Re-engineered work values:

* customers pay our salaries; help keep them happy
* all of our jobs depend on the value we create
* accept ownership for problems; help solve them
* we are all part of a team; a good manager builds teams
* the future is uncertain; constant learning is the key to future success.

We will now briefly discuss some of the main contemporary issues in OB, already mentioned earlier in the chapter. We will revisit these themes throughout the book as your knowledge of OB builds.

GLOBALIZATION

Globalization is not a new concept. The advantages and disadvantages – indeed the definition – of globalization have been the topic of much controversy for decades. We look at this debate in the 'counterpoint' section later in this chapter. For our purposes we will define globalization as the process of becoming more international in scope, influence or application. In a business context, globalization is characterized by networks that bind countries, institutions and people in an interdependent global economy. In terms of relevance for OB, one specific aspect of globalization that stands out is its sense of greater interconnectedness between people from other cultures. This can manifest itself both in evermore frequent travel to new countries as a routine part of many job roles and increasing exposure to people from other cultures working within *any one* workplace – consider for example the inherently multicultural makeup of London's twenty-first century workforce.

Globalization *brings a greater sense of interconnectedness between people from diverse cultures. It has also been defined as the process of becoming more international in scope, influence or application.*

OB IN ACTION

Forty years after Britain's first race relations legislation, organizations are increasingly sending employees on race awareness courses. A BBC report on the topic[38] identifies a variety of (sometimes contentious) learning methods used by trainers in this field. Jane Elliott runs day-long courses in race awareness training. Her approach is described as uncompromising, brusque and authoritative. One of her techniques involves splitting her class into two groups, one formed of blue-eyed participants; the other composed of a brown-eyed group. The blue-eyed group is then verbally abused by the other group (on the instructions of the trainer). Posters denigrating the group are pinned up in the training room – for example asking would you want your child to marry a 'bluey'? While most diversity training does not seek to recreate emotional distress a number of methods do require participants to reflect on the impact of their language, possibly using less confrontational techniques. The levels of appropriate workplace behaviour are also explored – another diversity training programme asked whether cracking blonde jokes should be tolerated. Diversity training is increasing in popularity – there are over 100 specialist trainers listed in one directory – but this development is not universally welcomed with some people claiming that such courses reinforce a sense of difference between groups rather than bringing them closer. In the US, millions of dollars are spent in discrimination litigation costs, so if this trend is repeated elsewhere there may be practical concerns indicating a further rise in diversity training, although the US is often characterized as a particularly litigious society.

In both cases globalization can impact on individual's work patterns and roles and on the nature of relationships within organizations.[37]

Success in the increasingly global business environment will depend on a new breed of 'global manager' with global management skills and competencies. Global management skills and competencies include a strong and detailed understanding of international business strategy and cross-cultural management, including a sensitivity to the existence and importance of cultural difference and an ability to manage a diverse workforce. The Effective Manager 1.2 section suggests 10 important attributes of the successful global manager:

It is important for managers to study and learn about the management and organizational practices of their counterparts in other nations. What is being done well in other settings may be of great value at home, whether that 'home' is Britain, the Netherlands, Sweden or anywhere else in the world. Whereas the world at large once looked mainly to North America, Japan and Germany for management insights, today we recognize that no one culture possesses all of the 'right' answers to our management and organizational problems.

EFFECTIVE MANAGER 1.2

Ten attributes of the global manager

The global manager is able to:
- be culturally sensitive and adaptable
- solve problems quickly and under different circumstances
- motivate and communicate well with people from different cultures
- understand different government and political systems
- manage and create a sustainable environment

- convey a positive attitude and enthusiasm when dealing with others
- manage business in both traditional and virtual environments
- view different economies as belonging to a single global market
- negotiate effectively in different business environments
- manage the 'triple bottom line' – society, economy and the environment.

OB IN ACTION

MADE WITH PASS!ON™

Dame Anita Roddick the late co-founder of the Body Shop organization (purchased by L'Oreal in 2006), was well-known for her distinctive views on the nature of business. Her vision of leadership – in her case of an environmentally aware, caring and successful organization – differed substantially from some conventional treatments of the topic. The external behaviour associated with leadership from her perspective involved 'going to every part of the organization, sitting in on meetings, going onto the factory floor, talking to everyone, educating and motivating staff, stretching their abilities and imagination. Communicating with customers, the community and the media. Developing a culture of being different.'[39] Strategies for implementing this vision which go beyond observable behaviour included: encouraging staff to question the status quo and encouraging dissonant feedback and devil's advocates.[40] This view of leadership – essentially personalized and interactive – differed from the command style that has been and continues to be prevalent in many work settings. However the *contingency approach* referred to earlier in the chapter counsels us against assuming that any one style of leadership will always be effective; the central message is that it all depends. Dame Anita's style apparently worked well in the context of the Body Shop; to what extent would it need to be re-evaluated in a more hierarchical setting, or in an organization with a very different *raison d'être* such as the armed forces? As we will see later in this chapter, one way of characterizing national cultures is *power distance,* which relates to people's perceptions of authority and hierarchy, so we might also question the acceptability of a participative management style in certain countries.

> ## COUNTERPOINT
>
> ## Globalization for good or evil?
>
> An article in the British magazine *Time Out*,[41] published in 2007, highlighted the downside of global migration patterns in particular the 'churn' of people into and out of the UK, focusing on the experience of incoming workers who find themselves on the lowest rungs of the labour market. The article noted that 'we eat the food they have picked and wear the clothes they have sewn; they clean our homes and offices and even wipe our children's noses. Many things Londoners take for granted – fresh fruit and veg in the supermarket, cheap designer fashions and affordable childcare – rely on the work of foreign migrants who are employed here, legally and illegally, often in poorly paid and dangerous jobs'. The words of 'Ana', 34. from Brazil provide an eloquent case in point:
>
> > I get up at 4.30 am to go to work at two cleaning jobs. The first begins at 6.30 and is in a college in Westminster. I get there by bus from my flat. I clean for two hours a day for £34 a week. Then I take a bus to Docklands, where I work in a business hotel cleaning rooms until 5pm. I'm paid £1.47 a room and we are expected to clean 18 rooms a day. On average I clean around 13 rooms as it's such hard work. We have to clean everything including the carpet, make the bed and clean the bathroom. There is no break and I usually don't eat as it would take up too much time. Occasionally I put some lunch in a bag and eat as I go along. There are about 15 cleaners but none of us say a word to each other during the day – we just don't have time.
> >
> > Sometimes the rooms are in a really bad state and everything is destroyed. People come here to take drugs and I often find syringes, condoms, blood and vomit in the rooms. When I've finished I feel pretty depressed.
> >
> > I arrived in London a year ago. I used to sell slimming products in Sao Paulo and I earned good money, but the company closed and I couldn't find another job. I also came here to send money home to my family. Sometimes I send as much as £50 a month. But usually it's difficult as it is so expensive to live here. I'm not happy, working so hard for so little money, and I'm looking for another job. Despite that my life is probably better here than it was in Brazil.
>
> ### Questions
>
> 1. Summarize the issues surrounding globalization as presented above, identifying both positive and negative aspects.
> 2. How would you characterize 'Ana's' psychological contract. How could her current employers improve her working experience?

THE CHANGING NATURE OF WORK

Work itself is changing rapidly due to globalization, advances in technology, the growth in the services sector, and especially an increasing reliance on knowledge to generate new products and services. These changes require workers with different skills to the workers of the past, including the ability to continuously learn new skills and adapt to changing needs. Managing such workers presents a number of new challenges for managers. We will look at some of the biggest changes in the following sections.

Technology

Technology has emerged as an ever-present, dominant force in our lives. Just as 100 years ago people could not have accurately predicted the technology that is commonplace now, so we cannot foresee all the technological advances ahead of us. Our predictions of the future are bounded by what we know to be real right now: it is difficult to 'think the unthinkable'. What is almost certain is that continuing change in information and communications technology will have massive implications for workers, managers and organizations alike.

High technology allows machines to do many routine chores more cheaply and accurately than people can; it makes available more information for planning and control to more people at all levels of organizational responsibility and it is driving change in organizational structures and ways of working. For example, the use of email has revolutionized office communication. It is a convenient medium among the more than 100 million email users worldwide.[42] However, email has potentially negative consequences in the workplace. The main problems are that written forms are more official, less easy to withdraw and suffer from the absence of other additional communication modes, such as body language and intonation of voice. In addition, there is a growing body of research that suggests email reduces a person's ability to build rapport and impairs the establishment of trust. These problems are exacerbated by cultural issues when email users are in different countries.[43] Nevertheless, email has proven to be a convenient communication medium that has changed work practices significantly. How many of us currently involved in white collar work begin our day by checking emails, either in the office, at home or even while travelling abroad?

Knowledge management

Another major driver of organizational change is the growth of the knowledge-based economy in which prosperity is built on 'intellectual capital' – the use of information in people's minds – rather than on physical resources. The OECD defines a **knowledge-based economy** as 'an economy in which the production, distribution and use of knowledge is the main driver of growth, wealth creation and employment across all industries – not only those industries classified as high tech or knowledge intensive.'[44]

Recognition of knowledge and the contribution that knowledge creation, distribution and use can make towards improved levels of performance and productivity is not new; economies have always relied on knowledge expansion and application through research and development to create new products and improvements in productivity. What is new is the speed at which knowledge is being created and the pace at which it is being transformed into new goods and services.

In a knowledge-based economy, the central questions for high-performing organizations are:

*A **knowledge-based economy** is an economy in which the production, distribution and use of knowledge is the main driver of growth, wealth creation and employment across all industries – not only those classified as high-tech or knowledge intensive.*

- What do we know and what is the currency of the knowledge we have?
- How do we organize to make best use of this knowledge?
- Who can add value to what we know?
- How quickly can we learn something new?
- How quickly can we deliver this new knowledge into the global marketplace?

Knowledge management *focuses on processes designed to improve an organization's ability to capture, share and diffuse knowledge in a manner that will improve business performance.*

Much knowledge resides within employees, including their skills, creativity and experience. It also exists in other areas such as the organization's systems, processes and structures, and in the relationships that organizations have with their customers, suppliers and other stakeholders. Knowledge management (KM), focuses on processes designed to improve an organization's ability to capture, share and diffuse knowledge in a manner that will improve business performance.

An important aspect of knowledge management is retaining people who possess the knowledge that the organization or the country needs. Workers are increasingly mobile and are taking their knowledge with them to their new workplaces across the globe. Such movement across national boundaries is commonly referred to as brain drain.

Brain drain *refers to a characteristic of today's skilled workforce whose members are now more mobile and prepared to take their knowledge with them to their new workplaces as they pursue opportunities across the globe.*

A study by professional service firm Harvey Nash and the Centre for Economic and Business Research indicates that the UK is heavily dependent on the contribution of migrant workers in the professional and managerial spheres. The journal *Personnel Today*, reporting the results of this study, indicates that in Britain, many organizations such as the National Health Service (NHS), would not be able to function effectively without their migrant workforces.[45] In the case of the NHS one striking statistic is that more than 30% of all nursing roles are taken by recent migrants to the UK.

THE CHANGING NATURE OF THE WORKFORCE

The composition of the workforce is changing. Managers must be aware of, and able to successfully manage in the context of, the following trends:[46]

- the size of the workforce is growing more slowly than in the past
- the average age of the workforce is rising
- more women are entering the workforce
- the proportion of ethnic minorities in the workforce is increasing
- the proportion of immigrants in the workforce is increasing
- workforce mobility is increasing
- 'labour packaging' is growing through short-term migrant labour importation in many Asian and Middle Eastern countries
- international careers and mobile managers are becoming commonplace
- international experience is becoming a prerequisite for career progression to many top-level management positions.

Perhaps the most notable change in the workforce is that it is more diverse than at any time in history. The term workforce diversity refers to the presence of demographic differences among members of a given workforce.[47] These differences include gender, sexual orientation, race and ethnicity, culture, age and able bodiedness.

In the sections below, we will look at the changing nature of the workforce in terms of culture, age and gender.

Culture

The workforce is becoming more multicultural as a result of migration and as workforces increasingly span more than one country. To take two examples, Australia and New Zealand are among the more multicultural countries in the world. Almost one in three members of the workforce in major Australian cities such as Sydney and Melbourne was born outside Australia. About one in three people in the Auckland region of New Zealand was born overseas. Managers – whether or not they are directly involved in international business – must be able to manage people from different cultures effectively and make the most of the advantages that a diverse workforce can bring. For example, diversifying the workforce can be used as a strategic advantage. A diverse workforce can provide business with a competitive advantage by capitalizing on language skills, cultural knowledge, business networks and knowledge of business practices in overseas markets and intelligence about overseas markets, including intimate knowledge of consumer tastes and preferences. Businesses can use the skills to improve productivity and innovation in the workplace, developing domestic niche markets and entering new, or increasing market share in, overseas markets.[48]

Research has shown that styles of leadership, motivation and decision making, and other management roles vary among different countries.[49] For example:

- Leadership. A study of international airlines found substantial differences in leadership styles despite the fact that the technology, types of jobs, skills required and basic operations are very similar from one company to another.[50]
- Motivation. Managers must avoid being parochial (where they fail to perceive difference due to limited horizons) or ethnocentric (in which case they believe that 'their way' is best). They cannot assume all people will be motivated by the same things and in the same ways as they are. Most of the popular theories of work motivation have been developed in the US. These theories may help explain the behaviour of North Americans but serious questions must be raised about how applicable they are to other cultures.[51] While North Americans, for example, value individual rewards, Japanese people prefer group rewards.
- Decision making. Latin American employees may feel uncomfortable with a boss who delegates too much authority to them. In France, research indicates that decisions tend to be made at the top of companies and passed down the hierarchy for implementation.[52] In other cultures, such as the Scandinavian countries contrastingly, employees

Workforce diversity *means a workforce consisting of a broad mix of workers from different racial and ethnic backgrounds, of different ages and genders and of different domestic and national cultures.*

prefer their managers to emphasize a participative, problem-solving approach. In Japan, many companies use the *ringi* system for making decisions. *Ringi* is a group decision approach whereby all affected company members affix their sign of approval to widely circulated written proposals. Culture may even play a role in determining whether a decision is necessary at all – that is, in whether the situation should be changed. Australians and New Zealanders tend to perceive situations as problems to be solved; others, such as Thai and Indonesian cultures, tend to accept situations as they are. Thus, an Australian is more likely to decide that a workplace problem exists and that something should be done about it.

The dimensions of culture

Geert Hofstede, a Dutch scholar and consultant, has identified five dimensions of national culture – power-distance, uncertainty avoidance, individualism–collectivism, masculinity–femininity and long-term–short-term orientation – which provide one way of understanding differences across national cultures.[53] Hofstede's five dimensions of national culture can be described as follows:

- Power-distance – the degree to which people in a country accept a hierarchical or unequal distribution of power in organizations. Indonesia, for example, is considered a high power-distance culture, whereas the Netherlands is considered a relatively low power-distance culture.
- Uncertainty avoidance – the degree to which people in a country prefer structured rather than unstructured situations. France, for example, is considered a high uncertainty avoidance culture, whereas Hong Kong is considered a low uncertainty avoidance culture.
- Individualism–collectivism – the degree to which people in a country focus on working as individuals more than on working together in groups, and the extent to which they are bonded into and identify with groups. The US, for example, is identified as one of the most strongly individualistic cultures, whereas China is considered a far more collectivist culture.
- Masculinity–femininity – the degree to which people in a country emphasize so-called masculine traits, such as assertiveness, independence and insensitivity to feelings, as dominant values (note the possibly stereotypical assumptions here). Japan, for example, is characterized as a highly masculine culture whereas Denmark is considered a more feminine culture. The Netherlands and the Scandinavian countries are, for Hofstede, the only societies that can be regarded as 'feminine'.
- A further so-called fifth dimension or long-term–short-term orientation was later developed by Hofstede in conjunction with Michael Bond.[54] Prompted by the success of many Asian economies from the 1980s onwards, this dimension identified a number of values including thrift and persistence, social obligations and tradition which together made up a long-term orientation. China, for example, is high on long-term orientation, whereas the US is, within this framework, more orientated towards the short term.

Continuing research on these cultural dimensions examines how countries can be grouped into clusters sharing generally similar cultures. Scholars are interested in such cluster maps as they try to determine how management practices can and do transfer across cultures. We will examine the validity of this approach termed the *etic* or comparative view of culture in Chapter 8, contrasting it with the *emic* view, which advocates deep understanding of individual cultures without recourse to comparison and categorization.

One such comparative grouping is shown in Figure 1.6. 'Anglo' countries tend to score quite low on the long-term–short-term dimension, whereas the Asian 'tigers' – Hong Kong, Singapore, South Korea and Taiwan – score quite high on this dimension. Hofstede and Bond argue that the long-term value and influence of Confucian dynamism may, at least in part, account for the surge of economic successes by these Asian nations. Chen (2004) suggests that cultural factors should also be considered when analysing economically difficult periods; for example the Asian recessions following 1997.[55]

Age

Europe's rate of population growth is falling. Italy has a fertility rate of 1.2 children per parent, which is amongst the lowest in the world. The country has also experienced high levels of unemployment in recent years. Trends also indicate the increasing age of many

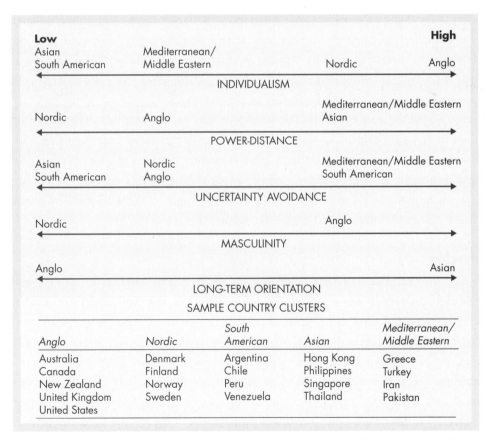

Figure 1.6: A sample of 'country clusters' based on Hofstede's five dimensions of national cultures.

populations. The percentage of over-65s was anticipated to rise from 15.4% of the EU population in 1995 to 22.4% by 2025.[56] Meanwhile Japan will have the most rapidly ageing population of any major power, and will experience an increasing shortage of labour. The ageing of the workforce has a number of important implications for organizations. These include:

- The possibility of a labour shortage – not enough workers with the right skills for the work that needs to be done.
- A loss of 'organizational memory' as the baby-boomer generation (born between 1946 and 1955) and the so-called shadow boomers (born between 1956 and 1964) reaches retirement age and leaves the workforce.
- An increasing representation of generations X (born after 1964) and Y (born after 1978) at senior levels within organizations as the baby boomer generation retires. The *modernization thesis* put forward by Ingelhart and Baker[57] suggests that the needs and preoccupations of this generation may move beyond a concern with material values to increasing 'quality of life' issues, coupled with a desire to engage with new forms of spirituality (in North America and Western Europe), while in Eastern Europe and other parts of the world we see a resurgence of traditional religious values.
- The need for new types of employment relationships to meet the needs of generations X and Y. For example, workers from generations X and Y are looking for different types of rewards for their work – they are less focused on just pay and job security. Vodafone, for example, meets this need by offering incentives such as giving workers the day off on their birthdays, allowing casual dress and giving them access to a health and wellbeing programme that includes such services as free massages.[58]
- Greater workforce mobility and less loyalty to the organization due to the different attitudes of members of generations X and Y. They expect to have a series of jobs and multiple careers over their working lives. This is in stark contrast to older generations who tended to work for one company, perhaps rising through the ranks over the years.
- The much higher levels of technical competence brought to the workplace by generation X and Y employees compared with their predecessors.

Gender

The past 40 years has been characterized by an increasing number of women entering the workforce, a breaking down of the traditional idea that some jobs are gender specific (for example, nurses are women, mechanics are men), and increasing – although for some still disappointing – numbers of women in senior positions within organizations. For example, in the Irish Republic statistics[59] showed that in 1998 only 3% of managing director posts were occupied by women in corporate Ireland. Across all categories of work organization, women constituted 8% of senior managers and 30% of middle managers. The picture is very obviously imbalanced. One of the greatest implications of increased female participation in the workforce is for organizations to learn how to manage work–family relations such as maternity leave. This will be discussed later. The increased female presence in the workforce has also influenced OB in terms of employer–employee relations.

THE CHANGING NATURE OF EMPLOYER–EMPLOYEE RELATIONS

The relationship between employers and employees is changing. There are changes in the ways that organizations view their members and in how people view employers. In many 'new' workplaces, employment is often cut and streamlined for operational efficiency, businesses have flatter and more flexible structures and the workforce is more diverse and dispersed. This is especially true of countries coming under the Anglo-Saxon model of capitalism.[60]

Globalization has significantly altered the employment relationship, creating challenges for organizations, managers and employees. Wage earners find themselves working at home for foreign employers. More senior executives are arriving at their positions with the benefit of 'overseas experience'. And more junior executives are being asked and encouraged to take on such assignments. Consequently, today's managers must be able to both 'think globally' and 'act locally' in pursuing their opportunities.

Human rights and social justice are increasingly pursued in the new workplace, just as they are in the world at large. All managers must deal with growing pressures for self-determination from people at work. Workers may increasingly want input into major decisions that have a direct effect on their working lives.[61] Many workers want more freedom to determine how and when to do their jobs. They want the benefits of increased participation accrued through workplace initiatives such as industrial democracy, job enrichment, autonomous work groups, flexible working hours and family-friendly workplaces. All of these initiatives are changing the nature of day-to-day human resource management.

To create value-adding human capital, the twenty-first-century manager must be well prepared to deal with not only the pressures outlined above but also pressures for:

- Employee rights. People in most cultural contexts expect their rights to be respected on the job as well as outside their work environment, including the rights of individual privacy, due process, free speech, free consent, freedom of conscience and freedom from sexual harassment.
- Job security. People expect their security to be protected, including security of their physical wellbeing (in terms of occupational safety and health matters, as well as economic livelihood), guaranteed protection against layoffs and provisions for cost-of-living wage increases.
- Employment opportunity. People expect – and increasingly demand – the right to employment without discrimination on the basis of age, sex, ethnic background or disabilities. Among these demands are concerns to further the modest but important gains made in recent years by women and other groups that have been marginalized in the workplace. The concept of the 'glass ceiling' has been introduced into management vocabulary to

describe the discriminatory barriers that women may face as they seek to advance their careers in organizations. Progress will be applauded, but it will not be accepted as a substitute for true equality of opportunity.

- Equity of earnings. People expect to be compensated to the same extent for the 'comparable worth' of their work contributions. The fact that certain occupations (such as nursing) have been traditionally dominated by women whereas others (such as carpentry) have been traditionally dominated by men is no longer accepted as justifying pay inequity. Equal pay for equal work, equity of rewards involving a comparison of inputs to output and other related issues such as money and motivation continue to be widely discussed topics.

We will now briefly examine a few of the major issues in the changing employment relationship.

WORK–LIFE BALANCE

Increasingly, workers are seeking balance between their work and the other aspects of their lives. Progressive organizations recognize the need to support their workforce to minimize stress levels and burnout, and to maximize work performance. Many companies recognize the increased pressures experienced in dual-income households, where both partners try to manage work and family commitments. Many companies are introducing initiatives to create a 'family-friendly workplace' to help employees better balance work and family commitments.

Workplace initiatives include work options such as job sharing, permanent part-time work and telecommuting, new leave provisions such as paid maternity and paid paternity leave, as well as supported childcare facilities.[62]

The Web site 'Where Women Want to Work' (**www.wherewomenwanttowork.com**)[63] identifies a number of specific initiatives that have been taken by business organizations in promoting work–life balance by focusing on parental responsibilities. The financial services provider HSBC offers its UK employees workplace nursery places and childcare vouchers for children up to 16 years old. This scheme is equivalent to a 6.5% pay increase for a typical clerical staff member and more for higher rate taxpayers. These vouchers can also be used to buy nursery care, nannies, au pairs, childminders and for after-school schemes and school nursery cover. Around half of the 57 000-strong HSBC's UK workforce has children under the age of 16 years. Staff can choose nursery places, childcare vouchers (or both) instead of salary. The company suggests that this improves employees' work–life balance, which benefits HSBC as well as the individual staff members.[64]

Questions

1. Summarize the business and ethical case for introducing or extending paternity leave in a country of your choice (research the actual legal position in that country first).
2. How could you explain Norway's preoccupation with this issue in the light of Hofstede's model of culture? See p. 31.

OB IN ACTION

But what about dad?

Most countries in the EU offer paid paternity leave, from two days in Spain to two weeks in France. Norway (which is not a EU member state), tops this particular list with four weeks, staking a claim to be the most family-friendly country in Europe.[65]

Norway introduced a four-week paternity quota in 1993. The provision set aside four weeks of the parental period for the father with the purpose of encouraging more fathers to take an active role in the care of children during the first year. These four weeks cannot be transferred to the mother and are lost if the father does not use them. The paternity quota may, in agreement with the employer be divided into several periods, although it must be taken within the overall benefit timescale (up to 43 weeks at full pay or up to 53 weeks at 0.8 of salary).

The percentage of eligible natural or adoptive fathers taking their paternity quota increased from 75% to 89% between 1997 and 2004, and was predicted to rise further following even more generous provisions introduced from 2005.

OUTSOURCING

As we have already seen, countries, cultures and peoples around the world are increasingly interconnected. One result is that it is increasingly possible to transfer jobs from one country to another. Job migration (the transfer of jobs from one country to another) and global outsourcing (the replacement of domestic jobs with contract workers in another country) has been an important phenomenon in recent years with a significant outflow of jobs to countries such as India, the Philippines and Russia, especially in IT-related jobs. With increasing use of virtual workspaces enabled by communications and information technology, it is easy to contract for many types of work anywhere in the world, at the lowest price. To remain competitive, organizations and workers themselves must continually change to achieve high performance.

OB IN ACTION

Outsourcing to India

India places a high value on education and many workers have one or two degrees. Through successful global marketing of its knowledge-based workforce, many companies in a variety of industries (IT, aerospace, finance, telecommunications)

are now outsourcing their work to India. Often the workers are shown video footage from the country they service; they watch local television shows via cable and partake in accent reduction courses, all in an effort to 'fit' with the culture they are servicing. One of the largest growth areas is finance. AXA Asia Pacific has its back-office functions and data entry work done in India, and part of the ANZ Bank's IT operations are also undertaken there. Organizations like GE Capital (which runs credit card operations for Coles Myer, Shell and Buyers Edge), HSBC Bank and American Express have relocated credit card fraud departments to India. This influx of new call centre jobs has proved to be very significant for India: in 1995 the Indian outsourcing sector turned over about US$100 million; by 2002 that figure had increased to US$2 billion.[66] Many companies outsource labour to developing countries, where skills are often high and labour costs are significantly cheaper. However, companies must carefully consider both internal (cost) and external (customer experience) factors when outsourcing services.

In the UK there has been a degree of negative publicity concerning call-centre operations in the Indian subcontinent and there is some evidence that the peak of the trend may be over. Powergen and Esure are returning their call centres to British locations, while a Natwest bank advertising campaign stresses that their call centres are in the UK. Some customers have failed to accept call centres that are not locally based (it is hoped this relates to actual quality of experience rather than xenophobic views), which could affect their trust in, and loyalty to, a certain brand, company or organization.

CASUALIZATION OF THE WORKFORCE

One of the key themes from the chapter so far has been that organizations and the environments in which they operate are rapidly changing. Organizations are seeking greater flexibility and adaptability to respond to these changes. Increasingly, organizations are seeking people who can adapt to changing needs. Another method of achieving this aim has been to change the composition of their workforce to consist of core workers and contingent (or peripheral) workers. The contingent workers are usually employed on a casual basis.

Casual work *is work where the number and schedule of work hours vary and there is little or no security of ongoing employment.*

Casual work is work where the number and schedule of work hours vary and there is little or no ongoing security of employment. Employing casual staff gives managers the ability to quickly increase or decrease the number of workers to meet demand but there are significant downsides for both employer and employees. For example, employees suffer a loss of job security and predictability of income; they may have less loyalty to their employer and they may be less likely to invest in new skills or knowledge that could benefit the employer. They may also not be well protected by health and safety measures. On 21 February 2004, 21 Chinese cockle pickers were drowned after being caught by the tide in Morecambe Bay in the north of England. Anyone who read transcripts of the mobile phone calls and text messages sent by some of these casualized workers as they awaited their death, cannot but be deeply moved and keen to avoid similar tragedies in future, in so far as anyone one can realistically interfere with the workings of this end of the labour market.

TELEWORKING

Teleworking means working from a location other than the organization's offices. It often refers to working from home. Teleworking has become increasingly feasible due to technology (for example, mobile phones, email) that allows easy communication with the office and co-workers. It is an increasingly widespread practice with a recent EU study[67] concluding that in Finland 16.8 % of the workforce were classified as teleworkers – the highest figure in an EU state. There are benefits to employees in terms of work–life balance (for example, saved travelling time and being able to work in their home environment), employees can become socially isolated and may miss out on opportunities for promotion and workplace interaction more generally – see Chapter 4 for a discussion of workers' 'social needs'.

Since the terrorist attack on the World Trade Center towers in New York on 11 September 2001, many companies have been reluctant to place all or most of their employees at one location. By having operations spread across different geographic locations – or even just different buildings – the risk of losing a large proportion of human, physical or intellectual resources in a terror attack or disaster such as an earthquake or fire is greatly reduced.

Telework principles relate to work conducted remotely from the central organization using information technology.

ETHICS AND VALUES

With an increasingly interconnected world, the growing representation of generation X and Y employees and employers, and a greater appreciation of the fragility of the natural environment, organizations, their members and the communities they exist within are placing more emphasis on ethical behaviour. The concepts of corporate social responsibility (that organizations have a responsibility to the societies that sustain them) and triple bottom-line reporting (that organizations need to consider society and the environment as well as their economic performance) are among the most prominent organizational responses to the increased emphasis placed on ethics and values.

Ethical behaviour is behaviour that is morally accepted as good and right, as opposed to bad or wrong, in a particular setting. Business scandals resulting in the collapse of high-profile companies such as Enron and Worldcom highlighted the importance of ethics in managerial behaviour. Today a trend is clear: there are increasing demands that government officials, managers, workers in general and the organizations they represent all act in accordance with high ethical and moral standards.

Ethical managerial behaviour is behaviour that conforms not only to legal requirements but also to broader social moral codes. Exactly what moral code governs a person's choices is a subject of debate.

Corporate social responsibility includes such things as providing employment, caring for the environment, contributing to charities and operating in a way that meets the society's needs. Corporate social responsibility for some should remain the responsibility

Ethical behaviour is behaviour that is morally accepted as 'good' and 'right' as opposed to 'bad' and 'wrong' in a particular social context.

Corporate social responsibility refers to the notion that corporations have a responsibility to the society that sustains them; and the obligation of organizations to behave in ethical and moral ways.

of individual companies, embedded in their own context, and not subject to regulation. The UK Confederation of British Industry (CBI) for example, states that corporate social responsibility should remain voluntary and market driven.[68]

An **ethical dilemma** occurs when a person must make a decision that requires a choice among competing sets of principles.

An **ethical dilemma** occurs when a person must make a decision that requires a choice among competing sets of principles. Such a situation may arise when a member of an organization decides whether to do something that could be considered unethical, but that benefits the person or the organization or both. Is it ethical, for example, to pay to obtain a business contract in a foreign country? Is it ethical to allow your company to dispose of hazardous waste in an unsafe fashion? Is it ethical to withhold information in order to discourage a good worker from taking another job? Is it ethical to conduct personal business on company time? Ethical dilemmas are common in life and at work. Research suggests that managers encounter such dilemmas in their working relationships not only with superiors and employees but also with customers, competitors, suppliers and regulators. Common issues underlying the dilemmas involve honesty in communications and contracts, gifts and entertainment, outright bribery, pricing practices and ending workers' employment; either individually or collectively.[69]

CONCLUSION

Organizational behaviour is relevant, topical and we trust will therefore be of interest to all readers. It should be possible to relate material from subsequent chapters to our own lives and our work experiences in particular. Knowledge within the field is drawn from a number of academic disciplines and researchers are very concerned to create a body of knowledge that is based on rigorous foundations, thereby rising above the commonsense level. By now you should also have an indication of why it is important for managers – and every other member of an organization – to have a good understanding of OB.

The message is clear: the successful twenty-first-century manager will have to make the behavioural and attitudinal adjustments necessary to succeed in dynamic times.

Tomorrow's managers can come from any country or culture and experience many placements and sample multiple locations in a wide ranging career. They will also increasingly be highly educated – possibly to postgraduate level – with a global focus, able to manage in both regulated and deregulated economies in an environment typified by rapid change. They would be surprised by anything more than a limited term, high-pressure appointment and their position will be results driven.

Your learning about OB may begin with this book and a module in a course as part of your formal education but it can and should continue in the future as you benefit from actual work experiences. Your most significant learning about OB may come with time as your career progresses but it will do so only if you prepare well and if you are ready to take maximum advantage of each learning opportunity that arises.

The terms 'lifelong learning' and 'recurrent learning' perhaps best conceptualize the learning and education of the future. The essence of these propositions is that education and learning should continue over the lifespan of the individual and should form part of actual work and life experiences. It is both a personal responsibility and a prerequisite for long-term career success. Day-to-day work experiences, conversations with colleagues and friends, counselling and advice from mentors, training seminars and workshops, professional reading and podcasts, and the information available in the quality press and television (also the Internet used selectively and with caution), all provide frequent opportunities for continual learning about OB. In progressive organizations, supportive policies and a commitment to extensive training and development are among the criteria for organizational excellence. The opportunities for lifelong learning and recurrent education are there; you must make the commitment to take full advantage of them at all times.

SUMMARY

LEARNING OBJECTIVE 1
Organizational behaviour defined

Organizational behaviour is the study of individuals and groups in work organizations. This body of knowledge can assist managers to interact effectively with their employees and help improve organizational performance. Effective managers need to understand the people on whom they rely for the performance of their unit. The complexity of this area can be illuminated by the performance equation, which views performance as the result of the personal and/or group attributes, the work effort they make and the organizational support they receive.

Some scholars within OB focus more on peoples' own understandings and subjective experiences of life within organizations. This approach to OB uses more qualitative research methods when studying organizations and the people who are affected by them. It stresses important differences between natural and social science and locates OB firmly within the latter category.

LEARNING OBJECTIVE 2
Why organizations exist

Organizations are collections of individuals working together to achieve a common purpose or goal. But not all people will work towards organizational goals as they may have their own agendas such as their career development. Organizations exist because individuals are limited in their physical and mental capabilities. By working together in organizations, collections of individuals are able to achieve more than any individual could by working alone. The purpose of an organization is to produce a product or to provide a service. To produce such outputs, organizations divide work into required tasks to organize the efforts of people to their best advantage. This process is termed 'division of labour'. Organizations can be portrayed as 'open systems' in that they obtain human and material inputs from their external environment, then transform these inputs into product outputs in the form of finished goods or services, which they then offer back to the external environment for consumption. If the environment values these outputs then the organization will continue to survive;

if not, then it may fail to obtain subsequent inputs for future production and it may ultimately cease to operate.

LEARNING OBJECTIVE 3
The role of people management

A manager is responsible for work that is accomplished through the performance contributions of one or more other people. The management process involves planning, organizing, leading and controlling. Managers should seek two key results for a work unit or work team: task performance, which is the quality and quantity of the work produced or the services provided by the work unit; and human resource performance, which is engendered through attraction, retention and development of a capable workforce over time. An effective manager's work unit achieves high levels of productivity and maintains itself as a capable workforce over time by keeping the psychological contract in balance. The psychological contract is based on individuals' expectations regarding what they and the organization expect to give and receive from each other as an exchange of values. In a 'healthy' psychological contract, the contributions made to the organization are believed to be in balance with the inducements received in return. The insights provided through the study of OB can help managers help others maintain healthy psychological contracts with their employers. They can also help managers to build and maintain work environments that offer their members a high quality of work–life, which is marked by participation, independence, equity and responsiveness.

LEARNING OBJECTIVE 4
Key issues affecting organizations

Globalization is the process of becoming increasingly international in perspective and interconnected with others worldwide. A managerial career in today's work environment is highly likely to bring contact with international issues and considerations (even when managers remain in their home countries). Managing to perform effectively in a globalized marketplace requires many new skills and competencies.

Changes to the nature of work are largely due to globalization, advances in technology, the growth in the services sector and, especially, an increasing reliance on knowledge to generate new products and services. These changes to the nature of work require workers and managers with new skills and abilities.

The workforce is becoming diverse: more multicultural, older, and there are more women working than ever before. Managing such a workforce requires new approaches.

Workers are seeking greater work–life balance. They are also seeking a greater variety of incentives for their work contribution. More workers expect to have a series of jobs or careers over their lifetime. Employers cannot and should not expect the same degree of loyalty as in the past. Employers are seeking a more flexible, adaptable workforce that can keep pace with the ever increasing speed of change in the marketplace. Outsourcing and the use of casual workers are among the ways organizations are responding to these needs.

Organizations are under increasing pressure to conduct themselves ethically and to acknowledge that they have a responsibility to the society that sustains them.

LEARNING OBJECTIVE 5
The need to understand OB

Learning about OB is both a personal responsibility and a prerequisite for long-term career success. The field of OB helps managers to deal with and learn from their workplace experiences. Managers who understand OB are better prepared to know what to look for in work situations, to understand what they find and to take (or help others to take) the required action.

Even if you are not in a managerial role and/or have no desire to be in one, insights gleaned from OB – and we hope from reading this book – will help you to understand your own experiences of working in and otherwise dealing with organizations. It is virtually impossible to avoid organizations!

CHAPTER 1 STUDY GUIDE

You can also test your understanding and access further resources at **www.wileyeurope. com/college/french**.

REVIEW QUESTIONS

1. What is organizational behaviour and why do managers need to understand it?
2. Identify *four* factors that accelerate organizational change. Use contemporary examples to bring your answer to life.
3. What is an effective manager? What are the competencies needed by an effective global manager?
4. What do you understand by the term 'psychological contract'? Give examples from your own life – either current or past – to show how well this concept works in explaining attitudes and behaviour.

RESEARCH QUESTIONS

1. Write a report to answer the following question. On the basis of identified changes in the business environment, how will people be managed within organizations in 2015? Include examples of both what you *expect* to occur in the period leading up to 2015 and what you would *wish* to happen. In answering this question support your arguments with material from at least one academic journal and one business publication. Please ensure your lecturer or tutor approves sources.
2. Provide a summary of the benefits of workplace diversity. In your report refer to possible negative consequences of diversity at work. Use at least three textbooks and Web site sources approved by your lecturer or tutor.

APPLICATION QUESTIONS

1. Why is human resource performance important to effective management? What negative effects on business performance may result from managers' neglect of people issues? Can managerial performance be measured using a single criterion? Explain your answer.

2. What is meant by the term 'global management'? What distinguishes it from other types of management?

3. How have developments in information technology changed the nature of the workplace and the practice of management? How do virtual organizations differ from more conventional forms?

4. Why is an understanding of cultural differences important to business? What are some steps that managers can take to develop greater cross-cultural awareness? How would you describe the culture into which you were born if you were attempting to attract foreign investment?

 RUNNING PROJECT

The running project appears at the end of each chapter in this book. By completing the exercises in the running project you will gain important insights into organizational behaviour and management in the new workplace. Each exercise requires you to collect and analyse information relating to the material discussed in that chapter.

The first step is to choose an organization to study. Remember that we will be asking you for information about a broad range of management approaches and processes at your chosen organization, so you must choose an organization for which this information is readily available. We suggest using one of the following approaches.

1. Choose a well-known company. This option means you are likely to have access to information through newspapers, magazines, the company's corporate Web site and your library's resources.

2. Better still, choose a smaller company that you can access directly. This approach has much to offer if management will agree to talk to you at length (remember that you'll need to talk to them regularly throughout your study of this book). For example, you might choose the company you work for. For this approach make sure you can secure substantial cooperation and information from your chosen company. Your lecturer/tutor may have some guidance for you before you make a decision . . . *please do not approach an organization before consulting with your academic tutor.*

3. Your instructor may provide suggestions on which company to study.

Your task for Chapter 1 is to choose the organization you will study and to obtain enough information about it to carry out the following instructions and answer the questions asked.

1. Identify the *stated* purpose or goals of the organization.
2. Draw the organization as an 'open system'. List the inputs, transformations and outputs.
3. What knowledge management processes does the organization have in place to provide feedback?
4. Describe the business environment affecting that organization both in terms of specific environment and general environment.

INDIVIDUAL ACTIVITY

Global awareness

As we noted in this chapter, the environment of business is becoming more global. The following assessment is designed to help you understand your readiness to respond to managing in a global context. You will agree with some of the following statements and disagree with others. In some cases, you may find it difficult to make a decision, but you should force a choice. Record your answers next to each statement using the following scale:

Strongly agree = 4
Somewhat disagree = 2
Somewhat agree = 3
Strongly disagree = 1

_____ 1. Although aspects of behaviour such as motivation and attitudes within organizational settings remain diverse across cultures, organizations themselves appear to be increasingly similar in terms of design and technology.

_____ 2. Spain, France, Japan, Singapore, Mexico, Brazil and Indonesia have cultures with a strong orientation towards authority.

_____ 3. Japan and Austria define male and female roles more rigidly and value qualities like forcefulness and achievement more than Norway, Sweden, Denmark and Finland.

_____ 4. Australia, the UK, the Netherlands, Canada and New Zealand have cultures that view people first as individuals and place a priority on their own interests and values, whereas Colombia, Pakistan, Taiwan, Peru, Singapore, Mexico, Greece and Hong Kong have cultures in which the good of the group or society is considered the priority.

_____ 5. The US, Israel, Austria, Denmark, Ireland, Norway, Germany and New Zealand have cultures with a low orientation towards authority.

_____ 6. The same manager may behave differently in different cultural settings.

_____ 7. Denmark, Canada, Norway, Singapore, Hong Kong and Australia have cultures in which employees tolerate a high degree of uncertainty but such levels of uncertainty are not well tolerated in Israel, Austria, Japan, Italy, Argentina, Peru, France and Belgium.

_____ 8. Societies while exhibiting national characteristics are composed of subcultures. Respond according to the 1–4 scale, also what do you understand by this term and give *two* examples.

For the interpretation of your results see page 51.

GROUP ACTIVITY

Management foundations

Objectives

1. To understand the skills and personal characteristics that are claimed to be indicators of success in the new workplace of the twenty-first century.
2. To assess your abilities in the 10 management foundations.
3. To select areas for development through planning.
4. To examine diversity within the class members' responses.

Total time: 10–20 minutes.

Step 1: Self-assessment

Rate yourself by placing a number from 1 to 7 on the line before each of the 10 management foundations to best describe how frequently you exhibit this behaviour. Be honest – you will not be asked to share your score in class.

Usually = 7
Frequently = 6
Often = 5
Sometimes = 4

Infrequently = 3

Seldom = 2

Rarely = 1

_____ 1. Resistance to stress. I get the job done under stressful conditions.

_____ 2. Tolerance for uncertainty. I get the job done under ambiguous and uncertain conditions.

_____ 3. Social objectivity. I act free of racial, ethnic, gender and other prejudices or biases.

_____ 4. Inner work standards. I personally set and work to high performance standards on my own.

_____ 5. Stamina. I work long, hard hours.

_____ 6. Adaptability. I am flexible and adapt to change.

_____ 7. Self-confidence. I am consistently decisive and display my personal presence.

_____ 8. Self-objectivity. I evaluate my personal strengths and weaknesses, and understand my motives and skills relative to tasks I need to do.

_____ 9. Introspection. I learn from experience, awareness and self-study. (I do not make the same mistake twice.)

_____10. Entrepreneurial orientation. I address problems and take advantage of opportunities for constructive change.

Finally, consider this question: 'If I asked my friends and co-workers to answer these questions for me, would they select the same frequencies that I did?' You may want to ask them to select scores for comparison.

Step 2: Best practice manager

Repeat the process of rating against the 10 management foundations but this time assess how frequently you consider a 'best practice' manager should exhibit these behaviours.

Step 3: Gap analysis

Compare your self-assessment ratings with those for the best practice manager. Identify any significant differences (greater than one point) in the two sets of ratings. Select the three management foundations in which the greatest gaps were evident when you compared the ratings.

Step 4: Self-development

Review the three management foundations with the greatest gaps (identified in Step 3). Develop some suggestions for self-improvement in each of these three areas.

Procedure

1. Discuss whether there is diversity, or whether all students selected the same foundations.

2. Beginning with those identified by the largest number of students, discuss how to improve performance against the management foundations.

3. Continue to discuss the foundations in priority order (from highest to lowest numbers identifies) until all ten are discussed, or the time runs out for the exercise.

IS HE NOT CLEAR THEN? (THE WORLD'S WORST AIRCRAFT ACCIDENT)

On 27 March 1977 the world's worst aircraft accident to date occurred in Tenerife. By supreme irony, and as if to mock those who fear flying, the accident took place on the ground, with two Boeing 747 'jumbo jets' colliding on the runway at the Canary Island's airport. The disaster killed 583 people.

The crash took place when a KLM Royal Dutch Airlines plane taking off, in the captain's mistaken belief that he had clearance to depart, crashed into a Pan American plane taxiing on the same runway. The accident took place in thick fog and the Pan American crew missed its correct turn-off from the runway, leaving them in the direct path of the other flight.

There were several technical reasons for the crash including the obscuring of a simultaneous radio call from both planes through mutual interference on the radio frequency. If either message had been heard it should have alerted the other crew to the true sequence of events and offered an escape route from the impending collision. However the underlying reasons for the crash were human and rooted in the work environment, attitudes and behaviour.

The KLM Captain, Jacob van Zanten, was returning to route flying after six months of training duties on a simulator and possibly still attuned to training conditions. He may also have been keen to take off quickly to keep within crew duty hours. At any rate he *perceived* an air traffic controller's (ATC) instructions on departure route and what to do when airborne as actual clearance to take off. There was an element of miscommunication when the KLM crew gave an ambiguous message which crash investigators subsequently heard as either 'we are at take-off' or 'we are uh taking off', (they were unable to decipher which). The ATC responded to this message with a terse 'OK' (a nonstandard term in this context). His follow-up message; 'stand by for take-off, I will call you' was never heard due to the radio interference caused by a transmission from Pan Am at that precise second. And yet there was still one final chance to avoid the crash. The Flight Engineer on the KLM plane heard the Pan Am crew's radio message that they would report when they had cleared the runway. He was heard on the cockpit voice recorder to query his captain's decision to take off asking; 'Is he not clear then?' On receiving the response 'what did you say?' from the captain, the Flight Engineer asked again 'Is he not clear, that Pan American?' However Captain Van Zanten responded decisively 'Oh yes!' and the Flight Engineer did not persist with his question as the plane continued to accelerate down the runway. Captain Van Zanten was one of the airline's most experienced pilots; he appeared on a magazine advertisement for the company and it

This case study is adapted from a number of sources. Transcripts of cockpit voice recordings were taken from Stewart, S. (1986), *Air Disasters*, Ian Allan: Shepperton.

was reported that when news of this disaster broke KLM attempted to contact him to give public statements before learning that, tragically, he was the captain of the crashed plane.

The subsequent enquiry into the crash made several conclusions that reflected the human factors underlying the disaster. A new phrase 'line up and wait' was introduced for planes ready to take off but not yet cleared. Key instructions would henceforth have to be read back, not merely acknowledged with a phrase like 'OK'. Interestingly the report also focused on hierarchical relations among air crew with a greater emphasis proposed for mutual agreement on decision making.

Question

What OB topics do you consider relevant to an explanation of the events surrounding this real-life disaster? Refer to the chapter headings in the index of this book when formulating your response.

SUGGESTED READING

Thompson, P. & McHugh, D. (2002), *Work Organizations,* 3rd edn, Palgrave Macmillan: Basingstoke. The authors provide an in-depth critical perspective on OB recommended for readers wishing to extend their study at advanced level.

Watson, T.J. (2006), *Organising and Managing Work,* 7th edn, FT Prentice Hall: Harlow. The author's approach is to focus on task and practice at work and to use concepts and theories from OB, and other academic areas in order to help make sense of them.

END NOTES

1. Unbeatable Gore marches fourth into top spot again, *Sunday Times,* 11 March 2007.
2. Ibid.
3. James, O. (2007), *Affluenza,* Vermilion: London.
4. Bolton, S. (2005), *The Sunday Times 100 Best Companies to Work For: Background, Methodology and Initial Findings for Dignity at Work,* Lancaster University, Management School Report: London.
5. Clegg, S., Kornberger, M. & Pitsis, M. (2005), *Managing and Organizations: An Introduction to Theory and Practice,* Sage: London, p. 193.
6. Bratton, J., Calliman, M., Forshaw, C. & Sawchuk, P. (2007), *Work and Organizational Behaviour,* Palgrave Macmillan: Basingstoke.
7. Mullins, L.J. (2005), *Management and Organizational Behaviour,* 7th edn, FT Prentice Hall: Harlow.
8. Knights, D. & Willmott, H. (2007), *Introducing Organizational Behaviour and Management,* Thomson: London, p. 36.
9. Mesure, S. (2006), Immigrants have boosted UK growth, *Independent,* 24 April.
10. Grey, C. (2005), *A Very Short, Fairly Interesting and Reasonably Cheap Book About Studying Organizations,* Sage: London, p. 7.
11. Lawrence, P.R. & Lorsch, J.W. (1967), *Organizations and Environment: Managing Differentiation and Integration,* Richard D. Irwin: Homewood, IL.

12. French, R. (2007), *Cross-Cultural Management in Work Organizations*, CIPD: London.

13. Muller, M. (1998), Human resource and industrial relations practices of UK and US multinationals in Germany. *International Journal of Human Resource Management*, **9** (4), 732–744.

14. Hendrick, H. (1983), Pilot performance under reversed stick conditions. *Journal of Occupational Psychology*, **56**, 297–301.

15. Ward, J. & Winstanley, D. (2006), Watching the watch: the UK fire service and its impact on sexual minorities in the workplace. *Gender, Work and Organization*, **13** (2), 193–219.

16. Goleman, D. (2000), *Working with Emotional Intelligence*, Bantam: New York.

17. Bar-On, R. (1997), *The Emotional Intelligence Inventory (EQi)*, Technical Manual, Multi Health System: Toronto.

18. Mayer, J.D. & Salovey, P. (1997), What is emotional intelligence? In *Emotional Development and Emotional Intelligence* (eds P. Salovey and D.J. Sluyter), Basic Books: New York.

19. See Watson (2006) [REF. Watson, T.J. (2006), *Organising and Managing Work*, 2nd edition, FT Prentice Hall: Harlow for an account of air cabin crews' behaviour in this regard – which included deliberately overturning coffee cups into obnoxious passengers' laps and lacing their drinks with laxative.

20. Vodafone Group, 'Vision and values', www.voda-fone.com/article/0,3029,CATEGORY_ID%253D30304%2526LANGUAGE_ID%253D0%2526CONTENT_ID%253D21016,00.html, accessed 4 October 2005.

21. Singtel, 'Company profile', http://home.singtel.com/-about_singtel/company_profile/vision_n_mission/companypro_visionmission.asp, accessed 9 March 2005.

22. Philips 'Our vision', www.philips.com/about/company/missionvisionvaluesstrategy/index.html, accessed 1 April 2007.

23. M. Wertheimer, address to the Kant Society, Berlin, 7 December 1924, reprinted in W.D. Ellis (1938), *Source Book of Gestalt Psychology*, Harcourt, Brace & Co: New York.

24. Braverman, H. (1974), *Labour and Monopoly Capital: The Degradation of Work in the Twentieth Century*, Monthly Review Press: New York.

25. A special report on European business. *The Economist*, **382**, 10 February 2007.

26. Kurosawa, S. (2005), Vulture tourists, *The Australian*, 24 October, p. 10.

27. Ibid.

28. Fish, A. & Wood, J. (1996), Cross-cultural management competence in Australian business enterprises. *Asia Pacific Journal of Human Resources*, **35** (1), 274–301.

29. Fayol, H. (1949), *General and Industrial Management*, Pitman: London.

30. Mintzberg, H. (1990), The design school: reconsidering the basic premises of strategic management. *Strategic Management Journal*, **11**, 176–195.

31. From vodafone.com.

32. Ibid.

33. Champion-Hughes, R. (2001), Totally integrated employee benefits, *Public Personnel Management*, **30**, (3); Joseph Sirgy, M., Efraty, D., Siegel, P. & Lee, D. (2001), A new measure of quality of work–life (QWL) based on need satisfaction and spill-over theories. *Social Indicators Research*, **55** (3), 241–302.

34. Ibid.

35. Rousseau, D.M. (2000), *Psychological Contract Inventory – Technical Report*, Carnegie Mellon University: Pittsburg.

36. Hammer, M. & Champy, J. (1993), *Re-engineering the Corporation*, HarperCollins: New York.

37. Schneider, S. & Barsoux, J.-L. (2003), *Managing Across Cultures*, FT Prentice Hall: Harlow.

38. Murza, M. (2005), *Ticking all the Boxes*, BBC News online, 12 December, see www.news.bbc.co.uk/1/hi/magazine/4521244.stm, accessed 8 November 2007.

39. *Belief Model for The Leadership of Anita Roddick*, www.mission-coach.co.uk/pages/belief, accessed 2 April 2007.

40. Ibid.

41. London's twenty-first century slave trade. *Time Out*, 26 March 2007.

42. Gottschalk, J. (2005), The risks associated with the business use of email. *Intellectual*

Property and Technology Law Journal, **17** (7), 16–18.

43. Eason, N. (2005), Don't send the wrong message, when email crosses borders, a faux pas could be just a click away, *Business 2.0,* **6** (7), 102; Harris, S. Uh oh. *Government Executive,* **37** (1), 66–71.

44. Organisation for Economic Cooperation and Development (1996), *The Knowledge Based Economy,* OECD: Paris.

45. Skilled migrant workers add £54bn to UK Economy. *Personnel Today,* 28 November 2006.

46. See also Workforce 2000 (1990), *Competing in a Seller's Market, Is Corporate America Prepared?* Tower Perrin/Hudson Institute: Indianapolis.

47. See Fernandez, J.P. (1991), Managing a diverse workforce. D.C Heath: Lexington, MA; O'Mara, J. (1991), *Managing Workplace 2000,* Jossey-Bass: San Francisco.

48. Department of Immigration and Multicultural and Indigenous Affairs, Productive diversity: Australia's competitive advantage, http://www.immi.gov.au/facts/07productive.htm, accessed 25 October 2005.

49. House, R.J., Javidan, M. & Dorfman, P. (2001), The Globe Project. *Applied Psychology: An International Review,* **50** (4), 489–505.

50. Rieger, F. & Wong-Rieger, D. (1985), Strategies of international airlines as influenced by industry, societal and corporate culture. *Proceedings of the Administrative Sciences Association of Canada,* **6** (8), 129–150. Hofstede, G. (1980), Motivation, leadership, and organization: do American theories apply abroad? *Organizational Dynamics,* **9** (Summer), 42–63. Adler, N. (2002), *International Dimensions of Organizational Behaviour,* 4th edn, South-Western College Publishing: Thomson Learning.

51. Maurice, M., Sorge, A. & Warner, M. Societal differences in organizing manufacturing units: a comparison of France, West Germany and Great Britain. *British Journal of Industrial Relations,* **18** (3), 318–333.

52. Hofstede, G. (2001), *Culture's Consequences,* 2nd edn, Sage: Thousand Oaks, CA.

53. Ibid.

54. Hofstede, G. & Bond, M. (1988), The Confucius connection: from culture roots to economic growth. *Organizational Dynamics,* **16** (4), 4–21.

55. Chen, M. (2004), *Asian Management Systems,* 2nd edn, Thomson: London.

56. *Europe's Ageing Workforce,* BBC News Online, 20 June 2002, www.news.bbc.co.uk/1/world/europe/2053581.stm, accessed 3 April 2007.

57. Ingelhart, R. & Baker, W. (2000), Modernization, cultural change and the persistence of traditional values. *American Sociological Review,* **65** (1), 19–51.

58. Vodafone Group, 'Working for Vodafone', www.vodafone.co.nz/aboutus/12.1.2.4_working.jsp?item=people&subitem=working, accessed 29 September 2005.

59. Report finds 'glass ceiling' obstructs women in management, http://eurofound.eu.eiro/2002./04/feature, accessed 3 April 2007.

60. Davis, E. & Lansbury, R. (1996), *Managing Together,* Longman: Sydney.

61. For a fuller analysis and some interesting cross-cultural comparisons see Needle, D. (2004), *Business in Context,* 4th edn, Thomson: London.

62. Albion, M.J. (2004), A measure of attitudes towards flexible work options. *Australian Journal of Management,* **29** (2), 275–294.

63. 'HSBC sets benchmark for staff childcare', www.wherewomenwanttowork.com/evidence/evidence 2.asp?id, accessed 5 April 2007.

64. *Engaging Employees: A Family Friendly Approach:* Employer of the Year Masterclass 2006, HSBC 20 June 2006.

65. International Labour Organisation (2006), Modern daddy: Norway's progressive policy on paternity leave, *World of Work Magazine,* no. 54.

66. Lawson, M. (2003), Making the switch from Dubbo to Delhi, *Australian Financial Review,* March, http://afr.com/specialreports/report 1/2003/03/20/FFXXYTV9DDD.html, accessed 10 March 2005; Agence France Presse (2005), India set to emerge as a major outsourcing hub for global aerospace industry, www.independent-bangladesh.com/news/feb/14/14022005bs.htm#A13, accessed 10 March 2005.

67. *Finland Leads Teleworking in Europe*, **http://netti.sak.fi.sak/englanti/atricles/teleworking.htm**, accessed 5 April 2007.

68. Confederation of British Industry position on CSR (2007), **http://cbi.org.uk/pdf/psdcsr1006.pdf**, accessed 8 November 2007.

69. Christy, R. & Brown, E. (2005), Ethics and diversity in human resource management, in *Managing and Leading People*, (eds D. Adam-Smith & C. Rayner), CIPD: London.

INTERPRETATION OF INDIVIDUAL ACTIVITY

All of the statements are true. Thus, your score should be close to 40. The closer your score is to 40, the more you understand the global context of organizational environments. The closer your score is to 10, the less you understand the global context. For development purposes you should note any particular items for which you had a low score and concentrate on improving your knowledge of those areas.

Journal Article

Extracts from:

RELOCATION DECISION-MAKING AND COUPLE RELATIONSHIPS: A QUANTITATIVE AND QUALITATIVE STUDY OF DUAL-EARNER COUPLES

Hélène Challiol and Karim Mignonac
(The full article can be found on this book's Web site: **www.wileyeurope.com/college/french.**)

SUMMARY

We present the results of two empirical studies of the relocation decision-making process of dual-earner couples. The first study is a quantitative survey of 155 management-level employees and focuses on the variables likely to moderate the influence of the spouse (partner) on the probability of accepting or turning down geographical mobility. The second complementary study is qualitative, consisting of 11 in-depth interviews of dual-earner couples; it attempts to identify the dynamics within the couple when making relocation decisions. We found that the couple's decision-making process in the face of a transfer proposition is above all a search for compromise solutions that are a function of the respective occupational and family roles within the couple as well as their expectations of how to organize their life as a couple. Copyright © 2005 John Wiley & Sons, Ltd.

INTRODUCTION

In the last two decades, corporations have become particularly concerned with the prospect of geographical mobility of employees as an instrument of flexibility and human resource management (Feldman, 2001). Paradoxically, it seems that, during this same period, employees have become increasingly reticent to accept this career strategy, despite the numerous advantages often associated with such mobility (Stroh, 1999). These findings have stimulated an impressive number of studies of the profile of the potentially mobile employee, by examining a wide range of individual and situational determinants of the willingness to relocate .... Most of the research on this issue sought primarily to better understand employees' expectations of different scenarios of geographical mobility, so that the corporation might use these results to propose relocation offers to those who are most mobile and/or develop programs to convince the more reticent. Up to now, however, the results fall far short of the effort deployed in studying this phenomenon. As Stroh (1999) pointed out, the significance of personal and career-related variables on an employee's willingness to move has generated somewhat inconclusive and at times contradictory results ....

The attitude of the spouse (or partner[1]) is one of the few explanatory factors found to be relatively constant, both in the direction and the significance of the results, across different

---

[1]We use the two terms, 'spouse' and 'partner' interchangeably throughout this article: *spouse* does not necessarily imply 'married,' nor *partner* that the couple is not formally married.

Reproduced with permission from the *Journal of Organizitional Behaviour*, **26**: 247–274(2005), © John Wiley & Sons, Ltd.

studies of relocation decision-making. Studies converge to show that the partner's own willingness to be mobile has a definite influence on the employee him or herself, whether the mobility is within the same country or involves moving to another country .... This finding, however interesting it may be, raises a number of other questions that researchers need to examine if we want to advance our understanding of the different dimensions of relocation decisions. For instance, we should be asking: Do male partners who object to relocation have a stronger influence on the decision than female partners? What are the most significant factors in determining whether a couple is willing or unwilling to accept a transfer to advance the male partner's career? How does the perception of gender roles within the couple influence the decision? How is the decision influenced by the overall income level of the husband or of the family as a whole? How much is the wife committed to her career and her employer? (Stroh, 1999, research questions 3 and 5). In addition, it would be worth studying the reciprocal relationships between the employee and his or her partner. This would greatly increase our understanding of career choices in general, and, more specifically, decisions about whether or not to accept a proposition of geographical mobility .... From this perspective, dual-earner couples are a particularly interesting object of study since their frequency is increasing relative to traditional couples (i.e., where the husband is the sole earner) and the career strategies and transitions of one member of the couple invariably affect the other partner, making career management by employers an even more sensitive issue ....

Our objective in this article is to gain a better understanding of the complex process of relocation decision-making by employees in dual-earner couples. To do this, we undertook two empirical studies with two independent samples of French management-level employees. The first study was quantitative and sought to establish whether the spouse's attitude toward mobility unconditionally influenced the employee's likelihood of accepting a relocation opportunity or whether it varied in function of various factors which we identify in a review of the research literature. The second study adopted a qualitative research design and complemented the first by providing a perspective on the initial results and attempting to isolate the dynamics of relocation decision-making within couples.

ORGANIZATIONAL CONTEXT

Both studies were conducted in France between 1999 and 2000. As for the socio-demographic characteristics of the French population, France has experienced many of the same fundamental changes in family living arrangements and employment patterns (i.e., increase in non-traditional living arrangements and the employment of women) as other countries at or near the same stage of economic development (Martin & Kats, 2003). Professional career paths in France, and more particularly those of management-level employees, have not changed radically, despite changes in objective career paths and the evolution of individual aspirations related to careers (Dany, 2003). France is a country where much is expected from its institutions, and behaviour remains prudent and, indeed, more 'obedient' than the new career literature suggests (e.g., boundaryless career theory). The generalizability of our results should therefore be tempered in the light of these various elements.

STUDY 1: AN EMPIRICAL TEST OF THE MODERATORS OF THE SPOUSE'S INFLUENCE ON THE EMPLOYEE'S RELOCATION DECISION

In adopting a hypothetical–deductive approach and a quantitative research design, this first study is in line with the majority of studies on relocation decision-making. However, this study focuses more directly on dual-earner couples and extends the field of investigation by attempting to identify the factors likely to moderate the influence of the spouse's willingness to move on the employee's likelihood of accepting a relocation opportunity.

Hypothesis 1a: The smaller the relative contribution of the partner to household income, the weaker the relationship between the partner's willingness to relocate and the employee's likelihood of accepting a relocation proposition.

Hypothesis 1b: The lower the job alternatives for the spouse, the stronger the relationship between the spouse's willingness to relocate and the employee's likelihood of accepting a relocation proposition.

Hypothesis 2a: The relationship between the partner's willingness to relocate and the employee's likelihood of accepting a relocation proposition is stronger when the partner is male rather than female.

Hypothesis 2b: The greater the partner's relative career priority, the weaker the relationship between the partner's willingness to relocate and the employee's likelihood of accepting a relocation proposition.

Hypothesis 3: The better the marital quality, the stronger the relationship between the partner's willingness to relocate and the employee's likelihood of accepting a relocation proposition.

METHOD

Participants and procedure

A total of 415 surveys and pre-stamped envelopes for sending back the replies were mailed to a randomly selected sample of French-speaking business graduates from a large university in southern France. Survey packages were sent directly to the prospective participants' private addresses, which were obtained from alumni directories. A cover letter accompanying the questionnaire explained the objective of the study and assured respondents of the confidentiality of any information they would provide. As an incentive for participation, informants were offered a copy of the study findings in exchange for returning their questionnaire. Surveys with usable data were returned by 240 respondents (57.8 per cent). After excluding returns from respondents living alone or in 'traditional' couples (in which the partner does not work), 155 completed questionnaires were retained for analyses.

The final sample of subjects averaged 36 years of age of whom 45.5 per cent were working in the southwestern region of France, 17.6 per cent in the east-central region and 24.9 per cent in Paris or its surrounding region. The great majority (93 per cent) were full-time employees, of whom 83.8 per cent were working in the private sector. They were employed in a variety of occupational fields, including finance/accounting/banking (31 per cent), marketing/sales (22 per cent), consulting/R&D/ IS (13 per cent), human resources/personnel (13 per cent), engineering/production (12 per cent), and administration (9 per cent). 43.5 per cent of the respondents indicated they had a mobility clause in their hiring contract.[2] Among participants, 50.4 per cent were female and 64.5 per cent were married—the others living in variously labeled conjugal arrangements ('divorced, living with a partner,' 'living together,' 'single, living with a partner,' etc.). 33 per cent of respondents had no children living at home or in close proximity, 27.5 per cent had one child, and 39.5 per cent had two or more children. 45.8 per cent had completed their bachelor's degree, 52.2 per cent a master's degree, and 2 per cent held a doctorate.

As for the partners, 56 per cent were salaried employees in private corporations, 24 per cent were government employees (including teachers), and 20 per cent were working in a profession (doctors, lawyers, psychologists, etc.); 77.2 per cent of partners were working full-time, and all possessed at least 2 years of post-secondary education.

Measures

Because the study was conducted in a French-speaking environment, all measures initially developed in English were taken from previous published studies that had used French translations of the scales, following a standard back-translation procedure. For each of the variables, a 7-point Likert-type scale was used to measure respondents' level of agreement or disagreement with each statement.

The dependent variable

Most of the research on relocation decision-making has used *willingness to relocate* as the dependent variable and has been based on the theory of reasoned action (Ajzen & Fishbein, 1980) or, its extension, the theory of planned behaviour (Ajzen, 1991). Since Brett and Reilly (1988) found a correlation of 0.32 ($p < 0.01$) between willingness to relocate (intent) and whether an employee had accepted a job transfer decision over a 5-year period (behaviour), this interpretative model has become the norm in this field of research .... We similarly used in our first, quantitative study a substitute variable for the actual decision to relocate. Following Stilwell et al. (1998), we used the variable *likelihood of accepting a transfer* (estimation) instead of *willingness to relocate* (intention). Sheppard, Hartwick, and

---

[2]The inclusion of geographical mobility clauses in labour contracts is becoming more and more commonplace in France and acceptance of the clause a condition of being hired. The employee whose contract contains such a clause cannot, in principle, refuse a change in work location. By refusing a transfer to the new work location, the employee will in principle be committing a breach of contract unless it can be shown that the employer has not been acting in the company's interests or has not given the employees sufficient prior notice to arrange their affairs.

Warshaw (1988, p. 327) underscored that 'although the responses to intention and estimation questions often involve similar considerations and are quite similar, there clearly are times where what one intends to do and what one actually expects to do are quite different.' We can therefore envisage that an employee does not have an initial intention to be mobile yet considers that it is probable that he will accept a mobility proposal (e.g., because of strong pressure by the employer, or for fear of losing one's job if it is refused). We can also envisage an employee indicating willingness to be mobile but finally judging that the probability of accepting this mobility is low because of different constraints, independent of the employee's own desires (e.g., the probable refusal of the spouse or the children to follow). Finally, Sheppard et al. (1988) suggest that a measure of behavioural probability is in itself better at predicting actual behaviour than a measure of willingness, since it takes all these factors just mentioned into account. In consequence of this, we followed this latter line of argument and operationalized *likelihood of accepting a transfer* by asking the following question: 'How likely are you to accept a transfer to a new geograph ic location?' (1 = very unlikely; 7 = very likely).

Moderators and independent variables

Marital quality. Marital quality was measured with a 7-item scale ($\alpha = 0.79$), adapted from Brett and Stroh (1995) and Ribbens (unpublished, 1994). Respondents were asked to indicate the frequency with which seven events occurred within their couple (planning for the future, quarrelling, confiding in each other, believing that things were going well between the two partners, regretting have committed oneself to one's partner, spending leisure time together, envisaging divorce or separation).

Perceived job alternatives for the spouse. We used five items adapted from the scale developed by Rusbult, Farrell, Rogers, and Mainous (1988) to assess the spouse's perceived ease of attaining other comparable or better opportunities by relocating (e.g., 'Would your partner be sure of finding work that would satisfy him (her) if he (she) was forced to quit his (her) work?' ($\alpha = 0.85$).

Spouse's career priority. The spouse's career priority was measured with one item developed specifically for this study: 'How would you characterize the priority of your partner's career in your couple?' (1 = My own career has priority over that of my partner; 7 = My partner's career has priority over my own career).

Spouse's willingness to relocate. One item was used to assess spouse's willingness to relocate: 'To what extent would your partner be willing to follow you if you had a proposition to relocate?' (1 = very very unwilling; 7 = very willing).

Employee's relative contribution to household income. The percentage of household income was estimated with the following question: 'What is your own contribution to the annual revenues (salary and other sources of revenue) as a proportion of all household revenue?'

Control variables

The following were used as control variables: age, job tenure, organizational tenure, number of years living in the same community, number of children at home, number of prior moves, contractual mobility clause.

In order to differentiate between the influence of the employee's willingness and that of the partner, a four-item scale developed specifically for this study was used ($\alpha = 0.75$): 'If you were alone, to what extent would you be willing to accept relocation under each of the following conditions: (a) for a better job in the same organization, (b) for the same job in the same organization, (c) for a better job in another organization, (d) for the same job in another organization?' (1 = very unwilling; 7 = very very willing).

RESULTS

Table 1 reports the means, standard deviations, and correlations between the variables in our study. The likelihood of accepting a transfer was found to be positively correlated to the employee's willingness to move, perceived job alternatives for the spouse, and spouse's willingness to move; likelihood of accepting a transfer was negatively correlated with gender, the career priority of the spouse, length of residence in current location, and job tenure.

Table 2 provides the results of the moderated hierarchical multiple regressions. As can be seen in Table 2, control variables (step 1) accounted for 17.9 per cent of the variance in predicting employee *likelihood of accepting a transfer*. With the exception of *employee willingness to move* ($\beta = 0.348$; $p < 0.001$), none of these variables was found to be significant. Step 2 explained a unique and significant additional 33 per cent of the variance in the equation. *Spouse's willingness to move* was found to be the strongest predictor ($\beta = 0.532$; $p < 0.001$), followed by *spouse's career priority* ($\beta = -0.201$; $p < 0.05$), and *perceived job alternatives for the spouse* ($\beta = 0.155$; $p < 0.05$) whereas *gender, employee's relative contribution to household income*, and *marital quality* were not significantly linked to employee likelihood of accepting a transfer. The addition of the interaction terms (step 3) explained a significant level of variance beyond that accounted by the other variables (R^2 change 6.1 = per cent; $p < 0.01$). Only the cross-product *spouse's career priority × spouse's willingness to move* was found to be significant. Thus, Hypothesis 2b was supported, while Hypotheses 2a, 1a, 1b, and 3e were not.

In order to clarify the nature of this interaction and its impact over the employee's relocation decision, the sample was divided into three groups. Group 1 consisted of employees who considered that their own career was more important than that of their partner ($n = 61$), Group 2 were those who considered their spouse's career as at least equally important as their own, ($n = 69$), and Group 3 were those who gave greater priority to their spouse's career than to their own ($n = 25$). The dependent variable was then regressed on scores of *the spouse's willingness to relocate* within each group. The resulting regression lines are depicted in Figure 1, which shows that employees with lower career priorities for themselves were less likely to relocate as the spouse's willingness to relocate decreased.

	Mean	SD	1	2	3	4	5	6	7	8	9	10	11	12	13	14
1. Age	35.97	6.16														
2. Gender[a]	1.36	0.48	−0.11													
3. Community tenure	13.00	12.27	0.34**	0.07												
4. Employee's contribution to household income	55.74	15.04	0.22**	−0.56**	0.01											
5. Number of children living at home	0.94	0.97	0.33**	−0.08	0.25**	0.02										
6. Organizational tenure	5.38	4.69	0.50**	−0.06	0.24**	0.20*	0.24**									
7. Job tenure	2.62	2.75	0.39**	−0.04	0.31**	0.02	0.06	0.40**								
8. Number of prior moves	2.22	2.32	0.38**	−0.05	−0.24**	0.13	0.13	0.14	−0.02							
9. Marital quality	5.70	0.83	0.03	0.21**	0.01	−0.25**	0.11	0.01	0.03	0.03						
10. Percieved job alternatives for the spouse	4.54	1.31	−0.08	0.02	−0.01	−0.12	0.02	0.05	−0.06	−0.02	0.10					
11. Spouse's career priority	4.41	1.31	−0.10	0.52**	0.04	−0.57**	0.03	−0.11	0.01	−0.07	0.18	0.12				
12. Contractual mobility clause	0.50	0.54	−0.03	−0.30**	−0.04	0.24**	−0.03	−0.02	−0.08	−0.08	−0.07	−0.13	−0.20*			
13. Spouse's willingness to move	4.36	1.65	−0.13	−0.24**	−0.08	0.03	−0.01	0.01	0.08	−0.09	0.16*	0.22**	−0.14	0.02		
14. Employee's willingness to move	5.05	1.37	−0.14	0.00	−0.17*	0.01	−0.11	−0.01	−0.14	0.14	−0.12	0.01	−0.08	0.12	0.25**	
15. Likelihood of accepting a transfer	4.40	1.47	−0.07	−0.23**	−0.21*	0.05	−0.05	−0.07	−0.17*	0.12	−0.04	0.17*	−0.26**	0.15	0.48**	0.36**

*$p < 0.05$; **$p < 0.01$.

[a]Coding: 0 = male; 1 = female.

$N = 153$–155 due to missing data.

Table 1: Means, standard deviations, and correlations between the variables.

	β	ΔR^2
Step 1: Control variables		
Age	0.043	
Community tenure	−0.131	
Number of children living at home	0.010	
Organizational tenure	−0.051	
Job tenure	−0.092	
Number of prior moves	0.012	
Contractual mobility clause[a]	0.033	
Employee willingness to relocate	0.348***	
R^2 change		0.179**
Step 2: Main effects		
Gender[b] (a)	−0.010	
Employee's contribution to household income (b)	−0.129	
Spouse's career priority (c)	−0.201*	
Perceived job alternatives for the spouse (d)	0.155*	
Marital quality (e)	−0.122	
Spouse's willingness to relocate (f)	0.532***	
R^2 change		0.330***
Step 3: Interaction terms		
a × f	0.212	
b × f	−0.070	
c × f	0.195**	
d × f	−0.039	
e × f	0.013	
R^2 change		0.061**
Total adj. R^2		0.505

*$p < 0.05$; **$p < 0.01$; ***$p < 0.001$.
Coefficients are standardized betas.
[a]Coding: 0 = no; 1 = yes; [b]Coding: 0 = male; 1 = female.
N = 149–155 due to missing data.

Table 2: Hierarchical regressions predicting employee decision to relocate.

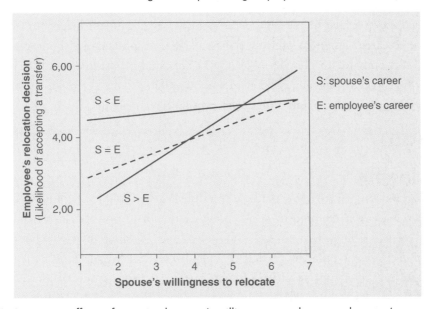

Figure 1: Interactive effects of perceived spouse's willingness to relocate and spouse's career priority on employee's decision to relocate.

Study 1: summary of results

Firstly, the results of this first study confirm the findings of previous research which identified the spouse's willingness to be geographically mobile as an essential variable intervening in the transfer decision by the employee .... Our results are also consistent with other research showing a direct effect of the spouse's career priority ... on the employee's transfer decision. Confirming the results of other studies, we also found a non-significant direct influence of gender ..., proportion of family revenue contributed by the employee ..., and marital quality ....

Our results also suggest that, among the variables studied, only the priority given to the careers of each member of the couple moderated the relationship between the willingness of the spouse to be mobile and the probability of accepting a transfer. In view of these results, we can hypothesize that the final decision by an employee in a dual-earner couple to accept (or reject) relocation could also be interpreted as the consequence of two elements: each member of the couple's willingness towards relocation, and, on the other hand, arriving at a compromise, relative to the weight assigned to the career priority of each member of the couple.

While this quantitative study certainly provided interesting results, these need to be interpreted cautiously. Given the limitations of the research protocol (see 'General Discussion' below), we cannot rule out the possibility that some of the relationships (or lack of relationships) are attributable to methodological artifacts. Moreover, the static nature of this research limits our insight into the dynamic nature of decision-making. We therefore decided to undertake a second study, to confirm, complement, and extend our understanding of relocation decision-making by dual-earner couples.

Study 2: qualitative investigation of the dynamics of couples' relocation decision-making

This second study is one of the few in the field of organizational behaviour adopting a qualitative research design to address the issue of decision-making about geographical mobility .... Compared to our survey (Study 1), this study constituted both triangulation across methods (i.e., reconciling qualitative and quantitative data ...) and complementarity (i.e., examining overlapping and different facets of a phenomenon ...).

METHOD

Participants

The population targeted by this study was double-earner couples within which one of the partners had been required to decide whether or not to accept relocation. With this in mind, we felt it important to seek out individuals of different ages who had made relocation decisions at different periods of their lives. This would allow us to take into account the impact of varying characteristics of the family situation on the distribution of roles between partners within a couple, as well as changes over time in gender role norms.

We should recognize, however, that studying the decision-making processes within a couple raises numerous methodological problems, which have already been described by researchers in the field of marketing, where the context of family consumer behaviour has been a focus of attention .... These problems result mainly from substantial differences between families. No research design, however rigorous, can control all the characteristics likely to influence behaviours within a family unit. Moreover, family decision-making occurs within an intimate, private social group, hard to observe and in which the researcher may find strong reticence to self-disclosure.

Given the purpose of this phase of our research and the problems we have just mentioned, we used a snowball sampling technique to identify participants. We diversified as much as possible the origin of the different circuits we used (circle of friends, professional contacts, those living in the same neighborhood) in order to ensure a broad spectrum of demographic and professional characteristics. Each of three initial interviewees from one of the sources just mentioned was asked to identify one or several other couples according to the following criteria: the person had to be a member of a dual-earner couple, having, on at least one occasion during the time they lived as couple, received a proposition to relocate, which may or may not have been accepted. We did not fix in advance the number of respondents to be interviewed; this was determined as a result of the richness and quality of data gathered during each interview. We decided to continue with these interviews until we believed we had reached the 'saturation' point ..., that is, little new or relevant information was retrieved from the latter interviews.

A total of 11 couples were formally interviewed. It should be noted that this sample was independent of the sample used in Study 1. During the course of these interviews, we identified 31 relocation decisions. Table 3 presents the ages and occupational status of each member of the 11 couples as well as the family situation in each case at the time of the interview. The initial of the first name of each partner is provided in Table 3 to help locate the couples in the sections that follow. Finally, the time between the different relocation decisions and the date of the interviews is given, in order to get a better idea of any *a posteriori* rationalization bias likely to have influenced the information we obtained in the interviews.

FINDINGS

Types of geographical mobility

In order to characterize relocation decision-making at the level of the couple, we judged it necessary to take account of: (1) the initial conjugal situation (living in the same accommodation or living in separate locations); (2) changes each partner decided to make about their place of work and place of residence; and (3) the conjugal situation after the decision-making process was completed. We should note that in the great majority of cases it was the male partner who was the decision initiator, with their female partner in the role of 'follower' (25 out of 31 decisions). This confirms results frequently reported in the literature ....

Initial and age of each member of the couple	Professional situation of each member of the couple	Couple's family situation	Time between relocation decision and interview
Her: B, (44) Him: S, (53) Couple code: B&S	Her: Regional correspondent for national daily paper Him: Manager, training center	Married, 2 children (aged 5 and 8) living at home + husband: 2 children (aged 20 and 22)	D1: 10 years; D2: 8 years; D3: 6 years; D4: 3 years; D5: 1 year
Her: A, (45) Him: B, (48) Couple code: A&B	Her: Magistrate Him: Air-traffic controller	Married, 3 children (the youngest 5 years old) living at home	D1: 8 years D2: several offers in last 8 years
Her: S, (35) Him: N, (36) Couple code: S&N	Her: Teacher Him: Supervisor in charge of ship repair yard	Married, 2 children (aged 2.5 and 5) living at home	D1: 6 years; D2: 1.5 years
Her: N, (32) Him: JP, (35) Couple code: N&JP	Her: Senior bank employee Him: Director, chartering office	Married, 2 children (aged 2.5 and 5) living at home	D1: 10 months
Her: V, (32) Him: S, (31) Couple code: V&S	Her: Director running human resources in a factory Him: Research engineer	Married, 1 child (aged 3 months)	D1: 4 years; D2: 2 years D3: 2 years; D4: 2 months
Her: P, (50) Him: J, (52) Couple code: P&J	Her: Professional consultant Him: Teacher	Married, 2 children (aged 19 and 23), one of whom is living at home	D1: 25 years; D2: 9 years
Her: F, (35) Him: G, (40) Couple code: F&G	Her: Teacher Him: Production director	Married, 3 children (aged 1.5, 4.5, and 9) living at home	D1: 11 years; D2: 2 years; D3: 1.5 years
Her: F, (57) Him: A, (58) Couple code: F&A	Her: Family-guidance counsellor and adult educator Him: Director, Training Center	Married, 2 children (aged 29 living separately and another deceased at age 14)	D1: 31 years; D2: 27 years; D3: 23 years
Her: I, (31) Him: P, (30) Couple code: I&P	Her: Counselling officer, human resources Him: Strategic counselling officer	Living as a couple, without children	D1: 7 years; D2: 5 years; D3: 2 years; D4: 10 months
Her: F, (55) Him: D, (56) Couple code: F&D	Her: Magistrate Him: Manager, sales department	Married, 3 children (aged 21, 24, and 27) living separately	D1: 27 years; D2: 20 years; D3: 15 years
Her: N (38) Him: F (40) Couple code: N&F	Her: Officer in charge of foreign sales Him: Human resources officer	Married, 2 children (aged 3 and 5) living at home	D1: 5 years; D2: 2 years

Table 3: Study 2: sample characteristics.

Analysis of the 31 decisions about which we obtained data allowed us to develop different scenarios (see Table 4):

- *Scenario 1* refers to relocation decisions as they have classically been conceived in the literature. Both members of the couple decided to change their place of work and place of residence and found themselves living together under the same roof in another geographical location after making the decision.
- *Scenario 2* represents decisions by one member of the couple to change both his or her place of work and of residence, while the partner only changed his or her place of

	Initial situation	Employee	Spouse	Situation finale	Couples included in this category[a]
Scenario 1 (13)[a]	Living together or in separate accommodation	Change of workplace and place of residence	Change of workplace and place of residence	Live together in another geographical location	B&S (2), S&N (1), N&JP (1) A&B (1), P&J (2), I&P (2), F&D (1), A&F (2), N&F (1)
Scenario 2 (8)	Living together	Change of workplace and place of residence	Does not change workplace but changes place of residence	Live together in another geographical location	B&S (1), S&N (1),V&S (2), F&G (3), F&D (1)
Scenario 3 (2)	Living together	Change of workplace and place of residence	Does not change workplace or place of residence	Continue to live in separate accommodation	B&S (1), I&P (1)
Scenario 4 (6)	Living together or in separate accommodation	Refusal to change of workplace and place of residence	Does not change workplace or place of residence	No change from original situation	B&S (1), V&S (2), A&B (1), A&F (1), N&F (1)
Scenario 5 (1)	Living together	Change of workplace but not place of residence	Does not change workplace or place of residence	Live together in the original location	F&D (1)
Scenario 6 (1)	Living in separate accommodation	Change of workplace and place of residence	Does not change workplace or place of residence	Continue to live in separate accommodation	I&P (1)

[a]The figures in parentheses correspond to the number of decisions made per couple concerning relocation.

Table 4: Types and number of decisions made by couples.

residence. This type of decision occurred either when one partner agreed to be relocated and the partner moved as well, rearranging her or his life to maintain the job held before their spouse's relocation, or the partner accepted the geographical move to be closer to the workplace of the partner.

- *Scenario 3* describes the situation in which one member of the couple decided to relocate, while the other did not follow. This meant the 'follower' either maintained the initial living arrangement and place of work or modified either the place of work or residence without, however, following their partner. The couple in this case changed from living together to living in separate locations.
- *Scenario 4* incorporated decisions to refuse a job opportunity that would require relocation. Whatever the initial situation of the couple (living together or separately) the decision-making process induced no change.
- *Scenario 5* concerns the decision to accept a change in the geographical location of work without thereby putting into question the life in common of the couple and the spouse's job. The employee accepted the relocation offer but did not move away from home, in this case travelling between the home and the workplace. The initial situation of the couple living together was therefore maintained.
- *Scenario 6* refers to the situation in which the two members of the couple are initially living separately and continue to do so after the relocation. One member of the couple accepted a geographical transfer without it being possible for the couple to live together in this new location. So here the decision did not require any change in the living arrangements of the two partners (maintaining separate accommodation) or in the spouse's work.

Analyzing relocation decisions on the basis of the couple's priorities

We proceeded to examine more closely the cases of attitude divergence between the partners (16 decisions) in order to understand how this divergence led in some cases to acceptance, in others to refusal, of the relocation proposition.

How attitude divergence between the partners was resolved was closely related to the way the partners reconciled their respective professional and family roles. Attitude divergence led the partners into a process of decision-making and of negotiation to arrive at a common decision. The time factor played a key role in this process. To reach the decision, the partners had to search out information and this led to putting into question their priorities. We found that the partners' attitudes were not entirely rigid and evolved throughout the time spent making the decision. These changes in attitudes resulted from the partners' evaluation of the potential solutions to resolve their attitude divergences. So, for example, if the 'follower' found a professional solution to accompany the spouse in her or his relocation, then his or her attitude towards the move would change. Consequently, the employee's attitude would evolve since the consequences of the relocation for the partner would no longer be evaluated in the same way.

We see therefore that, in the course of decision-making, the partners questioned their initial attitudes as a function of their priorities and the solutions that they developed when faced with deciding about relocation. We found that the partners' decision not only depended on the priority assigned to the career of each member of the couple, but also on the priority given to their family life and, more specifically, given to living together.

When attitude divergences arose between the partners, there were three priority systems available to understand the decision that was made.

(1) Relocation was accepted when the partners gave priority to the employee's career and their family life rather than giving priority to the career of the partner–follower (nine decisions)

In resolving their differences, some couples gave priority both to the employee to whom relocation was proposed and to their family life. From our analysis of the interviews, we see that in making the relocation decision priority could be given to the employee in two ways:

- *1st case.* The spouse's occupational status was precarious and changing the place of work would not make her or his work situation worse; it might even have improved it.
- *2nd case.* The partner might rearrange her or his working conditions and thereby maintain her or his professional situation, while at the same time changing the place of residence. This compromise was found in 5 of the 16 cases of divergence in our interviews. But the reorganization of working conditions of the partner was only possible when the new place of residence of the couple was not far away from the partner's place of work or when there were good transportation links and/or good communication links.

B: *'So we took a house half-way between and since I was then closer to* [the city from which he had been transferred] *I started living a different way, I was still working full-time, but I was supposed to be working at home 1 or 2 days a week in* [the city of origin], *no more than that because meantime I had my daughter.' (B&S 2)*

It is worth noting in this second case that the followers often justified the reorganization of their working conditions by their wish to give priority to their partner's career or to enable them to get out of an unsatisfactory working situation themselves.

V: *'One of the reasons I accepted the move is because I started working 2 years before S. In fact, when it came up, I'd already been working at* [name of the company] *where I'd carved out my place, I was known there, I felt good there. My job was going well, and so I wasn't thrilled with the idea of a lot of travelling, but to go and live in the countryside why not? And S, he had to go for it.' (V&S 1)*

In making these decisions, living together became essential to maintain the quality of the relationship between the couple as well as the life of the family.

F: 'I figure that if you don't live together, you're not a family. For me, the idea of geographical celibacy, I don't know how to do it and, what's more I don't want to. You know, we want to live as a family, we like being together, in any case, that's how we've set our priorities… I said to myself that if he ever goes to live in [the city to which he was to be relocated], even if it's long way away, and I've got to look after the house—well, I'm soon going to be free, him also, and then, well… we've only got the kids to hold us together. I find all that very dangerous, because a couple is very fragile and I don't want to get into taking these risks. And all that was part of my decision to go and live in [the city of destination].' (F&G 2)

In some cases, the transfer was also perceived as a way of improving marital life. So, as we found in one couple (S&N 1), the partner agreed to follow the employee despite the unattractiveness of the place that was being proposed, first because he refused the idea of living separately, and then because there was a possibility of keeping his job and changing his working conditions. Finally, the possibility for the spouse of having more time to devote to married life by accepting the transfer reinforced his attitude.

This type of decision is therefore based on a compromise which allows the employee to accept the proposed relocation, while minimizing its impact on the partner's career, and still allows them to live together.

(2) The transfer was accepted when both members of the couple gave higher priority to their professional lives than their family life (four decisions)

In certain cases, the employee accepts the transfer without the spouse's agreement. This type of decision occurred when the partners judged the impact of the relocation on their family life and their relationship as a couple was less important than the consequences of refusing to relocate would be for the employee and the consequences of agreeing to follow the partner being relocated would be for the spouse.

I: 'We told ourselves: OK, so we're separated but it wasn't clear how that could change our relationship. So it seemed we had to have jobs in the same place where we had both just graduated. It seemed right to maintain our balance, right then, so there wouldn't be any frustration.' (I&P 2)

Sometimes, but not always, this decision led the partners to live in separate accommodation. It could also lead to the employee traveling between his or her place of residence and the new place of work. This type of compromise allows couples to minimize the impact of the relocation on the two partners but often challenges their life together as a couple. This result tends to show that, beyond the quality of the marital relation, it would be appropriate in future research also to include the priority that the partners accord to living together as well.

(3) The relocation was rejected since the partners refused to give priority to one member of the couple over the career of the other and to put into question their family life (three decisions)

Relocation was refused if its consequences were considered as negative by the couple because, firstly, they considered it would put into question the follower's career and secondly, the follower refused to accompany the husband to the place of destination—or, at least, had a negative attitude to such a prospect. They believed that this would create a situation which would fall far short of their expectations of their life together as a couple and as a family. Then the decision adopted was, for the couples in our study, to refuse the offer, regardless of its potential benefits.

> V: 'S is more specialized than I am, so it was harder for him to find a job than for me. And also his looking for a job was taking longer than expected. I was under pressure, on my side, they wanted me to accept the post fast, they even wanted me to cut short my maternity leave. So, from the time S didn't have anything, and my company wasn't helping him, and was pressurizing us to decide, me, I said no.' (V&S 4)
>
> S: 'There was nothing wrong with it but despite that B said: "You can do what you want—if you want to go then off we go, but I'd prefer to stay in [the city of departure], only because of my job." She'd looked for work for me at [the city of destination] and there was nothing. Obviously, if I said "Let's go to [the city of destination]" we would get into a sort of power struggle, crabs clawing at each other there [the city of destination] with B getting depressed—or else we'd stay here, which after all wasn't too bad. But we've always tried to do things by consensus.' (B&S 5)

This type of decision therefore stemmed from the couple's inability to find a compromise which satisfied their respective expectations for their professional lives and their marital relations. Interestingly, one can note that maintaining the quality of the marital relationship took priority in this type of decision. This result is consistent with the analysis in terms of social exchange which posits that, in decision-making, the desire to maintain a satisfactory relationship with one's partner can be at least as important as satisfying one's own interests.

Summary of the results of Study 2

Our analysis demonstrates the complexity of the relocation decision in dual-earner couples. Just taking account of the respective attitudes of each partner toward the proposition of geographical mobility does not allow for a realistic prediction of the final decision. Even if the employee's negative attitude led to a rejection of the proposition in the cases we studied, this was not invariably the case for the partner. Despite a negative or mitigated attitude by the spouse the offer was nevertheless accepted in the majority of cases (in 13 out of 16 cases). So the influence of the spouse on the employee's final decision becomes, in the end, relative, as had been suggested in our first quantitative study.

This analysis in terms of the couple's priorities therefore provides elements of explanation of the relocation decisions when their attitudes diverge. We found that, beyond the career priorities of each member of the couple, the priority given to family life played a decisive role. Depending on the couple's priorities at the time of making the decision, attitude divergences between the partners were resolved by making different decisions. So we found that, for a transfer to be accepted, both partners had to find a solution that satisfied the priorities of both of them. While recognizing that some couples gave priority to their careers relative to their life as a family, others put the family before their professional lives. Where divergence arose, the partners sought a compromise that best satisfied the couple's priorities even if that might lead to one member of the couple accepting a decision that did not correspond to her or his initial attitude to relocation. This result calls for more attention to the values which underlie the exchange system between the partners—as proposed, moreover, by social exchange theory. If the economic or socio-cultural elements, particularly in terms of gender roles, may play a part in the partners' decision-making process, it is in fact the importance that the partners assign to these different elements which seems to be determinant.

GENERAL DISCUSSION

Our objective in this article was to understand better the process of mobility decision-making by employees living in dual-earner couples. Our results are consistent with those of other studies suggesting that the partner's influence on the ultimate decision is decisive. Nevertheless our findings provide a nuanced perspective on this influence by showing that a partner's *a priori* negative attitude does not invariably lead to the employee's rejection of the relocation offer. When attitudes diverge, a complex negotiation process is engaged to resolve the dilemma. This may take more or less time and may lead the couple to reconsider their initial respective attitudes. In this context, the couple's decision-making process about a relocation proposal becomes above all a search for compromise solutions: these are a function of both the respective distribution of their professional and family roles within the couple, and their expectations about how their marital life should be organized.

In the following sections, we discuss the implications of these results for theory and practice, as well as their limitations.

Theoretical implications

The results of our second study reveal a number of limitations of the quantitative non-longitudinal design used in Study 1 and in most other research on relocation decision-making. Of course, we agree with Spector (1994, p. 390) who pointed out that cross-sectional, self-report results can provide a useful 'first step in studying phenomena of interest.' Our Study 1 was conducted within this framework and enabled us to identify certain expected effects. Yet we believe that the results of this first research, in themselves, would have had less value if we had not been able to interpret and add to them in our second, qualitative study. Given the already impressive number of quantitative research studies that has examined relocation decision-making and their generally inconclusive results (Feldman, 2001; Stroh, 1999), it was clear that more elaborate research designs were needed to elucidate such a multi-parameter type of decision-making. So a qualitative approach, either standing alone or as a complement to quantitative research, would be very helpful in shedding new light on our understanding of this phenomenon (Bartunek & Seo, 2002).

Our research poses a challenge to the classical career paradigm insofar as the latter seeks to describe and provide an adequate explanation of the mobility of employees living in dual-earner couples. Our results clearly contradict the traditional image of career as a linear progression, by a male employee with a certain level of human capital, maximizing his choices, within a single organization. Rather, our results are closer to the more recent conceptualization of career ..., which integrates economic, social, and socio-demographic changes (e.g., two-job or two-career families are now the majority, not the exception). These models envisage a career more as a life path, in other words, as 'a series of initiatives and adaptations to employment, family, and community, and evolving not only with changes in individual interests or skills or the characteristics and requirements of one's employment context, but life experiences of oneself and of the people central to one's personal space' ....

Limitations of our research

Our findings need to be tempered in the light of the methodological limitations inherent in both our studies. The major limitation of our quantitative study is that it relied on cross-sectional and self-report data. Moreover we used a substitute variable—likelihood of accepting a transfer—instead of the actual decision concerning mobility. It is also appropriate to ask to what extent individuals who say they are willing to be geographically mobile would actually accept the move if it were proposed to them. Surprisingly, only three studies, to our knowledge, have addressed this critical question by adopting a multi-wave, longitudinal research design. The first found a 0.44 correlation between the intention of being geographically mobile one year and actual mobility a year later (Speare, 1974); the second reported a correlation of 0.32 between the two constructs measured 5 years apart (Brett & Reilly, 1988); and the third more recent study obtained a non-significant ($r = 0.22$) correlation between employees' intention to follow their company in the process of relocalization and actual mobility 4 months later (Sagie, Krausz, & Weinstein, 2001). Most of the research on the willingness to relocate has made reference to the first two research studies we have just mentioned to justify studying the determinants of the willingness to relocate as an adequate way of understanding the ultimate decision about relocation. In other words, the concept of willingness, and even more so, the probability of accepting a relocation proposition, has been taken as an acceptable substitute for the actual decision, just as the intention to quit one's job is frequently used as a substitute for actual turnover. But we should be extremely prudent about this usage (Dalton, Johnson, & Daily, 1999), given the small number of research studies incorporating these two measures and the fact that the correlations obtained are, in the end, relatively modest.

Another limitation of our research is that the variables concerning the spouse were obtained from the employee and not directly from the spouse. Some studies have shown that the partner's perception of her or his partner's attitudes is not always accurate .... Nevertheless, these studies generally show that the differences in perception diminish (1) as the relationship lasts longer, (2) when the partners possess a high degree of homogamy, and (3) when the decision has already been extensively discussed within the couple.

Also, given the characteristics of our sample (those questioned had passed an average of 7.7 years with their partner; the educational level of both members of the couple was equivalent, thus implying at least a certain degree of homogamy) and the type of decision we studied (research on dual-career couples has confirmed that the question of geographical mobility arises very early in these couples' lives and recurs often in managing the family–work interface ..., We can propose that, for our study, the repondents had a relatively good awareness of their partners' attitudes and that perceptual biases were minimized due to the sample characteristics and the type of decision studied. Yet, we need to acknowledge that it would have undoubtedly been better to obtain the information directly from the spouses, in particular with respect to the willingness to accept mobility and the perception of alternative job opportunities.

The major limitation on our qualitative findings is related to the small sample size and the selection of participants. Drawbacks of small snowball samples include their non-random, non-representative nature, which prevents direct generalization to a broader population. In particular, it should be noted that our sample was restricted to couples who were in stable relationships, both prior and subsequent to their transfers. While this enabled us to conduct interviews on sensitive issues, it also perhaps failed to identify certain variables which might have influenced our results. Despite such potential limitations, these sample issues may have been mitigated by two factors. First, we tried to obtain a wide range of experiences by targeting a diverse sample of couples. We achieved this with respect to age, background, family responsibility and job classifications. Second, the effects of the small sample size were lessened by the use of relocation decisions as a unit of analysis (i.e., we analyzed substantially more relocations decisions than there were participants).

Finally, our qualitative findings are based on retrospective evaluations which might have induced rationalization biases or simply forgetting the reasons for making relocation decisions. Recall bias and recall distortions are always a risk when using retrospective techniques. However, major and salient events such as geographical mobility are quite easy to remember and people can usually assign the actual date such decisions were made. Moreover, the couples corrected and supplemented each other during the interviews, indicating that recall and response biases were at least reduced.

REFERENCES

The references to go with this article can be found on www.wileyeurope.com/college/french.

QUESTIONS TO CONSIDER

1. What are the objectives of Challiol and Mignonac's study? Who might be interested in the findings contained in this article and why?
2. What do you think are the *two* most important findings that emerge from Challiol and Mignonac's study? Give reasons for your choice.
3. This study employs both quantitative and qualitative research methods. Outline possible advantages and disadvantages of any of the methods used, in terms of achieving the researchers' aims.

PART 2

INDIVIDUAL DIFFERENCES AND WORK PERFORMANCE

2 Individual attributes and their effects on job performance

3 Learning, reinforcement and self-management

4 Motivation and empowerment

5 Job design, goal setting and flexible work arrangements

Journal article: Makin, P.J. & Sutherland, V.J. (1994), Reducing accidents using a behavioural approach. *Leadership and Organization Development Journal*, **15** (5), 5–10.

In this section of the book we explore a range of topics comprising the psychological perspective on organizational behaviour, in which the essential focus is on the individual person. An important tradition within OB has identified links between individual attributes and behaviour at work. Some writers stress individual uniqueness based on our own life experiences but others have sought to group people by personality type or preferred styles of learning. This latter perspective has led to a preponderance of psychometric testing enabling organizations to identify and choose the 'right person', from their point of view. We will examine the validity of such psychometric predictions and also consider the important ethical considerations involved.

In the following chapters, we will highlight the importance of individual attributes within the performance equation. We will also delve into the specific topic areas of *perception* – the process by which we select, interpret and respond to information from the world around us – *personality, learning* and *motivation*. While we will show how individual attributes can impact on the way we work, this relationship is two-sided and in the chapter on job design, we indicate how the ways in which work is designed and organized will, in turn, impact on the individual worker and their attitudes.

CHAPTER
2

Individual attributes and their effects on job performance

LEARNING OBJECTIVES

After studying this chapter you should be able to:

- explain the individual performance equation

- comprehend the perceptual process and its importance in determining workplace attitudes and behaviour

- locate competency characteristics that distinguish individuals

- discuss personality characteristics that distinguish individuals

- identify competencies arising from values and attitudes, which enable managers to capitalize on workforce diversity in their organizations

- define and understand the nature of values and attitudes and their importance within organizational behaviour.

SLAYING THE DRAGONS

Dragons' Den is a popular television programme in which potential entrepreneurs present their ideas to a panel of business experts – the self-styled 'dragons'. If the dragons are sufficiently impressed by the presentation they can offer a contestant investment finance in return for a percentage of the new company. Contestants have approximately two hours to promote their ideas, although only a 5-minute extract is screened on air. The viewer sees this condensed version of the proposal followed by questioning by the dragons and negotiation on the value of the company and the dragons' potential stake. The programme originated

in Japan and by 2007 versions were screened in a number of countries including the UK, Israel and the Netherlands. It is possible that it may be rolled out to still more countries in future.

The judgements made on individual business ideas by the dragons are essentially based on *perception*. As such, although the dragons are comprised of experienced and successful figures from the world of business, their record in identifying good ideas, even when they are right in front of them, is less than perfect. One example of where quick perceptions did not predict future success can be seen in the case of Rachel Lowe and her board game *Destination,* screened in the British version of the show. This board game is based around the 'rules' of taxi journeys (collecting fares, obeying traffic rules and completing a working shift before fuel runs out). Based on Rachel's own experience as a taxi driver in Portsmouth, the game expanded to include versions set in other UK cities including London, Cardiff and Sheffield. The global nature of this venture has seen versions set in cities such as Dublin, Paris, Delhi and New York. In 2007 Rachel signed deals for a *Destination Hogwarts*, based on the Harry Potter books as well as a tie-up with Disney Pixar, so we can anticipate future editions such as *Destination* Finding Nemo and Monsters Inc.

Although *Destination* was the best-selling product at London's Hamleys toy store at Christmas 2004, Rachel's appearance on Dragons' Den, screened in January 2005 was, on her own admission, a less than happy experience. Three of the dragons questioned her awareness of the proposed market for the game and cast doubt on her financial forecasts. All of the dragons claimed that Rachel was unaware of the difference between gross and net profit. On the basis of their conclusions, they declined to take a stake in her company in exchange for investment finance. Yet, as we have seen, Rachel's idea was already taking off at the time of the programme and has continued to thrive. What lessons can we learn from the *Destination* story and its implications for the study of organizational behaviour?

First, as already noted, the dragons' view of Rachel and her business scheme was essentially based on perception. Their need for a quick assessment is typical of many business situations such as selection interviewing where decisions have to be made swiftly, in an artificial setting and on the basis of incomplete

Source: www.rtlgames.co.uk/enterthedragon.html, accessed 22 May 2007.

information. As we will see later in this chapter, such a situation holds potential dangers of perceptual errors such as overreliance on first impressions or of making judgements based on one overriding criteria. Both scenarios apply in the Dragons' Den example. One of the dragons, Doug Richard has stressed the need for contestants to encapsulate their idea: 'If you can't say, in one simple sentence, what makes you different, then you don't have a difference. If it's too complex to explain then it's probably too difficult to understand.'[1] Doug Richard is here basing his perception on a premise; that all good business ideas can be reduced to a single clear proposition. This underlying *value* position colours his perception. Rachel Lowe has explained her negative experience of Dragons' Den by pointing to the particular circumstances surrounding the programme stating that; 'I had no idea that what I was essentially going into was a business version of pop idol. I was interrogated at length about figures and sales forecasting – but had been stripped of my business plan before walking up those steps. 'You can't take that in with you' said the producer, 'it doesn't look good on camera.'[2] Here we see Rachel *attributing* her negative experience to external events – we will elaborate on this concept later in the chapter.

The *vignette* above illustrates the relevance of other OB concepts beyond perception. Reading Rachel Lowe's story, one is struck by her attributes and competencies. She exhibits specific *personality* characteristics including strong determination and perseverance noting that: 'although Dragon's Den was a traumatic experience for me, it gave me the incentive to step-up my mission to prove those dragons wrong – and that's exactly what I did!'[3] Her own work *values*, in combining the roles of student, taxi driver and mother of two can be seen as driving her on to achieve success. It is also possible to go beyond individually based explanations. For example Rachel's self-confessed dislike of numbers points to the need to structure an organization along the principle of division of labour, with other financial experts ideally complementing her creative vision. We address this topic under the heading of structure in Chapter 7. The importance of playing to one's strengths has relevance in this story, as one of the rules of the game in Dragons' Den is that irrespective of the quality of the business idea, if the numbers fail to convince then any deal is automatically off. However in this chapter we will primarily focus on individual factors which inform OB. Which factors are important in this regard?

Questions

1. Why might a short business presentation such as we see in *Dragons' Den,* or a job interview, not be a good predictor of subsequent performance?

2. A number of reality television programmes, such as *Big Brother* involve the 'eviction' of contestants from the programme by viewers. However the perceptions of viewers, as evidenced by their votes, often differs sharply from the perceptions contestants have of each other. How could we explain such discrepancies?

INTRODUCTION

Everyone is different from everyone else. Contemporary organizations are dealing with some key issues that a manager must address when attempting to influence individual performance. Accordingly, it is important that managers stop and ask what makes people different. In this chapter we will examine in detail three broad categories important in our study of organizational behaviour: individual perception, **competency** characteristics and **personality** characteristics. As students or as managers of people, it is extremely important to understand your own values and how they differ from those held by others. This is especially the case in pluralist societies increasingly common in Europe. In a pluralist society we particularly need to understand differences in perceptions across cultures.

Consequently, in this chapter we also examine **values** and **attitudes** as they relate to the workplace. These concepts: *perception, competencies, personality, values* and *attitudes* are critical to your understanding of individuality in the workplace.

A review of the concepts listed above also brings into focus some issues surrounding the nature of OB as a subject, as introduced in Chapter 1. Consider for example, from the topic of perception, the picture of a woman contained in the image below (Figure 2.1).

Figure 2.1: Old/young woman.

Do you see an old woman, a young woman or both in Figure 2.1? Differences in response to this picture, first published in 1915,[4] can be explained by *psychological factors,* for example the ways our sensory systems operate, leading some of us to see one image while others would perceive another – even when we are looking at the same object as in this case. However another important notion within perception is stereotyping, namely the tendency to attribute perceived group characteristics to individual members of that group. In order to understand a **stereotype**, we need to refer to the subject of *sociology.*

For example, Linehan,[5] in explaining the underrepresentation of women in international management roles, noted that women often found it difficult to secure international assignments due in part to concerns regarding their acceptability in a second culture. So stereotyped views within society (interestingly in this case originating in the 'home' location) contribute to the perpetuating of the **glass ceiling** phenomenon in international management.

Competency is the umbrella term for any task-related knowledge or skill possessed by an individual. Competencies could be technical or interpersonal.

Personality is the overall profile or combination of traits that characterize the unique nature of a person.

Values are global beliefs that guide actions and judgements across a variety of situations.

An **attitude** is a predisposition to respond in a positive or negative way to someone or something in your environment.

A **stereotype** is a view of an individual person or group that is derived from assumed wider characteristics, for example the view that Italians are emotional.

The **glass ceiling** refers to an invisible barrier that stops women from attaining senior positions within organizations. It can involve unstated or unofficial views of women and their roles at work.

Ergonomics *involves the application of scientific principles to the interaction between humans and their work environment including task and work areas, including physical layout, work systems and scheduling.*

In Chapter 1 we also suggested that OB research would need to employ a range of methods in order to capture the reality of people's working lives. Positivist style methods, for example, could be used to explore aspects of perception such as understanding of how our perceptual thresholds operate (consider for example how we screen out the sound of a ticking clock after a period of time). Such a topic is amenable to experimental study, maybe varying the audibility of clocks while exploring the impact of demographic variables such as age. Much work in the field of ergonomics might usefully be based on this type of positivist style research. In contrast, the interpretivist tradition could be used to highlight the deeper perceptions of workers – see, for example, the work by Kiely and Henbest[6] who conducted two extended case studies providing rich data on how female workers actually perceived sexual harassment, based on conversations with the workers in question – although these authors also used questionnaires to build up a broader view of this topic.

INDIVIDUAL PERFORMANCE FACTORS

In Chapter 1 we presented the organizational behaviour model that helps us explain and predict human behaviour in the workplace. As discussed, the performance equation (see Figure 1.1) views performance as the result of the personal attributes of individuals, the work effort they make and the organizational support they receive. The multiplication signs reinforce the key point that all three factors must be present for high performance to be achieved. Every manager must understand how these three factors can affect performance results.

We will use this equation as the theoretical guide for the material presented in this chapter. Notice that:

- individual attributes relate to a capacity to perform
- work effort relates to a willingness to perform
- organizational support relates to the opportunity to perform

Individual attributes

Several broad categories of attributes create individual differences that are important in the study of organizational behaviour. These include demographic or biographic characteristics (for example, gender, age or ethnic background); competency characteristics (aptitude/ ability, or what a person can do); personality characteristics (the features that affect an individual's characteristic behaviour); and the values, attitudes and perceptions that influence how we interpret the world. The relative importance of these topics depends on the nature of the job and its task requirements. When seeking to achieve organizational goals – or the goals of those who control organizations – individual attributes should ideally match task requirements to facilitate job performance (Figure 2.2).

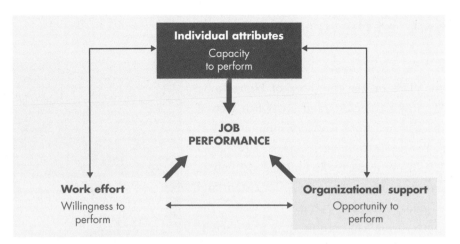

Figure 2.2: Dimensions of individual performance factors.
Source: Suggested by Melvin Blumberg and Charles D. Pringle, The Missing Opportunity in Organizational Research: Source implications for a theory of work performance, *Academy of Management Review*, Vol. 7, 1982, P. 565.

Work effort

To achieve high levels of performance, even people with the right individual attributes must have the willingness to perform; that is, they must display adequate work effort. For many reasons, different individuals display different levels of willingness to perform. Motivation to work describes the forces within an individual that account for the level, direction and persistence of effort expended on work. A highly motivated person will tend to work hard. Level of effort refers to the amount of energy that is put forth by the individual (for example, high or low level of effort to complete a task). Direction refers to an individual's choice when presented with a number of alternatives (for example, quality versus quantity) and persistence refers to the length of time a person is willing to persevere with a given action (trying to achieve a goal or alternatively abandoning it when it is found difficult to attain the goal). The topic of motivation and managers' role in this process is complex and will be analysed in depth in Chapter 4.

Motivation to work *refers to the forces within an individual that account for the level, direction and persistence of effort expended at work.*

Organizational support

The third component of the individual performance equation is organizational support.[7] Even people whose individual characteristics satisfy job requirements and who are highly motivated to exert effort may not be good performers because they do not receive adequate support in the workplace. Organizational behaviour researchers refer to such inadequacies as **situational constraints** and these may include poor time planning, inadequate budgets, problems with work technology ('the system is down again' is an all too common lament), unclear instructions, unfair levels of expected performance and inflexibility of procedures.

    Let us now turn to the first set of variables in our model – individual difference and attributes – and examine three topics in particular: *perception*, *competency* and *personality*.

Situational constraints *are organizational factors that do not allow workers to perform adequately.*

PERCEPTION AND ATTRIBUTION

The Bank of China tower building occupies a prominent place on the foreshore of Hong Kong Island. Its striking angles stand out when viewed across the harbour from Kowloon; illuminated at night it provides a stunning spectacle. Completed in 1990, in many respects the building symbolizes the emergence of Hong Kong as an important and thriving global financial centre. However the building has, from conception through to completion, attracted a large amount of controversy. In particular, some people have claimed that its angular shape goes against principles of *feng shui*, a Chinese belief system based on the need to secure harmony and balance, which has addressed the layout of individual buildings and indeed whole conurbations. Thus portions of the cross bars endemic to the tower's structure have been altered

to create diamond shapes rather than the earlier X shapes, which were considered inauspicious. When it was noted that the basic orientation of its sharp angles was towards Government House, the former headquarters of the last British Governor, Chris Patten, willow trees were reportedly planted in front of this older building in order to ward off any bad luck emanating from its new neighbour.

Perception *is the process through which people receive, organize and interpret information from their environment.*

This example illustrates, within the area of work and organization, the concept of perception, the process by which people select, organize, interpret, retrieve and respond to information from the world around them. This information is gathered from the five senses of sight, hearing, touch, taste, and smell. Mullins and Carter suggest that; 'perception is the root of all organizational behaviour; any situation can be analysed in terms of its perceptual connotation.'[8] We support this conclusion in this book as perception and reality are not necessarily the same thing. It is people's *perception* of reality that provides the fuel which drives their attitude formation and possibly their actual behaviour.

Through perception, people process information inputs into responses involving feelings and action. Perception is a way of forming impressions about oneself, other people, and daily life experiences. It also serves as a screen or filter through which information passes before it has an effect on people. The quality or accuracy of a person's perceptions, therefore, has a major impact on his or her responses to a given situation. It is therefore entirely appropriate that perception is the first substantive OB topic analysed in this book.

We perceive the world in different ways. One of the authors is familiar with the skyscrapers along the Hong Kong shore and regards the Bank of China tower as a beautiful building. But he does not have a lifelong knowledge of *feng shui*, which could cause him to perceive the building in a quite different way. No one perception is 'right' in any objective sense and, as can be seem from this example, the ways in which we view the world can be influenced by our cultural background, an important point to recognize in our increasingly interconnected business world.

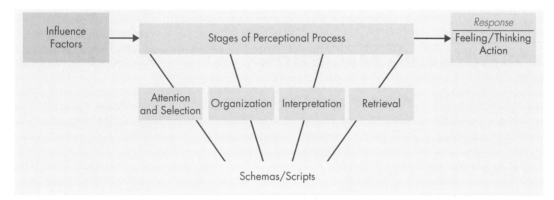

Figure 2.3: The perceptual process.

Within the OB arena, perceptual responses are also likely to vary within an organizational setting, for example between managers and subordinates. Consider Figure 2.4, which depicts contrasting perceptions of a performance appraisal between managers and subordinates.

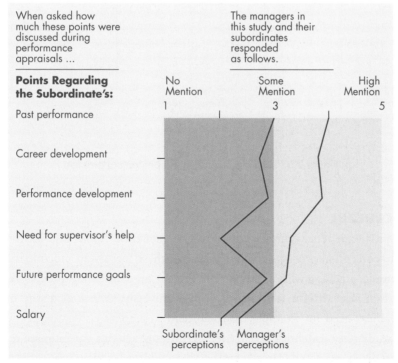

Figure 2.4: Contrasting perceptions between managers and their subordinates: the case of the performance appraisal interview.

Rather substantial differences exist in the two sets of perceptions. In this case, managers who perceive that they already give adequate attention to past performance, career development, and supervisory help are unlikely to give greater emphasis to these points in future performance appraisal interviews. In contrast, their subordinates are likely to experience continued frustration because they perceive that these subjects are not being given sufficient attention.

FACTORS INFLUENCING PERCEPTION

The factors that contribute to perceptual differences and the perceptual process among people at work, summarized in Figure 2.5, include characteristics of the perceiver, the setting, and the perceived.

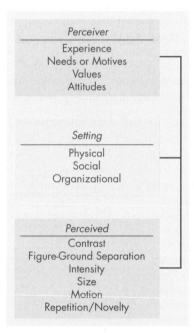

Figure 2.5: Factors influencing the perceptual process.

The perceiver

*A **perceptual set** comprises those factors that predetermine an individual's ability to perceive particular stimuli and respond in characteristic ways.*

A person's past experiences, needs or motives, personality, values and attitudes may all influence the perceptual process. Psychologists call these factors an individual's **perceptual set**. For example, a person with a strong achievement need will tend to perceive a situation in terms of that need. If you see doing well in a university course as a way to help meet your achievement need for example, you will tend to emphasize that aspect when prioritizing your study responsibilities, social life, recreational activities or intimate relationships. You are more likely to attend classes regularly than another student whose priorities reflect the importance of other needs. A person with a negative predisposition towards someone with red hair might react antagonistically if interviewing someone of this description for an employment post. Such a stance might be dysfunctional (the redhead might be the best qualified candidate); it is certainly unethical. However that interviewer's perceptual set may influence his or her attitudes – and consequently behaviour – at a subliminal level. These and other perceiver factors influence the various aspects of the perceptual process.

The setting

The physical, social, and organizational context of the perceptual setting also can influence the perceptual process. Hearing the word 'fire' might lead you to behave quite differently in a classroom than if you were a spectator at a military tattoo. The British television pro-gramme *Blackadder Goes Forth*, set against the backdrop of the First World War, made great comic play out of naming one of its characters Captain Darling. His superior officer, using the social convention of the time, called him by his surname each time they spoke. The juxtaposition of the word 'darling', popularly a term of endearment, with the formal military *milieu* of the programme, was used to considerable comic effect. The anomalous context, as perceived by the viewer, thus brought out a specific reaction.

The perceived

Characteristics of the perceived person, object, or event – such as contrast, intensity, size, motion and repetition or novelty—are also important in the perceptual process. For example, one main-frame computer among six PCs will be perceived differently from one of six mainframe computers. Five students talking in the back row of a lecture theatre will be

more easily perceived by the lecturer than 300 students quietly taking notes in the same room due to *contrast*. Intensity can vary in terms of brightness, colour, sound and move-ment. A bright red sports car stands out from a group of grey saloons; whispering or shouting stands out from ordinary conversation. This concept is known as figure-ground separation, and it depends on which image is perceived as the background and which as the figure. For an illustration, look at Figure 2.6. What do you see? Faces or a vase?

In the matter of size, very small or very large people tend to be perceived differently and more readily from average-sized people. Similarly, in terms of motion, moving objects are perceived differently from stationary objects. If you look out of a window on to a street, any moving vehicle will more readily capture your attention than those that are stuck in traffic or parked. Advertisers meanwhile hope that an advertisement's repetition or frequency will positively influence people's perception of a product. Finally, the novelty of a situation affects its perception. Tiger Woods' emergence as a world-class golf star may

Figure 2.6: Figure-ground illustration.

have led to him being perceived differently due to his mixed race ethnicity, as top players in the sport had previously been overwhelmingly white.

STAGES OF THE PERCEPTUAL PROCESS

So far we have discussed key factors influencing the perceptual process. Now we will dissect *stages* involved in processing the information that ultimately determines a person's perception and reaction, as shown previously in Figure 2.3.

The information-processing stages are divided into information attention and selection, organization of information, information interpretation and information retrieval.

Attention and selection

Our senses are constantly bombarded with so much information that if we don't screen it we quickly become incapacitated with information overload. Selective screening lets in only a tiny proportion of all the information available. Some of the selectivity comes from controlled processing – consciously deciding what information to pay attention to and what to ignore. In this case, the perceivers are aware that they are processing information. Think about the last time you were at a noisy restaurant and screened out all the sounds but those of the person with whom you were talking. If this occurred then that person is probably special to you. 'Cherry's cocktail party effect' describes a situation when you selectively perceive a communication because it is important to you – for example across a crowded room you hear your name; you are immediately alert because it is *your name* – and we are all, inevitably, the centre of our own universes!

In contrast to controlled processing, screening can also take place without the perceiver's conscious awareness. For example, you may drive a car without consciously thinking about the process of driving; you may be thinking about a problem you are having with your coursework instead. In driving the car, you are affected by information from the world around you, such as traffic lights and other cars, but you don't pay conscious attention to that information. Such selectivity of attention and automatic information processing works well most of the time when you drive, but if a nonroutine event occurs, such as a pedestrian running into the road, it is hoped that you can quickly shift back into controlled processing mode.

Controlled processing *refers, within the topic of perception, to conscious decisions made to pay attention to certain stimuli while ignoring others.*

Screening *is the umbrella term for the ways we selectively perceive objects and people.*

Organization

Even though selective screening takes place in the attention stage, it is still necessary to find ways to organize the information efficiently. Schemas help us do this. Schemas are cognitive frameworks that represent organized knowledge about a given concept or stimulus developed through experience.[9] A self schema contains information about a person's own appearance, behaviour and personality. For instance, a person with a decisiveness schema tends to perceive himself or herself in terms of that aspect, especially in circumstances calling for leadership.

Person schemas refer to the way individuals sort others into categories, such as types or groups, in terms of similar perceived features. The term 'prototype', or 'stereotype' is often used to represent these categories; it is an abstract set of features commonly associated with members of that category. Once the prototype is formed, it is stored in long-term memory; it is retrieved when it is needed for a comparison of how well a person matches the prototype's features. For instance, you may have a 'good worker' prototype in mind, which includes hard work, intelligence, punctuality, articulateness, and decisiveness; that prototype is used as a measure against which to compare a given worker. Stereotypes, may be regarded as prototypes based on such demographic characteristics as gender, age, able bodiedness, nationality or ethnic origin. Stereotyping has a generally negative connotation. But it is difficult to avoid in reality. It is one more manifestation of perceptual organization – we seek to close off meaning by taking short cuts in person perception. We are all truly unique, with an infinite number of individual differences. But in business settings, particularly in large organizations, it may not be realistic to truly know a co-worker (if such a thing is ever possible) and stereotyping offers us a way to define reality. A person may be female, Italian, in her twenties, a marketing executive and blonde – so we try to construct a complete mental picture of her by locating her within these groups and the assumptions we make about these groups. This simplifies the inherently complex activity of understanding a fellow human being and provides us with comforting predictions of her future behaviour – which may well turn out to be entirely false.

A script schema is defined as a knowledge framework that describes the appropriate sequence of events in a given situation.[10] For example, an experienced manager would use a script schema to think about the appropriate steps involved in running a meeting. Finally, person-in-situation schemas combine schemas built around persons (self and person schemas) and events (script schemas).[11] Thus, a manager might organize his or her perceived information in a meeting around a decisiveness schema for both himself or herself and a key participant in the meeting. Here, a script schema would provide the steps and their sequence in the meeting; the manager would push through the steps decisively and call on the selected participants periodically throughout the meeting to respond decisively. Note that, although this approach might facilitate organization of important information, the perceptions of those attending might not be completely accurate because the decisiveness element of the person-in-situation schema did not allow the attendees enough time for open discussion.

As you can see in Figure 2.3, schemas are not only important in the organization stage; they also affect other stages in the perception process. Furthermore, schemas rely

Schemas *are cognitive frameworks developed through experience.*

A prototype *is a perception of a person based on group characteristics, from which the individual person may diverge.*

Stereotyping *describes the process by which we attribute characteristics to an individual based on our understanding of wider groups, e.g. she is Italian therefore she is an emotional person.*

heavily on automatic processing to free people up to use controlled processing as necessary. Finally, as we will show, the perceptual factors described earlier as well as the distortions to be discussed shortly, influence schemas in various ways.

Interpretation

Once your attention has been drawn to certain stimuli and you have grouped or organized this information, the next step is to uncover the reasons behind the actions. That is, even if your attention is called to the same information and you organize it in the same way your friend does, you may interpret it differently or make different attributions about the reasons behind what you have perceived. For example, as a manager, you might attribute compliments from a friendly subordinate to his being an eager worker, whereas your friend might interpret the behaviour as insincere flattery. Cultural differences become important here. Hall's concept of low-context and high-context cultures,[12] incorporates differences in communication style including nonverbal communication. A manager on an interview panel from a low-context society such as Denmark could interpret lack of eye contact from an interviewee as evasiveness. However if that interviewee were from a high context country – China provides an example in Hall's model – they might regard eye contact as a from of rudeness and avoid it on the grounds of wishing to be polite. We cannot be aware of all such culturally derived nuances of behaviour. For example one of the authors was asked not to write comments on an essay by a Hindu student in red because the colour symbolized death in her culture; it was not surprising that he was previously unaware of this specific significance of red ink. However a good manager must be alert to the *possibility* of misinterpreting cues from people from

OB IN ACTION

The emergence of China as a major economic player has led to a plethora of guides for conducting business in that country and with Chinese nationals elsewhere. Such guides typically note the importance of nonverbal cues, which play an important role in communication within Chinese culture. Indirect communication is preferred over explicit spoken or written messages. The memoirs of ex-US President Richard Nixon record his initial difficulty in decoding messages from the Chinese Communist Party Chairman Mao Tse Tung during Nixon's visit to China in 1972. A double translation was needed; firstly from Mandarin to English, and secondly from the allegorical style of speech used by Mao into the direct information-based mode of language favoured by Nixon, before the latter statesman could comprehend what his counterpart had said. As noted before, in Hall's model China is a high-context culture whereas the US is low-context in this regard, so these perceptual misunderstandings might be expected.

other cultures – they cannot be parochial – or 'culture-blind' in the globalized twenty-first century business world. This is also, of course, true for other workers in nonmanagerial roles who operate either outside their own indigenous culture or in diverse multicultural work settings.

Retrieval

So far, we have discussed the stages of the perceptual process as if they all occurred at the same time. However, to do so ignores the important component of memory. Each of the previous stages forms part of that memory and contributes to the stimuli or information stored there. The information stored in our memory must be retrieved if it is to be used. This leads us to the retrieval stage of the perceptual process summarized in Figure 2.3.

All of us at times find it hard to retrieve information stored in our memory. More commonly, our memory decays so that only some of the information is retrieved. Schemas play an important role in this area. They make it difficult for people to remember things not included in them. For example, based on your prototype about the traits comprising a 'high-performing employee' (hard work, punctuality, intelligence, articulateness, and decisiveness) you may overestimate these traits and underestimate others when you are evaluating the performance of a subordinate whom you generally consider good. Thus, you may overestimate the person's decisiveness because it is a key part of your high-performance prototype.

Indeed, people are as likely to recall nonexistent traits as they are to recall those that are really there. Furthermore, once formed, prototypes may be difficult to change and tend to last a long time.[13] Most importantly this distortion can cause major problems in terms of performance appraisals and promotions, not to mention numerous other interactions both of a work and nonwork variety. At the same time, as we have seen such prototypes allow you to 'chunk' information and reduce overload. Thus, prototypes are a double-edged sword.

RESPONSE TO THE PERCEPTUAL PROCESS

Throughout this chapter, we have shown how the perceptual process influences numerous OB responses. Figure 2.3 classifies such responses into thoughts and feelings and actions. For example, in Korea the exchange of business cards holds deep symbolic meaning and there are a series of stages bound up in the process; cards should be held in both hands and read thoroughly, just two steps in what is a very important social interaction. Anyone new to Korea might hope that any mistake would be forgiven and understood by their hosts. Nonetheless as you cover the other OB topics in the book, you also should be alert to the importance of perceptual responses covering thoughts, feelings, and actions.

Common perceptual distortions

Figure 2.7 provides a summary of selected common kinds of distortions, some of which have already been referred to in this chapter. In all cases such distortions can render the

The **halo effect** within interpersonal perception occurs when our perception of another person is framed on the basis of a single striking favourable characteristic (the rusty halo phenomenon occurs when the characteristic is perceived negatively).

Selective perception refers to the ways in which we categorize and organize stimuli leading us to perceive the world in a unique way.

Projection involves projecting our own emotions or motives on to another person. It is an example of a perceptual error.

Contrast effects occur within the process of perception when an object or person is perceived due to it standing out from its surroundings or group.

A **self-fulfilling prophecy** occurs when a prophecy comes true simply because it has been made. For example, if we label people in a particular way, they will behave in the expected manner.

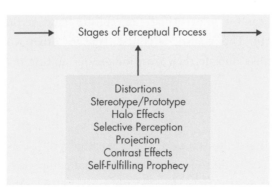

Figure 2.7: Distortions occurring in perceptual process stages.

perceptual process inaccurate and affect the lives of others in a profound way. These are stereotypes and prototypes, halo effects, selective perception, projection, contrast effects and self-fulfilling prophecy.

Stereotypes or prototypes

Earlier, when discussing person schemas, we described stereotypes, or prototypes, as useful ways of combining information in order to deal with information overload. At the same time, we pointed out how stereotypes can cause inaccuracies in retrieving information, along with some further problems. In particular, stereotypes obscure individual differences; that is, they can prevent managers, or indeed anyone else, from getting to know people as individuals and from accurately assessing their needs, preferences and abilities. Research results show the errors that can occur when stereotypes are relied on for decision making. Nevertheless, stereotypes continue to inform both attitudes and practice at senior management level.

Halo effects

A halo effect occurs when one attribute of a person or situation is used to develop an overall impression of the individual or situation. Like stereotypes, these distortions are more likely to occur in the organization stage of perception. Halo effects are common in our everyday lives. When meeting a new person, for example, a pleasant smile can lead to a positive first impression of an overall 'warm' and 'honest' person. Alternatively, someone dropping a chocolate ice cream on to their shirt just before being called into a selection interview may run the risk of negative perception on the part of interviewers; the single striking stain on clothing being an example of the 'rusty halo' variant of this effect. The result of a halo effect is the same as that associated with a stereotype, however individual differences are obscured.

Halo effects are particularly important in the performance appraisal process because they can influence a manager's evaluations of subordinates' work performance. For example, people with good attendance records tend to be viewed as intelligent and responsible; those with poor attendance records are considered poor performers. Such conclusions may or may not be valid. Equally you may question the wisdom of eating a chocolate ice cream

OB IN ACTION

Steven J. Karau, Associate Professor of Management at Southern Illinois University, has studied gender stereotyping in the US and Sweden. His study, conducted jointly with a Swedish academic Eric Hansen, involved asking college students in these two countries to correlate a number of traits as they perceived them to apply to men in general, women in general, or middle managers. His hypothesis, based on previous research, was that so-called manager traits overlapped more with male traits than female traits. This is termed the 'think manager – think male effect'.

However Karau's study found that the think manager – think male effect only held true for male raters – perhaps an expected finding – and that interestingly this effect was much less apparent in Sweden than in the US.

Steven Karau believes that his work can improve work opportunities for women stating that: 'my hope would be for organizations to rely more directly on people's qualifications and to become aware of potential contaminating factors in their judgements in order to make better hiring and promotion decisions such that every person has a chance to go as far as their talents will take them.'[14]

Here, we reiterate our previous message: both managers and employees need to be sensitive to stereotypes; they must also attempt to overcome them and recognize that an increasingly diverse workforce can be a truly competitive advantage. It is also illuminating to record the cultural differences thrown up by Karau's study. In Chapter 1 we saw that Hofstede's classifications of culture included the masculine/feminine dimension, with Sweden identified as a feminine society, so we may find some corroboration of Hofstede's work in this study.

just before an interview! Ultimately it is the manager's job to try to form true impressions rather than allowing halo effects to result in biased and erroneous evaluations.

Selective perception

Selective perception is the tendency to single out those aspects of a situation, person, or object that are consistent with one's needs, values or attitudes. Its strongest impact occurs in the attention stage of the perceptual process. This perceptual distortion was identified in a classic research study involving executives in a manufacturing company.[15] When asked to identify the key problem in a comprehensive business policy case, each executive selected problems consistent with his or her functional area work assignments. For example, most marketing executives viewed the key problem area as sales, whereas production people tended to see the problem as one of production and organization. These differing viewpoints would affect how the executives approached the problem; they might also create difficulties once these people tried to work together to improve things.

In a more recent study, 121 middle- and upper level managers attending an executive development seminar programme expressed broader views in conjunction with an emphasis on their own function. For example, a chief financial officer indicated an awareness of the importance of manufacturing and an assistant marketing manager recognized the importance of accounting and finance along with each of their own functions.[16] This more recent research demonstrated very little perceptual selectivity. The researchers were not, however, able to state definitively what accounted for the differing results.

These results suggest that selective perception is more important at some times than at others. Managers should be aware of this characteristic and test whether or not situations, events, or individuals are being selectively perceived. The easiest way to do this is to gather additional opinions from other people. When these opinions contradict a manager's own, an effort should be made to check the original impression.

Projection

Projection is the assignment of one's own personal attributes to other individuals; it is especially likely to occur in the interpretation stage of perception. A classic projection error is illustrated by managers who assume that the needs of their subordinates coincide with their own needs. Suppose, for example, that you enjoy responsibility and achievement in your work. Suppose, too, that you are the newly appointed manager of a group whose jobs seem dull and routine. You may move quickly to expand these jobs to help the workers achieve increased satisfaction from more challenging tasks because you want them to experience things that you, personally, value in work. But this may not be a good decision. If you project your needs onto the subordinates, individual differences are lost. Instead of designing the subordinates' jobs to best fit their needs, you have designed their jobs to best fit *your* needs. The problem is that the subordinates may be quite satisfied and productive doing jobs that seem dull and routine to you. Their own psychological contracts may lead them to be happy with the relative exchange between inputs and outcomes. Projection can be controlled through a high degree of self-awareness and empathy – the ability to view a situation as others see it. This of course ties in with the concept of emotional intelligence introduced in Chapter 1.

Contrast effects

Earlier, when discussing 'the perceived', we mentioned how a bright red sports car would stand out from a group of grey saloons because it contrasts with them. Here, we show the perceptual distortion that can occur when, for example, a person gives a talk following a strong speaker or is interviewed for a job following a series of mediocre applicants. We can expect a contrast effect to occur when an individual's characteristics are contrasted with those of others recently encountered who rank higher or lower on the same characteristics. Clearly, both managers and other employees need to be aware of the possible perceptual distortion the contrast effect may create in many work settings. It is emphatically not impossible to overcome this problem but awareness is necessary in the first instance.

Self-fulfilling prophecies

A final perceptual distortion that we consider is the self-fulfilling prophecy – the tendency to create or find in another situation or individual that which you expected to find in the first place. A self-fulfilling prophecy is sometimes referred to as the 'Pygmalion effect', named after a mythical Greek sculptor who created a statue of his ideal mate and then made her come to life.[17] His prophecy came true! Through self-fulfilling prophecies you also may create in the work situation that which you expect to find.

Self-fulfilling prophecies can have both positive and negative results for you should you be involved in managing others. Suppose you assume that your subordinates prefer to satisfy most of their needs outside the work setting and want only minimal involvement with their jobs. Consequently, you are likely to provide simple, highly structured jobs designed to require little involvement. Can you predict what response the subordinates would have to this situation? Their most likely response would be to show the lack of commitment you assumed they would have in the first place. Thus, your initial expectations are confirmed as a self-fulfilling prophecy. Self-fulfilling prophecies can have a positive side however. Students introduced to their teachers as star pupils do better on achievement tests than do their counterparts who lack such a positive introduction.

OB IN ACTION

A particularly interesting example of the self-fulfilling prophecy is shown in the research carried out by Eden and Shani in a military setting in Israel. One set of senior officers was told that, according to test data, some members of their assigned crews had exceptional abilities but others were only average. In reality, the crew members were assigned randomly, so that the two test groups were equal in ability. Later, the commanding officers reported that the so-called exceptional crew members performed

better than the 'average' members. As the study revealed, however, the commanders had paid more attention to and praised the crew members for whom they had the higher expectations.[18]

The self-fulfilling effects in the cases documented above argue strongly for managers to adopt positive and optimistic approaches to people at work. This is also shown by Manzoni and Barsoux[19] who identified the mirror image 'set up to fail' syndrome. Here managers were found to micromanage and control those employees perceived as weak (often on the basis of a single incident), which led to a downward spiral with such employees losing confidence, resulting in turn in depressed levels of performance.

MANAGING PERCEPTIONS

To be successful, managers must understand that everyone is different in terms of the ways they perceive the external world. In order to maximize their own performance, those who manage others should also be aware of the implications of the topic for themselves through an awareness of perceptual processes, the stages involved and the impact the perceptual process can have on their own and others' responses. They must also be aware of what roles the perceiver, the setting and the perceived have in the perceptual process. Particularly important with regard to the perceived is the concept of impression management – for managers and others.

Impression management

Impression management is a person's systematic attempt to behave in ways that will create and maintain desired impressions in the eyes of others. First impressions are especially important and influence how people respond to one another. Research demonstrates how quickly individuals on a selection panel make up their minds about individuals.[20] More generally, impression management is influenced by such activities as associating with the 'right people', doing favours to gain approval, flattering others to impress them, taking credit for a favourable event, apologizing for a negative event while seeking a pardon, agreeing with the opinions of others and downplaying the severity of a negative event.[21] In the 1960s an American social psychologist Erving Goffman[22] illuminated fascinating instances of how workers in the public eye – for example waiters – would consciously manipulate their own behaviour in view of what was expected by customers, partly in order to maximize gratuities. One can also argue that managers learn how to use these activities to enhance their own images and are sensitive to their use by their subordinates and others in their organizations. In this context, job titles are particularly important.

Distortion management

During the attention and selection stage, managers should be alert to balancing automatic and controlled information processing. Most of their responsibilities, such as performance assessment and clear communication, will involve controlled processing, which will take time away from other job responsibilities. Along with more controlled processing, managers need to be concerned about increasing the frequency of observations and about obtaining representative information rather than simply responding to the most recent information about a subordinate or a production order, for instance. In addition, managers should not fail to seek out disconfirming information that will help provide a balance to their typical perceptions.

The various kinds of schemas and prototypes and stereotypes are particularly important at the information organizing stage. Managers should strive to broaden their schemas or should even replace them with more accurate or complete ones.

At the interpretation stage, managers need to be especially attuned to the impact of attribution on information; we discuss this concept further in the next section. At the retrieval stage, managers should be sensitive to the fallibility of memory. They should recognize the tendency to rely too much on schemas, especially prototypes or stereotypes that may bias information storage and retrieval.

Throughout the entire perception process, managers and, once again we stress, all workers, should be sensitive to the information distortions caused by halo effects, selective perception, projection, contrast effects, and self-fulfilling prophecies, in addition to the distortions caused by stereotypes and prototypes.

ATTRIBUTION THEORY

Earlier in the chapter we mentioned attribution theory in the context of perceptual interpretation. Attribution theory aids in this interpretation by focusing on how people attempt to (1) understand the causes of a certain event, (2) assess responsibility for the outcomes of the event and (3) evaluate the personal qualities of the people involved in the event.[23] In applying attribution theory, we are especially concerned with whether one's behaviour has been internally or externally caused. Internal causes are believed to be under an individual's control – you believe Marie's performance is poor because she is lazy. External causes are seen as coming from outside a person – you believe Sarfraz's performance is poor because his machine has not been upgraded with the latest software.

The importance of attributions

According to attribution theory, three factors influence this internal or external determination: *distinctiveness, consensus*, and *consistency*. Distinctiveness considers how consistent a person's behaviour is across different situations. If Marie's performance is low, regardless of the technological capabilities of her computer, we tend to give the poor performance an internal attribution; if the poor performance is unusual, we tend to assign an external cause to explain it.

Consensus takes into account how likely all those facing a similar situation are to respond in the same way. If all the people using machinery like Sarfraz's perform poorly, we tend to give his performance an external attribution. If other employees do not perform poorly, we attribute his performance to internal causation.

Consistency concerns whether an individual responds the same way across time. If Marie has a batch of low-performance figures, we tend to give the poor performance an internal attribution. In contrast, if Marie's low performance is an isolated incident, we attribute it to an external cause.

Attribution errors

In addition to these three influences, two errors have an impact on internal versus external determination – the fundamental **attribution error** and the self-serving bias.[24] Figure 2.8 provides data from a group of healthcare managers. When supervisors were asked to identify, or attribute, causes of poor performance among their subordinates, the

Attribution errors *occur within the process of perception and relate to the reasons we attribute to events and behaviour. A common attribution error is to overemphasize the contribution of our own efforts and abilities when explaining our successes and to, contrastingly, attribute negative occurrences to outside influences such as bad luck.*

Cause of Poor Performance by Their Subordinates	Most Frequent Attribution	Cause of Poor Performance by Themselves
7	Lack of *ability*	1
12	Lack of *effort*	1
5	Lack of *support*	23

Figure 2.8: Healthcare managers' attributions of causes for poor performance.

supervisors more often chose the individual's internal deficiencies – lack of ability and effort – rather than external deficiencies in the situation, such as lack of support. This demonstrates the fundamental attribution error – the tendency to underestimate the influence of situational factors and to overestimate the influence of personal factors in evaluating someone else's behaviour. When asked to identify causes of their own poor performance however, the supervisors overwhelmingly cited lack of support – an external, or situational, deficiency. This indicates the self-serving bias – the tendency to deny personal responsibility for performance problems but to accept personal responsibility for performance success.

To summarize, we tend to overemphasize other people's internal personal factors in their behaviour and to underemphasize external factors in other people's behaviour. In contrast, we tend to attribute our own success to our own internal factors and to attribute our failure to external factors.

The managerial implications of attribution theory can be traced back to the fact that perceptions influence responses. For example, a manager who feels that subordinates are not performing well and perceives the reason to be an internal lack of effort is likely to respond with attempts to 'motivate' the subordinates to work harder; the possibility of

OB IN ACTION

Following the European Champions League soccer final on 17 May 2006, in which FC Barcelona defeated the London club side Arsenal 2–1, both Arsenal's then star striker Thierry Henry (he swapped clubs in 2007) and team manager Arsene Wenger attributed their side's defeat to decisions made by the match officials in the game. Henry was quoted as saying 'I don't know if the referee was wearing a Barcelona shirt because they kicked me all over the place. If the referee did not want us to win he should have said so from the off. Some of the calls were strange. I believe the referee did not do his job. I would have liked to see a proper referee'[25] Manager Wenger said.' My biggest regret is that the first [Barcelona] goal was offside. It's difficult to lose the game on a wrong decision. It was offside and it is proven on TV.'[26] Without going into the intricacies of the referee and his assistant's decision making, we have here – in the context of emotional reactions immediately following a dramatic sporting event – examples of attribution theory in action. And yet there were other factors influencing the result, including some missed chances to score by Arsenal players. Arsene Wenger acknowledged that his team had two or three good chances to increase their 1–0 lead in the course of the same interview cited here. The Barcelona coach Frank Rijkard contrastingly, emphasized the role of his team's goalkeeper Victor Valdes in the side's triumph, drawing attention to key saves made by that player. Here we see how attribution of success is related to internal factors, in this case a team member's skill.

changing external, situational factors that may remove job constraints and provide better organizational support may be largely ignored. This oversight could sacrifice major performance gains. Interestingly, because of the self-serving bias, when they evaluated their own behaviour, the supervisors in the earlier study indicated that their performance would benefit from having better support. Thus, the supervisors' own abilities or willingness to work hard were not felt to be at issue.

Attributions across cultures

Research on the self-serving bias and fundamental attribution error has been carried out in cultures across the world with varying results.[27] In Korea, for example, the self-serving bias was found to be negative; that is, Korean managers attribute workgroup failure to themselves to a far greater extent – 'I was not a capable leader' – rather than to external causes. In India, the fundamental attribution error overemphasizes external rather than internal causes for failure. Certain cultures, such as that of the US, tend to overemphasize internal causes and underemphasize external ones. Such overemphasis may result in negative attributions toward employees. These negative attributions, in turn, can lead to disciplinary action, negative performance evaluations, transfers to other departments, and overreliance on training, rather than focusing on such external causes as lack of workplace support.[28] Employees, too, take their cues from managerial misattributions and, through negative self-fulfilling prophecies, may reinforce managers' original misattributions. Employees and managers alike can be taught attributional realignment to help deal with such misattributions (see Effective Manager 2.1).[29]

EFFECTIVE MANAGER 2.1
Keys in managing perceptions and attributions

- Be self-aware.
- Seek a wide range of differing information.
- Try to see a situation as others would.
- Be aware of different types of schemas.
- Be aware of perceptual distortions.
- Be aware of self and other impression management.
- Be aware of attribution theory implications.

THE CRITICAL IMPORTANCE OF PERCEPTION

You may have wondered how the concept of perception was relevant to OB. We trust that you are now convinced that it is highly relevant. Individuals perceive the world in different ways. We are unique in the ways we select, organize, interpret and retrieve information from the environment. Our perceptions of the world predate our attitudes and conceivably our actual behaviour. The psychological contract, introduced as an important concept in Chapter 1 is essentially a perceptual mindset. We tend to perceive other people with reference to our own perceptual worlds, so an awareness of the nature of perception can help us to better understand other people. Such an ability is crucial to securing strong organizational performance.

COMPETENCY DIFFERENCES AMONG INDIVIDUALS

Competency
is the umbrella term for any task-related knowledge or skill possessed by an individual. Competencies could be technical or interpersonal.

The second category of individual attributes relates to competency. Competency is a broad concept relating to the aptitudes and abilities of people at work. Aptitude represents a person's capability to learn something. Ability reflects a person's existing capacity to perform the various tasks needed for a given job. Aptitudes are potential abilities, while abilities are the knowledge and skills that an individual already possesses.[30] In addition, emotional competence plays a role in the ability to handle work pressures.

In terms of our individual performance model, competency is an important consideration for a manager when selecting candidates for a job. Once people with the appropriate aptitudes or abilities have been selected, on-the-job and continuing education/training or professional development activities can be used to enhance their required job skills.

Many different aptitudes and abilities are recognized as relevant to work performance and some have been extensively researched in the workplace. As a result, various tests are currently available to measure individual capacity. We can categorize abilities as cognitive abilities, physical abilities and emotional intelligence.

Cognitive abilities

It is quite likely that you have taken some tests of cognitive abilities either during your education or when you were applying for a job. Some provide a measure of general intelligence or the 'G factor' (such as the Stanford-Binet IQ test); others represent capacity in more specific areas such as verbal comprehension, spatial ability, numerical ability and memory.[31] Researchers still disagree over the extent to which our intelligence is determined at birth. The consensus view is that genetics and life experience together shape our capacity, although we are all born with some limits to development in specific areas. Assessment of cognitive abilities is closely linked with the topic of learning covered in Chapter 3, so at this stage we will briefly note the importance of this area and assess it more fully in the next chapter.

Physical abilities

Tune in to the Olympics, Paralympics or European Athletics Championships and it is soon apparent that we all differ in terms of our physical abilities. Different sports require different levels of speed, strength, flexibility and stamina. The same is true of many different jobs. Firefighters need strength and stamina to withstand extreme physical conditions. Electricians need colour-perfect vision to work with electrical circuitry (about 10% of the male population is red-green colour blind whereas only a small proportion of females are). Manual dexterity has long been recognized as a crucial skill for people engaged in detailed work, such as microsurgery and jewellery making.

If a particular job has a certain physical requirement, it is important that it is measured objectively, rather than through the inappropriate use of stereotypes. But debates on the necessity of particular physical requirements can be difficult to resolve.

OB IN ACTION

In November 2006, the Supreme Court in Delhi was asked to rule on whether Indian Airlines could reasonably dismiss air cabin crew for being too fat. The Court was asked to consider the cases of 11 stewardesses who had been 'grounded' for allegedly carrying too much weight. One such victim, found to be 1.9 kg above her height/weight threshold, and faced with the prospect of losing her job, went on a crash diet but subsequently described her experience as personally demeaning and alien to the dignity of Indian culture. However an Indian Airlines spokesperson located the company's policy within the imperative of commercial survival. One competitor, Kingfisher Airlines, actively markets female cabin crew in scarlet shoes and short red skirts as part of its brand image. Indian Airlines also point to weight as an indicator of fitness, a company source noting that: 'Staff need to be fit enough to control crazy guys who are trying to take over the flight.'[32]

Emotional competence

Until fairly recently emotions were given very little attention by researchers in organizational behaviour. Generally speaking, emotions were seen as impediments to sound decision making and an ordered approach to workplace relations. This kind of thinking is quickly being replaced by a view that sees emotions as a normal part of our workplace experiences. In fact, recent research has revealed the centrality of emotions to all areas of human functioning.[33] For example, to make decisions we are guided by our values, which are in turn based on our emotions. Reasoning and emotion are intertwined.

Emotional intelligence, introduced in Chapter 1, is one aspect of our emotional functioning that complements cognitive forms of intelligence. It is a form of social intelligence that allows us to monitor and shape our emotional responses and those of others. For many people, it is even more important than cognitive intelligence for success in life. Daniel Goleman popularized the concept of emotional intelligence in 1995 with the publication of his book on the topic, although others had been researching the area for some time.[34]

We now turn to the specific dimensions that make up emotional intelligence. A sound place to start is with the research instruments that are under development to assess it. There are several of these and each has a slightly different way of constructing and defining the dimensions or components of emotional intelligence. The oldest and most well-researched was developed by Reuven Bar-On as a self-report instrument of emotional wellbeing.[35] It includes various measures of self-awareness and regard, interpersonal competence, adaptability, stress management and general mood state. An instrument that focuses more closely on awareness and management of emotions is the Multifactor Emotional Intelligence Scale, (MEIS).[36] Please also refer to this scale on our Web site: **www.wileyeurope.com/college/french**. The four dimensions on the MEIS are as follows:

- identifying emotions – awareness of, and the ability to identify, the emotions you and others are feeling
- using emotions – the capacity to weigh up the emotional aspects of values and attitudes when confronting problems and making decisions
- understanding emotions – the ability to understand complex emotions and to recognize how emotions pass through stages over time
- managing emotions – the ability to exercise self-control and self-regulation, and to empathize with and influence others.

Emotion management *is exercising emotional self-control and self-regulation influenced by the context in which individuals find themselves.*

Emotion management is an important organizational concern. Emotion can be viewed as a valuable resource to be harnessed in order to gain employee commitment (willingness) and a competitive advantage. Some researchers have the pessimistic view that emotion can be commodified via a 'commercialization of intimate life'.[37] Others celebrate the recognition of emotion as a vital part of organizational life, and harness these energies in a positive way to improve customer service and counteract employees' emotional exhaustion.[38]

Emotion is a lived interactional experience with an organizational dark side. For example, emotional burnout in front-line service work, the everyday stresses and strains of organizational life and the difficulty of working with bullies or harassers are realities that any employee can face. However, emotion cannot (and arguably should not) be controlled by the organization. Employees are social beings who enter the organization with life histories and experiences. They may take up organizationally prescribed roles, experience frustrations and often have to present themselves very differently to customers or clients. There is no clear divide between public and private worlds of emotion.[39]

Perhaps one of the most emotionally exhausting professions is nursing. Often nurses cannot show publicly their private emotions. For example, when a nurse cares for a particular patient during the process of dying, and especially when he or she has cared for this person for a long period of time, the nurse will experience a strong emotional response to the patient's death. At the same time, the nurse is likely to care for several other patients in the ward. In consideration of his or her other patients, the nurse cannot share these private emotions. Thus, to be effective, nurses need to be highly competent social actors and emotion managers.

Emotion constantly crosses boundaries between self and society, private and public, formal and informal. Employees continually juggle their mixed emotions in order to both enjoy and endure the rigours of organizational life.[40] Managing employee emotions in the workplace includes recognizing the potential transformative power of human action.

Managers also need to recognize the emotive forces that inhibit organizationally desirable behaviours. For this, managers themselves need to be emotionally competent. As is often the case in OB, this concept has attracted criticism from within the academic community, one commentator, viewing it as 'old wine in new bottles'[41] and questioning whether *qualities* of emotional intelligence – for example self-awareness – are actually different from *competencies* that they are held to affect – such as accurate self-assessment. However some evidence points to emotional intelligence as a powerful influence on job performance. One study[42] identified 10 emotional competencies as the prime distinguishing capabilities of successful teams operating in a chemical company in Germany.

RESEARCH IN OB

Look at the article by Kahn *et al.* on our Web site **www.wileyeurope.com/college/french** examining the topic of burnout amongst teachers in the US. Note the multifaceted nature of burnout including emotional exhaustion, cynicism and concerns with efficacy. It is also interesting to record Kahn *et al.*'s finding that emotional support from supervisors and co-workers was a particularly important factor in dealing with symptoms of burnout. As positive emotional support increased, emotional exhaustion, cynicism and worries concerning efficacy decreased. The healing effect of emotional support worked for all personality types (see the next section for a full discussion of this concept). This research study lends support to the validity of the performance equation discussed earlier, within this case, specific corroboration of the importance of organizational support.

PERSONALITY DIFFERENCES AMONG INDIVIDUALS

The third basic attribute of individuals is *personality*. We use the term personality to represent the overall profile or combination of characteristics that capture the unique nature of a person as that person reacts and interacts with others. Personality combines a set of physical and mental characteristics that reflect how a person looks, thinks, acts and feels. Understanding personality contributes to an understanding of organizational behaviour by helping us to see what shapes individuals, what they can do (competency) and what they will do (motivation). One might expect there to be a predictable interplay between an individual's personality and their tendency to behave in certain ways. A common expectation, for example, is that introverts (people who are more interested in their private thoughts and feelings than in their external environment) tend to be less sociable than extroverts. Personality is a vital individual attribute for managers to understand.

> **Personality** is the overall profile or combination of traits that characterize the unique nature of a person.

Personality determinants

An important question in looking at personality is what determines it. Is personality inherited or genetically determined? Or are personality attributes determined by experience?

You may have heard someone say something like 'she acts like her mother'. Or someone may argue that: 'Paulo is the way he is because of how he was raised' or indeed: 'Yasmin is a born leader'. These arguments illustrate the nature/nurture controversy – that is, is personality determined by heredity (or genetic endowment) or one's environment? Figure 2.9 shows that these two forces actually operate in combination. Heredity consists of those factors that are determined at conception, and includes physical characteristics and gender in addition to personality factors. Environment consists of cultural, social and situational factors.

Figure 2.9: Heredity and environmental links with personality.

Heredity

Psychologists acknowledge that the mind is made up of three domains: the cognitive domain (such as skills and learned behaviour), the affective domain (emotions) and the conative domain (instinctive approaches). Conative actions are those derived from striving instincts. Previous studies of components of the mind often ignored the notion of conation or instinct. Instinct is described as inherited patterns of unreasoned and unchangeable responses to particular actions and behaviours. At the beginning of modern psychology, both emotion and conation were considered central to its study. However, interest in these topics declined as measuring overt behaviour and cognition received more attention. The notion of instinct as the primary source of motivation was abandoned for several reasons, the common one being that this may place human beings on the same level as other animals.[43] Striving instincts are subconscious and immeasurable. They may nonetheless form an important component of the ways in which a person acts, or more pertinently, *the ways in which they would like to act.*

Psychodynamic theory

The pioneering work of Freud[44] put forward the view that personality is composed of thoughts and drives emanating from the **unconscious**. Freud's view was that our minds were firstly governed by the pleasure principle, or *id,* to use his own terminology. We are driven by this principle, which could manifest itself in sexual desire, need for nourishment or aggression (Freud was one of the psychologists who believed that human beings have a dark or 'shadow' side to their nature). The second aspect of our mental states was termed the *ego;* this essentially comprises the rational, problem-solving ways in which we consciously cope with our environments, governing the reality of our lives. The third element of our mental functioning is the *superego,* defined as our learned sense of how we should behave – or how we think other people think we should behave. This reflexive notion of behaviour involves our awareness of society's norms, which we learn through

The term **'unconscious',** *within Freud's theory of personality, refers to basic desires below the conscious level, which drive our behaviour and potentially conflict with values learned through socialization.*

childhood. So our individual personality evolves dynamically over time – hence the term psychodynamic.

Freud's theory of personality is also psychodynamic in that he identifies a series of *stages* through which all people progress in their childhood. He proposed that our experiences in our early years are important determinants of our adult behaviour. The stages, including the oral, anal, phallic and genital, refer to those areas of the body that form pleasure centres for the child. Freud believed that the stages correlate with specific ages in childhood and that overindulgence or deprivation at any stage will result in difficulties when that individual reaches adulthood. For example an anally retentive personality is associated with meanness and an excessive desire for control. If one accepts this reading of personality development it provides a novel (albeit for some a far-fetched) model for explaining behaviour in organizations.

There is considerable debate concerning the relative impact of heredity and environment – particularly childhood experiences on personality. The most general conclusion is that heredity sets the limits on just how much personality characteristics can be developed, whereas the environment determines development within these limits. The limits appear to vary from one characteristic to the next.

OB IN ACTION

In 2005, two British psychologists, Belinda Board and Katrina Fritzon[45] interviewed and administered psychological tests to 39 senior UK business executives. They compared these executives' psychological profiles with psychiatric patients at the high security Broadmoor prison, which is the abode of some of the country's most infamous criminals, including at least one of Britain's most notorious serial killers. Somewhat disturbingly, Board and Fritzon found that three out of 11 identified personality disorders (PDs) were more apparent in the executive sample than among the Broadmoor patients. These were:

- Histrionic PD manifestations which included charm, insincerity, manipulativeness and egocentricity.
- Obsessive-compulsive disorder (OCD). Here symptoms numbered perfectionism, dictatorial behaviour, excessive devotion (in these cases to work) and rigidity.
- Narcissistic PD involving lack of empathy for others, grandiosity and independence.

This interesting research may explain what has become known as 'toxic manager syndrome' – disturbingly, many people can personally confirm the existence of such figures. One can also speculate on what internal forces have driven such individuals on to their current career success. Maybe Freud's vision of the destructive side of human behaviour is not so fanciful after all!

The nomothetic (traits) approach to personality

Organizational behaviour literature typically stresses the way of understanding personality that centres on traits and characteristics. This so-called *nomothetic* approach is popular within the business studies canon, possibly because it enables students of business and practising managers to identify and classify personality according to recognizable characteristics. It is an approach that lends itself easily to adoption within work organizations in terms of policy and practice. In the US and UK, a desire to measure individual differences as part of selection and remuneration policies means that nomothetic assumptions concerning personality will be familiar to you if you have lived and worked in those countries. Research indicates that psychometric testing (a logical follow-on from the nomothetic view) is used more or less frequently in particular societies.[46] In Chapter 1 we noted that Hofstede distinguished between individually and group-oriented societies. There is less of a desire to focus on the identification of individual differences in societies stressing group cohesion – such as Portugal and Greece – so managers there may be less concerned with putting the nomothetic approach into operation at the workplace.

The essence of the nomothetic view of personality is that it can best be understood by identifying the ways in which our personality varies from others. It proposes that it is possible to identify a set of dimensions along which we can all be classified and compared. These dimensions are called *traits*. Furthermore the traits cluster in a consistent fashion to create types. For example, traits of practicality and risk taking are typically found together within a single personality and form part of the extravert type.[47] The nomothetic approach considers that personality is relatively unchanging; traits remain constant even in changing circumstances and can be captured through questionnaires and psychometric testing more generally.

In this section we will consider some of the personality traits that have been linked with behaviour in organizations. Firstly, we will outline the 'big five personality dimensions', and we will follow this with a discussion of other key characteristics that have attracted considerable research interest.

Psychometric testing *involves an attempt to extract an individual's key characteristics via controlled measures such as personality inventories.*

Nomothetic *approaches to understanding personality locate individuals within types on the basis of their traits. There is also a belief that personality is stable and unchanging, possibly as a result of inherited characteristics.*

Five key dimensions of personality

In a fascinating study of how we describe people's personalities, researchers identified 17 953 English-language terms that had been used over the years.[48] They sorted the terms into groups with similar meanings and finally distilled them into five key dimensions of personality. Research has generally confirmed the relevance of each dimension to behaviour in organizations:

- Extroversion–introversion: the degree to which individuals are oriented to the social world of people, relationships and events as opposed to the inner world (respectively). Extroverts tend to be outgoing, talkative and sociable, whereas introverts are generally quieter and happier spending time alone or with a few close friends.
- Conscientiousness: the extent to which individuals are organized, dependable and focused on detail, rather than disorganized, less reliable and lacking in perseverance.

- Agreeableness: the extent to which individuals are compliant, friendly, reliable and helpful, versus disagreeable, argumentative and uncooperative. One measure of this dimension is the Employee Reliability Scale.[49] Low-reliability individuals tend to be hostile towards rules, have feelings of detachment from others and are thrill-seeking, impulsive and socially insensitive. Those with high scores have favourable attitudes to teamwork, helping others, punctuality, and are more adaptable.

- Emotional stability: the degree to which individuals are secure, resilient and calm, versus anxious, reactive and subject to mood swings.

- Openness to experience: the extent to which individuals are curious, open, adaptable and interested in a wide range of things, versus resistant to change and new experiences, less open to new ideas and preferring routine.

It might be assumed that employers and human resource managers in particular, might commonly wish to recruit workers who are agreeable, stable and open to experience. While this would probably apply in most scenarios we should allow for the reverse being true. The nomothetic trait approach could be used in many ways by organizations: the essence of this approach is that it is possible to identify stable traits in a predictive way. The traits that are sought would vary according to the situation.

Locus of control

One influential facet of personality is found in Rotter's concept of locus of control, which measures the internal–external orientation of a person – that is, the extent to which a person feels able to affect his or her life.[50] This notion does not sit easily within the nomothetic approach and shows how our personalities are influenced by feelings and thoughts deriving from our early influences and experiences. It is nonetheless a useful illustration of the potential importance of identifiable features in explaining personality and the actions people pursue. Locus of control refers to the general conceptions people have about whether events are controlled by themselves primarily, which indicates an *internal orientation*, or by outside forces or their social and physical environment, which indicates an *external orientation*. Internals, or persons with an internal locus of control, believe they control their own fate or destiny. In contrast, externals, or persons with an external locus of control, believe much of what happens to them is beyond their control and is determined by environmental forces.

> **Locus of control** is the internal–external orientation – that is, the extent to which people feel able to affect their lives.

For example, 'internals' would agree with statements like 'people's misfortunes result from the mistakes they make' and 'by taking an active part in political and social affairs, people can control world events'. On the other hand, 'externals' would agree with statements such as 'many of the unhappy things in people's lives are partly due to bad luck' and 'as far as world affairs are concerned, most of us are the victims of forces we can neither understand nor control'.

In the work context, at the general level, internals seek more information, experience stronger job satisfaction, perform better on learning and problem-solving tasks, have greater self-control and are more independent than externals.

Authoritarianism/dogmatism

Both 'authoritarianism' and 'dogmatism' deal with the rigidity of a person's beliefs. A person high in authoritarianism tends to adhere rigidly to conventional values and to obey recognized authority. This person is concerned with toughness and power. People high in dogmatism see the world as a threatening place. They often regard legitimate authority as absolute, and accept or reject others according to how much they agree with accepted authority. Superiors possessing these latter traits tend to be rigid and closed.[51]

We may expect highly authoritarian individuals to present a special problem because they are so susceptible to obey authority that they may behave unethically in their eagerness to comply.[52] Authoritarianism has been directly linked with 'crimes of obedience' and unethical behaviour.[53] For example, authoritarianism is a required trait in military organizations throughout the world. One recent example of a crime of obedience was the abuse of Iraqi prisoners by US soldiers at Abu Ghraib, and there have been many historical examples including genocide in Cambodia and the 1968 My Lai massacre in Vietnam.[54]

However, authoritarianism is not confined to the military; for example, under instruction, Arthur Andersen employees shredded documents to cover up the impending corporate scandal that allegedly led to the demise of one of the US's largest accountancy organizations and sparked the ENRON scandal.[55]

Machiavellianism

Machiavellians *are people who view and manipulate others purely for personal gain.*

Another interesting personality dimension is Machiavellianism, which owes its origins to Niccolo Machiavelli. The very name of this sixteenth-century author evokes visions of a master of guile, deceit and opportunism in interpersonal relations. Machiavelli earned his place in history by writing *The Prince*, a nobleman's guide to the acquisition and use of power.[56] From its pages emerges the personality profile of a Machiavellian – that is, someone who views and manipulates others purely for personal gain.

Manipulation is a basic drive for some people in social settings. And although some people view manipulation of others as being deceitful and even sinful, others see manipulation as an important attribute for career success in an organization. Thus, it is easy to see why Machiavelli's ideas have been both so avidly read and so heavily criticized over the years.[57]

The idiographic approach to personality

The nomothetic approach to understanding personality predominates in business and management literature but we should also recognize the potential contribution of an alternative conception of the subject known as the *idiographic* view. It is also useful to locate

COUNTERPOINT

The windows to the soul – or a selection criterion?

Research published in 2007 by two Swedish academics concludes that patterns in individuals' irises can be an indicator of their personality. Mats Larsson who led this project at Orebo University in Sweden[58] claims that the genes involved in the development of this part of the eye also determine part of the brain's frontal lobe, which in turn is said to influence our personality. The eyes of 428 people were analysed and the personalities of these individuals 'tested'. Intricate patterns in the iris were found to be linked to personality features – for example densely packed crypts (the wavy lines radiating from the pupil) were associated with open and empathetic personality traits.

Mats Larsson and his team have not suggested possible applications of these findings. But it is conceivable that they could be used in the course of employee selection in future as the study is potentially strong on predictive validity – the extent to which findings predict future behaviour.

This study highlights the rise of genetic explanations of personality. In common with other scientific findings in the field of genetics, it brings forward important ethical issues.

Would you be happy to have your eyes scanned as part of a selection process and what would your reaction be if you were turned down for a job because of your eye markings? You might accept the judgement as scientifically valid or you could, alternatively, regard such a practice as an outrageous and unwarranted intrusion. More generally, what is your reaction to the possible use of genetic criteria such as this within business?

this tradition within a process-relational view of individuals.[59] Here people are conceived as having developing identities and enacting their worlds – in other words our personalities emerge and develop in the light of our experiences. Cooley an American psychologist writing in the early twentieth century, termed this idea the 'looking glass self'. We find this idea plausible in explaining our everyday lives. For example, If you tell jokes and people habitually laugh at your jokes, this will reinforce your self-image as a sociable extravert. If on the other hand your attempts to amuse are met with baffled silence or, even worse, disdain and abuse then your self-image is likely to change along with your behaviour. The famous psychologist Carl Rogers[60] found that adjusted individuals were able to cope with changes in their self-concept. A flexible notion of one's self, recognizing that it can change over time and in new circumstances, will result in positive feelings and a psychologically healthy person.

The idiographic approach to personality is less amenable to easy application within the workplace. Its central tenets are summarized below:

- individuals are unique complex entities and should not be located within typologies
- personality should be understood as a complete entity (one should not focus on particular traits)
- people's personalities; closely related to their self-image, can change – sometimes radically – due to experience.

*The **idiographic** approach to understanding personality focuses on individual uniqueness. It regards personality as potentially shifting according to an individual's self-image and experiences.*

The idiographic approach implies that one needs a deep understanding of any one individual in order to capture their personality. This, of course becomes difficult in an employee selection process that will probably be constrained by time and budget. But there are some methods that fall within this tradition. Thematic apperception tests (TATs), involve presenting someone with a photograph or other image, usually depicting a group of people, and asking him or her to imagine what is happening in terms of the dynamics between the people shown. It is claimed that TATs clearly evoke what is actually present in someone's mind although we are heavily dependent on people's honesty here. If their reaction was that they wanted to murder the people in the picture, how likely are they to reveal this thought if appointment to a desired job depends on it? Assessment centres are a collection of methods possibly including personality tests, group and team leadership activities, physical endurance tasks and work simulation. Such a combined range of measures administered over several days may go some way to creating a wider, more varied picture of someone's personality as it is manifested in different situations. Overall, idiographic approaches to personality are more closely associated with the *interpretivist* tradition in OB, set out in Chapter 1 and research methods aligning with that philosophical approach.

Individual differences and workplace diversity

Increasing diversity is creating unparalleled workplace challenges. Significant variations are occurring in skill levels, education, physical abilities, cultural backgrounds, lifestyles, personal values, individual needs, ethnicity and social values. This increasing diversity is changing the mix of skills required to manage the workforce effectively.

EFFECTIVE MANAGER 2.2

In a situation where you are asked to work with workplace diversity, for example implementing a diversity management programme:

- Examine current structures and processes – do they harbour any systemic biases to disadvantage some groups? Whose priorities do they reflect? Who is excluded (for example, from decisions made in corridors or on the golf course)?
- Take a long-term view – attitudes may need to change and this will not happen overnight.
- Obtain support for change from the top (commitment, resources, money, time), as nothing will change without it.
- Obtain the involvement of all those who will be affected by change.

The benefits of a workplace that is open to diversity are:

- With shortages of skilled labour in some occupational areas, recruitment of staff is easier for organizations that welcome diversity.
- Diverse workplaces have contacts with customers and business partners from a wider range of cultures and groups.
- Diverse perspectives bring creativity and innovation.
- Problems are solved using a wider range of ideas and perspectives.

Organizations that can incorporate the opportunities created by diversity into their business strategies and management practices can gain a significant competitive advantage.

Essentially, managers need to ensure that everyone in the organization is sensitive to individual differences and to seek innovative ways to match increasingly diverse workers with job requirements. This may mean developing innovative recruiting strategies to attract new sources of labour and creating flexible employment conditions to better use the increasingly diverse range of workers.

The organization also needs to use various aspects of education and training in working with diverse employees, using a broad range of programmes, from basic skills to workshops designed to encourage managers and employees to value those with different demographic backgrounds. Note that training should be ongoing. Some organizations involve managers in conducting the training, to help provide a feeling of responsibility for making workplace diversity successful.

Look at Figure 2.10, which depicts the performance equation, building on Figure 1.1 on p 11.

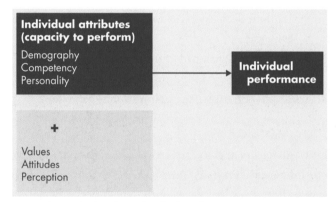

Figure 2.10: The individual performance equation.

Notice that we include two more important individual attribute variables:

- values
- attitudes

We will now discuss these variables in more detail.

VALUES

Values can be defined as broad preferences concerning appropriate courses of action or outcomes. As such, they reflect a person's sense of right and wrong, or what 'ought' to be.[61] 'Equal rights for all' and 'people should be treated with respect and dignity' are examples of values held by people. Values tend to influence attitudes and behaviour. If, for example, you value equal rights for all and you work for an organization that manifestly treats its managers much better than it does its other workers, you may form the attitude that your organization is an unfair place to work, and you may seek employment elsewhere.

Sources and types of values

People's values develop as a product of the learning and experiences they encounter in the cultural setting in which they live. Because learning and experiences differ from one person to another, value differences result. Such differences are likely to be deep seated and difficult (although not impossible) to change; many have their roots in early childhood and the way in which a person was raised.[62]

Psychologist Gordon Allport and his associates developed a classification of human values in the early 1930s.[63] However, although that classification had a major impact on the literature, it was not specifically designed for people in a work setting. More recently Meglino and associates have developed a values schema aimed at people in the workplace.[64] There are four values in this classification:

• achievement – getting things done and working hard to accomplish difficult things in life
• helping and concern for others – being concerned with other people and helping others
• honesty – telling the truth and doing what you feel is right
• fairness – being impartial and doing what is fair for all concerned.

The Meglino framework was developed from information obtained in the workplace, where these four values were shown to be especially important. Thus, the framework should be particularly relevant for studying organizational behaviour.

Importance of values

Values are important to managers and to the field of organizational behaviour because they have the potential to influence workplace attitudes, behaviours and outputs. In addition, values can be influential through value congruence, which occurs when individuals express positive feelings on encountering others who exhibit values similar to their own. When values differ, or are incongruent, conflicts may result over such things as goals and the means to achieve them. The Meglino value schema was used to examine value congruence between leaders and followers. The researchers found greater follower satisfaction with the leader when there was such congruence in terms of achievement, helping, honesty and fairness values.

Now turn to Table 2.1. The values reported here are based on responses from a sample of US managers and human resource professionals.[65] The responding organizational specialists were asked to identify the work-related values they believe to be most important to individuals in the workforce, both now and in the near future. The nine most popular values are listed in the table. Even though individual workers place their own importance on these values, and many countries have diverse workforces, this overall characterization is a good place for managers to start when dealing with employees in the new workplace.

However, we should be aware of applied research on value trends over time. Values change as the world is changing. For example, the 9/11 tragedies will have changed value ranking. When employees talk about security this is no longer assumed to be financial security but also personal security at work. Employment on the 79th floor of an office building may be more an issue of concern than it would have been before September 2001.

1 Recognition for competence and accomplishments	People want to be seen and recognized, both as individuals and teams, for their value, skills and accomplishments. They want to know that their contribution is appreciated.
2 Respect and dignity	This value focuses on how people are treated — through the jobs they hold, in response to their ideas, or by virtue of their background. The strong support for this value indicates that most people want to be respected for who they are; they want to be valued.
3 Personal choice and freedom	People want more opportunity to be free from constraints and decisions made for and about them by authorities. They want to be more autonomous and able to rely more on their own judgement. They wish to have more personal choice in what affects their lives.
4 Involvement at work	Large portions of the workforce want to be kept informed, included and involved in important decisions at work, particularly where these decisions affect their work and quality of life at work.
5 Pride in one's work	People want to do a good job and feel a sense of accomplishment. Fulfilment and pride come through quality workmanship.
6 Lifestyle quality	People pursue many different lifestyles and each person wants theirs to be of high quality. Work policies and practices have a great impact on lifestyle pursuits. The desire for time with family and time for leisure were strongly emphasised.
7 Financial security	People want to know that they can succeed. They want some security from economic cycles, rampant inflation or devastating financial situations. This appears to be a new variation on the desire for money—not continual pursuit of money, but enough to feel secure in today's world, enjoy a comfortable lifestyle and ride out bad times.
8 Self-development	The focus here is on the desire to improve continually, to do more with one's life, to reach one's potential, to learn and to grow. There is a strong desire by individuals to take initiative and to use opportunities to further themselves.
9 Health and wellness	This value reflects the ageing workforce and increased information on wellness. People want to organise life and work in ways that are healthy and contribute to log-term wellness.

Table 2.1: The top nine work-related values.

Source: Jamieson, D. and O'Mara, J., (1991), Managing workforce 2000, San Francisco, Jossey-Bass, pp. 28-29. Reproduced by permission of John Wiley & Sons, Inc.

ATTITUDES

Like values, attitudes are an important component of organizational behaviour. Attitudes are influenced by values but they focus on specific people or objects, whereas values have a more general focus. 'Employees should be allowed to participate' is a value. Your positive or negative feeling about your job as a result of the participation it allows, is an attitude. An attitude is a predisposition to respond in a positive or negative way to someone or something in our environment. When you say that you 'like' or 'dislike' someone or something you are expressing an attitude. One important work-related attitude is job satisfaction (see Chapter 5). This attitude expresses a person's positive or negative feelings about various aspects of their job and/or work environment.

Regardless of the specific attitude considered, it is important to remember that an attitude, like a value, is a concept or construct; that is, one never sees, touches or actually isolates an attitude. Rather, attitudes are *inferred* from the things people say (informally or formally) or do (their behaviour).

Components of attitudes

Study Figure 2.11 carefully. This shows attitudes as accompanied by antecedents and results. The beliefs and values antecedents in the figure form the cognitive component of an attitude: the beliefs, opinions, knowledge or information a person possesses. Beliefs represent ideas about someone or something and the conclusions people draw about them; they convey a sense of 'what is' to an individual. 'My job lacks responsibility' is a belief shown in Figure 2.11. Note that the beliefs may or may not be accurate. 'Responsibility is important' is a corresponding aspect of the cognitive component that reflects an underlying value. In Chapter 1 we introduced the concept of the psychological contract, we can now see that, as a belief it is essentially subjective – it is the individual's perception of the belief's reality that is most important.

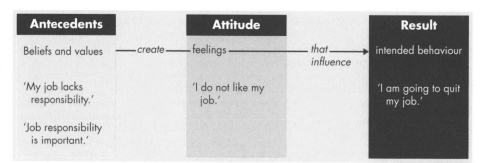

Figure 2.11: A work-related example of the three components of attitude.

The affective component of an attitude is a specific feeling regarding the personal impact of the antecedents. This is the actual attitude, such as 'I do not like my job'. The behavioural component is an intention to behave in a certain way based on specific feelings or attitudes. This intended behaviour is a predisposition to act in a specific way, such as 'I am going to quit my job'. In summary, the components of attitudes systematically relate to one another as follows:[66]

Beliefs and values → attitudes → behaviour.

Attitudes and behaviour

Look again at Figure 2.11. It is essential to recognize that the link between attitudes and behaviour is tentative. An attitude results in intended behaviour. This intention may or may not be carried out in a given circumstance. For example, a person with a favourable attitude towards unions would, one might assume, be likely to articulate positive opinions about unions. However, other practical factors in a given situation may override their intentions. For example, hearing a good friend say negative things about unions may lead to the suppression of the tendency to say something positive in the same conversation. The person has not changed his favourable attitude in this case, but nor has he carried out the associated intention to behave.

Even though attitudes do not always predict behaviour, the link between attitudes and potential or intended behaviour is important for managers to understand. Think about your work experiences or conversations with other people about their work. It is not uncommon to hear concerns expressed about someone's 'bad attitude'. These concerns typically reflect displeasure with the behavioural consequences with which the poor attitude is associated. As we will show in subsequent chapters, unfavourable attitudes in the form of low job satisfaction can result in costly labour turnover. Unfavourable attitudes may also result in absenteeism, tardiness and even impaired physical or mental health. One of the manager's responsibilities, therefore, is to recognize attitudes and to understand both their antecedents and their potential implications.

Attitudes and cognitive consistency

One additional avenue of research on attitudes involves cognitive consistency; that is, the consistency between a person's expressed attitudes and actual behaviour. Let us go back to the example depicted in Figure 2.11. A person in this illustration has an unfavourable attitude towards a job. She knows and recognizes this fact. Now assume that her intentions to leave are not fulfilled and that she continues to work at the same job each day. The result is an inconsistency between the attitude (job dissatisfaction) and the behaviour (continuing to work at the job).

Festinger, a noted social psychologist, uses the term **cognitive dissonance** to describe a state of inconsistency between an individual's attitudes and his or her behaviour.[67] Let us assume that you have the attitude that recycling rubbish is good for the economy but you do not recycle. Festinger predicts that such an inconsistency results in discomfort and a desire to reduce or eliminate it. There are three ways of achieving this reduction or elimination:

Cognitive dissonance *is a state of perceived inconsistency between a person's expressed attitudes and actual behaviour.*

- Changing the underlying attitude. You decide that recycling really is not a major priority for you as you now believe it has no impact on climate change.
- Changing future behaviour. You start recycling.
- Developing new ways of explaining or rationalizing the inconsistency. For example, recycling is good for the environment but you do not recycle because recycling bags and new rubbish collection procedures require more resources than are actually saved through recycling.

A new set of values and attitudes: global managerial competencies

The increasingly globalized nature of business, set out in Chapter 1, which often involves us dealing routinely with people from other cultures, means that managers and other workers must understand and respond to customers, governments and competitors from different parts of the world. To be successful, global managers in particular, must develop key global and cultural competencies: cultural self-awareness, cultural consciousness, ability to lead multicultural teams, ability to negotiate across cultures and a global mindset.[68]

- Cultural self-awareness. The starting pointing for cultural sensitivity is an understanding of the influence of one's own culture. A clear appreciation of one's own cultural values, assumptions and beliefs is a prerequisite for developing an appreciation of other cultures.[69]
- Cultural consciousness. A critical requirement for global managers is the ability to adapt to cultural requirements and manage cultural diversity.[70]
- The ability to lead multicultural teams. This requires working collaboratively with people with different cultural perspectives and developing cultural sensitivity.[71]
- The ability to negotiate across cultures. Global managers are required to negotiate with people from different countries and cultures. Negotiating styles and approaches vary substantially with each culture.[72]
- A global mindset. An essential global management competency has been described as 'global thinking', a 'global mindset' or a 'global perspective'. Managers need to appreciate the strategic implication of global business and develop a long-term orientation. A global mindset allows a manager to scan the global environment from a very broad perspective.[73]

Culture shock describes a series of stages experienced by people when they encounter a new cultural setting. It is normally depicted as a U-curve with initial elation followed by negative feelings, succeeded in turn by recovery and adjustment.

A re-evaluation of our own culturally derived values and attitudes may result in some psychological disorientation. Writers on cross-cultural management have drawn attention to the concept of **culture shock** in this context.[74] We see that many managers are able to cope with culture shock and emerge as even more effective performers. Note that the re-evaluation of their values and a recognition of cultural difference within the process of culture shock is necessary, if sometimes traumatic, if they are to succeed in their job roles. Here we have a potent illustration of the relationship between values, attitudes and job performance.

CONCLUSION

Thus far we have discussed individual differences in terms of perception, competency, personality, values and attitudes. All of these areas within OB are important in that they underlie so many of our routine experiences at work. For example, the way we perceive stimuli, whether these take the form of objects or other people, informs our attitudes and behaviour – perception is the springboard to what we do in our lives. An understanding of individual differences can also have a positive effect in terms of work and organizational performance. In this context turn back to the individual performance equation on p 11. Employees' capacity to perform depends on individual attributes (perception, competency and personality) that are influenced by values and attitudes. So an understanding of individual differences is critical to the study of OB and also helps us to understand some underpinnings of both individual and organizational performance.

SUMMARY

LEARNING OBJECTIVE 1
The individual performance equation

The individual performance equation views performance as the result of the personal attributes of individuals, the work efforts they put forth and the organizational support they receive. *Individual* performance factors are highlighted in the equation: performance = individual attributes × work effort × organizational support. Individual factors regarded as crucial within OB are our perceptual world, competency and personality characteristics. Work effort is reflected in the motivation to work. Organizational support consists of a wide range of organizational support mechanisms, such as work technology, resources and an enabling organizational structure that provide the opportunity for an individual to perform if they have the capacity and willingness.

LEARNING OBJECTIVE 2
The perceptual process

Individuals do not all perceive the world, including other people in it, in an identical fashion. This means that we select, organize, interpret and retrieve information from the environment in unique ways. Our perceptions are influenced by a number of factors, including social and physical aspects of the situation as well as personal factors such as needs, experience, values, attitudes and personality. An awareness of the perceptual process can help us more easily understand how other people may perceive a situation and enable us to minimize common perceptual distortions. Stereotypes are not always inaccurate but they frequently are, so should be avoided. You probably wish to be understood as an individual rather than a member of a wider category; other people will wish this too so an awareness of stereotyping can help us deal with others in a better way.

LEARNING OBJECTIVE 3
Competency characteristics of individuals

Competency characteristics among individuals consist of aptitude (the capability to learn something) and ability (the existing capacity to do something). Aptitudes are potential abilities. Abilities can be classified as cognitive abilities, physical abilities and emotional intelligence. We have argued that emotional intelligence is becoming increasingly prized in the workplace and is a very useful attribute for managers.

LEARNING OBJECTIVE 4
Personality characteristics of individuals

Personality captures the overall profile or combination of characteristics that represent the unique nature of a person as that person reacts and interacts with others. We expect there to be a predictable interplay between an individual's personality and a tendency to behave in certain ways. The nomothetic view of personality focuses on identifying and measuring traits important in organizational behaviour including, locus of control, authoritarianism/dogmatism, Machiavellianism, and the oft-cited 'big five' personality dimensions. The contrasting idiographic approach to this topic, emphasizes our individual uniqueness including an individual's self-concept. It allows for personality change in response to our experiences, so plays down the importance of fixed traits. This is conceivably a deeper view of personality in academic terms but is more challenging to put into operation in the organizational setting.

LEARNING OBJECTIVE 5
Capitalizing on workplace diversity

Increasing diversity is creating workplace challenges. Significant variations are occurring in skill levels, education, physical abilities, cultural backgrounds, lifestyles, personal values, individual needs and ethnic and social differences. Workplaces that are open to diversity can create competitive advantage. Specific cultural competencies are becoming increasingly relevant in the workplace and managers will need to possess these competencies even more in the future.

LEARNING OBJECTIVE 6
Values and attitudes

Values are global concepts that guide actions and judgements across a variety of situations. Values are especially important in organizational behaviour because they can influence performance outcomes directly. They can also have an indirect influence on behaviour by means of attitudes and perceptions. While treated as characteristics of individuals in this chapter, values can also reflect differences among various societal and organizational cultures – see also Chapter 8. Attitudes are influenced by values but focus on specific people or objects; in contrast, values have a more global focus. Attitudes are predispositions to respond in a positive or negative way to someone or something in one's environment. They operate through intended behaviour to influence actual behaviour or other variables.

CHAPTER 2 STUDY GUIDE

You can also test your understanding and access further resources at **www.wileyeurope. com/college/french**.

REVIEW QUESTIONS

1. Outline and explain the individual performance equation used in this chapter.
2. Identify the factors influencing an individual's capacity to perform. Why is each of these important?
3. Which factors influence the perceptual process and how do they do so?
4. List and briefly explain the dimensions of personality, put forward as the so-called big five traits.
5. Identify Meglino *et al.*'s four workplace values. Can you think of any additional values not included in their list?

APPLICATION QUESTIONS

1. Personality testing is widely used as a recruitment and selection strategy. What are the advantages and disadvantages of such a strategy and why? Please use examples in your answer.

2. The year is 2015 and you are employed by the 'Commission of Inquiry into the Ageing Workforce'. Your role is to prepare a report on current employment trends in relation to age; their broader implications for the economy and society and creative strategies to address problem issues. What would you write?

3. Colleges and universities are 'workplaces' for generating, acquiring and sharing new knowledge. There is great diversity within the student population, but this may not be used in the classroom teaching strategies that you experience. Develop a 'diversity management programme' suitable for use by teachers and lecturers in the classroom, which would reflect the diversity of the student group, and capitalize on its potential within this group to enhance learning. Explain the ideas behind your diversity management programme.

4. Explain the relevance of emotional intelligence and emotional management to the workplace. Illustrate your answer with examples.

5. What values and attitudes do you think individuals need to develop to become successful global managers? How do these values and attitudes differ from what a local manager must develop?

6. 'Workplace values and attitudes typically undergo significant change from one generation of workers to the next.' Do you agree? Explain and give examples.

RESEARCH QUESTIONS

1. Review the discussion of diversity in terms of the basic attributes of individuals in organizations. Write a report that answers the following questions.

   (a) Research and describe the current diversity of the workforce in a country of your choice.

   (b) Select at least five items for comparison and compare data on workforce diversity in the country identified in (a) with data from at least three other countries. Present your findings in a table. What were facilitators and barriers to the comprehensiveness of your analysis? Can you draw a conclusion on how well 'diversity' is understood in the countries you have looked at?

   (c) When comparing these different countries, can you conclude in overall terms whether country (a)'s workforce is more or less diverse than those of the other countries? Why or why not?

   (d) What is the implication of workforce diversity in terms of global business management?

2. Search the Internet for an organization in any of the transport, health, hospitality, banking or retail industries and notice the values that it espouses in its mission or goal statement and related materials. Do you think that these values are the most appropriate for this organization? Can you find any evidence that this organization is putting its values into practice? Does the organization monitor the values and attitudes of its staff to ensure alignment with corporate objectives and, if so, how?

RUNNING PROJECT

Using the information you have available about your organization, perform the following activities:

1. What does management look for in potential employees to ensure a good fit between employees and job requirements?
2. Assess the validity of selection methods chosen by the organization including any psychometric tests it uses.
3. How diverse is the workforce of your organization? Assess the strategies your organization has in place to encourage and benefit from workforce diversity.
4. Ascertain the importance the organization attaches to core values.

INDIVIDUAL ACTIVITY [75]

Personal values

For the following 16 items, rate how important each one is to you. Write a number between 0 and 100 on the line to the left of each item.

Not important				Important				Very important	
0	10	20	30	40	50	60	70	80	90	100

_____ 1. An enjoyable, satisfying job

_____ 2. A high-paying job

_____ 3. A strong intimate relationship

_____ 4. Meeting new people; social events

_____ 5. Involvement in community activities

_____ 6. Religion and spirituality

_____ 7. Exercising, playing sports

_____ 8. Intellectual development

_____ 9. A career with challenging opportunities

_____ 10. Nice cars, clothes, home etc.

_____ 11. Spending time with family

_____ 12. Having several close friends

_____ 13. Volunteer work for not-for-profit organizations, like a medical charity

_____ 14. Meditation, quiet time to think and contemplate.

_____ 15. A healthy balanced diet

_____ 16. Educational reading, and/or self-improvement programmes.

Below, transfer the numbers beside each of the 16 items to the appropriate column, then add the two numbers in each column.

Professional	Financial	Family	Social
1. _____	2. _____	3. _____	4. _____
9. _____	10. _____	11. _____	12. _____
Totals _____	_____	_____	_____

Community	Spiritual	Physical	Intellectual
5. _____	6. _____	7. _____	8. _____
13. _____	14. _____	15. _____	16. _____
Totals _____	_____	_____	_____

The higher the total in any area, the higher the value you place on that particular area. The closer the numbers are in all eight areas, the more well rounded you are – that is your values encompass a number of areas.

Think about the time and effort you put into your top three values. Is it sufficient to allow you to achieve the level of success you want in each area? If not, what can you do to change the situation? Is there any area in which you feel you should have a higher value total? If yes, which area? What can you do to realize this wish?

GROUP ACTIVITY [76]

Building a more positive self-concept

Objective
To develop a more positive self-concept.

Total time: 5–15 minutes.

Preparation
The objective of this activity is to develop a more positive self-concept. According to humanistic theory, the self-concept is important in the development of personality –

see our earlier summary of the idiographic approach to the topic. This may not be an easy exercise for you but it could result in improving your self-concept, which can have a major impact on your success in life.

Complete the following three-step plan for building a positive self-concept. You may be asked to share your plan with a person of your choice in class. (Your lecturer should tell you if you will be asked to do so.) If so, do not include anything you do not wish to share; write a second set of plans that you are willing to share.

Step 1: Identify your strengths and areas for improvement

What do you like about yourself? What can you do well (reflect on some of your accomplishments)? What skills and abilities do you have to offer people and organizations? What are the things about yourself or your behaviour that you could improve to help build a more positive self-concept?

Step 2: Set goals and visualize them

Based on your areas of improvement, write down some goals in a positive, affirmative format; three to five is recommended as a start. Once you achieve these goals, go on to others – for example, 'I am positive and successful' (not 'I need to stop thinking/worrying about failure') or 'I enjoy listening to others' (not 'I need to stop dominating the conversation'). Visualize yourself achieving your goals; for example, imagine yourself succeeding without worrying, or visualize having a conversation that you know you will have, without dominating it.

Step 3: Develop a plan and implement it

For each of your goals, state what you will do to achieve it. What specific action will you take to improve your self-concept by changing your thoughts or behaviour? Number your plans to correspond with your goals.

Procedure for group discussion

Break into teams of two or three members. Try to work with someone with whom you feel comfortable sharing your plan.

Using your prepared plan, share your questions and responses one at a time. It is recommended that you each share one question/answer before proceeding to the next. The choice is yours but be sure you get equal 'air time': for example, one person states 'what I like about myself' and the other person follows with their response. After you both share, go on to cover 'what I do well' and so on. During your sharing you may offer each other helpful suggestions but do so in a positive way; remember, you are helping one another build a more positive self-concept. Avoid saying anything that could be considered confrontational or critical.

MEDIZIN AG

Case Study

Medizin AG, is the fully owned German subsidiary of a large pharmaceutical company whose headquarters are in Canada. It manufactures a wide range of both prescription and 'over-the-counter' medicines. The company also invests heavily in research and development (R&D) in the hope of becoming a world player in pharmaceuticals.

The board of directors at Medizin AG at the German plant located in Gelsenkirchen are comprised of older males and this is also true of executive management posts within this subsidiary. The rest of the workforce consists of around 60 staff members, including highly qualified scientists and technicians involved with R&D, technically skilled pharmaceutical workers and a general factory workforce with seven different nationalities represented. In addition, administration is carried out by four female clerical officers.

Recently business has not been going well. Medizin AG has been finding it difficult to compete with overseas companies who manufacture medicines more cheaply, including strong competition from companies located in the Czech Republic, Portugal and Indonesia. At the moment, 95% of the skilled pharmaceutical workers in the plant are full-time permanent employees. To cut costs, senior managers have decided that the skilled pharmaceutical workers must work on a more flexible basis. The plan is to re-employ 50% of those workers as casual employees, which will result in a decrease in direct costs. The general factory workforce will be reduced by 30%. In addition, Medizin AG plans to set up an Internet business so that it can sell some products directly to the public, both in Germany and more widely, in the hope that it can cut more staff, including two of the clerical officers. These proposals will have to be discussed with the Works Council (including employee representatives) at the company within German codetermination law.

Questions

1. How are the employees at Medizin AG likely to perceive the proposed changes. Identify some ways in which perceptions could differ *within* the workforce.
2. What behaviours are you expecting from the skilled workers in response to the strategies proposed by the managers?
3. You are at the beginning of your studies in organizational behaviour. What additional knowledge about human behaviour (beyond that covered in this chapter) would help you to better understand the problems at Medizin AG and to propose suitable solutions?

Based on Drugs Inc, in J. Wood, R. Zeffane, M. Fromholtz & J. Fitzgerald (2006), *Organizational Behaviour: Core Concepts and Applications*, John Wiley & Sons: Milton, Queensland.

SUGGESTED READING

Arnold, J., Silvester, J., Patterson, F. *et al.* (2005), *Work Psychology, Understanding Human Behaviour in the Workplace*, 4th edn, FT Prentice Hall: Harlow. This book provides a useful outline of the nature of work psychology and the ways this discipline can be applied in a workplace setting.

Goffman, E. (1959), *The Presentation of Self in Everyday Life*, Penguin: Harmondsworth. This original source book contains numerous evocative examples of how workers present themselves to others by adopting roles and using fixed props as an actor would in a dramatic production.

END NOTES

1. www.uktv.co.uk/index.cfm/uktv. People, accessed 22 May 2007.

2. www.rtlgames.co.uk/enterthedragon.html, accessed 22 May 2007.

3. Ibid.

4. W.E. Hill (1915), *Puck*, 6 November.

5. Linehan, M (2005), Women in international management, in *International Human Resource Management: A Critical Text* (eds H. Scullion and M. Linehan). Palgrave Macmillan: Basingstoke.

6. Kiely, J. & Henbest, A. (2000), Sexual harassment at work: experiences from an oil refinery. *Women in Management Review*, **15** (2), 65–77.

7. Wagner, J.A. III & Hollenbeck, J.R. (1998), *Organizational Behaviour*, 3rd edn, Prentice Hall: Upper Saddle River, NJ, p. 59.

8. Mullins, L.J & Carter, L. (2007), *Management and Organizational Behaviour*, FT Prentice Hall: Harlow, p. 209.

9. Cronshaw, S.F. & Lord, R.G. (1987), Effects of categorization, attribution and encoding processes in leadership perceptions. *Journal of Applied Psychology*, **72**, 97–106.

10. Ibid.

11. Hunt, J.G. (1991), *Leadership: A New Synthesis*, Sage: Newbury Park, CA.

12. Hall, E.T (1990), *Understanding Cultural Differences*, Intercultural Press: Yarmouth, ME.

13. Hunt, J.G, Baliga, B.R & Peterson, M.P. (1988), Strategic Apex leader scripts and an organizational life cycle approach to leadership and excellence. *Journal of Management Development*, 7, 61–83.

14. See www. news.siu.edu/news/August06/080 306sm6063, accessed 26 May 2007.

15. Dearborn, D.W. & Simon, H.A. (1958), Selective perception: a note on the departmental identification of executives. *Sociometry*, **21**, 140–144.

16. Walsh, J.P. (1988), Selectivity and selective perception: an investigation of managers' belief structures and information processing. *Academy of Management Journal*, **24**, 453–470.

17. Sterling Livingston, J. (1969), Pygmalion in management. *Harvard Business Review*, July/ August, 81–89.

18. Eden, D. & Shani, A.B. (1982) Pygmalion goes to boot camp. *Journal of Applied Psychology*, **67**, 194–199.

19. Manzoni, J.-F. & Barsoux, J.-L. (2002), *The Set Up to fail Syndrome: How Good Managers Cause Great People to Fail*, Harvard Business School Press: Boston, MA.

20. Anderson, N. & Shackleton, V. (1993), *Successful Selection Interviewing*, Blackwell, Oxford.

21. Gardner, W.L & Martinko, M.J. (1988), Impression management in organizations. *Journal of Management*, June, 332.

22. Goffman, E. (1959), *The Presentation of Self in Everyday Life*, Penguin: Harmondsworth.

23. Kelley, H.H. (1972) Attribution in Social Interaction, in *Attribution: Perceiving the Causes of Behaviour* (eds E.E. Jones, DE. Kanouse, H.H., Kelley *et al.*), General Learning Press: Morristown, NJ.

24. Harvey, J.H. & Weary, G. (1984), Current issues in attribution theory and research. *Annual Review of Psychology*, **35**, 427–459.

25. http://soccernet.espn.go.com/news/story, accessed 26 May 2007.

26. Ibid.

27. Steers, R.M., Bischoff, S.J. & Higgins, L.H. (1992), Cross cultural management research. *Journal of Management Inquiry,* December, 325–326.

28. Crant, J.M. & Bateman, T.S. (1993), Assignment of credit and blame for performance outcomes. *Academy of Management Journal,* February, 7–27.

29. Fosterling, F. (1985), Attributional retraining: a review, *Psychological Bulletin,* November, 496–512.

30. Smith, E. (2005), Measurement of human potential, *Journal of Workplace Learning,* **17** (1/2), 7.

31. Spearman, C. (1927), *The Abilities of Man,* Macmillan: New York.

32. Gentleman, A. (2006), India grounds hostesses who are 'too fat to fly', *Observer,* 5 November.

33. Herkenhoff, L. (2004), Culturally tuned emotional intelligence: an effective change management tool? *Strategic Change,* **13** (2), 73.

34. Goleman, D. (2000), *Working with Emotional Intelligence.* Bantam: New York.

35. Bar-On, R. (2001), Emotional intelligence and self-actualization, in *Emotional Intelligence in Everyday Life: A Scientific Inquiry* (eds J. Ciarrochi, J. Forgas & J.D. Mayer), Psychology Press: New York.

36. Mayer, J.D. & Salovey, P. (1997), What is emotional intelligence? In *Emotional Development and Emotional Intelligence* (eds P. Salovey & D.J. Sluyter), Basic Books: New York.

37. Hochschild, A. (2003), *The Commercialization of Intimate Life,* University of California Press: Berkeley, Los Angeles.

38. Kinnie, N., Hutchinson, S. & Purcell, J. (2000), Fun and surveillance: the paradox of high commitment management in call centres. *International Journal of Human Resource Management,* **11** (5), 967–985.

39. Bolton, S. (2005), *Emotion Management in the Workplace,* Palgrave Macmillan: Basingstoke.

40. Stock, R. (2003), Watch those emotions – they're the new IQ, *Sunday Star Times* (Wellington, New Zealand), 21 December.

41. Woodruffe, C. (2001), Promotional intelligence, *People Management,* **7** (1), 26–29.

42. Goleman, D. (1999), *Working with Emotional Intelligence,* Bloomsbury: London.

43. Kolbe, K. & Kolbe, D. (1999), Management by instinct leads the way to change, www.kolbe.com/info_center/articles.cfm, accessed 9 November 2007.

44. Freud, S. (1935), *A General Introduction to Psychoanalysis,* Carlton House: New York.

45. Board, B.J. & Fritzon, K. (2005), Disordered personalities at work, *Psychology, Crime and Law,* **11** (1), 17–32.

46. Perkins, S.J. & Shortland, S.M. (2006), *Strategic International Human Resource Management,* 2nd edn, Kogan Page: London.

47. Eysenck, H.J. (1970), *The Structure of Human Personality,* 3rd edn, Methuen: London.

48. Allport, G. & Odbert, H. (1936), Trait names: a psycholexical study. *Psychological Monographs,* **47**, 211–214.

49. Hogan, J. & Hogan, R. (1988), How to measure employee reliability, *Journal of Applied Psychology,* **74**, 273–279.

50. Rotter, J.B. (1966), Generalized expectancies for internal versus external control of reinforcement, *Psychological Monographs,* **80**, 1–28.

51. Hellriegel, D., Slocum, J.W. Jr & Woodman, R.W. (2004), *Organizational Behaviour,* 11th edn, West: St Paul.

52. Wagner, J.A. III & Hollenbeck, J.R. (1995), *Management of Organizational Behaviour,* Prentice Hall: Englewood Cliffs, NJ, Ch. 4.

53. Hamilton, V.L. & Kelman, H.C. (1990), *Crimes of Obedience: Towards a Social Psychology of Authority and Responsibility,* Yale University Press: London.

54. Kelman, H.C. (2005), The policy context of torture: a social-psychological analysis, *International Review of the Red Cross,* **87** (857).

55. Waldmeir, P. (2005), Anderson conviction overturned, *Financial Times* (London), 1 June, p. 15.

56. Machiavelli, N. (1961), *The Prince,* trans. George Bull, Penguin: Harmondsworth.

57. Cyriac, K. & Dharmaraj, R. (1994), Machiavellianism in Indian management, *Journal of Business Ethics,* **13** (4), 281–286.

58. Larsson, M., Pederson, N.L & Stattin, H. (in press), Associations between iris characteristics and personality in adulthood, *Biological Psychology*.

59. Watson, T.J. (2006), *Organising and Managing Work*, 2nd edn, FT Prentice Hall: Harlow.

60. Rogers, C.R. (1947), Some observations on the organization of personality, *American Psychologist*, **2**, 358–368.

61. Jacob, P.E., Flink, J.J. & Schuchman, H.L. (1962), Values and their function in decision making, *American Behavioral Scientist*, **5** (9), 6–38.

62. Rokeach, M. & Ball Rokeach, S.J. (1989), Stability and change in American value priorities, 1968–1981, *American Psychologist*, May, 775–784.

63. Allport, G., Vernon, P.E. & Lindzey, G. (1931), *Study of Values*, Houghton Mifflin: Boston, MA.

64. Meglino, B.M., Ravlin, E.C. & Adkins, C.L. (1992), The measurement of work value congruence: a field study comparison, *Journal of Management*, **1** (1), 33–43.

65. Jamieson, D. & O'Mara, J. (1991), *Managing Workforce 2000*, Jossey-Bass: San Francisco, pp. 28–29.

66. Fishbein, M. & Ajzen, I.(1975), *Belief, Attitude, Intention, and Behaviour: an Introduction to Theory and Research*, Addison-Wesley: Reading, MA.

67. Festinger, L. (1957), *A Theory of Cognitive Dissonance*, Stanford University Press: Palo Alto, CA.

68. Cant, A.G. (2004), Internationalizing the business curriculum: developing intercultural competence, *Journal of American Academy of Business*, **5** (1/2), 177–182.

69. Adler, N.J. (2002), *International Dimensions of Organizational Behaviour*, 4th edn. South-Western College Publishing, Thomson Learning: Cincinnati, OH.

70. McCall, M.W. & Hollenbeck, G.P. (2002), *Developing Global Executives: the Lessons of International Experience*, Harvard Business School: Boston, MA.

71. Schneider, S. & Barsoux, J.-L., (2003), *Managing Across Cultures*, 2nd edn, FT Prentice Hall: Harlow.

72. Hyman, R. (2003), Varieties of capitalism, national industrial relations systems and transnational challenges, in *International Human Resource Management* (eds A.-W. Harzing & J. van Ruysseveldt), Sage: London.

73. Bartlett, C.A. & Ghoshal, S. (1998), *Managing Across Borders: The Transnational Solution*, 2nd edn, Random House: London.

74. French, R. (2007), *Cross-Cultural Management in Work Organizations*, CIPD: London.

75 Lussier, R.N. (1993), Human Relations in Organizations: a skill building approach (2nd edn), Homewood, IL, Richard D. Irwin. © The McGraw-Hill Companies, Inc. Reproduced by permission.

76. Ibid.

CHAPTER
3

Learning, reinforcement and self-management

LEARNING OBJECTIVES

After studying this chapter you should be able to:

- identify the various general approaches to learning
- explain organizational behavioural modification and how reinforcement strategies are involved in it
- discuss social learning theory and behavioural self management
- examine modern forms of learning
- discuss the concept of the learning organization.

A PUNISHMENT OR A REWARD?

Bob Segers works for a major US car manufacturer based in Chicago. The company has operated a quality management approach for the last decade, in which each 'cell' (or department) is responsible for its own output standards and quality checking. His performance has recently changed, resulting in a poorer standard of quality of his work. As well as letting himself down, he is also letting the production team down.

His team leader (cell leader) calls him over for a chat, and simply says 'Bob, take the day off tomorrow.' (Bob takes the following day off, and receives his full pay for the day.) There is no extra cover arranged to fill the gap that Bob's absence will create.

This example illustrates the difficulties involved in attempting to change employees' behaviour. In this instance, how could Bob perceive the order to stay home from his team leader and to what extent is having the next day off seen as a punishment? There could also be cultural dimensions to this topic area. How would the instruction given by this team leader be perceived by a fellow worker in Spain, France, UK, China or another country – more of a punishment than a reward?

INTRODUCTION

This chapter will focus on learning that takes place primarily within the workplace or in workplace-related activities. The concept of reinforcement and learning theories will then be considered, leading to an exploration of the concept of self-management.

THE NATURE OF LEARNING

The growth of literature surrounding workplace learning, knowledge management and core competence in the workplace is testament to the need to link learning with competitive advantage. According to Hamel,[1] 'A company's value derives not from things, but from knowledge, know-how, intellectual assets, competencies – all embodied in people.' Similarly, if an organization's expertise (skill set, knowledge, capabilities, core competence and so forth) is standing still, then the company will not improve and, by definition, will not remain competitive.

Some organizational philosophies may still be based upon a predominantly instructional training approach whereby remedial action needs to take place to put something right. However, if it isn't broken and no fixing is needed, then no development activity will take place. Training interventions therefore only take place when the need is significant or the consequences deemed important (like essential health and safety training).

Contrary to this philosophy is the lifelong learning approach within organizations, adopting a much more developmental approach to training *and* development. If employees are seen as an important asset within the organization, then they need to be developed and nurtured, so that this asset can be maximized.

Malone[2] defines training as 'a planned and systematic way of improving a person's knowledge, skills and attitudes so that he or she can perform the current job more competently' (p. 76). Malone's definition of development is 'the process of preparing a person to take on more onerous responsibilities or equip him or her for future promotion within the organization' (p. 76). The same author's definition of learning is 'the process which brings about persistent change in behaviour. Learning gives a person increased competence to deal successfully with his or her environment as by acquiring knowledge, skills and attitudes' (p. 152).

Learning can be defined more simply as a relatively permanent change in behaviour that occurs as a result of experience. The critical question for the management of organizations is as to how this impacts upon performance.

Learning relies upon the acquisition of the requisite skills or competencies to perform a task, job or role. Whereas performance includes learning and the motivation to engage in behaviour appropriate to apply to learning.

Learning can occur at various levels within an organization – at individual, group, team, department, division level or throughout the organization. This chapter concentrates primarily on individual learning but the importance of team learning and organizational learning cannot be underestimated.

It would be foolhardy to think that all learning in organizations is planned, systematic, structured and predictable. There are four general approaches to learning that have differing philosophical and historic principles:

- classical and operant conditioning
- cognitive learning
- social learning
- modern approaches to learning.

Each approach offers useful insights into understanding organizational behaviour.

Lifelong learning adopts the philosophy that we learn throughout our lives, and that learning does not cease when we reach a certain age.

Organizational learning is the process of acquiring knowledge and using information to adapt successfully to changing circumstances.

CLASSICAL CONDITIONING AND OPERANT CONDITIONING

Behaviourists, such as Pavlov, and Skinner emphasize 'behaviour' as their central focus, not thoughts or feelings. Their emphasis is upon observation of behaviours.

Classical conditioning is a form of learning through association that involves the manipulation of stimuli to influence behaviour. Pavlov, a Russian psychologist, taught dogs to salivate at the sound of a bell by ringing the bell when feeding the dogs. The sight of the food naturally caused the dogs to salivate. Eventually, the dogs 'learned' to associate the bell ringing with the presentation of meat and to salivate at the ringing of the bell alone. Such 'learning' through association is so common in organizations that it is often ignored until it causes considerable confusion. Look at Figure 3.1.

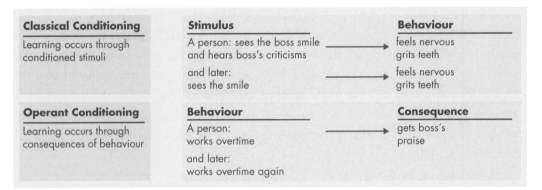

Figure 3.1: Differences between classical and operant conditioning approaches for a boss and subordinate.

A **stimulus** is something that incites action.

The key is to understand a stimulus and a conditioned stimulus. A **stimulus** is something that incites action and draws forth a response (the meat for the dogs). The trick is to associate one neutral potential stimulus (the bell ringing) with another initial stimulus that already affects behaviour (the meat). The once-neutral stimulus is called a *conditioned stimulus* when it affects behaviour in the same way as the initial stimulus. In Figure 3.1, the boss's smiling becomes a conditioned stimulus because of its linkage to his criticisms.

Operant conditioning is the process of controlling behaviour by manipulating its consequences.

Operant conditioning, popularized by B.F. Skinner, is an extension of the classical case to much more practical affairs.[3] It includes more than just a stimulus and a response behaviour. **Operant conditioning** is the process of controlling behaviour by manipulating its consequences. Classical and operant conditioning differ in two important ways. First, control in operant conditioning is via manipulation of consequences. Secondly, operant conditioning calls for examining antecedents, behaviour and consequences. The *antecedent* is the condition leading up to or 'cueing' behaviour. For example, in Figure 3.1, an agreement between the boss and the employee to work overtime as needed is an antecedent. If the employee works overtime, this would be the *behaviour*, while the *consequence* would be the boss's praise.

The **law of effect** refers to Thorndike's observation that behaviour that results in a pleasant outcome is likely to be repeated; behaviour that results in an unpleasant outcome is not likely to be repeated.

A boss who wants a behaviour, such as working overtime, to be repeated must manipulate the consequences. The basis for manipulating consequences is E.L. Thorndike's law of effect.[4] The law of effect is simple but powerful: behaviour that results in a pleasant outcome is likely to be repeated, while behaviour that results in an unpleasant outcome is not likely to be repeated. The implications of this law are rather straightforward. If, as a supervisor, you want more of a behaviour, you must make the consequences for the individual positive.

Note that the emphasis is on consequences that can be manipulated rather than on consequences inherent in the behaviour itself. Organizational behaviour research often emphasizes specific types of rewards that are considered by the **reinforcement** perspective to influence individual behaviour. *Extrinsic rewards* are positively valued work outcomes that are given to the individual by some other person. They are important external reinforcers or environmental consequences that can substantially influence a person's work behaviours through the law of effect. Figure 3.2 presents a sample of extrinsic rewards that managers can allocate to their subordinates.[5] Some of these rewards are contrived, or planned, rewards that have direct costs and budgetary implications. Examples are pay increases and cash bonuses. A second category includes natural rewards that have no cost other than the manager's personal time and efforts. Examples are verbal praise and recognition in the workplace.

Reinforcement *is the administration of a consequence as a result of behaviour.*

Contrived Rewards: Some Direct Cost		Natural Rewards: No Direct Cost	
refreshments	promotion	smiles	recognition
piped-in music	trips	greetings	feedback
nice offices	company car	compliments	asking advice
cash bonuses	paid insurance	special jobs	
merit pay increases	stock options		
profit sharing	gifts		
office parties	sport tickets		

Figure 3.2: A sample of extrinsic rewards allocated by managers.

Reinforcement strategies

We now bring the notions of classical conditioning, operant conditioning, reinforcement and extrinsic rewards together to show how the direction, level and persistence of individual behaviour can be changed. This combination is called OB Mod after its longer title of **organizational behaviour modification**. OB Mod is the systematic reinforcement of desirable work behaviour and the nonreinforcement or punishment of unwanted work behaviour. OB Mod includes four basic reinforcement strategies: positive reinforcement, negative reinforcement (or avoidance), punishment, and **extinction**.

Organizational behaviour modification *is the systematic reinforcement of desirable work behaviour and the nonreinforcement or punishment of unwanted work behaviour.*

B. F. Skinner and his followers advocated **positive reinforcement** – the administration of positive consequences that tend to increase the likelihood of repeating the desirable behaviour in similar settings. For example, a Texas Instruments manager nods to a subordinate to express approval after she makes a useful comment during a sales meeting. Obviously, the boss wants more useful comments. Later, the subordinate makes another useful comment, just as the boss hoped she would.

Extinction *is the withdrawal of the reinforcing consequences of behaviour.*

To begin using a strategy of positive reinforcement, we need to be aware that positive reinforcers and rewards are not necessarily the same. Recognition, for example, is both a reward and a potential positive reinforcer. Recognition becomes a positive reinforcer only if a person's performance later improves. Sometimes, rewards turn out not to be positive reinforcers. For example, a supervisor might praise a subordinate in front of other group members for finding errors in a report. If the group members then give the worker the silent treatment, however, the worker may stop looking for errors in the future. In this case, the supervisor's 'reward' does not serve as a positive reinforcer.

Positive reinforcement *is the administration of positive consequences that tend to increase the likelihood of repeating the behaviour in similar settings.*

*The **law of contingent reinforcement** is the view that for a reward to have maximum reinforcing value it must be delivered only if the desired behaviour is exhibited.*

*The **law of immediate reinforcement** states that the more immediate the delivery of a reward after the occurrence of a desirable behaviour, the greater the reinforcing effect on behaviour.*

***Shaping** is the creation of a new behaviour by the positive reinforcement of successive approximations to the desired behaviour.*

***Continuous reinforcement** is a reinforcement schedule that administers a reward each time a desired behaviour occurs.*

***Intermittent reinforcement** is a reinforcement schedule that rewards behaviour only periodically.*

To have maximum reinforcement value, a reward must be delivered only if the desired behaviour is exhibited. That is, the reward must be contingent on the desired behaviour. This principle is known as the law of contingent reinforcement. In the Texas Instruments example, the supervisor's praise was contingent on the subordinate's making constructive comments. Finally, the reward must be given as soon as possible after the desired behaviour. This is known as the law of immediate reinforcement.[6] If the TI boss waited for the annual performance review to praise the subordinate for providing constructive comments, the law of immediate reinforcement would be violated.

Now that we have presented the general concepts, it is time to address two important issues of implementation. First, what do you do if the behaviour approximates what you want but is not exactly on target? Second, is it necessary to provide reinforcement each and every time? These are issues of shaping and scheduling, respectively.

If the desired behaviour is specific in nature and is difficult to achieve, a pattern of positive reinforcement, called shaping, can be used. Shaping is the creation of a new behaviour by the positive reinforcement of successive approximations leading to the desired behaviour. For example, new machine operators in the Ford Motor casting operation in Ohio must learn a complex series of tasks in pouring molten metal into the casting in order to avoid gaps, overfills, or cracks.[7] The moulds are filled in a three-step process with each step progressively more difficult than its predecessor. Astute master craftspersons first show neophytes how to pour the first step and give praise based on what they did correctly. As the apprentices gain experience they are given praise only when all of the elements of the first step are completed successfully. Once the apprentices have mastered the first step, they progress to the second. Reinforcement is given only when the entire first step and an aspect of the second step are completed successfully. Over time, apprentices learn all three steps and are given contingent positive rewards immediately for a complete casting that has no cracks or gaps. In this way, behaviour is shaped gradually rather than changed all at once.

Positive reinforcement can be given according to either continuous or intermittent schedules. Continuous reinforcement administers a reward each time a desired behaviour occurs. Intermittent reinforcement rewards behaviour only periodically. These alternatives are important because the two schedules may have very different impacts on behaviour. In general, continuous reinforcement elicits a desired behaviour more quickly than does intermittent reinforcement. Thus, continuous reinforcement would be important in the initial training of the apprentice casters. At the same time, continuous reinforcement is more costly in the consumption of rewards and is more easily extinguished when reinforcement is no longer present. In contrast, behaviour acquired under intermittent reinforcement lasts longer upon the discontinuance of reinforcement than does behaviour acquired under continuous reinforcement. In other words, it is more resistant to extinction. Thus, as the apprentices master an aspect of the pouring, the schedule is switched from continuous to intermittent reinforcement.

As shown in Figure 3.3, intermittent reinforcement can be given according to fixed or variable schedules. *Variable schedules* typically result in more consistent patterns of desired behaviour than do fixed reinforcement schedules.

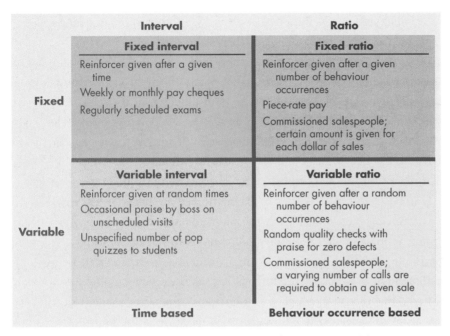

Figure 3.3: Four types of intermittent reinforcement schedules.

Fixed-interval schedules provide rewards at the first appearance of a behaviour after a given time has elapsed. *Fixed-ratio schedules* result in a reward each time a certain number of the behaviours have occurred. A *variable-interval schedule* rewards behaviour at random times, whereas a *variable-ratio schedule* rewards behaviour after a random number of occurrences. For example, as the apprentices perfect their technique for a stage of pouring castings, the astute masters switch to a variable-ratio reinforcement.

A second reinforcement strategy used in OB Mod is negative reinforcement or avoidance – the withdrawal of negative consequences, which tends to increase the likelihood of repeating the desirable behaviour in similar settings. For example, a manager at McDonald's regularly nags a worker about his poor performance and then stops nagging when the worker does not fall behind one day. We need to focus on two aspects here: the negative consequences followed by the withdrawal of these consequences when desirable behaviour occurs. The term 'negative reinforcement' comes from this withdrawal of the negative consequences. This strategy is also sometimes called *avoidance* because its intent is for the person to avoid the negative consequence by performing the desired behaviour. For instance, we stop at a red light to avoid a traffic ticket, or a worker who prefers the day shift is allowed to return to that shift if she performs well on the night shift.

A third OB Mod strategy is punishment. Unlike positive reinforcement and negative reinforcement, punishment is intended not to encourage positive behaviour but to discourage negative behaviour. Formally defined, punishment is the administration of negative consequences or the withdrawal of positive consequences that tend to reduce the likelihood of repeating the behaviour in similar settings. The first type of punishment is illustrated by a fast-food manager who assigns a tardy worker to an unpleasant job, such

Negative reinforcement *is the withdrawal of negative consequences, which tends to increase the likelihood of the behaviour being repeated in similar settings; it is also known as avoidance.*

Punishment *is the administration of negative consequences that tend to reduce the likelihood of repeating the behaviour in similar settings.*

as cleaning the toilets. An example of withdrawing positive consequences is a fast-food manager who docks the employee's pay when she is tardy.

Some scholarly work illustrates the importance of punishment by showing that punishment administered for poor performance leads to enhanced performance without a significant effect on satisfaction. However, punishment seen by workers as arbitrary and capricious leads to very low satisfaction as well as low performance.[8] Thus, punishment can be handled poorly, or it can be handled well. Of course, the manager's challenge is to know when to use this strategy and how to use it correctly.

Finally, punishment may be offset by positive reinforcement received from another source. It is possible for a worker to be reinforced by peers at the same time that the worker is receiving punishment from the manager. Sometimes the positive value of such peer support is so great that the individual chooses to put up with the punishment. Thus, the undesirable behaviour continues. As many times as an experienced worker may be verbally reprimanded by a supervisor for playing jokes on new employees, for example, the 'grins' offered by other workers may well justify continuation of the jokes in the future.

Does all of this mean that punishment should never be administered? Of course not. The important things to remember are to administer punishment selectively and then to do it right.

The final OB Mod reinforcement strategy is *extinction* – the withdrawal of the reinforcing consequences for a given behaviour. For example, Jack is often late for work, and his co-workers cover for him (positive reinforcement). The manager instructs Jack's co-workers to stop covering for him, withdrawing the reinforcing consequences. The manager has deliberately used extinction to get rid of an undesirable behaviour. This strategy decreases the frequency of or weakens the behaviour. The behaviour is not 'unlearned'; it simply is not exhibited. As the behaviour is no longer reinforced, it will reappear if reinforced again. Whereas positive reinforcement seeks to establish and maintain desirable work behaviour, extinction is intended to weaken and eliminate undesirable behaviour.

Figure 3.4 summarizes and illustrates the use of each OB Mod strategy. They are all designed to direct work behaviour toward practices desired by management. Both positive and negative reinforcement are used to strengthen the desirable behaviour of improving work quality when it occurs. Punishment is used to weaken undesirable behaviour leading to high error rates and involves either administering negative consequences or withdrawing positive consequences. Similarly, extinction is used deliberately to weaken undesirable behaviour leading to high error rates when it occurs. Note also, however, that extinction is used inadvertently to weaken the desirable behaviour of low error rates. Finally, these strategies may be used in combination as well as independently.

Reinforcement and employee rights

Whilst the effective use of reinforcement strategies can help manage human behaviour at work, these approaches are also susceptible to a range of criticisms.

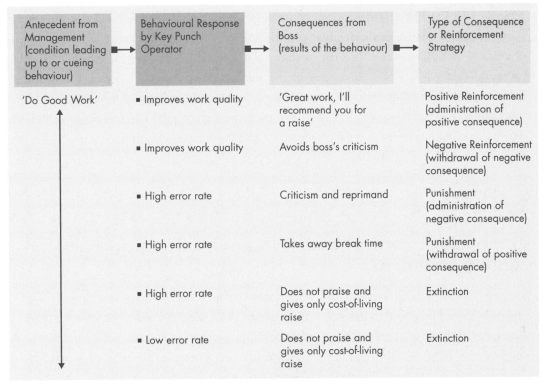

Antecedent from Management (condition leading up to or cueing behaviour)	Behavioural Response by Key Punch Operator	Consequences from Boss (results of the behaviour)	Type of Consequence or Reinforcement Strategy
'Do Good Work'	▪ Improves work quality	'Great work, I'll recommend you for a raise'	Positive Reinforcement (administration of positive consequence)
	▪ Improves work quality	Avoids boss's criticism	Negative Reinforcement (withdrawal of negative consequence)
	▪ High error rate	Criticism and reprimand	Punishment (administration of negative consequence)
	▪ High error rate	Takes away break time	Punishment (withdrawal of positive consequence)
	▪ High error rate	Does not praise and gives only cost-of-living raise	Extinction
	▪ Low error rate	Does not praise and gives only cost-of-living raise	Extinction

Figure 3.4: Applying reinforcement strategies.

RESEARCH IN OB

Look at the article by Makin and Sutherland at the end of Part 2 of this book. Note how these researchers have applied a behavioural approach to a real-life organizational problem, in this case reducing accidents at work. They showed how employees were encouraged to report the full range of accidents and accident-related activities by using positive rewards – reporting was in itself regarded as a positive behaviour and rewarded accordingly. As a result of this intervention, the company in question experienced a significant drop in work-related accidents, resulting in a far safer working environment.

Managerial use of these approaches is not without criticism, however. For example, some reports on the 'success' of specific programmes involve isolated cases that have been analysed without the benefit of scientific research designs. It is hard to conclude definitively whether the observed results were caused by reinforcement dynamics. In fact, one critic argues that the improved performance may well have occurred only because of the goal setting involved – because specific performance goals were clarified and workers were individually held accountable for their accomplishment.

Another major criticism rests with the potential value dilemmas associated with using reinforcement to influence human behaviour at work. For example, some critics may argue

Burnout *is a psychological concept associated with the experience of long-term exhaustion or diminished interest usually within the workplace.*

that the systematic use of reinforcement strategies leads to a demeaning and dehumanising view of people that stunts individual growth and development. A related criticism is that managers abuse the power of their position and knowledge by exerting external control over individual behaviour. Advocates of the reinforcement approach attack the problem head on: they agree that behaviour modification involves the control of behaviour, but they also argue that behaviour control is part of every manager's job. The real poser is how to ensure that manipulation is done in a positive and constructive fashion.

OB IN ACTION

To what extent does control over the environment impact upon the ability to learn?

According to Ramirez,[9] the ability of humans to learn is impaired if they feel as though they cannot control their environment. Seligman's controversial experiments on dogs in the 1960s and 1970s led by accident to the concept of 'learned helplessness'. Seligman[10] set up experimental laboratories, whereby dogs were restrained in a harness and administered several shocks, which were paired with a conditioned stimulus (as in traditional classical conditioning experiments). The dogs were then placed in a shuttle box. They could avoid shocks by jumping over a barrier. These experiments then turned to operant conditioning. Only about a third of all dogs in the experiments (out of the 150 total sample), failed to jump the barrier and hence avoid the shock. Seligman argued that this prior exposure to inescapable shock had interfered with the dogs' ability to learn, even though escape and therefore avoidance of shock was possible.

Learned helplessness can take part in everyday working life, where employees feel that they have

little control over their working environment. An organization that employs constant change may elicit certain psychological states in its employees.

Consider for example the case of **burnout**. Within the medical profession in the UK, high rates of burnout have been encountered with nurses.[11] Whilst there is a line of argument to link burnout with clinical depression and specific types of personality traits, employees in certain high stress occupational areas are more susceptible to burnout. Burnout may result in an employee simply not being able to face their work or place of work anymore, they have simply 'had enough'. Like Seligman's dogs, employees simply give up.

Questions

1. To what extent does Seligman's work negate the work of behaviourists such as Pavlov and Skinner?
2. Can you identify examples of 'learned helplessness' in the workplace which you have either observed or experienced yourself.

COGNITIVE LEARNING

Cognitive learning is learning that is achieved by thinking about the perceived relationship between events and individual goals and expectations. The process motivation theories reviewed in Chapter 4 help to illustrate how this learning perspective is applied to the work setting. These theories are concerned with explaining how and why people decide to do things by examining the ways in which people come to view various work activities as perceived opportunities to pursue desired rewards, to eliminate felt inequities and the like. These cognitive explanations of learning differ markedly from the behaviourist explanations of operant conditioning.

Cognitive learning *is a form of learning achieved by thinking about the perceived relationship between events and individual goals and expectations.*

Social learning

Social learning is learning that is achieved through the reciprocal interactions among people, behaviour and environment. Social learning theory is expressed in the work of Albert Bandura[12] and uses such reciprocal interactions to integrate operant and cognitive learning approaches; that is, environmental determinism and self-determinism are combined. Behaviour is seen not simply as a function of external antecedents and consequences, or as being caused by only internal needs, satisfaction or expectations (see Chapter 4), but as a combination of the two. Social learning theory stresses our capacity to learn from re-enforcement and punishments experienced by other people and ourselves. Figure 3.5 illustrates and elaborates on this reciprocal interaction notion.

Social learning *is learning that is achieved through the reciprocal interaction between people and their environments.*

In Figure 3.5, the individual uses modelling or vicarious learning to acquire behaviour by observing and imitating others. The person then attempts to acquire these behaviours by modelling them through practice. The 'models' could be the person's parents, friends or even well known celebrities. In the work situation, the model may be a manager or co-worker who demonstrates desired behaviours. Mentors or senior workers who befriend more inexperienced protégés can also be very important models.

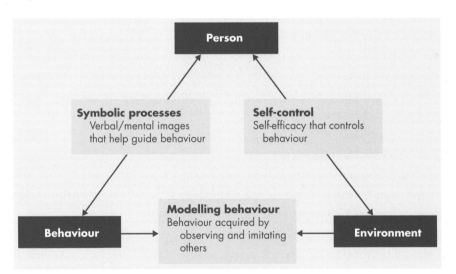

Figure 3.5: Social learning model.
Source: Adapted form Kreitner, R. and Luthans, F. (1984) *Organizational Dynamics*, Autumn, P.55.

Although mentors or role models may come from diverse sources, the shortage of appropriate mentors or role models is often a concern in the contemporary workplace. Indeed, some have argued that a shortage of mentors for women in management is a major constraint on their progression up the career ladder. It is also a leading reason why many women are leaving the corporate world and moving into self-employment.[13]

Case Study

COACH JACKSON CRACKS THE WHIP

There is an awful lot of laughter at Cardiff Athletics Stadium, which is surprising given it is 10.30 and Tim Benjamin is already out on the track training.

But the Welsh 400 m runner has quickly learnt that when you hire Colin Jackson as your coach you can expect a high rate of laughter per lap. Jackson sits on the high jump crash mat, screwing in the spikes of Benjamin's new racers: 'You'll never normally see me doing this, I'm doing it under duress. I'm only going to put them in half-way so you trip up when you're running,' Jackson jokes to Benjamin. The pair have comfortably settled into their new coach–athlete relationship after their first winter training together.

Jackson, a double world 110 m hurdle champion, offered to coach Benjamin, 25, and 400 m hurdler Rhys Williams, 23, last September after a persuasive coffee with Britain's former javelin world champion, Fatima Whitbread. 'She told me it was a real waste when I knew so much about athletics but wasn't passing it on – and she was right,' explains Jackson, 40.

'I just didn't think I would find any athletes who I would be happy to commit my time and effort to.' As it happened, they found him. Williams, who won European bronze in 2006, came to him for technical advice on his hurdling. Benjamin left his coach Tony Lester, sold his flat and was packed and ready to fly out to America – before Jackson put in the call and brought him home to Cardiff. 'It's been awesome,' said Benjamin, who was on the same Welsh Commonwealth Games and Great Britain teams as Jackson in 2002 and 2003. 'He knows a lot about track and field and I bring the experience of 400 m to him. We have a very good relationship.' So is 'Jackson the coach' akin to a fiery Alex Ferguson or an ice-cool Sven-Goran Eriksson?

'He's Colin Jackson,' Benjamin answers with more than a little awe. 'He's a really cool guy. I've never seen him in a mood or sad. He brings fun and enjoyment to training. He doesn't shout at me but I know what he expects of me.'

Jackson, who held the 110 m hurdle world record for almost 13 years, sets his standards high and wasted no time telling his new charges they were a long, long way below them. 'You've heard how brutal I can be?' joked Jackson. 'I can be very brutal when it's needed.' What Jackson identified in both Benjamin and Williams was a lack of general fitness and conditioning that he described as 'shocking'. He set about devising a new training schedule which included three gym sessions a week and less rest periods between repetition runs on

---

Source: **http://news.bbc.co.uk/sport1/hi/athletics/6696173.stm**, accessed 27 November 2007.

the track. 'On my first day of training he asked me to do 600 sit-ups,' said Benjamin, who admits to being pushed so hard by Jackson that he vomited on the track. 'He can do 600 sit-ups and that is why in his eyes I was poorly conditioned, but it doesn't mean I wasn't fit under Tony Lester. I just wasn't up to Colin's standard.

'I couldn't do it then but I can now and I feel physically stronger. I've put on more muscle and so this season I'm getting used to a different way of running.'

Jackson's exacting standards are a relic of his career-long relationship with no-nonsense coach Malcolm Arnold, who now coaches British sprinters Jason Gardener and Craig Pickering. 'There are lots of elements that I use that are definitely Malcolm Arnold,' says Jackson, who looks very un-Arnold standing trackside in his stylish jeans and black wind cheater.

'The professionalism and the way I try to communicate with my athletes come from Malcolm wanting his athletes to be thinkers and to take responsibility.' Jackson also plans to plunder the expertise of double Olympic 400 m hurdle champion Ed Moses and five-time Olympic gold-medal winning sprinter Michael Johnson. And after winning 11 individual medals at major championships, Jackson will also rely on his own experiences in guiding Benjamin and Williams.

'I feel very strange because the training is so different,' says Benjamin, whose fears look pretty unfounded as he blitzes through 300 m in 36 seconds on a relaxed training run. 'The reason I changed coaches two years before an Olympics is because things don't happen overnight and this first year may not go as I want it to. 'But next year my goal, and Colin's as my coach, is to get an individual Olympic medal in Beijing.' While Benjamin is definite about what he wants to gain from his new coach, Jackson's own incentives are less clear.

The Welshman, who is a television pundit and presenter for the BBC, does not receive any kind of financial support from UK Athletics to coach Benjamin and Williams. He does not charge them, just as Arnold did not charge him.

'What am I getting out of it? I couldn't honestly tell you,' says Jackson, stumped for once. 'Every day we are here at the track and my life revolves around these guys now. It's like having kids, trust me.

'But we are having a huge amount of fun and it gives me great pleasure. I didn't think I would enjoy it as much as I have.' Jackson notoriously failed to win an Olympic gold medal but if he ended up coaching a champion would that go some way to making amends?

'No, not at all,' he says. 'I helped my training partner (Mark McKoy) win the Olympic gold that I was supposed to win so coaching kids won't make me feel much better. 'But if Tim and Rhys deliver what they are capable of then they should win gold medals – and if they do it will all be down to them.'

Questions

1. In spite of the negative comments about coaching, why is Jackson still carrying on in this role?
2. How will both Benjamin and Williams learn from Jackson?

Self-efficacy and social learning

The symbolic processes depicted in Figure 3.5 are also important in social learning. Words and symbols used by managers and others in the workplace can help communicate values, beliefs and goals and therefore serve as guides to a person's behaviour. A 'thumbs up' or other symbol from the boss, for example, lets you know your behaviour is appropriate.

At the same time, an individual's self-control is important in influencing his or her behaviour. Self-efficacy is an important part of such self-control. People with high self-efficacy believe that:

- they have the necessary ability for a given job
- they are capable of the effort required
- they are motivated to perform the required behaviour
- no outside events will hinder them from obtaining their desired performance level.[14]

In other words, high self-efficacy people believe they can manage their environmental cues and consequences and their cognitive processes to control their own behaviour. People with low self-efficacy believe that, no matter how hard they try, they cannot manage their environment well enough to be successful. If you feel self-efficacious as a student, for example, a low grade on one test will encourage you to study harder, talk to the lecturer or do other things to enable you to perform well the next time. In contrast, a person low in self efficacy might drop the course or give up studying.

Even people who are high in self-efficacy do not control their environment entirely. As a manager, you can have an impact on the environment and other factors shown in Figure 3.5 (even though the impact is less than in the operant approach). This is especially the case in influencing another person's self-efficacy. A manager's expectations and peer support can go far in increasing a worker's self-efficacy and feelings of control.

EFFECTIVE MANAGER 3.1

Points for managers to consider in applying social learning theory[15]

- Identify appropriate job behaviours.
- Help employees select an appropriate behavioural model for behavioural modelling.
- Work with employees to meet the requirements of the new behaviours.
- Structure the learning situation to enhance learning of the necessary behaviours.

- Provide appropriate rewards (consequences) for workers who perform the appropriate behaviours.
- Engage in appropriate managerial actions to maintain the newly learned behaviours.

SOCIAL LEARNING THEORY AND BEHAVIOURAL SELF-MANAGEMENT

Social learning theory is applied in the workplace to encourage employees to help manage or lead themselves. Table 3.1 shows some possible self-management strategies. Notice how these strategies build on social learning theory to emphasize both behavioural and cognitive focuses. Their use is designed to enhance self-efficacy and the worker's feeling of self-control. For example, 3M (the company that manufactures Post-It notes) encourages employees to apply behavioural self-management actions (such as those listed in Table 3.1) wherever possible. People are encouraged to 'work outside the box' to facilitate new product innovations.[16] Many high-profile sporting organizations throughout the world use sports psychologists to teach players the strategies listed in Table 3.1.[17]

Behaviour	Strategy
	Behaviour-focused strategies
Self-setting goals	Setting goals for your own work efforts
Managing cues	Arranging and altering cues in the work environment to facilitate your desired personal behaviours
Rehearsing	Physically or mentally practising work activities before you actually perform them
Self-observing	Observing and gathering information about specific behaviours that you have targeted for change
Self-rewarding	Providing yourself with personally valued rewards for completing desirable behaviours
Self-punishing	Administering punishments to yourself for behaving in undesirable ways (This strategy is generally not very effective.)
	Cognitive-focused strategies
Building natural rewards into tasks	Redesigning where and how you do your work to increase the level of natural rewards in your job. Natural rewards that are part of, rather than separate from, the work (that is, the work, like a hobby, becomes the reward) result from activities that cause you to feel: – a sense of competence – a sense of self-control
Focusing thinking on natural rewards	Purposely focusing your thinking on the naturally rewarding features of your work
Establishing constructive thought patterns	Establishing constructive and effective habits or patterns in your thinking (for example, a tendency to search for opportunities rather than obstacles embedded in challenges) by managing your: – beliefs and assumptions – mental imagery – internal self-talk

Table 3.1: Self-management strategies.

Self-management is a social learning theory that can be applied by behaviour-focused strategies and cognitive-focused strategies. However, self-management for an organizational member includes managing inconsistencies between individual and organizational expectations and goals.

It is evident that self-management includes self-reflection or introspection, where individuals contemplate their thoughts, feelings and actions. In the organizational context, self-reflection can lead to the discovery of incongruence between organizational goals and personal expectations. These **intrapersonal conflicts** often involve actual or perceived pressures from incompatible goals or expectations of the following types. *Approach conflict* occurs when a person must choose between two positive and equally attractive alternatives. An example is having to choose between a valued promotion in the organization or a desirable new job with another organization. *Avoidance conflict* occurs when a person must choose between two negative and equally unattractive alternatives.

An example is being asked either to accept a job transfer to another town in an undesirable location or to have your employment with an organization terminated. *Approach–avoidance conflict* occurs when a person must decide to do something that has both positive and negative consequences. An example is being offered a higher paying job but one whose responsibilities will entail unwanted demands on your time.

This chapter has emphasized workers as individuals. However, many of the self-management strategies can also be extended to self-managed teams, which are discussed later in the book. Managers are seeking strategies designed to increase the use of human potential in the workplace. Many Western organizations have experienced the downsizing of the past decade, and now they are giving increased attention to new approaches designed to increase worker productivity. Organizations are being designed to have flatter structures, provide increased worker empowerment and offer greater opportunities for self-management – all strategies designed to increase the use of the workplace's human resource.

> **Intrapersonal conflict** *is conflict that occurs within the individual as a result of actual or perceived pressures from incompatible goals or expectations.*

EXPERIENTIAL LEARNING THEORY

'The best way to learn things is by doing them' is the tenet of experiential learning theory. Through reflection, people can draw conclusions and possibly then act differently (learn). Kolb[18] argues that learning is an iterative process and involves a learning cycle, whereby individuals experience, interpret, generalize and test things.

Individuals may have a preference for any of the four aspects included in this model. Some individuals spend little or no time reflecting on their experiences, and may repeat the same mistakes time and time again, whilst others may spend too much time reflecting and not actual complete very much in practical terms. A balance of the four aspects may provide a more suitable approach to learning.

Kolb has extended his research to link the learning cycle with personality types. For further reading, please see Kolb, D. (1984), *Experiential Learning*, Prentice Hall: Englewood Cliffs, NJ.

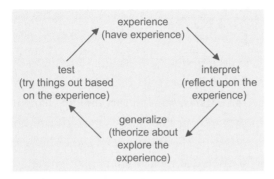

Figure 3.6: Kolb's experiential learning cycle.
Source: Kolb, D. (1984) *Experiential Learning*, Englewood Cliffs, NJ, Prentice-Hall.

MODERN FORMS OF LEARNING

There can be little doubt that the rate of technological advance in this millennium is phenomenal, and continues to increase in speed and complexity. The growth of e-learning and blended learning continues to fascinate academics and professional bodies, like the Chartered Institute of Personnel and Development (UK).

In the CIPD's 2005 *Learning and Development Survey*, they found that over half of respondents (Companies) (54 %) reported that they use e-learning, and a further 39 % said they had plans to introduce it in the coming year.[20] According to the CIPD, the following are the major listed uses of e-learning:

- IT training (70 %)
- technical training (45 %)
- health and safety (34 %)
- induction (33 %).[21]

E-learning is utilized less for:

- management training (23 %)
- interpersonal skills training (13 %)
- diversity (9 %)
- foreign languages (7 %)
- team building (3 %).

Having access to information and data is important but it needs to attract the recipient's attention and interest. Other forms of e-learning such as **blended learning** may prove attractive to employers and employees alike.

The question arises as to the reasons behind these findings and, more importantly, how e-learning is fully evaluated as a learning process.

E-learning is 'Learning that is delivered, enabled or mediated using electronic technology for the explicit purpose of training in organizations.'[19]

Blended learning is an approach that blends, mixes, or combines online learning with classroom instruction, coaching or mentoring.[22]

THE LEARNING ORGANIZATION

The human race has experienced more rapid changes since the early 1980s than in the rest of humanity's existence. During the next 20 years or so, this pace of change is likely to accelerate. The challenge for organizations in this rapidly changing environment is to be flexible and adaptable enough to cope because not only growth but, perhaps more importantly, organizational survival depends on these responses. This section introduces the concepts of the learning organization and the teaching organization.

The 'learning organization' was popularized by Peter Senge in his book, *The Fifth Discipline*.[23] He argued that a learning organization is a medium to enhance the development and use of knowledge at an individual level and, consequently, at an organizational level. Such knowledge will lead to organizational change. Learning organizational models are attempting to harness this potential for change in order to achieve competitive advantage.

Organizational learning *is acquiring or developing new knowledge that modifies or changes behaviour and improves organizational performance.*

Organizational learning refers to the process of becoming a learning organization and can be conceptualized as acquiring or developing new knowledge that modifies or changes behaviour and improves organizational performance. Underlying the concept of a learning organization is a belief that organizations can be transformed by improving communication processes and techniques so as to enrich relationships among members.

Creating a learning organization

Managers can create a learning organization by:[24]

- building a powerful shared vision of future growth that will provide the focus for learning and a benchmark for future achievements
- developing strategies and action plans that will inspire the commitment of all personnel to achieve the future goals of the organization
- making extensive use of a continuous process of consultation to achieve consensus and unity of thought
- encouraging continual renewal of all organizational structures and processes
- employing systems thinking to ensure the organization focuses on both internal and external factors driving the change
- creating self-directed teams of employees that are supported to make decisions at appropriate levels.

The degree to which an organization can successfully create a learning environment can be measured by examining:

- the relationship between the employee and the organization
- the value placed on the employee and their organizational contribution
- employee ownership and acceptance of responsibility, and
- employee empowerment.

OB IN ACTION

Airline soars with new e-learning environment

For Cathay Pacific Airways, the move to e-learning is part of a larger cultural shift away from passenger participation toward employee initiative. Integral to this is the development of 'Learner's World'.

Cathay Pacific executives invested a large amount of money in its e-business as part of its plan to be Asia's leading e-business airline. The key principle around Learner's World is for employees to be enabled to control their own performance development.

According to Graham Higgins, manager of Cathay Pacific's learning and development team, the concept of flexible benefits was critical. 'We need to give them (employees) choice, control and the ability to tailor the learning process to their own needs.' Higgins chose NetDimension's Enterprise Knowledge Platform (EKP) as the airline's learning management system. This system enrols students, tracks their progress, delivers tests and reports costs, and can do so in any language. The flexibility of the software was commended by Higgins.

One example quoted is how staff keep themselves familiarized with airport layouts, so that if they have to be pulled out in an emergency, incident or disruption, they will know their way around. Higgins stated that they created a virtual tour using 3-D imagery, so that an employee can refresh their memory by walking virtually through the restricted and nonrestricted areas of the airport.

The trick for Cathay Pacific was to get employees to buy into the process voluntarily. The process

therefore had to be of interest to employees, for example, the creation of an online travel desk, where staff can enter their comments on hotels that they have stayed in. This process proved very popular because of the frequency of staff travel and the need for feedback.

EKP was just the first part of the process for Cathay Pacific and, according to Higgins, they are now looking to personalize issues and seek collaboration form training managers on course content and methodology, so that employees take charge of their learning, drive their careers forward and improve customer service.

In the near future, NetDimensions, with direct input from Cathay Pacific will unveil a new Web-based exam environment that features high-level security, publishing and assessment capabilities.

Questions

1. To what extent is Cathay Pacific doing anything different in terms of employee learning?
2. What impact will 'testing' have upon employees' willingness to participate and commit to 'Learners World'?

Single-loop learning *is learning by rote, with an emphasis on memorization rather than comprehension.*

Double-loop learning *is learning that involves innovation and creativity, by going beyond the basic line of questioning and thinking outside of the box.*

Knowledge management *is the way in which organizations access, capture and distribute the tacit and explicit knowledge so as to increase their effectiveness, efficiency and competitiveness.*

The amount of learning that takes place is important to individuals, teams and organizations but the depth of learning is also important. Adaptation from learning may be an important factor in gaining competitive advantage. The concepts of **single-loop learning** and **double-loop learning** are important factors to consider.

Single-loop learning is more of a passive approach to learning and may be linked more readily to an operational focus, whereas double–loop learning involves deeper questioning (a more critical approach) as to why certain actions or activities take place in the way that they do. Double-loop learning may also occur more readily in a strategic context. Another differentiator may be that single-loop learning operates more effectively in a static, safe environment, where organization change is marginal, as opposed to a rapidly changing, complex environment for double-loop learning. Organizations wishing to maximize their employees' knowledge and competences need to consider how learning takes place and what mechanisms they have to support it.

Organizations may have in place various infrastructures, like strategic human resource development strategies and plans, **knowledge management** systems, group development plans, personal development plans (for individuals), as well as competence-based learning approaches and mechanisms. The question arises as to how these are translated into output and performance, continuous improvement and motivational drivers. Creating a 'learning culture' will depend on the whole organizational infrastructure and should not just simply be a company wish or mantra in the mission statement.

Certain preconditions are essential if a successful learning environment is to be created through these new communication processes:[25]

- *Trust.* All organizational members must believe they can rely on an individual's word (spoken or written). Trust permeates all organizational relationships and strongly influences all aspects of coordination and control. Managerial actions – such as encouraging supportive rather than defensive behaviour, aligning goals among and between organizational members, managing information flows and avoiding stereotyping – assist in building a trusting environment.
- *Commitment.* The company must develop an emotional and intellectual commitment to its actions and achievements.
- *Perceived organizational support.* Organizational support reinforces a bond between the organization and its employees and creates a sense of involvement with organizational objectives. An emphasis on relationship building and organizational support also reinforces the growth of trust and commitment.

LEARNING SUMMARY

What do the terms 'learning' and 'learning organization' mean? In common usage, people generally equate them with acquiring facts. However, acquired information needs to be interpreted and translated into usable knowledge. For organizations, knowledge acquisition

EFFECTIVE MANAGER 3.2

Managers in action

Garvin argues that managers need to follow the four steps set out below in pursuit of building a learning organization:[26]

1. Foster an environment that is conducive to learning. There needs to be time for reflection and analysis so that strategic plans can be considered, customer needs considered, assessing of work systems. Management need to free up opportunities for employee learning. Training in brainstorming, problem solving, evaluating experiments and other core learning skills can make employees doubly productive.

2. Open up boundaries and stimulate the exchange of ideas. Conferences, meetings, project teams, crossing boundaries and or linking with customers and suppliers ensure a fresh flow of ideas and ultimately the consideration of competing perspectives.

3. The creation of learning forums is the next step. Programmes or events need to be designed with explicit learning goals in mind, such as strategic reviews, systems audits, and international benchmarking reports. Employees are required to wrestle with new knowledge and consider its implications.

4. Move learning higher on the organizational agenda, shifting away from continuous improvement toward a commitment to learning, resulting in the 3Ms – meaning, management and measurement of learning.

is tied up with systems for codifying and disseminating information. But the real meaning of learning is much broader than this. It encompasses the subtle changes that take place when people, individually or collectively, reinterpret or *reframe* their experiences and modify their behaviour accordingly.

Learning organizations can only enable competitive advantage via learning if 'knowledge' exists and can be identified as important to the organization. In addition, this knowledge then needs to be *transferable* and a learning organization needs to transfer it better than comparable organizations.[27]

Knowledge acquisition and transfer are problematic as gaining knowledge tends to be self-referential (based on what is known within the organization). Knowledge sharing is vitally important to a learning organization, as having a 'shared vision' underpins the collective nature of the organizational learning process. The problem is that when an organization's members are all moving the same way, they may very well move in the wrong direction and 'actively damage the future direction of the company'.[28] This means that despite all intentions of being 'open' to external feedback and responsive to specific and general organizational environments, organizational decision making is likely to be reactive. This reactivity is in direct contrast to an organizational learning process that is meant to be proactive. Therefore, knowledge development to enable competitive advantage, on the scale anticipated by learning organizations, is somewhat idealistic. The process may legitimate ineffective and circular processes and may hinder the desire to become a learning organization – it is unlikely that transformation will occur.

Difficulties may also occur with learning and well-intentioned attempts to create a 'learning organization' because existing mental models limit our ability to be adaptive.[29] Mental models can provide a link between individuals and collectives as they provide a context for interpretation of knowledge. Recent research in the UK, regarding the role of strongly held mental models in a team environment suggested that individual and organizational mental models may ultimately prevent desired creativity for innovation.[30] Strongly shared mental models are potentially 'closed' to new stimuli; little new knowledge can emerge and radically different and creative ideas are likely to be rejected. Hence, behaviour modification is unlikely to be achieved.

Learning is a subjective process encompassing the absorption of new knowledge through emotional, intuitive and reflective filters and mental models. Real learning is a lifelong process and requires the skills of self-management, self-knowledge and self-evaluation.

THE TEACHING ORGANIZATION

The 1990s saw the rise to prominence of the learning organization. Learning is a necessary competence but it is insufficient to assure market leadership. The companies that have outperformed competitors and increased shareholder returns have been those able to move beyond being learning organizations to become teaching organizations.

A teaching organization aims to pass on learning experiences to others, thereby allowing the organization to achieve and maintain success.

The two types of organization have many similarities. Fundamental to both is the common objective that every person within the organization continually acquires new knowledge and appropriate skills. However, the distinguishing aspect of a teaching organization is its ability to be more agile and to build more continuity into its successes. This is a direct consequence of a teaching organization's added focus on passing on learning experiences and knowledge; that is, a teaching organization aims to convey learning experiences to others, thereby allowing the organization to achieve and maintain success. Leaders in teaching organizations feel responsible for sharing their knowledge with other staff as a means of helping the organization to develop a knowledge base rapidly and accurately, infused with hands-on experience.

The constant focus on developing people to become leaders allows a teaching organization to become more agile and responsive to changes because its members are always armed with the necessary knowledge and knowhow to deal with new situations. An added benefit is the continuity of smooth leadership successions, preventing the potential disruption that a leadership change can entail.

CONCLUSION

Developing core work skills and ensuring lifelong learning for all is a massive undertaking for any country, even the richest ones, and can only be achieved over a very long time frame, if ever. It is a target that is continually moving out of reach.[31]

The requirement for countries and organizations will be how to maximize development and, by definition, learning of their inhabitants/employees. A sophisticated understanding of how people learn will assist in this process. The motivation to learn and develop may be expected to come from within individual employees rather than being imposed upon them from above. The ideal scenario for an employer is that its employees are self-starters, do not require much supervision, are receptive to learning and change and manage to be innovative and creative at the same time. The organization's role is to help nurture the employees' talent so as to produce the desired outputs.

SUMMARY

LEARNING OBJECTIVE 1
Four general approaches to learning

Learning is a relatively permanent change in behaviour resulting from experience. It is an important part of reward management. The four general approaches to learning are classical conditioning, operant conditioning, cognitive learning and social learning. Modern managers need to understand the principles of cognitive learning, which relate to the motivational theories discussed in Chapter 4, to operant conditioning, which is achieved when the consequences of behaviour lead to changes in the probability of its occurrence, and to social learning.

LEARNING OBJECTIVE 2
Organizational behaviour modification and reinforcement strategies

Reinforcement is the means through which operant conditioning takes place. Its foundation is the law of effect, which states that behaviour will be repeated or extinguished, depending on whether the consequences are positive or negative. Reinforcement is related to extrinsic rewards (valued outcomes that are given to the individual by some other person) because these rewards serve as environmental consequences that can influence people's work behaviours through the law of effect.

Organizational behaviour modification uses four reinforcement strategies to change behaviour: positive reinforcement, negative reinforcement (avoidance), punishment and extinction. Positive reinforcement is used to encourage desirable behaviour; the administration of positive consequences tends to increase the likelihood of a person repeating a behaviour in similar settings. Positive reinforcement should be contingent (administered only if the desired behaviour is exhibited) and immediate (as close in time to the desired behaviour as possible).

Negative reinforcement, or avoidance, is used to encourage desirable behaviour; the withdrawal of negative consequences tends to increase the likelihood that a person will repeat a desirable behaviour in similar settings.

Punishment is the administration of negative consequences or the withdrawal of positive consequences, which tends to reduce the likelihood of a given behaviour being repeated in similar settings. Punishment is used to weaken or eliminate undesirable behaviour, but problems can occur. One must therefore be especially careful to follow appropriate reinforcement guidelines (including the laws of contingent and immediate reinforcement) when using it. Punishment is likely to be more effective if combined with positive reinforcement.

Extinction is the withdrawal of the reinforcing consequences for a given behaviour. It is often used to withhold reinforcement for a behaviour that has previously been reinforced. This is done to weaken or eliminate the undesirable behaviour. It is an especially powerful strategy when combined with positive reinforcement.

LEARNING OBJECTIVE 3
Social learning theory and behavioural self-management

Social learning theory advocates learning through the reciprocal interactions among people, behaviour and environment. Therefore, it combines operant and cognitive learning approaches. Behavioural self-management builds on social learning theory to emphasize both behavioural and cognitive foci with a special emphasis on enhancing a worker's self-efficacy and feeling of self-control. Self-management is useful in treating workers both as individuals and as part of self-managed teams.

LEARNING OBJECTIVE 4
Modern forms of learning

E-learning has changed the way that individuals and organizations can access and distribute knowledge and learning. Due to societal changes in the way that communication occurs, employees may begin to learn 'outside normal working time'. E-learning may not suit all types of learning activity or intervention but it can allow greater flexibility in terms of access. Blended learning involves a combination of online learning with classroom instruction, or possibly other supportive interventions like coaching or mentoring.

LEARNING OBJECTIVE 5
Learning organizations and teaching organizations

A learning organization is one in which members recognize the importance of communicating new knowledge for the benefit of the organization. Such an environment can be encouraged if trust, commitment and a perception of organizational support exist. A teaching organization is highly similar to a learning organization; the difference lies in the focus on continuity in the passing on of necessary knowledge and knowhow from leaders to other members of the organization. This ensures that a teaching organization is always agile and able to maintain its success.

CHAPTER 3 STUDY GUIDE

You can also test your understanding and access further resources at **www.wileyeurope .com/college/french**.

REVIEW QUESTIONS

1. Explain the 'law of effect'.
2. What are extrinsic rewards and how are these related to learning and reinforcement?
3. Distinguish between 'negative reinforcement' and 'punishment'. Summarize the main features of a learning organization.

APPLICATION QUESTIONS

1. Describe the classical conditioning process and provide examples of its impact on behaviours and emotions.
2. Mentoring, based on social learning theory, is often used to teach less experienced managers new skills. Discuss the operation and efficacy of mentoring programmes in the contemporary workplace.
3. Punishment strategies should be used sparingly by managers. Explain why.
4. What are some cultural issues to consider when using incentives for the purpose of achieving greater performance?
5. Critically analyse the difference between 'a learning organization' and 'organizational learning'

RESEARCH QUESTIONS

1. As you have read in this chapter, punishment is a management tool that continues to be used in the workplace despite increasing concerns about its effectiveness. Using the library and other resources you have access to, research the following questions and either write a 1000-word report on your findings, or complete a 20-minute presentation of your findings to the class. Thinking of your own workplace (or one you are familiar with):
   (a) How frequently is punishment used? Give examples.
   (b) Explain the behavioural and emotional response to punishment.
   (c) How does punishment prevent undesirable behaviour from reoccurring?
   (d) Do you think that punishment has a place in modern workplaces? Why or why not?
2. Find an organization online that publicizes its employee rewards. How does the organization motivate its employees? Would you like to work for this organization? Why or why not? Compare your answer with those from others in your class and discuss why your answers may be the same or different

RUNNING PROJECT

Complete the following activities for your organization:
1. Identify at least one example of each of the four approaches to learning.

2. Describe the formal and informal mentoring processes in place. If there aren't any, why are they thought unnecessary?

3. What extrinsic rewards does management use?

4. How does management deal with unwanted work behaviour exhibited by employees?

5. Identify whether your organization exhibits elements of a learning or teaching organization. Describe them. If the organization is not a learning or teaching organization, has this disadvantaged the organization?

INDIVIDUAL ACTIVITY

What, when and how I learn[32]

Objective

To gain a greater understanding of what, when and how individuals learn.

Total time: 40 minutes.

Instructions

Think of *four* different things that you have learned that were, and still are, important to you. Now, for each one, think carefully about *what* you learned, *when* you learned, *how* you learned and, lastly, what it was that most *helped you learn it*. To help you with this, you might like a few ideas. What you learned and when are straightforward, but how and what helped most are a little more complicated!

In terms of the 'how' part of the question, think about this. Did you learn whatever it was by reading about it, being told about it, being shown how to do it, by trial and error, by practising it, by thinking about it, from film or video or any other medium, by research or by a combination of these or any other ways of learning? Were you taught by somebody else or did you learn it on your own? Were you in a group? Was the process formal or informal and did you have to undergo some kind of testing or accreditation? Did you learn in a way not given here? If so, what was it?

For the part of the question that asks what helped you learn, decide which factors you believe most helped you to learn. Was it your interest? Did you have a particularly inspiring teacher or instructor? Was there some kind of reward or sanction to be applied if you did or did not succeed? Or perhaps it was a target that you set yourself? Is there anything else that you can define that caused you to *want* to learn, helped you to keep learning and supported your successful learning? It will be worthwhile considering which factors were internal (that is, from within yourself) and which were external – from the job, peer pressure, fashion or anything else.

Now fill out the following table. To think about how you leave, place a tick under the heading that describes you best.

To obtain a better understanding of how you learn, think about these questions:

- How do I learn best – alone, in a group, with an instructor, from books, by doing, by watching, by any other way or by a lot of different ways?
- What makes me want to learn?
- What gets me started on learning?
- What keeps me learning?
- What stops me learning?
- How do other people affect my learning?

Now reflect on how you learn. How can you improve the way you are learning?

	Always	Most times	Seldom	Never
I memorize things easily				
I work out the meaning of things				
I notice what is around me				
I ask questions and think about the answers				
I use sources of information (the media, libraries, etc.)				
I measure what I find out against things I know				
I see links between things				
I choose how best to do things				
I use information and experience to choose solutions				
I act when I have decided				
I think about consequences				
I select important bits of information				
I enjoy learning new things				
I share what I learn				

GROUP ACTIVITY

Getting creative with remuneration

Objectives

1. To provide an experience of choices faced by managers when they make remuneration decisions
2. To help you review some of the theoretical issues involved in attempts to motivate employees though learning, reinforcement and flexible benefit plans
3. To apply these issues in a realistic and practical work setting

Total time: 30 minutes

Instructions

In groups, you are to select a remuneration package that best fits each of the following employees' needs (they are listed under the employee profiles). When you have finished, one member of each group will report to the class their groups' remuneration selections for each employee. In the report the speaker must justify each selection made by using relevant theory and case knowledge.

Employee profiles

'The Nut House' is altering its pay structure to a more creative and flexible one to assist with employee motivation. However, each employee has at least 40 per cent of their package as a base salary. At the moment, all packages are paid as salary, and no performance bonuses are paid. Any additional hours worked by employees are not paid; instead, they receive time-in-lieu, which is to be taken one day at a time, on a Tuesday or Wednesday.

Fred

Fred is a middle manager who has been with the organisation for eight years. During that time he has never had a pay rise or a promotion. Fred is not skilled and obtained his position on the basis of bringing several very large customers to the organisation. Fred is unhappy at work. Fred has an aggressive manner when communicating with people. Fred has expressed no interest in learning new skills. Current salary package = €45000.

Huong

Huong is an administrative officer who has been with the organisation for two years. She was looking for a slower-paced life where she could do her job and spend more time on her hobbies. Huong is well respected and an excellent worker who is keen to expand her knowledge at every opportunity. Current salary package = €23 000.

Carlos

Carlos is a middle manager who has been in the organisation for six years. Carlos is highly skilled and cannot be replaced easily; he is one of the hardest workers in the organisation and puts in long hours on the job. He is very well respected by everyone in the organisation and clients adore him. He never seems to take the time-in-lieu that he has accumulated. Carlos is looking for another job, where he can spend more time at home and to have an opportunity to undertake training and development. Current salary package = €58 000.

June

June is a 63-year-old lady who has been with the organisation since anyone else can remember. She worked two days per week. Although June is very good at her job, she has been taking more and more time off due to illness and other 'personal reasons', which is beginning to frustrate other members of staff. Current salary package = €13 000.

Kim

Kim is a 25-year-old marketing graduate who has worked in the sales department for three years. Kim intends working hard and being an executive by the time she is 30 years old. She has high aims that involve earning a lot of money, travel and driving a luxury car. Her current performance is average: she makes the sales margins, but there are also some complaints about her lack of customer service. Current salary package = €30 000.

Flexible options

Following are some of the more usual benefits available. This is not an exhaustive list and you may choose any other options that you think appropriate for the individual; be as creative as you can.

- Base salary
- Superannuation top-ups (no more than 20 per cent of total package)
- Gym membership €380
- Four-day working week €1 300
- Part-time university education €1 300
- Performance-linked salary
- Car allowance €6 500 (tax free)
- Provision of lunch €2 300

- 25 per cent pay cut per annum, for every fifth year off with full pay
- Holiday accommodation vouchers up to €1 300
- Skill-based salary
- ASX 100 shares of the employee's choice €3 300
- Medical benefits: single €1 300, family €2 600
- Mobile phone €780
- Child-care/elder-care payments up to €2 600 per annum per child/elder

TRAINING AT CONVERGYS CONTACT CENTRES, INDIA

Background

Convergys is the world's largest operator of call or contact centres. It was established in its current form in 1998 and grew out of the US Cincinnati Bell telecommunications company. Revenue in 2005 was $2.58 billion and there are four operating divisions: customer management (the contact centre business), employee care (outsourced personnel activities, including payroll, benefits, learning and recruitment), information management (IT outsourcing, with specialisms in billing platforms) and finance and accounting (the outsourcing business recently acquired from Deloitte).

Currently Convergys operates over 65 contact, service and data centres worldwide. The largest number of service centres (54) is in North America where the company was founded. There are seven centres in India (the subject of this case study), and six in the Philippines. Total capacity in India is some 6 000 'seats', which, given shift-working arrangements, means that some 9 000 people are employed by Convergys in the country.

Programmes (the term used to describe a discrete activity centred around a product, service or market) are delivered for overseas clients. Convergys operates 'third party' centres for clients as opposed to 'captive centres' where a contact centre is established in India solely to meet the needs of the overseas parent company. The challenge therefore is to ensure that staff have both the technical and business knowledge to assist the client's customers and the communication skills and empathy so that this is put across in a way that leaves a positive and favourable impression.

Recruitment and retention

In its centres of operation (three in Gurgaon on the outskirts of Delhi, and one each in Mumbai, Bangalore, Pune Thane and Hyderabad) Convergys is a prominent employer. The largest centre at Gurgaon, for example, has over 2 000 agents (the term used for the staff who deal with client calls). As has been well observed, India has a current surfeit of capable and ambitious young people leaving its education system. Though the recruitment market is becoming more competitive, Convergys remains an 'employer of aspiration' for those who wish to work for the leader in the global contact centre business.

The majority of staff are young, mainly in their early 20s and half are female. Given that the majority of calls come from North America much of the work takes place from evening until early morning and the company puts a lot of resources into providing meals, transport and security. For many staff it will be their first job since leaving full-time education. Much of the initial induction is therefore focused on the transition to work – what the company offers and what is expected from the employee. Retention rates can be a

Case Study

This material has been taken from the "Helping People Learn – case studies" (2008) section of the website: **www.cipd.co.uk**, with the permission of the publisher, the Chartered Institute of Personnel and Developement, London. The author is Martyn Sloman.)
Source: **www.cipd.co.uk/helpingpeoplelearn/_casestudies/_intcnvrgys.htm**.

problem: some people leave after a transitory period to move on to a different career or into higher education. Others simply 'don't know why they joined'. However, given the need for staff to acquire the knowledge and skills demanded by clients Convergys puts a considerable effort into training, as Gyan Nagpal, Organizational Development Director based in Gurgaon puts it: 'If an organization engages with its staff, offering them a career with prospects and progression, they will stay and develop.'

Initial training

After the initial induction, which typically lasts two days, the new agent will be supervised through two training modules. Both last three or four weeks and it can therefore be up to seven weeks before the new joiner takes their first customer facing call.

The first module is designed to increase 'cultural sensitivity' to the country where the calls will originate, and to understand the context in which the client operates. All staff have English as a spoken language, and dealing with variations in accent is an issue in two respects. First, the agent needs to be comfortable understanding the caller's accent: five different groups of accents have been identified from North American callers alone. The second issue is the agent's accent – an element of 'accent neutralization' can be needed. Although, as Gyan Nagpur puts it: 'A person can't change their accent in three weeks even if it was necessary. We emphasize the need for clarity and encourage our agents to speak more slowly.'

Those modules are delivered in the classroom in groups of approximately 20 people, with feedback offered from the trainer and peers. Recording devices and audio support the programme. The second module, which is, again, classroom based, also introduces technology-based training screens. The module is focused on the client's products and systems and the questions that are likely to arise. Much of the detail is determined by the client's requirements and, whereas some clients are keen to avoid any situation where a customer sees a difference in approach between the client's home staff and the agent in India, others are less concerned. The nature of the client's product often determines the depth of understanding that the agents need to have.

Before they can deal with the client's customers over the phone, all agents must acquire both the generic skills of client handling and the specific knowledge to answer the underlying request. Agents are brought up to speed in an efficient and timely way: driving minimum 'time to competence' measures is an important consideration.

Ongoing support: the role of the team leader

Convergys's contact centres operate a relatively flat management structure and the normal progression for the agents is to the role of team leader: typically a team leader will have 15 to 20 direct reports. Team leaders are invariably chosen from high performing agents, so their technical understanding of contact centre work will be good. However for many the management of staff will be a new challenge.

From start to finish, the training period for new team leaders can be as long as 90 days. The classroom component of this training is delivered in five day modules. Critical elements include the modules that focus on staff development – one of the five day modules is mainly centred on coaching – and modules on tools that the team leader will use to monitor and drive performance. Feedback to agents regarding their call-handling capability is critical to the team and to the business's success and the team leader must have the skills and confidence to perform this task.

As part of the preparation for the new role, during this 90-day period, team leaders are required to undertake 13 modules of online e-learning (from two to four hours each). The majority of the modules have been specifically developed by Convergys, as the organization increasingly deploys e-learning as a preferred means of training delivery within a blended approach. Convergys acquired Digitalthink, a US-based e-learning organization in 2004, and has used these skills to deploy a learning portal that is available for Convergys agents throughout the world.

Convergys recognizes that the quality and motivation of its agents is critical to the success of the organization. The delivery of focused training in a cost effective, globally consistent fashion drives higher standards of service from Convergys' centres, whilst simultaneously reducing turnover and the associated bottom-line costs.

Questions

1. How would you describe the type of training that Convergys offer in terms of learning theory?
2. How would you evaluate the way in which Convergys carry out their training?

SUGGESTED READING

Harrison, R. (2005), *Learning and Development*, CIPD: London. This book provides a useful combination of theory and practice. It takes a contemporary approach and provides a range of useful perspectives on individual and organizational learning.

END NOTES

1. Hamel, G. (2005), MT master class, *Management Today*, 1 July, 22.

2. Malone, S.A. (2003), *Learning About Learning: An A to Z of Training and Developmental Tools and Techniques*, CIPD: London.

3. For some of B.F. Skinner's work see Skinner, B.F. (1948), *Walden Two*, Macmillan: New York. Skinner, B.F. (1953), *Science and Human Behaviour*, Macmillan: New York. Skinner, B.F. (1969), *Contingencies of Reinforcement*, Appleton-Century-Crofts: New York.

4. Thorndike, E.L. (1911), *Animal Intelligence*, Macmillan: New York, p. 244.

5. Adapted from Luthans, F. & Kreitner, R. (1985), *Organizational Behaviour Modification and Beyond*, Scott, Feresman: Glenview, IL.

6. Both laws are stated in Miller, K.L. (1975), *Principles of Everyday Behaviour Analysis*, Brooks/Cole: Monterey, CA, p. 122.

7. Example based on Price, B. & Osborn, R. (1999), *Shaping the Training of Skilled Workers*, working paper, Department of Management, Wayne State University: Detroit, MI.

8. Korukonda, A.R. & Hunt, J.G. (1989), Pat on the back versus kick in the pants: an application of cognitive inference to the study of leader

reward and punishment behaviour. *Group and Organizational Studies,* **14** (3), 299–324.

9. Ramirez, E., Maldonado, A. & Martos, R. (1992). Attribution modulate immunization against learned helplessness in humans. *Journal of Personality and Social Psychology,* **62**, 139–146.

10. Seligman, M. E. P. and Maier, S. F. Learned helplessness: theory and evidence. *Journal of Experimental Psychology: General,* **105**, 3 (1976) 46.

11. Cordes, C.L. and Dougherty, T.W. (1993), A review and integration of research on job burnout. *Academy of Management Review,* **18** (4), 621–654.

12. Bandura, A. (1977), *Social Learning Theory,* Prentice Hall: Englewood-Cliffs, NJ.

13. Mattis, M. (2004), Women entrepreneurs: out from under the glass ceiling, *Women in Management Review,* **19** (3), 154.

14. Peterson, T. & Amn, R. (2005), Self efficacy: the foundation of human performance. *Performance Improvement Quarterly,* **18** (2), 5–18.

15. See Zalesny, J.D. & Ford, J.K. (1990), Extending the social information processing perspective: new links to attitudes, behaviours and perceptions. *Organizational Behaviour and Human Decision Processes,* **47**, 205–246. Gist, M.E., Schwoerer, C. & Rosen, B. (1989), Effects of alternative training methods on self-efficacy and performance in computer software training. *Journal of Applied Psychology,* **74**, 884–891. Sutton, D.D. & Woodman, R.W. (1989), Pygmalion goes to work: the effects of supervisor expectations in a retail setting. *Journal of Applied Psychology,* **74**, 943–950. Gist, M.E. (1989), The influence of training method on self-efficacy and idea generation among managers. *Personnel Psychology,* **42**, 787–805.

16. Manz, C.C. & Sims, H. Jr (1990), *Superleadership,* Berkley Books: New York.

17. Kolb, D. (1984), *Experiential Learning,* Prentice Hall: Englewood Cliffs, NJ.

18. McLean, T. (2000), How to find the right frame of mind. *Financial Times,* 22 April, p. 22. Johnson, A. and Gilbert, J. (2004), The psychological uniform: using mental skills in youth sport. *Strategies,* **18** (2), 5–9. Improving the performance of expert workers. *Journal for Quality and Participation,* **27** (1), 9–11.

19. CIPD Web site: www.cipd.co.uk/subjects/lrn-anddev/elearning/elearnprog.htm?IsSrchRes=1, accessed 29 November 2007.

20. Ibid.

21. CIPD Annual Training Survey, 2005, www.cipd.co.uk/subjects/training/general/trdev2005.htm, accessed 30 November 2007.

22. Allison, R. (2002), *The ASTD E-Learning Handbook,* McGraw-Hill: New York.

23. Senge, P. (1992), *The Fifth Discipline,* Random House: Sydney.

24. Barker, R.T. & Caramata, M.R. (1998), The role of communication in creating and maintaining a learning organization: preconditions, indicators and disciplines. *Journal of Business Communication,* **35** (4), 443–467.

25. Blackman, D. & Henderson, S. (2005), Why learning organizations do not transform. *The Learning Organization Journal,* **12** (1), 42–56. Lee-Kelley, L. & Blackman, D. (2005), More than shared goals: the impact of mental models on team innovation and learning. *Journal of Innovation and Learning,* **2** (1), 11–25. Blackman, D. (2001), Is knowledge acquisition and transfer realisable? *Electronic Journal of Radical Organization Theory,* **7** (1), www.mngt.waikato.ac.nz/research/ejrot.

26. Garvin, D.A. (1993), Building a learning organization. *Harvard Business Review,* July-August, pp. 78–91.

27. Blackman, D. & Henderson, S., op. cit.

28. Ibid.

29. Lee-Kelley, L. & Blackman, D., op. cit.

30. Ibid.

31. 'Learning and Training for work in the knowledge society' 2003:13 International Labour Office. Geneva.

32. Extracted from National Institute of Adult Continuing Education, 'Your life, your work, you future', www.niace.org.uk/research/edp/leonmatall2.doc, accessed 30 November 2007.

CHAPTER 4

Motivation and empowerment

LEARNING OBJECTIVES

After studying this chapter you should be able to:

- discuss the complexities of motivating and empowering today's workforce
- explain the difference between the two main types of motivation theories – content and process.
- outline the major theoretical contributions from the content theories of motivation of Maslow, Alderfer, McClelland and Herzberg
- explain the process theories of motivation, including equity theory and expectancy theory
- explain how managers can use an integrated model of content and process motivation theories to enhance productivity and human resource maintenance
- explain how self-concept and personal values may add to our understanding of individual motivation
- explain how pay can be used as an extrinsic reward to motivate employees
- discuss empowerment and explain how the empowerment process works.

IT'S GOT TO BE A REAL SMILE

David Smith, Head of Human Resources at the supermarket chain Asda, headquarters in Leeds, UK, claims you can feel the warmth as soon as you enter an Asda store: 'Our store is a community. Staff are encouraged to chat to each other and the managers to get to know the staff. How can you treat people with respect unless you understand them?'

Asda has mystery shoppers measuring that warmth. They check on the friendliness of the staff, eye contact, use of the customer's name at the checkout, even smiles. And, says Smith:' It's got to be a real smile. We have a sense that people in the Asda family live the values. That's what makes the business go. Life is much more than what people get paid. It's what does the boss think of me? What do my colleagues think of me?'

What Asda is trying to achieve in its company culture requires employees' emotional investment. It's the first to admit it doesn't pay its 133,000 British employees particularly well; instead it lavishes them with 'bursting with pride' and 'thank you' certificates. There are 'listening groups', 'huddles' and 'colleagues' circles' aimed at encouraging what Smith calls a 'sense of ownership'. There are countless competitions including 'Oscars' for work 'above and beyond the call of duty'.

At the Asda superstore in York, the 'colleagues' pass a full length mirror on their way to the shop floor; above it, a big sign asks: 'Are you ready for the Asda stage?'

It's easy to be sceptical about such schemes but it seems to work. On her coffee break, 'Kath' complains bitterly about her pay and how her workload as a supervisor has increased. But she admits she is still working for Asda after 20 years: 'I like my job. I'm left to get on with it. The managers do actually speak to you now. The quarterly meetings when they tell you how the store is doing and what's going on are good fun. You come out with a positive attitude.'

Questions

1. How might the giving of 'thank you' notes motivate workers to do a better job?
2. Why despite being unhappy with her salary does 'Kath' remain motivated in her job?

Source: Bunting, M. (2006), *Willing Slaves*, HarperCollins: Oxford. Reprinted by permission of HarperCollins Publishers Ltd. Further permission received by A.P. Watt Ltd. on behalf of M. Bunting.

INTRODUCTION

One of the keys to effective management lies in harnessing the motivation of employees in order to achieve the organization's goals and objectives, but how do managers achieve this? Is there a simple formula such as the 10-step approach suggested in Effective Manager 4.1 or is there one key ingredient that motivates all individuals? Many managers still believe that the key to motivation is money; people work for money therefore higher pay equals higher productivity. Research over 50 years into the subject of employee motivation provides evidence that, although money can motivate individuals, motivation depends on a wide variety of variables, which could include, age, gender, socio-economic circumstances, job design and culture. The case study from Asda would support the view that motivation is a complex issue involving a combination of both intrinsic and extrinsic factors yet the pressure on organizations such as Asda to harness this motivation into employee productivity has never been greater because of the intensity of competition created by globalization, demographic changes and technological development. This chapter discusses several motivation theories and the concept of empowerment in terms of how they may contribute towards increasing productivity and the quality of working life as well as considering how motivation and pay are linked. The theories in this chapter are an important foundation for the ideas to be developed throughout the rest of this book.

EFFECTIVE MANAGER 4.1

Ten ways to motivate your staff:

- Keep them involved.
- Push autonomy, but be available.
- Tell them when they're doing well.
- Keep the buzz quotient high…
- …but see the upside of mellow.

- Take them out for lunch.
- Introduce flexible working.
- Promote only talented people.
- Hold a good bash once in a while.
- Do your own job well.[1]

Before looking at the separate theories, two key points should be made. First, motivation to work refers to forces within an individual that account for the level, direction and persistence of effort expended at work. Within this definition of work motivation:

- level refers to the amount of effort a person puts forth (for example, a lot or a little)
- direction refers to what the person chooses when presented with a number of possible alternatives (for example, to exert effort on achieving product quality or product quantity)
- persistence refers to how long a person sticks with a given action (for example, to try for product quantity or quality and to give up when it is difficult to attain).

Second, motivation to work (or willingness to perform) is one of three components of the individual performance equation (the other two are the capacity to perform and organizational support), which were presented in Chapters 1 and 2. High performance in the workplace depends on the combination of these three individual performance equation factors (as will be emphasized later in the chapter when motivation theories are integrated).

Motivation to work *refers to the forces within an individual that account for the level, direction and persistence of effort expended at work.*

MOTIVATING AND EMPOWERING THE WORKFORCE

Each employee is different, each organization's workforce may have different characteristics, and at different times or in different locations there may be different circumstances that affect motivation and empowerment strategies in different ways. In order to meet the challenge of motivating employees, managers must be concerned with the context in which this is being done. Managers also need to understand the challenges of the work effort–motivation cycle.

Organizations that fail to recognize contextual factors and their implications for workplace motivation risk losing their best people to more exciting, satisfying or rewarding opportunities elsewhere. Managers also need to understand the challenges of the work effort–motivation cycle, creating a positive organizational climate in which employees are motivated to achieve high levels of work performance.

This challenge is examined in more detail in Figure 4.1. The figure shows how an individual's willingness to perform is directly related to the needs, expectations and values of the individual and their link to the incentives or aspirations presented by the organization's reward system. Rewards fulfil individual goals such as financial remuneration and career advancement.

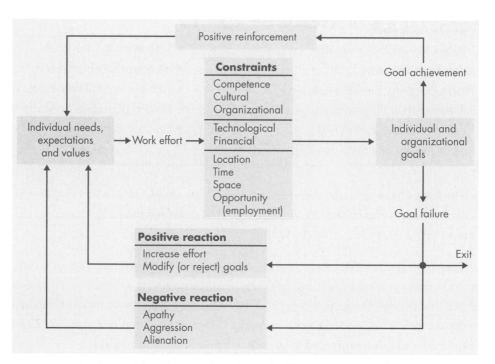

Figure 4.1: Understanding the work effort–motivation cycle.

The degree of effort expended to achieve these outcomes will depend on:

- the individual's willingness to perform, and his or her commitment to these outcomes in terms of the value attached to a particular outcome
- the individual's competency or capacity to perform the tasks
- the individual's personal assessment of the probability of attaining a specific outcome
- the opportunity to perform (which is central to empowerment, discussed later in the chapter).

A number of organizational constraints or barriers, if not minimized, may restrict levels of individual performance.

Figure 4.1 shows that if the outcome or goal is attained then the individual experiences a reduction in pressure or tension and goal attainment positively reinforces the expended effort to achieve the outcome. As a result of this positive experience, the individual may repeat the cycle. On the other hand, if the outcome is frustrated after a reasonable passage of time (for example, when no career progression has occurred) then the individual experiences goal frustration and arrives at a decision point. The individual is presented with three alternatives:

- exit from the organization
- renew attempts at goal achievement, or modify or abandon the goals
- adopt a negative response to the frustration experience and perform at below-optimum level.

The challenge for managers is to create organizations in which the opportunities to perform through competency building and empowerment are maximized and the impediments to performance are kept to a minimum to avoid the negative consequences of goal frustration. Of course, as we outlined in Chapter 1, not all of us are managers or aspire to be. However, with the subject of motivation we have a prime example of why OB is relevant to everyone. Who among us has no interest in why we do the things we do? Figure 4.1 shows the complexity of the work motivational process and emphasizes the importance of individual needs, expectations and values as key elements of this process. Some of these issues are addressed in the rest of this chapter. The following case demonstrates that strategies used by employers to motivate their staff to improve performance can be varied.

OB IN ACTION

Civil servants at a municipal office in Bangkok, Thailand are being encouraged to take an afternoon nap to boost motivation and productivity. Lights go out just after noon in a designated 'nap room', which has soft music, sweet-smelling flowers and rules barring employees from using mobile phones and talking. Of 200 employees at the capital's Pathumwan district municipal office about 20 regular 'nappers' reported to the Associated press that they felt 'fresher and brighter' after their midday snooze. A bizarre idea you may think, however it may be catching on in Europe. Proctor and Gamble have installed a sleep pod at their Weybridge site in the UK which employees can use for 20-minute power naps. The pod has a visor to block out sunlight and external sounds and can play music on speakers or headphones. Since its introduction the pod has been in use for most of the time.[2]

CONTENT AND PROCESS MOTIVATION THEORIES

The two main approaches to the study of motivation, developed since the 1950s and still widely promoted today, are known as the content and process theories. A more recent approach, based on personal values and self-concept, is presented later in the chapter.

Content theories *of motivation offer ways to profile or analyse individuals to identify the needs that are assumed to motivate their behaviours.*

Content theories are primarily concerned with what it is within individuals or their environment that energizes and sustains behaviour. In other words, what specific needs or motives within an individual or their environment energizes individual behaviour? We use the terms 'needs' and 'motives' interchangeably to mean the physiological or psychological deficiencies that one feels a compulsion to reduce or eliminate. If you feel very hungry (a physiological need), you will feel a compulsion to satisfy that need by eating. If you have a need for recognition (a psychological need), you may try to satisfy that need by working hard to please your boss. Content theories are useful because they help managers to understand what people will and will not value as work rewards or need satisfiers.

Process theories *of motivation seek to understand the thought processes that take place in the minds of people and how these act to motivate their behaviour.*

The process theories strive to provide an understanding of the thought or cognitive processes that take place within the minds of individuals to influence their behaviour. Thus, a content theory may suggest that security is an important need. A process theory may go further by suggesting how and why a need for security could be linked to specific rewards and to the specific actions that the worker may need to perform to achieve these rewards. Process theories add a cognitive dimension by focusing on individuals' beliefs about how certain behaviours will lead to rewards such as money or promotion; that is, the assumed connection between work activities and the satisfaction of needs.[3]

CONTENT THEORIES

Maslow, Alderfer, McClelland and Herzberg proposed four of the better-known content theories. Each of these content theories has made a major contribution to our understanding of work motivation. Some have provided a basis for more complex theorizing in later years.

Higher-order needs *are esteem and self-actualization needs in Maslow's hierarchy.*

Lower-order needs *are physiological, safety and social needs in Maslow's hierarchy.*

Maslow's hierarchy of needs theory

Abraham Maslow's 'hierarchy of needs' theory (Figure 4.2) identifies five distinct levels of individual needs from self-actualization and esteem at the top (higher-order needs) to social, safety and physiological requirements at the bottom (lower-order needs). Maslow assumes that some needs are more important (potent) than others and must be satisfied before other needs can serve as motivators. Thus, the physiological needs must be satisfied before the safety needs are activated and the safety needs must be satisfied before the social needs are activated and so on.

The physiological needs are considered the most basic; they consist of needs for such things as food and water. Individuals try to satisfy these needs before turning to needs at the safety level, which involve security, protection, stability and so on. When these needs are active, people will look at their jobs in terms of how well they satisfy these needs.

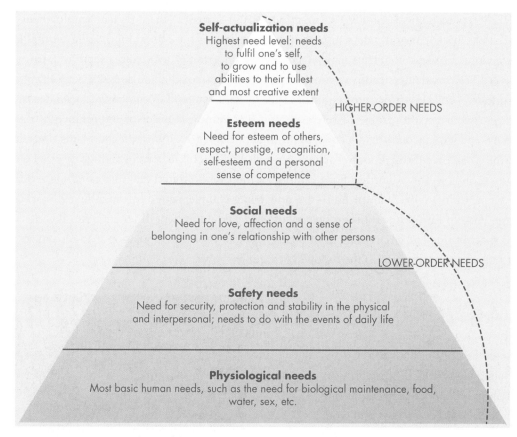

Figure 4.2: Higher-order and lower-order needs in Maslow's hierarchy of needs.

The social needs of a sense of belonging and a need for affiliation are activated once the physiological and safety needs are satisfied. The higher-order needs depicted in Figure 4.2 consist of the esteem and self-actualization needs – that is, being all that one can be. Here, challenging work and recognition for good performance assume centre stage.

Maslow: the research

Whilst Maslow's theory has proved popular with managers there is limited research evidence to support his theory, in fact Maslow himself even questioned its applicability to organizational behaviour.[4] Some research suggests that there is a tendency for higher-order needs to increase in importance over lower-order needs as individuals move up the managerial hierarchy.[5] However other studies, such as one of Greek R&D professionals, suggest that individuals still place the greatest emphasis on lower-order needs (particularly money) even though they were fully achieving higher-order needs.[6] Other studies report that needs vary according to a person's career stage,[7] the size of the organization.[8] and even geographic location.[9] Generally, there is no consistent evidence that the satisfaction of a need at one level will decrease its importance and increase the importance of the next higher need.[10]

To what extent does Maslow's theory apply only to Western culture? In many developing nations, the satisfaction of lower-order needs, such as basic subsistence and survival needs, consumes the entire lifetimes of many millions of individuals, with little opportunity to progress to higher level need satisfaction. But in societies where regular employment is available, basic cultural values appear to play an important role in motivating workplace behaviour. In those countries high in Hofstede's uncertainty avoidance, such as Japan or Greece, security tends to motivate most employees more strongly than does self-actualization. Workers in collectivist-oriented countries such as Pakistan tend to emphasize social needs.[11] In general, a person's frame of reference will determine the order of importance of their needs, and societal culture influences that frame of reference.[12] With the increasing diversity of the workforce throughout Europe we must also be careful to consider ethnic or other cultural groups within countries. For example, in the UK the traditional mix of ethnic groups – Asian, Chinese, black and white – are now being complemented by the influx of workers from Eastern European ethnic groups; all of whom could present different cultural contexts for motivation. The circumstances of different sections of the population may also make a difference to motivation, as the following example shows.

ERG theory *categorizes needs into existence, relatedness and growth needs.*

Existence needs *arise from desire for physiological and material wellbeing.*

OB *IN ACTION*

In the Jinjian Garment Factory in Shenzen, China, workers are predominantly unskilled peasants who are willing to come to the province to work for low wages, endure crowded living conditions and work uneven seasonal hours (up to 12 hours a day for 28 days of the month in peak season). Production pressures have led the company to try penalizing workers by deducting pay for quality deficiencies, especially because there appears to be a deliberate slowdown in rate among them.[13] However, due to

a shortage in experienced workers caused by high employee turnover, the company is now looking for other ways to motivate and retain its employees.

Alderfer's ERG theory

Relatedness needs *refer to the desire for satisfying interpersonal relationships.*

Growth needs *relate to the desire for continued personal growth and development.*

Clayton Alderfer's ERG theory (Figure 4.3) is also based on needs but is more flexible than Maslow's theory in three basic respects.[14] First, the theory collapses Maslow's five need categories into three: existence needs relate to a person's desire for physiological and material wellbeing; relatedness needs represent the desire for satisfying interpersonal relationships; and growth needs are about the desire for continued personal growth and development. Second, where Maslow's theory argues that individuals progress up a needs hierarchy as a result of the satisfaction of lower-order needs (a satisfaction–progression process), ERG theory includes a 'frustration–regression' principle, whereby an already satisfied lower-level need can become activated when a higher level need cannot be satisfied. Thus, if a person is continually frustrated in their attempts to satisfy growth needs, relatedness needs will again surface as key motivators. Third, according to Maslow, a person focuses on one need at a time. In contrast, ERG theory contends that more than one need may be activated at the same time.

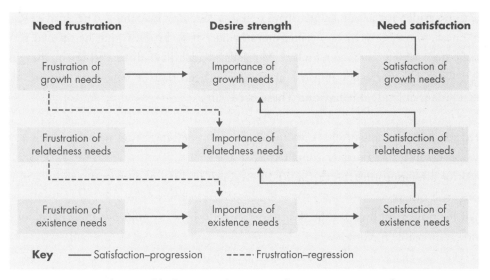

Figure 4.3: Clayton Alderfer's ERG theory: satisfaction–progression, frustration–regression components of the ERG theory.

Source: Marc J Wallace, Jr, and Andrew D Szilagyi, Jr, Managing Behaviour in Organizations, 1982. Scott Foresman & Company, Glenview, IL.

ERG: the research

Research appears to provide better supporting evidence for ERG theory than Maslow's theory. However, the research is relatively limited includes disclaimers[15] and additional research is needed to support its validity. One article provides evidence for the ERG need categories and reports additional findings – for example, growth needs were greater for respondents with more highly educated parents, and women had lower strength of existence needs and higher strength of relatedness needs than men.[16] The combined satisfaction–progression and frustration–regression principles provide the manager with a more flexible approach to understanding human needs than does Maslow's strict hierarchy. Importantly, Alderfer's theory emphasizes that performance constraints outside the control of the individual (see Figure 4.1), or innate disposition (such as lack of competence or low intrinsic work motivation) may cause a decline in effort or negative behaviour. Managers thus need to examine the workplace environment continually to remove or reduce any organizational constraint that will restrict opportunities for personal growth and development.

McClelland's acquired needs theory

In the late 1940s, psychologist David I. McClelland and his colleagues began experimenting with the Thematic Apperception Test (TAT) as a way of measuring human needs.[17] The TAT, as mentioned in Chapter 2, is a projective technique that asks people to view pictures and write stories about what they see. It is normally associated with personality testing. McClelland, however, used it to collect data on motivation. In one case, McClelland showed three executives a photograph of a man sitting down and looking at family photos arranged on his work desk. One executive wrote of an engineer who was daydreaming about a family outing scheduled for the next day. Another described a designer who had picked up an idea for a new gadget from remarks made by his family. The third described an engineer who was intently working on a bridge-stress problem that he seemed sure to solve because of his confident look.[18] McClelland identified three themes in these TAT stories, with each corresponding to an underlying need that he believes is important for understanding individual behaviour. These needs are:

- **need for achievement** (nAch) – the desire to do something better or more efficiently, to solve problems, or to master complex tasks
- **need for affiliation** (nAff) – the desire to establish and maintain friendly and warm relations with others
- **need for power** (nPower) – the desire to control others, to influence their behaviour, or to be responsible for others.

McClelland's basic theory is that these three needs are acquired over time, as a result of life experiences. Individuals are motivated by these needs, which can be associated with different work roles and preferences. The theory encourages managers to learn how to identify the presence of nAch, nAff, and nPower in themselves and in others and to create work environments that are responsive to the respective need profiles of different employees.

McClelland: the research

The research lends considerable insight into nAch, in particular. McClelland's theory challenges and rejects the research of other psychologists such as Erikson[19] who suggest that the need to achieve is a behaviour that is only acquired and developed during early childhood: if it is not obtained then it cannot easily be learned or achieved during adult life. McClelland maintains that the need to achieve is a behaviour that an individual can acquire through appropriate training in adulthood. For example McClelland trained business people in Kakinda, India, to think, talk and act like high achievers by having them write stories about achievement and participate in a business game that encouraged achievement. The business people also met with successful entrepreneurs and learned how to set challenging goals for their own businesses. Over a two-year period following these activities, the people from the Kakinda study engaged in activities that created twice as many new jobs as those who did not receive training.[20]

Other research also suggests that societal culture can make a difference in the emphasis on nAch. Anglo-American countries such as the UK, the US, Canada and Australia (countries weak in uncertainty avoidance and high in masculinity) tend to follow the high nAch pattern. In contrast, strong uncertainty, high femininity countries, such as Portugal and Chile, tend to follow a low nAch pattern. There are two especially relevant managerial applications of McClelland's theory. First, the theory is particularly useful when each need is linked with a set of work preferences (Table 4.1). Second, if these needs can truly be acquired, it may be possible to acquaint people with the need profiles required to succeed in various types of jobs. For example, McClelland found that the combination of a moderate to high need for power and a lower need for affiliation enables people to be effective managers at higher levels in organizations. Lower nAff allows the manager to make difficult decisions without undue worry of being disliked.[21] High nPower creates the willingness to have influence or impact on others, though misuse of that power may result in sabotage by those mistreated or prevented from rising to the top of the organization.[22] Other more recent studies have found that the satisfaction of these needs particularly self esteem had a significant influence on the job performance of senior managers.[23]

Individual needs	Work preference	Example
High need for achievement	Individual responsibility; challenging but achievable goals; feedback on performance	Field salesperson with a challenging quota and the opportunity to earn individual bonus; entrepreneur
High need for affiliation	Interpersonal relationships; opportunities to communicate	Customer service representative; member of a work unit that is subject to a group wage bonus plan
High need for power	Influence over other persons; attention; recognition	Formal position of supervisory responsibility; appointment as head of special task force or committee

Table 4.1: Work preferences of persons high in need for achievement, affiliation and power.

Herzberg's two-factor theory

Frederick Herzberg took a different approach to examining motivation. Using a 'critical incident' interviewing technique, Herzberg simply asked workers to comment on two statements:[24]

- 'Tell me about a time when you felt exceptionally good about your job.'
- 'Tell me about a time when you felt exceptionally bad about your job.'

After analysing nearly 4000 responses to these statements (Figure 4.4) Herzberg and his associates developed the two-factor theory, also known as the motivator–hygiene theory. They noticed that the factors identified as sources of work dissatisfaction (subsequently called 'dissatisfiers' or 'hygiene factors') were different from those identified as sources of satisfaction (subsequently called 'satisfiers' or 'motivator factors').

According to Herzberg's two-factor theory, an individual employee could be simultaneously both satisfied and dissatisfied because each of these two factors has a different set of drivers and is recorded on a separate scale. According to Herzberg's measurement the two scales are:

The motivator–hygiene theory distinguishes between sources of work dissatisfaction (hygiene factors) and satisfaction (motivators); it is also known as the two-factor theory.

1. Satisfaction   No satisfaction
2. Dissatisfaction   No dissatisfaction

Effective managers have to achieve two distinct outcomes as discussed below: to maximize the job satisfaction of the people who work for them and, similarly, to minimize their job dissatisfaction.

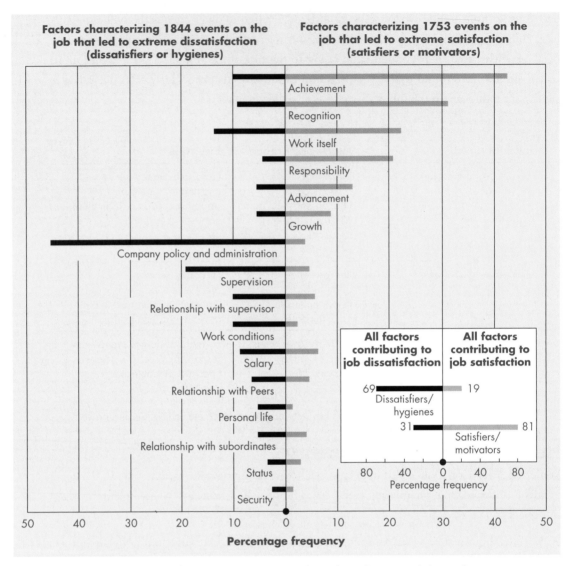

Figure 4.4: Herzberg's two-factor theory: sources of satisfaction and dissatisfaction as reported in 12 investigations.

Source: Reprinted by permission of Harvard Business Review. Adapted from Herzberg Z., One more time: how do you motivate employees? *Harvard Business Review*, September/October 1987 © 2002 Harvard Business School Publishing Corporation. All Rights Reserved

Satisfiers or motivator factors

Motivators
(motivator factors)
are satisfiers that
are associated
with what people
do in their work.

Job content
refers to what
people do in their
work.

To improve satisfaction, a manager must use **motivators** as shown on the right side of Figure 4.4. These factors are related to job content – that is, what people do in their work. Adding these satisfiers or motivators to people's jobs is Herzberg's link to performance. These are also known as intrinsic rewards and cover such things as sense of achievement, recognition and responsibility. According to Herzberg, when these opportunities are absent workers will not be satisfied and will not perform well. Building such factors into a job is an important topic and it is discussed at length in the next chapter.

Dissatisfiers or hygiene factors

Hygiene factors are associated with the job context; that is, they are factors related to a person's work setting. Improving working conditions (for example, special offices and air conditioning) involves improving a hygiene or job-context factor. It will prevent people from being dissatisfied with their work but will not make them satisfied. Table 4.2 shows other examples of hygiene factors in work settings.

As Table 4.2 shows, salary or money is included as a hygiene factor. This is perhaps surprising and is discussed further in the next section.

Hygiene factors *are dissatisfiers that are associated with aspects of a person's work setting.*

Job context *refers to a person's work setting.*

Hygiene factors	Examples
Organizational policies, procedures	Attendance rules
Holiday schedules	
Grievance procedures, Performance appraisal methods	
Working conditions	Noise levels Safety
Personal comfort, Size of work area	
Interpersonal relationships	Co-worker relations, Customer relations Relationship with boss
Quality of supervision	Technical competence of boss
Base salary	Hourly wage rate or salary

Table 4.2: Sample hygiene factors found in work settings.

Money: motivator or hygiene factor

Herzberg found that low salary makes people dissatisfied but that paying people more does not satisfy or motivate them. It is important to bear in mind that this conclusion derives from data finding that salary had considerable cross-loading across both motivators and hygiene factors (see the bars that cross the central vertical line at zero percentage frequency in Figure 4.4). Because most of the variance could be explained within the hygiene or job context group of factors, Herzberg concluded that money was not a motivator. The theme of money as an extrinsic reward is discussed more fully later in the chapter.

Herzberg: the research and practical implications

There has been much debate on the merits of the two-factor theory.[25] While Herzberg's continuing research and that of his followers support the theory, some researchers have used different methods and are unable to confirm the theory. It is therefore criticized as being method-bound – that is, supportable only by applying Herzberg's original method. This is a serious criticism because the scientific approach requires that theories be verifiable when different research methods are used. Perhaps the most powerful critique was offered by Vroom who postulated that the critical incident method used by Herzberg may have resulted in respondents generally associating good times in their jobs with things under their personal control, or for which they could give themselves credit. Bad times, on the other hand, were more often associated with factors in the environment, or under the control of management.[26]

Herzberg's theory has also met with other criticisms:

- the original sample of scientists and engineers probably is not representative of the working population
- the theory does not account for individual differences (for example, the impact of pay according to gender, age and other important variables)
- the theory does not clearly define the relationship between satisfaction and motivation.[27]

Such criticisms may contribute to the mixed findings from research conducted outside the US. In New Zealand, for example, supervision and interpersonal relationships were found to contribute significantly to satisfaction and not merely to reducing dissatisfaction. Certain hygiene factors were cited more frequently as satisfiers in Panama, Latin America and a number of countries other than the US. In contrast, evidence from countries such as Finland tends to confirm US results.[28] In view of globalizing workforces these distinctions may have significant importance for managers endeavouring to motivate their employees.

OB IN ACTION

Hugh Symons Communications, the mobile phone airtime distributor, introduced an online bonus scheme five years ago as a cost-effective way to reward and recognize the efforts of its employees in its 850 retail outlets across the UK. Previously the company had only rewarded its top three employees several times a year, but this was seen to be a poor distribution of the reward budget. Not only was it regarded as demotivational for the employees who narrowly missed out but it provided no incentive for those employees who felt they had no chance of receiving a bonus. 'The problem is when you have a large number of employees involved and you only have three gifts, the vast majority are left with nothing, even if they have put the effort in', says Theresa Williams, head of marketing. The new online scheme has proved to be a success and popular with employees as it allows more employees to be rewarded as when needed through the purchase of online points which employees can then convert to prizes, thus giving the company greater flexibility to reward more of its employees without committing to a big spend. There are a vast number of prizes and employees are not restricted to single rewards. 'Choice is important, employers should not dictate to staff what they are rewarded with. Choice can make motivation schemes much more cost effective' Williams explained.[29]

However, the theory does have value. For example, it may help to identify why a focus on job environment factors (such as special office fixtures, piped-in music, comfortable lounges for breaks high base salaries and other monetary-based rewards schemes) often do not motivate. This has led to many companies rethinking these types of schemes as the above example demonstrates. It also draws strong attention to the value of job design and motivation as discussed in the next chapter.

PROCESS THEORIES

The various content theories still emphasize the 'what' aspect of motivation – that is they try to look for ways of improving motivation by dealing with deprived needs. They do not emphasize the thought processes concerning 'why' and 'how' people choose one action over another in the workplace. For this, we must turn to *process motivation theories*. Two well-known process theories are equity theory and expectancy theory.

Equity theory

Equity theory is based on the phenomenon of social comparison and is best known through the writing of J. Stacy Adams.[30] Adams argues that when people gauge the fairness of their work outcomes compared with those of others, felt inequity is a motivating state of mind. That is, when people perceive inequity in their work, they experience a state of cognitive dissonance and they will be aroused to remove the discomfort and to restore a sense of felt equity to the situation. Inequities exist whenever people feel that the rewards or inducements they receive for their work inputs or contributions are unequal to the rewards other people appear to have received for their inputs. For the individual, the equity comparison or thought process that determines such feeling is:

Individual rewards/individual inputs ⟷ comparison ⟷ Others' rewards/others' inputs

Equity theory is based on the phenomenon of social comparison and posits that because people gauge the fairness of their work outcomes compared with others, any perceived inequity will result in an unpleasant feeling that the individual will be driven to remove through a variety of possible actions.

Resolving felt inequities

A felt negative inequity exists when individuals feel that they have received relatively less than others have in proportion to work inputs. Felt positive inequity exists when individuals feel that they have received relatively more than others have.

Both felt negative and felt positive inequity are motivating states. When either exists, the individual will likely engage in one or more of the following behaviours to restore a sense of equity:

Felt negative inequity exists when individuals feel they have received relatively less than others have in proportion to work inputs.

- change work inputs (for example, reduce performance efforts)
- change the outcomes (rewards) received (for example, ask for an increase in salary)
- act to change the inputs or outputs of the comparison person (for example, get a co-worker to accept more work)
- change the comparison points (for example, compare self with a different co-worker)
- psychologically distort the comparisons (for example, rationalize that the inequity is only temporary and will be resolved in the future)
- leave the situation (for example, change departments or quit).

Felt positive inequity exists when individuals feel they have received relatively more than others have.

Equity theory predicts that people who feel either under-rewarded or over-rewarded for their work will act to restore a sense of equity.

Adams's equity theory: the research

The research of Adams and others, accomplished largely in laboratory settings, lends tentative support to this prediction.[31] The research indicates that people who feel overpaid (feel positive inequity) have been found to increase the quantity or quality of their work, while those who are underpaid (feel negative inequity) decrease the quantity or quality of their work. The research is most conclusive about felt negative inequity. It appears that people are less comfortable when they are under-rewarded than when they are over-rewarded, which is hardly surprising. These feelings of inequity can still be felt even when the person has left their job, as in the case of Bridget Bodman below.

 **IN ACTION**

Bridget Bodman, a former accountant at manufacturing company API group received £25 000 in an equal pay case in November 2006 supported by the UK's Equal Opportunities Commission. Bridget's case was unusual as she used her successor's salary to make the claim. In most equal pay cases a claimant is required to produce a 'comparator' – pointing to someone doing a similar role, at the same time, on higher pay. Bridget found out that her male successor had a higher salary (£8 000) and was paid a £8 640 car allowance and additional benefits that she had not received. API in defending the claim stated that these differences were due to other material factors and not sex discrimination.

Whilst Bridget's case is unusual in that she compared herself against her successor the statistics in Europe show a continuing pay gap (17 % in the UK in 2006) between men's and women's pay. Under UK and European law pay differentials between sexes can still exist if there is a genuine reason for the difference, such as market forces.[32] Thus employers have been able to justify salary differences, because male employees negotiate higher salaries on appointment but how does this affect people's motivation to work if they feel that they are being unfairly rewarded? What would you do if you were in Bridget's situation? In contrast, the Wimbledon (UK) tennis championship bowed to pressure to equalize the prize money for male and female players in 2007 despite the fact that the men's singles matches were the best of five sets whereas the women only played three.[33]

Managing the equity dynamic

Figure 4.5 shows that the equity comparison intervenes between a manager's allocation of rewards and their impact on the work behaviour of staff. Feelings of inequity are determined solely by the individual's interpretation of the situation.

Figure 4.5: The equity comparison as an intervening variable in the rewards, satisfaction and performance relationship.

Thus, it is incorrect to assume all employees in a work group will view their annual pay rise as fair. It is not how a manager feels about the allocation of rewards that counts;

it is how the recipients perceive the rewards that will determine the motivational outcomes of the equity dynamic. Fairness in this context also focuses on both distributive justice – the perceived fairness of the amount of the reward employees received and procedural justice – the perceived fairness of the process used to determine the distribution of awards among employees. Research mainly carried out in the US found that workers place greater emphasis on the perceived fairness of the system rather than the actual pay rise itself.[34] Another study of senior managers supports this view and goes further in suggesting that they place little value on comparisons with other employees and are only concerned about whether the system has fairly rewarded them for their performance.[35] The challenge for management is, then, in creating a process that is seen to be fair because perceived equity can foster job satisfaction and performance. In contrast, rewards that are received with feelings of negative inequity can damage these key work results. The burden lies with the manager to take control of the situation and make sure that any negative consequences of the equity comparisons are avoided, or at least minimized, when rewards are allocated.

Distributive justice *refers to perceived fairness of how rewards are allocated.*

Procedural justice *refers to perceived fairness of the process used to determine the distribution of rewards.*

EFFECTIVE MANAGER 4.2

Higher-Order Needs

Self-Actualization

Highest need level; need to fulfill oneself; to grow and use abilities to fullest and most creative extent.

Esteem

Need for esteem of others; respect, prestige, recognition, need for self-esteem, personal sense of competence, mastery.

Lower-Order Needs

Social

Need for love, affection, sense of belongingness in one's relationships with other persons.

Safety

Need for security, protection, and stability in the physical and inter-personal events of day-to-day life.

Physiological

Most basic of all human needs; need for biological maintenance; need for food, water and sustenance.

- Recognize that an employee is likely to make an equity comparison with colleagues when especially visible rewards, such as pay, promotions and so on, are being allocated.
- Anticipate felt negative inequities.
- Communicate to each individual your evaluation of the reward, an appraisal of the performance on which it is based, and the comparison points you consider to be appropriate.

Steps for managing the equity process

Managing the equity dynamic across cultures can become very complex. Western expatriates working in multinational corporations typically adopt an individual frame of reference when making equity comparisons. For local employees in Eastern cultures, the value placed on rewards and the weighting attributed to a specific outcome may vary considerably from Western norms. The group, not the individual, is the major point of reference for such equity comparisons and if a multinational corporation tries to motivate by offering individualized rewards employees may not respond as expected.[36]

Expectancy *is the probability that the individual assigns to work effort being followed by a given level of achieved task performance.*

Instrumentality *is the probability that the individual assigns to a level of achieved task performance leading to various work outcomes.*

Valence *represents the values that the individual attaches to various work outcomes.*

Expectancy theory *argues that work motivation is determined by individual beliefs about effort–performance relationships and the desirability of various work outcomes from different performance levels.*

Expectancy theory

Victor Vroom's expectancy theory[37] seeks to predict or explain the task-related effort expended by a person. The theory's central question is: 'What determines the willingness of an individual to exert personal effort to work at tasks that contribute to the performance of the team and the organization?' Figure 4.6 illustrates the managerial foundations of expectancy theory. Individuals are viewed as making conscious decisions to allocate their behaviour towards work efforts and to serve self-interests. The three key terms in the theory are as follows.

- Expectancy: the probability that the individual assigns to work effort being followed by a given level of achieved task performance. Expectancy would equal '0' if the person felt it was impossible to achieve the given performance level; it would equal '1' if a person was 100% certain that the performance could be achieved.
- Instrumentality: the probability that the individual assigns to a given level of achieved task performance leading to various work outcomes that are rewarding for them. Instrumentality also varies from '1' (meaning the reward outcome is 100% certain to follow performance) to '0' (indicating that there is no chance that performance will lead to the reward outcome).
- Valence: the value that the individual attaches to various work reward outcomes. Valences form a scale from –1 (very undesirable outcome) to +1 (very desirable outcome).

Expectancy theory argues that work motivation is determined by individual beliefs about effort–performance relationships and the desirability of various work outcomes from different performance levels. Simply, the theory is based on the logic that people will do what they can do when they want to.[38] If you want a promotion and see that high performance can lead to that promotion, and that if you work hard you can achieve high performance, you will be motivated to work hard.

Multiplier effects and multiple outcomes

Vroom posits that motivation (M), expectancy (E), instrumentality (I) and valence (V) are related to one another by the equation: $M = E \times I \times V$.

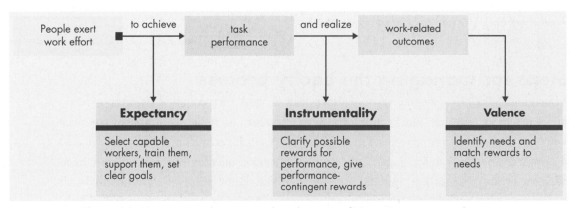

Figure 4.6: Key terms and managerial implications of Vroom's expectancy theory.

This relationship means that the motivational appeal of a given work path is sharply reduced whenever any one or more of these factors approaches the value of zero. Conversely, for a given reward to have a high and positive motivational impact as a work outcome, the expectancy, instrumentality and valence associated with the reward must all be high and positive.

Suppose a manager is wondering whether the prospect of earning a merit pay rise will be motivational to a subordinate. Expectancy theory predicts that motivation to work hard to earn the merit pay will be low if individuals:

- feel they cannot achieve the necessary performance level (expectancy)
- is not confident a high level of task performance will result in a high merit pay rise (instrumentality)
- places little value (valence) on a merit pay increase
- experiences any combination of these.

Expectancy theory is able to accommodate multiple work outcomes in predicting motivation. As shown in Figure 4.7, the outcome of a merit pay increase may not be the only one affecting the individual's decision to work hard. Relationships with colleagues may also be important, and they may be undermined if the individual stands out from the group as a high performer. Although merit pay is both highly valued and considered accessible to the individual, its motivational power can be cancelled out by the negative effects of high performance on the individual's social relationships with colleagues. One of the advantages of expectancy theory is its ability to help managers account for such multiple outcomes when trying to determine the motivational value of various work rewards to individual employees.

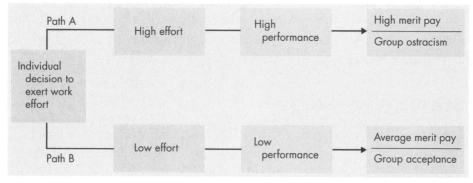

Figure 4.7: An example of individual thought processes as viewed by expectancy theory.

Vroom: managerial implications

The managerial implications of Vroom's expectancy theory are summarized in Table 4.3. Expectancy logic argues that a manager must try to understand individual thought processes, then actively intervene in the work situation to influence them. This includes trying to maximize work expectancies, instrumentalities and valences that support the organization's production purposes. In other words, a manager should strive to create a work setting in which the individual will also value work contributions serving the organization's needs as paths towards desired personal outcomes or rewards.

Expectancy term	The individual's question	Managerial implications
Expectancy	'Can I achieve the desired level of task performance?'	Select workers with ability; train workers to use ability; support individual ability with organizational resources; identify performance goals.
Instrumentality	'What work outcomes will be received as a result of the performance?'	Clarify psychological contracts; communicate performance–reward possibilities; confirm performance–reward possibilities by making actual rewards contingent on performance.
Valence	'How highly do I value the work outcomes?'	Identify individual needs or outcomes; adjust available rewards to match these.

Table 4.3: Managerial implications of expectancy theory.

In terms of outcome valence, the manager can identify individual needs or outcomes important to each individual, then try to adjust available rewards to match these. In this sense the theory can be universally applied. Each individual may be different, though different cultural patterns of values will affect valence of rewards across cultures. It may also be possible to change the individual's perceptions of the valence of various outcomes, as shown in Effective Manager 4.3.

EFFECTIVE MANAGER 4.3

Tips for influencing the perceived valence of work outcomes:
- find out the currently valued outcomes for each employee
- determine the outcomes that are currently available to them
- discuss how well the two sets match, and examine similarities between each individual's list and your list
- show how some available outcomes may be more desirable or less undesirable than the worker thinks (for example, promotion may be available but the employee currently does not desire it because he or she feels uncomfortable with it).

Vroom: the research

There is a great deal of research on expectancy theory and good review articles are available.[39] Although the theory has received substantial support, the terminology used by psychologists is often difficult to understand and apply. Rather than suggesting that the underlying theory is inadequate, researchers indicate that problems of method and measurement may cause their inability to generate more confirming data. Thus, while awaiting the results of more sophisticated research, experts seem to agree that expectancy theory is a useful insight into work motivation.

One of the more popular modifications of Vroom's original version of the theory distinguishes between extrinsic and intrinsic rewards as two separate types of possible work outcomes.[40] Extrinsic rewards are positively valued work outcomes that the individual receives from some other person in the work setting. An example is pay. Workers typically do not pay themselves directly; some representative of the organization administers the reward. In contrast, intrinsic rewards are positively valued work outcomes that the individual receives directly as a result of task performance; they do not require the participation of another person. A feeling of achievement after accomplishing a particularly challenging task is one example. The distinction between extrinsic and intrinsic rewards is important because each type demands separate attention from a manager seeking to use rewards to increase motivation.

Extrinsic *rewards are positively valued work outcomes that the individual receives from some other person in the work setting.*

Intrinsic *rewards are positively valued work outcomes that the individual receives directly as a result of task performance.*

INTEGRATING CONTENT AND PROCESS MOTIVATION THEORIES

Each of the theories presented in this chapter is potentially useful for the manager. Although the equity and expectancy theories have special strengths, current thinking argues for a combined approach that points out where and when various motivation theories work best.[41] Thus, before leaving this discussion, we should pull the content and process theories together into one integrated model of individual performance and satisfaction.

First, the various content theories have a common theme, as shown in Figure 4.8. Content theorists disagree somewhat as to the exact nature of human needs but they do agree that:

$$\text{Individual needs} \xrightarrow{\text{activate}} \text{tensions} \xrightarrow[\text{influence}]{\text{that}} \text{attitudes and behaviour.}$$

The manager's job is to create a work environment that responds positively to individual needs. Poor performance, undesirable behaviours and/or decreased satisfaction can be partly explained in terms of 'blocked' needs, or needs that are not satisfied on the job. The motivational value of rewards (intrinsic and extrinsic) can also be analysed in terms of 'activated' needs to which a given reward either does or does not respond. Ultimately, managers must understand that individuals have different needs and place different importance on different needs. Managers must also know what to offer individuals to respond to their needs and to create work settings that give people the opportunity to satisfy their needs through their contributions to task, work unit and organizational performance.

Maslow	Alderfer	McClelland	Herzberg
Needs hierarchy	**ERG theory**	**Acquired needs theory**	**Two-factor theory**
Self-actualization	Growth	Need for achievement	Motivators and satisfiers
		Need for power	
Esteem			Hygienes and dissatisfiers
Social	Relatedness	Need for affiliation	
Safety and security			
Physiological	Existence		

Figure 4.8: Comparison of content motivation theories.

Porter and Lawler's model

Figure 4.9 is a model that goes further to integrate content and process theories. The model, as proposed by Lyman W. Porter and Edward E. Lawler, is an extension of Vroom's original expectancy theory.[42] The figure is based on the individual performance equation (see Chapter 2). Individual attributes and work effort and the manager's ability to create a work setting that positively responds to individual needs and goals all affect performance. Whether a work setting can satisfy needs depends on the availability of rewards (extrinsic and intrinsic). The content theories enter the model as the manager's guide to understanding individual attributes and identifying the needs that give motivational value to the various work rewards allocated to employees. Managers are also interested in promoting high levels of individual satisfaction as a part of their concern for human resource maintenance. Motivation performance and satisfaction can all occur when rewards are allocated on the basis of past performance (that is, when rewards are performance contingent) but motivation can also occur when job satisfactions result from rewards that are felt to be equitably allocated. When felt negative inequity results, satisfaction will be low and motivation will be reduced. Thus, the integrated model includes a key role for equity theory and recognizes job performance and satisfaction as separate but potentially interdependent work results.[43]

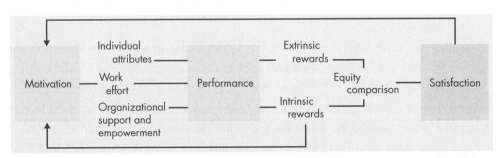

Figure 4.9: Predicting individual work performance and satisfaction: an integrated model.

SELF-CONCEPT AND PERSONAL VALUES

In recent years a new body of work has developed to explain other dimensions of motivation that do not seem to be covered by content and process theories. For example, people often offer their services voluntarily or engage in altruistic deeds for no anticipated rewards (intrinsic or extrinsic). Personal value systems and the idea of self-concept underlie this approach. **Self-concept** is the concept that individuals have of themselves as physical, social and spiritual or moral beings.

Self-concept is the concept that individuals have of themselves as physical, social and spiritual or moral beings.

The self-concept approach comes from personality theory. It focuses on using the concept of the self as an underlying force that motivates behaviour, which gives it direction and energy and sustains it. Self-concept is derived from many influences including family, social identity and reference groups, education and experience. Generally speaking, these aspects of personality are a guide to our behaviour and help us to decide what to do in specific situations. So, for example, young people may choose to study medicine or dentistry at university, or to enter the family business, because that is what was always expected of them and has therefore become an important part of their identity. Rewards such as money and status may be secondary considerations. Many acts are done out of a sense of responsibility, integrity or even humour, which relate to the self-concept aspect of personality.[44] This sort of approach would help to explain the nurse who waits with the relatives of a critically injured patient for hours after his/her shift is completed; or the person who works the shift of a friend who is studying for exams. It may also explain why more employees seek to work for ethical employers.

OB IN ACTION

In the romantic comedy *Two Weeks' Notice*, Sandra Bullock plays a smart but idealistic Harvard lawyer working in legal aid who, despite her desire to change the world, is persuaded by millionaire George Wade (Hugh Grant) to join his property company, promising that she can run the firms' *pro bono* programme. Yet a year later she is unhappy. The Christmas bonus and excellent healthcare plan offer little or no incentive and she finds that the firm does not share her social and environmental values, so she hands in her notice.

This may be Hollywood fluff but *Two Weeks' Notice* does highlight the growing concern of employees, nine out of 10 according to the 2004 poll in the UK by Mori, with employers' ethical stance and corporate social responsibilities. Tracy Maxed, HR manager at organic wholesalers Abel & Cole, confirms this finding. 'I've worked in the organic industry for 15 years and there's definitely an interest for people from all walks of life to drop out of the rat race and into a feel-good environment – even if it means less money and status,' she says. As an employer Abel & Cole offers a range of green perks. There is a quarterly £300 bonus for all employees if the company meets its reduction in waste targets; a strictly no suits policy and, each day, employees take turns in cooking lunch using organic ingredients.[45]

In contrast to a focus on needs or cognitive thought processes to explain motivation, the self-concept approach relies on other ways of understanding motivation to explain the full range of motivated behaviour. People may also draw on the values they hold and the way that these values are a guide to behaviours that seem right or appropriate for them. For example, people internalize values that are espoused by the professional group (or the organization) to which they belong. Behaviours consistent with such values might include saving lives and property at considerable personal risk, exposing unethical financial practices despite censure from management, facing personal hardship or leaving a well paid job because the company's values differ from their own as the following article demonstrates.

Having identified many content and process theories and an integrated model of these two approaches, as well as the ideas of self-concept and personal values in motivation, it is a good time to reflect on how managers may be able to realistically implement all these in the workplace. The following 'Counterpoint' raises some points about the complexity and difficulties of motivating employees.

▶ COUNTERPOINT

Knowing and engaging our workers?

When managers or scholars discuss workplace motivation, they tend to talk about it as if work, and a single workplace, is the only place where people exert effort towards fulfilling needs, achieving rewards and/or living life according to their self-concept. The idea that you can get to know your employees and work out what motivational needs they have, then find ways to help them satisfy those needs, can overascribe the importance of work in motivating people and simplify the complex circumstances and working arrangements that exist in today's workforce.

It is to be expected that employers would want some return on their motivational strategies. To do so employers need to invest time, money and other resources into employees who are 'engaged' with the company. The idea of 'employee engagement' helps to link up motivation with the workplace attitudes of organizational commitment, job satisfaction and advocacy (those who speak highly of their own organization as an employer and of its products, services and brand). Studies in the US and Canada reveal that companies with disengaged employees have significant productivity losses, while those with engaged employees have higher revenue, customer loyalty and profits.[46]

The idea that in the new-style workplace employees are all engaged may be problematic because many remain for only a short time, have links with more than one organization and/or have mixed feelings about their employment. These include an increasing number of casual or part-time employees, who in turn include the 'well-heeled itinerants' who are working multiple jobs (such as some university academics who hold three or more concurrent jobs).[47] Loosely engaged professionals often move from one contracted job to another, many working as free agents. Older workers may be torn between the pressures to continue working, at least part-time, and their desire to retire. At the other end of the age spectrum, a recent British survey of generation Y employees (those born between 1978 and 1994) found that they were very likely to change jobs if their expectations were not met in an organization.[48] People who work remotely or operate in a virtual workplace may lack engagement with the organization. For example, 4000 software consultants at Wipro, an Indian IT company, operate from and between customer sites outside of India.[49]

Also, it is important to remember that people do not spend all their lives at work and other things in their lives may drive behaviour as much as their work. Whether they play sport, work in their gardens, act in a voluntary capacity in a community organization or pursue further study, they are involved in motivation outside the workplace.

Questions

1. How might an employee's needs be satisfied outside the workplace and, if this occurs, how would it affect the needs that employees seek to satisfy in the workplace?

2. Why might casual employees, those with multiple jobs, older employees, generation Y workers, and virtual and professional workers be less engaged than other employees and what could an employer do to seek to motivate these different cohorts?

MANAGING PAY AS AN EXTRINSIC REWARD

In the next chapter we discuss more fully the nature of intrinsic motivation and job satisfaction, in this chapter we will now look more closely at pay as an extrinsic reward. As we have already said extrinsic rewards are positively valued work outcomes that the individual receives from some other person. Pay is an especially complex extrinsic reward. It can help organizations attract and retain highly capable workers and it can help satisfy and motivate these workers to work hard to achieve high performance but if workers are dissatisfied with the salary pay can also lead to strikes, grievances, absenteeism, turnover and sometimes even poor physical and mental health. The various aspects of pay make it an especially important extrinsic reward.[50]

Multiple meanings of pay

To use pay effectively as a reward a manager must understand why it is important to people. Various OB theories recognize multiple meanings of pay and the potential of these meanings to vary from one person or situation to another. When it comes to the relationship between pay and job satisfaction, for example, each of the following theories (which were discussed in general earlier in the chapter) offers a slightly different perspective.

According to Maslow's hierarchy of needs theory, pay is a unique reward that can satisfy many different needs. It is used directly to satisfy lower-order needs, such as the physiological need for food, and it is of symbolic value in satisfying higher-order needs, such as ego fulfilment.

According to McClelland's acquired needs theory, pay is an important source of performance feedback for high-need achievers. It can be attractive to persons with a high need for affiliation when offered as a group bonus and it is valued by the high need-for-power person as a means of 'buying' prestige or control over others.

According to Herzberg's two-factor theory, pay in the form of base wage or salary can prevent dissatisfaction but cannot lead to motivation (although merit pay rises given as special rewards for jobs done well can cause increased satisfaction and motivation). However, Herzberg's research does show that pay crossloads across both his hygiene and motivating factors. This finding recognizes that many of the respondents in Herzberg's research perceived money as a motivating factor.

Expectancy and equity theories, as well as the various reinforcement strategies, give additional insight into the multiple meanings of pay and their potential relationships to job performance. These ideas (summarized in Table 4.4) show how pay can serve as a motivator of work effort, when properly managed. This phrase is the real key; for pay to prove successful as a reward that is truly motivational to the recipient, it must be given:

• contingent on the occurrence of specific and desirable work behaviours, and
• equitably.

Merit pay and a variety of emerging creative pay practices are applications that need to be dealt with in more detail.

Theory	The meaning of pay
Equity theory	Pay is an object of social comparison. People are likely to compare their pay and pay increases with those received by others. When felt inequity occurs as a result of such comparisons, work effort may be reduced in the case of negative inequity, or increased in the case of positive inequity.
Expectancy theory	Pay is only one of many work rewards that individuals may value at work. When valence, instrumentality and expectancy are high, pay can be a source of motivation. However, the opportunity to work hard to obtain high pay will be viewed in the context of other effort–outcome expectancies and the equity dynamic.
Reinforcement theory	Pay is one of the extrinsic rewards that a manager may use to influence the work behaviour of employees. Through the techniques of operant conditioning, pay can be used as a positive reinforcer when the laws of contingent and immediate reinforcement are followed.

Table 4.4: The multiple meanings of pay as viewed from a performance perspective.

Merit pay

Edward Lawler's research has contributed greatly to our understanding of pay as an extrinsic reward. His research generally concludes that for pay to serve as a source of work motivation, high levels of job performance must be viewed as the path through which high pay can be achieved.[51] Merit pay is defined as a compensation system that bases an individual's salary or wage increase on a measure of the person's performance accomplishments during a specified time period. That is, merit pay is an attempt to make pay contingent on performance.

For some time now, research has supported the logic and theoretical benefits of merit pay but it also indicates that the implementation of merit pay plans is not as universal or as easy as we may expect.[52]

To work well, a merit pay plan must.

- be based on realistic and accurate measures of individual work performance
- create a belief among employees that the way to achieve high pay is to perform at high levels
- discriminate clearly between high and low performers in the amount of pay reward received
- avoid confusing 'merit' aspects of a pay increase with 'cost-of-living' adjustments.

These guidelines are consistent with the basic laws of reinforcement and the guidelines for positive reinforcement discussed in Chapter 3.

However, total quality management guru W. Edwards Deming has long been a critic of pay-for-performance schemes. Deming argues that, because performance is difficult to measure, all employees should receive a traditional salary or wage, and that all future pay rises should be administered uniformly across the company to encourage cooperation and teamwork. There are potential problems in linking pay to performance. However, many human resource experts and headhunters emphasize the importance of rewarding high performers for a private company's ability to attract top talent in a competitive global marketplace.

Merit pay is a compensation system that bases an individual's salary or wage increase on a measure of the person's performance accomplishments during a specified time period.

Paying for performance

The concept of linking pay with performance is controversial. Most employers would agree that quality employees deserve higher pay than underperforming employees. However, exactly what constitutes a 'quality employee' is problematic. Performance measurements are largely based on the perceptions of immediate supervisors; they are subjective and not based on specific criteria, and therefore can cause a sense of unfairness for many employees. In addition the low inflation economies that exist in Western Europe create more problems because the difference between an average and high performing employee may only translate into a 2–3 % difference in the pay increase. So is pay a motivator? In summary it depends on a number of factors some of which are outlined in the following counterpoint.

COUNTERPOINT

But it's all about money deep down isn't it?

The link between money and motivation remains complex and inconclusive. This lack of clear evidence is compounded by the problem that when asked employees often understate the importance of pay; that is to say, it is much more important in people's actual choices and behaviours than it is in their self-reports of what motivates them.[53] It is also evident that the link between money and motivation depends on a number of other variables such as time, career stage, level in the organization, age and culture. One longitudinal study, found that employees' motivational preferences vary over time with today's workers placing greater emphasis on more extrinsic factors with 'good wages' still being the top motivator for the majority of employees.[54] Another, in the hospitality industry, found that where jobs offer no variety and little intrinsic job satisfaction employees are overwhelmingly motivated by money alone.[55] In Britain 83% of human resources directors believed that younger employees were more motivated by flexible hours and career development programmes than by more traditional benefits such as money.[56] This was supported in a survey by the DTI that found that over 46% of respondents would chose flexible working over money as a benefit[57] and although money was reported to be the main motivator for young people in the Far and Middle East, work ethic and mastery were ranked higher in North and South America.[58] Robbins suggests that money can be considered to act as a 'scorecard' that enables employees to assess the value their employer places on them in comparison to others and as a medium of exchange allowing employees to purchase whatever 'needs satisfying' things they desire.[59] Other research develops this comparative concept further arguing that it's not absolute salary but comparative salary that motivates employees. Put simply, it doesn't matter so much what you are paid, more how much you are paid in comparison to others.[60] This concept is the basis of equity theory, which we have already discussed in this chapter.

Questions

1. How much does money motivate you in your choice of job?
2. Would you change jobs for an increase in salary alone?
3. Would you change jobs in order to work more flexibly even if it meant a cut in salary?

Creative pay practices

So how can employers effectively use financially based rewards to motivate their staff? Merit pay plans are but one attempt to enhance the positive value of pay as a work reward and to use it as a positive reinforcer but some argue that merit pay plans are not consistent with the demands of today's organizations because they fail to recognize the high degree of task interdependence among employees, as illustrated particularly in total quality management programmes. Still others contend that the nature of any incentive scheme should be tied to the overall organizational strategy and the nature of the desired behaviour; for example the pay system of an organization that needs highly skilled individuals who are in short supply should emphasize employee retention rather than performance.[61]

Many organizations facing increased competition, in an attempt to become more competitive by getting more from their workers, use varying creative incentive schemes either singly or in combination. Such nontraditional practices are becoming more common in organizations with increasingly diverse workforces and a growing emphasis on total quality management or similar setups.[62] These creative schemes can include skill-based pay, gainsharing plans, lump-sum pay increases, bonus share schemes and flexible benefit plans. Table 4.5 below depicts & variety of remuneration methods available to employers.

Pay practice	Description
Skill-based pay	A pay system that rewards people for acquiring and developing job-relevant skills that relate to organizational needs.
Gain-sharing plans	A pay system that links pay and performance by giving workers the opportunity to share in productivity gains through increased earnings.
Lump-sum pay increases	A pay system in which people elect to receive their annual wage or salary increase in one or more lump-sum payments.
Bonus share schemes	A share plan to reward high-performing executives.
Flexible benefit plans	Pay systems that allow workers to select benefits according to their individual needs.

Table 4.5: Creative pay practices.

There is a growing trend away from rewarding performance solely by financial outcomes. Many companies are now incorporating nonfinancial outcomes, such as a flexible benefit plan, into this performance-based pay equation. Additional criteria such as improved customer service, employee satisfaction with managerial style and increased market share are being added to the equation to obtain a clearer and more comprehensive profile of the measurement of effective managerial performance.[63] The following 'OB in action' looks at how the effectiveness of incentives varies with different cultural and economic contexts.

 **IN ACTION**

Can performance incentives work for China?

The use of incentives to motivate employees to increase performance is a typically Western concept. Hence we cannot assume that the concept of incentives is considered in the same manner in other areas of the world and, in some cases, it could be considered offensive to entice workers to perform better.

For example, in China, traditionally employees are paid according to the legislated national wage scales as a blue- or white-collar worker, with little differences in pay between workers and their supervisors. Bonuses are usually paid to a group that exceeded predetermined performance targets and the individual members of that group benefit from the bonus. Attempts to introduce individual performance-based incentives are becoming more common. However, it has been suggested that this will be a very difficult transition due to the deep-rooted collectivism in the Chinese culture.

Diverse opinions about performance incentive schemes in the West and the East have significant consequences for Chinese multinational corporations (MNCs) operating in countries such as Australia, New Zealand, the US or the UK. This means that individual wages for comparable positions across different countries will be very different. In addition to deep-seated cultural underpinnings, differences arise from complex legal and economic issues. For example, one major legal issue is that in Australia, Chinese firms have to pay holiday pay, which is an unknown concept in China. In addition, Chinese MNCs in Western countries compete with the local labour market and are generally forced to offer higher wages to attract better-skilled staff. Further, the art of negotiating a wage contract is very much

a Western concept and avoided by Chinese executives. Interestingly, Chinese head offices appear to be unaware of salary practices that are in place overseas, as these are often determined locally by the subsidiaries and are not necessarily declared.

What happens to those Chinese nationals who elect to work for MNCs outside China? The dilemma for Chinese MNCs is that they need to conform to international standards while still being faithful to their national practices. Many organizations do this by treating their global employees differently, based on their national backgrounds and managerial status. Hence, Chinese MNCs use a mixture of fixed and flexible performance-based payments for their non-Chinese workers, while retaining standard wages for their expatriate Chinese employees. This may not be an ideal situation in terms of equity, which may be the reason for the apparent ignorance of global diverse wage practices at the head office.

Nevertheless, Chinese MNCs are found to conform to international best practice; they are found to be internally equitable, externally competitive and actively enabling organizations to optimize their total wages packages.[64]

EMPOWERMENT

Empowerment *is the process by which managers delegate power to employees who therefore have an enhanced view of their work and role within the organization.*

Much of the motivational theory discussed in this chapter has addressed the question of what management can do to ensure employees positively contribute to the achievement of organizational goals. This chapter has emphasized the influence of extrinsic rewards such as pay in motivating staff to perform; however in the workplace in the twenty-first century workers may not just be searching for money but also for recognition, involvement and a heightened sense of self-worth. The employer is often looking for a 'can do' mentality among employees that lessens the need for managerial control.

Empowerment can meet these requirements. Empowerment is the process by which managers delegate power to employees to motivate greater responsibility in balancing the achievement of both personal and organizational goals. The key question for managers is how to facilitate employees' individual and joint contributions to the organization and their own development. Empowerment focuses on liberating, not controlling, human energy, and on balancing the achievement of personal and organizational goals. Managers commonly attempt these processes by delegating more power to employees and encouraging them to take on leadership roles in the organization.

The concept of empowerment is founded on the belief that everyone has an internal need for self-determination and a need to cope with environmental demands directly. This suggests that appropriate empowerment strategies can raise the perception of low self-efficacy. Self-efficacy refers to a person's belief that they can perform adequately in a situation. It refers to a state of mind or mentality,[65] which is why its relationship with empowerment strategies is important. Empowerment strategies are designed to improve self-efficacy by providing employees with greater autonomy and by increasing knowledge and control over factors directly related to job performance.

Self-efficacy *refers to a person's belief that they can perform adequately in a situation.*

Some work on empowerment has identified the following stages (see Figure 4.10) in the empowerment process:[66]

- *Stage 1:* Identify the conditions contributing to low self-efficacy. This could include organizational factors (such as poor communication systems and an impersonal bureaucratic climate); supervisory style factors (such as authoritarianism, an emphasis on failure or lack of communication of reasons for action or inaction); reward factors (such as rewards that are not performance based, or the low incentive value of rewards) and job design factors (such as unclear roles, unrealistic goals, low levels of participation and low job enrichment).

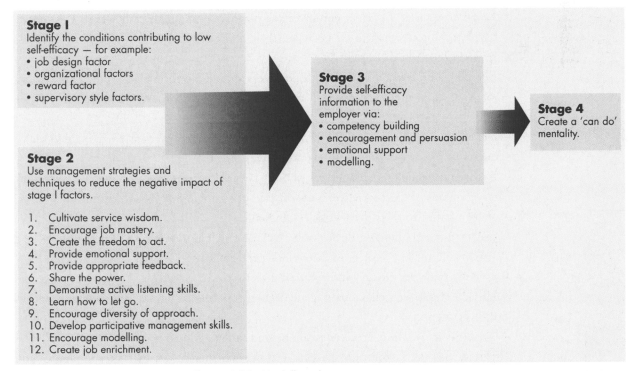

Stage 1
Identify the conditions contributing to low self-efficacy — for example:
- job design factor
- organizational factors
- reward factor
- supervisory style factors.

Stage 2
Use management strategies and techniques to reduce the negative impact of stage 1 factors.

1. Cultivate service wisdom.
2. Encourage job mastery.
3. Create the freedom to act.
4. Provide emotional support.
5. Provide appropriate feedback.
6. Share the power.
7. Demonstrate active listening skills.
8. Learn how to let go.
9. Encourage diversity of approach.
10. Develop participative management skills.
11. Encourage modelling.
12. Create job enrichment.

Stage 3
Provide self-efficacy information to the employer via:
- competency building
- encouragement and persuasion
- emotional support
- modelling.

Stage 4
Create a 'can do' mentality.

Figure 4.10: Modelling the empowerment process.

- *Stage 2:* Employ empowerment strategies and techniques that help to vest substantial responsibility in the hands of the individual who is closest to the problem requiring a solution.
  - *Cultivate a 'service wisdom'.* Trained and multiskilled employees should be able to handle nonroutine situations, to understand the bigger picture and how their role affects other employees and the achievement of organizational goals.
  - *Encourage job mastery.* Provide coaching, training and appropriate experiences to ensure successful job performance.
  - *Create a freedom to act.* Treat employees as if they own their jobs, devolving power so employees can adequately resolve problems. Managers should set appropriate boundaries to the freedom to facilitate successful employee job performance without creating inappropriate licence.
  - *Provide emotional support.* Employees must feel that if they act within the designated boundaries then managers will support their actions even if they make mistakes. Such support helps reduce stress and anxiety through clearer role definition, task support and concern for employee wellbeing.
  - *Provide appropriate feedback.* Employees need regular and detailed feedback so they know how they are performing against managerial expectations.
  - *Share the power.* Share as much power as possible, allowing for employee experience, education and task difficulty.
  - *Demonstrate active listening skills.* Learn to listen to feedback from experienced employees because the person performing the task often has the best ideas on process improvement.
  - *Learn how to let go.* Treat employees as partners and equals rather than as subordinates and know when to let go when their work is successfully helping the business move in the right direction.
  - *Encourage diversity of approach.* Employees should have the discretion to use various job styles and methods provided they meet agreed organizational standards for the work.
  - *Develop participative management skills.* Encourage employees to participate in major decisions that affect their daily working lives directly.
  - *Encourage modelling.* Employees should be able to observe and model their work on examples of 'best practice' performance in particular skills and competency-based areas relevant to their own work assignments.
  - *Create job enrichment.* Enrich jobs by making employees more accountable and responsible for key aspects of their work performance.
- *Stage 3:* Provide self-efficacy information directly to the employee. This stage focuses on modifying employee behaviour and increasing the self-efficacy belief. Four approaches have been identified:
  - *Competency building.* Structure training and organizational learning so that employees acquire new skills through successive, moderate increments in task complexity and responsibility.

- *Encouragement and persuasion.* Use verbal feedback and other persuasive techniques to encourage and reinforce successful job performance.
- *Emotional support.* Provide emotional support for employees and minimize emotional arousal states such as anxiety, stress and the fear associated with making mistakes. Mistakes should be seen as part of the learning process.
- *Modelling.* Allow employees to observe workers who perform successfully on the job.

Both stages 2 and 3 are designed to remove and eradicate the conditions identified in stage 1, and to develop the positive feelings of self-efficacy within the individual employee.

- *Stage 4.* Create a 'can do' mentality and an empowering experience for the employee. If stages 2 and 3 are successful then they will increase the employee's effort–performance understanding. As we saw earlier in the chapter, expectancy theories of motivation are essential for high and sustained levels of performance. Here, performance is linked directly to the positive mentality of the individual.

RESEARCH IN OB

In view of the potential importance of this topic for individual worker satisfaction, wellbeing and organizational performance, it will be no surprise to readers to learn that there is a rich body of research within OB attempting to demonstrate the relative validity of models of motivation discussed in this chapter. You may wish to look at our Web site **www.wileyeurope.com/college/french** and in particular at the article by Kuvaas examining the links between commitment, different forms of pay administration and motivation among knowledge workers in Norway. Typical of research in this field, Kuuvas's study points to the complexity of the topic, noting several links between reward and employee attitude.

CONCLUSION

Theories and models of motivation often contain quite different underlying assumptions on how similar and different humans are in terms of work motivation. They also appear at times to pose different questions – content theories focusing on *what* motivates whereas process theories look at *how* we come to be motivated or not by examining links between our expectations (including equitable treatment) and behaviour. An integrated model comprising elements of both traditions may help in terms of predicting behaviour and enhancing performance. The relationship between pay and motivation is complex and recent work has stressed empowerment as an important concept within this subject area.

SUMMARY

LEARNING OBJECTIVE 1
Motivating and empowering today's workforce

In the contemporary world a key challenge is to motivate and empower workers towards productive performance. With ageing populations, labour shortages and mobile workforces, organizations will need to understand how to motivate and empower employees in order to attract and retain them and to enhance performance.

LEARNING OBJECTIVE 2
Difference between content and process motivation theories

There are two main types of motivational theories – content and process. Content theories examine the needs that individuals have. Their efforts to satisfy those needs are what drive their behaviour. Process theories examine the thought processes that people have in relation to motivating their behaviour.

LEARNING OBJECTIVE 3
Content theories of motivation

The content theories of Maslow, Alderfer, McClelland and Herzberg emphasize needs or motives. They are often criticized for being culturally biased and caution should be exercised when applying these theories in non-Western cultures.

Maslow's hierarchy of needs theory arranges human needs into a five-step hierarchy: physiological, safety, social (the three lower-order needs), esteem and self-actualization (the two higher-order needs). Satisfaction of any need activates the need at the next higher level and people are presumed to move step by step up the hierarchy. Alderfer's ERG theory has modified this theory by collapsing the five needs into three: existence, relatedness and growth. Alderfer also allows for more than one need to be activated at a time and for a frustration–regression response. McClelland's acquired needs theory focuses on the needs for achievement (nAch), affiliation (nAff) and power (nPower). The theory argues that these needs can be developed through experience and training. Persons high in nAch prefer jobs with individual responsibility, performance feedback and moderately challenging goals. Successful executives typically have a high nPower that is greater than their nAff. Herzberg's two-factor theory treats job satisfaction and job dissatisfaction as two separate issues. Satisfiers, or motivator factors such as achievement, responsibility and recognition, are associated with job content. An improvement in job content is expected to increase satisfaction and motivation to perform well. In contrast, dissatisfiers, or hygiene factors such as working conditions, relations with co-workers and salary, are associated with the job context. Improving job context does not lead to more satisfaction but is expected to reduce dissatisfaction.

LEARNING OBJECTIVE 4
Process theories of motivation

Process theories emphasize the thought processes concerning how and why people choose one action over another in the workplace. Process theories focus on understanding the cognitive processes that act to influence behaviour. Although process theories can be very useful in explaining work motivation in crosscultural settings, the values that drive such theories may vary substantially across cultures and the outcomes may differ considerably.

Equity theory points out that people compare their rewards (and inputs) with those of others. The individual is then motivated to engage in behaviour to correct any perceived inequity. At the extreme, feelings of inequity may lead to reduced performance or job turnover. Expectancy theory argues that work motivation is determined by an individual's beliefs concerning effort–performance relationships (expectancy), work–outcome relationships (instrumentality) and the desirability of various work outcomes (valence). Managers, therefore, must build positive expectancies, demonstrate performance-reward instrumentalities and use rewards with high positive valences in their motivational strategies.

LEARNING OBJECTIVE 5
Integrating content and process motivation theories

The content theories can be compared, with some overlap identified. An integrated model of motivation builds from the individual performance equation developed in Chapter 2 and combines the content and process theories to show how well managed rewards can lead to high levels of both individual performance and satisfaction.

LEARNING OBJECTIVE 6
Self-concept, personal values and motivation

Theories that focus on self-concept and personal values seek to describe motivation that cannot be readily explained by content and process theories. Self-concept is an aspect of personality that describes the concept individuals have of themselves as physical, social and spiritual or moral beings. This self-conception guides their behaviour. Personal values can guide behaviour in the same way.

LEARNING OBJECTIVE 7
Managing pay as an extrinsic reward

Managing pay as an extrinsic reward is particularly important as pay has multiple meanings – some positive and some negative. As a major and highly visible extrinsic reward, pay plays a role in reinforcement and in the motivation theories. Its reward implications are especially important in terms of merit pay.

LEARNING OBJECTIVE 8
Empowerment and the empowerment process

Empowerment is the process by which managers delegate power to employees to motivate greater responsibility in balancing the achievement of personal and organizational goals. For employees who experience low self-efficacy, managers can implement strategies to improve the employees' feelings of self-worth and their capacity to improve their performance.

CHAPTER 4 STUDY GUIDE

You can also test your understanding and access further resources at **www.wileyeurope.com/college/french**.

REVIEW QUESTIONS

1. Define 'work motivation' and identify the role of motivation in the individual performance equation.
2. Compare the 'needs' in Alderfer's and McClelland's theories of motivation.
3. Explain the key differences between the expectancy and the equity theories of motivation.
4. Describe each of the four stages in the empowerment process.

APPLICATION QUESTIONS

1. What challenges might there be in motivating (a) young unskilled workers and (b) highly talented and experienced middle-aged workers?
2. Assuming that an organization successfully retains its older employees, what can it do to motivate them?
3. 'It is impossible to know what employees want but if you give them good salaries or wages they can use the money to find ways to fulfil their own needs. Employers do not need to worry about anything else.' Discuss this statement.
4. Explain the application of the integrated model of motivation to each of the following occupational groups at an early career stage: police officers and marketing research professionals.
5. Discuss ways in which (a) a major retail store could empower its retail assistants in their jobs and (b) a bank could empower its cashiers in their work.
6. Imagine that you are the manager of a small furniture design and manufacturing company. Several of the staff members have complained that the rewards and benefits provided by the company are inequitable. What practical steps can you take to evaluate current policies and practices, or to ensure that perceptions of inequity are rectified?
7. Turn back to the 'OB in action' 'Can Performance Incentives work for China?' What are some of the cultural issues to consider when using incentives for the purpose of achieving greater performance?
8. What are some of the ethical issues to consider when linking pay and performance?

RESEARCH QUESTIONS

1. 'The need theories of motivation are culturally based.' Discuss this statement, examining in detail one of the need theories of motivation. In answering this

question, you are encouraged to read an original work of the theorist associated with the theory you chose, such as David McClelland's *The Achieving Society,* or the works of Douglas McGregor and Abraham Maslow given in the 'suggested reading' for this chapter.

2. Many companies in the service sector – large hotels and resorts, for example – are implementing empowerment strategies to improve the quality of service provided to residents and guests. Search the Internet for an example of such a company, with particular emphasis on strategies used to empower front-line staff.

RUNNING PROJECT

Using the information you have available about your organization, answer the following questions:

1. How does management try to motivate employees?
2. Based on your answer to question 1, does this vary between permanent and casual or part-time employees? How and why?
3. To what extent does management use money, both wages/salary and performance-based pay, as a motivator?
4. Are the self-concepts or personal values of individuals likely to have an impact on their efforts at work?
5. How does the organization manage the equity process?
6. How does management empower the organization's employees?

INDIVIDUAL ACTIVITY

Are you motivated to work hard at your studies?

Complete the questions in this exercise, based on your work as a university or college student. This exercise should help to explain the level of effort you put into your studies at university or college, while also clarifying the way the expectancy theory of motivation is intended to work.

Never   Sometimes   Often   Always

1. Spending twice as many hours on an assignment results in a higher grade.
2. Studying consistently throughout the semester leads to better results.
3. Participating in class activities enhances my understanding of the subject or improves my grades.
4. Being organized helps me handle the demands of being a student.

Connection 2: Instrumentality (probability that your performance will result in various rewards and outcomes)

How likely are you to receive the following rewards if you work hard (put in the hours, study consistently, participate, try to be organized)?

	Never	Not very likely	Fairly likely	Very likely

1. A better academic record/transcript
2. More/better employment options
3. Peer acceptance
4. Sense of accomplishment
5. Building my knowledge/skills
6. Feeling good about myself
7. Avoidance of pressure and stress
8. A 'pat on the back' from my parents/family
9. Reward — holiday, dinner out etc.
10. Other (specify)

Connection 3: Valence (value of the reward outcome to you)

How important are each of the following rewards to you?

	Not important	Moderately important	Fairly important	Very important

1. A better academic record/transcript
2. More/better employment options
3. Peer acceptance
4. Sense of accomplishment
5. Building my knowledge/skills
6. Feeling good about myself
7. Avoidance of pressure and stress
8. A 'pat on the back' from my parents/family
9. Reward — holiday, dinner out etc.
10. Other (specify)

After you have completed the questions, review your answers in the light of what expectancy theory tells us about motivation:

- What do your answers in the 'expectancy' section tell you about your level of confidence in your abilities, or the things that have discouraged/encouraged you in the past?
- Refer to your responses in the 'instrumentality' section. What do they tell you about the rewards you experience from your studies? Are they predominantly extrinsic, intrinsic or a mix of both?

- Compare the rewards you experience (or expect to experience) from your studies with the rewards you value from the 'valence' section. How well do they match one another? Are there any rewards that you value highly but do not expect to receive?
- Assess the 'multiplier effect' to explain the level of effort you put into your studies. Compare your results with those of others in the class. If your motivation to study is low, what can you do to improve it?

GROUP ACTIVITY

What do you want from a job – motivators or hygienes? [67]

Objectives

1. To help you better understand how job factors affect motivation.
2. To help you realize that people are motivated by different factors.
3. To better understand Herzberg's motivation theory and determine whether you agree with it.

Total time: 10–30 minutes.

Preparation

Complete the following 'Motivators or hygienes' assessment before coming to class. Most workers want job satisfaction. The following 12 job factors may contribute to job satisfaction. Rate each according to how important it is to you. Place a number on a scale of 1 to 5 next to each factor.

Very important	Somewhat important		Not important	
5	4	3	2	1

_____ 1. An interesting job

_____ 2. A good boss

_____ 3. Recognition and appreciation for the work I do

_____ 4. The opportunity for advancement

_____ 5. A satisfying personal life

_____ 6. A prestigious or status job

_____ 7. Job responsibility

_____ 8. Good working conditions (nice office)

_____ 9. Sensible company rules, regulations, procedures and policies

_____ 10. The opportunity to grow through learning new things

_____ 11. A job I can do well and at which I can succeed

_____ 12. Job security

To determine if hygienes or motivators are important to you, place your scores below.

Hygiene factors		Motivational factors	
	Score		Score
2.	_____	1.	_____
5.	_____	3.	_____
6.	_____	4.	_____
8.	_____	7.	_____
9.	_____	10.	_____
12.	_____	11.	_____
Total points	_____	Total points	_____

Add each column vertically. Did you select hygienes or motivators as being more important to you?

Procedure for group discussion

1. Break into groups of five or six members and discuss the job factors selected as important by group members. Come to a consensus on the three factors that are most important to the group. If the group has other factors not listed in the activity, you may add them.

2. Select a representative from your group to write the group's three most important job factors on the board.

3. The lecturer can then identify the most important job factors for the entire class.

4. Are the class selections motivators or hygiene factors? As a class, discuss whether you agree with Herzberg's two-factor theory.

LONDON ELECTRICITY GROUP GIVES A HELPING HAND TO EMPLOYEE MOTIVATION

Case Study

London Electricity (LE) Group's staff-volunteering programme, Helping Hands, made an impact right from its introduction – not only by contributing to communities, but also by building employee motivation, skills and a common identity across the business. The group is committed to sustainability and corporate responsibility (CR), understanding that this can both benefit the communities in which the company operates and drive fundamental business performance. Corporate community investment is part of this wider CR approach and includes encouraging employee volunteering with a focus on education and employability.

Active in the community

London Electricity Group has always been active in the community. The catalyst for board-level support and strategic direction, however, was a Business in the Community Seeing is Believing visit in Southwark, London, when the chief executive and other top managers were brought face-to-face with pressing social issues, and recognized the potential role of education and employability for neighbourhood renewal.

In May 2001, LE Group launched Helping Hands, its first formal group-wide employee-volunteering scheme, which included the offer to all employees of two days' paid work time for volunteering. By the end of the first year, LE Group had achieved over 24 % staff involvement across the group, rising to an impressive 50 % within the Sunderland customer-service centre, at Doxford, all in line with the aim that Helping Hands becomes an important part of the corporate culture.

Business benefits of volunteering

The group executive understands the business benefits of volunteering and the company is committed to being a respected employer because the acquisition and retention of a talented and satisfied workforce is fundamental to business success. LE Group believes that Helping Hands directly contributes towards this. Feedback so far indicates that the programme is having a positive effect on motivation within the company and is also helping to build key skills. The scheme is seen as a dynamic and evolving initiative.

LE Group has four key stated corporate values, one of which is to excel in corporate responsibility and to work for sustainable development. Helping Hands is contributing to this. The objectives for the programme are to:

* complement existing training and management development
* support and enhance the company's existing community investment

Source: Viewpoint (2003), *Human Resource Management International Digest,* **11** (4), 35–37. Reproduced by permission of Emerald Insight.

- improve its contribution to specific social and economic issues, especially education, homelessness and regeneration; and
- enhance the company's reputation among its stakeholders.

The programme has been driven both through the clear executive leadership and the natural take-up by employees.

Dedicated team

Helping Hands, along with the wider corporate community investment, is managed by a small dedicated team, and delivered throughout the group by a network of coordinators within business units. The volunteering policy and information on getting involved are set out in publications and on an intranet, which includes a database of volunteering opportunities. Helping Hands works through partnerships to meet its aims and objectives. Schools are close to offices and are all in education action zones, releasing matched public-sector funding from regeneration budgets, through primary school and secondary school volunteering programmes.

Skill development is a fundamental objective. Senior managers, managers and graduates are all asked to contribute towards a community project through in-house training programmes. These range from team challenges to mentoring and enterprise programmes with schools. Community involvement is included in employee performance appraisals and career-development plans.

A central community-affairs budget of almost £500 000 is supplemented by charitable gifts and community investment within business units. The actual level of total community investment across the group in 2001 reached 1.6 % of pretax profits, and was included in the company's first corporate-responsibility report in 2002. The report involved a new measurement regime including the London benchmarking group model and the business impact review group.

Positive impact on society

Helping Hands is designed to encourage and raise the capacity of employees to make a positive impact on society, specifically through education and employability. In its first eight months, 4 665 hours of paid work time was completed. Of this, almost 60 % was directed towards volunteering in more than 30 primary and secondary schools, all in education action zones. This leveraged more than £42 500 from various public regeneration budgets. More than 140 children benefited from literacy and numeracy programmes, and 65 children were mentored. The value of this work in schools has been recognized in an Ofsted school-inspection report. Employees have also taken on team challenges, such as developing school play areas and decorating classrooms. The company's Sunderland customer-service centre has pioneered a graduate programme that matches university graduates within LE Group with high potential year 11 pupils, to raise their aspirations and motivation. The company also arranges activity days at primary and secondary schools, which promote the workplace relevance of basic numeracy and literacy skills. Community activities also tackle adult employability and lifelong learning. Interview-skill days are held for tenants from the Aylesbury estate in Southwark – principally for mothers keen to get back to work – with some participants taken on for short-term work placements. The company also looks for opportunities to link the education and employability activity, Helping Hands volunteering and sponsorship.

Increased loyalty to the company

LE Group recognizes the value of an active community programme to drive business performance by building a vibrant workforce and customer base. Some 90% of volunteers confirm that doing so makes them feel more positive about working for the company, on the basis of the skills gained, the sense of responsibility and increased motivation. Senior managers have had the opportunity to apply problem-solving and strategy skills in entirely new contexts.

Helping Hands was put together in conjunction with the company's employer group – a team of senior executives who look at how to acquire, retain and develop a talented workforce. The programme also helps to build the company's group identity across business units, which is a major priority as the company grows across geographical locations and cultures. The scheme also encourages communication and team building within departments. Finally, Helping Hands and the broader community programme is a major factor driving positive media coverage for the company. The LE Group chief executive, Vincent de Rivaz, commented: 'Along with the rest of the executive, I am committed to finding ways in which all parts of the group can play a positive role in the community. It is no longer enough just to give cash – to give our skills and time is one of the most important ways we are able to have an impact and to make our contribution to the sustainable improvement of our community.'

Questions

1. How do you think the Helping Hands programme contributes to employee motivation?
2. In what ways may these types of volunteering schemes satisfy higher-order needs as described by Maslow?
3. In what ways has the scheme been of benefit to the employer and the employees who have taken part and how might you sell these to other employers?
4. Is there a relationship between such volunteering schemes and work performance and, if so, what is it?

SUGGESTED READING

All OB books devote considerable time and space to motivation as a topic and many provide remarkably similar coverage. One recent textbook takes an innovative approach by locating motivation within the domain of leaders and leadership, with use of interesting examples and images. This is:

Clegg, S., Kornberger, M. & Pitsis, T. (2005), *Managing and Organizations*, Sage: London.

END NOTES

1. *Management Today* Brainfood: Ten Ways To... Motivate your staff, 16 January 2006, p14

2. *Personnel Today*, January 2007 and *Personnel Today*, 14 June 2007, p. 14

3. Campbell, J.P., Dunnette, M.D., Lawler, E.E. III & Weick, K.E. Jr, (1970), *Managerial Behaviour Performance and Effectiveness*, McGraw-Hill: New York, Chapter 15.

4. Maslow, A.H. (1943), A theory of human motivation. *Psychological Review*, 50 (4), 370–396.

5. Porter, L.W. (1963), Job attitudes in management: II. Perceived importance of needs as a function of job level. *Journal of Applied Psychology*, 47 (April), 141–148.

6. Manolopoulos, D. (2006), What motivates R&D professionals? Evidence from decentralized laboratories in Greece. *International Journal of HRM*, 11, 4 April, 616–647.

7. Hall, D.T. & Nougaim, K.E. (1968), An examination of Maslow's need hierarchy in an organizational setting. *Organizational Behaviour and Human Performance*, 3, 12–35.

8. Porter, L.W. (1963), Job attitudes in management: IV. Perceived deficiencies in need fulfillment as a function of size of company. *Journal of Applied Psychology*, 47 (December), 386–397.

9. Ivancevich, J.M. (1969), Perceived need satisfactions of domestic versus overseas managers. *Journal of Applied Psychology*, 54 (August), 274–278.

10. Wahba, M.A. & Bridwell, L.G. (1974), Maslow reconsidered: a review of research on the need hierarchy theory. Academy of Management Proceedings, 514–520. Lawler, E.E. III & Shuttle, J.L. (1973), A causal correlation test of the need hierarchy concept. *Organizational Behaviour and Human Performance*, 7, 265–287.

11. See Adler, N.J. (1991), *International Dimensions of Organizational Behaviour*, 2nd edn. PWS-Kent: Boston, MA, p. 153. Hodgetts, R.M. & Luthans, F. (1991), *International Management*. McGraw-Hill: New York.

12. Adler, op. cit., Ch. 11.

13. Huang, T., Liang, J. & Beamish, P.W. (2006), Jinjian Garment Factory: motivating go-slow workers, in *Cases in Organizational Behaviour* (ed. Gerard H. Siejts). Sage: Thousand Oaks, CA, pp. 30–35.

14. See Alderfer, C.P. (1969), An empirical test of a new theory of human needs. *Organizational Behaviour and Human Performance*, 4, 142–175. Alderfer, C.P. (1972), *Existence, Relatedness, and Growth*. The Free Press: New York. Schneider, B. & Alderfer, C.P. (1973), Three studies of need satisfaction in organizations. *Administrative Science Quarterly*, 18, 489–505.

15. Tracy, L. (1984), A dynamic living systems model of work motivation. *Systems Research*, 1, 191–203; Rauschenberger, J., Schmidt, N. & Hunter, J.E. (1980), A test of the need hierarchy concept by a Markov model of change in need strength. *Administrative Science Quarterly*, 25, 654–670.

16. Alderfer, C.P. & Guzzo, R.A. (1979), Life experiences and adults enduring strength of desires in organizations. *Administrative Science Quarterly*, 24, 347–361.

17. Sources pertinent to this discussion are McClelland, D.C. (1961), *The Achieving Society*. Van Nostrand: New York. McClelland, D.C. (1962), Business, drive and national achievement. *Harvard Business Review*, 40 (July/August), 99–112. McClelland, D.C. (1966), That urge to achieve. *Think*, (November/December), 19–32. Litwin, G.H. and Stringer, R.A. (1966), *Motivation and Organizational Climate*. Division of Research, Harvard Business School: Boston, MA, pp. 18–25.

18. Harris, G. (1971), To know why men do what they do: a conversation with David C. McClelland. *Psychology Today*, 4 (January), 35–39.

19. Erikson, E.H. (1963), *Childhood and Society*, 2nd edn. Vintage: New York.

20. Miron, P. & McClelland, D.C. (1979), The impact of achievement motivation training in small businesses. *California Management Review*, (Summer), 13–28.

21. McClelland, D.C. & Burnham, D.H. (1976), Power is the great motivator. *Harvard Business Review*, **54** (March/April), 100–110. McClelland, D.C. & Boyatzis, R.E. (1982), Leadership motive pattern and long-term success in management. *Journal of Applied Psychology*, **67**, 737–743.

22. Kelly, C.M. (1987), The interrelationship of ethics and power in today's organizations. *Organizational Dynamics*, **5** (Summer). Farrell, C. (1986), Gutfreund gives Salmon's young lions more power. *Business Week*, **32** (20 October). Solomon, J. (1987), Heirs apparent to chief executives often trip over prospect of power. *Wall Street Journal*, **29** (24 March 1987).

23. Arnolds, C.A. & Boshoff, C. (2003), Compensation, esteem, valence and job performance: an empirical assessment of Alderfer's ERG theory. *International Journal of Human Resource Management*, **13** (4 June), 687–719.

24. The complete two-factor theory is well explained by Herzberg and his associates in Herzberg, F., Mausner, B. & Synderman, B.B. (1967), *The Motivation to Work*, 2nd edn. John Wiley & Sons: New York. See also Herzberg, F. (1968), One more time: how do you motivate employees? *Harvard Business Review*, **46** (January/February), 53–62.

25. See House, R.J. & Wigdor, L.A. (1967), Herzberg's dual-factor theory of job satisfaction and motivation: a review of the evidence and a criticism. *Personnel Psychology*, **20** (Winter), 369–389. Kerr, S., Harlan, A. & Stogdill, R. (1974), Preference for motivator and hygiene factors in a hypothetical interview situation. *Personnel Psychology*, **27** (Winter), 109–24.

26. Vroom, V.H. (1963), *Work and Motivation*. John Wiley & Sons, Ltd: Chichester.

27. See King, N. (1970), A clarification and evaluation of the two-factor theory of job satisfaction. *Psychological Bulletin*, (July), 18–31. Dunnette, M., Campbell, J. & Hakel, M. (1967), Factors contributing to job satisfaction and job dissatisfaction in six occupational groups. *Organizational Behaviour and Human Performance*, (May), 143–174. House & Wigdor, op. cit.

28. Adler, op. cit., Ch. 6. Adler, N.J. & Graham, J.T. (1989), Cross cultural interaction: the international comparison fallacy. *Journal of International Business Studies*, (Fall), 515–537. Herzberg, F. (1987), Workers' needs: the same around the world. *Industry Week*, (27 September), 29–32.

29. See Employee benefits September 2006: Centaur www.employeebenefits.co.uk

30. See, for example, Adams, J.S. (1963), Toward an understanding of inequality. *Journal of Abnormal and Social Psychology*, **67**, 422–436. Adams, J.S. (1965), Inequity in social exchange, in *Advances in Experimental Social Psychology*, vol. 2 (ed. L Berkowitz). Academic Press: New York, pp. 267–300.

31. See Toronto Sun Publishing Corporation, *Wall Street Journal*, 9 March 1990, pp. B1–B2.

32. See for example Ferandez v. the Parliamentary Commission, *IRLR* 22 2004 and Nelson v. Carrilon Services, *IRLR* 428 2003.

33. See the Equality and Human Rights commission Web site, www.equalityhumanrights,com/pages/eocdrcre.aspx

34. Folger, R. & Konovsky, M.A. (1989), Effects of procedural and distributive justice on reactions to pay raise decisions. *Academy of Management Journal*, **32**, 135–148.

35. Adler op. cit.

36. Dowling, P., Schuler, R. & Welch, D. (1994), *International Dimensions of Human Resource Management*. Wadsworth: Melbourne.

37. Vroom, V.H. (1964), *Work and Motivation*. John Wiley & Sons: New York.

38. For an excellent review see Mowday, R.T. (1987), Equity theory predictions of behaviour in organizations, in *Motivation and Work Behaviour*, 4th edn (eds Richard M. Steers & Lyman W. Porter). McGraw-Hill: New York, pp. 89–110.

39. Salancik, G.R. & Pfeffer, J. (1978), A social information processing approach to job attitudes and task design. *Administrative Science Quarterly*, **23** (June), 224–253.

40. See Mitchell, T.R. (1974), Expectancy models of job satisfaction, occupational preference and effort: a theoretical, methodological, and empirical

appraisal. *Psychological Bulletin*, **81**, 1053–1077. Wahba, M.A. & House, R.J. (1974), Expectancy theory in work and motivation: some logical and methodological issues. *Human Relations*, **27** (January), 121–147. Connolly, T. (1976), Some conceptual and methodological issues in expectancy models of work performance motivation. *Academy of Management Review*, **1** (October), pp. 37–47. Mitchell, T. (1980), *Expectancy-value Models in Organizational Psychology, in Expectancy, Incentive and Action* (ed. N. Feather). Erlbaum: New York.

41. Mitchell, T.R. (1982), Motivation – new directions for theory, research and practice. *Academy of Management Review*, **7** (January), 80–81.

42. Porter, L.W. & Lawler, E.E. III (1968), *Managerial Attitudes and Performance*, Richard D. Irwin: Homewood, IL.

43. This integrated model is not only based on the Porter and Lawler model but is consistent with the kind of comprehensive approach suggested by Evans in a recent review. See Evans, M.G. (1986), Organizational behaviour: the central role of motivation, in Hunt, J.G. & Blair, J.D. (eds), (1986) Yearly review of management. Journal of Management, **12**, 203–222.

44. For further explanation of alternatives to process and content theories of motivation, see Leonard, N., Beauvais, L. & Scholl, R. (1999), Work motivation: the incorporation of self-concept-based processes. *Human Relations*, **52** (8), 969–998. McKenna, R. (2000), Identity, not motivation: the key to employee-organisation relations, in *Management and Organizational Behaviour* (eds R. Wiesner & B. Millett). John Wiley & Sons: Brisbane, pp. 35–45.

45. Employee benefits, op.cit.

46. Samson, K. (2004/5) Research off the map. *HR Monthly*, (December/January), 34–35.

47. Macken, D. (2004), My job-juggling career. *The Weekend Australian Financial Review*, (6–7 March), p. 25.

48. YOYOY (2006), *IRS Employment Review*, issue 845, 4.

49. Lui, J. (2004). Asia Pacific 25: not by price alone. *Managing Information Strategies*, (special annual issue), 73–86.

50. Spinelli, M.A. & Gray, G.R. (2003), How important is compensation for job satisfaction of retail trainers? Some evidence. *Employee Benefit Plan Reviews*, **58** (5), 29.

51. Lawler, E.E. III (1981), *Pay and Organizational Development*, Addison-Wesley: Reading, MA.

52. Lawler, E.E. III (1971), *Pay and Organizational Effectiveness*. McGraw-Hill: New York. Lawler (1981), op. cit. Lawler, E.E. III (1987), The design of effective systems, in *Handbook of Organizational Behaviour* (ed. Jay W. Lorsch), Prentice Hall: Englewood Cliffs, NJ.

53. Rynes, S., Gerhart, B. & Minette, K. (2004), The importance of pay in employee motivation: discrepancies between what people say and what they do. *Human Resource Management*, **43** (4), 381–394.

54. Wiley, C. (1997), What motivates employees according to 40 years of motivation surveys. *International Journal of Manpower*, **18** (3), 263–280.

55. Weaver, T. (2003), Theory M: motivating with money. *Conrell HRA Quarterly*, **29** (3), 40–45.

56. YOYOY (2006), op. cit.

57. See DTI (2003) Balancing Work and Family Life: Enhancing Choice and Support for Parents. HMSO: London. More people want flexible hours than cash, company car or gym. DTI (2002), HMSO: London.

58. Furnham, A., Kirkaldy, B.D. & Lynn, R. (1994) National attitudes to competitiveness, money and work amongst young people: first, second and third world differences. *Human Relations*, **47** (1), 119–132.

59. Robbins, S.P. (1996), *Organizational Behaviour*. Prentice Hall: Englewood Cliffs, NJ.

60. Furnham, A. & Booth, T. (2006), Just for the money: what really motivates us at work. Cyan Books: London.

61. Pearce, J.L. (1987), Why merit pay doesn't work: implications from organizational theory, in *New Perspectives on Compensation* (eds David B. Balkin & Luis R. Gomez-Mejia). Prentice Hall: Englewood Cliffs, NJ, pp. 214–224. Lawler, E.E. III (1989), Pay for performance:

making it work. *Compensation and Benefits Review*, **21** (1), 55–60.

62. See Boyle, D.C. (1992), Employee motivation that works. *HR Magazine*, **37** (10), 83–9.

63. Weinberg, N. (2002), Hidden treasure, *Forbes*, 28 October, p. 58.

64. Shen, J. (2004), Compensation in Chinese multinationals. *Compensation and Benefits Review*, **36** (1), 5–26.

65. Gist, M.E. (1987), Self-efficacy: implications in organizational behaviour and human resource management. *Academy of Management Review*, **12**, 472–485. Bandura, A. (1987), Self-efficacy mechanism in human agency. *American Psychologist*, **37**, 122–147.

66. Conger, J.A. & Kanungo, R.N. (1988), The empowerment process: integrating theory and practice. *Academy of Management Review*, **13** (3), 471–482.

67. Lussier, R.N. (1993), Human Relations in Organizations: a skill building approach (2nd edn). Homewood, IL, Richard D. Irwin. © The McGraw-Hill Companies, Inc. Reproduced by permission.

CHAPTER

5

Job design, goal setting and flexible work arrangements

LEARNING OBJECTIVES

After studying this chapter you should be able to:

- explain the concept of intrinsic motivation
- compare and contrast the alternative job design strategies and link them to intrinsic work rewards
- discuss the job characteristics model employing job diagnosis techniques as a newer approach to job enrichment
- explain how goal-setting theory is linked to job design
- discuss how flexible work arrangements contribute to workforce flexibility.

A QUESTION OF BALANCE

The nature of work, the design of jobs and arrangements concerning when and where we work are undergoing change. Flexible work arrangements can sometimes be difficult to implement but, as is the case for the Foreign and Commonwealth Office (FCO) of the UK government, the gains for both the employer and employee can be substantial.

Life for employees at the FCO is rarely dull but at times days can be long and arduous. The government department deals with people worldwide, so it runs almost a 24-hour operation, which can mean that many employees work long hours with little flexibility. As a result the FCO has developed a reputation for working hours that do not fit in with family life. In April 2003 the FOC introduced a formal flexible-working scheme for all employees. This was partly in response to government legislation but also, as Maria Forsyth, the FCO diversity policy officer, commented, 'we wanted to extend the option of requesting flexible working to all staff regardless of criteria defined by the legislation.'

Flexible work options on offer are part-time working, job share, term-time only working, compressed hours and home working. Job sharing is the most popular option. For example, Mara Yamaauchi, a manager in the HR directorate, chose to job share so that she could reduce her hours and spend more time training for her athletics career. Compressed hours is also a very popular option, with whole teams working compressed hours but varying their days off. Forsyth comments that this has boosted morale as well as motivation. Employees still work long days but now they are rewarded with time off work. In addition to these formal schemes a number of employees have taken advantage of informal flexible working that is widely operated in the FCO. This tends to involve staggering start and finish times and ad hoc days working at home but also employees now have the option to take time off in lieu rather than paid overtime if they have worked excessive hours.

Home and remote working are now much more readily available as part of the scheme after the IT department was able to create a secure laptop, which is modified to ensure that no one other than the author has access to the laptop's content. This has meant that the FCO has been able to retain valuable employees who have moved abroad to accompany their FCO partners in their jobs as well as attracting employees who do not wish to work in London. Coupled with the scheme is a range of other benefits to attract and retain workers, including additional paid leave for 'domestic emergencies' and a career break scheme that can extend up to 10 years.

So what are the benefits? Flexible working practices are seen to lead to more motivated, happier and more productive workers who take less sick leave, have reduced absenteeism and experience less stress.

Questions

1. How has the introduction of flexible working practices assisted in the recruitment and retention of staff at the FCO?
2. How do these more flexible working arrangements help employees deal with their work–life balance?
3. In what ways do you think jobs might have been redesigned in order to accommodate a remote worker or job sharer?

Source: Adapted from Charlotte Wolff (2005), Foreign Office give stamp of approval to work–life balance, *IRS Employment Review,* 24 June, issue 826 and also FCO Web site.

INTRODUCTION

Our society and the nature of workplaces are continuously changing, generating forces that impact upon how workers experience their work and their workplaces. Within the workplace, there is a deeper appreciation of how the job itself can affect an individual's motivation and job satisfaction. Organizations have moved well beyond simply trying to improve worker performance by offering limited extrinsic rewards such as higher wages or promotion. There is more focus now on responding to the intrinsic rewards that employees get from doing their jobs and on the goals that can help to guide and motivate them in their work. Designing the work to maximize employee outcomes is fundamental to this process.

In Chapter 4 we discussed motivation in relation to intrinsic and extrinsic rewards. We also emphasized various aspects of reinforcement and different kinds of pay plans as extrinsic rewards. In this chapter we give special emphasis to intrinsic rewards and how to use job design, goal setting and flexible work arrangements to improve intrinsic job satisfactions. The theoretical aspects of job design are explained and job design theories or approaches (such as job characteristics, socio-technical, socio-information and multiskilling) are examined to demonstrate how the design of jobs can have an impact on workers. The alignment and achievement of organizational goals through a process of goal setting is also considered as these affect employees' jobs and their motivation, satisfaction and performance within them. Finally, a discussion of flexible work arrangements explores how the very arrangements in which workers are employed are being reconsidered and modified. These new arrangements take into account the demands that employees make; they enhance the quality of their working lives and also enhance their capacity to work productively for their organizations.

INTRINSIC MOTIVATION

Intrinsic work rewards were defined in Chapter 4 as those rewards that an individual receives directly as a result of task performance. One example is the feeling of achievement that comes from completing a challenging project. Such feelings are individually determined and integral to the work. The individual is not dependent on an outsider, such as a manager, to provide these rewards or feelings.

This concept is in direct contrast to extrinsic rewards, such as pay and conditions, which are externally controlled. The unique nature of intrinsic rewards can be seen when a social worker says: 'My working conditions are bad and my co-workers are boring but I get a sense of satisfaction out of helping my clients.'[1]

Intrinsic work rewards,[2] are a very important part of motivating and satisfying employees in the workplace. Herzberg's two-factor theory of motivation in Chapter 4 particularly draws attention to the importance of intrinsic job content factors in improving satisfaction in the job (while extrinsic job context factors can lead to dissatisfaction). His ideas will be discussed further in this chapter when job enrichment is considered. Intrinsic work rewards play a key part in effective job design. The example above illustrates that people can be motivated simply because they enjoy the experience of accomplishing tasks. This is described as intrinsic motivation, which is a desire to work hard solely for the pleasant experience of task accomplishment.

Intrinsic motivation *is a desire to work hard solely for the pleasant experience of task accomplishment.*

When we discussed extrinsic rewards in Chapter 4, we saw the manager as responsible for allocating extrinsic rewards such as pay, promotion and verbal praise to employees and for controlling general working conditions. To serve in this capacity, a manager must be good at evaluating performance, knowing what rewards employees value and giving these rewards to employees contingent upon work performance.

Managing intrinsic work rewards presents an additional challenge for the manager. Still acting as an agent of the organization, the manager must design jobs for individual employees so that intrinsic rewards become available to them as a direct result of feedback gained from working on assigned tasks. That is not to say that every manager should design every job to provide every employee with the maximum opportunity to experience intrinsic work rewards. This chapter will help you to understand:

- when people may desire intrinsic work rewards
- how to design jobs for people who desire greater intrinsic work rewards
- how to motivate those people who do not desire intrinsic work rewards.

JOB DESIGN

A job is one or more tasks that an individual performs in direct support of an organization's production purpose. Well designed jobs can facilitate both the quality of task performance and job satisfaction, partly through intrinsic motivation. Additional aspects of human resource performance, such as absenteeism, commitment and turnover, may also be influenced.

Job design involves the planning and specification of job tasks and the work setting designated for their accomplishment. This definition includes both the specification of task attributes and the creation of a work setting for these attributes. It includes all the structural and social elements of the job and their impact on employee behaviour and performance. The objective of job design is to help make jobs meaningful, interesting and challenging. For the organization it is essential that jobs are properly designed in order to reduce stress, improve performance and enhance motivation and job satisfaction so that they can compete effectively in the global market.[3] The manager's responsibility is to design jobs that will motivate the individual employee. Figuratively speaking, this is properly done when:

Individual needs + task attributes + work setting → performance and satisfaction.

Between 1900 and 1950 there were many developments in management theories that ranged from scientific studies of job efficiency to studies that were more concerned with the human response to the job. Four major approaches to job design were identified. Each approach was prescriptive in nature and assumed that all workers would respond to the strategies in the same manner. None of these approaches made allowance for variation in the motivational potential of the individual worker. The approaches were:

- job simplification
- job enlargement
- job rotation
- job enrichment

Job design is the planning and specification of job tasks and the work setting in which they are to be accomplished.

Job simplification

Job simplification involves standardizing work procedures and employing people in clearly defined and specialized tasks. The machine-paced car assembly line is a classic example of this job design strategy.

This approach, deriving from the scientific managers such as Frederick Taylor, involves simplified jobs that are highly specialized and usually require an individual to perform a narrow set of tasks repetitively. The potential advantages include increased operating efficiency (which was the original intent of the job simplification approach), low-skill and low-cost labour, minimal training requirements and controlled production quantity. Some possible disadvantages of this 'deskilling' include loss of efficiency due to low-quality work, high rates of absenteeism and turnover, and the need to pay high wages to get people to do unattractive jobs. For most people, simplified job designs tend to be low in intrinsic motivation. The jobs lack challenge and lead to boredom. In Chapter 1 we saw how Braverman went further in his analysis of deskilling, seeing it as a deliberate strategy by owners and managers of organizations to strengthen their own power position relative to that of workers. In Chapter 10 we examine the strategic contingencies model of power, which suggests that power accrues to those who are in control of key attributes or tasks central to the organization's functioning and survival. Deskilled workers within this framework have sharply reduced potential power.

In today's high-technology age, a natural extension of job simplification is complete automation – allowing a machine to do the work previously accomplished through human

Job simplification involves standardizing work procedures and employing people in clearly defined and specialized tasks.

effort. This approach increasingly involves the use of robots and sophisticated computer applications based on expert systems and artificial intelligence. The Walgreens pharmacy chain in the US increased the rate of packing shipments from its distribution centre to its stores by more than 800 % with its use of robots.[4] More recently, computer applications such as menus on call centre help lines and the directed prompts and menus of bank cash machines have replaced tasks previously done by human effort.

Job enlargement

Job enlargement
involves increasing task variety by combining into one job tasks of similar skill levels that were previously assigned to separate workers.

Job enlargement emerged in the 1950s when many managers sought a job design strategy to reduce the boredom associated with the job simplification approach. The aim is to increase the breadth of a job by adding to the variety of tasks performed by a worker. Task variety is assumed to offset some of the disadvantages of job simplification, thereby increasing job performance and satisfaction for the individual. Job enlargement increases task variety by combining into one job two or more tasks previously assigned to separate workers. The only change in the original job design is that a worker now does a greater variety of tasks.

Often job enlargement has not lived up to its promise. For example, if a graphic designer who has been designing business brochures and posters is also given the task of preparing book-cover layouts, the job has been enlarged even if the same basic technique of using computer design software is used. The designer's supervisor would still secure the business, conduct meetings with the client and oversee the tasks, so there is no more responsibility. Job enlargement may add variety and alleviate boredom with mundane tasks but there may be limits to how much it might stimulate and satisfy the designer.

Job rotation

Job rotation
involves increasing task variety by periodically shifting workers among jobs involving different tasks at similar levels of skill.

Like job enlargement, job rotation increases task variety but generally it does so by periodically shifting workers among jobs involving different tasks at similar skill levels. Job rotation can be arranged around almost any time period, such as hourly, daily or weekly schedules. For example, a nurse may be rotated on a monthly basis, looking after geriatric patients one month, surgical patients the next and rehabilitation patients each third month. However, as with job enlargement, the results have sometimes been disappointing. If a rotation cycle takes employees through a series of the same old jobs, the employees simply experience many boring jobs instead of just one. The nurse may still be doing the same repetitive tasks of checking pulses and taking blood pressure and temperatures in each ward. In different wards there may be different tasks such as checking and changing wound dressings or feeding patients in geriatrics, but overall the tasks may still seem routine.

Job rotation may decrease efficiency because people spend more time changing but it can add to workforce flexibility. Staff can be moved from one job to another and this is currently often the primary purpose of job rotation. Employers have a more adaptable workforce to accomplish work tasks when employees are on holiday or sick leave; or when they move from the organization.

Perhaps the greatest weakness in the application of job rotation in the 1950s was that workers tended to be rotated horizontally (expanding the scope of the job) – that is, across tasks that demanded similar skill profiles. In other words, just as with enlargement, there was a **horizontal loading** of tasks, which means that the breadth of the job is increased by the addition of a variety of tasks. Research (for example in Denmark) continues to show that, although job-rotation schemes are widely used, they do little to enhance employee motivation and job satisfaction because of this horizontal loading.[5] Since the mid-1970s, job rotation has become an important part of work experience and corporate acculturation. New employees are often rotated around the company and across different divisions to gain a better understanding of the corporate structure and corporate work and communication networks. Many graduate training programmes in the UK include what is known as 'Cook's Tour' of planned job rotation as part of their training programme allowing graduates to experience all aspects of the business including a period spent working on the shop floor before being given their first substantive appointment. Job rotation can often involve **vertical loading**, which enables increasing job depth by adding responsibilities, like planning and controlling, which were previously held by supervisors. Such experience often contributes to employee development and helps overcome many limitations of the earlier approaches to job rotation. China, for example, has used rotation schemes to send employees from central urban locations into rural areas to keep in touch with the needs of rural communities.[6] Global companies in China such as Kone, Standard Chartered and Schering all offer job rotation as a feature of employment on their careers pages.[7] Vertical loading is a key aspect of job enrichment.

> **Horizontal loading** *involves increasing the breadth of a job by adding to the variety of tasks that the worker performs.*

> **Vertical loading** *involves increasing job depth by adding responsibilities, like planning and controlling, previously held by supervisors.*

Job enrichment

Frederick Herzberg, whose two-factor theory is discussed in Chapter 4, suggests that it is illogical to expect high levels of motivation from employees whose jobs are designed according to the rules of simplification, enlargement or rotation (with horizontal loading). Herzberg asks, '[Why] should a worker become motivated when one or more "meaningless" tasks are added to previously existing ones or when work assignments are rotated among equally "meaningless" tasks?'[8] Rather than pursuing one of these job design strategies, Herzberg recommends that managers practise job enrichment.

Job enrichment is the practice of building motivating factors into job content. This job-design strategy differs from the previous ones in that it seeks to expand job content by adding planning and evaluating duties (normally performed by the manager) to the employee's job. The changes that increase the 'depth' of a job involve vertical loading of the tasks, as opposed to the horizontal loading involved in job enlargement and much job rotation.

> **Job enrichment** *is the practice of building motivating factors into job content.*

The seven principles guiding Herzberg's approach to job enrichment are listed in Table 5.1. Each principle is an action guideline designed to increase the presence of one or more motivating factors. Remember, in the job enlargement and rotation strategies, managers tend to retain all responsibility for work planning and evaluating; in contrast, the job enrichment strategy involves vertical loading, which allows employees to share in these planning and evaluating responsibilities, as well as doing the actual work.

On the face of it, job enrichment seems appealing. However, it has some problems:

- Little, if any, diagnosis of the jobs is undertaken before they are redesigned.
- Cost-benefit data concerning job enrichment are not often reported and it may not always be worth it. Much of the time it is expensive to implement, especially if work flows need to be redesigned and facilities or equipment changed.
- Situational factors specifically supporting job enrichment have often not been systematically assessed.
- Many reports of the success of job enrichment have been evangelical in nature – that is, the authors overstate benefits and understate problems. There are few reported failures in the literature, possibly as a result of such bragging.
- Evaluations of job enrichment programmes too often have not been conducted rigorously using the appropriate scientific method.
- Many trials of job enrichment have been undertaken with hand-picked employees, rather than a random sample of employees representing differing skill profiles and job environments.
- Job enrichment theory fails to recognize and emphasize that individuals may respond differently to job enrichment and that not all individuals will like it.
- Job enrichment falls into that category of workplace innovations that is much talked about but not widely practised. Despite the plethora of literature defining job enrichment, only a small number of case studies have actually been reported.[9]

Principle	Motivators involved
1. Remove some controls while retaining accountability	Responsibility and achievement
2. Increase the accountability of individuals for their own work	Responsibility and recognition
3. Give a person a complete natural unit of work (module, division, area and so on)	Responsibility, achievement and recognition
4. Grant additional authority to employees in their activities; provide job freedom	Responsibility, achievement and recognition
5. Make periodic reports directly available to the worker rather than to the supervisor	Recognition
6. Introduce new and more difficult tasks that the individual has not previously handled	Growth and learning
7. Assign to individuals specific or specialized tasks; enable them to become experts	Responsibility, achievement, recognition and advancement

Table 5.1: Herzberg's principles of job enrichment.

The various strategies of job design are summarized on a continuum in Figure 5.1. This figure shows how the strategies differ in their degree of task specialization and as sources of intrinsic work rewards. The availability of intrinsic rewards is lowest for task attributes associated with simplified jobs, and highest for enriched jobs. Task specialization is higher for simplified jobs and lower for enriched jobs.

The four basic approaches to job design (simplification, enlargement, rotation and enrichment), as shown in Figure 5.1, have provided vital insights into the complexity of effective job design. Collectively, they are an important platform for later theorists. However, the common factor underlying these approaches is that they are 'static'; that is, they assume that all individuals will respond in the same, positive manner to these approaches. They fail to recognize the 'dynamic' nature of individual behaviour – that workers can and will respond in a variety of ways to the implementation of any innovative job design approach. To be effective, a manager needs to be able to understand, identify and predict how an individual employee will respond to any job redesign approach.

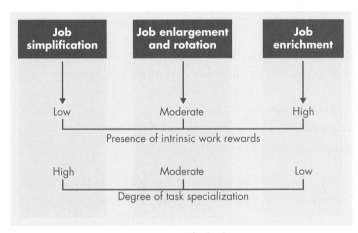

Figure 5.1: A continuum of job design strategies.

THE JOB CHARACTERISTICS MODEL

Pioneering work by Turner and Lawrence and Hulin and Blood in the 1960s began to look at the role of individual differences in job design.[10] They were trying to understand how an individual would respond to job redesign. That work led to the diagnostic approach – a technique developed by Richard Hackman and Greg Oldham and which is the basis of their job characteristics model (sometimes abbreviated to JCM). This model addresses job design in a contingency fashion.[11] The diagnostic job design approach, which generated considerable research in the 1980s, recognizes that there will be differences in the way any group of individuals responds to a change in the design of their jobs.

The current version of this newer approach to job enrichment, as depicted in Hackman and Oldham's job characteristics model, is shown in Figure 5.2. Five core job characteristics are identified as task attributes of special importance in the diagnosis of job design.

*The **job characteristics model** identifies five core characteristics (skill variety, task identity, task significance, autonomy and job feedback) as having special importance to job designs.*

A job that is high in these core characteristics is said to be enriched. The core job characteristics are:

- Skill variety – the degree to which the job requires an employee to undertake a variety of different activities and use different skills and talents.
- Task identity – the degree to which the job requires completion of a 'whole' and identifiable piece of work (that is, it involves doing a job from beginning to end with a visible outcome).
- Task significance – the degree to which the job is important and involves a meaningful contribution to the organization or society in general.
- Autonomy – the degree to which the job gives the employee substantial freedom, independence and discretion in scheduling the work and determining the procedures used in carrying it out.
- Job feedback – the degree to which carrying out the work activities results in the employee obtaining direct and clear information on how well the job has been done.

Hackman and Oldham state further that three critical psychological states must be realized for people to develop intrinsic work motivation. These are:

- experienced meaningfulness in the work
- experienced responsibility for the outcomes of the work
- knowledge of actual results of the work activities.

These psychological states represent intrinsic rewards that are believed to occur and to influence later performance and satisfaction when the core job characteristics are present in the job design.

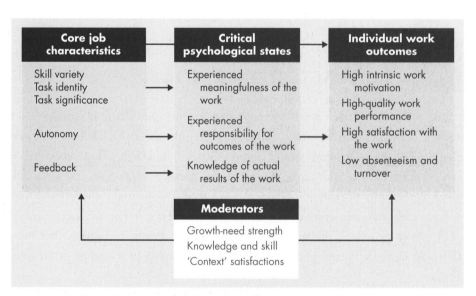

Figure 5.2: Job design implications of job characteristics theory.

Source: Adapted from: Hackman, J. R. & Oldham, G. R. (1975). Development of the Job, Diagnostic Survey. *Journal of Applied Psychology* 60, 159–170: 161. Reproduced by permission of Richard Hackman.

INDIVIDUAL DIFFERENCES: MODERATORS OF THE JOB CHARACTERISTICS MODEL

The job characteristics model recognizes that the five core job characteristics do not affect all people in the same way. Unlike many earlier theories of job design, the job characteristics model recognizes individual differences in response to changes in job design. A number of factors will influence the manner in which any individual employee responds to changes in the design of his or her job. These factors are called 'job design moderators'. Figure 5.2 shows three important individual difference moderators:

- Growth-need strength. This is the degree to which a person desires the opportunity for self-direction, learning and personal accomplishment at work. It is similar to Maslow's esteem and self-actualization and Alderfer's growth needs. The theory predicts that people strong in growth-need will respond positively to enriched jobs, experiencing high internal motivation, high growth satisfaction, high-quality performance and low absenteeism and turnover. On the other hand, people low in growth-need will have negative reactions and will find enriched jobs a source of anxiety. They are likely to be at risk of being 'overstretched' in the job and possibly balking at doing the job.[12]
- Knowledge and skill. Those with the knowledge and skill needed for performance in an enriched job are predicted to respond positively to the enrichment. Once again, we see how important a sense of competency or self-efficacy can be to people at work.
- Context satisfaction. This is the extent to which an employee is satisfied with the kind of contextual factors emphasized by Herzberg. For example, those satisfied with salary levels, supervision and working conditions are more likely than their dissatisfied colleagues to support job enrichment.

This list of moderators of the work outcome relationship of the job characteristics model is not intended to be exhaustive because many other variables (such as high-order needs and workers' value systems) have also been examined as potential moderators of reactions to these job dimensions.[13] In general, people whose capabilities match the requirements of an enriched job are likely to experience positive feelings and to perform well; people who are inadequate or who feel inadequate in this regard are likely to have difficulties.

The following 'OB in Action' looks at the increasing importance of having jobs that will attract and retain talented global workers.

For the organization that invests in talented employees it is important to be sure that the job offered is sufficiently enriched, satisfying and motivating to retain the employees into the future, although this cannot, of course, be guaranteed as talented workers may continue to seek new opportunities. For example, president of ANZ China Andrew McGregor says that the bank's really good people are headhunted at least weekly. At ANZ China (in locations such as Shanghai), many Chinese workers have gained 'Western' experience in the bank. In order to retain these workers, he tries to promote exchanges with Australian bank workers to enhance their global experience. In the context of mobile global workers there will also be a need to consider cultural differences for workers from different backgrounds in any job placement or design. McGregor, for example, has found that, although his Chinese workers adapt to less hierarchical organizational structures, it is difficult to foster feedback and open discussion with them because of their respect for people in higher positions.[18] One might expect this given Hofstede's findings on cultural differences set out in Chapter 1.

The shortage of knowledge workers is also being exacerbated by the demographic changes in particular the likely brain drain as the 'baby boomers' near retirement,[19] and the underutilization of part-time workers, particularly women, in the workforce through the 'hidden brain drain.' The UK's Equal Opportunities Commission argued that the incidence of flexible working practices needs to be extended in order to take full advantage of these often highly qualified and experienced workers.[20] These themes are explored later in the chapter.

OB IN ACTION

Attracting and retaining talented global workers

Increasing levels of globalization involving international companies and markets are now part of the business world we operate in. Workers are also increasingly mobile and there are skills shortages in many countries and global competition for knowledge workers. The so-called 'brain drain' has caused major shortages of information technology and e-business professionals in many countries, particularly in Western Europe. In the UK highly skilled foreign workers are increasingly being used to plug the gaps in healthcare, IT and managerial work where recruitment difficulties are acute. At the other end of the scale, with other labour shortages, there is an increasing trend towards using unskilled migrant workers from Eastern Europe to do jobs in the agricultural and hotel and catering industries that UK workers don't want to do.[14] Skills shortages have also contributed to the trend of shifting business activities to overseas locations. As an illustration of this trend, many banks and other major organizations have outsourced call centre operations to India, and to a lesser extent to the Philippines and China.[15]

There can be considerable incentives for mobile workers to move to where the best jobs can be found – there is often competition between countries for the best workers. In India the expansion of the financial services market has meant that there has been increasing competition for English speaking graduates which has led to severe skills shortages and annual turnover rates in call centres as high as 150%.[16] Attracting 'talent' and retaining good employees is widely discussed in contemporary business literature because of its importance to organizational success but job design is also important in this context. Knowledge-based economies can contribute towards changing job design so that organizations can offer jobs that will attract the most talented workers. These workers are often highly qualified and can afford to seek out jobs that offer them meaning, responsibility and opportunities for personal advancement and improvement. Survey evidence in the UK suggests that if job rotation schemes are not present these workers will simply move on.[17]

TESTING AND THE MOTIVATING POTENTIAL SCORE

Hackman and Oldham developed the job diagnostic survey questionnaire to test each of the dimensions in their job characteristics model, as shown in Figure 5.2. They also developed a motivating potential score (MPS) to summarize a job's overall potential for motivating those in the workplace. You can calculate this score using the following formula:

MPS = (variety + identity + significance) /3 × autonomy × feedback

The scores for each of the dimensions come from the job diagnostic survey and show the great importance of autonomy and feedback in providing the results shown in Figure 5.2. The MPS is especially useful for identifying low-scoring jobs that may benefit most from redesign.

*A **job diagnostic survey** is a questionnaire used to examine each of the dimensions of the job characteristics model.*

*A **motivating potential score** is a summary of a job's overall potential for motivating those in the workplace.*

The research

Considerable research has been done on the job characteristics approach. The approach has been examined in a variety of work settings, including banks, dentists' offices, telephone companies, and such organizations as IBM and Texas Instruments. Job-design studies using this approach have also been reported in the Netherlands[21] and the UK.[22]

A comprehensive review of the approach shows that:[23]

- On average, job characteristics affect performance but not nearly as much as they affect satisfaction.
- It is important to consider growth-need strength. Job characteristics influence performance more strongly for high growth-need employees than for low growth-need employees. The relationship to growth-need is about as strong as that to job satisfaction.
- Employee perceptions of job characteristics are different from objective measures and from those of independent observers. Positive results are typically strongest when an overall performance measure is used, rather than a separate measure of quality or quantity.

Effective Manager 5.1 summarizes some guidelines for implementing a job enrichment programme and for reviewing the process.

EFFECTIVE MANAGER 5.1

GUIDELINES FOR IMPLEMENTING A PROGRAMME OF JOB ENRICHMENT

Consider a job to be a candidate for job enrichment only when evidence exists that job satisfaction and/or performance is either deteriorating or open for improvement. Use a diagnostic approach and proceed with actual job enrichment only when:

- employees view their jobs as deficient in one or more of the core job characteristics

- extrinsic rewards and job context are not causing dissatisfaction
- cost and other potential constraints do not prohibit job design changes necessary for enrichment
- employees view core job characteristics positively
- employees have needs and capabilities consistent with new job designs.

Whenever possible, conduct a careful evaluation of the results of job enrichment to discontinue the job design strategy (if necessary) or to make constructive changes to increase its value. Expect that enrichment will also affect the job of the supervising manager because duties will be delegated. Do not feel threatened or become anxious or frustrated. If needed, get help for required personal work adjustments.

Experts generally agree that the job diagnostic approach that is the basis for Hackman and Oldham's job characteristics model is useful. A series of implementation concepts for the enrichment of core job characteristics is outlined in Figure 5.3 and some impacts of enriching core job characteristics are listed in Table 5.2. However, these experts urge caution in applying the technique, emphasizing that it is not a universal panacea for job performance and satisfaction problems. It can fail when job requirements are increased beyond the level of individual capabilities and/or interest. It can also raise issues of changes in remuneration – if employees are taking on more responsibility, should they be paid more? In summary, jobs high in core characteristics (especially as perceived by employees) tend to increase both satisfaction and performance, particularly among high growth-need employees. The following 'Counterpoint' looks at how job enrichment may overtax employees and increase the imbalance between the working and personal lives of employees (work–life balance is also discussed further later in the chapter).

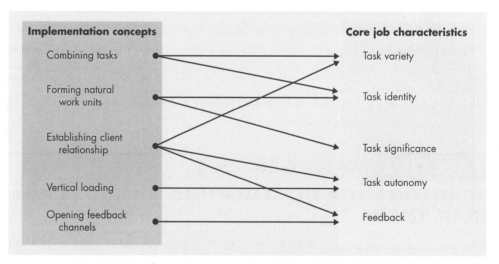

Figure 5.3: Implementation concepts and the core job characteristics.

Source: Derived from: Hackman, J. R., Oldham, G. & Purdy, K., (1975) A new strategy for job enrichment, *California Management Review*, **17**(4): 62.

	Enriched	Unenriched
Skill variety	Decided own strategy for performing task and changed strategy at will.	Were provided with explicit instructions for task to perform and strategy to use (e.g. 'first, open letters').
Task identity	Formed into groups of ten; performed all necessary operations on a certain proportion of customer requests.	As an individual, performed just one of these operations on all requests.
Task significance	Were briefed about importance of their jobs and how they fitted into the organization as a whole.	Received no formal instruction.
Autonomy	Chose length and timing of breaks. Performed own inspections at intervals they determined.	Except for breaks, stayed at workplace throughout the day. Had work periodically checked by inspectors.
Feedback	Saw productivity posted on scoreboards at end of each day.	Received no specific information about performance level.

Table 5.2: Sample core job characteristics for enriched and unenriched jobs.

▶ *COUNTERPOINT*

Enrichment and work–life balance in the 'real world'

The notion of job design and job enrichment transforming the working lives of people is commendable. However, in reality there are much more complicated factors involved and the job experience for many people, although perhaps more stimulating, challenging and satisfying, may also be much more stressful and difficult.

The suggestions for job enrichment in Table 5.2 look very reasonable. The opportunity for developing more skills, for completing more parts of the task, for having autonomy and feedback and viewing your job as significant in the organization are commendable. Many people are experiencing enriched jobs in many organizations. More skills are acquired and required to do the job. Jobs are less routine and more autonomous and people take responsibility for much of their own work. They are often given a sense of identity with the task and

feel their work is significant. But how does this fit into the real world of longer working hours and pressures for balance between work and home?

While endeavouring to improve jobs on the one hand, it would appear that organizations can also be major contributors to making individual workers' lives very difficult. In many countries people are being required to work longer hours. In the EU long working hours are still a key feature of working life for many workers, with workers in Eastern and Southern Europe (particularly in the hospitality and construction industry) working the longest at more than 45 hours per week; for example 64% of workers in Romania work in excess of 45 hours per week and senior managers in all member states typically work more than 48 hours.[24] In Australia the difference between perception of working life and the reality was clearly illustrated by a survey of young graduates. The survey found that 58% of employers expected graduates to work up to 50 hours a week with very few (8%) paying overtime. In contrast only 45% of graduates had any expectation that they would be required to work these hours.[25] Companies might talk actively about enriched jobs and work–life balance but we need to take some stock of how these changes really affect people. Given more responsibility in enriched jobs, many people will work harder to do what is required for the job, even when it involves working longer hours. A number of studies in the UK and across Europe all show that although working longer hours improves pay prospects it does not improve career prospects and has a significant affect on work satisfaction, feelings of wellness and work–life balance.[26] However, increasing hours were also linked to increasing employee consultation, involvement in decision making, career opportunities and awareness of organizational direction. It seems that when there is some 'say' in their work and a desire for career success, workers may be more prepared to work long hours and sacrifice some balance between their work and home lives.[27]

Questions

1. How and why would an enriched job cause an employee to work longer hours?
2. What responsibility do managers have to ensure their employees do not work excessive hours and experience excessive stress?
3. Is there any value in organizations providing flexible work arrangements if, at the same time, they are encouraging employees (intentionally or unintentionally) to work longer hours?

SOCIO-TECHNICAL JOB DESIGN

Socio-technical job design *is the design of jobs to optimize the relationship between the technology system and the social system.*

Technology can sometimes constrain the ability to enrich jobs. Socio-technical job design recognizes this problem and seeks to optimize the relationship between the technology system and the social system. This is achieved by designing work roles to integrate with the technology system. Best known is the semiautonomous work group approach, by which self-managed or autonomous work teams perform a job previously done on the assembly line (these teams are discussed in Chapter 6).

It is difficult and costly to modify technology in an existing factory, and to change work practices and job design across the entire organization, so the socio-technical approach often works more effectively in a 'greenfield' site (that is, a new site with no established work practices).

Since the mid-1990s some managers have begun to question the costs of maintaining and developing this socio-technical approach in some factories because of the rising costs associated with rapid knowledge obsolescence and multiskilling the workforce. However, this is not always a problem, or organizations can take action to minimize this effect. For example, while Boeing has different cockpits on its different aircraft, Airbus's strategy is to have the same cockpit on all the models in its fleet. This means that pilots require much less reskilling when they move between different aircraft models. More research on the costs and benefits of the approach in contemporary environments and of strategies to minimize problems is needed to address such criticisms.

SOCIAL INFORMATION AND JOB DESIGN

Gerald Salancik and Jeffrey Pfeffer have reviewed the literature on the job diagnostic approach to job design.[28] They question whether jobs have stable and objective characteristics that individuals perceive and to which they respond predictably and consistently. As an alternative, their social information-processing approach argues that individual needs, task perceptions and reactions are a result of socially constructed realities. Thus, social information in the workplace influences employees' perceptions of the job and their responses to it (see Chapter 2 for a fuller discussion of the topic of perception). It is much like a student's perception of a class. Several of the student's friends may tell her that the lecturer is bad, the content is boring and the class requires too much work. The student may then think that the critical characteristics of the class are the lecturer, the content and the workload and that they are all bad. All of this may take place before the student has even set foot in that class and may substantially influence the student's class perception and response, regardless of the characteristics in the job characteristics approach.

The **social information-processing approach** *argues that individual needs, task perceptions and reactions are a result of socially constructed realities.*

Research on the social information-processing approach provides mixed results. Essentially, the results show that social information processing does influence task perceptions and attitudes, but the kinds of job characteristics described earlier remain very important.

MULTISKILLING

Multiskilling programmes help employees become members of a flexible workforce and acquire an array of skills needed to perform multiple tasks in a company's production or customer-service function. The cross-training and multiskilling of employees allow them to assume broader responsibilities so they are better equipped to solve problems. When a team member is absent there is always someone who can take over the role. When suggestions for process improvements are required, members of the team have the requisite skills and expertise to make highly valued contributions. The training programme in the example below illustrates this.

 **IN ACTION**

A training initiative to broaden the skills of staff at the Marriott's Marble Arch Hotel in London UK has helped employees become more flexible. The training scheme, which was offered to all 150 staff, enabled them to develop the skills needed in different departments thus improving their ability and enabled them to become more flexible through the introduction of multiskilling. This was mutually

beneficial as it allowed staff to move across departments but also increased opportunities and readiness for promotion or movement sideways within the organization. The scheme that helped the hotel win a British Hospitality Association 'Excellence through People Award' has now been incorporated into the induction process. All new staff now receive a two-week cross-training programme, which gives them the skills and flexibility to be able to work in a range of departments. The scheme is also available to staff looking to develop skills.[29]

Multiskilling is an innovative work practice that has helped improve organizational performance by 30% to 40% in some cases. Strong links between a multiskilled workforce and improved productivity have been identified. More recently, the skills matrix has been used to measure employees' skill levels and compare them to the desired levels, which are often an upward-moving target.

Overall, employees in a flexible workforce benefit from having a challenging and varied work experience, more control over their work environment, higher skill levels, higher pay opportunities and greater marketability in the job market.

GOAL-SETTING THEORY

Goal setting
is the process of developing, negotiating and formalizing an employee's targets and objectives.

A reasonable question for any employee to ask an employer is: 'What is it you want me to do?' Without clear and appropriate goals, employees may suffer a direction problem and be unable to channel their work energies towards the right goal. The case of 'Sarah' set out in the next OB in Action box illustrates this.

Similar problems are found in many workplaces. Proper setting and clarification of task goals can eliminate, or at least reduce, these and other problems. Goal setting involves building challenging and specific goals into jobs and providing appropriate performance feedback.

OB *IN ACTION*

Sarah sought help from New Zealand coaching company Blue Chip because she was having trouble getting results from some of her teams whose job it was to implement projects. After personal coaching and analysis of the problem, Sarah came to realize that it was her own lack of confidence about some jobs that was being reflected in her teams' performance. When she knew what the job was about she was able to communicate requirements confidently to her team. However, when she was out of her depth with a project and not confident that she could deliver, she failed to find out from the client enough about th... oroject t... not v... ed s... her te... he

identified the problem and learnt how to handle it, Sarah was able to stop, ask the right questions of the client and then retain her focus on the task. This allowed her to clarify goals and task requirements and confidently lead and direct her teams to success.[30]

obje
incl
imp
Lock
dicti
vides

otiating and formalizing the targets or ...mplishing'.[31] Expanding job design to ... each individual. These task goals are ...nance. Over a number of years, Edwin ... concerning this link. This set of pre- ...ocke's research and that of others pro-...ons:[32]

1. Di
   be
   see
   An

   ...rformance than are less difficult ones ... outcomes. However, if the goals are ...ip with performance no longer holds. ...unattainable.

2. Spe
   or
   bett

   ...formance than are no goals or vague ...refrigerators a month should lead to ...l.

3. Tas
   perf
   peo... ...stand and if they are ... or off course in their efforts; for

   ...to motivate people towards higher ...performance goals. Feedback lets

   example, think about how eager you are to find out how well you have done in an examination.

4. Goals are most likely to lead to higher performance when people have the abilities and the feelings of self-efficacy required to accomplish them. Individuals must believe that they are able to accomplish the goals and feel confident in their abilities.

5. Goals are most likely to motivate people towards higher performance when they are accepted and there is commitment to them. One way of achieving such acceptance or commitment is by participating in the goal-setting process. You then feel a sense of 'ownership' of the goals. However, Locke and Latham report that goals assigned by someone else can be equally effective. The assigners are likely to be influential authority figures. Also, the assignment implies that the employee can actually reach the goal. Third, assigned goals are often a challenge. Finally, assigned goals help define the standards people use to attain personal satisfaction with their performance.[33] According to Locke and Latham, assigned goals only lead to poor performance when they are curtly or inadequately explained.[34]

GOAL SETTING: FOLLOW-UP RESEARCH

Research using and extending the five predictions discussed is now quite extensive. Indeed, there is more research for goal setting than for any other theory related to work motivation.[35] Nearly 400 studies have been conducted in several countries, including Australia, the UK, Germany, Japan and the US.[36] Locke and Latham and their associates have been at the forefront of this work and have recently integrated their predictions into a more comprehensive framework that links goals to performance. We show a simplified version of the Locke and Latham framework in Figure 5.4.

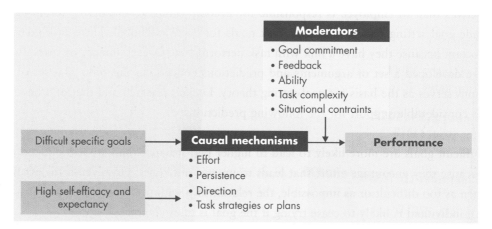

Figure 5.4: Simplified Locke and Latham goal-setting framework.

Source: Adapted from Locke, E. A. & Latham, G. P., (1990) Work motivation and satisfaction: light at the end of the tunnel, *Psychological Science*, 1(4): 244. Reproduced by permission of Blackwell Publishing.

Starting at the left we see the difficult, specific goals mentioned earlier in predictions 1 and 2. These are joined by high self-efficacy (mentioned in prediction 4 and emphasized in Chapters 2 and 4) and high expectancy (discussed as a part of expectancy motivation theory in Chapter 4). The argument is that these factors operate through the linking mechanisms of effort, persistence, direction, and task strategies or plans to affect performance. At the same time, the moderators of goal commitment (prediction 5), feedback (prediction 3), ability (prediction 4), task complexity and situational constraints also operate to strengthen or weaken the relationship between goals and performance.

Locke's predictions concerning goal setting are still relevant. However, they have now been embedded in the simplified framework in Figure 5.4. That framework includes some ideas discussed in the motivation chapter and relates to concepts from expectancy theory, as shown in our discussion in the previous paragraph of the role of expectancy and self-efficacy. Further, although our simplified framework does not show it, Locke and Latham argue that the instrumentality concept from expectancy theory (that is, that performance leads to rewards) operates through the link between challenging goals and valued rewards.[37] Again, the basic tenets of expectancy theory prove useful in explaining work behaviour. This relationship has sometimes led to the treatment of goal-setting theory as a process motivation theory, in addition to the equity and expectancy theories discussed in Chapter 4. Furthermore, the task-complexity notion discussed earlier suggests a link with job enrichment. As more enrichment is built into a job, the job becomes more complex and probably calls for new task strategies or plans. Finally, Locke's fourth prediction links goal-setting theory with ability as an individual attribute and with self-efficacy, which is so important in social learning theory.[38]

GOAL SETTING AND MBO

When we speak of goal setting and its potential to influence individual performance at work, the concept of management by objectives (MBO) immediately comes to mind. This approach has been widely used in many large organizations in both the public and private sectors.[39] In Europe and the US many senior executives have performance-based contracts that identify clear goal-achievement milestones for each year.

Management by objectives involves managers working with their employees to establish performance goals and plans that are consistent with higher level work unit and organizational objectives.[40] When this process is followed throughout an organization, MBO helps to clarify the hierarchy of objectives as a series of well-defined means–end chains.

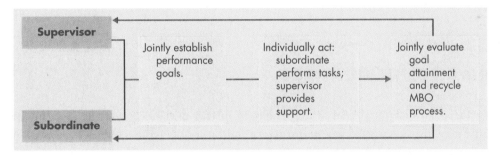

Figure 5.5: The management by objectives (MBO) process.

Figure 5.5 shows a comprehensive view of MBO. The concept is consistent with the notion of goal setting and its associated principles (as already discussed). Notice how joint supervisor–employee discussions are designed to extend participation from the point of initial goal establishment to the point of evaluating results in terms of goal attainment. Key issues for mutual goal setting are summarized in Effective Manager 5.1.

In addition to the goal-setting steps previously discussed, a successful MBO system calls for careful implementation. This means that the previous steps are translated into the kinds of strategies or plans, mentioned earlier, that will lead to goal accomplishment. Employees must have freedom to carry out the required tasks; managers may have to do considerable coaching and counselling. As with other applied organizational behaviour programmes, managers should be aware of MBO's potential costs as well as its benefits.

EFFECTIVE MANAGER 5.2

Key issues for mutual goal setting in an MBO programme

- What must be done? Start with higher level goals, job descriptions stating tasks to be performed, outcomes expected, necessary supplies and equipment and so on.
- How will performance be measured? Time, money or physical units may often be used to measure performance. If the job is more subjective, emphasize behaviours or actions believed to lead to success.
- What is the performance standard? Start with previous performance or the average perform-ance of others doing this job. Where these

measures do not exist, use mutual supervisor–subordinate judgement and discussion.
- What are the deadlines for the goals? Discuss deadlines in terms of daily, weekly or longer terms.
- What is the relative importance of the goals? Not all goals are equally important. The manager and employee should decide the goal ranking together.
- How difficult are the goals? Watch especially for high task complexity and multiple goals. Come up with a clearly agreed decision.

Despite substantial research based on case studies of MBO success, such research has not always been rigorously controlled and it reports mixed results.[41] In general, and as an application of goal-setting theory, MBO has much to offer. But it is not easy to start and keep going. MBO may also need to be implemented organization-wide if it is to work well.[42]

KEY PERFORMANCE INDICATORS

Key performance indicators *are standards against which individual and organizational performance can be measured.*

The concept of individual goal setting has been further developed over the past few years to introduce the concept of **key performance indicators** (KPIs) – standards against which individual and organizational performance can be measured.

Such measurement is a step in the benchmarking process taken by companies wanting to achieve superior performance in a formal and structured way. High performance has been linked to improved business performance, which has been strongly associated with improve-ments in recognizing and using an organization's key performance indicators. In the UK the government's national standard for HR activity 'Investors in People' (IIP) is underpinned by the concept of KPIs. Investors in People is a continuous improvement activity designed to help organizations of any size or type to achieve their business objectives through its people investment. IIP involves companies achieving 10 KPIs in order to gain the award. Although the award is not prescriptive as it encourages organizations to achieve the standard in their own way. Over 30 000 have done so since the scheme began in 1993.[43]

The use of such indicators in employee remuneration packages has been popular.[44] Using performance appraisal's, an employee's pay is structured according to their achieve-ment of individual key performance indicators that cascade down from organizational ones. The individual's contribution to the organization can thus be measured because the indicators provide a benchmark against which an employee can be judged. The use of performance appraisals holds employees accountable for their achievements.

A key performance indicator must therefore be Specific, Measurable, Achievable, Realistic and Time-framed (SMART).[45] It depends on the nature of the employee's job, the industry in which the employee works, the strategic direction and goals of the company, and the bottom line of the organization.

The common use of key performance indicators to measure quantifiable targets also extends to qualitative issues, such as staff initiative and communication skills. For example, the Australian National Maritime Museum's KPIs include quantitative targets, such as number of visitor interactions, as well as qualitative ones, such as reputation (assessed by focus groups).[46]

FLEXIBLE WORK ARRANGEMENTS

Attempting to enhance worker satisfaction through job redesign involves mostly intrinsic factors related to doing the job. Employee satisfaction (as well as avoidance of dissatisfaction) can also be achieved by changing job conditions, such as the timing or number of working hours and work location. For example, the employee may experience a more acceptable working environment (extrinsic change) if working hours are flexible enough to allow the achievement of other (personal) goals. This, in turn, may affect the employee's levels of work motivation and performance (intrinsic changes) because they are more satisfied with their job environment. The key drivers and practices of flexible work arrangements are now presented.

MAJOR DRIVERS OF CHANGING WORK ARRANGEMENTS

Since the mid 1990s the European Employment Strategy has been driving through changes that focus on the introduction of more flexible working practices. 'Policies on career breaks, parental leave and part-time work as well as flexible working arrangements which serve the interest of both employers and employees are of particular importance.'[47] In the spring of 2000, the UK Government launched its work–life balance campaign in order to promote the benefits of more flexible working practices. In the baseline survey carried out by a government department as part of this initiative, it was found that 91% of those responding felt that: 'people work their best when they can balance their work and other aspects of their lives.'[48]

Organizations that use flexible strategies in the workforce have the potential to reap many benefits including:

• higher retention of staff and thus higher retention of organizational knowledge
• less absenteeism

- more capacity to meet peak demand and more capacity to service client demands outside normal hours
- more contented, productive, committed and motivated employees
- more diverse and qualified workforces.[49]

Flexible work practices can assist individual workers to deal with their work in the context of the following drivers.

CHANGING FAMILY LIFESTYLES AND WORK–LIFE BALANCE

Work–life balance *refers to a concern which people have with balancing work hours with other responsibilities including caring for children or adults. It has become a key issue for employers with the advent of 24/7 societies and customers' expectations of where and when services should be provided for them.*

The prevalence of households where both partners are working (dual-income families) and the rising number of one-parent families, along with increasing hours worked, exacerbate the problems of balancing work and non work pressures. At the heart of the European strategy is the growing concern about demographic changes, the detrimental effects of long working hours and the view that work–life balance isn't just for mothers but for all employees. Substantial benefits can be gained for both employees and employers in considering the work–life balance for workers in very many different ways, as the following examples show.

Even simple measures can reduce the pressures on staff as they struggle to fulfil personal and work goals in the limited time available to them. For example, car parts manufacturer Autoliv has set up a prayer room in its workplace to assist its many Muslim workers to participate in necessary religious activities.[50]

OB IN ACTION

In 2004 MSN UK (part of Microsoft) won the working families' Employer of the Year Innovation and Opportunity Now's New Member Award for its project to reduce excessive working hours and encourage a flexible working culture. From none in the beginning, 85% of employees now work flexibly, including 45% of men and all of the leadership team. This has improved staff morale and increased productivity with the business growing by 66% since the changes. MSN have implemented a formal work–life balance policy which includes a range of measures including home working, flexitime, compressed working and flexible location working. This has been coupled by a cultural change programme with senior management working more flexibly and through the company providing support with employee assistance and wellbeing programmes. MSN say that not only do they have a happier and more productive workforce but the policy has helped to retain key people and reduce stress at work.[51]

OCCUPATIONAL STRESS

One of the major adverse influences on job satisfaction and work performance is the increasing incidence of **stress** at work.[52] With the emphasis on cost cutting and downsizing that has prevailed over the past few decades, where employees in many organizations are expected to 'do far more with less'. In Europe the introduction of the Working Time Directive in 1998 was intended to reduce the maximum number of hours employees should work; however, as already mentioned, many workers throughout Europe still work long hours. In the UK survey evidence found that over 50 % of employees worked some hours in addition to their fixed or standard hours (an additional nine hours average for full-time workers)[53] and many professional workers were still working more than 48 hours per week often with unpaid overtime.[54] The real working conditions of so many employees, with increased pressure to work harder and longer, are associated with rising levels of work stress and burnout, thus it is not surprising that headlines such as 'stress at work is the biggest problem in European companies' are becoming more prevalent.[55] Three recent European studies support this view concluding that the main causes of workplace stress are related to deficiencies in the design and management of work.[56] Some organizations are responding by offering extended breaks from the workplace, such as sabbatical leave, to help employees cope more effectively.[57] Others as discussed later in this chapter are beginning to see the benefits of offering their employees more flexible working arrangements.

Stress is a state of tension experienced by individuals facing extraordinary demands, constraints or opportunities.

CHANGING LEVELS AND MODES OF EMPLOYMENT

Throughout the 1980s and into the 1990s, rising levels of unemployment dominated and impacted on work security and workload. More recently, unemployment figures have stabilized or decreased (though there is some dispute about the way in which figures are measured). For example, in Europe in 2006 unemployment was 8 % of the workforce, with the Eastern block countries such as Poland (14 %) having even higher rates. Unemployment rates for women in the UK were less that those for men which may be a reflection of the significant increase in part-time working in the EU since 2002 with 17.8 % of the work force now working part-time; in the UK alone some 7.3 million people now work part-time. This shift away from permanent full-time work is also reflected in the rise of fixed term contract and agency employees working within Europe (13.9 %). It is also suggested that this is a reflection of the increasing emphasis being placed on work–life balance and demographic changes in particular the ageing work force in Europe.[58] These changes are also leading to labour shortages in some areas and the encouragement of free movement of migrant workers within the EU. For example in Italy there is already a severe shortage of nurses, which has resulted in immigration laws being relaxed for care workers and in Sweden there is growing concern that 60 % of all nurses are over 44 years of age.[59]

AGEING POPULATION AND CHANGING RETIREMENT PATTERNS

The population in Western European is ageing (16% over the age of 65)[60] and yet the labour market participation rates are declining sharply for men and women from their mid-50s onwards.[61] This means increasing pressure on social services, so flexible work options are being explored to retain the productive skills of many older workers while simultaneously offering them a new balance between work and lifestyle. In the UK, the proportion of people aged 65 and over has increased from 13% in 1971 to 16% in 2006 while, conversely, the numbers under 16 have fallen from 25% to 19%. Employees aged 50 or over now form 27% of the UK workforce.[62] These statistics, coupled with the introduction of the legislation on ageism in October 2006, have led many UK employers into rethinking their retirement strategies. As these trends continue it will be even more critical to retain as many older employees as possible in the workforce. Survey evidence from Mori and the CIPD indicated that respondents were more than willing to work beyond retirement providing they could work more flexibly.[63] Offering them part-time work, phased retirement or contracted work will also help to retain older workers.[64] The home improvements chain B&Q has for a long time been a champion of the older worker but UK employers as diverse as the Nationwide Building Society, Derby City Council and the Ministry of Defence have all introduced practical measures to support the recruitment and retention of older workers.[65] This trend is also reflected in Europe: Polyfelt in Austria, Dell Inc. in Slovenia, Zemat in Poland and Volvo in Sweden are just a few of the companies that have strategies under way.[66] The following examples illustrate some of these.

OB IN ACTION

Asda is now the biggest UK employer of the over-50s with 20% of its workforce in that age range. Asda supports and values a diverse workplace, which includes older workers who have often been seen as less effective than their younger colleagues, yet at Asda the over-50s continually receive the best customer feedback. Asda believe that 'older, more mature employees would bring with them an immense treasure of knowledge and life skills to the workplace.' Increasing the number of older workers has led to a more flexible and better motivated workforce with lower levels of absenteeism and a decrease in staff turnover and increased levels of performance and job satisfaction. ASDA's strategy to recruit and retain older workers began in 1999 with the 'to be best for the over-50s' policy. In essence this offered older workers a package of leave benefits including 'Benidorm leave' (perhaps a rather stereotypical view of older workers' preferred holiday destinations) and grandparents' leave allowing older workers' to take unpaid leave for extended holidays and the birth of a grandchild. Since then a full range of flexible measures have been introduced to the whole workforce, including flexitime, home working, 'v' time and flexible retirement.[67]

In the Netherlands the financial services company Achmea have developed an elaborate set of age-aware and life-course related HR policies aimed at all workers not exclusively older workers. These include flexible working schemes, health management programmes and training development schemes that are related to age. For example workers over 40 are given up to 10 days of paid study leave per year and workers over 57 years may bank hours in order to reduce their working week without reducing their pay.[68]

CHANGING TECHNOLOGY AND THE CAPACITY TO WORK REMOTELY

Information technology enables many changes to the way in which work is organized and located. Work can often be location independent and in reality there may be no need for the employee and the employer to meet regularly. Teleworking and working remotely from the office have been extensively discussed over many years[69] and, despite a slow takeup, have been increasing in popularity.

Telework *principles relate to work conducted remotely from the central organization using information technology.*

TYPES OF FLEXIBLE WORK ARRANGEMENTS

As already mentioned the introduction of more flexible working patterns figure highly on the European Employment Strategy,[70] and in the UK The Employment Act of 2002 gave parents and carers the right to request more flexible working from their employer. Some of the important work options to emerge from the trends already outlined include a compressed work week, annualized hours, zero hours, flexitime, job sharing and teleworking or remote working. Employers are increasingly recognizing the business case for introducing more flexible working patterns[71] but, more importantly here, nearly all these options are designed to influence employee satisfaction and to serve as both extrinsic and intrinsic motivating devices by helping employees to balance the demands of their working and nonworking lives. In our fast-changing society these arrangements are becoming more important as a way of dealing with our increasingly diverse workforce.

THE COMPRESSED WORK WEEK

A compressed work week is any scheduling of work that allows a full-time job to be completed in fewer than the standard five days (the assumed five day norm may however in itself be an outdated concept). The most common form of compressed work week is the

A compressed work week *is any scheduling of work that allows a full-time job to be completed in fewer than the standard five days.*

'4–40'; that is, 40 hours of work accomplished in four 10-hour days, but can include other forms such as nine days in a fortnight. In the UK this pattern of work is more common in the public sector, for example Medway Council allows employees to work nine days over a fortnight (74 hours), but is becoming more widespread with one fifth of employers reporting they operate compressed hours for some staff. This may often be as part of a wider flexible working package; the bank Lloyds TSB in the UK allows staff to compress their working week into fewer than five days,[72] and the chemical firm Bayer also have a compressed working week as one of their flexible working options.[73] Added time off is the key benefit for the employee with the individual often benefiting from increased leisure time, more three-day weekends, free week days to pursue personal business and lower commuting costs. The organization can benefit, too, through reduced energy consumption during three-day shutdowns, lower employee absenteeism, improved recruiting of new employees, and the extra time available for building and equipment maintenance, although results are inconsistent.[74]

The potential disadvantages of the compressed work week include increased fatigue from the extended work day and family adjustment problems for the individual and, for the organization, increased work scheduling problems and possible customer complaints due to breaks in work coverage. One study found that reaction to the compressed work week was most favourable among employees who had participated in the decision to compress the work week, who had had their jobs enriched as a result of the new schedule, and who had strong higher-order needs. The enrichment occurred because fewer employees were on duty at any one time and job duties were changed and enriched to accommodate this reduction.[75] A further interesting finding is employees' seeming reluctance to subsequently seek employment under the typical standard-hours model of five days/40 hours, once they have experienced the lifestyle changes associated with a compressed work week.[76]

ANNUALIZED HOURS

Annualization *is a scheme whereby employees' working time and pay is scheduled and calculated over a period of a year.*

Annualization or 'annualized hours' schemes allow employees' working time (and pay) to be calculated and scheduled over a period of a year. Pay is equalized each month but working hours vary. Annualization is a means of achieving working time flexibility, which has proved increasingly popular in a number of European countries in recent years, and which has been promoted by EU policy and recommendations.[77] In Denmark, 67% of employees in the private sector have access to this work pattern,[78] meanwhile in Finland, 14% of workers in the private sector had annualized contracts.[79] In the UK, 5% of workers in 2004 were engaged on annual hour's contracts.[80] For example ground staff at Aberdeen City Council work 1924 hours a year,[81] whilst the bank Alliance and Leicester introduced annualized contracts for their branch staff that accommodated staff preferences, including school term time only working, with an agreed fixed number of working hours to be scheduled throughout the year.[82]

OB IN ACTION

Thomas Sanderson, the UK's leading supplier of conservatory blinds and patio awnings introduced annual hours to cope with its sales peaks and troughs that typically occur twice a year. Under the old contract employees were being paid for a fixed 43 hour week regardless of demand where staff would typically be under occupied during quiet periods while the company would need to pay overtime for busy periods. The new annualized hours programme has reduced the need to pay overtime has given staff increased time off and has helped drive staff retention according to Nigel Campkin Executive Director.[83]

Such a system can reduce the need for overtime, match staff to fluctuating workloads such as those caused by seasonal demand, can reduce absenteeism since options for taking time off are available and can remove the need for bringing in casual staff. Other benefits to the employer include improved productivity, multiskilling, improved team working and higher morale and motivation. Employees report increased job satisfaction, improved team working, 'usable' leisure time as well as work–life balance improvements.[84]

ZERO-HOURS CONTRACTS

A zero-hours contract can be defined as an arrangement where the worker is not guaranteed any work at all but in some way is required to be available as and when the employer needs that person. Wide-ranging flexibility is the main motive for employing workers on zero-hours contracts. In the UK many employers (around 22 %) use zero-hours contracts in order to deal with work fluctuations, particularly seasonal variations. In mainland Europe though there is little evidence for this pattern of work. Woolworth's for example has around 15 % of its workforce on zero-hours contracts, a large proportion of whom have previously been employed by the company on other contracts but who no longer want to commit themselves to regular working hours, or students who are available to work in university holidays.

The advantages of this type of working for the employer are reduced costs and greater flexibility. For many workers this is a very flexible arrangement with a good degree of choice over when and whether or not they work. However, in reality employers have been criticized for treating employees on zero-hours contracts less favourably than other staff in terms of pay and conditions of service.[85] For many adopting a critical perspective within OB, zero-hours contracts constitute a clear case of significant exploitation of workers.

JOB SHARING

Another alternative work pattern is **job sharing**, whereby one full-time job is assigned to two or more people, who then divide the work according to agreements made between or among themselves and with the employer.[86] Under this scheme a job can be 'shared',

Job sharing *is the assignment of one full-time job to two or more persons, who divide the work according to agreements made between themselves and the employer.*

which may require a high degree of coordination and communication between job-sharing partners, or it may be 'split', which requires little cooperative interaction and coordination. Some jobs require a careful job-sharing approach, whereas in other cases a job split approach can work effectively. Work options such as job sharing and permanent part-time help facilitate a better balance between work and family life. Job sharing often entails split weeks, with each person working half a week or split days with each person working half a day, although it may also be a weekly or monthly arrangement.

Job sharing has a lot to offer for the creation of a family-friendly workplace. Yet in the UK only 2% of employees are employed on a job-sharing basis.[87] Organizations benefit from job sharing when they are able to attract talented people who would otherwise be unable to work. For example in the teaching profession, two members of staff are able to teach one class. Whilst many organizations in the UK report that any employee can ask to job share; in practice it is more common in the public sector and tends to be concentrated in secretarial/clerical and administrative positions.[88]

Burnout *is a negative felt emotion relating to one's work. It is characterized by emotional exhaustion, cynicism and doubts regarding self-efficacy.*

Some job sharers report less **burnout** and claim to feel recharged each time they report for work. Finding the right partnership is very important however, because the 'sharers' must work well with each other.[89] A more recent and somewhat controversial development of this scheme is 'family job sharing', which has been introduced by Macdonald's. Here husbands, wives, children and grandparents can job share and swap shifts without notifying management in advance. Introduced to help to tackle the problem of absenteeism, this type of workplace flexibility could increase job satisfaction and help workers to achieve a better work–life balance.[90]

FLEXIBLE WORKING HOURS OR FLEXITIME

Flexible working *hours (flexitime) is any work schedule that gives employees daily choice in the timing of work and nonwork activities.*

There is much debate as to what actually constitutes flexible working with some commentators including part-time working within their definitions. True flexible working allows employees to 'exercise a choice in relation to personal circumstances and work demands but compatible with the achievement of business objectives'[91] but in reality this translates into a more limited daily flexitime 'that gives employees daily some choice in the timing of work and nonwork activities.'[92] Flexitime is perhaps the most widely adopted work option in Western economies, although data about it are not always clear. In Europe in 2004 there were sharp differences in practice; in northern European countries workers can choose to adapt working time to their needs to a large extent (around half of employees say they can do so with or without certain limits), which is in sharp contrast to southern and eastern European countries, where more than 75% of employees have no possibility whatsoever of adapting their work schedules, as they are set by the company.[93] Other evidence suggest that flexible working, particularly part-time working and flexi-time is widespread in Europe and set to increase further.[94] In the UK survey evidence is often contradictory, on the one hand one survey stated that less than one in two workers have any control over their working hours,[95] with the TUC finding that this lack of flexibility was as high as 77%,[96] and on the other 37% of employers now have flexitime schemes.[97] What is perhaps of more concern is the number of workers who have lower job satisfaction because they cannot work more flexibly. In 2007 the EOC reported that 6.5 million UK workers could be using their skills more fully if more flexible working was available in the UK. Often considered a problem limited to working mothers the EOC findings show that this 'skills drain' affects almost as many men as women and more nonparents than parents.[98] This research supports earlier research that many workers are stuck in jobs for which they are overqualified and in which they do not use all their skills, because they lack the opportunity to work more flexibly.[99] The potential advantages of flexible working are listed in Table 5.3.

Organizational benefits	Individual benefits
Lower absenteeism	More time for leisure and personal business, e.g. dentist, bank and better timing of commuting
Reduced tardiness	Less commuting time
Reduced turnover	Higher job satisfaction
Higher work commitment	Greater sense of responsibility
Higher performance	Easier personal scheduling

Table 5.3: Organizational and individual benefits of flexible working hours.

Proponents of flexible working argue that the discretion it allows workers in scheduling their own hours of work encourages them to develop positive attitudes and increased commitment to the organization. Research tends to support this position.[100] The growing demand for working hours flexibility in the UK is clearly reflected in a number of surveys. In a survey for the EOC nearly half the working population 52 % of men and 48 % of women say they wanted to work more flexibly;[101] more than 1 in 10 employees (2.3 million) according to the TUC reported they would like to work fewer hours;[102] in a CIPD survey 45 % of respondents had changed their jobs in order to work more flexibly,[103] and a DTI survey found that 46 % of the 4 000 job seekers surveyed would choose flexible working as the benefit that they would most look for in their next job, with a third stating their preference for this over an increase in salary of £1 000 per year.[104]

However, there can be many other ways of assisting employees through the provision of reduced working hours. For example, many women are keen to resume work in a part-time capacity after maternity leave or older workers no longer wishing to work full time. Being able to do this is not always easy, with some organizations being more and others less supportive, as the following example of Tesco and British Airways demonstrate.

OB IN ACTION

Tesco supermarket chain in the UK employs thousands of part-time workers. Wherever possible, Tesco endeavours to accommodate the needs of all its workers. For example, when women return to work after maternity leave they are given the

option to change their working hours if they desire it. Many of them return to a three or four-hour shift in the evenings and then move to day shifts as their children grow older. School hours and term-time only working are just some of the other options available to the whole workforce. Older workers are also encouraged, such as Dick Stanners aged 84, who, at the age of 80, came out of retirement and now works part time as a personal shopper in Tesco's Crawley store.[105]

Jessica Starmer, a British Airways pilot who wanted to work part-time to look after her two young daughters won a three-year campaign against the airline in March 2007 after taking her case to an employment tribunal. Jessica had been fighting to work part-time since 2004, when the airline refused to let her reduce her hours by 50% to look after her oldest daughter but continued to work for the organization, working 75% of full-time hours while she took her case to court. Jessica is just one of 171 females who make up the total of 3100 pilots worldwide and yet 23 other pilots are allowed to work 50% part-time. Jessica said that she regretted having to take legal action but hoped that her case would lead to a change in attitude for other women 'There is so much research out there proving that if they are allowed to work flexibly, mothers make committed, dedicated and loyal employees' she commented.[106]

The 'OB in action' section invokes some interesting potential questions including what would could be done to consider Jessica's proposal fully and properly, what advantages and disadvantages for the employer might be possible in such a scenario when a full-time employee wants to come back from maternity leave to part-time work and what strategies could one take to maximize the outcomes for both the employee and the organization?

REMOTE WORKING AND THE VIRTUAL OFFICE

It is now clear that the traditional office is no longer the sole focal point of employee activity.[107] Advances in communication and information technology, as well as changing attitudes towards trusting employees, are leading to more work being undertaken in 'virtual offices' remote from the central workplace. Workers can work from home, work while travelling on a train, in a hotel overseas or many other locations. Despite lack of physical proximity to each other, workers in different locations are able to interact extensively with each other. There are numerous options and forms of teleworking. The most common is working from home but other options enable workers to work from well-equipped hotels, resorts, offices, telecentres and vehicles. All these options involve telework principles whereby a worker is enabled, in various ways but especially through information technology, to work remotely from the central organization (see also p. 244).

There are many examples of successful teleworking as the following three demonstrate.

OB IN ACTION

Teleworking was introduced at the Unity Trust Bank in the UK in 1999. Business development managers based in London and regional offices were given the choice to work from home. The main reason for the introduction of the scheme was to save costs; however, other benefits have been increased productivity and worker satisfaction partly because they are able to determine their own working hours. One teleworker explained that it had benefited her family life in that she could take her children to school in the morning and pick them up in the afternoon which was previously impossible. The scheme has since been extended to other staff.[108]

Malta Telecommunications Agency is the agency responsible for the regulation of the Maltese telecommunications sector. An ad hoc type of teleworking is being used by senior managers and professional staff at the agency because these workers often need to work away from their main office and to save office space.[109]

SAGA Holidays is an international tour operator specializing in holidays for older people. At present, various teleworking activities are in use within the company due to the nature of the work. As employees are constantly dealing with people and requests have to be handled efficiently and effectively, all staff members need access to laptop/notebook computers and mobile phones. This enables them to offer services from wherever they are, avoiding reliance on an office.[110] In all three of these cases, workers report increased satisfaction with work and no desire to return to the traditional office environment.

Further definition is required of those who qualify as remote workers in any statistical count of such workers and data collection must become more accurate. Although teleworking has expanded substantially over the past decade, much of this can be accounted for by the inclusion of sales staff and 'white van men' whose jobs have always taken them on the road but who can now keep in touch with their base using a laptop and mobile phone. Teleworking also tends to be concentrated amongst professional and managerial staff that can be 'trusted' to work from home.[111]

Trying to gain an accurate picture is difficult as surveys differ on who they count as teleworkers. In Europe just over 11% of employees usually or sometimes work from home. While the proportion of employees who usually work from home is higher for women the share of those sometimes working from home is higher for men. The share of home-based teleworking is considerably higher in the original 15 member states (EU15). The highest percentages can be found in the Netherlands, Denmark, France and Sweden. In the Netherlands, 9% of employed people work more than one full day each week in home-based teleworking. Just over half (51%) of teleworkers in the EU15 feel that, without the option to telework from home, they could not do their job as well as they can with telework and 27% would have to reduce their working hours per week.[112]

Teleworkers work in virtual workplaces or offices. In virtual workplaces, productivity can rise substantially as a result of fewer interruptions and a quieter, more focused environment. The virtual office can offer more flexible work schedules, allowing employees to do work when and where they are most productive, whether early in the morning or late in the evening. It also fosters better customer service because virtual workers are constantly in the field in direct contact with their clients.

It is vital to match the right people to remote work. They must have disciplined work habits (or a facility to acquire them) and the knowledge and technical skills to be able to work effectively without supervision. They must also be motivated to continually improve their work skills on their own and to know when to call on outside support. Use of email, Internet and software for work and work meetings is involved. Employees will benefit by saving in commuting time and expense and reducing personal expenditure on lunches, work clothes, laundry and so on. However, they may feel isolated from other employees and the workplace. They may be overlooked for training opportunities and promotions because they do not have a presence in the workplace. Managers and colleagues often do not believe that employees can work effectively at home without being supervised. However survey evidence in the UK showed that teleworkers are more productive and the quality of work had increased.[113] Employees may be expected to work harder to prove the effectiveness of the arrangement and/or because working at home blurred the hours of attending to home and work duties. There can also be an expectation that being at home means workers can work at any time.[114] It can be unclear who should bear the cost of infrastructure for telework in the home (computers, printers, wireless or Internet broadband, air-conditioning, heating, lighting, etc.). It does appear that workers are often not knowledgeable enough to provide adequate data security and that technology failure can be a strong cause for terminating telework arrangements (with inability to download large files being an example of the problems that arise).[115]

OB IN ACTION

Roy Hanrahan, with a background in marine engineering and industrial relations, was able to enjoy the benefits of teleworking when offered a job by Telecom in New Zealand. Roy's role was to help former employees who had been seconded to a contractor to carry out design, building and maintenance work. He was to help them with their grievances, mediations and so forth and to help them decide issues for themselves. As a teleworker, Roy enjoyed being able to wear casual clothes at home. He also had free use of a company car and was required to travel often (and could enjoy his wife's company). He was allocated a desk in the HR section but was not required to attend meetings. Instead of being measured in terms of how many hours he works, Roy is assessed in terms of whether he gets the job done so he can, if he can manage it, work fewer hours and have more time for his own life.[116] Heather Jones, who is a communications manager for IBM, works two days at home and three days at the office. She has been able to maintain the benefits of working in the workplace (collegiate atmosphere and involvement in meetings and social events) but has also been able to be around to watch her 14-month-old child's development (such as when she started walking).[117]

When an employee becomes a teleworker, advantages accrue to the community through the reduction of travel, traffic and pollution, as well as by returning patterns of consumption to local neighbourhoods instead of city centres.[118] For the organization, advantages include increased employee productivity and satisfaction; lower costs in providing office space and parking (providing ICT in the home or elsewhere can be much cheaper) and access to a larger pool of highly skilled workers, many of whom may not be willing to cope with the demands of the traditional office environment (those in carer roles or with a physical disability, for example). The potential business costs and problems may include insurance, security, office safety, remote support and supervision. Insurance issues involving the home office can be complex because responsibilities are not always clear. Others are data confidentiality and security, because employees often have confidential client information in their home office and must be responsible for security and backing up data to the main office's network.[119]

RESEARCH IN OB

Access our Web site **www.wileyeurope.com/ college/french** for an interesting research article by Golden, examining how teleworking impacts on relationships with managers, co-workers and family and how these, in turn, affect job satisfaction. One can anticipate other studies going on to examine similar topics given the importance of this contextual development.

CONCLUSION

The twenty-first century work environment is subject to rapid and significant change. Job design, technological developments and radically altered work patterns such as virtual, remote and teleworking have resulted in new and, for many, exciting ways of organizing our working and nonworking lives.[120] There is considerable pressure on those people who run organizations to facilitate ways of working that both motivate employees and are cost effective. Workers' performance can be seen as strongly related to the context in which they carry out their tasks and roles.

SUMMARY

LEARNING OBJECTIVE 1
Intrinsic motivation

Intrinsic motivation is the desire to work hard solely for the pleasant experience of task accomplishment. It builds upon intrinsic work rewards, or those rewards that an individual receives directly as a result of task performance. They are self-motivating and do not require external reinforcement. Together these can be important components of job design.

LEARNING OBJECTIVE 2
Job design strategies and intrinsic work rewards

In theory, job design involves the planning and specification of job tasks and the work setting in which they are to be accomplished. The manager's responsibility is to fit individual needs with task attributes and the work setting so both performance and human resource maintenance are facilitated. Job design strategies include four broad alternatives. Job simplification standardizes work procedures and employs people in clearly defined and specialized tasks. Job enlargement increases task variety by combining two or more tasks previously assigned to separate workers. Job rotation increases task variety by periodically rotating employees among jobs involving different tasks. Job enrichment builds motivating factors into job content by adding planning and evaluating duties. The intrinsic work rewards made available by these strategies range on a continuum from low (job simplification) to high (job enrichment).

LEARNING OBJECTIVE 3
The job characteristics model and the diagnostic approach to job enrichment

The job characteristics model and the diagnostic approach to job enrichment recognize that not everyone wants an enriched job. Rather, they consider those with high and low growth needs and related concerns. They then look at the effect of five core job characteristics (ranging from skill variety to feedback from the job itself) on intervening critical psychological states that influence motivation, performance and satisfaction. The socio-technical approach to job design is also known as the semi-autonomous work group. The impact and role of technology is viewed as a factor in designing jobs, and steps are taken to optimize the relationship between technology and the social system to which employees belong. The social information-processing model argues that individual needs, task perceptions and reactions are a result of social constructions of reality. Multiskilling promotes the learning of a wide array of skills needed to perform multiple tasks within a company. Employees who are multiskilled are better equipped to shoulder greater responsibilities and to take over when another employee is absent.

LEARNING OBJECTIVE 4
Goal-setting theory and job design

Goal setting is the process of developing, negotiating and formalizing the targets or objectives that an employee is responsible for accomplishing. It includes predictions that link it to job design and that serve as the basis for goal-setting theory. These predictions emphasize challenging and specific goals, knowledge of results, ability, a feeling of self-efficacy to accomplish the goals and goal commitment or acceptance. A managerial technique that applies goal-setting theory is management by objectives (MBO). A manager and subordinate agree on individual goals that are consistent with higher level ones. A process is then implemented to monitor and assist the subordinate in task accomplishment, and the subordinate's performance is evaluated in terms of accomplished results. If implemented well, many positive aspects of goal-setting theory can be realized from MBO but effective MBO systems are difficult to establish and maintain. Key performance indicators provide a benchmark against which employees' goals can be measured.

LEARNING OBJECTIVE 5
Flexible work arrangements

There are a number of flexible work arrangements. The compressed work week allows full-time work to be completed in less than five days. Flexible working hours allow employees a daily choice in timing work and nonwork activities. Job sharing occurs when two or more people divide one full-time job according to an agreement among themselves and the employer. Flexitime, annual hours, job sharing and teleworking are all designed to enable workers to balance the competing demands on their time of work, leisure and education. These flexible work arrangements are becoming more important as a way of obtaining the services of an increasingly diverse workforce requiring a family-friendly workplace in our rapidly changing society. Information and communication technologies have had a significant impact on organizational design. The capabilities of this technology and lessening costs mean that the technology can often be taken with the worker or to the worker. This enables workers to work while travelling to and/or from their homes. Such teleworking allows work to be conducted remotely from the central organization using information technology. These methods have several potential benefits, especially for those with childcare or other care duties, or for those with physical disabilities. For all employees it can involve reductions in employee expenditure on travel to work, lunches and work clothes, as well as saving on time. The potential costs are increased isolation of employees, and poorer communication and knowledge sharing, as well as costs like insurance and establishment of home offices. Data confidentiality and security and local government zoning laws can also present potential problems.

CHAPTER 5 STUDY GUIDE

You can also test your understanding and access further resources at **www.wileyeurope .com/college/french.**

REVIEW QUESTIONS

1. What is the difference between intrinsic rewards and extrinsic rewards?
2. Explain the difference between job enlargement and job enrichment.
3. List and define the core job characteristics.
4. Explain the differences between job sharing and voluntary reduced work time.

APPLICATION QUESTIONS

1. Consider a situation in which you performed a duty for someone – for example, doing an assignment, doing a job for your supervisor or even doing a favour for a friend. List the rewards you obtained from completing the duty. Distinguish between the intrinsic and extrinsic rewards.
2. Assume you are a university lecturer in this subject. You are designing an assignment for students. Consider the assignment design as being a job design. Use the job characteristics model to design an assignment that will maximize the intrinsic motivation for students doing the assignment. Explain the advantages of your assignment design.
3. Think about and explain how much your current 'job' (studying at college or university) involves social information processing. Provide two examples.
4. In view of the listed predictions on goal setting provided in this chapter, how would you set goals for yourself in completing a subject in your course? How do you think your tutor could be involved in this process of goal setting for you?

5. Consider the principles of teleworking. How much of your study requires you to be located at your college or university and how much of it do you undertake remotely? Explain the role that information technology plays in enhancing this process. Discuss, based on your experience as a student, whether you think you would work effectively as a teleworker or telecommuter in the workforce.

6. Think about a job with which you have some familiarity (for example, a bank clerk, shop assistant or your teacher). Explain what advantages or disadvantages you would see for (a) that person, (b) the employer and (c) you as the customer if that person was working flexible hours.

RESEARCH QUESTIONS

1. Many organizations have strongly developed conditions to support workplace flexibility for employees. Find two organizations in your community and investigate what flexible work arrangements they provide for their employees, and evaluate their apparent effectiveness.

2. Hewitt Associates, a global HR outsourcing company, announces each year the 'best employers' list for countries such as China, Hong Kong, India, the Philippines, Malaysia, Singapore, Thailand, Australia and New Zealand – and for Asia in general. In 2004, for Australia and New Zealand, Sales Force topped the list, with Bain International, Cisco Systems, Flight Centre and Seek ranking as highly commended. Analyse the characteristics of these 'best' employers (from your country of interest) in terms of their jobs and job-related practices. (Note that there are other relevant or similar awards, such as *Fortune* magazine's awards for work–life balance.)

RUNNING PROJECT

Try to find the answers to the following questions about your organization:

1. Has the nature of work, including the technology used and/or the formal educational qualifications required for positions at the organization increased over the past 10 years? If so, has there been a corresponding change in job design and rewards? Explain. If not, why have the requirements increased? Do the requirements seem to match the job?

2. What intrinsic rewards do the employees at the organization obtain from their work? If you have direct access to the organization it might be useful to speak directly with the employees.

3. Have any of the four approaches to job design been implemented? What was the outcome?

4. How does the organization set goals for its employees? How does it communicate these goals and assess whether they are being met?

5. Describe any flexible work arrangements the organization offers its employees. Assess the outcomes of these arrangements for both employees and the organization.

INDIVIDUAL ACTIVITY[121]

Job design preference

Instructions

People differ in what they like and dislike about their jobs. Listed below are 12 pairs of jobs. For each pair, indicate which job you would prefer. Assume that everything else about the jobs is the same – pay attention only to the characteristics actually listed for each pair of jobs. If you would prefer the job in column A, indicate how much you would prefer it by putting a check mark in a blank to the left of the neutral point. If you would prefer the job in column B, check one of the blanks to the right of neutral. Check the neutral blank only if you find the two jobs equally attractive or unattractive. Try to use the neutral blank sparingly.

Column A

1. A job that offers little or no challenge.

   Strongly   Neutral   Strongly

2. A job that pays well.

   Strongly   Neutral   Strongly

3. A job that often requires you to make important decisions.

   Strongly   Neutral   Strongly

4. A job with little security in a somewhat unstable organization.

   Strongly   Neutral   Strongly

5. A job in which greater responsibility is given to those who do the best work.

   Strongly   Neutral   Strongly

Column B

A job that requires you to be completely isolated from co-workers.

A job that allows considerable opportunity to be creative and innovative.

A job in which there are many pleasant people to work with.

A job in which you have little or no opportunity to participate in decisions that affect your work.

A job in which greater responsibility is given to loyal employees who have the most seniority.

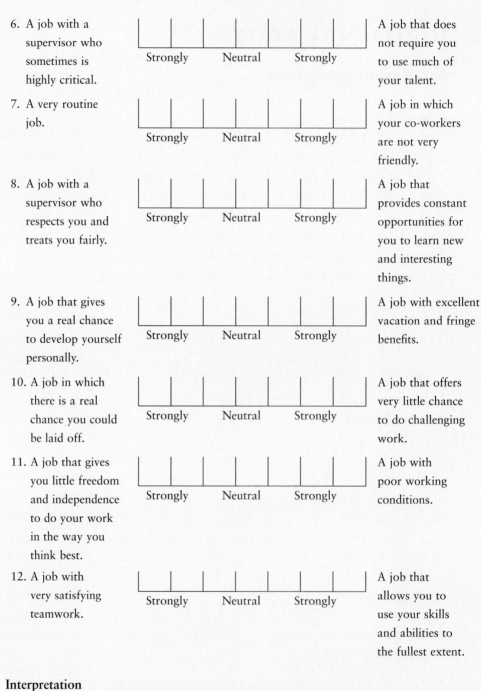

6. A job with a supervisor who sometimes is highly critical.

Strongly   Neutral   Strongly

A job that does not require you to use much of your talent.

7. A very routine job.

Strongly   Neutral   Strongly

A job in which your co-workers are not very friendly.

8. A job with a supervisor who respects you and treats you fairly.

Strongly   Neutral   Strongly

A job that provides constant opportunities for you to learn new and interesting things.

9. A job that gives you a real chance to develop yourself personally.

Strongly   Neutral   Strongly

A job with excellent vacation and fringe benefits.

10. A job in which there is a real chance you could be laid off.

Strongly   Neutral   Strongly

A job that offers very little chance to do challenging work.

11. A job that gives you little freedom and independence to do your work in the way you think best.

Strongly   Neutral   Strongly

A job with poor working conditions.

12. A job with very satisfying teamwork.

Strongly   Neutral   Strongly

A job that allows you to use your skills and abilities to the fullest extent.

Interpretation

People differ in their need for psychological growth at work. This instrument measures the degree to which you seek growth-need satisfaction. Score your responses as follows:

For items 1, 2, 7, 8, 11 and 12 give yourself the following points for each item:

1	2	3	4	5	6	7
Strongly prefer A			Neutral			Strongly prefer B

Add up all of your scores and divide by 12 to find the average. If you score above 4.0, your desire for growth-need satisfaction through work tends to be high and you are likely to prefer an enriched job. If you score below 4.0, your desire for growth-need satisfaction through work tends to be low and you are unlikely to be satisfied or motivated by an enriched job.

For items 3, 4, 5, 6, 9 and 10, give yourself the following points for each item:

7	6	5	4	3	2	1
Strongly prefer A			Neutral			Strongly prefer B

Source: Reprinted by permission from Hickman, J. R. & Oldham, G. R. (1974), *The Job Diagnostic Survey: An Instrument for the Diagnosis of Jobs and the Evaluation of Job Redesign Projects*, technical report 4, Yale University, Department of Administrative Sciences: New Haven, CT.

GROUP ACTIVITY

Aligning personal goals with organizational goals

Objectives
1. To help you develop a framework that will enable you to distinguish between personal goals and organizational goals.
2. To develop an understanding of the 'big picture'.

Total time: 20–30 minutes.

Procedure
1. In the context of your current course, list your personal goals for the course. These could take the form of what you hope to learn from the class, what grade you hope to obtain, or how you plan to apply the lessons you learn to your personal life.
2. Placing yourself in the position of the instructor, list objectives you think he or she would have for this class.
3. Compare your lists from steps 1 and 2 (that is, your personal goals and class objectives). Identify the areas in which the two lists align and those in which they differ. Where there are differences, consider why these differences exist.
4. In groups of three or four, attempt to map out the big picture – that is, the goals of the class – and suggest how you can align your personal goals with this big picture.

Case Study

TELEWORKING AT BRITISH TELECOM

British Telecom (BT) is one of the largest employers of 'flexible workers' in the UK. Nearly 2 000 teleworkers at BT were surveyed as part of a EU wide project on sustainable working. Perhaps the most striking finding from this survey was that a large majority of the respondents say they work longer hours than they did in their office-bound existence. Yet they also say their quality of life has improved. In some cases this can equate to more than 15 extra hours per week and many say that they work from home when they would be too ill to go into the office.

The profile of the respondents to the survey follow that typically found in the UK of middle aged men in managerial or sales jobs. They work largely from home or spilt their time between home, BT offices and clients premises. Only 8 % still have a main office and only 1 % a dedicated office desk.

British Telecom has particularly encouraged middle management and above to work remotely because they tend to be motivated, are able to organize their work and are not paid overtime. For the managers themselves 77 % said that they choose to do so because they had more flexibility about when and where they worked. It also appears that they get more work done because the home is quieter than the office. 'I'd forgotten what it was like to read documents without my fingers in my ears', said one respondent who had previously worked in an open-plan office.

Improved quality of life is one of the key benefits with teleworkers no longer being out of the house for over 12 hours per day they can also combine work with doing the shopping or ironing or taking children to school. This leaves them with more 'quality time' in the evening and at weekends and less stress in their relationship. Some say that their female partners have been able to return to work as a result. 'I can hand out the washing and prepare the evening meal when I finish work', says one worker. The downside to this can be lack of social interaction and knowledge exchange with fellow workers as well as the feeling of isolation and the fear that not being seen in the office will hinder future advancement.

Questions

1. Why do you think that teleworkers report greater satisfaction with work despite working longer hours?
2. Would you accept a home-based job on graduation? What are your reasons for your choice?
3. Consider an office based job with which you are familiar. How would this need to be redesigned in order to allow the job occupant to work remotely?
4. What issues exist for the organization in managing the remote worker and how can they be addressed effectively?

Source: Adapted from Maitland, A. (2002), Inside track: a long day at home, *Financial Times*, 21 October and EU's Sustel project Web site, **www.sustel.org.**

SUGGESTED READING

It is useful to recognize that topics contained in this chapter can be viewed from the perspective of human resource management (HRM) as well as from an OB vantage point. Look at relevant sections of the following book for an HRM treatment of the issue of flexibility at work:

Harris, L. (2003), Home-based Teleworking and the Employment Relationship: Managerial Challenges and Dilemmas. *Personnel Review*, **32** (4), 422-437.

This journal article points to a range of practical implications when introducing teleworking, and highlights the need for effective managerial interventions.

Pilbeam, S. & Corbridge, M. (2006), *People Resourcing Contemporary HRM in Practice*, 3rd edn, FT Prentice Hall: Harlow.

END NOTES

1. Aldag, R.J. & Brief, A.P. (1977), The intrinsic-extrinsic dichotomy: toward conceptual clarity, *Academy of Management Review*, **2**, 497–498.

2. See Tosi, H.L., Rizzo, J.R. & Carroll, S.J. (1990), *Managing Organizational Behaviour*, 2nd edn. Harper & Row: New York, Ch. 8.

3. Garg, P. & Renu, R. (2006), New model of job design: motivating employees' performance. *Journal of Management Development*, **25** (6), 572–587.

4. Based on an example presented in Lawler, E.E. III (1973), *Motivation in Work Organizations*. Brooks/Cole: Monterey, CA, pp. 154–155.

5. Eriksson, T. & Ortega, J. (2006), The adoption of job rotation: testing theories, *Industrial and Labour Relations Review*, **59** (4), 653–666.

6. *Hong Kong Standard*, August 1990, p. 6.

7. Kone China, 'Careers – working at Kone', www.kone.com (viewed 9 January 2006); Standard Chartered, 'Careers – building your career' (2006), www.standardchartered.cn/career/byc_tra.html (viewed 9 January 2006); Schering China, 'Career – FAQs', www.schering.com.cn (viewed 9 January 2006).

8. Herzberg, F. (1968), One more time: how do you motivate employees? *Harvard Business Review*, **46** (January/February), 53–62.

9. See Hackman, J.R. (1975) On the coming demise of job enrichment, in *Man and Work in Society*, (eds E.L. Cass & F.G. Zimmer), Van Nostrand: New York.

10. See Hulin, C.L. and Blood, M.R. (1968), Job enlargement, individual differences, and worker responses, *Psychological Bulletin*, **69**, 41–55. Blood, M.R. & Hulin, C.L. (1967), Alienation, environmental characteristics and worker responses, *Journal of Applied Psychology*, **51**, 284–290. Turner, A.N. & Lawrence, P.R. (1965), *Industrial Jobs and the Worker: An Investigation of Responses to Task Attributes*, Harvard Graduate School of Business Administration: Boston, MA.

11. For a complete description and review of the research, see Hackman, J.R. & Oldham, G.R. (1980), *Work Redesign*. Addison-Wesley: Reading, MA.

12. See Hackman, J.R., Oldham, G., Janson, R. & Purdy, K. (1975), A new strategy for job enrichment. *California Management Review*, **17** (4), 60.

13. See discussion on research into job design moderators in Luthans, E. (1985), *Organizational Behaviour*. McGraw-Hill: New York.

14. *Foreign Labour in the United Kingdom: Patterns and Trends* (2001), Labour Market Trends.

15. Maiden, M. (2005), Banks want to do the mess for less', *Sydney Morning Herald*, Business and Money section, 5–6 February, p. 46.

16. Wusterman, L.A. (2005), A Passage to India; off-shoring in financial services, *IRS Employment Review*, Issue 831.

17. Berry, M. (2005), Employees sure to walk out if opportunity doesn't knock. *Personnel Today*, 19 April.

18. Rance, C. (2005), The long march. *HR Monthly*, April, 22–29.

19. Brain drain likely as baby boomers near retirement, *Personnel Today*, 4 October 2006.

20. *Britain's Hidden Brain Drain*, (2005), Equal Opportunities Commission: Landon.

21. Van der Vegt, G., Emms, B. & Van de Vliert, E. (1998), Motivating effect of task and outcome interdependence in work teams. *Group and Organisation Management*, 23 (2), 124–143.

22. Lee-Ross, D. (1998), A practical theory of motivation applied to hotels. *International Journal of Contemporary Hospitality Management*, 10 (3).

23. See Hackman, J.R. and Oldham, G. (1975), Development of the job diagnostic survey. *Journal of Applied Psychology*, 60, 159–170.

24. European Foundation for the Improvement of Living and Working Conditions, (2005), Fourth European Working Conditions Survey, www.eurofound.europa.eu.

25. Graduates not in the real world. *HR Monthly*, December 2004–January 2005, p. 7.

26. European Foundation for the Improvement of Living and working Conditions, (2005), op. cit.

27. Langford, P. & Parkes, L. (2005), Debunking the myths around work–life balance. *Human Resources*, 3 May, p. 14.

28. See Salancik, G. & Pfeffer, J. (1977), An examination of need–satisfaction models of job attitudes. *Administrative Science Quarterly*, 22, 427–456. Salancik, G. & Pfeffer, J. (1978), A social information processing approach to job attitude and task design. *Administrative Science Quarterly*, 23, 224–253.

29. Adapted from Marriot Hotel wins Excellence Through People Award. *Personnel Today*, (2001), 13 November.

30. Byrne, C. (2005), Getting to know me! *Management Woman*, April, p. 21.

31. Locke, E.A., Shaw, K.N., Saari, L.M. & Latham, G.P. (1981), Goal setting and task performance: 1969–1980. *Psychological Bulletin*, 90 (July/November), 125–152. See also Latham, G.P. & Locke, E.A. (1979), Goal setting – a motivational technique that works. *Organizational Dynamics*, 8 (Autumn), 68–80. Latham, G.P. & Steele, T.P. (1983) The motivational effects of participation versus goal-setting on performance. *Academy of Management Journal*, 26, 406–417. Erez, M. & Kanfer, F.H. (1983), The role of goal acceptance in goal setting and task performance. *Academy of Management Review*, 8, 454–463.

32. Ibid.

33. See Locke, E.A. & Latham, G.P. (1990), Work motivation and satisfaction: light at the end of the tunnel. *Psychological Science*, 1 (4) (July), 240–246.

34. Ibid.

35. Ibid.

36. For a complete review of goal-setting theory and research see Locke, E.A. & Latham, G.P. (1990), *A Theory of Goal Setting and Task Performance*. Prentice Hall: Englewood Cliffs, NJ.

37. See Locke, E.A. & Latham, G.P. (1990), Work motivation and satisfaction. *Psychological Science*, July, p. 241.

38. Ibid., pp. 240–246.

39. Schuster, F. & Kendall, K. (1974), Where we stand – a survey of Fortune 500. *Human Resources Management*, Spring, pp. 8–11.

40. For a good review of MBO, see Raia, A.P. (1974), *Managing by Objective*, Scott Foresman: Glenview, IL. The criticisms are summarized well in Kerr, S. (1976), Overcoming the dysfunctions of MBO. *Management by Objectives*, 5 (1).

41. Pinder, C.C. (1984), *Work Motivation Theory, Issues, and Applications*, Scott Foresman: Dallas, TX, p. 169.

42. Based on Cypress Semiconductor Corporation, *Harvard Business Review* (July/August 1990), pp. 88–9.

43. Investors in People UK (2006), see www.investorsinpeople.co.uk.

44. Roberts, P. (1998), Sharing the secrets of success. *Australian Financial Review*, 3 July, p. 42.

45. Moodie, A.-M. (1998), Career surfing now the new wave. *Australian Financial Review*, 22 May, p. 58.

46. Australian Maritime Museum, 'Strategic plan 2003–2006', www.anmm.gov.au/stratplan.htm.

47. EU Directive 1995, cited in Hardy, S. and Adnett, N. (2002), The parental leave directive; towards a family friendly social Europe? *European Journal of Industrial Relations,* **8** (2), 157–172.

48. Work–life Balance – Changing Patterns in a Changing World, (2000), DfEE: London.

49. The Work and Age Trust, 'Flexible employment', www.eeotrust.org.nz/worklife/flex_employment.shtml, p. 6.

50. Foster, C. (2005), Tackling the long-hours culture, *Equal Opportunities Review,* 1 April.

51. Wells, J. (2004), *Just Rewards,* Allen & Unwin: Sydney, p. 37.

52. Arnold, J., Cooper, C.L. & Robertson, I.T. (2004), *Work Psychology: Understanding Human Behaviour in the Workplace,* 5th edn, FT Prentice Hall: Harlow.

53. DfEE, (2000), *Work–life Balance; Results from the Baseline Survey,* HMSO: London.

54. CIPD Survey (2000), *Married to the Job,* CIPD: London.

55. Stress is becoming the biggest problem in European companies. *Financial Times,* 8 May 2000.

56. European Foundation for the Improvement of Living and Working Conditions (2001), *Third European Survey on Working Conditions,* EU0101292F. Cox, T., Griffiths, A. & Rial-Gonzalez, E. (2000), *Research on Work-related Stress.* Armstrong, J. (2001), *Workplace Stress in Ireland,* ICTU.

57. Wood, J. & Duffie, J. (1982), Sabbatical: a strategy for creating jobs. *New Ways to Work Newsletter,* **2** (1), 5–6. Wood, J. & Duffie, J. (1982), Sabbatical: a strategy for creating jobs (part II). *New Ways to Work Newsletter,* **2** (2–3), 5–6.

58. European Foundation for the Improvement of Living and Working Conditions (2007), *Annual Review of Working Conditions in Europe 2006–7.* European Foundation for the Improvement of Living and Working Conditions.

59. See www.eurofound.europa.eu/.

60. Eurostat (2006), *Statistics in Focus: Population and Social Conditions 2006.*

61. European Industrial Relations Review (2006), *Report seeks to encourage flexible working,* Issue 384/1/1.

62. Kersley, B., Alpin, C., Forth, J. *et al.* (2006), Inside the Workplace Findings from the 2004 Workplace Employment Relations Survey, Routledge: London.

63. 'Flexible working a top priority for UK workers', press release, 3 October 2005, www.manpower.co.uk. Chartered Institute of Personnel and Development, (2005), *Tackling Age Discrimination in the Workplace,* October. CIPD: London.

64. IRS Employment Review (2005), *Extending Working Life,* Issue 838.

65. *IRS Management Review* (2001), Employing Older Workers; The Practice, Issue 21.

66. European Foundation for the Improvement of Working Conditions, (2007), www.eurofound.europa.eu/.

67. Foster, C. (2004), ASDA–valuing the over 50s. *Equal Opportunities Review,* Issue 34, n.p.

68. Achmea, The Netherlands. 'Flexible working practices, training and development, health and well-being exit policy', www.eurofound.europa.eu/areas/populationandsociety/cases/.

69. Nilles, J. (1976), *The Telecommunications-transportation Tradeoff: Options for Tomorrow,* John Wiley & Sons: New York.

70. Hardy, S. & Adnett, N. (2002), The parental leave directive; towards a family friendly social Europe? *European Journal of Industrial Relations,* **8** (2), 157–172.

71. DfEE (2000), *Work–life Balance – changing Patterns in a Changing World,* HMSO: London.

72. *IRS Employment Review* (2002), The way we work now, Issue 755.

73. Bayer's staff free to choose own working hours, *Personnel Today,* 28 May, 2006.

74. Latack, J.C. & Foster, L.W. (1985), Implementation of compressed work schedules: participation and job redesign as critical factors for employee acceptance. *Personnel Psychology,* **38**, 75–92.

75. Cohen, A.R. & Gadon, H. (1978), Alternative Work Schedules: Integrating Individual and Organizational Needs. Addison-Wesley: Reading, MA, pp. 38–46. See also Pearce, J.L.

& Newstrom, J.W. (1980), Toward a conceptual clarification of employee responses to flexible working hours: a work adjustment approach. *Journal of Management*, **6**, 117–134.

76. Wood, J. (1977), *Altered Work Week Study*, unpublished PhD thesis, Department of Educational Administration, University of Alberta, Canada.

77. Report for the European Foundation for the Improvement of Living and Working Conditions, (2007), *Annualized hours in Europe*. European Foundation for the Improvement of Living and Working Conditions: Dublin.

78. Danish Employers' Federation, Danish *Arbeydsgiverforening*.

79. Confederation of Finnish Industry, *Teollusus y a tyon*.

80. Incomes Data Services Report (2004), *Annual Hours*, February.

81. *The way we work now*, Issue 755 (2002), IRS Employment Review.

82. IRS Management Review (1998), *Variable-hours Schemes*, Issue 9.

83. www.smart-workforce.com.

84. Whittam, J. & White, K. (2005), Managing working time: annual hours, *Personnel Today Management Resources One Stop Guide*, 1 October. IRS Management Review (2005), *Variable-hours Schemes*, Issue 9.

85. Ibid.

86. Wood, J. & Wattus, G. (1987), The attitudes of professionals towards job sharing, *Australian Journal of Management*, **12** (2), 103–121.

87. IRS Employment Trends (1998), *Two heads are better than one: a survey of job sharing*, Issue 661.

88. Ibid.

89. Job shares can mean two brains for the price of one. *Management Today*, August 1998, p. 10.

90. Adler, R. (2006), Beware the risks of job sharing, *Personnel Today*, 28 February.

91. Pilbeam, S. & Corbridge, M. (2006), *People Resourcing: HRM in Practice*, 3rd edn, FT Prentice Hall: Harlow.

92. France aims to make job sharing work, *The Australian*, 23 August 1996.

93. Parent-Thirion, A., Fernández Macías, E., Hurley, J. & Vermeylen, G. (2005) *Fourth Euroean Working Conditions Survey*. European foundation for the improvement of living and working conditions: Dublin.

94. Brewster, C., Mayne, L. & Tregaskis, O. (1997), Flexible working in Europe, *Journal of World Business*, **32** (2), 133–151.

95. Doyle, J & Reeves, R. (2003), *Time Out, The Case for Time Sovereignty*, The Work Foundation: London.

96. *Challenging Times: Flexibility and Flexible Working in the UK* (2006), Trade Union Congress: London.

97. Ibid

98. *Working outside the box*, Equal Opportunities Commission report, 2007.

99. Equal Opportunities Commision (2005), Flexible working for all should be the norm, *Equal Opportunities Review*, IRS Issue 146, 1 October.

100. Pearce, J.L., Newstrom, J.W., Dunham, R.B & Barber, A.E. (1989), *Alternative Work Schedules*, Allyn & Bacon: Boston.

101. *Working outside the box*, Equal Opportunities Commission report, 2007.

102. *Challenging Times: Flexibility and Flexible Working in the UK* (2006), Trade Union Congress: London.

103. CIPD report (2002), *Work, Parenting and Careers*, CIPD: London.

104. Department of Trade and Industry (2005), *More People Want Flexible Hours than Cash, Company Car or Gym*. DTI: London.

105. See www.tescocorporate.com.

106. Pidd, H. (2007), Woman BA pilot wins flexible working flight. *Guardian*, 10 March.

107. Gray, M., Hodson, N. & Gordon, G. (1993), *Teleworking Explained*, John Wiley & Sons: New York.

108. McIlroy, R. (2001), 'Teleworking in action at Unity Trust Bank', www.Eurofound.europa.eu/.

109. Ibid.

110. Ibid.

111. Crail, M. (2006), Teleworking: where reality and urban myth collide, *IRS Employment Review*, issue 80, 1 December.

112. Third European Working Conditions survey (2003), *European Foundation for the Improvement of Living and Working Conditions*: Dublin.

113. Crail, M. (2006), Teleworking: where reality and urban myth collide, *IRS Employment Review*, issue 80, 1 December.

114. Australian Telework Advisory Committee (ATAC) (2005), *Telework in Australia*, (II), March, pp. 17–18.

115. Ibid., pp. 19–20.

116. 'Flexible employment', www.eeotrust. org.nz/.

117. Long, C. (2004), No workplace like home, *Sydney Morning Herald*, 30 October.

118. 'Telework New Zealand, alternatives and choices', www.telework.co.nz/Alternatives.htm.

119. Kepczyk, R.H. (1999), Evaluating the virtual office, *Ohio CPA Journal*, **58** (2), 16–17.

120. Third European Working Conditions survey (2003), *European Foundation for the Improvement of Living and Working Conditions*.

121. Hackman, J.R. and Oldham, E.R., The job diagnostic survey: as instrument for the diagnosis of jobs and the evaluation of job redesign projects; technical report 4, New Haven, CT, Yale University Dept. of Administrative Sciences and Hackman, J.R. and Oldham, E.R. (1975), Development of the Job, Diagnostic Survey: *Journal of Applied Psychology*, **60**:159–70. Reprinted by permission.

Journal Article

REDUCING ACCIDENTS USING A BEHAVIOURAL APPROACH

Peter J. Makin and Valerie J. Sutherland

Despite the evident success of behavioural approaches to various organizational problems (see Luthans and Martinko, 1987), in a number of different contexts (Walsh *et al.*, 1993), it remains, in the authors' opinion, under-utilized. One reason for this possible under-utilization is suggested by attribution theory. This theory describes the way people assign causality for events, whether they be safety-related or more general. In particular, it is concerned with explanations for peoples' behaviour, and how people attribute the causes for such behaviour.

ATTRIBUTION THEORY

When we seek to understand why individuals behave the way they do, there are two major types of explanation that people use. Behaviour can be perceived as being caused by factors that are either *internal* or *external* to the individual. Internal factors are those that can be seen as being "within" the individual. Examples include things such as personality traits, attitudes, and moods. In fact, the original title for these factors was "dispositional". An explanation of a person's behaviour using an internal attribution would see the behaviour as being caused by, for example, their negligence, or them being foolhardy, or even "accident-prone". External factors, on the other hand, are those that are part of the external "situation". Behaviour that is perceived as being caused "externally" would place emphasis on the individual reacting to events in the environment, rather than being driven by their personality or attitudes. For example, many people explain any mistakes they make while driving, on the situation – "the road signs were inadequate", rather than their own carelessness – "I wasn't paying attention".

How people make such attributions, and the factors that influence the attributions they make, is a complex process (see Hewstone, 1989). However, there do appear to be certain "biases" which predispose people towards the making of certain attributions. The example given above concerning the attributions for driving errors, highlights a very common "bias". When asked to describe the causes for their own behaviour people are more likely to provide an explanation in terms of them reacting to the situation. As evidence for the validity of this explanation, individuals will often point out that other people, as well as themselves, regularly undertake this pattern of behaviour. The reason for using the behaviour of others as evidence for an external cause is simple. If most people, despite their differing personalities and attitudes, behave the same way in the same situation, then the cause is likely to be external.

The "actors" in a situation are likely to attribute external factors as influencing their behaviour, especially when that behaviour is seen as being undesirable. Outside observers, on the other hand, also seeking to explain the same behaviour are more likely to suggest an internal explanation, such as "carelessness".

This common bias has been called, by some psychologists, the "Fundamental Attribution Error" (Nisbett and Ross, 1980). Put simply, there is a strong tendency for people to underestimate the effects of the situation when seeking to explain the behaviour of others (but not themselves). (It is interesting that this bias appears to have some cultural determinants. It is more pronounced in the highly individualistic Western societies, with their emphasis on personal responsibility.)

Applied to safety, the fundamental attribution error manifests itself in a tendency to seek explanations that emphasize individual responsibility, rather than situational variables, as the prime cause of accidents. The role of "situational" determinants is correspondingly down-played. This tendency is further strengthened by organizational and legal pressures. If a particular individual can be held personally responsible for an accident, e.g. they were "negligent or careless", the organization and its safety systems are absolved of any blame (Makin and Sutherland, 1991).

This desire, to blame a person rather than the situation, is apparent after disasters. When the official reports into, for example, the sinking of *The Herald of Free Enterprise* or *The Marchioness*, were published it was interesting to note the reaction of the victims' relatives. In each case there was a chorus of complaints to the effect that the reports were inadequate, linked with a demand that "someone" be identified whose actions "caused" the disaster.

Recognizing this natural tendency to underestimate the power of the situation to influence behaviour, the behavioural approach to safety adopts a predominantly *external* approach to the causes and cures of accidents. It places a major emphasis on those factors in the situation that either encourage or discourage behaviour that is likely to lead to accidents. It correspondingly places far less emphasis on internal factors such as personality or attitudes as determinants of behaviour. This may be summed up as follows:

Proposition 1: When seeking to explain and change behaviour, concentrate on the situation, and the behaviour it encourages, rather than the personality or attitudes of the people involved.

A BEHAVIOURAL APPROACH TO THE CAUSES OF ACCIDENTS

In seeking to explain the cause of accidents in terms of situational factors, the behavioural approach draws on the body of psychological theory known as *Organizational Behaviour Modification*, (OBMod for short: (see Luthans and Kreitner, 1985)). Like most theories its details are fairly complex, but the basic principle is easily understood. Indeed, it might even be called "common sense". Put simply, if a particular pattern of behaviour is rewarded, it will occur more often. If it is punished, it will occur less frequently. Unfortunately these simple "common sense" facts are often overlooked by organizations.

Accidents continue to happen, despite the expressed desire of management to reduce them. One possible reason, we believe, lies in the way that company policies influence the way people behave. Despite the best of possible motives the system of rewards often encourages the very behaviour that management would like to discourage. The authors have numerous examples, from their own experiences, of organizations doing precisely this. A common example is the allocation of annual budgets within organizations. Most organizations urge all their departments to be as efficient as possible and to save money. If, at the end of the financial year, an efficient department has heeded this advice and is under-spent on its budget what happens? In our experience the surplus is often clawed back by the financial administrators and the following year's budget is cut. The department has been punished for doing precisely what was asked of it! A more subtle mistake occurs when organizations reward the achievement of "ultimate objectives" without taking into account the behaviour required to reach those objectives. In doing so they sometimes inadvertently reward behaviour that is incompatible with the objective. What needs to be rewarded is the behaviour required to achieve specific goals. This distinction can be illustrated with an example which, we believe, has parallels with what happens in industry. Some time ago the international health organizations undertook a concerted campaign to eradicate smallpox. Most cases of the disease occurred in the "third world" and the "front line troops" for the campaign were health visitors. Each of these had a geographical area for which they were responsible. In order to motivate the health visitors a bonus scheme was introduced. Arguing that the final objective was the eradication of smallpox, a scheme was devised whereby each visitor was rewarded according to the absence of smallpox in their area. However, although the visitors consistently earned good bonuses, smallpox remained endemic. When considered from the health visitors' perspective the reasons for this apparently paradoxical situation becomes clear. If you are rewarded for the lack of cases, the incentive is to turn a blind eye. When in doubt don't report! The system is obviously open to abuse. Management finally realized this potential for abuse, and the reward system was turned on its head. Instead of being rewarded for the *absence* of cases, visitors were now rewarded for *finding* cases. The results were dramatic, undiscovered cases now came to the attention of the authorities and could therefore be treated. As is well known, smallpox is now considered to be completely eradicated. However, we doubt if this would have been the case had the original reward system not been changed.

We believe that the same sort of well-intentioned error is happening in many organizations, particularly in relation to safety. Companies are, quite rightly, put under pressure from regulatory authorities to reduce accidents. The most common measure of this is "lost-time accident free periods". While this is laudable as an ultimate objective, it is not, we believe, where the emphasis should be placed. As a result of the use of this measure, the goal on the shop floor becomes "report as few accidents as possible". The pressure is on workers to turn a blind eye to minor accidents, and especially near accidents. Even the reporting of fairly serious injuries may be discouraged. This pressure is intensified by the common practice of rewarding such accident free periods. In the case of a minor incident (or a potentially major incident that fortunately came to nothing), all the pressures are towards influencing the worker not to report.

We believe there are two conclusions that can be drawn from the examples given above.

First, ensure that the organizational systems are not, inadvertently, rewarding the very behaviour they are seeking to discourage, and vice versa.

Second, and perhaps most importantly:

Proposition 2: Concentrate on specific, observable behaviour, and not ultimate objectives.

"Traditional" approaches to safety often, as we have seen, try to encourage the goal of accident reduction. The behavioural approach concentrates on encouraging safe behaviour. This should then lead naturally to a reduction in accidents. Organizations often believe that they do indeed encourage the desirable behaviour (i.e. a good accident record) but, as we have argued above, this is often counter-productive. The behaviour that needs to be encouraged should be very specific, e.g. the wearing of hard hats, safety footwear etc. Individual managers, charged with the responsibility for ensuring good safety practices, often use discipline and punishment for non-compliance, rather than rewarding compliance. Managers rarely congratulate individuals for wearing their hard hat, but rather punish those who do not.

Unfortunately for managers (and perhaps society in general), the ways in which rewards and punishment influence behaviour are not the same. For rewards to be effective in maintaining behaviour they need occur only every so often. (Think of the fruit machine as an example.) Punishment, on the other hand, has to fulfil two criteria if it is to be effective. It must occur *every time* the behaviour occurs, and *as soon as possible* after the behaviour. This may help us understand why hangovers rarely have a long-term influence over drinking. The rewards of drinking to excess are immediate, while the punishing hangover is somewhere in the future. In addition, you may sometimes escape without having a hangover. (Interestingly, one way of treating alcoholics is to use drugs that produce an unpleasant effect immediately any alcohol is consumed.) In the context of safety, many behaviours can be identified where the punishment is perceived as being either so improbable, or so remote, that it has little effect on behaviour. The potential loss of hearing caused by the failure to wear ear defenders does little to influence their usage, especially among younger workers, to whom the effects are so remote as to be almost unimaginable (Zohar and Fussfield, 1981).

It should be apparent that the conditions for using punishment or discipline effectively are very limited. Managers and other individuals with responsibility for enforcement are rarely in a position where they can monitor people all the time. The difficulties associated with the effective use of punishment lead us, therefore, to:

Proposition 3: Schemes should concentrate on the encouragement of desirable behaviour rather than trying to use discipline to eliminate the undesirable.

Combining the three propositions outlined above leads us to an approach to safety that may be summed up as:

> The modification of situational factors in the work-place so as to encourage specific behaviours that are related to safe working practices.

This approach was implemented in a factory manufacturing cellophane.

BEHAVIOURAL "INTERVENTION"

The production process ran on a continuous shift system which operated on a 10-day cycle. The factory had a workforce of approximately 550. Although the majority of these were in the "core" production process they were supported by various maintenance and administrative functions. These included "blue collar" departments such as engineering maintenance, and "white collar" departments, predominantly offices. With one minor exception, the study involved all the organization's employees on site.

The organization had a continuing and active commitment to safety. The site had a full-time safety officer and had, since 1964, an active safety committee which included both shop-floor and management representatives. At senior management level the chief executive of the site, who had recently been appointed, was committed to improving safety. The organization had an on-site surgery staffed during the day by a nurse. At night cover was provided by trained first-aiders. The company's commitment to safety was perhaps best illustrated by the fact that all management meetings within the organization, at whatever level, started with safety as the first item on the agenda. In addition, the company was a subsidiary of a large multi-national organization with a main board director with responsibility for safety. Long-term safety targets were set for each subsidiary company and heavy financial penalties were levied for accidents, especially those resulting in lost time.

In the past, efforts to improve safety had been reactive, rather than proactive, involving correcting dangerous situations after accidents. These approaches had, over a period of some years, led to an overall 10 per cent year-on-year reduction in accidents. Indeed, at the time of the commencement of the behavioural approach approximately three months had passed since the last "lost time accident", and the workforce had received portable fire extinguishers in recognition of this achievement. Despite all its efforts, however, the organization had reached a base level of minor accidents, below which it was proving difficult to drop further. New safety campaigns produced some reduction in accidents, but these were not being maintained.

IMPLEMENTATION

The first step in implementing a behavioural approach requires the identification of the specific behaviours that are to be encouraged. This information was gained largely from two sources. First, an analysis was carried out of all accident records for the past two years. The second source of information was indepth, semi-structured interviews, averaging half an hour in length, with a random sample of approximately 15 per cent of the workforce.

It is generally accepted that many minor accidents go unreported and it was thought that these interviews would help in discovering such behaviours.

From these interviews, together with the data from the accident record, a checklist was constructed for each department, comprising those behaviours most commonly associated with accidents. Examples of these behaviours included "goggles worn when using nail gun", "cut-resistant gloves worn when cutting" and "long gloves must be used when recovering viscose from acid". Each of these became a checklist item. Many were related to the use of PPE (Personal Protective Equipment). These checklists were then refined, using the managers in each of the departments who were asked for feedback on the appropriateness of each of the items. In addition, the departmental safety committees also aided in this refinement.

A member of each department within the factory was then trained to act as an observer, using the checklist. Further refinement of the checklists was undertaken in the light of the experiences of these observers. The observers were asked to undertake, at random times during the shift, at least one survey of their own department using the checklist. Each checklist item was scored as to the number of times safe or unsafe behaviour was observed. These were the only figures recorded. The employees were assured that no names would be recorded. In line with the policy of rewarding desirable, rather than punishing undesirable behaviour, it was stressed that no disciplinary action would follow from the results of these observations. The checklists took, on average, about 10 minutes to complete. The observers used the checklists for a minimum of four weeks, both to establish a baseline, and to allow both observers and the observed to become familiar with the procedure.

Having identified the specific behaviours, the next step was to identify methods of encouraging checklist related behaviours. In other studies encouragement has been through the use of tangible rewards, such as money or time off work, which have been shown to influence behaviour. However, some of the most powerful rewards are those that occur naturally. For example, there is considerable evidence to show that the achievement of self-set goals has a highly motivating effect. In order for this to happen, however, individuals must be given feedback as to their level of performance. It was decided that this procedure, of goal setting plus feedback, would be used.

During the period in which the baselines were being measured display boards were produced for each of the eight departments, and an enlarged copy of the relevant checklist was publicly displayed in each department. At the end of the four-week period the baseline data were entered on the board in graphical form. (The data were presented in a format which presented the number of safe behaviours as a percentage of total observed behaviours.) Each shift in each department then attended a "goal setting" meeting at which the purpose and philosophy of the approach was explained. Particular emphasis was placed on the fact that no individual worker could be identified in the behavioural observations, and that no disciplinary action would follow as a result of the observations. The results of the baseline observations were then presented and each group was asked to agree on a target that was "difficult yet achievable" for improvement in safety behaviours. The goals for different shifts in the same department were averaged and the result entered as a solid line on each of the boards.

Following the goal setting meetings the boards were placed in display positions in the respective departments. Observations were continued at the same rate as that during the baseline period and the results were plotted on the boards every Friday. Observations and plotting was carried out for 16 weeks. At the end of this 16-week block new observers were trained and new checklists developed. Behaviours that were reaching 100 per cent safety were removed and new behaviours substituted.

RESULTS

Following the introduction of the scheme there was an immediate and dramatic reduction in the level of accidents, to a figure less than half that of the same period in the previous year. For the 16-week period prior to the introduction of the scheme there were 142 accidents reported. In the 16 weeks of the intervention phase this was reduced to 64. The decline has continued since that time. During the fifth block of 16 weeks there were 46 accidents. The figures for lost time accidents has also continued to fall. In the year prior to the introduction of the programme there were 22 lost time accidents; for 1993 there were three. The organization is currently training its sixth batch of observers. By the end of that block, therefore, the scheme will have been in place almost two years. It is now part of the organization's culture.

PROBLEMS AND BENEFITS

Practical problems

The major problems encountered were of a practical nature. One of the central tenets of the scheme is that responsibility for safety is devolved to those most affected i.e. the shopfloor workers. This requires that they become involved in the scheme and actively participate, for example in the generation of the checklists and the setting of goals. This participative ethos was somewhat different from the normal systems within the organization, and on occasions this became apparent. For example, the researchers allowed the organization to undertake the recruitment of volunteers for training as observers. When the training started it became apparent that the volunteers had, in fact, been chosen by management and instructed to attend "a training course on safety". None of the volunteers had any information as to what the course entailed. As will be discussed later, the ethos of the scheme differs, in some respects, from the traditional, hierarchical, nature of the organization. This difference means that the consultants needed to retain control, at least initially, over the communication with the workforce of information regarding the scheme.

Organizational problems

The introduction of a new safety scheme, especially one which places a heavy emphasis on shopfloor participation, cannot be done in isolation. Any change of this magnitude will also have effects on the way the organization is managed. The introduction of the scheme becomes, in fact, organizational development. An issue that commonly arises in these circumstances concerns change, particularly resistance to change. So it was in the present study. Resistance was encountered from workers, observers and managers.

There had been a recent history of redundancy, which did not help in establishing trust between the workforce and the consultants. Redundancies had quickly followed their last contact with consultants. Apart from the interviews, the first substantial contact we had was with the potential observers. Despite some early resistance from the potential observers this was not as strong as might have been expected. Given that the volunteers for training as observers were, in fact, conscripts, there were surprisingly few drop-outs from the training course. Of the 48 observers initially trained, only five felt unable to act as such. There was also resistance at middle management levels. However, the resistance here was mostly passive, expressed as a lack of involvement. Although we have no quantitative data to support our view, we suspect that the resistance arose because of a fear of being by-passed. In the authors' experience such feelings are not uncommon in a programme that is attempting to devolve some elements of decision making and control to the workforce. This was especially so for the managers of blue-collar workers. The resistance among the work-force was most forcibly expressed by blue-collar workers during the goal-setting meetings. It was originally intended that the observers would conduct the meetings and that managers would be present to demonstrate their commitment to the programme. In the event many observers felt uncomfortable undertaking such a presentation, and the responsibility fell on the researcher, one of whom was present at each of the meetings. Resistance ranged from passive non-involvement to outright hostility, almost entirely directed at management. This hostility often started with a discussion of unresolved safety issues, quickly broadening out into other areas of criticism. The researchers had to manage these meetings with some tact, allowing time for legitimate grievances to be discussed fully, yet keeping the meeting on track. In the researchers' view there is little doubt that their status as independent "outsiders" assisted this process. It is doubtful if an internal facilitator could have avoided involvement in the debate. Again, although there is no quantitative evidence, the researchers feel that their university affiliation also helped them to be perceived as independent. Throughout the programme it was referred to, by all concerned, as the "UMIST" safety initiative.

Benefits

The most obvious benefit was the reduction in the level of accidents, reported above. However, there were other benefits associated with the scheme.

The introduction of a participative scheme involving the workforce meant that many issues regarding safety that had been ignored re-emerged. For example an accident "near miss" reporting system that had fallen into disuse was resurrected. The reporting system of these near misses was changed slightly. To each report a detachable slip was attached which was returned to the originator of the report to show what action was to be taken as a result of the report and whose responsibility it was. These changes reinforced the message that management had started actively listening to the workforce again, and were acting upon what they heard.

Our impression is also that the climate within the organization improved over the course of the intervention. Shopfloor workers seemed more ready to comment on issues, including those other than safety, and management appeared more willing to listen. More importantly perhaps, they also appeared more ready to act on the information provided by the workforce. The resurrection of the near miss reporting procedure was such an example. It had been moribund for a long time. Management complained that no near misses were reported, the workers that if they reported incidents they were never acted upon.

Perhaps a more tangible expression of the lowered level of resistance was expressed in the second phase of observer training. An essential feature of the programme is that it is intended to be ongoing "in perpetuity". Another feature is that it was intended that eventually everyone in the factory would act as an observer. To this end new observers need to be trained on a regular basis. The training of the second group of observers took place towards the end of the first 16-week "intervention" phase. Although one of the researchers was present during the training, the organization expressed a desire to "fly solo" as soon as possible, and ran this training course themselves. It was noticeable that there were many genuine volunteers for this course, including some managers who wished to become more involved.

CONCLUSIONS

Perhaps the most obvious conclusion is that the behavioural approach has been remarkably successful in reducing accidents. Over a period of slightly more than three months the accident rate was reduced by 55 per cent. It is currently (February 1994) running at 32 per cent of its initial level.

Although the success of the scheme is obvious there are, we believe, other factors that at least contributed to this success and that may be essential if similar schemes are to succeed.

As others have pointed out, the nature of any new programme, whether safety related or otherwise, will interact with, and have an impact on, organizational climate and culture (Zohar and Fussfeld, 1981; Mawhinney, 1992). This will, inevitably, produce changes in the way the organization functions. In our experience at least the initial stages of the change need to be undertaken by independent consultants. Mention has been made of the resistance to the programme and we believe it likely that an "internal change agent" would have been viewed with suspicion. Indeed, there is a danger they would have been sucked into the arguments concerning management actions or inaction.

The organization needs to be aware that the scheme will need a high level of support from all levels of management. Past experience shows that *active* management support, especially at the highest level is essential to ensure success. In the present case the support of the new chief executive was willingly offered, and there is little doubt that his more participative approach helped reinforce that of the programme. He regularly visited the shopfloor to look at the safety boards. In addition, it was his practice to have lunch in the canteen with various shopfloor workers. This open demonstration of approachability undoubtedly influenced the change in climate.

The organization needs to be aware that participation by the workforce in one area of their jobs will inevitably raise expectations regarding participation elsewhere. However, we believe that such changes can only be beneficial.

Evidence for this has been provided in a number of ways. Currently the organization is undertaking a hazard spotting programme and employees are attending work in their own time to undertake this exercise. Signs of this improved employee commitment is also evident elsewhere. The behavioural approach has recently been extended to the area of quality improvement. Although the new work is at a very early stage, the enthusiasm and commitment of the workforce is self-evident and the initial results are extremely encouraging.

Perhaps the major conclusions that can be drawn from our work are, therefore:

- the behavioural approach does work
- in order for it to maintain its efficacy over the longer term, it is essential that there is commitment to the scheme *from the top*, and that the changes produced are absorbed into the organization's culture
- everyone must be involved.

(The early stages of the study reported here were carried out by a team led by the two authors. The authors would like to acknowledge the contributions of the other members of the team, Dominic Cooper and Robin Phillips.)

REFERENCES
The references to go with this article can be found on **www.wileyeurope.com/college/french**

QUESTIONS TO CONSIDER
1. To what extent does the study by Makin and Sutherland confirm principles of behaviour modification? Give reasons for your conclusions.
2. How could a hypothetical problem of university students failing to undertake required reading prior to classes be addressed by applying principles of both behaviour modification and behavioural self-management?

PART 3

MANAGING GROUP DYNAMICS AND TEAM PERFORMANCE

6 Groups and teams

Journal article: Schouteten, R. (2004), Group work in a Dutch home care organization: does it improve the quality of working life? *International Journal of Health Planning and Management*, 19, 179–194.

Groups and teams form a key part of life in work organizations. Most activities taking place within organizations are dependent on coordination and cooperation that can only be achieved by people working together. In the twenty-first century competitive pressures have led to a renewed concern on the part of managers to ensure that groups and teams perform to their full potential. At the same time, psychologists typically point to individuals' social needs; in other words many people seek to become members of groups and gain satisfaction and enjoyment from interacting with other humans. We have devoted an entire part of this book to the topic of groups and teams, which we believe, underlies its importance within OB. There is a strong body of evidence showing that individuals are affected by group membership, often behaving in atypical and surprising ways. Stanley Milgram's work on group conformity showing how many people were willing to administer what they believed to be fatal electric shocks if they thought other group members were also doing so, provides a striking example of this phenomenon. This in itself would justify an extended analysis of group and team working. In contemporary organizations it is moreover, critically important to understand how groups and teams contribute to organizational effectiveness. While their effect is potentially positive, we will also point out the possible negative or dysfunctional aspects of group working.

CHAPTER
6

Groups and teams

LEARNING OBJECTIVES

After studying this chapter you should be able to:

- define groups and teams and understand the differences between them
- understand and explain how effective group and team working can contribute to organizational performance
- define the dynamics and process that occur within groups
- explain the key features of intergroup dynamics and why it is important that managers understand them
- explain the factors that affect team performance and cohesion
- discuss the range of teambuilding activities and approaches
- describe the main types of teams that exist in an organization.

TEAMWORK IN THE FAST LANE

Formula One racing works at a speed and intensity that would leave more conventional businesses absolutely breathless. With only a week separating some of the meetings, there is no time to spare as the vast caravan is loaded into trucks and shipped across the world. For three race meetings – in Brazil, Japan and China – everything from hospitality suites to team workshops has to be air-freighted. As an industry, F1 is remarkable. It is the third most-watched sport in the world after the Olympic Games and World Cup football. In 2003, 162 million television viewers tuned into the races, and each event draws about 212 000 spectators. Team budgets can exceed $300 million (£173 million) with a workforce of 1 000 in the bigger teams. The sums of money involved are dazzling. In 2004 almost half the $1.8 billion revenue that flowed into F1 came from car manufacturers, with Toyota's $170 million the biggest contribution and top drivers such as Michael Schumacher being paid more than $30 million a year.

The pressure is intense. A team's whole reputation and success can turn on a pit stop lasting about seven seconds. A bungled pit stop can make a mockery of all the organizational and engineering talent poured into a successful team. When the replacement wheel flew off Nigel Mansell's Williams in the pit lane a few years ago it cost him the world championship. Managing all this requires distinct skills and organizational ability. But how can they consistently maintain performance in such a competitive, high-pressure environment? F1 teams have to provide achievements in innovation, communications, rapid decision making and leadership that would be of great value to a more conventional business. Mark Jenkins, business strategy professor at Cranfield School of Management, argues that 'this industry encapsulates many of the challenges faced by today's managers across many different types of organization and sector.'

These challenges included more learning and teaching, he said, as well as working with global and virtual teams, managing across boundaries, stepping up innovation and creativity and effective execution of strategy. Combined, these would create sustained levels of performance that competitors would be unable to match. 'There's a lot that business can take away from this,' he added. It was with this in mind that Jenkins with his colleagues Richard West and Ken Pasternak came together to design and deliver a management-development course for the international law firm Freshfields Bruckhaus Deringer. Hugh Crisp, chief executive of Freshfields, said one feature that emerged was the usefulness of F1 techniques in coaching people to learn and adapt quickly. The firm has 2 400 lawyers working from 27 offices in 17 countries and teamwork is very important. 'A lot of people depend on each other', said Crisp.

Each two-day residential course is attended by 20 associates. The programme's emphasis is on evaluating return on capital. The aim is to find out whether it is worthwhile for a company to get involved

Source: Adapted from Eglin, R. (2005), Going flat out for teamwork. *Sunday Times*, 24 July. See also Jenkins, M., Pasternak, K. & West, R. (2005) *Performance at the Limit: Business Lessons from Formula 1 Motor Racing*, Cambridge University Press: Cambridge.

in F1. For one exercise, the young lawyers carried out a full wheel change on a real Ferrari. They had to study a video of a pit stop and work out how they were going to do it. There was some concern that the women among them would find it a bit macho, but they were as enthusiastic as the men. Crisp said they were all amazed at how light the car was. 'The wheels were about a third of the weight of an ordinary car and there was only one nut per wheel.' The parallel between assembling a cooperative group of lawyers and a high-powered F1 team proved very close.

Three-times world champion Sir Jackie Stewart is quoted as saying: 'Formula 1 is entirely teamwork-related.' Another top driver, Jensen Button, said after his first podium place at the Malaysian Grand Prix for BAR-Honda in 2004: 'There was a lot of emotion. Feelings you can't fully explain rush in as you realize you have done something with the team that so many people had worked hard to achieve.' A successful elite motor-racing team has to master all the features that inspire modern management. Without mastery of the 'soft' management features that bring close, informal working relationships all the way from star drivers such as the Schumacher's and Alonso's to the workshop cleaners, the enterprise will not work.

Questions

1. How does team working influence the performance of Formula One teams?
2. In what groups do you participate and how could they benefit from better team working?

INTRODUCTION

Gathering in groups has always been a characteristic of human behaviour. We work in groups in our families, neighbourhoods, communities and educational systems. Individuals seldom, if ever, behave without being influenced by the groups to which they belong. In organizations most activities that take place require some degree of coordination and co-operation that can only be achieved through individuals working together in groups and teams. The workplace in the twenty-first century places great value on change and adaptation. As the Formula One team vignette shows, organizations are continually under pressure to find new ways of operating in the quest for higher productivity, total quality and service, customer satisfaction and better quality of working life. The challenge of remaining competitive in a global market has led to organizations restructuring with flatter structures, wider spans of control and general reductions in the layers of management and increasing empowerment of employees. All of these aspects lead to a greater need for organizations to tap the full potential of groups and teams more creatively as critical organizational resources. There is no doubt that an organization's success depends in a significant part on the performance of its internal networks of groups and teams. To meet competitive demands in challenging environments, the best organizations mobilize groups and teams in many capacities in the quest to reach their full potential as high-performance systems. Most organizational goals cannot be achieved by members working alone (Formula One drivers owe their racing success to their supporting team); thus most employees spend an increasing amount of work time working with others in groups. It is therefore essential that leaders in organizations understand the nature of groups and teams and how to harness the behaviours that will lead to better performance and effectiveness if they are to meet the challenging global business environment that exists today. This chapter will help you understand groups and teams and how they work, how they contribute to effective organizational performance and will provide you with the knowledge and skills to work in and manage groups and teams better.

GROUPS IN ORGANIZATIONS

There is no doubt that groups can be important sources of performance, creativity and enthusiasm for organizations but it takes great leadership to achieve these results consistently. Just putting people together does not guarantee success; the pathways to such success all begin with an understanding of groups in organizations.

WHAT IS AN EFFECTIVE GROUP?

There is no single agreed definition of what constitutes as a group. One of the most popular definitions by Schein defines a group in psychological terms 'as any number of people who interact with one another; are psychologically aware of one another; and perceive themselves to be a group.'[1] Handy puts this more simply 'as any collection of people who perceive themselves as a group.'[2] However neither of these definitions encapsulate *why* people form groups at work, so perhaps a better definition here is that a group is a collection of two or more people who interact with one another regularly to achieve common goals. In a group within this definition, members

A group is a collection of two or more people who interact with each other regularly to achieve common goals.

- are mutually dependent on one another to achieve common goals and
- interact regularly with one another to pursue those goals over a sustained period of time.[3]

Groups are important resources that are good for both organizations and their members. They help organizations to accomplish important tasks. They also help to maintain a high-quality workforce by satisfying needs and expectations of their members. Consultant and management scholar Harold J. Leavitt is a well-known advocate for the power and usefulness of groups.[4] He describes 'hot groups' that thrive in conditions of crisis and competition and whose creativity and innovativeness generate extraordinary returns.[5]

An effective group is one that achieves high levels of task performance, member satisfaction and team viability. With regard to task performance, an effective group achieves its performance goals – in the standard sense of quantity, quality and timeliness of work results. For a formal workgroup, such as a manufacturing team, this may mean meeting daily production targets. For a temporary group, such as a new policy working party, this may involve meeting a deadline for submitting a new organizational policy to the managing director. With regard to member satisfaction, an effective group is one whose members believe that their participation and experiences are positive and meet important personal needs. They are satisfied with their tasks, accomplishments and interpersonal relationships. With regard to team viability, the members of an effective group are sufficiently satisfied to continue working well together on an ongoing basis and/or to look forward to working together again at some future point in time. Such a group has all-important long-term performance potential.

Effective groups are groups that achieve high levels of both task performance and human resource performance.

OB IN ACTION

Marks and Spencer (M&S), one of the UK's leading high street retailers has over 520 stores and employs over 75 000 people. While millions of customers visit M&S stores every week, the company has, nonetheless, expressed a wish to create an ever stronger customer focus. The company's strategy in this regard has involved setting up self-managing teams in order to facilitate a partnership approach to customer service allowing quick response to customer needs. This approach has allowed small teams of staff to make decisions about their area of the store without recourse to senior management. As part of this team approach, the 'it's not my job' syndrome has been discarded with the whole team taking responsibility

for their work. A key element of this has been the ability of teams to roster their own working hours in consultation with line managers to suit both the business and their own needs and expectations, taking full advantage of the company's range of flexible working options. The company assert that this approach has had a positive impact on staff morale and retention and ultimately on business performance.[6]

GROUP SYNERGY AND GROUP ACCOMPLISHMENTS

Synergy *is the creation of a whole that is greater than the sum of its parts.*

When groups are effective, they help organizations accomplish important tasks. In particular, they offer the potential for synergy – the creation of a whole that is greater than the sum of its parts. When synergy occurs, groups accomplish more than the total of their members' individual capabilities. Group synergy is increasingly required in order that organizations become and remain competitive and achieve long-term high performance in the dynamic twenty-first century business environment. There are several benefits that groups can bring to organizations. Groups can have performance advantages over individuals acting alone in three specific situations:[7]

- when there is no clear 'expert' in a particular task or problem
- when problems are complex, requiring a division of labour and the sharing of information
- when creativity and innovation is required because groups tend to make riskier decisions.

Groups are important settings where people learn from one another and share job skills and knowledge. The learning environment and the pool of experience within a group can be used to solve difficult and unique problems as well as develop and share competencies. Groups are also important sources of need satisfaction (discussed in Chapter 4) for their members. Opportunities for social interaction within a group can provide individuals with a sense of security, can provide emotional support for group members in times of special crisis or pressure and can help them experience self-esteem and personal involvement through group working.

At the same time that they have enormous performance potential, however, groups can also have problems. One concern is social loafing, also known as the Ringlemann effect, named after the German psychologist who first popularized the phenomenon. It is the tendency of people to work less hard in a group than they would individually.[8] In Ringlemann's specific example, people were asked to pull on a rope as hard as they could, first alone and then in a group.[9] He found that on average, productivity dropped as more people joined the rope-pulling task. He suggested that people may not work as hard in groups because their individual contributions are less noticeable in the group context and they prefer to see others carry the workload. Some ways for dealing with social loafing or preventing its occurrence include the following:

Social loafing is the tendency of people not to work as hard in groups as they would individually.

- define roles and tasks to maximize individual interests
- raise accountability by making individual performance expectations clear and identifiable
- tie individual rewards to their performance contributions to the group.

Formal and informal groups

Before exploring the role of groups at work in further detail it is necessary to distinguish between particular *types* of group. A formal group is an official group that is designated by formal authority to serve a specific organizational purpose to which employees are formally assigned. A typical example is a work project headed by a manager and consisting of one or more subordinates. The organization creates such a group to perform a specific task, which typically involves the use of resources to create a product such as a report, decision, service or commodity. The head of a formal group is responsible for the group's performance, but all members contribute the required work. Managers are typically seen as playing a key linchpin role that ties groups horizontally and vertically with the rest of the organization.[10] For example a manager of a bank branch may be 'in charge' of the bank but will also be a member of another group in which he/she isn't the head.

Formal groups are 'official' groups that are designated by formal authority to serve a specific purpose.

Formal groups may be permanent or temporary. Permanent workgroups often appear on organization charts as departments (for example, the sales and marketing department), divisions (for example, the consumer products division), or teams (the customer services team). Such groups can vary in size from very small departments or teams of just a few people to large divisions employing 100 or more people. As permanent workgroups, they are each officially created to perform a specific function on an ongoing basis. They continue to exist until a decision is made to change or reconfigure the organization for some reason. In contrast, temporary workgroups are task groups specifically created to solve a problem or perform a defined task. They often disband once the assigned purpose or task has been accomplished. Examples are the many temporary committees and task forces that are important components of any organization.[11] Indeed, today's organizations tend to make more use of cross-functional teams or working parties for special problem-solving efforts.

The HR manager, for example, might convene a task group to investigate the possibility of implementing flexible working for all employees. Usually, such temporary groups appoint a head who is held accountable for results. Another common form is the project team that is formed, often cross-functionally, to complete a specific task with a well-defined end point. Examples include installing a new computer system and introducing a new product modification.

Informal groups *are groups that emerge unofficially and are not formally designated as parts of the organization.*

Informal groups emerge without being officially designated by the organization. They form spontaneously through personal relationships or special interests, not by any specific organizational endorsement. Friendship groups, for example, consist of persons with natural affinities for one another. They tend to work together, smoke cigarettes together outside work premises, take lunch breaks together and even socialize outside of the workplace. Interest groups consist of persons who share common interests. These may be job-related interests, such as a desire to learn more about computers, or nonwork interests, such as leisure pursuits or sports. Informal groups often help people get their jobs done. Through their network of interpersonal relationships, they can do things more quickly and assist each other in ways that formal lines of authority fail to provide. They also help individuals satisfy needs such as social and security needs that are thwarted or otherwise left unmet in a formal group.

STAGES OF GROUP DEVELOPMENT

Whether one is part of a formal or informal group, the group itself, as shown in many research studies, will pass through a series of life cycle stages.[12] Depending on the stage the group has reached, the leader and members can face very different challenges. The five stages of group development (see Figure 6.1) have been described as follows:[13]

- Forming stage. In the forming stage of group development, the primary concern is the initial entry of members into the group. Individuals may ask a number of questions as they begin to identify with other group members and with the group itself. Their concerns may include: 'What can the group offer me?' 'What will I be asked to contribute?' People are interested in getting to know each other and discovering what is considered acceptable behaviour, in determining the real task of the group, and in defining group rules.
- Storming stage. The storming stage of group development is a period of high emotion and tension among the group members. During this stage, hostility and infighting may occur and the group typically experiences many changes. Alliances or cliques may form as individuals jockey for position and compete to impose their preferences on the group. Outside demands, including premature expectations for performance results, may create uncomfortable pressures. In the process, membership expectations tend to be clarified and attention shifts toward obstacles standing in the way of group goals. Individuals begin to understand one another's interpersonal styles and efforts are made to find ways to accomplish group goals while also satisfying individual needs.

- Norming stage.. The norming stage of group development, sometimes called initial integration, is the point at which the group really begins to come together as a coordinated unit. The turmoil of the storming stage gives way to a precarious balancing of forces. With the pleasures of a new sense of harmony, group members will strive to maintain positive balance. Holding the group together may become more important to some than successfully working on the group's tasks. Minority viewpoints, deviations from group directions and criticisms may be discouraged as group members experience a preliminary sense of closeness. Some members may mistakenly perceive this stage as one of ultimate maturity. In fact, a premature sense of accomplishment at this point needs to be carefully managed as a stepping stone to the next – higher level of group development.

- Performing stage. The performing stage of group development, sometimes called total integration, marks the emergence of a mature, organized, and well-functioning group. The group is now able to deal with complex tasks and handle internal disagreements in creative ways. The structure is stable, and members are motivated by group goals and are generally satisfied. The primary challenges are continued efforts to improve relationships and performance. Group members should be able to adapt successfully as opportunities and demands change over time.

- Adjourning stage. A well integrated group is able to disband, if required, when its work is accomplished. The adjourning stage of group development is especially important for the many temporary groups such as project teams that are increasingly common in the new workplace. Members of these groups must be able to convene quickly, do their jobs on a tight schedule, and then adjourn – often to reconvene later if needed. Their willingness to disband when the job is done and to work well together in future responsibilities, group or otherwise, is an important long-run test of group success.

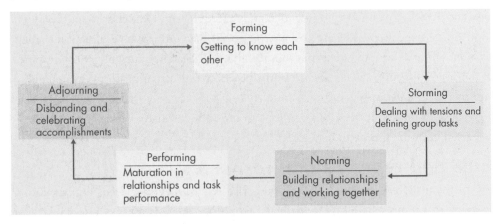

Figure 6.1: Five stages of group development.

FACTORS THAT AFFECT GROUP PERFORMANCE

One way to gain a better understanding of what it takes to become effective as a group and remain so is to view the group as an open system see Figure 6.2. This perspective depicts a group as an open system that interacts with its environment to transform group resource inputs into outputs. The environment here will consist of other individuals and groups with whom the group interacts within the organization. The group needs these resources in order to operate. The quality and strength of the input resources will affect the quality of the group output and long-term group effectiveness. A truly effective group will use resources in order to achieve its own goal but also help other groups attain theirs. Key group inputs include the nature of the task, goals, rewards, resources, technology, membership characteristics and group size.

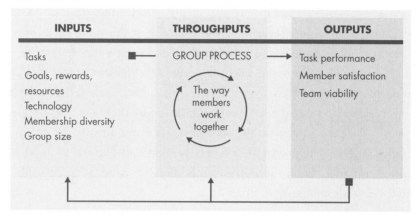

Figure 6.2: The work group as an open system transforming resource inputs into product outputs.

Nature of the group task

The tasks that groups are asked to perform can place different demands on them, with varying implications for group effectiveness. The technical demands of a group's task include its difficulty and information requirements. The social demands of a task involve relationships, individuals identifying with the task and agreement on how to achieve it. Tasks that are complex and technically demanding require unique solutions and more information processing; those that are complex in social demands involve difficulties reaching agreement on goals or methods for accomplishing them. Simply put, the more complex the task the more difficult it is for the group to be effective.[14] In order to master complexity, group members must apply and distribute their efforts broadly and actively cooperate to achieve desired results, in turn this can lead to group members experiencing high levels of satisfaction with the group and its accomplishments.

Goals and rewards and resources

Many of the insights discussed in Chapter 4 with regard to goals, needs and rewards can be applied to groups as well as individuals. Appropriate goals and well-designed reward systems can help establish and maintain the 'motivation' for the group members to work hard together in support of collective accomplishments. Conversely a group's performance, just like individual performance, can suffer when goals are unclear, insufficiently challenging or arbitrarily imposed. It can also suffer if goals and rewards are focused too much on individual-level instead of group-level accomplishments. Similarly it can suffer if adequate budgets, the right facilities, good work methods and best procedures as well as the right technology are not available.

Membership characteristics

The attributes of individual group members are also important inputs that may affect the way the group operates and its achievements. A group must have the right skills and competencies available for problem solving and to perform the task. Although talents alone cannot guarantee desired results, they establish an important baseline of performance potential. It is difficult to overcome the performance limits that result when the input competencies are insufficient to the task at hand. For example if there is too much personal conflict it may distract the group's resources away from the task to be accomplished. In homogeneous groups, where members are very similar to one another, members may find it very easy to work together, however they may still suffer performance limitations if their collective skills, experiences and perspectives are not a good match for complex tasks. In heterogeneous groups, whose members vary in age, gender, race, experience, culture, and the like, a wide pool of talent and viewpoints is available for problem solving. But this diversity may create difficulties as members try to define problems, share information and handle interpersonal conflicts. These difficulties may be quite pronounced in the short run or early stages of group development. Once members learn how to work together, however, research confirms that diversity can be turned into enhanced performance potential.[15] Diversity certainly presents a challenge for groups and teams in the future.

Researchers' identify what is called the diversity–consensus dilemma. This is the tendency for increasing diversity among group members to make it harder for group members to work together, even though the diversity itself expands the skills and perspectives available for problem solving.[16] The challenge to group effectiveness in a culturally mixed multinational team, for example, is to take advantage of the diversity without suffering process disadvantages.[17] The following 'counterpoint' provides another perspective on a phenomenon called 'homophily' that may also have an impact on group and in particular team working.

Homogeneous groups *are groups whose members have similar backgrounds, interests, values, attitudes and so on.*

Heterogeneous groups *are groups whose members have diverse backgrounds, interests, values, attitudes and so on.*

The **diversity–consensus dilemma** *refers to a tendency for diversity in group membership to make it harder for people to work together even though diversity itself expands a group's problem-solving capacity.*

Group size

The number of members in a group can also have an impact on group effectiveness. In larger groups more people are available to divide up the work and accomplish needed tasks. This can boost performance and member satisfaction. However, as a group continues to grow in size, communication and coordination problems often set in, such as increases in dissatisfaction, turnover, absenteeism and social loafing. Even logistical matters, such as finding time and locations for meetings, become more difficult for larger groups and can damage performance.[18] A good size for problem-solving groups is between five and seven members. A group with fewer than five may be too small to adequately share responsibilities. With more than seven, individuals may find it harder to participate and offer ideas. Larger groups are also more prone to possible domination by aggressive members and have tendencies to split into coalitions or subgroups.[19] Groups with an odd number of members may be more effective where speed of decision is paramount because they can use majority voting in to order resolve disagreements. But when careful deliberations are required and the emphasis is more on consensus, such as in jury duty or very complex problem solving, even-numbered groups may be more effective unless an irreconcilable deadlock occurs.[22]

COUNTERPOINT

Too friendly to be effective?

As the old proverb goes, 'birds of a feather flock together.' Paul Davis has conducted research into the phenomenon of 'homophily' and its impacts in the workplace, including its effect in groups and teams. Homophily, a term coined in 1964 by Lazarfield and Merton, describes the tendency of people to be with others who are similar to themselves in age, social background, ethnicity, gender, interests, geographic location and perhaps in other ways.[20]

We often draw attention to the need for diversity or heterogeneity in teams, so it can be seen that problems may arise when people cluster in smaller groups within a team. Doing this may undermine the benefits of diversity that might be gained in the team as it might inhibit the range of life experiences, ideas, opinions and attitudes that could be brought to the team process. There is another aspect to this phenomenon. Teambuilding encourages trust, camaraderie and working closely together, so it is possible that team members may become close and homophilic on the basis of their teams. That is, they may tend to cluster in their teams in other contexts, which could inhibit their capacity to gain from networking and/or working with others outside the team to achieve team tasks.

Davis's research showed that managers at a conference who did not know each other tended to sit next to people who were like themselves (based on outward features such as age, gender or cultural background). In another five-day workshop for a company, his research showed that people were

six times more likely to arrive and sit with people from their own work area rather than with those from other work areas. They were slow to come back from breaks and on average 25 minutes a day were lost through this. Additionally, work was often rushed, not taken seriously and of low quality. People spent some of their time 'off task' and sometimes the bare minimum on the task. When Davis intentionally mixed them up on the final day of the workshop, 14 out of 17 people were unhappy with the change and some were openly hostile. Yet they returned from breaks quicker (on average wasting only 12 minutes), spent more of the allotted time completing required tasks and produced better quality outcomes. A survey of the participants revealed that they achieved more away from their friends on the last day and were more focused. They networked more, took the workshop more seriously, and put more effort into it. Only two of the 17 said they got nothing out of the change on the fifth day. The participants themselves acknowledged that they behave differently when they work with people with whom they have a lot in common.[21]

Questions

1. If homophily can affect team/group performance as described, should organizations pull back from the trend towards team-based management?
2. How can organizations build diverse but cohesive and effective teams?
3. What role is there for team leadership in managing the phenomenon of homophily?

Group and intergroup dynamics

The effectiveness of any group as an open system (depicted earlier in Figure 6.2) requires more than the correct inputs. It always depends also on how well members work together to use these inputs to produce the desired outputs. When we speak about people 'working together' in groups, we are dealing with issues of group dynamics – that is, the forces operating in groups that affect the way members relate to and work with one another.

George Homans described a classic model of group dynamics involving required and emergent behaviours. Required behaviours are those formally defined and expected by the organization.[23] For example, they may include such behaviours as punctuality, respect for customers and helping colleagues. Emergent behaviours are those that are derived from personal initiative in addition to what the organization asks of them. Emergent behaviours often include things that people do beyond formal job requirements and that help get the job done – for example, telephoning an absent member to keep him informed about what happened during a group meeting. Emergent behaviours are essential because it is unlikely that required behaviours will specify all the demands that arise in a work situation.

The term intergroup dynamics refers to the dynamics that take place between two or more groups. Organizations would ideally operate as cooperative systems in which the various groups are willing and able to help one another as needed (this may not, of course, automatically occur in reality). An important managerial responsibility, therefore, is to make sure that groups work together to benefit the whole organization. Competition between groups can stimulate them to work harder, become more focused on key tasks, develop more internal loyalty and satisfaction, or achieve a higher level of creativity in problem solving. Japanese companies, for example, often use competitive themes to motivate their workforces. At Sony workers once rallied around the slogan: 'beat Matsushita whatsoever.'[24] Conversely intergroup conflict may lead to group members focusing more on their animosities toward the other group than on the performance of important tasks.

Group dynamics are the forces operating in groups that affect group performance and member satisfaction.

Required behaviours are those contributions the organization formally requests from group members as a basis for continued affiliation and support.

Emergent behaviours are those things that group members do in addition to, or in place of, what is formally asked of them by the organization.

Intergroup dynamics are the dynamics that take place between groups, as opposed to within groups.

GROUP COMMUNICATION AND DECISION MAKING

Within groups communications and decision making are important functions. However they are also important processes in the organization as a whole and for this reason they are dealt with within subsequent chapters in this book. It is important for us to acknowledge here that the dynamics of groups will affect the quality of decision making and communication and also that the functioning of groups (both in terms of task performance and group maintenance) will be affected by decision making and communication. One particular problem that can occur with group decision making is 'groupthink', when members of a highly cohesive group seek to conform and then come to think alike and/or become unwilling to be critical of one another's ideas and suggestions. This can result in poor and sometimes very costly decision errors. This and other group decision-making issues are discussed at length in Chapter 10. In terms of communication, the structure of groups and how group members work on tasks – that is, in an interactive, coactive or counteractive way – will relate closely to the types of communication networks that exist in the group: decentralized, centralized or restrictive, respectively.

TEAM WORKING

In most literature and in organizations themselves the terms 'group' and 'team' are often interchangeable. Guzzo and Dickson argue that it is sometimes impossible to make a distinction between the two and thus it is pointless to attempt to do so.[25] But is there a difference between the two or is this a simple matter of wording? Whilst we have seen a group is made of individuals who see themselves and are seen as a social entity, a team is a small number of people with complementary skills, who are committed to a common purpose, performance goals and approach for which they hold them themselves mutually accountable.[26] Work groups can also be teams but they do not become a team just because that is what someone calls them. The essence of a team is *shared commitment*. Without it groups perform as individuals; with it they become a powerful unit of *collective performance*. Another important distinction is that whereas a group relies on its members to contribute to group performance and sometimes achieves synergy, an effective team is always worth more than the sum of its parts. Some suggest that groups and teams form a continuum. Groups, at one end, are collections of people whose individual efforts combine 'additively' towards the achievement of a goal. Teams, at the other end, are collections of people whose efforts combine synergistically towards the achievement of the team's particular goals as well as the goals of the organization.[27] Teams can be extremely powerful when they work well but transforming a group of individuals into a team that can function well in any of the following settings can be hard work.[28]

*A **team** role is a pattern of behaviour characterizing the ways one team member interacts with others.*

Types of teams

First, there are *teams that recommend things*. Established to study specific problems and recommend solutions to them, these teams typically work with a target completion date and disband once their purpose has been fulfilled. They are temporary groups including working parties, ad hoc committees, project teams and the like. Members of these teams must be able to learn quickly how to work well together, accomplish the assigned task and make good action recommendations for follow-up work by other people. Second, *there are teams that run things*. Such management teams consist of people with the formal responsibility for leading other groups. These teams may exist at all levels of responsibility from the individual work unit composed of a team leader and team members to the top-management team composed of a CEO and other senior executives. Teams can add value to work processes at any level and offer special opportunities for dealing with complex problems and uncertain situations. Key issues addressed by top-management teams include, for example, identifying overall organizational purposes, goals and values; formulating strategies; and persuading others to support them.[29] Third there are *teams that make or do things*. These are functional groups and work units that perform ongoing tasks, such as marketing or manufacturing. Members of these teams must have good long-term working relationships with one another, solid operating systems and the external support needed to achieve effectiveness over a sustained period of time. They also need energy to keep up the pace and meet the day-to-day challenges of sustained high performance.

The nature of teamwork

All teams need members who believe in team goals and are motivated to work actively with others to accomplish important tasks, whether those tasks involve recommending things, making or doing things, or running things. Indeed, an essential criterion of a true team is that the members feel 'collectively accountable' for what they accomplish.[30] This sense of collective accountability sets the stage for real teamwork, with team members actively working together in such a way that all their respective skills are well utilized to achieve a common purpose.[31] A commitment to teamwork is found in the willingness of every member to 'listen and respond constructively to views expressed by others, give others the benefit of the doubt, provide support, and recognize the interests and achievements of others.'[32] Although such teamwork is essential for any high-performance team, developing and sustaining it are challenging leadership tasks (see Effective manager 6.1). The fact is that it takes a lot more work to build a well-functioning team than simply assigning members to the same group and then expecting them to do a great job.[33]

High-performance teams have special characteristics that allow them to excel at teamwork and achieve special performance advantages:

High-performance teams *excel in teamwork while achieving performance advantages.*

- High-performance teams have strong core values that help guide their attitudes and behaviours in directions consistent with the team's purpose. Such values act as an internal control system for a group or team that can substitute for outside direction and supervisory attention.
- High-performance teams turn a general sense of purpose into specific performance objectives. Whereas a shared sense of purpose gives general direction to a team, commitment to specific performance results makes this purpose truly meaningful. Specific objectives such as reducing the time of getting the product to market by half provide a clear focus for solving problems and resolving conflicts. They also set standards for measuring results and obtaining performance feedback. And they help group members understand the need for collective versus purely individual efforts.
- Members of high-performance teams have the right mix of skills, including technical skills, problem-solving and decision-making skills, and interpersonal skills.
- High-performance teams possess creativity. In the new workplace, teams must use their creativity to assist organizations in continuous improvement of operations and in continuous development of new products, services and markets.

The 'OB in action' section on South African Breweries shows how a high-performance team culture can be disseminated throughout an organization.

OB IN ACTION

Eighteen billion drinks is a lot of liquid, yet that is what South African Breweries (SAB) one of the world's top four brewers sells in a year. In South Africa alone, its share of the market is 98% for beer and 57% for all alcohol consumed. In the past decade SAB has almost doubled its production in South Africa to 2.5 billion litres and halved its workforce to 7000 following a switch to high-performance team working. New structures and an emphasis on quality, performance management and social responsibility have formed the basis of major change and rapid expansion.

The process began with the identification of the organization's core values in consultation with the whole workforce (people, growth and reputation) and the identification of strategic plans that enabled the alignment of individual and team goals to the business strategy and encourage a climate of change. Jobs were redesigned, bringing in a four-tier team structure consisting of regional executive teams, departmental teams, unit or section teams and shift teams. These were all multiskilled autonomous teams that were self sufficient in operating machinery, problem solving, quality control and maintenance and there was a new emphasis on team accountability. Later on there was a further shift in teamworking structures,

which abolished traditional functional reporting lines and introduced autonomous and multiskilled working practices to the whole organization. Each team is now fully responsible for all its systems and the whole range of its products. Coaching and performance management are built into the team structure as well as identification of individual development needs to ensure continued team effectiveness.

Although there has been considerable investment in training and development with some teams undertaking an intensive three months' training programme in order to achieve the right skills and to work in different ways, the net result is a more efficient and effective team-based organization that met its long term goal of being one of the top five brewers in the world.[34]

TEAMBUILDING

Teamwork doesn't always happen naturally in a group. It must be nurtured and supported; it is something that team members and leaders must continuously work hard to achieve. In sports teams, for example, coaches and managers focus on teamwork when building new teams at the start of each season but even experienced teams often run into problems as a season progresses. Members slack off or become disgruntled; some have performance 'slumps'; some are traded to other teams. Even world-champion teams have losing streaks, and the most talented players can lose motivation at times, quibble among themselves and end up contributing little to team success. When these things happen, the owners, managers and players are apt to examine their problems, take corrective action to rebuild the team and restore the teamwork needed to achieve high-performance results.[35]

Workgroups and teams have similar difficulties. When newly formed, they must master challenges as members come together and begin the process of growing and working together as they pass though the various stages of group development. Even when they are mature, most work teams encounter problems of insufficient teamwork at different points in time. This is why the process known as teambuilding is so important. This is a sequence of planned activities designed to gather and analyse data on the functioning of a group and to initiate changes designed to improve teamwork and increase group effectiveness.[36] When done well and at the right times, teambuilding is a good way to deal with teamwork difficulties when they occur or to help prevent them from developing in the first place.

The action steps and process of continuous improvement highlighted in Figure 6.3 are typical of most teambuilding approaches. The process begins when someone notices that a problem exists or may develop with team effectiveness. Members then work together to gather data relating to the problem, analyse these data, plan for improvements and implement the action plans. The entire teambuilding process is highly collaborative. Everyone is expected to participate actively as group operations are evaluated and decisions are made on what needs to be done to improve the team's functioning in the future. This process can and should become an ongoing part of any team's work agenda. It is an approach to continuous improvement that can be very beneficial to long-term effectiveness.

> **Teambuilding** *is a sequence of planned action steps designed to gather and analyse data on the functioning of a group and to implement changes to increase its operating effectiveness.*

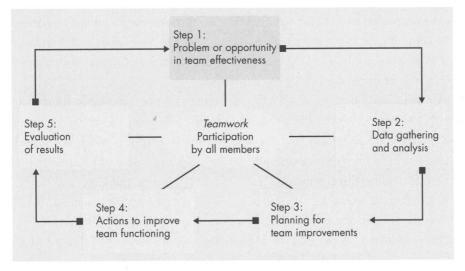

Figure 6.3: The teambuilding process.

Teambuilding is participatory and it is data based. Whether the data are gathered by questionnaire, interview, nominal group meeting or other creative methods, the goal is to get good answers to such questions as: 'How well are we doing in terms of task accomplishment?' 'How satisfied are we as individual members with the group and the way it operates?' There are a variety of ways for such questions to be asked and answered in a collaborative and motivating manner.

Approaches to teambuilding

For most teams, teambuilding will take place as part of continuous improvement in the work place. Managers, team leaders and group members take responsibility for regularly engaging in the teambuilding process. This may be as simple as having regular meetings that implement the teambuilding steps or having a formal review of team progress. In all cases team members commit themselves to continuously monitoring group development and accomplishments and making the day-to-day changes needed to ensure team effectiveness. Such continuous improvement of teamwork is essential to the themes of total quality and total service management so important to organizations today.

However not all teambuilding is done at work, it may involve, (particularly where there are problems, or at the formation stage) taking the team away from the work environment. This could result in structured 'away day/s' involving a formal review of the team's operation and performance, or may involve some form of 'outward bound' or fun experience such as 'paint balling', in order to improve team cohesion and effectiveness. Formal away days are often facilitated by consultants and involve group members working intensively on a variety of assessment and planning tasks that have been initiated by a review of team functioning, using data gathered through surveys, interviews and other means.

Using outdoor activities as a basis of teambuilding is a very popular method of teambuilding that can be done on its own or in combination with other approaches. Here group members are given a variety of physically challenging tasks that must be mastered through teamwork. By having to work together in the face of difficult obstacles, team members are supposed to experience increased self-confidence, more respect for others' capabilities and a greater commitment to teamwork. For a group that has never done teambuilding before, outdoor experience can be an exciting way to begin; for groups familiar with teambuilding, it can be a way of further enriching the experience.

One of the most high profile Outward Bound training schools is John Ridgeway's School of Adventure, which was founded in 1969 by round-the-world yachtsman and ex-army officer John Ridgeway and his wife Marie. The school, which is situated in the remote highlands of north-west Scotland, ran for 35 years a series of challenging outdoor courses encapsulating three principles 'self-reliance', 'positive thinking' and 'leave people and places better than you find them', which over 12 000 people attended. In 1993 the school was the subject of a British television documentary, made by Channel 4, in which a camera crew followed 24 top executives from Rockwood International, aged between 28 and 50, while they endured the toughest management course in the country. The managers were expected to jump into icy seas, camp on a deserted island and climb mountains in gale-force winds. For some participants this was an experience they never wanted to repeat and the programme led to much debate and research into the value and ethics of such training programmes.[37]

Today outdoor teambuilding encompasses a whole range of experiences including treasure hunts, sailing adventures, high wire courses and circus performances. Undoubtedly, taking part in these type of events can be hugely enjoyable and promote a temporary sense of wellbeing, camaraderie among team members, but this type of event, argues Simon

Hollingsworth, Executive Chairman of Value Based Leadership, should not be confused with properly thought-through and objective based teambuilding. He further argues that the key to successful teambuilding is to have clear objectives that are tied in with business strategies and performance management systems and he criticizes many events for not having structured review sessions that link the experiences back to the realities of the workplace and subsequent action plans.[38] Where this does take place, there can be real value for the team as the 'OB in action' section on Roche Products shows.

OB IN ACTION

With a new team under his direction, Martin Woollard, manager of the UK Clinical Projects Group from the pharmaceutical company Roche Products, decided action was needed 'to help the team bond and allow me to better understand the team dynamics.' After some research he approached corporate teambuilding firm City Challenge about holding an event in the city of Oxford. Everyone taking part was asked in advance about their own personal and team objectives for the session and on the day trained facilitators started the session by analysing and discussing the day's goals. With a series of challenges based around Oxford's academic, literary and theatrical history, the Roche Products teams, among other things, had to find pubs made famous by the fictional policeman Inspector Morse. At the end of the day, informal discussions were held to discuss the immediate lessons learned while a detailed report was sent to Woollard, with suggestions for continuing team development. He says: 'It was hard work, but we had fun at the same time and learned some valuable lessons. It gave me an insight into the many varied members of my team and I am building on some of the issues which came out of the day, both in monthly team meetings and one-to-one sessions with individuals.'[39]

In addition to its general emphasis on improving teamwork and group effectiveness, teambuilding is useful for:

- clarifying core values to guide and direct the behaviour of members
- transforming a broad sense of purpose into specific performance objectives
- developing the right mix of skills to accomplish high-performance results
- enhancing creativity in task performance.

Improving team working

Team working is a key feature of many contemporary workplaces, but multiple and shifting memberships can cause complications. Team leaders and members alike must be prepared to deal positively with issues such as introducing new members, handling disagreements on goals and responsibilities, resolving delays and disputes when making decisions and reducing friction and interpersonal conflicts. Given the complex nature of group dynamics, teambuilding in a sense is never complete. Something is always happening that creates the need for further leadership efforts to help improve team processes.

Entry of new members

Difficulties are likely to occur when members first get together in a new group or work team, or when new members join an existing one. Problems arise as new members try to understand what is expected of them while dealing with the anxiety and discomfort of a new social setting. New members, for example, may worry about:

Participation – 'will I be allowed to participate?'
Goals – 'do I share the same goals as others?'
Control – 'will I be able to influence what takes place?'
Relationships – 'how close do people get?'
Processes – 'are conflicts likely to be upsetting?'

Edgar Schein points out that people may try to cope with individual entry problems in self-serving ways that may hinder group operations.[40] He identifies three behaviour profiles that are common in such situations. The *tough battler* is frustrated by a lack of identity in the new group and may act aggressively or reject authority. These individuals want to understand their role in the group. The *friendly helper* is insecure, suffering uncertainties of intimacy and control. This person may show extraordinary support for others, behave in a dependent way and seek alliances in subgroups or cliques. The friendly helper needs to know whether he or she will be liked. The *objective thinker* is anxious about how personal needs will be met in the group. This person may act in a passive, reflective and even single-minded manner while struggling with the fit between individual goals and group directions. The problems of integrating new members into existing teams can pose significant problems as the 'OB in action' section on expectation and newcomer performance in groups shows.

OB IN ACTION

Expectation and newcomer performance in groups

As the importance of teams in organizations is increasing, and as more of these teams are temporary and cross-functional types, the problem of managing newcomer entry and integration into groups becomes increasingly important as well. Gilad Chen and Richard J. Klimoski tested a model of newcomer effectiveness in work teams with a special focus on the performance of knowledge workers. They studied the effects of leaders' expectations on newcomer performance, the effect of newcomers' personal expectations on their performance, and related influences of self-efficacy, work

characteristics and empowerment. Through survey research of some 70 work teams in three IT organizations in the US, Chen and Klimoski found that:

- newcomers' problems often develop within an organization and have mixed consequences
- self-efficacy was positively related to their performance expectations

- these expectations were positively related to newcomer empowerment, and
- this empowerment was positively related to newcomer role performance.

They conclude that work characteristics, social exchanges and newcomer empowerment help to explain the effectiveness of newcomers in groups. They suggest that this research should be extended to other types of teams, including management teams and production teams.[41]

TASK AND MAINTENANCE LEADERSHIP

Research suggests that the key to high-performance team working is the successful balancing of the needs of the task with the needs of the team (team maintenance).[42] Whilst the formally appointed group leader should help fulfil these needs, all members should also contribute helpful activities. This sharing of responsibilities for contributions that move a group forward, called distributed leadership, is an important characteristic of any high-performance team. Figure 6.4 describes group task activities as the various things members do that directly contribute to the performance of important group tasks. They include initiating discussion, sharing information, asking others for information, clarifying something that has been said and summarizing the status of a deliberation.[43] A group will have difficulty accomplishing its objectives when task activities are not well performed. In an effective team, by contrast, members each pitch in to contribute important task leadership as needed.

Distributed leadership is the sharing of responsibility for fulfilling group task and maintenance needs.

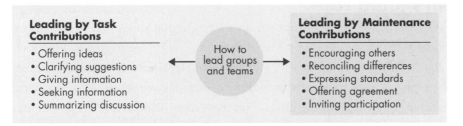

Figure 6.4: Task and maintenance leadership in group team dynamics.

Maintenance activities support the social and interpersonal relationships among group members. A team member can contribute maintenance leadership by encouraging the participation of others, trying to harmonize differences of opinion, praising the contributions of others, and agreeing to go along with a popular course of action. When maintenance leadership is poor, members become dissatisfied with one another, the value of their group membership diminishes, and emotional conflicts may drain energies otherwise needed for task performance. In an effective group, by contrast, maintenance activities help to sustain the relationships needed for team members to work well together over time.

Maintenance activities are activities that support the emotional life of the group as an ongoing social system.

In addition to helping meet a group's task and maintenance needs, group members share the additional responsibility of avoiding *disruptive behaviours* that harm the group process. Full participation in shared leadership of a team means taking individual responsibility for avoiding the following types of behaviours and helping others do the same:

- being overly aggressive toward other members
- withdrawing and refusing to cooperate with others
- horsing around when there is work to be done
- using the group as a forum for self-confession
- talking too much about irrelevant matters
- trying to compete for attention and recognition.

ROLES AND ROLE DYNAMICS

*A **role** is a set of expectations for the behaviour of a person holding a particular office or position.*

In groups and teams, new and old members alike need to know what others expect of them and what they can expect from others. A role is a set of expectations associated with a job or position on a team. The roles that individuals perform in a group have an important effect on its development and cohesiveness. Within a typical group activity, such as a team meeting, members will show a consistent preference for certain behaviours and not for others. Research into the nature of team roles suggests that these roles can be categorized into those that support the task, such as problem solving and those that support the team, such as resolving conflict. Early research by Benne and Sheats suggests that the roles performed in high-performing teams could be classified into three broad headings: group task roles, group building and maintenance roles, and individual roles. They argue that individual roles, such as dominating or avoiding need to be replaced with maintenance, building or task roles before the group can become a truly effective team.[44]

Belbin's team roles

Whilst there are many other models for identifying group roles, one of the most popular and influential is that developed by Meredith Belbin.[45] After many years of research effort, Belbin concluded that groups made up of for example, similar personalities or entirely of creative people were less successful than those comprised of a range of roles undertaken by various members. He initially identified eight team roles, which, upon further development, were expanded to nine. A team role is described by Belbin as a pattern of behaviour, characteristic of the way in which one team member interacts with another, whose performance serves to facilitate the progress of the team as a whole. He argues that it is these nine roles that team members need to fulfil if the team is to be effective and successful. For each team role Belbin identifies the strengths of the contribution but also its particularly weaknesses (see Table 6.1). Clearly not all teams consist of nine people taking on one role but, regardless of team size, Belbin argues that members are able to perform two or three roles depending on the circumstances. Belbin calls these 'back up team roles', which individuals can perform if needed. For example if the most junior team members cannot take on their preferred role of leaders, then they may look to contribute as team workers; however, as they become more senior in the organization their natural preference for a leadership role will become more dominant in group working situations.

Belbin's model has proved to be popular with HR professionals partly because he developed a practical questionnaire the 'Self-Perception Inventory', which he designed to

Team role	Descriptors	Strengths	Allowed weaknesses
Completer-Finisher(CF)	Anxious, conscientious, introvert, self-controlled, self-disciplined, submissive and worrisome.	Painstaking, conscientious, searches out errors and omissions, delivers on time.	Inclined to worry unduly. Reluctant to delegate.
Implementer (IMP)	Conservative, controlled, disciplined, efficient, inflexible, methodical, sincere, stable and systematic.	Disciplined, reliable, conservative and efficient, turns ideas into practical actions.	Somewhat inflexible. Slow to respond to new possibilities.
Team Worker (TW)	Extrovert, likeable, loyal, stable, submissive, supportive, unassertive, and uncompetitive.	Co-operative, mild, perceptive and diplomatic, listens, builds, averts friction, calms the waters.	Indecisive in crunch situations.
Specialist (SP)	Expert, defendant, not interested in others, serious, self-disciplined, efficient.	Single-minded, self-starting, dedicated; provides knowledge and skills in rare supply.	Contributes on a narrow front only. Dwells on technicalities.
Monitor Evaluator (ME)	Dependable, fair-minded, introvert, low drive, open to change, serious, stable and unambitious.	Sober, strategic and discerning, sees all options, judges accurately.	Lacks drive and ability to inspire others.
Co-ordinator (CO)	Dominant, trusting, extrovert, mature, positive, self-controlled, self-disciplined and stable.	Mature, confident, a good chairperson, clarifies goals, promotes decision making, delegates well.	Can be seen as manipulative. Offloads personal work.
Plant (PL)	Dominant, imaginative, introvert, original, radical-minded, trustful and uninhibited.	Creative, unorthodox, solves difficult problems.	Too preoccupied to communicate effectively.
Shaper (SH)	Abrasive, anxious, arrogant, competitive, dominant, edgy, emotional, extrovert, impatient, impulsive, outgoing and self-confident.	Challenging, dynamic, thrives on pressure, has drive and courage to overcome obstacles.	Prone to provocation. Offends people's feelings.
Resource Investigator (RI)	Diplomatic, dominant, enthusiastic, extrovert, flexible, inquisitive, optimistic, persuasive, positive, relaxed, social and stable.	Extrovert, communicative, explores opportunities, develops contacts.	Over-optimistic. Loses interest after initial enthusiasm.

Table 6.1: Team Role Descriptors, Strengths and Allowed Weaknesses.

Source: Belbin R.M., (1993) *Team Roles at Work*, Butterworth Heinemann, p.22. Reproduced by permission of Belbin Associates.

help individuals assess their best team roles, which training professionals have used to aid teambuilding in a variety of settings;[46] but also because research broadly supports his perception that the most effective teams have balance and diversity.[47] In fact one of Belbin's key principles is that 'no one's perfect but a team can be'. Thus Belbin stresses the benefits of diversity in teams and argues that his questionnaire is purely the starting point for teambuilding and development. There are varying views of how to build an effective team, the following Effective Manager section gives some suggestions.

EFFECTIVE MANAGER 6.1

How to build an effective team

1. Instil a sense of purpose – make sure all team members know why they are there and how their role fits into the organization's strategy.
2. Ensure that all organizational processes and procedures support team working – for example, the sharing of good practice.
3. Recruit people into teams not only for their specific skills, but also because they complement and challenge those already there
4. Get the right leaders – team leaders have a vital role to play in the creation of high performing teams so chose those who will guide rather than dominate the team.
5. Ensure teams have succession plans in place so that team members can develop into team leaders and can see the wider organizational picture
6. Let them have fun! Spend time and effort maintaining the team including socializing and time away from the task in order to improve morale and strengthen relationships.
7. Involve everyone in target setting.
8. Review team performance regularly.[48]

Role ambiguity, role conflict and role overload/underload

Role ambiguity *is the uncertainty about what other group members expect of a person.*

Role overload *occurs when too much is expected of individuals within their role designation.*

Role conflict *occurs when a person is unable to respond to the expectations of one or more group members.*

When team members are unclear about their roles or experience conflicting role demands, performance problems can occur. Unfortunately, this is a common problem in groups but it is also one that can be managed when leaders and members are able to identify role ambiguities and conflicts and to take action to clarify role expectations. Role ambiguity occurs when a person is uncertain about his or her role. To do any job well, people need to know what is expected of them. In new group or team situations, role ambiguities may create problems as members find that their work efforts are wasted or unappreciated by others. Even in mature groups and teams, the failure of members to share expectations and listen to one another may at times create a similar lack of understanding. Being asked to do too much or too little as a team member can also create problems. Role overload occurs when too much is expected and the individual feels overwhelmed with work; role underload occurs when too little is expected and the individual feels underutilized. Members of any group typically benefit from having clear and realistic expectations regarding their expected tasks and responsibilities.

Role conflict occurs when a person is unable to meet the expectations of others. The individual understands what needs to be done but for some reason cannot comply. The resulting tension can reduce satisfaction and affect both an individual's performance and relationships with other group members. There are four common forms of role conflict.

1. *Intra-sender role conflict* occurs when the same person sends conflicting expectations.
2. *Inter-sender role conflict* occurs when different people signal conflicting and mutually exclusive expectations.
3. *Person-role conflict* occurs when one's personal values and needs come into conflict with role expectations.
4. *Inter-role conflict* occurs when the expectations of two or more roles held by the same individual become incompatible, such as the conflict between work and family demands.

It is not only the job of the team leader but of team members to help clarify team roles and expectations in order to ensure that the team is performing effectively. This may involve negotiation of these expectations between team members. The starting point may be to agree group norms and terms of reference.

GROUP NORMS

The norms of a group or team represent ideas or beliefs about how members are expected to behave. They can be considered as 'rules' or 'standards' of conduct.[49] Norms help clarify the expectations associated with a person's membership in a group. They allow members to structure their own behaviour and to predict what others will do. They help members gain a common sense of direction and they reinforce a desired group or team culture. When someone violates a group norm, other members typically respond in ways that are aimed at enforcing the norm. These responses may include direct criticisms, reprimands, expulsion and social ostracism.

Managers and team leaders should help their groups adopt positive norms that support organizational goals. A key norm in any setting is the performance norm, which conveys expectations about how hard group members should work. Other norms are important too – for example, norms regarding attendance at meetings, punctuality, preparedness, criticism, and behaviour are needed. Groups also commonly have norms regarding how to deal with supervisors, colleagues, and customers, as well as norms establishing guidelines for honesty and ethical behaviours. Norms are often evident in the everyday conversations of people at work. The following examples show the types of norms that operate with positive and negative implications for groups and organizations.[50]

- Ethics norms – 'we try to make ethical decisions, and we expect others to do the same' (positive); 'don't worry about inflating your expenses, everyone does it here' (negative).
- Organizational and personal pride norms – 'it's a tradition around here for people to stand up for the company when others criticize it unfairly' (positive); 'in our company, they are always trying to take advantage of us' (negative).
- High-achievement norms – 'on our team, people always try to work hard' (positive); 'there's no point in trying harder on our team, nobody else does' (negative).

- Support and helpfulness norms – 'people on this committee are good listeners and actively seek out the ideas and opinions of others' (positive); 'on this committee it's dog-eat-dog and save your own skin' (negative).
- Improvement and change norms – 'in our department people are always looking for better ways of doing things' (positive); 'around here, people hang on to the old ways even after they have outlived their usefulness' (negative).

TEAM COHESIVENESS

Cohesiveness
is the degree to which members are attracted to and motivated to remain part of the group.

The cohesiveness of a group or team is the degree to which members are attracted to and motivated to remain part of it.[51] Persons in a highly cohesive group value their membership and strive to maintain positive relationships with other group members. In this sense, cohesive groups and teams are good for their members. In contrast to less cohesive groups, members of highly cohesive ones tend to be more energetic when working on group activities, less likely to be absent and more likely to be happy about performance success and sad about failures. Cohesive groups generally have low turnover and satisfy a broad range of individual needs, often providing a source of loyalty, security and esteem for their members.

Cohesiveness tends to be high when group members are similar in age, attitudes, needs and backgrounds. It also tends to be high in groups of small size, where members respect one another's competencies, agree on common goals and work on interdependent tasks. Cohesiveness tends to increase when groups are physically isolated from others and when they experience performance success or crisis.

Cohesive teams are good for their members. Members of highly cohesive teams are concerned about their teams' activities and achievements. In contrast to members of less cohesive teams, they tend to be more energetic when working on team activities, they are less likely to be absent and they tend to be happy about performance success and sad about failures. Cohesive teams generally have stable memberships and foster feelings of loyalty, security and high self-esteem among their members; they satisfy a full range of individual needs. Sometimes tough experiences and survival of them, as well as isolation, can be very influential in developing high team cohesiveness as shown in the 'OB in action' example set out below.

One can question how taking part in extreme challenges such as this might help team cohesion and effectiveness and, conversely, whether there could be negative aspects for the organization and the individual resulting from participation in such a project.

Cohesive groups or teams may or may not necessarily be good for an organization. The critical question is: 'how does cohesiveness influence performance?' Figure 6.5 helps answer this question by showing the relationship between team cohesiveness and team performance. Typically, the more cohesive the team, the greater the conformity of members to team norms. As you would expect, the performance norm is critical for any team. Thus, when the performance norm is positive, high conformity to it in a cohesive team should have a beneficial effect on task performance; when the performance norm is negative in a highly cohesive team, undesirable results may be experienced.

OB IN ACTION

Lynn Skelly, a 42-year-old American, doesn't so much multitask as multi-country. He heads the UK arm of American Express Bank and also part of the bank's global business, with staff reporting from all over the world. Working alongside Lynn is his senior associate Sue Salter, who fulfils an executive assistant role. Sue, 52, joined American Express in the 1980s. In addition to supporting Lynn, from managing his diary to sitting in on high level meetings, Sue's role involves a lot of projects such as dealing with the staff magazine but one recent project more than put her working relationship with Lynn to the test as their roles were reversed.

Sue assembled a team of nine people from the bank, including herself and Lynn, to take part in a gruelling trek across the Namibian desert to raise money for the Prince's Trust, the youth charity. Taking part in the challenge, which also involved abseiling down rocks, was entirely Sue's idea and she easily persuaded her boss to join: 'I played on the guilt factor. I told him that if I could do it at my age, he could certainly do it', she says. 'The challenge itself took six days but we were away for 10 and before we went we trained for six months, following an intensive training programme that involved a lot of running and cycling. We managed to raise more than £28 000 between us and we all felt the most incredible sense of achievement.'[52]

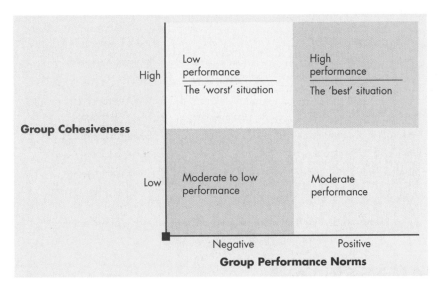

Figure 6.5: How cohesiveness and conformity to norms affect group performance.

Notice in Figure 6.5 the performance implications for various combinations of cohesiveness and norms. Performance is highest in a very cohesive team with positive performance norms. In this situation, members encourage one another to work hard on behalf of the team. The worst situation for a manager is a highly cohesive team with negative performance norms. Again, members will be highly motivated to support one another but the organization will suffer as the team restricts its performance consistent with the negative norm. Between these two extremes are mixed situations, in which a lack of cohesion fails to ensure member conformity to the guiding norm. The strength of the norm is reduced and the outcome is somewhat unpredictable but is most likely to be on the moderate or low side.

Influencing team cohesiveness

Look again at Figure 6.5. How would you feel with a team that falls into any cell other than the high-performance one? To deal with these possibilities a manager must recognize that there will be times when steps should be taken to build cohesiveness in a team, such as when the team has positive norms but low cohesiveness. There may be other times when steps must be taken to reduce cohesiveness, such as when the members of a highly cohesive team are operating with negative performance norms and when previous efforts to change these norms have failed. Managers must be prepared to deal with both situations. As shown in Figure 6.6, managers can take steps to increase or decrease team cohesiveness. These include making changes in team goals, membership composition, interactions, size, rewards, competition, location and duration. Trust is a very important ingredient for team cohesiveness and performance. The higher the level of trust in a team, the greater the cohesiveness, satisfaction and effectiveness. The genuine sharing of information can also greatly contribute to the building of trust; this simple act can demonstrate a strong commitment to the team.

How to Decrease Cohesion	TARGETS	How to Increase Cohesion
Create disagreement	Goals	Get agreement
Increase heterogeneity	Membership	Increase homogeneity
Restrict within team	Interactions	Enhance within team
Make team bigger	Size	Make team smaller
Focus within team	Competition	Focus on other teams
Reward individual results	Rewards	Reward team results
Open up to other teams	Location	Isolate from other teams
Disband the team	Duration	Keep team together

Figure 6.6: Ways to increase and decrease group cohesiveness.

EFFECTIVE MANAGER 6.2

Managing conflict in team situations[53]

- Giving ample recognition to each member of the team.
- Focusing on a win–win situation, in which both the individual and the team benefit.
- Establishing a team charter that states the responsibilities of each team member.
- Mediating personal differences, allowing all team members an opportunity to express their views.
- Finding areas of agreement to allow team members to focus on team goals rather than areas of conflict.
- Helping team members to address personal behaviours that will facilitate change.

Conflict is frequently an unavoidable part of teamwork. It is not necessarily detrimental and can lead to creative solutions. However, if not managed, it can destroy team cohesiveness. Effective Manager 6.2 gives some guidance on how to manage conflict in team situations.

TYPES OF WORKPLACE TEAMS

There is no easy formula to tell us exactly what category a particular team may fit into, or for giving a precise picture of the types of teams that operate in organizations and how successful they are. However, we do know that managers in contemporary organizations are adopting many innovative ways of better using teams as effective components of organizations. The watchwords of these approaches are empowerment, participation and involvement. More recently, technology enables physically remote membership of teams. The following OB in action illustrates some aspects of these approaches.

OB IN ACTION

Some time ago, Mahmood Mohajer, a production supervisor at a Digital plant, realized that his work team was two weeks behind in an important production run. In the past, Mahmood would have immediately put everyone on an overtime schedule. This time, he did things differently. He first met with the production teams and outlined the problem. He then asked them to come up with a solution. 'It was a real risk', he says of the approach. 'I was so nervous I had to trust them.'

Mahmood got the team's response the following Monday. Everyone decided to work the entire weekend to catch up on the production schedule. They had accepted responsibility for meeting the production goals and came up with a way of doing so that would meet their needs as well as those of the firm. It was still an overtime schedule but somewhat different from the one Mahmood might have set. Yet, theirs would also work... perhaps even better than his. Because it was their idea, team members were highly motivated to make their solution a real success.

Mahmood says that his new team approach requires a 'coaching' rather than a 'policing' role. One of his workers told him, 'We wanted to tell you how to fix some problems before, but you wouldn't listen to us'.[54]

The four most common types of teams are outlined in the following section: employee involvement teams, problem-solving teams, self-managing teams and virtual teams. Despite classifying them into types, it must be accepted that every team is different and may have features that overlap the types discussed here. For instance, it is possible to have a problem-solving team that is also an employee involvement team or a self-managing team that is also a virtual team. You will come across many other terms to describe teams and/or types of teams, such as cross-functional teams and world-class teams.

Employee involvement teams

Employee involvement teams are teams of workers who meet regularly outside their normal work units for the purpose of collectively addressing important workplace issues.

Many of the creative developments applied to the use of teams in organizations fall into the category of employee involvement teams. This term applies to a wide variety of settings in which teams of workers meet regularly outside their normal work units for the purpose of collectively addressing important workplace issues. The goals of an employee involvement team often relate to total quality concepts and the quest for continuous improvement in all operations. Typically consisting of five to 10 members, these teams regularly spend time discussing ways to enhance quality, better satisfy customers, raise productivity and improve the quality of work–life.

Employee involvement teams are mechanisms for participation. They allow workers to gain influence over matters affecting them and their work. They also allow the full advantages of team decision making to become a part of everyday organizational affairs. These advantages include bringing the full extent of worker know-how to bear on problems and gaining the commitment of these workers to implement fully any problem-solving approaches that may be selected.

For employee involvement to succeed, traditional managers like Mahmood Mohajer must make commit to participation and empowerment. The opportunities for the workers to have an influence on what happens to them must be real. When accomplished, true employee involvement offers the potential for contributing positively to performance accomplishments in the new workplace. It also offers employees the advantages of filling higher-order needs such as achievement, recognition and growth (see Chapter 4).

Problem-solving teams

Quality circles are groups of workers who meet periodically to discuss and develop solutions for problems relating to quality, productivity or cost.

Some teams are created for the specific purpose of generating solutions to problems, for example, quality circles, task forces and autonomous work teams. Developed as a means of generating ideas that would raise product quality by reducing defects and error rates, quality circles were a precursor to the total quality movement.[55] A quality circle is a small group of people who meet periodically (for example, for an hour or so once per week) to discuss and develop solutions for problems relating to quality, productivity or cost.

For the circles to be successful, members should receive special training in information-gathering and problem-analysis techniques. Quality circle leaders should emphasize democratic participation in identifying and analysing problems and choosing action alternatives. After proposed solutions are presented to management, implementation should be a joint effort between the quality circle and management.

Quality circles cannot be looked on as panaceas for all of an organization's ills, however. Indeed, a number of conditions must be met to keep quality circles from becoming just another management 'gimmick'. These include the following:

- an informed and knowledgeable workforce
- managerial willingness to trust workers with necessary information
- the presence of a 'team spirit' in the quality circle group
- a clear emphasis on quality in the organization's goals
- an organizational culture (see Chapter 8) that encourages participation.

The task force is another kind of team created to solve problems. Task forces are temporary, created with a relatively well-defined task to fulfil. They have a more limited time horizon than that of quality circles; once the task is accomplished the task force is disbanded.

Teams may be formed to solve important problems or to develop new ideas. The intention is to remove these teams from the pressures and demands of day-to-day work. However, it is important to acknowledge that some teams are so intensely involved in their task that individual needs and group maintenance activities are neglected. In this sense, they would fail to live up to the criteria of being high performing and trusting over a long period.

Task forces *are temporary teams created to fulfil a well-defined task within a fairly short period of time.*

Virtual teams

Alongside the changing trends towards teamwork in organizations, other important developments have resulted in the emergence of virtual teams. A virtual team is one whose members work interdependently towards the achievement of a common goal across space and time.[56] Such teams can also work across organizational boundaries. They have developed in the context of new forms of organizational structures, the rapid and ongoing advances in information and communication technologies (ICTs) and globalization. Virtual teams rely particularly on ICTs to enable communication and team activity because they are physically separate. The degree of separation may range from being on separate floors of a large building to being located in different countries around the world. While those in the same building might get together more often, their dislocation from each other and the availability of technology allow them to work together remotely. The following example from Glaxo-SmithKline shows how virtual team working is becoming more prevalent in organizations.

*A **virtual team** is one whose members work interdependently towards the achievement of a common goal across space and time.*

OB IN ACTION

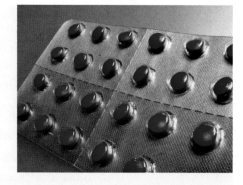

Imagine your organization is given the task of preparing for a global flu pandemic. Not an easy assignment – especially when you have 100 000 employees in 119 countries. Yet this was the situation that GlaxoSmithKline (GSK), the pharmaceutical giant, found itself in two years ago when workers in Philadelphia needed to brief their counterparts all over the world. 'It was a complicated exercise and very difficult to do remotely,' says Elaine Macfarlane, the vice-president of corporate identity and communications at GSK. 'We set up same-time meetings to allow employees to access their foreign colleagues' computer screens, walking them through what was expected of them.'

Welcome to collaborative working. Forget cozy team huddles – you don't need to be able to see your colleagues to work with them. 'The intranet is a powerful tool in our business,' Macfarlane says. 'People said they wanted to work together without getting on a plane. That's when we introduced web-conferencing.' This is one of a range of virtual collaborative tools used by GSK. Secure databases allow external stakeholders to access data, while the company's virtual workspace knows no limits. 'I can be in London at six in the morning delivering a presentation to a colleague in Tokyo,' Macfarlane says.[57]

There is a range of such virtual teams, including network teams, parallel teams, project or product-development teams, work or production teams, service teams, management teams and action teams. The most typical technologies used by such teams are direct email, email via list servers, specialized group software or 'groupware', videoconferencing and audio-conferencing.[58] Duarte and Snyder explain seven critical success factors for such teams: [59]

- supportive human resource policies including career development, rewards for cross-boundary work and results and provision of resources for virtual work
- training and on-the-job education and development, especially in the use of the communication technology
- standard organizational and team processes including clarification of goals, costing, planning, reporting and controlling
- provision and maintenance of necessary electronic collaboration and communication technology
- organizational culture that allows free flow of information, shared leadership and collaboration
- leadership support that values teamwork, communication, learning and capitalizing on diversity
- team-leader and team-member competencies for operating in a virtual and cross-cultural environment.

In some ways virtual teams are no different from other teams, and many teams may have elements of the 'virtual team' present. However, virtual teams do face particular risks because of the context in which they operate. The 'OB in action' section on emailing instead of talking highlights one problem that virtual teams face.

Virtual teams also differ from other teams in the following crucial areas:

- Dependence on technology. Participation may be inhibited if a team member is uncertain of the technology or if equipment is inadequate.
- Absence of nonverbal cues in communication. Misunderstandings in communication may occur as words are read or heard in the absence of facial expression and body gestures, for example.
- Place of interaction. Outside the context of a particular place and often a particular culture or subculture there may be fewer initial shared assumptions and values among team members.
- Timing of interaction. Communication may be synchronous (real time) or asynchronous as members respond in their own time.
- Degrees of public and private communication. In a team that physically meets there is more chance that conflict, domination and other aspects of human interaction are visible and unavoidable, whereas in virtual teams it is possible that private communications between some team members, in addition to full team shared communications, may influence behaviour.

- Recording of the group process. The electronic media used tend to record the group process automatically, whether or not the participants desire it, which may sometimes lead to team members exhibiting extra caution about what they are willing to 'say' in writing.[60]

IN ACTION

Emailing instead of talking face-to-face impedes team bonding for virtual teams

Remote workers who use email to contact colleagues instead of speaking to them face-to-face are damaging trust and teamwork in the workplace, according to research conducted by Cisco Systems and occupational psychologists Pearn Kandola. Virtual teams struggle to replicate the teamwork of people based in close proximity and the problem is worsened by the frequent or exclusive use of email. They suggest that when workers contact each other only by email it can take two weeks before relationships are as socially grounded as those based on face-to-face interaction. The delay is even longer within multicultural virtual teams; they can take up to 17 weeks to establish the same levels of trust achieved by a team of the same culture.

'Through globalization, virtual teams are becoming a common feature in many organizations', said Carolyn Shearsmith, occupational psychologist at Pearn Kandola. 'But they often struggle to be as successful as co-located teams. Our research shows that the media selected for a specific communication, whether it is instant messaging or video conferencing, is almost as important as the content.'[61]

Virtual teams can bring together a range of members with diverse contributions without requiring that those members be located in the same place. They have the ability to transcend borders and organizational structures. However, as for any other team, there are many other requirements for team success. Hackman[62] argues that virtual teams have the same needs and potential problems as any other team (as discussed throughout this chapter) but that it is even harder to create the right conditions for success in virtual teams.

Self-managing teams

Many organizations across the world have moved towards the concept of self-managed work teams in which employees work together as equals to solve problems and improve operations. Every self-managed team needs members with three different strengths:

- technical or functional expertise
- problem-solving and decision-making skills
- interpersonal skills.[63]

Self-managing teams are small groups of people empowered to manage themselves and the work they do on a day-to-day basis. They are also referred to as 'self-directed teams' or 'autonomous'. Typically, a self-managing work team is one in which the members themselves:

Self-managing teams *are small groups of people empowered to manage themselves and the work they do on a day-to-day basis.*

- make decisions on how to divide up tasks within the team
- make decisions on scheduling work within the team
- are able to perform more than one job for the team
- train one another in jobs performed by the team
- evaluate one another's job performance on the team
- are collectively held accountable for the team's performance results.

What differentiates self-managing teams from more traditional work groups is the fact that their members have substantial responsibility for a wide variety of decisions involved in the accomplishment of assigned tasks. Indeed, the very purpose of the self-managing work team is to take on duties previously performed by traditional supervisors – that is, such things as quality control, work scheduling and even performance evaluation. The example of BDM illustrates these features.

OB IN ACTION

Becton Dickinson Medical (BDM) based in Singapore manufactures hypodermic syringes, needles and cannulas, and other similar supplies for pharmaceutical industries. It prides itself on achieving its goals through mutual trust and respect and, accordingly, manages its 300-plus employees in teams. These are self-managing teams though subdivided into a steering team, resource teams and process teams. As their name suggests, resource teams provide resources and are focused on achieving technical improvements, better quality, cost reduction and improvements in waste management and efficiency. Their members come from across the organization, offering a range of skills and expertise. The process teams directly produce the products and their members include technicians, programmers, auditors, storemen, clerks and administrative assistants. Team leaders encourage participation, decision making and focus on performance, targets and evaluation of results. They have authority and responsibility to prioritize their activities, change methods and procedures, to meet standards, safety and customer requirements, to schedule their own activities and maintenance and many other aspects of their work.[64]

Well-designed, step-by-step methods of developing self-managed work teams can move authority and responsibility to all levels, allow employees to manage their own activities and help managers feel more comfortable with the process of empowering employees. This typically assumes that the proper foundations have been laid and the proper culture exists to allow an organization to begin this process.[65]

The establishment and implementation of the concept requires a number of steps. These may include:

- learning about the self-managing work team concept
- conducting a readiness assessment to determine if teams are right for the culture

- communicating to employees the organization's vision and values as they relate to empowerment and teams
- taking the organization through the workplace redesign process
- implementing the redesign
- evaluating the progress of self-managing work teams.

Organizing into self-directed work teams requires planning, selecting the right team members and leaders, designing teams for success, training continually, and carefully managing the shift of power and responsibilities from leaders to team members.

Self-managing teams operate with fewer layers of management than do traditional organizational structures (see also Chapter 7). Research shows that, in comparison with individuals with no participation in a team, members of self-directed teams are significantly more likely (than nonmembers) to report that teams have increased profits, improved customer service and boosted the morale of both employees and management.[66]

When self-managing teams are embedded within an organization, a number of benefits are expected. Among the advantages that may be realized are:[67]

- improved productivity and production quality, and greater production flexibility
- faster response to technological change
- fewer job classifications and fewer management levels
- lower employee absenteeism and turnover
- improved work attitudes.

Because a self-managing team really does manage itself in many ways, there is no real need for the former position of supervisor. Instead, a team leader usually represents the team when dealing with higher-level management. The possible extent of this change is shown in Figure 6.7, where the first level of supervisory management has been eliminated and replaced by self-managing teams. Note also that many traditional tasks of the supervisor have been reallocated to the team. Thus, for persons learning to work in such teams for the first time, and for those managers learning to deal with self-managing teams rather than individual workers, the implications can be quite substantial. Perhaps the most important prerequisite is for team members' jobs to be interdependent. Administrative systems must be able to record performance based on team accomplishments. At the same time, these systems should also enable rewards to be given to team members over time periods that may vary depending on the nature of team assignments. Self-managed work teams differ from traditional work groups in that the team, rather than the first-line supervisor, controls the critical management processes that typically include:

- planning
- organizing
- directing
- staffing.

Typically these teams move through five stages of development as they grow from new creations to mature, fully functioning groups over a period. To reach a fully functioning stage teams may need to undergo training that includes communication, administrative and technical skills. Progressive levels of training in these areas through each of the stages of development become the driving force for team growth and development.

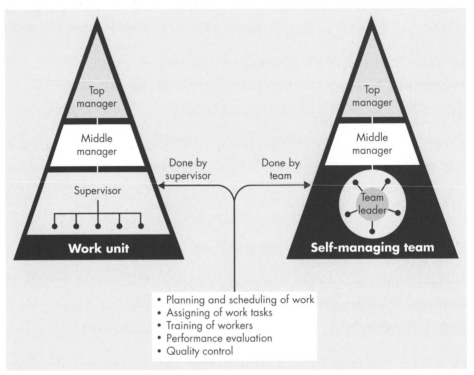

Figure 6.7: Organizational and management implications of self-managing work teams.

TEAM LEADERSHIP

Contemporary research recommends moving beyond self-managed teams to self-leading teams. Self-leading team members should have more freedom and authority to make decisions, independent of external supervision. Leaders should not compromise team membership processes by imposing control, but rather encourage and facilitate the team's self-managing capacity.[68] This capacity for self-leading is not just anchored in the joint actions of team members but also rests on the development of individuals within the team who are better equipped to self-manage and self-lead. Such an approach appreciates that team members are competent individuals who may be willing and interested in playing a role in the strategic direction of the organization as well as influencing their own specific work performance. If self-leading teams are also oriented towards the organization's strategy, they will be able to operate effectively on the organization's behalf without constant referral to higher-level leaders.

A distinguishing feature of self-leading teams is that workers perform work more for the natural (intrinsic) rewards that are built into the task than to receive externally administered rewards. However, self-leading, team-based work systems can only work under two fundamental conditions:

- a significant involvement of the workforce in determining the direction of the organization as well as pursuing that direction
- an opportunity for the work teams to influence that direction, especially as it relates to their specific work performance.

RESEARCH IN

To gain a clear, in-depth view of one example of the many pieces of research carried out in the area of groups and teams, look at the article by Schouteten at the end of Part 3 of this book. Here the author investigates the implementation of group work in care homes in the Netherlands. He shows how group work was conceived as a solution to increased workloads in what had been perceived as an unattractive sector and also how it contributed to an improvement in the quality of working life (QWL) in selected organizations.

You may also wish to access our Web site **www. wileyeurope.com/college/french** and read the article by Arizeta, Swailes and Senior who provide a comprehensive analysis, based on research, of the validity of Belbin's team role model.

CONCLUSION

The study of groups and teams is pivotal within OB. If we believe that people have social needs for affiliation then we must pay close attention to academic work in this subject area, both to explain attitudes and behaviour at work and as a means to enhance worker performance and achievement of organizational goals or, more accurately, the goals of the dominant coalition within organizations. We have set out the distinctions between groups and teams and examined different types of both categories and the ways in which groups and teams develop. Groups and teams have both potential advantages and dangers within the workplace. Managers need to have an understanding of groups and teams in order to deploy them effectively.

SUMMARY

LEARNING OBJECTIVE 1
Groups and teams

A group is a number of people who interact with one another for a common goal whereas a team is a group of people who function as a unit. Groups can be both formal or 'official groups' that are created by the organization or informal or 'unofficial' groups which emerge spontaneously. A team is a small group of people with complementary skills who work together as a unit to achieve a common purpose for which they hold themselves collectively accountable.

LEARNING OBJECTIVE 2
Effective group and team working

Group effectiveness occurs when groups are able to achieve high levels of both task performance and human resource maintenance. Within groups, synergy occurs when a group is able to accomplish more than its members would accomplish individually. However, disruptive or negative behaviours such as social loafing (when individual members do not work as hard as they might otherwise) sometimes occur. Groups can be viewed as open systems interacting with their environments. Group effectiveness involves success in transforming a variety of inputs to the group (such as organizational setting, nature of the task, group membership characteristics and size) into group outputs (task performance and human resource maintenance) through the group process. The group processes or group dynamics represent the internal processes of the group.

Teams operate on three levels so that members engaged in team tasks are also concerned with individual needs and the maintenance of the team. Teams can operate to make or do things, or to run things in an organization. The most effective teams have members with a balance of complementary skills and strengths so that they can achieve synergy.

LEARNING OBJECTIVE 3
Group process and dynamics

Group dynamics are the forces operating within groups that affect task performance and human resource maintenance. They are the internal processes through which members work together to accomplish the transformation of group inputs into group outputs. The terms 'group dynamics' and 'group processes' are often used interchangeably. The behaviours within groups may be required or they may be emergent, additional behaviours. All groups pass through various stages in their life cycles. Five different stages of group development pose somewhat distinct management problems. Groups in the forming stage have problems managing individual entry. The storming stage introduces problems of managing expectations and status. Groups in the norming stage have problems managing member relations and task efforts. Groups in the performing stage encounter problems managing continual improvement and self-renewal. Groups in the adjourning stage have problems managing task completion and the process of disbanding. Group norms or standards of behaviour will impact upon the behaviour of all group members. Group roles relating to particular positions in the group describe the expected behaviours for individuals in those roles. Emotions and patterns of communication and decision making are also elements of group dynamics.

LEARNING OBJECTIVE 4
Intergroup dynamics

Intergroup dynamics are the forces that operate between two or more groups. Although groups are supposed to cooperate in organizations, things do not always work this way. Groups can become involved in dysfunctional conflicts and competition. Sometimes, the origins of these conflicts lie in work flow interdependencies; at other times, the origins can be traced to differing group characteristics. Such things as status, time and goal orientations, reward systems and resource availabilities can all make a difference in the way in which groups work together. Managers must be aware of the potential for problems in intergroup relations and know how to deal with them, even as they recognize that some competition can be good. The disadvantages of intergroup competition can be reduced through management strategies to direct, train and reinforce groups to pursue cooperative actions instead of purely competitive actions.

LEARNING OBJECTIVE 5
Team performance and cohesiveness

An important aspect of any team is the set of norms within which it operates. Norms are rules or standards of member behaviour; they are ideas or beliefs about what is appropriate behaviour for team members. Norms identify the way in which 'loyal' members are supposed to behave. As such, they can exert a major influence on teams when members adhere to them. The clarification of roles is important for all members of work teams. Individuals have a preferred team role as well as backup roles that they can perform in order to contribute to team effectiveness. Role ambiguities and conflicts create anxieties and stress, and can detract from performance and personal satisfaction. Cohesiveness is a measure of the attractiveness of a team for its members. In a highly cohesive team, members value their place in the team and are very loyal to it. Thus, an important rule of thumb is that members of highly cohesive teams conform to team norms. Consequently, the combination of the team performance norms and level of cohesiveness can reveal a lot about its performance potential. The most favourable situation for any manager or team leader is to be in charge of a highly cohesive team with positive performance norms; the positive norms point behaviour in desired directions and the high cohesiveness creates desires to live up to the expectations set by these norms. Good managers are able to influence team cohesiveness in ways that support the accomplishment of long-term team effectiveness.

LEARNING OBJECTIVE 6
Teambuilding approaches

Teambuilding is a series of planned action steps designed to gather and analyse data on the functioning of a team. It is also about implementing changes to increase the team's operating effectiveness. Teamwork occurs when members of a team work together in a way that represents certain core values, all of which promote the use of skills to accomplish common goals. Teambuilding is thus a way of building the capacity for teamwork and high performance. The teambuilding process is participative and engages all team members in identifying problems and opportunities, planning appropriate actions, making individual commitments to implement these actions, and conducting appropriate evaluation and feedback activities. Teambuilding can involve brainstorming to generate uninhibited ideas, facilitators to raise self-awareness and group awareness, and training to develop team skills. Some specific teambuilding processes are away days, continual improvement and outdoor experiences.

LEARNING OBJECTIVE 7
Types of teams

An employee involvement team is any team whose members meet regularly outside of their formal task assignments to address important work-related problems and concerns. Most typically, these teams deal with issues involving total quality management and the quest for continual improvement in operations. Popular types of problem-solving teams are the quality circle, the task force and the autonomous work team. The latter was the precursor to the self-managed work team. A self-managing team is a work group whose members collectively take responsibility for performing the group task and making many of the 'supervisory' decisions relating to task performance on a day-to-day basis. The team members, in the full sense of the word, 'manage' themselves. The traditional level of supervisory management is eliminated and in its place the work team agrees to accept responsibility for self-management. Members of this team will plan, complete and evaluate their own work; they will collectively train and evaluate one another in task performance; they will share tasks and responsibilities and they may even determine one another's pay grades. Such teams are based on the concept of empowerment and offer another creative way to allow people to become more involved in important decisions affecting their work. Under the right circumstances, self-managing teams can contribute to improved productivity for organizations and improved quality of working life for their members. Virtual teams have members who work interdependently towards common goals even though they are not together in the same place at the same time.

CHAPTER 6 STUDY GUIDE

You can also test your understanding and access further resources at **www.wileyeurope.com/college/french**.

REVIEW QUESTIONS

1. Outline the different types of groups that can exist in organizations and provide your own example of each.
2. Explain the key differences between teams and groups and the reasons organizations might wish to instigate teams.
3. Explain how the size of a group or team might affect group processes and effectiveness.
4. Explain the difference between the forming and performing in the group development stages
5. What are the likely performance outcomes for a highly cohesive team and how can team cohesion be increased or decreased?
6. Compare and contrast employee involvement teams and self-managed teams.

APPLICATION QUESTIONS

1. If groups are to create positive synergy in the accomplishment of organizational tasks, what must managers do to overcome disruptive behaviours?

2. Until recently your group of seven members has been operating successfully and you felt that it was achieving high levels of effectiveness. However, since two members left your team (and the organization) to go to other jobs and you replaced them with two new members (one from outside the organization and one from another organizational section) there is less group cohesion and more conflict. Discuss the reasons why these changes might have occurred and use theories and concepts about groups to explain them.

3. Your organization operates with four key groups: corporate services, sales, finance and production. Recently there have been problems with achieving its production targets because there is a shortage of workers; the corporate services group has been unable to replace departing employees rapidly enough. Sales is unhappy because they are unable to meet orders for stock, and finance is becoming increasingly stressed about the lack of cash flow in the business. What are the likely work flow relationships between each group and why might they cause problems?

4. Your team leader is always pushing your work group to work harder, to be more productive and to be the most successful production team in the company. You and your fellow team members just laugh at him and get on with your work. You feel you are all productive and there's no need to work any harder. You get your weekly pay and working harder won't change that. What is the likelihood that the team could be more productive and what could the manager do to improve productivity?

5. Your organization produces linen household goods. In the production of those goods, groups of 15–20 employees typically work in a production unit with a supervisor who gives them frequent directions about what is required. The organization has decided to go towards a model of self-managing teams after trialing it successfully in the finance and the human resources departments. What are the likely changes that employees will face in changing to this way of working and how should management introduce the changes?

6. Your team is very close and members of the team will do anything to help each other out, including covering up for each other if there is a crisis or poor performance. What issues are there for the performance of the group?

7. You have a team of seven that operates in several different cities in your country. Your country is ethnically diverse and the level of knowledge of technological

advances in communication and information technology is uneven across different ethnic groups owing to their socioeconomic position in society. Since the success of the team depends on using new technology to communicate, what can you do to encourage full and equal participation by team members and what will you do to build them into a team?

RESEARCH QUESTIONS

1. Search the Web site of a major company looking for depictions of the company structure – either an organizational chart or lists of sections and departments in the company. Use this information to draw up a profile of formal groups within the organization, labelling different types of groups and links between them. Analyse the groups as much as you can from the information available, in terms of their likely features (size, homogeneity, position roles within them, resources, goals and decision-making functions). Repeat the process for another company and compare the two.

2. Search for at least two teambuilding consultants on the Internet. Look for what sorts of teambuilding processes they offer. What do they promise for organizations that use their services? How do their programmes compare with each other?

RUNNING PROJECT

Complete the following tasks relating to your organization:

1. Refer back to any earlier work you did on the structure of your organization. Also try to obtain an organizational chart for the organization. Describe how the organization uses groups to structure the workplace. Which of these groups, if any, could be described as teams?

2. Choose one group in the organization and draw a diagram of the group as an open system. List the most important outputs of the group and explain how the manager, group leader or group members would know whether the group is effective at any given time.

3. Choose two different groups within the organization. Describe how these groups work with each other. If you have direct access to the organization, ask management how it deals with intergroup conflict.

4. What types of teams exist in your organization? Try to find an example of each of the following: self-managing teams, virtual teams, employee involvement teams and problem-solving teams? Explain why they exist and how team members work together.

INDIVIDUAL ACTIVITY

Identifying norms that influence teams

Objectives

1. To help you determine the norms operating in an organization
2. To assess the strength of response to particular norms
3. To help clarify the importance of norms as influences on team behaviour

Total time: 60 minutes.

Procedure

1. Choose an organization that you have worked for or of which you are closely aware.
2. Insert each of the statements below into the following question:

If an employee in your organization were to [insert statement here], most other employees would, too.

Statements:

(a) show genuine concern for the problems that face the organization and make suggestions about solving them (organizational/personal pride)

(b) set very high personal standards of performance (performance/excellence)

(c) try to make the work group operate more like a team when dealing with issues or problems (teamwork/communication)

(d) think of going to a supervisor with a problem (leadership/supervision)

(e) evaluate expenditures in terms of the benefits they will provide for the organization (profitability/cost effectiveness)

(f) express concern for the wellbeing of other members of the organization (colleague/associate relations)

(g) Keep a customer or client waiting while looking after matters of personal convenience (customer/client relations)

(h) criticize another employee who is trying to improve things in the work situation (innovativeness/creativity)

(i) actively look to expand their knowledge to be able to do a better job (training/development)

(j) be perfectly honest in answering this questionnaire (candour/openness).

3. For each statement in point 2 above, indicate your response in terms of A, B, C, D or E.
   A Strongly agree or encourage it.
   B Agree with it or encourage it.

C Consider it unimportant.

D Disagree with or discourage it.

E Strongly disagree with or discourage it.

Evaluation

Review your results to decide whether the organization is likely to provide a suitable environment for effective teams.

GROUP ACTIVITY

Analysing your groups

Objective

To show the relevance and pervasiveness of formal and informal groups within your lives:

- in your 'organizational' environment at university/college
- outside that environment (social and other organizations).

Procedure

Working individually, list all of the various groups to which you belong currently. Working in groups:

1. Discuss the groups you have listed as individuals and place them into categories – formal or informal.
2. Are there some types of groups to which you all, or several of you, belong? Why?
3. What conclusions can you draw about the number of groups to which you individually and collectively belong?
4. Do you behave differently in different groups?

TEAM TACTICS – LESSONS FROM FOOTBALL FOR THE BUSINESS WORLD

Creating a world-class football squad involves more than just throwing talented players together. It's about building an effective team. The objectives in football are clear: score more goals than the opposition and you will take home a trophy. The best clubs spot talent early and will follow an ever-evolving group of players, sometimes for years. The clubs are constantly building relationships in the knowledge that they may want to sign a player two, three or four years down the line. Football managers have a clear view of what they are looking for in a player and how each individual will fit in with the team style. If the team is leaking goals, the manager will seek a strong centre back. If it is lacking creativity, an attacking midfield player could be the answer.

Getting the right mix of talent and ability is crucial. Too many 'ball-winners' and the team will not score many goals. Players must have the desire to make the group work well. If there are too many 'prima donnas' and things do not go well then people start being defensive and blame others. Often, most creativity comes from taking a risk on an unknown player. Glenn Hoddle, when he was England football coach, took a risk when he included Michael Owen in the England squad at the World Cup in 1998, and Sven Goran Eriksson took an even bigger risk in 2006 with Theo Walcott – a young player who had yet to play a competitive game in the English Premiership. Players with fancy footwork, such as France's Zinedine Zidane and Brazil's Ronaldinho, may grab all the headlines, but great teams also feature players who serve important but less visible roles, like Claude Makelele or Gilberto Silva, who marshal the midfield for France and Brazil. Many clubs make the mistake of focusing only on the talented top 2% or 3% of the team – forgetting the hard-working people below. Alert managers know that they must communicate the importance of working together as a team – that no one is bigger than the club. If someone is acting out of line, no matter how big a star they are, that needs to be addressed. Manchester United's manager, Sir Alex Ferguson, was prepared to sacrifice star players Roy Keane and David Beckham for the good of the team after a series of isolated incidents, for example. On a practical level, this is simply getting rid of an obstructive element. But it also sends a strong message that this behaviour will not be tolerated.

Winning football teams are constantly talking – both on and off the pitch. Senior players will give advice and encouragement and keep the squad focused on the game. 'Half time' is reserved for a frank evaluation of the play to date. Do we need to change tactics, push more men forward in search of an equalizer, or sit back and defend the lead? All teams should take time out to review performance.

Even the most successful clubs lose talent because it is not being developed, just look at the number of players who leave a club because they don't get enough first-team football. This is a big problem with Chelsea, and Real Madrid, which has top international players who don't get a game every week.

Adapted from Bentley, R. (2006), Talent management: Team tactics, *Personnel Today Magazine*, 27 June 2006. Reproduced by permission of Reed Business Information.

Case Study

A canny substitution at the right time can completely turn the game around, injecting the team with renewed enthusiasm. Sir Alex Ferguson did just that with Manchester United in the 1999 Champions League final when substitutes Teddy Sheringham and Ole Gunnar Solskjaer both scored in the dying minutes to win the game 2-1. So how do football managers stay on top of the game? Here are some simple steps that good managers and teams follow:

• Keep a cool head under pressure. Composure is vital in high-pressure matches. When Beckham kicked out against Argentina's Diego Simeone at the World Cup in 1998 and was sent off, it arguably lost England the match and the chance of winning the title.
• Be unpredictable. Walcott was unpredictable for his own team mates and the opposition. This could be the real stuff of creativity. For him, being on a team at that level really brought him on.
• Foster diversity. Creativity is most common in diverse teams – be it age, style, gender, ethnicity or cultural background. Well managed, this will lead to higher levels of innovation and performance. The key is to get a team to learn how to work together and to have a positive attitude towards difference. Differences can be uncomfortable but when worked through in a positive, supportive way, they foster creativity and innovation.

The most important element of managing a top team is to keep knowledge evolving. In football, as soon as the full-time whistle blows, the manager and coach will review the match to see what the team is doing well and what it is doing badly. The best managers in football were not necessarily the best players. Sir Alex Ferguson, Arsène Wenger and José Mourinho were good footballers, but not star players. So what does that tell you? Really good football managers understand what they are good at and what they are bad at and will buy in the people they need.

Questions

1. What key lessons can be learnt about teambuilding from football and other sporting teams?
2. How might knowledge of Belbin's team roles help team development in sporting and other teams?
3. Why are football managers' always blamed for the poor performance of their team and how does this differ if at all from other working situations?
4. Explain the role of the leader in fostering effective team working?

SUGGESTED READING

Fineman, S., Sims, D & Gabriel, Y. (2005), Us and Them, in *Organizing and Organizations*, 3rd edn, Sage: London. This provides a distinctive take on the topic, including some illuminating first-hand accounts of working in groups.

END NOTES

1. Schein, E.H. (1988), *Organizational Psychology,* 3rd edn, Prentice Hall: Englewood Cliffs, p. 145.

2. Handy, C. (1993), *Understanding Organizations,* Penguin Books: Harmondsworth.

3. For a good discussion of groups and teams in the workplace, see Katzenbach, J.R. & Smith, D.K. (1993), The discipline of teams. *Harvard Business Review,* March/April, 111–120. See also Stewart, G.L., Mane, C.C. & Sims, H.P. (1999), *Team Work and Group Dynamics,* John Wiley & Sons Ltd: New York.

4. Leavitt, H.J. & Lipman-Blumen, J. (1995), Hot groups. *Harvard Business Review,* July/August, 109–116.

5. See, for example, Lawler, E.E. III (1986), *High-Involvement Management,* Jossey-Bass: San Francisco.

6. Employer of the Year Awards – Valuing Work–Life Balance, *Equal Opportunities Review,* issue 96, 2001.

7. Shaw, M.E. (1976), *Group Dynamics: The Psychology of Small Group Behaviour,* 2nd edn. McGraw-Hill: New York.

8. Latané, B., Williams, K. & Harkins, S. (1978), Many hands make light the work: the causes and consequences of social loafing. *Journal of Personality and Social Psychology,* 37, 822–832. Weldon, E. & Gargano, G.M. (1985), Effort in additive task groups: the effects of shared responsibility on the quality of multi-attribute judgments. *Organizational Behaviour and Human Decision Processes,* 36, 348–361. George, J.M. (1992), Extrinsic and intrinsic origins of perceived social loafing in organizations. *Academy of Management Journal,* March, 191–202. Duncan, W.J. (1994), Why some people loaf in groups while others loaf alone. *Academy of Management Executive,* 8, 79–80.

9. Kravitz, D.A. & Martin, B. (1986), Ringelmann rediscovered. *Journal of Personality and Social Psychology,* 50, 936–941.

10. Likert, R. (1961), *New Patterns of Management.* McGraw-Hill: New York.

11. For a good discussion of task forces see Ware, J. (1977), Managing a task force. Note 478–002. Harvard Business School.

12. See, for example, Bradford, L.P. (1997), *Group Development,* 2nd edn. Jossey-Bass: San Francisco.

13. Heinen, J.S. & Jacobson, E. (1976), A model of task group development in complex organization and a strategy of implementation. *Academy of Management Review,* 1, October, 98–111. Tuckman, B.W. (1965), Developmental sequence in small groups. *Psychological Bulletin,* 63, 384–399. Tuckman, B.W. & Jensen, M.A.C. (1977), Stages of small group development revisited. *Group and Organization Studies,* 2, 419–427.

14. Herold, D.M. (1979), The effectiveness of work groups, in S. Kerr (ed.), *Organizational Behaviour.* Wiley: New York, p. 95; see also the discussion of group tasks in Manz, S. & Sims (1999), op. cit., pp. 142–143.

15. Ilgen, D.R., LePine, J.A. & Hollenbeck, J.R. (1997), Effective decision making in multinational teams, in *New Perspectives on International Industrial/Organizational Psychology* (eds P.C. Earley & M. Erez), New Lexington Press: San Francisco. Watson, W. (1993), Cultural diversity's impact on interaction process and performance. *Academy of Management Journal,* 16.

16. Argote, L. & McGrath, J.E. (1993), Group processes in organizations: continuity and change, in *International Review of Industrial and Organizational Psychology* (eds C.L. Cooper & I.T. Robertson). Wiley: New York, pp. 333–389.

17. See Ilgen, D.R., LePine, J.A. & Hollenbeck, J.R. (1997), op. cit., pp. 377–409.

18. Katzenbach, J.R. & Smith, D.K. (1993), op. cit.

19. Thomas, E.J. & Fink, C.F. (1969), Effects of group size, in *Readings in Organizational and Human Performance* (eds L.L. Cummings & W.E. Scott), Irwin: Homewood, IL, pp. 394–408.

20. Davis, P. (2005), Mix to match. *HR Monthly,* September, 42–43.

21. Ibid.

22. Shaw, M.E. (1976), op. cit.

23. Homans, G.C. (1950), *The Human Group.* Harcourt Brace: New York.

24. Producer power. *The Economist,* 4 March, 1995, p. 70.

25. Gizzo, R.A. & Dickson, M.J. (1996), Teams in organisations: recent research on performance and effectiveness. *Annual Review of Psychology,* 47, 307–338.

26. Katzenbach, J.R. & Smith, D.K. (1999), *The Wisdom of Teams: Creating the High Performance Organisation,* HarperCollins: New York.

27. Senior, B. & Swailes, S, (2004), The dimensions of management team performance: a repertory grid study. *Journal of Productivity and Performance Management,* 53 (4), 317–333.

28. Katzenbach, J.R. & Smith, D.K. (1993a) The discipline of teams. *Harvard Business Review,* (March/April), 111–120. Katzenbach, J.R. & Smith, D.K. (1993b), *The Wisdom of Teams: Creating the High-Performance Organization,* Harvard Business School Press: Boston, MA.

29. See also Katzenbach, J.R. (1997), The myth of the top management team. *Harvard Business Review,* 75 (November/December), 83–91.

30. Katzenbach, J.R. & Smith, D.K. (1993a) op. cit. and (1993b) op. cit.

31. For a good overview, see Stewart, G.L., Manz, C.C. & Sims, H.P. (1999), *Team Work and Group Dynamics,* John Wiley & Sons, Ltd: New York.

32. Katzenbach, J.R. & Smith, D.K. (1993a) op. cit., p. 112.

33. Developed from ibid. (1993a), pp. 118–119.

34. Johnson, R. (2000), The Beverage Report. *People Management,* 30 March.

35. For an interesting discussion of sports teams see Fagenson-Eland, E. (2001), The National Football League's Bill Parcells on winning, leading, and turning around teams. *Academy of Management Executive,* 15 (August 2001), 48–57. Nancy Katz (2002), Sports teams as a model for workplace teams: lessons and liabilities. *Academy of Management Executive,* 15, 56–69.

36. For a good discussion of teambuilding, see Dyer, W.D. (1995), *Teambuilding,* 3rd edn. Addison-Wesley: Reading, MA.

37. See Channel 4 programme, *Cutting Edge: Exposure,* 1993, see http://ftvdb.bfi.org.uk/title/484281.

38. See Simon Hollingsworth in *Personnel Today,* 29 June 2007

39. Bentley, R. (2006), The cook, the ape and the Da Vinci Code. *Training and Coaching,* 26 July.

40. Developed from a discussion by Schein, E.H. (1969), *Process Consultation.* Addison-Wesley: Reading, MA, pp. 32–37. Schein, E.H. (1988), *Process Consultation,* Vol. I. Addison-Wesley: Reading, MA, pp. 40–49.

41. Chen, G. & Klimoski, R.J. (2003), The impact of expectations on newcomer performance in teams as mediated by work characteristics, social exchanges and empowerment. *Academy of Management Journal,* 46, 591–607.

42. The classic work is Bales, R.F. (1958), Task roles and social roles in problem-solving groups, in *Readings in Social Psychology* (eds E.E. Maccoby, T.M. Newcomb & E.L. Hartley). Holt, Rinehart & Winston: New York.

43. For a good description of task and maintenance functions, see Gabarro, J.J. & Harlan, A. (1976), *Note on Process Observation,* Note 9-477-029, Harvard Business School.

44. Benne, K.D. & Sheats, P. (1948), Functional roles of group members. *Journal of Social Issues,* 4, 41–49.

45. Belbin, R.M.(1981), *Management Teams: Why they Succeed or Fail.* Butterworth-Heinemann: Oxford. Belbin, R.M. (1993), *Team Roles at Work.* Butterworth-Heinemann: Oxford.

46. Manning, T., Parker, R. & Progson, T. (2006), A revised model of team roles and some research findings. *Journal of Industrial and Commercial Training,* 38 (6), 287–296.

47. See Fisher, S.G., Hunter, T.A. & Macrosson, W.D.K. (2000), The distribution of Belbin team roles among UK managers. *Personnel Review,* 29 (2), 124–140. Belbin, R.M., op. cit. p. 22.

48. Hollington, S. (2007), How to build an effective team. *People Management,* 28 June, 11–12.

49. See Feldman, D.C. (1984), The development and enforcement of group norms. *Academy of Management Review,* 9, 47–53.

50. See Allen, R.F. & Pilnick, S. (1973), Confronting the shadow organization: how to select and defeat negative norms. *Organizational Dynamics,* Spring, 13–17. Zander, A. (1982), Making Groups Effective, Jossey-Bass: San Francisco, Ch. 4. Feldman, D.C. (1984), op. cit.

51. For a summary of research on group cohesiveness, see Shaw, M.E. (1971), *Group Dynamics.* McGraw-Hill: New York, pp. 110–112, 192.

52. See Renshaw, R. (2007), Passing the teamwork test. *The Times,* 27 June 2007. Reprodcued by permission of NI Syndication.

53. Guzzo, R.A. & Salas, E. (eds) (1995), Team Effectiveness and Decision Making in Organizations. Jossey-Bass: San Francisco.

54. Example from (1989) Time to toss tradition? *Enterprise,* Autumn, 35–39.

55. See K. Ohmae (1982), Quality control circles: they work and don't work. *Wall Street Journal,* 29 March, p. 16. Steel, R.P., Mento, A.J., Dilla, B.L. *et al.* (1985), Factors influencing the success and failure of two quality circles programs. *Journal of Management,* **11** (1), 99–119. Lawler, E.E. III & Mohrman, S.A. (1987), Quality circles: after the honeymoon. *Organizational Dynamics,* **15** (4), 42–54.

56. Lipnack, J. & Stamps, J. (2000), *Virtual Teams,* 2nd edn, John Wiley & Sons Ltd: New York, p. 18.

57. See Ford, E. (2007), Team work gets results. *The Times,* 28 June 2007. Reprodcued by permission of NI Syndication.

58. Elwyn, G., Greenhalgh, T. & Macfarlane, F. (2001), *Groups: A Guide to Small Group Work in Healthcare, Management, Education and Research,* Radcliffe Medical Press: Abingdon, pp. 203–206.

59. Duarte, D. & Tennant Snyder, N. (2001), *Mastering Virtual Teams,* revised edition, Jossey-Bass: San Francisco, pp. 4–23.

60. Elwyn, G., Greenhalgh, T. & Macfarlane, F. op. cit., pp. 206–214.

61. See James Brockett People Management Online, 21 September 2006, www.CIPD.co.uk.

62. Hackman, J.R. (2002), *Leading Teams: Setting the Stage for Great Performances,* Harvard Business School Press: Boston, MA, pp. 130–132.

63. Katzenbach, J.R. & Smith, D.K. (1993), The discipline of teams. *Harvard Business Review,* March/April, p. 112.

64. Spring Singapore, 'Self-managing teams in Becton Dickinson Medical (Singapore)', Productivity Digest, December 2000, www.spring.gov. sg/portal/newsroom/epublications/pd/2000_12/ index_IP.html, accessed 27 November 2007.

65. Lacy, L. (1992), Self-managed work groups step-by-step. *Journal for Quality and Participation,* **15** (3), 68–73.

66. Gordon, J. (1992), Work teams – how far have they come? *Training,* **29** (10), 59–65.

67. Developed in part from Wellins, R.S., Byham, W.C. & Wilson, J.M. (1992), Proactive teams achieve inspiring results. *World Executive's Digest,* October, 18–24.

68. Stewart, G.L. & Barrick, M.R. (2000), Team structure and performance: assessing the mediating role of intrateam process and the moderating role of task type. *Academy of Management Journal,* April, 135–148.

Journal Article

GROUP WORK IN A DUTCH HOME CARE ORGANIZATION: DOES IT IMPROVE THE QUALITY OF WORKING LIFE?

Roel Schouteten

SUMMARY

Home care in the Netherlands is facing a trend towards increasing workloads, giving it the image of an unattractive sector to work in. To deal with increasing workloads and their effects, many solutions have been developed, including the concept of team or group work. This paper will address the possibilities, conditions and effects involved in the implementation of group work in home care as a means of improving the quality of working life (QWL) in this sector. To this end I have studied QWL in three jobs in two organizations for home care, one of which implemented group work. This comparison concludes that jobs in the team-based organization are more complete and challenging, bringing more job decision latitude, but also higher work pressure. Copyright © 2004 John Wiley & Sons, Ltd.

INTRODUCTION

Workloads due to work intensification are increasingly becoming a serious problem (SCP, 1998; CBS, 2002). In Europe the Netherlands lead when it comes to workload, with a growth rate of workload above the European average (Houtman *et al.*, 1999). These workloads are often attributed to organizations pursuing flexibility, quality and efficiency (Cartwright and Cooper, 1997; Cooper, 1998; Oeij *et al.*, 1998; Sauter and Murphy, 1995). The home care sector in the Netherlands, in particular, is being affected by developments towards greater workloads, such as governmental decisions about the sector, shortage of personnel and increasing complexity in the need for home care (Breedveld, 2003; Broekhuis and Van der Vaart, 2002; Morée and Vulto, 1995; Van Noort, 2002; Vulto and Morée, 1996). To increase competition in the home care market and to improve the quality of home care, the government has stimulated a change from a non-profit home care sector towards a more market-oriented one (from supply-directed towards demand-directed). Increased professionalization and scaling-up of the sector (Meloen, 2000) has led to a change of working methods and to less personal care. Standardization and increased bureaucracy have brought about higher work loads and alienation of many, mostly intrinsically motivated workers. Though efficiency may have increased, competition in the sector and the quality of home care have not (Breedveld, 2003). Another effect has been that home care is increasingly seen as an unattractive sector to work in and be trained for (De Geus *et al.*, 2000). There are also the implications of increased medical knowledge, which has made more patients with more complicated care needs eligible for home care, raising the demand for more and different knowledge and skills from

---

Reproduced from *International Journal of Health Planning and Management*, **19**, 179–194(2004) © John Wiley & Sons, Ltd. Reproduced by permission.

care takers (De Jonge *et al.*, 1995). These developments have made workload and quality of working life (QWL) important issues in the home care sector.

Many solutions have been developed to deal with increasing workloads and its consequences, such as absenteeism, labor turnover, decreasing commitment and satisfaction, ranging from coping strategies (Cartwright and Cooper, 1997) to organizational change (Van der Zwaan, 1999). One such approach seeking to improve both the quality of working life and that of the organization (efficiency, profitability, flexibility, competitiveness), is the concept of team or group work (Procter and Mueller, 2000: 8). Working in teams has become ever more important in discussions about organizations and the organization of work (Harley, 2001; Procter and Mueller, 2000; Sundstrom *et al.*, 1990). However, the effects on QWL are controversial (see, e.g. Harley, 2001). This paper addresses the question whether the introduction of teamwork in an organization for home care improves QWL.

This question is also interesting, because literature on teamwork has an important bias, i.e. most discussions tend to be on the automotive industry, and especially on final car assembly, the most labor-intensive part of the production process (Benders *et al.*, 1999; Procter and Currie, 2002). This may create the impression that the automotive industry is the leading sector using group work. Benders *et al.*, however, show that manufacturing industries (including the automotive sector) are not the leading users of group delegation. In contrast, as their study shows, it is the nonprofit sector that is clearly leading, followed by service industries (Benders *et al.*, 1999: 19). For that reason, they urge researchers focus on non-profit sectors to find examples of team-based work. Only more recently, studies of teamwork in service settings have begun to emerge (Procter and Mueller, 2000). In service settings the nature of work is less straightforward than in manufacturing, and the organizational context is different. Since organizational structure and the nature of work are important determinants of the success of group work, we need to understand what teamwork in service settings looks like and whether it achieves its objectives.

An earlier study on teamwork in the Netherlands home care sector (Van Asch *et al.*, 2000) showed that the incidence of working in teams in this sector is increasing, yielding some positive results, such as a better image and increased worker commitment. However, this study was rather limited, and the question remains as to what level teamwork in the home care sector is possible and what the effects are on QWL. I will try to answer this question by comparing QWL in two organizations, of which one had implemented a form of teamwork. This means that the two organizations differ in work organization, although they offer similar services to their clients. Using theoretical notions on QWL and team work, as will be presented in the following sections, I will compare the two organizations and describe the differences in work organization and the extent to which they determine QWL.

TEAMWORK

Teamworking or group work has had a long history (Benders and Van Hootegem, 1999; Buchanan, 2000), with an abundance of literature (Benders *et al.*, 1999), and the term 'team' has been used in all kinds of meanings (Benders and Van Hootegem, 2000).

According to Buchanan, teamworking as a management idea has been rediscovered over and over again, and it can be described as an 'eager and enduring embrace' (Buchanan, 2000: 25). During the 1960s and 1970s teamwork in the form of autonomous group working was embraced by the QWL movement, and by the end of the 1970s it appeared to have some global reach, generating a significant volume of published output (Buchanan, 2000). In this period, the main managerial concern was with the implications of boredom for job satisfaction, productivity, absenteeism and labor turnover. In the 1980s management motives changed towards competitive advantage, particularly with respect to quality of product and customer service. More and more, teams are seen as a solution for organizational problems (Hut and Molleman, 1998). They are considered to be a viable means in dealing with growing complexity (for instance resulting from the introduction of new technologies) and variability increase caused by customization (diversified quality production, shorter product life cycles, and more customer service) (De Sitter *et al.*, 1997; Van der Zwaan, 1999).

This direct relationship with organizational performance carries along a number of implications for the way in which organizations are structured and managed (Procter and Mueller, 2000). Adapting organizational output characteristics (as the basis of organizational design) to changing environments requires simple organizations with complex jobs (instead of complex organizations with simple jobs; De Sitter *et al.*, 1997; Van Beinum *et al.*, 1968). In this sense, teamwork is a management strategy for the organization of work. And for it to be successful, fundamental changes must take place in an organization's structure and the nature of work (Procter and Currie, 2002).

As a management idea, there are two main traditions of teamworking (Benders and Van Hootegem, 1999), i.e. the idea of autonomous work groups, based on sociotechnical theory, and the idea of teamworking in Japanese industry, respectively. The sociotechnical concept of autonomous work teams is based on Trist and Bamforth's study of post-war British coal-mining industry (1951). In this industry, automation led to the development of the 'long-wall' method of coal-getting; a mass production system that replaced the autonomous, multi-skilled groups that had operated under the 'hand-got' system. Under the 'long-wall' regime one cycle of coal-getting was divided over three working shifts per day, each responsible for one subtask of the entire cycle. Underground working conditions (a breakage in the layers of coal), however, forced the workers to adapt to new and changing circumstances, resulting in the 'composite short-wall' method, based on multi-skilled, self-selecting groups, responsible on one shift for the whole cycle of coal-getting. From this observation emerged the theoretical development (initially at the Tavistock Institute of Human Relations) of the concept of autonomous work groups as known today in the Sociotechnical Systems Design (Buchanan, 2000).

Basic principle of a sociotechnical organizational design is the idea of a 'joint optimization' of the social and technical subsystems in organizations and simultaneously achieving employees' and organizational goals. Autonomous work groups are the means to reach this goal. Although the notion of sociotechnical teams was picked up in different countries (mostly in North-Western Europe) and different labels have been used, the common denominator is the idea that teams should have a considerable degree of responsible autonomy (Benders and Van Hootegem, 1999). Consequently, Benders and Van Hootegem define sociotechnical teams as: 'a group of workers, generally between 4 and 20 persons, responsible for a rounded-off part of the production process, and entitled to take certain decisions autonomously' (1999: 615).

Teamworking in Japanese industry is not this clearly defined, because it can take a variety of forms (Procter and Mueller, 2000; Sey, 2001). Moreover, in Japan, teamworking is perceived as a quite natural way of working. It is not a form of work organization designed apart from the workplace, but it is the work practice accomplished by management and workers through their experience in the workplace and their striving for a good work performance (Morita, 2001). For that reason, it did not warrant any special attention for a long time. Attention for this form of Japanese work organization was fuelled by the publication of *The Machine that Changed the World* by Womack *et al.* (1990). These (Western) authors used the term 'team' to describe the work groups in a Japanese work organization in 'lean' factories, emphasizing the advantages of running production with the lowest possible level of inventories. They claim that 'it is the dynamic work team that emerges as the heart of the lean factory' (1990: 99).

Morita (2001) distinguishes four characteristics of the Japanese work organization, i.e. multi-skilled workers, worker's continuous skill development, the 'one team, one task' principle and the role of supervisors. The first three show a resemblance to the characteristics of sociotechnical teams, but the supervisor's role is important in distinguishing Japanese teams from sociotechnical teams, particularly as regards team autonomy, which is important in the sociotechnical definition. If the supervisor is considered to be a part of the team (team 'leader'), the team scores high on autonomy. If the supervisor is not considered to be part of the team (team 'foreman'), the team scores low on autonomy. Due to a limited empirical understanding of the exact role of the supervisor in the Japanese work organization, it is difficult to label Japanese teams autonomous (Benders and Van Hootegem, 1999).

As a result, the term 'team' is often used in the 1990s, though its meaning depends on the context in which it is used. In this paper I will follow the approach that Benders *et al.* (1999, 2001) chose for their EPOC study on group work in Europe. They use the term 'group work' to overcome the lack of consensus about the term teamwork, as has been presented before. Group work, in their definition, denotes the autonomous form of teamwork (Benders *et al.*, 2001). They use two criteria to determine the level of group work in organizations, i.e. coverage and intensity. Coverage refers to the proportion of employees involved in group decision making, whereas intensity refers to the number of decision rights assigned to the groups in the organization. The latter is a measurement of autonomy or job decision latitude. The EPOC study shows that it is sensible to distinguish two types of teamworking, i.e. group work (the autonomous form) and teamwork (with limited autonomy). This distinction is based on the level of group delegation (distribution of decision rights) and the complexity of the organization, which can be used to determine the type of teamworking in the team-based organization in this study.

TEAMWORK AND QWL

Being the dependent variable in this study, QWL is a function of job content and can be defined as the balance between control need and control capacity (De Sitter *et al.*, 1997). Ashby's 'Law of requisite variety' (1969), implies that control capacity should be located where the need for control arises. This resembles Karasek's (1979) balance between job demands (control need) and decision latitude (control capacity). Important job characteristics in achieving this balance are the 'wholeness' of the work process, responsible autonomy, and worker's multiplicity of skills (Trist and Bamforth, 1951). This means that a job consisting of complete tasks and sufficient control capacity to conclusively deal with control need is considered as 'good' QWL. Complete tasks consist of a coherent set of executing, preparing and supporting tasks with varying levels of difficulty. Hacker (1989) uses the term Vollständige Arbeitstätigkeiten (complete tasks or functioning activities) to describe this kind of work: it appeals to various types and levels is skills and knowledge.

With regard to this definition of QWL, working in teams is considered to allow for job enlargement and enrichment (Molleman, 1994). Moreover, working in teams may improve the possibilities for employee participation and autonomous decision making. Harley summarizes this positive account on teamwork as follows, 'teamwork "empowers" workers by providing them with the opportunity for increased control over their work' (2001: 722). For that reason, it is argued that workers are more positively disposed to workplace management, more committed to the organization and able to use their skills and capabilities (Harley, 2001). In addition, the more challenging jobs offer more learning opportunities and motivation to develop new behaviour patterns (Karasek, 1979), all of which improve organizational performance.

These positive accounts on teamwork, however, tend to neglect any negative effects. For instance, more and more difficult (control) tasks may cause work intensification and higher work pressure (Findlay *et al.*, 2000; Van Klaveren and Tom, 1995). Another negative effect of increased employee participation and empowering employees in group or teamwork is the emergence of new forms of control which assist management in extracting labor from employees via work intensification (Marchington, 2000). Teamwork possibly 'substitutes autocratic and visible management control with the subtler moral and social controls of peer pressure, which are less visible and much less easily challenged' (Buchanan, 2000: 32; see also Procter and Mueller, 2000). Harley concludes that, 'from this perspective, any discretion associated with teamwork is illusory and may well mask increased managerial control of production, albeit via team members monitoring their own and others' performance' (2001: 725). These possible negative effects may have a negative influence on QWL in team-based organizations.

METHODOLOGY

To establish the effect of introducing teamwork in the organization for home care, it is important to determine the degree of group work in this organization. To assess this, I have used the measures of the EPOC study, i.e. coverage and intensity. Coverage is measured as the proportion of employees involved in group decision making. Intensity is measured as the number of decision rights assigned to the groups in the organization. Benders *et al.* (2001: 206) use eight decision rights that can be delegated:

– Allocation of work
– Scheduling of work
– Quality of work
– Time keeping
– Attendance and absence control
– Job rotation
– Coordination of work with other internal groups
– Improving work processes

Using these two criteria the authors distinguish three levels of group delegation (GD): 'group-based' organizations, 'medium GD', and 'weak GD' respectively. The authors speak of group work when coverage is more than 70% and at least four decision rights are assigned to groups. When coverage is under 30% and only one to three decision rights are assigned to groups, the authors speak of 'weak GD'. 'Medium GD' occurs in all other situations. 'Medium GD' can be classified as teamwork, but not as group work.

For a comparison between a team-based organization and a traditional one, it is important to acknowledge that the group of non-team based organizations is not a homogeneous one, since important differences exist between non-team workers in a Tayloristic setting, and non-team workers with a great deal of individual autonomy (Steijn, 2001). For instance, craftworkers, university professors, business consultants or independent plumbers are not team workers, but they do have a great deal of autonomy. Mixing these workers with Tayloristic non-team workers blurs the effects of teamworking on several dependent variables (outcomes). Consequently, it is important to determine to what extent workers in the non-team based organization have individual autonomy. Using two criteria (team versus non-team and low versus high autonomy), Steijn (2001) distinguishes four work systems (see Figure 1), i.e. Tayloristic, Professional, 'Lean' team and 'Sociotechnical' team. This arrangement in four analytical constructions can be used for indicating the systems to be compared.

The next section describes to what level the team-based organization meets the criteria of Benders *et al.* (2001), and how the traditional organization can be classified as Tayloristic or professional, using Steijn's criteria (2001).

	Low autonomy	High autonomy
Non-teamwork	Tayloristic	Professional
Teamwork	'Lean' team	'Sociotechnical' team

Figure 1: Four work systems according to Steijn (2001: 193).

The dependent variable in this study, i.e. QWL, was measured by conducting so-called WEBA-analyses (Vaas *et al.*, 1995). The WEBA-method is developed by government order for measuring well-being at work, which is an obligation for all organizations under the Dutch Occupational Health and Safety Act. In this Act, well-being at work is defined using Hacker's (1989) concept of complete tasks and Karasek's (1979) balance between job demands and decision latitude. Since I use the same definition for QWL in this paper, the WEBA-method is excellently suited for this research. Hacker's and Karasek's notions were combined in a list of seven characteristics of 'good jobs' (Vaas *et al.*, 1995), i.e.

1. Completeness of work: in addition to primary executing tasks, a job should contain preparing and supporting tasks.
2. Difficulty of work: a job should contain a variety of difficult and easy tasks. The criterion for difficulty is the variety and level of mental processing needed to complete the job. The level of education is not important.
3. Monotony of work: the job should consist of non-monotonous tasks. Monotonous tasks are defined as short-cyclical tasks that repeat themselves within 90 s and take up a great deal of the daily tasks.
4. Workplace autonomy: the worker should be able to decide upon work pace, order and methods.
5. Interaction potential at work: the ability to ask direct colleagues for help with problems.
6. Presence of organizing tasks: the ability to ask superiors or other departments for help with problems.
7. Information provision: the worker should get enough information with respect to the work to be done (What? How? How much? When?). This information should also be on time, complete and reliable.

With different job levels in both organizations I have used these characteristics to confront problems in work (control need) with the opportunities to deal with them (control capacity). Using the decision rules in the WEBA-method, each characteristic can be labeled 'sufficient', 'marginally sufficient' or 'insufficient' respectively. This gives a so-called 'profile of well-being' indicating the risks per job as regards wellbeing at work (see Table 1). Since this profile is based on WEBA only, it is hard to interpret without the underlying job descriptions. In drawing conclusions about QWL, these detailed job descriptions contain vital information about the results 'sufficient', 'marginally sufficient', and 'insufficient' per characteristic. This is important to take note of, since WEBA's decision rules on control capacity are very strict or rigid. Autonomy, interaction potential and organizing tasks nearly always score 'insufficient'. For instance, if one or more problems in the work (control need) cannot be solved with either autonomy, interaction potential or organizing tasks, these three characteristics automatically score 'insufficient', even if they do not result in workload. Hence the need of a detailed job description as background information for a proper comparison. This information will also be used in the next section to describe the differences in work organization between the two organizations.

	Traditional organization	Team-based organization
Home help		
Completeness of the work	Sufficient	Sufficient
Monotony of the work	Sufficient	Sufficient
Difficulty of the work	Insufficient	Insufficient
Workplace autonomy	Marginally sufficient	Insufficient
Interaction potential	Insufficient	Insufficient
Organizing tasks	Insufficient	Insufficient
Information provision	Marginally sufficient	Marginally sufficient
District nurse		
Completeness of the work	Marginally sufficient	Sufficient
Monotony of the work	Sufficient	Sufficient
Difficulty of the work	Insufficient	Marginally sufficient
Workplace autonomy	Insufficient	Insufficient
Interaction potential	Insufficient	Insufficient
Organizing tasks	Insufficient	Insufficient
Information provision	Sufficient	Marginally sufficient
Specialized district nurse		
Completeness of the work	Sufficient	Sufficient
Monotony of the work	Sufficient	Sufficient
Difficulty of the work	Insufficient	Marginally sufficient
Workplace autonomy	Insufficient	Insufficient
Interaction potential	Insufficient	Insufficient
Organizing tasks	Insufficient	Insufficient
Information provision	Insufficient	Marginally sufficient

Table 1: Profiles of wellbeing for the three jobs in the two organizations (WEBA method).

One problem, however, is that WEBA determines QWL at job level, not at an organizational level. This also complicates comparing QWL at an organizational level, since there are only three job levels that both organizations employ. The job levels in home care have been laid down in the Collective Labor Agreements, but the incidence of different job levels in both organizations differs. Although both organizations mostly employ home helps, one organization offers more specialized care than does the other. The three job levels that both organizations employ are: home help, district nurse and specialized district nurse, respectively. Home helps perform caring tasks (washing and dressing clients) and domestic tasks (shopping, cleaning, cooking). District nurses are responsible for the care for (chronically) sick, disabled and elderly people in their home situation. The most important tasks are nursing and caring, such as injecting insulin, bandaging legs, eye dripping, washing and dressing clients, and preparing medicines. Specialized district nurses are responsible for specialized nursing activities at the clients' homes, such as wound treatment and giving injections. They are also responsible for a radiophone service for emergencies. These three jobs will be judged on QWL in both organizations, but first the different work organizations will be described.

ORGANIZING THE WORK

Both organizations offer their clients similar services, varying from domestic care by home helps to nursing activities by (specialized) district nurses. The more specialized the job, the more nursing activities it contains. A home help is not allowed to conduct any nursing activities, which are reserved for properly educated and qualified workers. Additionally, the jobs differ in autonomy. According to regulations in the Collective Labor Agreements, workers at the lower levels (home helps) are more tied to the assistance protocol and prescribed procedures, whereas workers at higher levels (district nurses) are allowed to deviate from these procedures by taking action at their own discretion. Consequently, more specialized jobs are more complex and demanding than home help jobs.

Although both organizations offer similar services and have uniform job levels prescribed by the Collective Labor Agreements, they differ in work organization. The next two sections offer an overview of the work organization in both organizations.

The traditional organization for home care

In the traditional organization most employees work alone and at clients' homes, receiving their assignments from the central office, which coordinates all care activities. They sometimes meet with colleagues and superiors at the central office to discuss work progress, district nurses meeting more often (once a week) than home helps (once a month). In addition to the caring activities assigned to them, employees keep record of their working hours, which will be used for payment, planning and budgeting.

Despite the fact that a great deal of the work is prescribed, this organization cannot be classified as Tayloristic. Admittedly, home helps (mostly lower-educated) work according to well-defined and tight job descriptions, carrying out decisions taken by superiors at central office. On the other hand, specialized employees (higher educated) have a high degree of individual autonomy to act at their own discretion and deviate from the assistance protocol. Though home helps are the largest occupational group in the organization, a rather large group shows professional characteristics (cf. Steijn, 2001).

The team-based organization for home care

In the team-based organization, workers in the same jobs form teams. For that reason, they are functional teams. Each team, in cooperation with a manager from central office, is responsible for the care of a well-defined set of clients in a certain region. Within each team, workers are responsible for caring activities as well as one or more extra activities regarding (personnel) planning, education, quality or logistics. Workers are expected to rotate over these extra tasks. Dependent on the nature of the extra activities, the responsible team members frequently contact office managers, such as account managers, personnel consultants or planners. Besides, within a team, workers help each other or take over tasks in the event of too much work or illness.

In terms of coverage and intensity of group delegation (Benders *et al.*, 2001) these teams can be classified as group work. All caring and nursing workers work in teams, whereas only a small number of central office managers and staff are not members of a particular team. Five of the eight decision rights (Benders *et al.*, 2001) are assigned to the teams, i.e. allocation of work, scheduling of work, time keeping, job rotation and coordination of work with other internal groups (for instance with other job levels for other types of care for specific clients). Though the idea is that team members frequently contact office managers on these decision rights, most decisions are actually taken at team level. In this respect, the office manager operates as a kind of team leader (compare the Japanese team leaders as described in Benders and Van Hootegem, 1999).

With regard to team development it is important to note that, at the time of the research, the new structure had been operational in this organization for only two years, and that changes were still taking place. This means that not all teams had worked as a team for a long period of time and that some were still in a transitional phase.

These descriptions clearly show the differences between the two work organizations. The major difference is that workers in the team-based organization make up teams responsible for a well-defined set of clients, whereas workers in the traditional organization work solitarily, receiving their assignments from a central office. In addition, workers in the team-based organization have more and additional tasks apart from those laid down in the Collective Labor Agreements. There is also an important point of similarity: in both organizations workers have quite a large degree of individual autonomy to take action at their own discretion and deviate from the assistance protocol. Going by these descriptions of the work organization and the theoretical notions on QWL, I tend to expect higher QWL scores in the team-based organization, since they offer workers more complete tasks, more responsibilities and more interaction potential for solving problems. In order to test this hypothesis, the next section presents the profiles of well-being for three job levels.

RESULTS: QUALITY OF WORKING LIFE

Table 1 presents the results of the WEBA-analyses on the three jobs (as 'profiles of well-being') in the two organizations. At first sight, there seem to be few differences in the profiles of well-being. However, a closer investigation of the job descriptions (resulting from WEBA) offers more detailed information on the scores.

Home helps

In both organizations the jobs of home helps are short cyclical and highly routine. Even the extra tasks in the team-based organization can be performed routinely after a short period of settling in. This means that the difficulty of work is low, i.e. that the work is not challenging, resulting in the score 'insufficient' in both organizations. As to the balance between control need and control capacity, the home helps in both organizations face similar problems (control need), i.e. clients appealing for more care than they are scheduled for; working overtime; workers working alone, which complicates interaction with colleagues or superiors.

A remarkable point of difference between jobs in the two organizations is the extra tasks workers in the team-based organization are responsible for. Though these extra tasks may make the jobs more complete and less monotonous, they also do cause extra problems (work pressure) resulting in increasing control need. The need for consulting and tuning with team members and office managers, in particular, will increase, which may cause additional tuning problems (De Sitter *et al.*, 1997). The added advantage of extra tasks is that less caring activities are planned, allowing extra activities to be scheduled in a way that offers relief of the busy caring activities.

District nurses

In both organizations district nurses face similar problems (control need), i.e. a lack of institutionalized feedback (because of the solitary nature of the work), unpredictable client behaviour, and fluctuating workloads (because both organizations offer customized care). District nurses in the team-based organization, however, are better equipped to deal with these problems. The extra tasks make the work more complete, offering opportunities to level the workloads. In addition, since extra tasks require more functional interaction with colleagues and superiors, more opportunities for feedback are available. Limited accessibility of colleagues and superiors, however, can make consultation difficult. This is especially problematic, since the extra tasks require sufficient and timely exchange of information. In conclusion, though extra tasks make the job of district nurse in the team-based organization more complete and challenging, they can make consultation with colleagues and superiors problematic.

Specialized district nurses

This job is similar to that of a district nurse, with only one major difference: the former is more hectic, since in both organizations, in addition to their caring and nursing tasks, specialized district nurses are in charge of a radiophone service for emergencies. This makes these jobs in the two organizations very similar, which also holds for their profiles of wellbeing. The only difference is that the job of specialized district nurse is more complete and challenging, more so in the team-based than in the traditional organization.

DISCUSSION

Determining the effects of teamwork on QWL in home care, the profiles of wellbeing, suggest that the differences between the QWL scores in the team-based and conventional organizations are rather limited. At all job levels work in the team-based organization is more complete (i.e. more preparing and supporting tasks, entailing more responsibilities and decision rights) and, consequently, more challenging. On the other hand, the balances between control need and control capacity are fairly similar: only few problems that cannot be solved, which results in a fairly good balance between control need and control capacity for the jobs in both organizations.

A first reason for the minor differences in QWL in the two organizations is that work pressure in the team-based organization is higher, due to the number and difficulty of the extra tasks. In other words, though the extra tasks may make jobs more complete and challenging, serving as buffers when workload fluctuates, they also entail extra work pressure as work is intensified (Harley, 2001). To achieve a higher QWL, more control need will require more control capacity to level the balance. In the team-based organization this is not (yet) the case.

Another explanation is that the jobs in this study are highly professional, i.e. district nurses, specialized district nurses and, to a lesser extent, home helps in both organizations have a high degree of professional autonomy (control capacity), which suffices to solve most problems in the work. Admittedly, the profiles of well-being score insufficiently on autonomy (see Table 1), but this is due to the strict decision rules of the WEBA instrument.[†] Job descriptions clearly show high levels of autonomy for jobs in both organizations. The only pitfall is that geographical dispersion of the places of work makes it hard to call in help from colleagues (interaction potential) or superiors (organizing tasks). Both organizations suffer from these difficulties to the same extent. Consequently, teamwork in the team-based organization is mainly concerned with delegation of decision rights in the form of extra activities to teams of employees. Though these activities may alter the composition of the tasks (more preparing and supporting tasks), the content of the caring and nursing activities remains unchanged.

Linked to this is a third explanation: teamwork in this organization does not alter the output characteristics of the work. Jobs in both organizations lead to the same services to customers. In other words, the team-based organization failed to go through the transitional stage of changing the organization's structure and the nature of the work, which is essential for a successful introduction of teamwork as a management strategy for the organization of work (Procter and Currie, 2002) and enhancement of QWL. In this study, the team-based organization still offers the same services to their customers, and care takers still perform the same tasks, plus some extra ones. Note, however, that in the current situation, it is difficult to change the nature of work, because the different jobs are to a great extent prescribed in Collective Labor Agreements.

[†]The WEBA instrument uses very strict decision rules for control capacity (autonomy, interaction potential and organizing tasks; in this order). If any of the problems in the work (control need) cannot be solved with autonomy, the score is 'insufficient'. If that problem cannot be solved with interaction potential, that score will also be 'insufficient'. If, next, that problem cannot be solved with organizing tasks, either, the score will be 'insufficient' and the problem will lead to work stress. However, if all problems in the job can be solved with, for instance, organizing tasks, then there are no problems resulting in work stress, but the scores for autonomy and interaction potential will still be 'insufficient'. Therefore, I prefer to look at the three characteristics of control capacity taken together for the final judgement, using the detailed job descriptions for nuanced information.

Although this analysis shows that the differences in work design do not result in differences in QWL in terms of balance between control need and control capacity, it does show that the extra tasks in the team-based organization offer opportunities for more complete and challenging jobs. They bring more influence and responsibility for the workers on such points as planning, scheduling, and job rotation, offering more scope for meaningful commitment (a prerequisite for QWL according to De Sitter (1980)), job satisfaction and motivation.

CONCLUSION AND IMPLICATIONS

The comparison between the traditional and the team-based organization for home care as regards QWL shows that jobs in the team-based organization are more complete and challenging, bringing more job decision latitude, but also higher work pressure. The discussion bears out, on the one hand, that changing the organizational design by introducing teamwork in the home care sector is a complicated matter, attributable to the prescribed nature of the work as well as the geographical dispersion of work places. On the other hand, it is evident that the introduction of extra preparing and supporting tasks for care takers, as in the team-based organization in this study, offers opportunities for completer and more challenging jobs. From this conclusion arise a number of implications for handling workloads in this sector.

Firstly, if working in home care is made more challenging by increasing job decision latitude, more people may be interested in a career in this sector, which will lower the shortage of personnel, as has been argued in the introduction.

Secondly, more challenging and motivating jobs are an important instrument to stop further erosion of the quality of home care. As has been stated in the introduction, the emphasis on demand-driven home care has led to standardization of work processes and increased bureaucracy, at the expense of care for the customer (Meloen, 2000). This emphasis on standardization in health care organizations encourages an assembly line form of practice that constrains the care givers' ability to respond to their clients' unique situations and needs (Weinberg, 2003). To overcome this, motivated and satisfied employees are needed. According to Aiken *et al.* (1994) organizational arrangements, such as status, autonomy and control, along with teamwork and collegiality, are important for the well-being of nurses as well as patients. They affect nurses' behaviours on behalf of patients, enhancing patient outcomes (Aiken *et al.*, 1994) and reducing burnout in nurses (Aiken and Sloane, 1997). As a result, teams responsible for a well-defined set of clients, as in the team-based organization in this study, can improve the quality of care and QWL, since the focus is again on clients, which enhances the well-being of both care givers and clients.

Consequently, although the kind of teamwork in the team-based organization in this study may not alter the organization of work, it may help to overcome the erosion of the quality of home care. However, a warning is in place: studies on carefully planned restructuring strategies in health care organizations aimed at humanizing the workplace show conflicting results (see Weinberg, 2003: 14). These studies often fail to assess or report the actual effects restructuring may have on organizational arrangements that influence employees' attitudes and behaviours (such as status, autonomy and control). That is why the introduction of teamwork in home care organizations needs close assessment of the well-being of both employees and clients.

Another complicating factor in the introduction of teamwork in the home care sector is the growing occurrence of co-production, i.e. informal care from self, family, friends, etcetera. Co-production is another answer to growing rationalization and standardization in the sector. Where professional care takers spend ever less time and unique attention to their clients, non-professionals take over part of this care, which raises questions about the responsibility for the quality of care. Whereas this study shows that increasing decision latitude by delegating responsibilities to groups of care takers may improve the quality of care, more adjustment to, and cooperation with, non-professional care takers may be counterproductive and even harm the quality of care. Professional and non-professional care takers may have different or even contradictory ideas about what is 'good' care. These problems complicate an organizational design in which groups of (professional) care takers are responsible for the care for a well-defined set of clients. The need of increased coordination between the different professional and non-professional care takers is contrary to the principle of teamwork that coordination between teams or with others should be reduced to a minimum.

Another result of the growing occurrence of co-production is that it changes the demand for care. If non-professionals take over the easier tasks, only the more complicated care is left to the professionals. Not only will this alter the kind of care that home care organizations offer to their clients, but also the nature of work in these organizations. As a result, these changing circumstances will force organizations to change and adapt their organizational design. This development will add to the demand for customized care and is one of the major challenges for home care organizations.

ACKNOWLEDGEMENT

The author would like to thank Jos Benders for his comments on an earlier draft of this article.

REFERENCES

The references to go with this article can be found on www.wileyeurope.com/college/french.

QUESTIONS TO CONSIDER

1. Why does Schouten conclude that jobs in the team-based organization studied are more complete and challenging?
2. Summarize the methodology employed by Schouten in this study. Do you think the study's findings are likely to prove valid? Give reasons for your conclusions.

PART 4

MANAGING ORGANIZATIONAL PROCESSES AND PERFORMANCE

Journal article: Ryan, M.K. & Haslam, S.A. (2005), The glass cliff: evidence that women are over-represented in precarious leadership positions. *British Journal of Management*, **16**, 81–90.

In this section of the book we shift our focus to the organizational level. We will first examine features of organizations such as their *structure* and *culture*. In a sense our study of organizations at this macro-level can lead us to conclude that organizations are entities in their own right; in other words they are more than the sum of their parts. Nonetheless, whereas all organizations may be understood by reference to structure and culture, each organization is unique in these regards and its characteristic shape, values and beliefs will have been developed by individual actors through an emerging process of negotiation. In this way, the macro-level analysis contained in this part of the book links back to earlier sections dealing with individual attributes and group and/or team dynamics.

We also address several processes intrinsic to work organizations, namely *leadership*, *power and politics* and *change*. We argue that an understanding of these concepts is crucial to making sense of the reality of organizations. These are dynamic (constantly changing) processes, which involve interplay between the members of organizations and are subject to impact from events and trends in wider society. We have argued for the adoption of a contingency perspective in these and other subject areas; in other words no one model or perspective can always result in organizational effectiveness; rather, different types of leadership influence strategy and approach to change and their success depends on the particular situation.

CHAPTER

7

Organizational structure and design

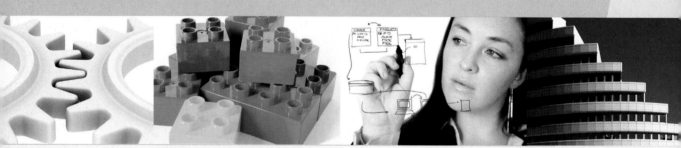

LEARNING OBJECTIVES

After studying this chapter you should be able to:

- define and compare organizational design and structure and discuss the relationship between them
- explain the basic factors that impact upon designing organizational structures and what organizational designs may emerge
- describe the different types of organizational goals and different methods of controlling and coordinating the activities of organizational members
- define vertical specialization and explain what is meant by chain of command, unity of command and span of control
- describe and compare different patterns of horizontal specialization used by organizations
- describe some of the emerging forms of organization design and their implications for the individuals within them.

AN AVOIDABLE TRAGEDY?

The world's worst chemical disaster occurred in Bhopal in the early hours of 3 December 1984, resulting in the death of 2500 people[1] and permanent injury to 100 000 people.[2] The cause of this disaster at the Union Carbide Plant in India is still in debate, with Union Carbide arguing that it was industrial sabotage by a disgruntled employee.

Eckerman argues that the causes were twofold – economic pressures (affecting safety procedures) and plant design (linked to the policies and systems in place).

Initially, operators at the plant had to be either science graduates or hold a diploma in engineering, but later, eight weeks of training was deemed to be sufficient to commence work. Workers and operators were given more responsibility than their training and competence equipped them to cope with. In 1982 most of the original operators had resigned and workers from other plants were asked to undergo training, which by that stage comprised 14 days in total. These new recruits were asked to take charge of a regular plant operator's position independently. Workers' knowledge was affected by acts of secrecy, with manuals kept in safe custody and the plant operating manual only available in English.

During the training period, technicians were treated as casual labourers and, even after training, only paid an hourly rate. Technicians who accepted a job at the Bhopal Plant received formal documentation informing them that they would undergo 6 months of training, but in practice, after 5 weeks of instruction, they were asked to stop the training and take on a fully fledged plant operator's role.

Operators who demonstrated unquestioning loyalty were invariably selected before others for promotions. Demands by workers for extra safety measures led to warnings that appointments could be terminated. There were lapses of safety measures, with some contract workers carrying out dangerous work without safety equipment and others routinely exposed to toxic chemicals.

There were reductions in personnel from 1983 to 1984 in order to lower costs. Early retirement was encouraged. Three hundred temporary workers were laid off and another 150 permanent workers were put into a pool to be assigned jobs as needed. The operating shifts were cut from 12 to 6 and the maintenance shifts from six to two. The positions of second shift supervisor and third shift maintenance supervisor had been eliminated just a few days before the disaster. On the night of 3 December 1984 there were no trained engineers on site. The responsible production supervisor who was on duty had been transferred from a Carbide battery plant only a month before.

On the night of the disaster, the supervisor from the day shift had left instructions on flushing the pipes leading from the tanks to the vent gas scrubber. However, he forgot to mention that the slip bends should have been placed at the end of the pipes. Then the worker cut off the water and the supervisor told him to clean the filters. When the worker turned on the water, it came out of only three of the four drain-cocks. The worker was told that the night shift worker would turn off the water. The ensuing result is one of terrible tragedy and loss of life.

Source: Adapted primarily from Eckerman, I. (2006), The Bhopal disaster 1984 – working conditions and the role of trade unions. *Asian-Pacific Newsletter on Occupational Health and Safety*, **13**, 48–49.

Questions

1. To what extent was this tragedy attributable to poor job design and training?
2. Could this tragedy have been avoided by appropriate organizational design linked to job responsibilities?
3. How could the organization have put in place safety measures and procedures to avoid individual sabotage?

INTRODUCTION

*An **organization** is a collectivity with a relatively identifiable boundary, a normative order, ranks of authority, communications systems, and membership coordinating systems; this collectively exists on a relatively continuous basis in an environment and engages in activities that are usually related to a set of goals; the activities have outcomes for organizational members, the organization itself and society.[3]*

Every organization needs to decide how to divide its work or activities, how to coordinate all work-related activities and how to control these activities to ensure that goals are achieved. The organization must consider its external environment and the internal systems and processes used to transform inputs to outputs. These differences help to explain, for example, why a football club is different from a manufacturing company. A manager of any organization must ensure consistency between the structure of the organization, the scale of its operations, the tasks at hand, the needs of all stakeholders and the strategic direction of the organization. This consistency between structure and operations distinguishes successful organizations from less successful ones.

In this chapter we will first explain the difference between organizational structure and organizational design and then consider the various factors that may impinge upon the design; that is, the scale of the organization, the technology it uses, its environment and its strategy. Collectively they will all influence how the structural elements are combined into a suitable design for the organization. Certain emerging forms of organizational design are presented at the end of the chapter but we must remember that every organization will be unique.

The basic structural attributes of organizations include the different types of goals that organizations develop and implement. They also involve the techniques used to effect control and coordination within organizations. Other structural considerations relate to how the organization allocates authority and manages the chain of command, how labour is divided into organizational units. These elements are, in essence, the building blocks of structure. They reflect various choices that can be made when organizing how work is to be done and goals are to be achieved. Understanding all these elements is necessary to predict how they affect employee behaviour.

ORGANIZATIONAL STRUCTURE AND DESIGN

Organizational structure and organizational design are very closely related. The process of choosing and implementing a structural configuration is referred to as organizational design.[4] Organizational executives should adjust the structural configuration of their organizations to best meet the challenges faced at any given point in time.

Formal structure shows the intended configuration of positions, job duties and lines of authority among different parts of the enterprise. This structure emerges from the process of designing the organization. It reflects the goals of the organization and also reflects the contingency factors that impact on the organization design, such as the organization's size, environment, technology and strategy. The formal structure also involves the decisions that are made about who has authority, how the organization and its members will be divided up to achieve tasks and how activities will be controlled and coordinated. We emphasize the word 'formal' simply because the intentions of organizational designers are not always fully realized. While no formal structure can provide the detail needed to show all the activities within an organization, it is still important because it provides the foundations for managerial action; that is, it outlines the jobs to be done, the people (in terms of position) who will perform specific activities and the ways in which the total task of the organization will be accomplished.

Organization charts are diagrams that depict the formal structures of organizations. A typical chart shows the various positions, the position holders and the lines of authority that link them to one another. The top half of Figure 7.1 is a partial organization chart for a small regional university.

Organizational design *is the process of choosing and implementing a structural configuration for an organization. The formal structure is the intended configuration of positions, job duties and lines of authority among the component parts of the organization.*

Organization charts *are diagrams that depict the formal structures of organizations.*

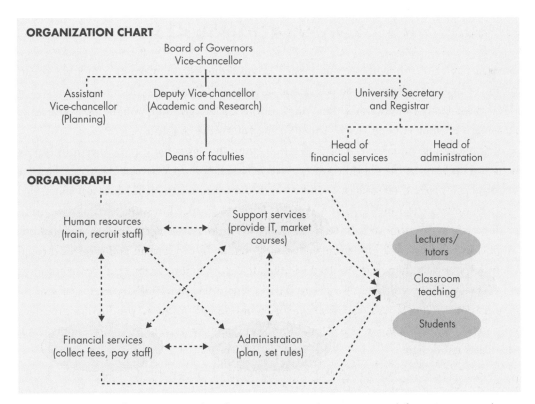

Figure 7.1: A partial organization chart for a university and an organigraph for university teaching.

Source: Organigraph developed from 'Organigraphs: drawing how companies really work' by Mintzberg, H. and Van der Heyden, L., *Harvard Business Review*, September/October 1999, pp. 87–94. Copyright © 1999 by the Harvard Business School Publishing Corporation, all rights reserved. Reprinted by permission of Harvard Business Review.

The chart allows university employees to locate their positions in the structure and to identify the lines of authority linking them with others in the organization. In this figure, the head of financial services reports to the registrar and secretary, who reports to the vice-chancellor (the chief executive officer of the university). Such charts predominate in representing organizational structures. However, there has been some criticism that they only show lines of authority and the division of the organization into different units. An alternative means of mapping organizational activities has been developed by Mintzberg and Van der Heyden. Their organigraphs show how an organization works, what it does, and how people, products and information interact. This can bring more insight, or at least a different perspective, to explaining the behaviour of people in organizations. The bottom half of Figure 7.1 shows a simple organigraph for teaching in a university.

In summary, organizational design involves the choices made about how to structure the organization, and the implementation of those choices. The formal structure explains in more detailed ways how the structural elements are configured. The terms 'organizational structure' and 'organizational design' are sometimes used interchangeably. Since organizational design is a structural configuration, the reasons for this are quite apparent. In the following sections, we will examine basic ways of understanding the design choices and structural features of organizations.

FACTORS INFLUENCING ORGANIZATIONAL DESIGN

Some particular factors will have an impact on the choices made when designing the organization: scale, technology, environment and strategy. This analysis will identify the way in which these factors impact and their implications on design. Some of the possible design outcomes that may emerge are described at the end of the chapter.

The more individuals in an organization, the more possible interconnections among them and the less the likelihood of direct interpersonal contact between everyone. Thus, as organizations grow, their structure is likely to become more complex. More advanced electronic communication methods and policies, rules and procedures are used as substitutes for direct supervision, both to save money and to ensure consistency. Larger organizations can be more efficient, with potential economies of scale in production and services through repetition, but then there is more need to break tasks down into parts, to allocate authority and to make sure everything and everyone is acting in a coordinated way to achieve the organization's goals. Larger organizations often have more products, production processes, geographic locations and so on. This additional complexity calls for more sophisticated organizational designs.

TECHNOLOGY

Organizations are said to arrange their internal structures to meet the dictates of their dominant 'technologies' or work flows; this is known as the technological imperative.[5]

Technology is the combination of resources, knowledge and techniques that creates a product or service output for an organization. The match between structure and technology is important for the successful design of organizations. Thompson[6] and Woodward[7] present different classifications that illustrate the possible diversity in technology and these are shown in Table 7.1. For example, Woodward's successful small-batch and continuous-process plants have flexible structures with small work groups at the bottom; more rigidly structured plants are less successful. In contrast, successful mass production operations are rigidly structured and have large work groups at the bottom.

*The **technological imperative** is the idea that if an organization does not adjust its internal structure to the requirements of the technology, it will not be successful.*

***Technology** is the combination of resources, knowledge and techniques that creates a product or service output for an organization.*

Thompson	
Intensive technology	Involves a team of highly interdependent specialists using a variety, but no certain, techniques to produce the desired outcomes for nonroutine problems or situations. Because the problem is unique there are no standard operating procedures and there must be mutual adjustments to deal with it. Examples include the team in a hospital emergency room and a research development laboratory.
Mediating technology	Links parties that want to become interdependent, such as wholesalers who link producers and retailers. Also, banks link creditors and depositors, and store money and information to facilitate such exchanges. Interdependent depositors and creditors rely on each other through pooled activity of the bank. If one creditor defaults on a loan, no one depositor is injured.
Long-linked technology	The way to produce the desired outcomes is known so the task is broken into sequential, interdependent steps. An example is the high-volume car assembly line.
Woodward	
Small-batch	A variety of custom products, such as tailored suits, are made to fit customer specifications. The machinery and equipment used are generally not elaborate, but considerable craftsmanship is often needed. For example, producing a unique marketing campaign or television movie.
Continuous-process	Producing a few products with considerable automation in an ongoing process. Examples include automated chemical plants and oil refineries.
Mass production	Similar to Thompson's long-linked technology; produces one or a few products using an assembly-line type of system. The work of one group depends on that of another, the equipment is typically sophisticated and the workers are given detailed instructions. Cars and refrigerators are produced in this way.

Table 7.1: Thompson's and Woodward's classifications of technology.

There are other possible technologies that can be described. For example, with more flexible manufacturing systems there is a trend towards more 'mass customization', where custom adjustments are possible even in a mass production process. Such a process would allow an infinite variety of goods and services unique to customer requirements.

ENVIRONMENT

An effective organizational design reflects powerful external forces as well as the desires of employees and managers. There are two main sets of parameters we can use to explain the environment. First, as open systems, organizations need to receive various inputs from their environment and sell various outputs to their environment. Environments can be labelled as either:

- General – that is, the set of cultural, economic, legal–political and educational conditions found in the areas in which the organization operates. These can include different global economies and markets.
- Specific – which involves the mix of owners, suppliers, distributors, government agencies and competitors with which it interacts.

Another basic concern in analysing the environment of the organization is its complexity. Environmental complexity is the estimated magnitude of the problems and opportunities in the organization's environment, as evidenced by the combination of the following three main factors that emerge uniquely, in the context of each organization, from the general and specific environments:[8]

- *Environmental richness*. The environment is richer when the economy is growing and improving, customers are spending more and investors investing more; when individuals are improving their education and others the organization relies upon are also prospering. Organizational survival is easier, there is more dynamism and there are more opportunities for change. The opposite is decline, which occurs in economic recession. Typically, workers may be laid off and the number of working units and managers may be reduced.
- *Environmental interdependence*. The link between external interdependence and organizational design is often subtle and indirect. The organization may coopt powerful outsiders onto its board of directors, and/or adjust its design strategy to absorb or buffer the demands of a more powerful external element. For example, it may include a public relations unit to deal with public pressures or to lobby government for policy change. Because of increasing internationalization, many organizations face a number of 'general environments' and maintain highly complex and diffuse interdependencies with them.
- *Uncertainty and volatility*. In times of change, investments quickly become outmoded and internal operations no longer work as expected. The obvious organizational design response to uncertainty and volatility is to opt for a more flexible structure. However, these pressures may run counter to those that arise from large size and technology and the organization may continue to struggle while adjusting its design a little at a time.

OB IN ACTION

Pause for thought!

To what extent do environmental influences, including internal ones, affect the organization? Mobach[9] argued that 'Organizations do not only use their building to sit dry and comfortable, but in many cases they actively seek to structure the work, improve the performance, and express their corporate identity through architectural design. It appears that organization and architecture have a lot in common.' Mobach goes on to argue that a building construction (or reconstruction) can support organizational design or change and improve current organizational processes and outcome.

To what extent does ergonomics have an impact when considering a holistic approach to organizational design? Why have some institutions, such as banks, adopted more open-plan architectural layouts for their business, and to what extent does this layout affect organizational culture?

OB IN ACTION

Going global

Businesses are increasingly engaging with global markets. This affects both the markets to which they sell their goods and services and also the labour market they rely on to produce them. The implications for businesses can be significant in terms of opening up new markets, or seeking favourable alliances or outsourcing arrangements. But moving into new countries means moving into new environments too, which can add to the diversity of political, cultural and economic scenarios that the business managers and employees must understand and succeed in.

According to an international survey conducted by PricewaterhouseCoopers (PwC), offshore expansion is an increasing trend among banks and financial services companies, with more than 80% of financial services companies offering some form of offshore operation. Such offshore operations involve setting up a business in a foreign country, setting up a joint venture, or outsourcing their business to another company in the foreign country. India and China are the two most popular countries for such outsourcing, especially in IT functions. Others include Ireland, Romania and the Philippines. Outcomes are not always favourable, however, with more than 15% of the respondents dissatisfied with the cost savings they achieved.[10]

STRATEGY

Organizational strategy *is the process of positioning the organization in its competitive environment and implementing actions to compete successfully.*

Organizational strategy is the process of positioning the organization in its competitive environment and implementing actions to compete successfully. The study of linking strategy, organizational design and performance has a long tradition in organizational analysis. While it cannot be covered extensively here, the important point is that the organization's strategy will be driving its goals and vision, and an organizational design must be established to achieve the vision. For example, an organization may be endeavouring to become a market leader by having the cheapest or best value-for-money product. Alternatively, it may be trying to differentiate its product from others. In other words, the degree to which the organization's strategy is aiming to produce standardized products, and the narrow or broad scope of the organization's business, may impact on the design choices that are made.

Another issue of strategy involves the organization building on and refining its unique experience and competencies; that is, competency-based strategies. Business practices that have built up over time and proved a key to the success of a business or the competence of employees may well be factors upon which the business should focus and make design decisions. For example, the design may need to be flexible and allow employees the scope to make decisions, such as where the organization is trying to capitalize on employee creativity in innovating new products. In other cases, it may be more important to have relatively rigid, formalized structures with more rules and controls.

ORGANIZATIONAL GOALS, CONTROL AND COORDINATION

The first of the structural building blocks are organizational goals. In an organization, people are organized into a structure in order to work together to achieve organizational goals. This involves breaking people and tasks up into units, allocating authority and making other decisions about how things are done. Two other components of structure are control and coordination, which provide ways of ensuring that these subdivided activities can be brought together to achieve the organizational goals.

ORGANIZATIONAL GOALS

Organizations may be viewed as entities with goals. The goals they pursue are multifaceted and often conflict with, or overlap, one another. These goals are common to individuals within an organization though their reasons for involvement in the organization are partly about serving their own individual interests. There are two types of organizational goals. The first centres on how the organization intends to serve particular groups in society, or with social responsibility, serve society as a whole. The second focuses on organizational survival.

Organizations are inevitably involved in some 'type of business', whether or not it is profit-oriented. They operate to provide products, services, infrastructure or wealth, for example. Output goals define the organization's type of business, and are the basis of the mission statements that organizations often use to indicate their purposes. These can form the basis for long-term planning and strategies and may help prevent huge organizations from diverting too many resources to peripheral areas.

Output goals *are the goals that define the organization's type of business.*

Some organizations may provide benefits to the society as a whole but most target their efforts towards a particular group or groups. The main recipients of the organization's efforts are the primary beneficiaries.

Primary beneficiaries are particular groups expected to benefit from the efforts of specific organizations.

Political organizations serve the common good, while culturally based organizations such as churches may emphasize contributions to their members. Social service organizations such as hospitals are expected to emphasize quality care to patients In Japan, long-time workers are typically placed at the centre of the organization with an expectation that through them and their secure employment there will be economic growth for the country. Many larger organizations have found it useful to review, clarify and state carefully their type of business.

In the process of serving society there is an expectation of corporate social responsibility; that is, the organization or corporation has an obligation to behave in ethical and moral ways. Organizations contributing to societal goals are given broader discretion and may obtain some control over resources, individuals, markets and products at lower costs. Organizations are typically expected to take action to improve society in a socially responsible way, or at least to avoid damaging it. Social responsibility is exhibited towards small and large social beneficiaries for a range of reasons, both altruistic and related to the organization's reputation. It is important for organizations to maintain society's trust and confidence if they wish to avoid negative impacts on their operations.

Organizations also face the immediate problem of just making it through the coming years. Systems goals are concerned with the internal conditions that are expected to increase the organization's survival potential. The list of systems goals is almost endless because each manager and researcher links today's conditions to tomorrow's existence in a different way. However, for many organizations the list includes growth, productivity, stability, harmony, flexibility, prestige and, of course, human resource maintenance. For some businesses, analysts consider market share and current profitability to be important systems goals. Other studies suggest that innovation and quality also may be considered important.

Systems goals *are goals concerned with conditions within the organization that are expected to increase organizational survival.*

In a practical sense, systems goals represent short-term organizational characteristics that higher-level managers wish to promote. Systems goals must often be balanced against one another; for instance, a productivity and efficiency drive may cut the flexibility of an organization. Different parts of the organization may be asked to pursue different types of systems goal. Higher-level managers, for example, may expect to see their production operations strive for efficiency, while pressing for innovation from their research and development laboratory and promoting stability in their financial affairs. Systems goals provide a 'road map' to assist in linking together various units of an organization to assure its survival. Well-defined systems goals are practical and easy to understand, focusing the manager's attention on what needs to be done.

CONTROL

Control *is the set of mechanisms used to keep actions and outputs within predetermined limits.*

Control is one of the basic management functions and is involved with ensuring the organization achieves what it is intended to achieve. Control is the set of mechanisms used to keep actions and/or outputs (based on predetermined organizational goals) within predetermined limits. Control deals with setting standards, measuring results against standards and instituting corrective action.

The control process that is used in activities such as accounting and production is depicted in Figure 7.2.

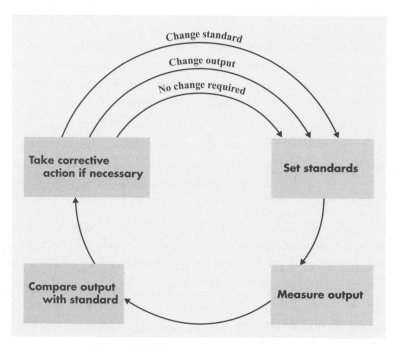

Figure 7.2: The business control process.

Note the iterative nature of the process; in other words, controlling activities within an organization is an ongoing process. Note also that once the actual output is compared with the objective or standard that has been set, the manager may need to decide whether to adjust the standard (if it proves unrealistic or unachievable) or produce a different level of output in step with the standard. For a given project, actual expenditure (output) may be exceeding the budget (standard), so the manager will need to take measures to reduce ongoing costs for the project in some way.

While controls are needed in all organizations, just a few controls may go a long way. Astute managers need to be aware of the danger of too much control in the organization, as noted in Effective Manager 7.1.

EFFECTIVE MANAGER 7.1

Signs of too much control

Astute managers look for the signs that too much control or inappropriate controls have been placed on their units. They look for:

- too much emphasis on one measured goal to the exclusion of all others
- too much emphasis on the quick fix and an unwillingness to look for underlying causes of problems or new opportunities
- a tradition of across-the-board cuts rather than reductions linked to demands, constraints and opportunities
- too many vague and unrealistic expectations that breed defeat
- raising of quotas without reward for employees, particularly after employee suggestions for change are implemented.

Output controls

Developing targets or standards, measuring results against these targets and taking corrective action are all steps involved in developing output controls. Output controls focus on desired targets and allow managers to use their own methods for reaching defined targets. Most modern organizations use output controls as a part of an overall method of managing by exception; that is, when identification of a problem triggers corrective actions. Such controls are popular because they promote flexibility and creativity, as well as facilitating dialogue about corrective action.

Output controls *are controls that focus on desired targets and allow managers to use their own methods for reaching defined targets.*

There is an important link between controls and goals but it is not necessarily simple or one way. The links are complex and encompassing. Goals define what is to be achieved and they influence the controls set in place to ensure that the goals are met. Controls may also have an impact on goals. For example, output goals may be revised if targets cannot realistically be met. Controls over the manner in which tasks are done may also have an impact on an organization's systems goals, especially if there is little choice over the controls. For example, an organization may be obliged to comply with certain requirements of government legislation such as those relating to workplace safety, or with the requirements of an allied organization such as a supplier, major customer or alliance partner.

Process controls

Few organizations run on output controls alone. Once a solution to a problem is found and successfully implemented, managers do not want the problem to recur, so they institute process controls. Process controls attempt to specify the manner in which tasks will be

Process controls *are controls that attempt to specify the manner in which tasks will be accomplished.*

accomplished. There are many types of process control, but three groups have received considerable attention.

POLICIES, RULES AND PROCEDURES

Most organizations have a variety of policies, rules and procedures in place at any time. Usually, we think of a policy as a guideline for action that outlines important objectives and broadly indicates how an activity is to be performed. A policy allows for individual discretion and minor adjustments without direct clearance by a higher-level manager. Many organizations have a stated policy towards cultural diversity, for example, which not only outlines their goals for increasing the diversity of the workforce but also specifies the procedures to be used in recruiting staff. Bear in mind that a policy is a statement of intent only and relies on employees following the rules and procedures.

Rules and procedures are more specific, rigid and impersonal than policies. They typically describe in detail how a task or series of tasks is to be performed. They are designed to apply to all individuals under specified conditions. Most car dealers, for example, have detailed instruction manuals for repairing a new car under warranty. They must follow strict procedures to obtain reimbursement from the manufacturer for warranty work that they have undertaken.

Other examples of rules and procedures include requirements for employees to:

- have someone countersign approval for payments
- wear certain apparel for certain jobs
- follow particular steps for cleaning equipment (such as coffee machines) or conducting regular maintenance checks (such as of electrical equipment).

Rules, procedures and policies are employed as substitutes for direct managerial supervision, leaving managers to focus on exceptional incidents or unique problems. Under the guidance of written rules and procedures, the organization can specifically direct the activities of many individuals. It can ensure virtually identical treatment across even distant work locations. McDonald's hamburgers and fries, for example, taste much the same whether they are purchased in Greece, London, Hong Kong, Moscow or Sydney, simply because the ingredients and the cooking methods follow standardized written rules and procedures.

FORMALIZATION AND STANDARDIZATION

Formalization refers to the written documentation of rules, procedures and policies to guide behaviour and decision making. It is often used to simplify jobs: for example, written instructions allow individuals with less training to perform comparatively sophisticated tasks. Formalization is the written documentation of work rules, policies and procedures.

Written procedures may also be available to ensure a proper sequence of tasks is executed, even if this sequence is only performed occasionally.

Most organizations have developed additional methods for dealing with recurring problems or situations. Standardization is the degree to which the range of allowable actions in a job or series of jobs is limited. It involves the creation of guidelines so similar work activities are repeatedly performed in a similar fashion and employees know what they can and cannot do. In some cases there may be no need for formalization and standardization; rules and regulations may unnecessarily hinder workers' progress in their jobs.

Standardization *is the degree to which the range of actions in a job or series of jobs is limited.*

In other cases they may be vital for ensuring equity, fair treatment of clients or safety. Typically, a worker's job requirements and limits are clearly defined in a job description and these often form part of a broad pattern of jobs. However, if you wanted highly creative workers to be innovative in the development of a new product, for example, putting them into straitjacketed jobs might not gain the desired behaviours from them.

OB IN ACTION

Working to rule[11]

Consider the following comparisons of the definitions of the term 'work to rule' for the four countries below, and then review the questions provided.

Greece: *aperyía zílou*
Form of industrial action in which employees, having previously agreed between themselves to do so, collec-

tively exhibit exaggerated care in the execution of work. In practice, the effect is to reduce output or to hinder the functioning of services. Working to rule, which has not been encountered in Greece, is a lawful form of strike although the element of a cessation of work is absent. As it constitutes strike

action, it would mean the loss of pay throughout its duration.

Netherlands: *stiptheidsactie*
A form of industrial action in which employees collectively slow down the pace of work through exaggeratedly meticulous observance

of rules and regulations. It is therefore mostly used in situations where voluminous and detailed sets of working rules are to be found, which mainly tends to be in the public sector. A work to rule is also seen as a less aggressive form of action than, for example, a strike or sit-in and its use reflects a less serious degree of dissension between employer and employees.

Sweden: *paragrafarbete* Situation in which employees follow all rules and regulations to the letter while working. This usually means that the work is  performed with more meticulous care and hence more slowly than usual, possibly but not necessarily in conjunction with a go-slow, which results in delays. Working to rule is done openly and is usually a way of exerting pressure on the employer, in which case it often constitutes a form of industrial action. As such, it is lawful if organized by a union but this is never so in practice. Working to rule is extremely rare in Sweden.

UK: *work to rule*

A form of collective industrial action in which workers collectively slow down the pace working through scrupulous and detailed observation of orders, works rules or health and safety regulations. This form of action is most frequently used in the public  service sector, where large and detailed sets of working rules are often found. Despite the fact that such action involves conforming to rules it may be held by the courts to constitute a breach of contract by the employees concerned.

Questions

1. Organizations and governments produce policies on the basis that people are rational, responsible and rule/law abiding. How would we operate different working practices in the four different countries?

2. What are the implications for management in dealing with employees who work to rule?

QUALITY MANAGEMENT

Another way to institute process controls is to establish a quality management process. Quality management emerged from the total quality management (TQM) movement founded by W. Edwards Deming. The heart of Deming's approach is to institute a process approach to continual improvement based on statistical analyses of the organization's operations. All levels of management are to be involved in the quality programme; managers are to improve supervision, train employees, retrain employees in new skills and create a structure that will push the quality programme. The emphasis is on training, learning and consistency of purpose, which appear to be important lessons and all organizations need to be reminded of this constantly.

COORDINATION

In order to enhance the operation of the organization, there must be ways to get all the separate activities, people and units working together. Coordination is the set of mechanisms that an organization uses to link the actions of its units into a consistent pattern. The greater the specialization in the organization, the greater the need for effective coordination. Much of the coordination within a unit is handled by its manager. Smaller organizations may rely on their management hierarchy to provide the necessary consistency but as the organization grows, managers become overloaded. The organization then needs to develop more efficient and effective ways of linking work units to one another. Coordination methods can be personal or impersonal.

Personal methods of coordination

Personal methods of coordination produce synergy by promoting dialogue, discussion, innovation, creativity and learning, allowing the organization to address the particular needs of distinct units and individuals simultaneously. Perhaps the most popular of the wide variety of personal methods is direct contact between and among organizational members. Typically, this involves the development of an effective informal network of contacts within the organization; for example, direct personal communication and email.

Committees, although generally costly and sluggish, are effective for mutual adjustment across unit heads, for communicating complex qualitative information and for helping managers whose units must work together to adjust schedules, work loads and work assignments to increase productivity. Task forces are typically formed with limited agendas, and involve individuals from different parts of the organization identifying and solving problems that cut across different departments. Another personal method of coordination involves developing a shared set of values that allows organizational members to predict accurately the responses of others to specific events. There is no magic involved in selecting the appropriate mix of personal coordination methods and tailoring them to the individual skills, abilities and experience of employees. Managers need to know the individuals involved and their preferences.

Effective Manager 7.2 provides some guidelines for understanding how different personal methods can be tailored to match different individuals.

EFFECTIVE MANAGER 7.2

Selecting personal coordination styles

The astute manager must recognize the following important differences in matching up workers:

- individuals and representatives of departments often have their own views of how best to move towards organizational goals
- some individuals emphasize immediate problems and move towards quick solutions; others stress underlying problems and longer term solutions

- given that each department develops its own unique vocabulary and standard way of communicating, the coordination method chosen should recognize such potential differences and include many opportunities for direct exchange
- there are often pronounced departmental and individual preferences for formality.

Source: Adapted from Lawrence, P. R. and Lavsch, J. W., *Organization and environment, Managing differentiation and Integration*, Homewood, IL, Richard D. Irwin, 1967.

Impersonal methods of coordination

Impersonal coordination methods are often refinements and extensions of process controls, with an emphasis on formalization and standardization. Most larger organizations have written policies and procedures, such as schedules, budgets and plans, which are designed to mesh the operations of several units into a whole. Some other examples of impersonal methods of coordination are:

- cross-departmental work units that coordinate the efforts of diverse functional units
- management information systems (MIS) that coordinate and control the operations of diverse subordinate units. These are computerized substitutes for schedules, budgets and the like. In some firms, MIS still operate as a combined process control and impersonal coordination mechanism. In the hands of astute managers, MIS become an electronic network, linking individuals throughout the organization. Using decentralized communication systems, supplemented with the telephone, fax machine and email, a manager can greatly improve coordination.

Two broad types of organizational design that reflect the degree of control and coordination in an organization (as well as the allocation of authority, which is considered in the next section) are mechanistic and organic. A mechanistic design is an organizational structure that tends to emphasize authority and control, as well as specialization in jobs. Organizations of this type stress rules, policies and procedures, specify techniques for decision making and emphasize well-documented control systems backed by a strong middle management and supported by a centralized staff. In an organic design there is more flexibility in how things are done, with fewer rules and procedures; there is even flexibility in how elements of the structure can change quickly in response to changing circumstances. More responsibility is placed in the hands of workers, who are seen as competent and/or expert at what they do.

VERTICAL SPECIALIZATION

Vertical specialization
is a hierarchical division of labour that distributes formal authority and establishes how critical decisions are made.

In most larger organizations, there is a clear separation of authority and duties by hierarchical rank. This separation represents vertical specialization, which is a hierarchical division of work that distributes formal authority and establishes where and how critical decisions will be made. This division creates a hierarchy of authority, and a chain of command, that arranges work positions in order of increasing authority. We will also discuss another form of division of labour in the next section on horizontal specialization.

The distribution of formal authority is evident in the responsibilities typically allocated to managers. Top managers or senior executives plan the overall strategy of the organization and plot its long-term future. Middle managers guide the daily operations of the organization, help formulate policy, and translate top management decisions into more specific guidelines for action. Lower-level managers supervise the actions of employees to ensure implementation of the strategies authorized by top management and compliance with the related policies established by middle management. When allocating authority or specializing vertically, one feature of organizational structure can be explained. That is, those organizations that have many levels in their hierarchies can be described as tall. Others that have very few levels can be described as flat.

We also consider organizations in terms of how centralized or decentralized they are. The degree of centralization of decision-making authority is high if discretion to spend money, recruit people and make similar decisions is retained further up the hierarchy of authority. The more such decisions are delegated, or moved down the hierarchy of authority, the greater is the degree of decentralization.

Applying these characteristics to mechanistic and organic designs we can make the following general (but not the only possible) observations about design. Visually, mechanistic organizations tend to have a tall hierarchy and may resemble a tall, thin pyramid with centralized decision-making senior staff at the top. Taller or more vertically specialized structures have more managers per worker. This may mean closer and tighter control over workers, with formal communication through several layers of hierarchy that can be slow and distorted. People might get frustrated waiting for approval in tall structures and feel unable to take responsibility for their own work.

Mechanistic design emphasizes vertical specialization, hierarchical levels, tight control and coordination through rules, policies and other impersonal methods.

Organic design is an organizational structure that emphasizes horizontal specialization, an extensive use of personal coordination and loose rules, policies and procedures.

Organic organizations are more likely to have a flatter structure because more responsibility is delegated down to workers. Flatter organizations with fewer layers of hierarchy and authority and fewer managers generally permit submanagers and employees more discretion; they decentralize decision-making and loosen control.

IN ACTION

Empowered or enslaved?

During the 1980s the concept of 'empowerment' was popular in various companies, including the automobile industry in the UK. The organization chart was deliberately turned upside down to demonstrate graphically the change in company philosophy, culture and approach. An example of a car-servicing garage is shown in Figure 7.3.

The case in question involves a garage in South Wales (UK) dealing with customer service and repairs. Traditionally in this company, when

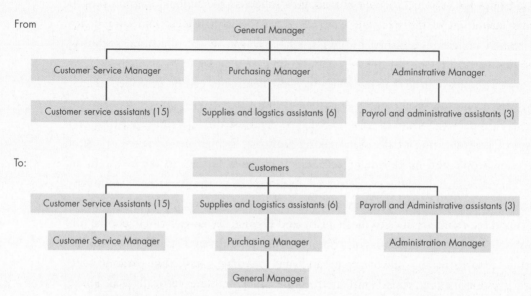

Figure 7.3: Inverted organization chart for a car-servicing garage.

customer service assistants encountered problems, they consulted their manager for a decision. Any problem that incurred a cost in excess of £500 required the general manager's approval. A month after the empowerment policy was brought in, Stephen Williams, one of the customer service assistants on the front desk, was confronted by an angry customer, asking for a replacement rear windscreen wiper to be put on their car. Stephen looked at the organizational chart that both he and customers could see (clearly and proudly displayed at the customer service desk) and duly replaced the wiper free of charge. A few minutes later, he was called into his manager's office and told that he should have sought permission before taking the decision that he did. Stephen challenged this approach stating that he was empowered to take this decision. His manager clarified that he was empowered to take the decision provided that it did not incur any charge to the organization.

Questions

1. What do you think Stephen's perception of the reversed organizational chart is likely to be?
2. What is the customer services manager's role under the new 'structure'?

Generally speaking, greater decentralization provides higher subordinate satisfaction and a quicker response to problems and may give workers a sense of ownership and greater levels of motivation in their work. Decentralization also assists in the on-the-job training of employees for higher-level positions.

Australia's leading accommodation Web site is an example of an organization that has made decisions about authority allocations.

Wotif.com began in 1999 when its founder and CEO Graeme Wood was asked to help a hotelier fill vacant rooms. He pioneered the selling of last-minute accommodation via the Internet. Now Wotif.com has 6000 hotels (or similar accommodation venues) on its books in 36 global locations and the Web site attracts nearly two million user sessions a month (translating into more than 100 000 monthly bookings). There are 100 employees internationally in Brisbane, Canada, New Zealand, Singapore and the UK. Wood has maintained a flat structure in the organization, with a focus on participation. He believes in keeping lines of communication completely open – a casual and accessible organization structure where anyone can talk to anyone else whenever they like.

Two other organizational characteristics that emerge from vertical specialization (though other factors might also contribute) are unity of command and span of control.

UNITY OF COMMAND AND SPAN OF CONTROL

As already indicated, with vertical specialization, executives, managers and supervisors are hierarchically connected through the 'chain of command'. Individuals are expected to follow their supervisors' decisions in the areas of responsibility outlined in the organization chart. Traditional management theory suggests that each individual should have one supervisor and each unit should have one leader. Under these circumstances there is a unity of command. Unity of command is considered necessary to avoid confusion, to assign accountability to specific individuals and to provide clear channels of communication up and down the organization. Unity of command, in a traditional hierarchy, is a readily understood approach for employees. A single boss makes life easier and less ambiguous but it could mean more hierarchical control, impersonality and rigid communication channels.

Unity of command is the situation in an organization where each worker has a clear reporting relationship to only one supervisor.

When vertically specializing the organization, decisions are made about the number of individuals that each manager directly supervises. To reduce the costs of having many managers, as is the case in flatter organizations, a manager may be given many employees to supervise, though the number any single manager can realistically manage is obviously limited. The concept of the number of individuals reporting to a supervisor is called the span of control.

Span of control may have a considerable impact on both manager behaviour and employee behaviour. If a supervisor has a wide span of control with many subordinates to supervise, it is more likely that the employees will have freedom to do the job their own way (autonomy). This may be suitable if they are highly experienced and/or in a very creative role. Control may be looser and people may have a higher satisfaction level (but not necessarily a higher performance level).

Span of control is the number of individuals reporting to a supervisor.

Narrower spans of control are expected when tasks are complex, when employees are inexperienced or poorly trained, and/or when tasks call for team effort.

Unfortunately, narrow spans of control yield many levels in the organizational hierarchy. The excessive number of levels is not only expensive (typically requiring more managers), but also makes the organization unresponsive to necessary change. A research study based on data collected from 74 manufacturing organizations found that differentiating mechanisms such as high job specialization and narrow spans of control led to poor integration of design manufacturing processes.[12]

HORIZONTAL SPECIALIZATION

Horizontal specialization *is the division of labour through the formation of work units or groups within an organization.*

Control, coordination and vertical specialization are only part of the picture. Managers must divide the total task into separate duties and group similar people and resources. Different groups or people do different parts of the larger operation. Look again at Figure 7.1 and note the two work groups reporting to the university secretary and registrar. Horizontal specialization is the division of labour that establishes work units or groups within an organization; it is often referred to as the process of departmentalization. In the following section we will examine three forms of horizontal specialization – by function, division and matrix – and also look at some 'mixed' or 'hybrid' forms that can emerge.

Line personnel are work groups that conduct the major business of the organization. Staff personnel are groups that assist the line units by performing specialized services for the organization.

Prior to doing this it is valuable to consider the difference between the terms 'line' and 'staff'. In an organization line personnel conduct the major business that directly affects the organization. In universities, academic staff, or in factories the workers who make the goods, are line workers. In contrast, staff personnel assist the line units by providing specialized expertise and services, such as accounting, human resources and public relations. The dotted lines on the organization chart depicted in the top of Figure 7.1 denote staff relationships, whereas the solid lines denote line relationships (teaching in the faculties is the major business of the university).

Line personnel are likely to feel more directly involved with the operations of the organization, especially if they can clearly see their part in achieving the organization's goals (task significance and task identity from the job characteristics model are particularly relevant). However, a common behavioural consequence is that there tend to be different perspectives between the line and staff groups. Staff personnel are often accused of interfering with line work with their unnecessary forms and procedures (although often they are trying to accomplish important things such as financial audits, legal compliance, payrolls and so on). Line personnel say they just want to get on with the job and lower-level managers, in particular, resent the demands or requirements of staff personnel. Inter-group and interpersonal conflict can be common (see Chapter 6).

DEPARTMENTALIZATION BY FUNCTION

Grouping individuals by skill, knowledge and action yields a pattern of functional departmentalization, and represents the most commonly used arrangement.

Figure 7.4 shows the organization chart for a supermarket chain, where each department has a technical specialty considered necessary for efficient operation. The organization is divided into four main functional groups – financial services, customer and marketing services, distribution and logistics, and company support services – and within each of these groups employees in different sections or departments undertake separate and

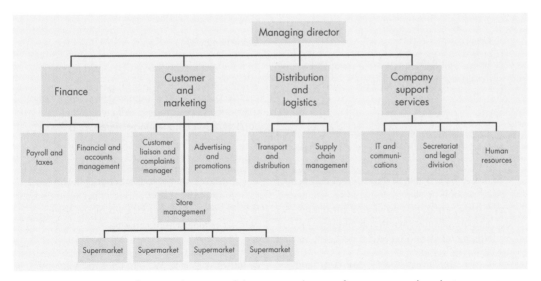

Figure 7.4: A functional pattern of departmentalization for a supermarket chain.

specialized tasks. In business organizations generally, marketing, finance, production and personnel are important functions. In many small organizations, this functional pattern dominates; for instance, Apple Computer used this pattern early in its development. Functional units or departments are often criticized as encouraging functional 'silos' that stand alone for too much of the time and discourage cooperative and coordinated behaviours. People working in functional departments tend to develop narrow interests, limited perspectives, competitive behaviours, unique language and cultures and a propensity to pass problems on to other sections.

Table 7.2 summarizes the advantages (and disadvantages) of a functional pattern. With all these advantages, it is not surprising that the functional form is extremely popular, being used in most organizations, despite some disadvantages. Organizations that rely on functional specialization may expect the following tendencies to emerge over time:

- an emphasis on quality from a technical standpoint
- rigidity with respect to change, particularly if change within one functional area is needed to help other functional areas
- difficulty in coordinating the actions of different functional areas, particularly if the organization must continually adjust to changing external conditions.

DEPARTMENTALIZATION BY DIVISION, GEOGRAPHY AND CUSTOMER

Alternatively, a divisional departmentalization may group individuals and resources by products, services and/or clients/customers. Figure 7.5 shows a divisional pattern of organization grouped around products (automotive parts such as transmissions and engines), regions (European, Asia-Pacific and South American) and customers (government accounts,

Advantages	Disadvantages
1. It can yield clear task assignments that are consistent with an individual's training.	1. It may reinforce the narrow training of individuals and lead to boring and routine jobs, e.g. accounts processing. Communication across technical areas is difficult, and conflict between units may increase. Lines of communication across the organization can become complex.
2. Individuals within a department can easily build on one another's knowledge, training and experience. Facing similar problems and having similar training facilitates communication and technical problem solving.	2. Complex communication channels can lead to 'top management overload'. Top management may spend too much time and effort dealing with cross-functional problems.
3. It provides an excellent training ground for new managers, who must translate their academic training into organizational actions.	3. Individuals may look up the organizational hierarchy for direction and reinforcement rather than focusing on products, services or clients. Guidance is typically sought from functional peers or superiors.
4. It is easy to explain. Most employees can understand the role of each unit, even though many may not know what individuals in a particular function do.	

Table 7.2: Major advantages and disadvantages of functional specialization.

corporate accounts and university/college accounts) for three divisions of a large international organization. This pattern is often used to meet diverse external threats and opportunities.

Many larger, geographically dispersed organizations that sell to national and international markets use departmentalization by geography. The savings in time, effort and travel can be substantial, and each territory can adjust to regional differences.

Divisional departmentalization is the grouping of individuals and resources by product, service and/or client. Departmentalization by geography is the grouping of individuals and resources by geographical territory. Departmentalization by customer is the grouping of individuals and resources by client.

Organizations that rely on a few major customers may organize their people and resources by client. The idea is to focus attention on the needs of the individual customer. To the extent that customer needs are unique, departmentalization by customer can also reduce confusion and increase synergy. Organizations expanding internationally may also divisionalize to meet the demands of complex host-country ownership requirements.

The major advantages and disadvantages of divisional specialization are summarized in Table 7.3. In organizations in which satisfying the demands of outsiders is particularly important, the divisional structure may provide the desired capabilities. This pattern can

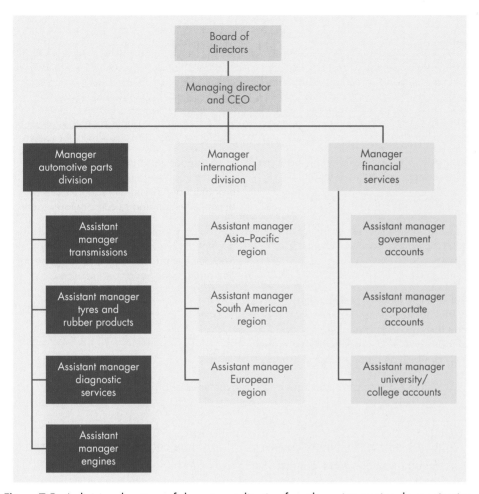

Figure 7.5: A divisional pattern of departmentalization for a large international organization.

help improve customer responsiveness for organizations that operate in many territories, produce quite different products and services, serve a few major customers or operate internationally. Organizations that rely on divisional specialization can generally expect the following tendencies to occur over time:

- an emphasis on flexibility and adaptability to the needs of important external units
- a lag in the technical quality of products and services compared with that of functionally structured competitors
- difficulty in achieving coordination across divisions, particularly where divisions must work closely or sell to each other.

Branch Offices

Having geographically remote offices or branches can be an important part of doing business in different locations (nationally or internationally). However, there can be problems in keeping in contact with head office. As Sean Spence (business mentor and consultant)

Advantages	Disadvantages
1. It provides adaptability and flexibility in meeting the demands of important external groups.	1. It does not provide a pool of highly trained individuals with similar expertise to solve problems and train new employees.
2. It allows for spotting external changes as they are emerging.	2. It can lead to a duplication of effort as each division attempts to solve similar problems.
3. It provides for the integration of specialized personnel deep within the hierarchy.	3. Divisional goals may be given priority over the health and welfare of the overall organization; divisional organizations may have difficulty responding to corporation-wide threats.
4. It focuses on the success or failure of particular products, services, clients or territories.	4. Conflict problems may arise when divisions attempt to develop joint projects, exchange resources, share individuals or 'transfer price' one another for goods and services.
5. To the extent that this pattern yields separate 'business units', top management can pit one division against another; for instance, Procter & Gamble has traditionally promoted friendly competition among product groups.	

Table 7.3: Major advantages and disadvantages of divisional specialization.

says: 'Mutual contempt is highly corrosive.' He recommends regular visits to the branch offices to maintain face-to-face contact. Such visits can be very effective.

DEPARTMENTALIZATION BY MATRIX

*A **matrix** structure is a combination of functional and divisional patterns in which an individual is assigned to more than one type of unit.*

From the aerospace industry, a third, unique form of departmentalization was developed; it is now called a **matrix structure**.[13]

In the aerospace industry projects are technically complex and they involve hundreds of subcontractors located throughout the world. Precise integration and control is needed across many sophisticated functional specialties and corporations. This is often more than a functional or divisional structure can provide. Thus, departmentalization by matrix uses both the functional and divisional forms simultaneously.

Figure 7.6 shows the basic matrix arrangement for an aerospace programme. Note the *functional* departments (production, marketing and engineering) and the *project* efforts representing the two elements of the matrix structure.

Workers and supervisors in the middle of the matrix have two bosses – one functional and one a project boss. For example, if you are one of the people in the marketing function and in the Vulcan project, you would report to the marketing manager but you would also report to your Vulcan project manager. Thus, the matrix breaks the 'unity of command' principle that is central to bureaucratic hierarchy. Each person in a project team has two

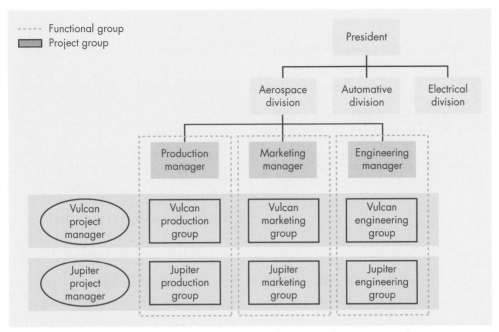

Figure 7.6: A matrix pattern of departmentalization in an aerospace division.
Source: Hodgetts, R. and Luthans, F., (1997) *International management*, McGraw-Hill, New York.

bosses. The project manager will be responsible for the person's contribution to the project. The department manager will be responsible for the person's:

• general career development
• pay
• promotion prospects within the organization
• contributions to the work of the department if/when there are gaps in their project team duties.[14]

It is also possible that some people in such an industry work outside this matrix structure. As you can see from the figure, there may be some people who work in the functional departments (production, marketing and engineering) but who are not necessarily also in a project team.

The major advantages and disadvantages of the matrix form of departmentalization are summarized in Table 7.4. The key disadvantage is the loss of unity of command. Individuals can be unsure as to what their jobs are, to whom they should report for specific activities and how various managers are to administer the effort. It can also be an expensive method because it relies on individual managers to coordinate efforts deep within the organization.

In Figure 7.6, note that the number of managers almost doubles compared with the number in either a functional or a divisional structure. Despite these limitations, the matrix structure provides a balance between functional and divisional concerns. Many problems can be resolved at the working level, where the balance between technical, cost, customer and organizational concerns can be rectified.

Advantages	Disadvantages
1. It combines strengths of both functional and divisional departmentalization.	1. It is expensive.
2. It helps to provide a blending of technical and market emphasis in organizations operating in exceedingly complex environments.	2. Unity of command is lost (because individuals have more than one supervisor).
3. It provides a series of managers able to converse with both technical and marketing personnel.	3. Authority and responsibilities of managers may overlap, causing conflicts and gaps in effort across units and inconsistencies in priorities.
	4. It is difficult to explain to employees.

Table 7.4: Major advantages and disadvantages of a matrix structure.

Many organizations also use elements of the matrix structure. Special project teams, coordinating committees and task forces, for example, can be the beginnings of a matrix. A large advertising firm could use project teams for major client contracts. Yet, these temporary structures can be used within a predominantly functional or divisional form without upsetting unity of command or recruiting additional managers.

MIXED FORMS OF DEPARTMENTALIZATION

As the matrix concept suggests, it is possible to departmentalize by two different methods at the same time but the matrix form is not the only possibility. Organizations often use a mixture of departmentalization forms; it may be desirable to divide the effort (group people and resources) by two methods at the same time to balance the advantages and disadvantages of each. Consider the example in Figure 7.7.

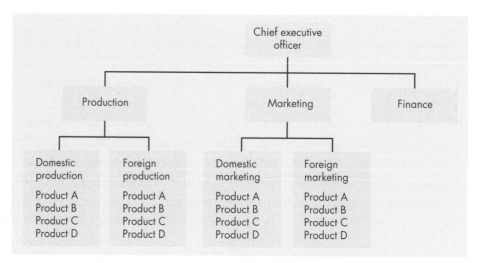

Figure 7.7: Partial organization chart showing a mixed form of departmentalization.
Source: Hodgetts, R. and Luthans, F., (1997), *International Management*, New York, McGraw-Hill Companies Inc. Reproduced by permission.

Notice that this organization has overall functional units (that is, production, marketing and finance) but that work is divided on a divisional basis (that is, domestic and foreign) within each functional area. Thus, departmentalization can take different permutations. Another example might be a geographically departmentalized organization that has functional departments within each major geographical area.

OB IN ACTION

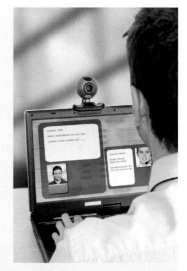

Pierre Lafarge was born in Switzerland and speaks French, German, Spanish, Italian and English fluently. As a recent business studies graduate, he went for an interview in Belgium in order to secure employment with one of the largest global human resources (HR) consulting firms, with their headquarters based in Strasbourg.

He realized after securing the job as a HR advisor that he was interviewed by a recruitment agency working for the global HR firm. There was a formal induction for the post, with a two-week intensive work-related induction delivered in Dubai. Pierre received an employment contract and an email account. He was charged with assisting with the running of client accounts, based in Hong Kong, Los Angeles, Brussels, Paris, Sofia and London.

He was notified that the organization adopts a matrix structure, with each account managed by a regional manager (based in the city mentioned) as well as a client account manager (there are several hundred client accounts and over 40 client account managers). Client account managers tend to be very mobile and typically operate from at least four countries.

Communication within the company tends to occur via electronic email, but where needed, video conferencing is arranged. There are a series of 'virtual office' sites, where messages can be left and work coordinated between employees. Contact with clients tends to be via telephone networks but face-to-face contact is allowed when client account managers authorize visits to clients.

Questions

1. To whom does Pierre go when he has a problem with his work?
2. What sort of problems is Pierre likely to face within the current organizational structure?

EMERGING FORMS OF ORGANIZATIONAL DESIGN

Every organization will develop a unique design in response to its scale, technology, environment and strategic aims and in terms of the choices it makes about goals, control, coordination and vertical and horizontal specialization. Other factors may also have an impact on design, such as the history of the organization, sudden changes, mergers and acquisitions and geographical locations.

In this section, we will consider some recognizable types of organizational design in the contemporary world. They are not necessarily new or unimagined but they do illustrate some generally occurring design trends for organizations. Common forms are the simple design, the bureaucracy, the divisionalized organization and the conglomerate. However, there are distinctions in the design of organizations even within these categories; for example, variations in the degree of organic or mechanistic design in bureaucracies. Figure 7.8 illustrates these popular basic designs. Other forms of organization design also emerge, such as alliances, virtual organizations, core-ring designs and adhocracies. These, and their impact on the people working within such organizations, will be briefly examined.

THE SIMPLE DESIGN

*A **simple design** is a configuration involving one or two ways of specializing individuals and units.*

The simple design is a configuration involving the specialization of individuals and units. That is, vertical specialization and control typically emphasize levels of supervision without elaborate formal mechanisms (such as rule books and policy manuals) and the majority of the control based with the manager. One or two ways of organizing departments are used, and coordination mechanisms are often personal.

The organization visually resembles a 'pyramid' with few staff individuals or units (see the simple design at the top of Figure 7.8).

The simple design is appropriate for many small organizations, such as family businesses, retail stores and small manufacturing companies,[15] as these have few people, little necessity for coordination, specialized tasks and hierarchical control. The strengths of the simple design are simplicity, flexibility and responsiveness to the desires of a central manager (in many cases, the owner). A simple design relies on the manager's personal leadership, so this configuration is only as effective as the senior manager.

THE BUREAUCRACY

The simple design is a basic building block of all organizations. However, as the organization grows, additional layers of management and more specialized departments are added. Line and staff functions are separated and the organization may begin to expand its territorial scope. In this way, larger organizations become much more structurally complex than small ones.[16]

A bureaucracy is an ideal form of organization whose characteristics include a division of labour, hierarchical control, promotion by merit with career opportunities for employees, and administration by rule.

The nature of the organization changes as layers of management increase, as the division of labour and coordination mechanisms become more elaborate, and as formal controls are established. In addition to the single, senior manager there are other 'levels' of management exercising varying degrees of authority.

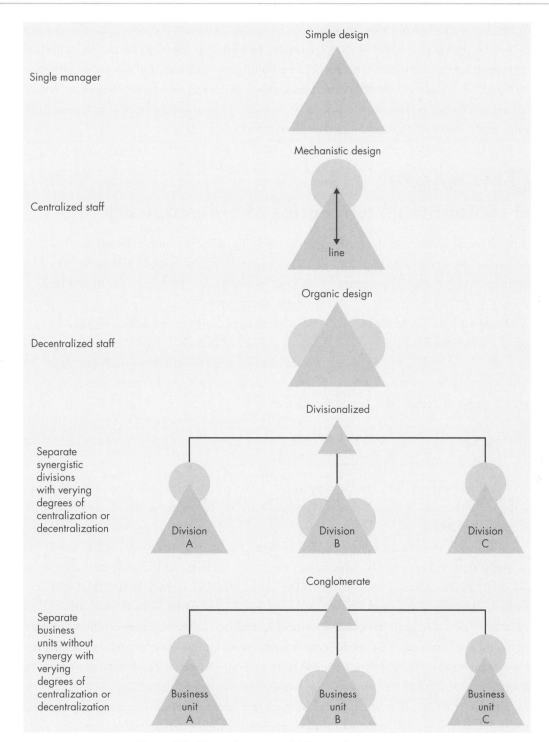

Figure 7.8: Visual depiction of different design options.

The famous German sociologist Max Weber suggested that large organizations would thrive if they relied on legal authority, logic and order.[17] Weber argued that relying on a division of labour, hierarchical control, promotion by merit with career opportunities for employees, and administration by rule was a superior option to the simple design. While

Weber knew the bureaucracy he was designing was an ideal type and that it could not always be perfect, he believed that efficiency, fairness and more freedom for individual expression within the organization would be important outcomes. Bureaucracies are often criticized for being too rule-bound and procedural and some organizations seek to reduce the impact of this, as the following example illustrates. Effective Manager 7.3 also indicates some of the dysfunctional tendencies of bureaucracies.

EFFECTIVE MANAGER 7.3

The natural dysfunctional tendencies of a bureaucracy

All large organizations must systematically work to minimize the dysfunctional characteristics of the modern bureaucracy. Among these dysfunctions are tendencies to:

* overspecialize and neglect to mitigate the resulting conflicts of interest resulting from specialization
* overuse the formal hierarchy and emphasize adherence to official channels rather than problem solving

* assume senior managers are superior performers on all tasks and rulers of a political system, rather than individuals who should help others reach goals
* overemphasize insignificant conformity that limits individual growth
* treat rules as ends in and of themselves rather than as poor mechanisms for control and coordination.

All large organizations are bureaucratic to some extent, although there are variations in the ways they are designed. The following discussion shows some possible variations to bureaucratic design.

Machine bureaucracies (characterized by mechanistic design features, as in Figure 7.8) are popular in industries with large-scale operations, such as banks, insurance companies and government offices. However, when the organization is viewed as too rigid and centralized, employees may feel constrained and the organization may be hindered in its capacity to adjust to external changes or new technologies. The inherent problems of such mechanistic command-and-control type structures are often overlooked by companies that try to resolve problems by frequent restructuring instead of fundamental changes in design.

On the other hand, a professional bureaucracy often relies on organic features in its design.[18] Universities, hospitals, consulting firms, libraries and social services agencies typically adopt this design. A professional bureaucracy looks like a broad, flat pyramid with a bulge in the centre for the professional staff (refer again to Figure 7.8, organic design). Power rests with knowledge and the experience of professionals but control is enhanced by the standardization of professional skills and the adoption of professional routines, standards and procedures. Given that this design emphasizes lateral relations and coordination, centralized direction by senior management is less intense. Although not as efficient as the mechanistic design, this design is better for problem solving, serving individual customer needs and detecting external changes and adjusting to new technologies (but sacrifices responsiveness to central management direction).[19]

The balance of technological and environmental demands can have an impact on the 'mix' of mechanistic and organic features in a bureaucracy. A bureaucracy can have an organic core with a mechanistic shell. While the technology of the organization may call for an organic design to promote flexibility, creativity and innovation, there may be environmental demands that lead to the development of a series of top-level and mechanistic staff units (for example, in response to powerful external groups). This strange design of mechanistic staff units at the top with organic line units towards the middle and bottom of the organization can protect the organization externally, while allowing responsible internal operations (see Figure 7.9).

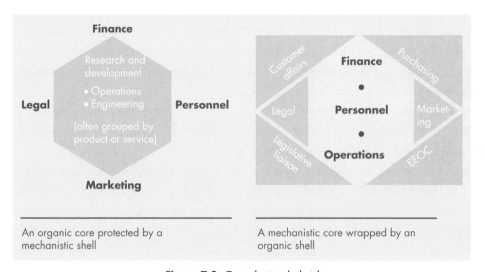

An organic core protected by a mechanistic shell

A mechanistic core wrapped by an organic shell

Figure 7.9: Two design hybrids.

A bureaucracy can also have a mechanistic core with an organic shell. Very large organizations with technologies that call for mechanistic designs and economies of scale are vulnerable to environmental uncertainty and volatility. A partial solution to the problem

RESEARCH IN OB

Many research studies have sought to indicate the relative appropriateness of different organizational forms to diverse settings and environments. Look at our Web site: www.wileyeurope.com/college/french for one such example. In their study, Ranamujam and Rousseau examine the extent to which organizational arrangements in hospitals affect their success. The researchers approach the topic recognizing that hospitals can in many cases fall far short in applying state-of-the-art clinical knowledge and management practices. Here we have an example of academic research that focuses on a critically important practical area.

is to wrap these inflexible cores within organic staff units. The staff units often attempt to change the external conditions by moderating the volatility in the specific environment and to absorb or buffer as many changes as possible. This latter option is found most often in organizations that must balance efficient production with flexible marketing and design operations. The assembly line is mechanistically structured, yet products may be designed by more organically structured teams.

DIVISIONALIZED ORGANIZATIONS

Divisionalized design *is an organizational structure that establishes a separate structure for each business or division.*

Many very large organizations find that neither the mechanistic nor the organic designs are suitable for all their operations. Adopting a machine bureaucracy would overload senior management and yield too many levels of management,[20] but adopting an organic design would mean losing control and becoming too inefficient. Even in the same industry, some business activities may call for an organic structure, whereas others call for a mechanistic one. The solution is the divisionalized design, by which the organization establishes a separate structure for each business or division.

The classic divisional organization was created for General Motors by Alfred Sloan, who divided the company's operations into divisions for designing and producing Chevys, Oldsmobiles, Pontiacs, Buicks and Cadillacs.[21]

Each division was treated as a separate business; each business competed against the others. In the divisionalized organization, all the businesses are coordinated by a comparatively small centralized team that provides support such as financial services and legal expertise. Senior line management provides direction and control over the presumably 'autonomous' divisions. In very large organizations, this approach can free top management to establish strategy and concentrate on large, long-term problems. Divisional heads run their own businesses and compete for resources, yet each enjoys the support (financial, personnel, legal and so on) of the larger parent.

This structure is expensive because many similar staff and support units must be developed for each division but it allows the organization greater flexibility to respond to different markets and customers. However, tension between divisional management and senior management is often apparent. It is difficult for corporate executives and corporate staff to allow the divisions to operate as independent businesses. Over time, senior staff may grow in number and force 'assistance' on the divisions. Further, because divisions compete for common resources, coordination across divisions is also often difficult.

THE CONGLOMERATE

Organizations that own several unrelated businesses are known as conglomerates. The line between the divisionalized form and the conglomerate can often be confusing. For our purposes, the key question is whether there is synergy among the various businesses owned by the corporation. Synergies are potential links, as between computers and information systems, or between financing and vehicle rentals, that create an entity with an output greater than its individual parts. If there is synergy, we would call the organization divisionalized; if there is little synergy, the organization is a conglomerate.

Conglomerates *are organizations that own several unrelated businesses.*

Pure conglomerates have not done particularly well in the US, mainly because substantive knowledge of the various businesses is often needed for them to be successfully managed.[22]

Most scholars would argue against conglomerates and for a more synergistic approach but Wesfarmers has proved to be an exception. Highly diverse conglomerates are not popular because it is believed that they do not have the capacity to sustain advantage in a number of nonsynergistic areas. Wesfarmers is a corporate company with multiple business units in diverse and unrelated areas (for example, hardware, insurance and fertilizers), meaning there are fewer opportunities to capitalize on common areas of competency and expertise. Wesfarmers successfully 'parents' those different businesses but maintains a centralized control through an integrated system focused on shareholders. Important planning processes, project evaluation, performance measurement and remuneration are all used in this way. In effect, Wesfarmers incubates the businesses until a buyer comes along to buy the business and make use of synergistic opportunities with their own, existing, businesses.[23]

THE CORE-RING ORGANIZATION

The pressure to enhance productivity in the last decades of the twentieth century encouraged many organizations to 'downsize' or reduce their number of employees. While this trend appears to have slowed, possible large-scale reductions in employee numbers still make headlines, as the following example shows.

In mid-2005, Kimberly-Clark announced plans to cut 6 000 jobs (around 10 % of its workforce) and sell 20 plants (17 % of its manufacturing facilities). Most of the plant closings were to be in North America and Europe. The move was part of a strategy to strengthen its diaper and healthcare businesses and to expand its presence in emerging markets (such as India and China). The restructuring was designed to achieve economies of scale in existing manufacturing plants.[24]

The widespread practice of downsizing has led to the increased popularity of an organizational design known as the core-ring organization. The major driver behind this new core-ring organization is the greater need for flexibility in production. An organization adopting a core-ring design (Figure 7.10) takes on a two-tiered structure, in which the inner core workforce represents the high value-adding members of the organization.

These employees often have higher job security, higher salaries and better career paths. The second tier of this structure is also known as the flexible ring and it is made up of a contingent workforce. Contingent workers in this outer ring may supply specialized services to the organization on an ongoing basis and, as a result, have a relatively stable employment

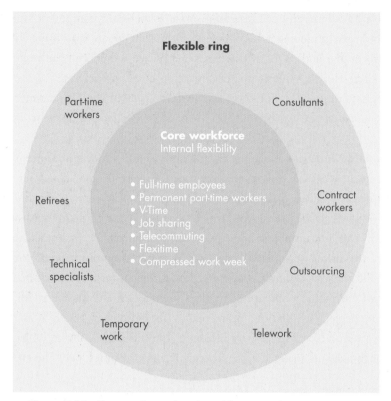

Figure 7.10: Core and peripheral workforce employment options.

relationship with the core organization (as least for the duration of their contracts). Traditionally, such services would be contained within the core of a large bureaucratic organization but in the core-ring organization services such as cleaning, information technology and specialist consultants can be more cost-effectively contracted or outsourced.

The largest component of the outer ring consists of lower skilled, casual employees. Such employees typically experience lower job security, relatively lower pay and a lack of available career paths.[25]

Workers in this peripheral category may actually receive a higher hourly rate of pay than that of some core workers in the organization but on-costs such as holiday loadings, training costs, sick leave and other fringe benefits do not apply to them because they are employed on a just-in-time basis. From the casual employee's point of view, their employment can be very 'precarious' with little certainty about having a steady income, where the next day's work is coming from and whether the family can enjoy a holiday together (as they may be called in for work).

Such workers are temporary; fluctuations in the size of this outer ring depend on prevailing levels of demand for the organization's products. These fluctuations may be due to changes in economic prosperity, market competition or other factors. For the organization, the core-ring design offers a flexible and cost-effective structure to adapt quickly to such variations in demand for a particular product. When product demand rises, the ring or contingent workforce can be rapidly expanded at short notice, given the high levels of unemployment in most OECD countries over the past decade. Given that organizations no longer expect demand patterns to be constant throughout the year, if demand falls, the contingent workforce can be cut back at short notice depending on the nature and the level of the work required.

COUNTERPOINT

Structure for the people – a workers' market?

Organizational designs have often placed more emphasis on getting outcomes for the organization than considering how the structure benefits the people within it. Designs such as the core-ring model, where workers are seen as human just-in-time inventory to be called upon or dispensed with on demand, reinforce this view. It appears that the main reason for casualized labour is the organization's bottom line. Casual employees cost less in terms of overheads, rights and benefits (such as leave and superannuation). While there are varying arguments about whether people are dissatisfied or not with being casual, there should perhaps be some concern about whether they are sufficiently productive, committed and motivated. It appears that having casual workers is one of very few ways employers can reduce fixed costs to compete in a global market. But for the workers themselves there is lack of job security and for the organizations there is potentially high turnover, recruitment and training costs.[26]

Designs do take into account how people might behave but they are less seriously focused on designing the organization to suit the preferences of its workers. If structural designs benefit the employees and increase their satisfaction and commitment (such as through empowerment and decentralized decision making) it is a bonus but the key reason for such changes is ultimately productivity and performance. The fact that the increased productivity or performance might be related to job satisfaction in some way helps to justify the designs but ultimately getting the most out of the workers is the driving aim of organizational design decisions.

However, with ageing populations and increasing labour shortages expected in a number of areas, organizations are now finding that they must respond to the expectations and requirements of valuable workers and potential workers. In any case, the on-call casuals may not always be so readily available.

There is increasing speculation about the ways in which organizations might endeavour to fulfil worker expectations (at least in the areas where they have trouble gaining required workers). With increasing acceptance that many employees are not happy at work, or that they want better work–life balance and/or less stress, organizations must reconsider the needs and satisfactions of workers in relation to the organizational design, just as we do with job design. We need to ask the following types of questions of our workers: Does the functional unit provide you with sufficient development and stimulation? Does the structure impede the way you can effectively relate to customers? Do you fulfil your needs for achievement and power? Can you manage stress and work–life balance in this position? These questions and many others could, in effect, reflect a customer-focus on employees. In recent years, businesses have been conditioned to a 'shortage of jobs' scenario, with a pool of workers keen to get those jobs. Now, there is a trend towards a demand-driven labour market (where good workers are in demand) and organizations must compete for the best of them, just as they would for customers.

Questions

1. How do casual workers experience their work in organizations? What implications are there for their commitment to the organization and their motivation/satisfaction with it?

2. What features of organizational design and structure, as discussed in this chapter, would act as a motivator to you as a worker?

3. Can organizations design themselves so that they may attract and retain the right sorts of people, who will be satisfied and committed to stay? Why or why not?

THE ADHOCRACY

*An **adhocracy** is an organizational structure that emphasizes shared, decentralized decision making, extremely horizontal specialization, few levels of management, the virtual absence of formal controls, and few rules, policies and procedures.*

The influence of technological considerations can be clearly seen in small organizations and in specific departments within large ones. In some instances, managers and employees simply do not know the appropriate way in which to service a client or to produce a particular product. This is the extreme of Thompson's intensive type of technology and may be found in some small-batch processes where a team of individuals must develop a unique product for a particular client. Mintzberg suggests that the 'adhocracy' may be an appropriate structure at these technological extremes.[27]

An adhocracy is characterized by:

- few rules, policies and procedures
- very decentralized, shared decision making among members
- extreme horizontal specialization because each member of the unit may be a distinct specialist
- few levels of management
- virtually no formal controls.

The adhocracy is particularly useful when an aspect of the organization's technology presents two problems: first, the tasks facing the organization vary considerably and provide many exceptions, as in a hospital and, second, when problems are difficult to define and resolve.[28]

The adhocracy places a premium on professionalism and coordination in problem solving, especially in solving technical problems. As such, adhocracies are often used as a supplement to other designs to offset their dysfunctional effects.[29]

Organizations use temporary task forces, special committees and even contracted consulting firms to provide the creative problem identification and problem solving that the adhocracy promotes. Lotus Development Corporation, for instance, creates autonomous departments to encourage talented employees to develop software programmes. Allied Chemical and 3M also set up quasi-autonomous groups to work through new ideas.

OTHER STRUCTURAL ARRANGEMENTS

Many other forms of organizational design are emerging or exist. They often involve alliances of two or more organizations, or networks of several organizations or of businesses within larger organizations. Some of these are now discussed and may be useful in describing some organizational or part-organizational designs.

Strategic alliances are announced cooperative agreements or joint ventures between two independent organizations. Often these agreements involve corporations that are headquartered in different nations.[30]

Strategic alliances *are announced cooperative agreements or joint ventures between two independent organizations.*

In high-technology areas, such as robotics, semiconductors, advanced materials (ceramics and carbon fibres) and advanced information systems, a single company often does not have all the knowledge necessary to bring new products to the market. Often the organizations with the knowledge are not even in the same country. In this case, the organizational design must go beyond the boundaries of the organization into strategic alliances. New Zealand company Comvita is one example of a company that collaborates in alliances. It has signed an agreement with a UK wound-dressing manufacturer to produce its innovative wound dressings (they combine alginate or seaweed fibres with medical-grade manuka honey).[31] Another purpose for alliances is to provide goods in the supply chain.

Alliances exist in other forms in other countries. In Europe, for example, they are called informal combines or cartels; competitors work cooperatively to share the market, decrease uncertainty and create more favourable outcomes for all. The legality of such arrangements may vary between countries, depending on trade practices, laws and other regulations.

In Japan, strategic alliances among well-established organizations in many industries are quite common and linked in a network of relationships called a *keiretsu*. For example, organizations may be linked to each other directly via cross-ownership and through historical ties to one bank, such as with the Mitsubishi group. Alternatively, a key manufacturer may be at the hub of a network of supplier organizations, with long-term supply contracts and cross-ownership ties, such as Toyota. Similar arrangements exist elsewhere. The network organization involves a central organization that specializes in a core activity, such as design and assembly. It works with a comparatively small number of participating suppliers on a long-term basis for both component development and manufacturing efficiency. Chrysler is a leader in the development of these relationships.

A network organization is a delayered organization aligned around the complementary competencies of players in a value chain.

More extreme variations of this network design are also emerging to meet apparently conflicting environmental, size and technological demands simultaneously. Organizations are spinning off staff functions to reduce their overall size and concentrate their internal design on technological dictates. Network organizations are delayered and flexible, with freer and less formal communication, control and coordination. Activities are geared towards alignment with the value chain in the industry, with an array of complementary competencies and resources brought together to achieve the objectives of the network.[32]

Kaplan and Norton[33] refer to the 'Velcro Organization', which can be 'pulled apart then reassembled in new ways to respond to changing opportunities'.

Organizations have to be flexible to demands of the market that they are operating in, have an external as opposed to internal focus, and act speedily when required. Moss-Kanter[34] uses the metaphor of large organizations being clumsy and slow to manoeuvre in her book *When Giants Learn to Dance*. We can imagine giants stepping on toes and being awkward. Agility and speed are important qualities to organizations operating in a complex and turbulent market. Similar analogies could be made likening large organizations to large oil tankers requiring several kilometres to stop or turn round.

VIRTUAL ORGANIZATIONS

Executives do not just face prospects for growth, more complex operations technology, new IT capabilities, or a more complex environment one at a time. For some firms, all of these internal and external contingencies are changing simultaneously and changing dramatically. Facing dramatic changes across the board, how do firms keep sufficient consistency in the pattern of their actions and yet co-evolve with their environment? That is, what is the design option when everything is changing and changing quickly?

A virtual organization is an ever shifting constellation of firms, with a lead corporation, that pool skills, resources, and experiences to thrive jointly.

There is no simple answer but we can start by saying that firms do not do it alone. Some executives have started to develop what are called virtual organizations.[35] A virtual organization is an ever-shifting constellation of firms, with a lead corporation, that pool skills, resources and experiences to thrive jointly. This ever-changing collection most likely has a relatively stable group of actors (usually independent firms) that normally include customers, competitors, research centres, suppliers and distributors. There is a lead organization that directs the constellation because this lead firm possesses a critical competence that all need. This critical competence may be a key technology or access to customers. Across time, members may come and go, as there are shifts in technology or alterations in environmental conditions. It is also important to stress that key customers are an integral part of a virtual organization. Not only do customers buy but they also participate in the development of new products and technologies. Thus, the virtual organization coevolves by incorporating many types of firms.

The virtual organization works if it operates by some unique rules and is led in a most untypical way. First, the production system yielding the products and services customers desire needs to be a partner network among independent firms where they are bound together by mutual trust and collective survival. As customer desires change, the proportion of work done by any member firm might change and the membership itself might change. In a similar fashion, the introduction of a new technology could shift the proportion of work among members or call for the introduction of new members. Second, this partner network needs to develop and maintain:

- an advanced information technology (rather than just face-to-face interaction)
- trust and cross-owning of problems and solutions and
- a common shared culture.

Developing these characteristics is a very tall order but the virtual organization can be highly resilient, extremely competent, innovative and efficient – characteristics that are usually tradeoffs. The virtual organization can effectively compete on a global scale in very complex settings using advanced technologies.

The role of the lead firm is also quite unusual and actually makes a network of firms a virtual organization. The lead firm must take responsibility for the whole constellation and coordinate the actions and evolution of autonomous member firms. Executives in the lead firm need to have the vision to see how the network of participants will both effectively compete with a consistent enough pattern action to be recognizable and still rapidly adjust to technological and environmental changes. Executives should not only communicate this vision and inspire individuals in the independent member firms but also treat members as if they were volunteers. To accomplish this across independent firms, the lead corporation and its members also need to rethink how they are internally organized and managed.

Based on a synthesis of successful management experiments by General Electric and its partners, a group of consultants and scholars put together a list of the changes firms need to consider if they are to compete globally in rapidly changing technical settings.[36] They used the buzz words of GE and labelled their package the 'boundaryless organization'. In essence, the challenge to management is to eliminate barriers vertically, horizontally, externally and geographically that block desired action. Specifically, an overemphasis on vertical relations can block communication up and down the firm. An overemphasis on functions, product lines, or organizational units blocks effective coordination. Maintaining rigid lines of demarcation between the firm and its partners can isolate it from others. And, of course, natural cultural, national and geographical borders can limit globally coordinated action. The notion of a boundaryless organization is not to eliminate all boundaries but to make them much more permeable. We think the development of permeable boundaries is a key characteristic of all members of a virtual organization.

The notion of a virtual and boundaryless organization is very different from the conditions found in and across most corporations. A movement toward cooperating to compete and removing barriers calls on firms to learn.

EFFECTIVE MANAGER 7.4

Managing a virtual project

The following needs to be carried out:
- establish a set of mutually reinforcing motives for participation, including a share in success
- stress self-governance and make sure that there is a manageable number of high quality contributors
- outline a set of rules that members can adapt to their individual needs
- encourage joint monitoring and sanctions of member behaviour
- stress shared values, norms and behaviour
- develop effective work structures and processes via project management software
- emphasize the use of technology for communication and norms about how to use it.

CONCLUSION

In spite of all the learned knowledge that is available about designing organizations, in the end it all comes down to people and the impact that culture has on organizational structure. The tripodic relationship between strategy, structure and culture cannot be underestimated. This perspective may focus to some extent upon internal issues but the external interface, together with all its unknowns and complexities makes designing organizations (and constantly redesigning organizations) a highly challenging task.

SUMMARY

LEARNING OBJECTIVE 1
Formal structure and organizational design

Organizational design is the process of choosing and implementing a formal structural configuration (that is, a formal structure) for an organization. The structure is typically represented on an organizational chart. Structure defines the configuration of jobs, positions and lines of authority of the various component parts of the organization.

LEARNING OBJECTIVE 2
Factors for organizational design

Four main factors can be said to affect organizational design – scale, technology, environment and strategy. Scale is important since the number of people and the degree of division of labour and authority will have an impact on the complexity of the organization and the need for compensatory control and coordination mechanisms. Major distinctions in technology are the Thompson (intensive, long-linked, mediating) and Woodward (small batch, mass production, continuous processing) classification systems. The technology of the organization will have some impact on the chosen structure. Environmental differences have a large impact on the type of organizational design that works best. Both the general environment (background conditions) and specific environment (key actors and organizations) are important, as is environmental complexity (richness, interdependence, and uncertainty and volatility in the organization/environment). The organizational design must support the strategy if it is to prove successful. Strategy positions an organization in its competitive environment. Strategies such as differentiating the business, or leading the market in price and value, or based on competency, can have an impact on the organizational design.

LEARNING OBJECTIVE 3
Goals, control and coordination

Organizational goals include both output and systems goals. Output goals relate to the type of business the organization is engaged in; they are concerned with satisfying primary beneficiaries and corporate social responsibility. Systems goals establish a basis for organizational survival and prosperity. Control is the set of mechanisms the organization uses to keep action and/or outputs within predetermined levels.

Output controls focus on desired targets and allow managers to use their own methods for reaching the desired target. Process controls (such as policies, rules, procedures, formalization and standardization) attempt to specify the manner in which tasks will be accomplished. Coordination is the set of mechanisms that an organization uses to link the actions of separate units into a consistent pattern. Coordination methods can be impersonal (such as centralized staff units) or personal (such as network development and task forces). Organizational designs, overall, can be said to be mechanistic (involving many levels of authority, high levels of control and impersonal coordination) or organic (breakup of work horizontally; personal coordination and loose control).

LEARNING OBJECTIVE 4
Vertical specialization

Vertical specialization is the hierarchical division of labour that specifies formal authority and a chain of command. The organization's hierarchy can be said to be tall or flat, relating to the number of levels of management or authority in the organization. Organizational authority can also be centralized (concentrated at the top or centre or the organization) or decentralized (where decision making is pushed down to lower-levels of the organization). Unity of command defines the situation in which each worker has a clear reporting relationship to only one supervisor. It lessens confusion and provides clear channels of communication. Span of control indicates the number of individuals reporting to a supervisor. Wide spans of control mean the supervisor supervises many people, whereas a supervisor with a narrow span of control will have few employees.

LEARNING OBJECTIVE 5
Horizontal specialization

Horizontal specialization is the division of labour that results in various work units or groups in the organization. The distinction between line and staff units can be particularly relevant to horizontal departmentalization. Line personnel conduct the major business of the organization while staff personnel assist in performing specialized supportive services. Three main types of 'departmentalization' are functional, divisional and matrix departmentalization. Each structure has advantages and disadvantages. Organizations may successfully use any type, or a mixture, as long as the strengths of the structure match the needs of the organization's goals.

LEARNING OBJECTIVE 6
Implications of emerging forms of work organization

Each organization's design will be unique. Smaller organizations often adopt a simple structure; larger organizations often adopt a bureaucratic form. The bureaucracy is an ideal form based on legal authority, logic and order rather than on individual supervision or tradition. Whilst most larger corporations are bureaucracies, they differ in the degree and combination of mechanistic and organic features.

Divisionalized organizations establish a separate structure for each business or division in the organization so that there is emphasis on coping with the particular aspects of that part of the business but also overall synergy. Conglomerates are organizations that own several unrelated businesses that do not have inherently synergistic advantages. Within divisionalized or conglomerate organizations each business can develop different design features. The core-ring organization involves an inner core, relatively permanent, workforce with higher job security, higher salaries and better career paths. There is also a flexible outer ring of workers employed on a part-time or casual basis as required. They tend to have lower job security, lower pay and a lack of career paths. This approach enables the organization to achieve economies by adapting its employment levels to suit the circumstances. The adhocracy is a structural form that emphasizes shared, decentralized decision making, extreme horizontal specialization, few levels of management and few formal controls. Other organization designs include strategic alliances, networked organizations, virtual organizations and franchises.

CHAPTER 7 STUDY GUIDE

You can also test your understanding and access further resources at **www.wileyeurope. com/college/french**.

REVIEW QUESTIONS

1. Compare control and coordination and explain two types of each.
2. Explain the difference between mechanistic and organic organizations.
3. Explain and compare the types of technology identified by Thompson and Woodward.
4. What is a core-ring organization and why does it have an impact on the workforce?

APPLICATION QUESTIONS

1. Demonstrate the purpose of an organizational chart in terms of depicting horizontal and vertical specialization in an organization.
2. From the perspective of an employee, how might it be to work in the following situations (compare the choices in each of (a), (b) and (c)?
   (a) A functionally departmentalized organization compared to a functionally departmentalized organization with project teams in a matrix structure.
   (b) An organization that is highly decentralized compared with one that is highly centralized.
   (c) An organization that uses a mass production technology compared to a small batch organization.
3. In a large organization employing mostly highly educated professionals, what do you think might be the best approaches to achieving control over those professionals? Explain your answers.

4. Many organizations are becoming flatter, reducing levels of hierarchy and widening the span of control. What advantages and disadvantages would there be in this approach for an organization that relied on its employees to make judgements on customers' requests (for example, for loans, insurance claims or special consideration of circumstances in social welfare cases)?

5. What form of hybrid design might be necessary for an organization that is very large and must reach economies of scale, but also needs to adapt to environmental uncertainty? Explain your answer.

6. How would you describe the technology and organizational forms used in the following (it is acceptable to describe a mix of technologies and forms)? Explain your reasons.

   (a) an organization making a Hollywood movie
   (b) a large company building prefabricated homes and later assembling them on customers' land
   (c) a firm of solicitors and barristers
   (d) a multinational mining and steel producer

RESEARCH QUESTIONS

1. Find two local organizations. Try to choose two different-sized organizations that have different processes – for example, retail and service industries. It would be best to avoid organizations that are branches of a bigger organization, as this would complicate your research. Give a brief overview of these two organizations and what they do and then compare and contrast them in terms of the following criteria: goals, control methods, vertical specialization, horizontal specialization and coordination methods. Also assess and compare the scale, environment, technology and strategy of the organizations to consider how this may have affected the design of the organizations.

2. Search the Web site of a major retail chain, analysing the chain in terms of the following elements of organizational structure:

   • statements of goals (output/system goals)
   • explanations or diagrams of the formal structure of the organization (organizational charts, number of layers in the hierarchy, span of control, apparent centralization/decentralization)
   • different groups/sections in the organization (type of specialization into divisions or departments, line and staff personnel, casual and permanent components of the staff).

Assuming there are different business units within the organization, analyse the range of businesses or business units in the 'organization' and draw conclusions based on whether you find them synergistic (or not synergistic) in the design of the entire organization.

RUNNING PROJECT

Complete the following activities for your chosen organization.

1. Identify the organization's goals. These might include formal, written goals as well as less obviously stated goals. Try to identify output goals and systems goals.
2. Refer to the organizational chart for your organization. From this chart, and from everything else you know about how the organization functions, construct an organigraph for the organization. Do you think the organizational chart or the organigraph is most useful in understanding the structure of the organization? Why?
3. How is the organization departmentalized? Explain how and why this is appropriate (considering types of departmentalization and issues such as line and staff personnel).
4. How does technology and environment affect the organizational design of your organization?
5. What are the likely implications of the design and structure of the organization on the employees?

INDIVIDUAL ACTIVITY

Vertical and horizontal specialization: organizing XYZ Paper Company

XYZ does not have an organizational chart. The following is a list of its management position titles. Develop an organizational chart by dividing the total task into separate duties, grouping similar people and resources together in a division of labour that establishes specific work units/departments. Draw your organizational chart using both the job title and the letter in each box.

A sales manager
B accountants
C engineering department

D vice-president of personnel

E president

F credit manager

G product A manager (facial tissue, paper towels, napkins, etc.)

H product B supervisor

I vice-president of finance

J advertising manager

K vice-president of manufacturing

L quality-control manager

M product A supervisor

N product A sales supervisor

O purchasing manager

P training manager

Q data-processing manager

R vice-president of marketing

S product B manager (writing paper, envelopes, etc.)

T sales supervisor product B

U assistant to the president

After completing the organizational chart, answer the following questions.

1. What is the span of control for the president and each vice-president? Is it broad or narrow?
2. Identify the line and staff units and consider whether XYZ uses standardization.
3. What type of departmentalization does your organizational chart have?
4. Use the following criteria to consider whether the organizational design tends towards being organic or mechanistic.

Mechanistic	Organic
Stable predictable environment	Innovative unpredictable environment
Strict formal lines of authority	Flexible informal lines of authority
Centralized authority	Decentralized authority
Extensive use of managerial techniques	Minimal use of managerial techniques
Many rules and procedures	Few rules and procedures
Specialist jobs	Generalist jobs
Formal and impersonal coordination and control	Informal and personal coordination and control
Large batch or mass production technology	Made-to-order or long-run process technology
Functional departmentalization	Divisional departmentalization

GROUP ACTIVITY

Assessing organizational structure and design

Objectives
To develop and refine your understanding of the basic design and structural characteristics of various organizations.

Total time: 60–90 minutes.

Procedure
1. In groups of five, choose an organization with which you are reasonably familiar. Develop a list of its basic structural elements using a chart or table to record all discussion on each of the attributes.
2. Address the following concerns.[38]
   (a) Product. What is the core business and the products/services that your organization provides to customers (or clients, members)? Are its products of real social value? What technologies are used to produce its products/services?
   (b) Workplace. Is the workplace safe? Is the business finding ways to involve workers in the decision-making process?
   (c) Environment. For example, if you have chosen a manufacturer, does the business protect air, water and so on? If you have chosen a financial business, does it use environmental responsibility when investing or underwriting?
   (d) Community. What kind of commitment does it have to its local and national community? Does it apply some standards to immigrant workers?
3. Suggest an organizational design that best suits your organization. Discuss why you chose it over other designs (it could be an improved design, or if you think the existing design is best you need to justify it).

Wrap up
Present your team findings to the class.

DEFENCE FORCE RECRUITING

It has been described as Australia's largest recruiting exercise contract and it is arguably the only recruitment contract of its kind in the world. In 1997, with an eye on costs, the Australian Defence Force (ADF) began a review of its recruitment functions in the army, navy and air force. Its recommendations included investigating and trialing an outsourced recruitment programme.

Fast forward to 2005 and ADF recruiting is now a collaboration between the ADF and a civilian recruitment and change management consultancy known as Defence Force Recruiting (DFR), a business unit of Manpower. It is the first time that ADF uniformed staff have worked in collaboration with civilian staff under a civilian organization's management structure.

This extraordinary partnership evolved from a transition and change management programme that took place over two years across the nation.

Talk to the people involved and they'll say it was one of the most complex organizational and culture change opportunities in the Australian business environment. And so far, the results are promising. As well as reducing costs the new arrangement has fostered a positive shift in culture. The new business improvement services structure encompassing human resources, learning and development, and quality, has been instrumental in creating an innovative culture where continuous improvement and learning is encouraged and supported throughout the organization.

Given the spread of the defence forces and the importance of a consistent national approach, DFR was created as an organization with a 'local national' approach. The organization is managed from a central headquarters with each regional office empowered to direct their resources as they see fit. Each area manager is encouraged to manage their business as if it were their own, with support and guidance available from headquarters if needed. Central requirements of the recruitment function such as target allocation, budget allocation and support for systems, processes and people are managed by headquarters.

Continuous improvement is a contractual requirement with ISO 9001/2000 selected as the quality system for DFR. The contract also requires a percentage decrease in the cost of services.

The collaborative nature of DFR means that each group plays to its strengths. Civilian staff perform the majority of the management, planning and administration functions while the ADF staff, and a small number of civilian staff, perform the shared function of candidate attraction, counselling and interviewing.

Each candidate is tested against medical and psychological standards provided by the military. These tests are undertaken by staff from the psychology services function and medical staff from the group's major teaming partner, Health Services Australia.

The final decision on whether a candidate is invited to join the defence force is made by an ADF member from the same service applied for. Enlistment of candidates and the

Case Study

Source: Latham, S. (2005), On Manoeuvres. *HR Monthly*, April, 30–34. Reproduced by permission of Scott Latham, Vantage Point Solutions, Australia.

appointment of officer candidates is a function retained by the ADF and is carried out by the senior military recruiting officer at each location.

A key feature of the organization's structure is that the staff perform their functions in operational cells, not roles.

Culturally, this approach to workplace relations emphasizes integrative yet individualistic systems. The manager in DFR is supported by the organizational structure to concentrate on employee participation, HR flow – of candidate and worker, reward systems and work organization – as opposed to reporting, representation, strategy and other hierarchical structural requirements. The operational worker in DFR can be used in a range of roles and functions to support the manager's mission.

The organization provides coaching, mentoring and flexible working environments, and the cells structure creates the environment where staff become skilled 'all-rounders' who are easily retrained and redeployed. This gives the DFR workforce the operational ability to be flexible and responsive.

Questions

1. What are the goals of the DFR and how does the structure support the achievement of the goals?
2. What type of horizontal specialization approach is used in the organization and how effective is it likely to be?
3. The defence forces are typically considered to have rule-bound, centralized and hierarchical organizations whereas DFR is said to be flexible and responsive. Discuss the differences between the 'typical' defence force (such as army or navy) and DFR, and the probable impacts on the defence-force personnel who now operate in DFR.

SUGGESTED READING

Crowther, D. & Green, M (2004), *Organizational Theory*, CIPD: London. These authors provide a summary of the development of organizational theory across time and in different contexts. As such, they illuminate the ways in which forms of organizational structures are themselves located in time and space.

END NOTES

1. Rice, A. (2006), Bhopal revisited – the tragedy of lessons ignored. *Asian-Pacific Newsletter on Occupational Health and Safety*, 13, 46–47.
2. Eckerman, I. (2006), The Bhopal disaster 1984 – working conditions and the role of trade unions. *Asian-Pacific Newsletter on Occupational Health and Safety*, 13, 48–49.
3. Hall, R.H. (1996), *Organizations – Structures, Processes and Outcomes*, 6th edn, Prentice Hall: Englewood Cliffs, NJ, p. 30.

4. Osborn, R.N., Hunt, J.G. & Jauch, L.R. (1984), *Organization Theory: Integrated Text and Cases,* Krieger: Melbourne, FL, pp. 123–215.

5. Woodward, J. (1965), *Industrial Organization: Theory and Practice,* Oxford University Press: London.

6. Thompson, J.D. (1967), *Organization in Action,* McGraw-Hill: New York.

7. Woodward, J., op. cit.

8. See Osborn, R.N. & Baughn, C.C. (1988), New patterns in the formation of US/Japanese cooperative ventures. *Columbia Journal of World Business,* **22,** 57–65.

9. Mobach, M.P. (2007), A critical systems perspective on the design of organizational space. *Systems Research and Behavioural Science,* **24,** 69–90.

10. Shifting business offshore growing. *Sydney Morning Herald,* 15 September 2005.

11. See: www.eurofound.europa.eu/emire/ UNITED%20KINGDOM/WORKTORULEEN. html,www.eurofound.europa.eu/emire/ SWEDEN/ANCHOR-PARAGRAFARBETESE. html,www.eurofound.europa.eu/emire/NETHER LANDS/WORKTORULE-NL.html,www.eurofound.europa. eu/emire/GREECE/WORKTORULEGR.html (accessed 10 July 2007). Adapted from Deming, W.E. (1982), Improvement of quality and productivity through action by management, *Productivity Review* (Winter 1982), 12–22; Deming, W.E. (1982), *Quality, Productivity and Competitive Position,* MIT Center for Advanced Engineering: Cambridge, MA.

12. Liker, J., Collins, P. and Hull, F. (1999), Flexibility and standardization: test of a contingency model of product design-manufacturing integration. *Journal of Product Innovation Management,* **16,** (3), 248–267.

13. For a discussion of matrix structures see Davis, S., Lawrence, P., Kolodny, H. & Beer, M. (1977), *Matrix,* Addison-Wesley: Reading, MA.

14. Open University, The effective manager. Unit 9: organizations. (United Kingdom, 1984), p. 19.

15. See Mintzberg, H. (1983), *Structure in Fives: Designing Effective Organizations,* Prentice Hall: Englewood Cliffs, NJ.

16. For a comprehensive review see Scott, W.R. (1987), *Organizations: Rational, Natural, and Open Systems,* 2nd edn, Prentice Hall: Englewood Cliffs, NJ.

17. Weber, M. (1947), *The Theory of Social and Economic Organization,* translated by A.M. Henderson & H.T. Parsons, The Free Press: New York.

18. Mintzberg, H., op. cit.

19. See Osborn, R.N., Hunt, J.G. & Jauch, L.R., op. cit., for an extended discussion.

20. See Clark, P. & Starkey, K. (1988), *Organization Transitions and Innovation-design,* Pinter Publications: London.

21. Osborn, R.N., Hunt, J.G. & Jauch, L.R., op. cit.

22. Ibid.

23. Kerin, P. (2005), The gold Wesfarmers. *Business Review Weekly,* 1–7 September, p. 32.

24. Kimberly-Clark to cut jobs. *Sydney Morning Herald,* 25 July 2005, www.smh.com.au/articles/- 2005/07/25.

25. Champy, J. (1995), *Reengineering Management,* HarperCollins: Glasgow. Michael Hammer & Steven Stanton, *The Engineering Revolution: A Handbook,* HarperCollins: New York. Morgan, R. & Smith, J. (1996), Staffing the New Workplace, CCH: Chicago, IL.

26. Parker, L. op. cit. pp. 20–25.

27. Mintzberg, H., op. cit.

28. Perrow, C. (1986), *Complex Organizations: A Critical Essay,* 3rd edn. Random House: New York.

29. Osborn, R.N., Hunt, J.G. & Jauch, L.R., op. cit.

30. See Ettlie, J. (1990), Technology drives a marriage. *Journal of Commerce,* 16 March, p. 6.

31. Comvita: healing with honey in the UK. *National Business Review,* 14 July 2005, www. nbr.co.nz.

32. Luthans, F. (2002), Organizational Behaviour, 9th edn, McGraw-Hill: Boston, MA, pp. 117–119.

33. Kaplan, R.S. & Norton, D.P. (2006), How to implement a new strategy without disrupting your organization. *Harvard Business Review,* March, 100–109.

34. Moss-Kanter, R. (1992), *When Giants Learn to Dance,* Routledge: New York.

35. The discussion of the virtual organization is based on Hedberg, B., Hahlgren, G., Hansson, J. & Olve, N. (2001), *Virtual Organizations and Beyond,* John Wiley & Sons, Ltd: New York.

36. This treatment of the boundaryless organization is based on Ashkenas, R., Ulrich, D., Jick, T. & Kerr, S. (1995), *The Boundaryless Organization: Breaking through the Chains of Organizational Structure,* Jossey-Bass: San Francisco.

37. This set of prescriptions is drawn from Kerr, S. & Ulrich, D. (1995), Creating the boundaryless organization: the radical reconstruction of organizational capabilities. *Planning Review,* **23,** 41–46.

38. Exercise adapted from *Mother Jones Magazine,* June 1985.

CHAPTER

8

Organizational culture

LEARNING OBJECTIVES

After studying this chapter you should be able to:

- define the concept of organizational culture and be aware of its importance within the study of organizational behaviour (OB)

- explain the levels of cultural analysis in organizations and the notions of dominant cultures, subcultures and cultural diversity

- identify common types of organizational culture as outlined in existing literature

- be aware of possible functions of organizational culture and links with performance

- discuss alternative and critical perspectives on organizational culture

- consider the interrelationships between organizational and national culture.

'THE WORLD OF WORK COULD BE SUCH A DIFFERENT PLACE': ?WHAT *IF!* INNOVATIONS COMPANY

The innovations company ?What *If!*, which works with clients to release creative potential of the client's people, products and brands, could not reasonably be described as having a conventional work environment.[1] For example many of the 300 plus workforce have distinctive job or role designations.

Matt Kingdon, ?What *If!*'s chairman, enjoys the title of Chief Enthusiast, while Sally-Ann Stuke, whose job encompasses employment issues, is the People Person. Now in its 15th year, ?What *If!* has five global bases in London, Manchester, New York, Sydney and Shanghai. They work with some of the world's most admired companies and their ever expanding team of 300 carry out innovation projects in over 40 countries.

?What *If!* has also given a good deal of thought to the physical environment in which employees work. Their four offices, built on the sites of former glassworks and school sites, are open plan, creating an atmosphere of space and also colour and light. In 2008 they will move to a renovated Police Station to house their expanding team of innovators under one roof. Staff hot desk, encouraging flexibility of working patterns. There is also a large kitchen area with food and drink stocked by the company each day for staff and clients to enjoy.

This organization has also developed a strongly distinctive set of values; love, passion, action, bravery, and freshness. Sally-Ann, a former dancer with a degree in dance and media, notes that these values connect to both her working and personal life and claims that working in ?What *If!* has resulted in her seeing the world differently.

The distinctiveness of ?What *If!*'s working practices extend to the ways in which they reward staff, which go far beyond salary and other financial benefits. Employees are offered free yoga and pilates courses and annual check ups at Well Woman or Man clinics. In 2007 a new benefits package was rolled out for the UK business; including an in-house GP, Physiologist, dental care, more leave and friends and family counselling service, and an attractive pension package. The company has increased paternity leave and introduced leave for adoption and fostering and also for those undergoing IVF treatment. ?What *If!* also extended their carers' leave entitlement to include people who care for elders or dependants. They were delighted when London Business School included ?What *If!* in their diversity report as 'gold standard'.

In a recent friends and family survey, respondents commented: *'it's a real values-led organization and it recognizes that its people have lives outside work'* and *'they really care for their people – if only more employers could see how valuable this is then the world of work could be such a different place'*.

Source: ?What *If!* and Braham, Michelle. "Cool cutting-edge offices mean work, rest and some play". **www.timesonline.co.uk** January 19 2005, **http://www.timesonline.co.uk/tol/life_and_style/career_and_jobs/secretarial/article413732.ece**, accessed June 28 2007. © NI Syndication, London 19th January 2005. Reproduced by permission of NI Syndication / Times Online and ?What *If!*

This depiction of language, symbols, physical layout, values, beliefs and ways of behaving set out here capture the essence of this company's organizational culture; in the case of ?What *If!*, a highly distinctive and unusual one. Do such things matter or are they simply surface or even shallow manifestations of style? Sally-Ann Stuke certainly thinks that the organizational culture she evokes has practical benefits, noting the positive impact of informality and 'groovy décor' in fostering trust amongst workers. Interestingly it seems that the culture is appropriate to the setting in which it operates and is linked to effectiveness; as Sally-Ann indicates: 'Underneath all the frilly stuff there is a central iron rod running through the company where people deliver impact for their clients'.

INTRODUCTION

Organizational culture is defined as 'the system of shared values and beliefs that develops within an organization and guides the behaviour of its members.' As we see from the example of ?What *If!*, the concept deals with nonquantifiable or even invisible aspects of organizational life – the so-called 'soft stuff'. But that does not mean that its importance should be minimized or even dismissed, as we shall attempt to show in this chapter. It is in fact a topic of much contemporary interest within OB, although the concept of culture has only recently been applied to organizations and the field of business studies more generally; significant contributions by Peters and Waterman,[2] and Schein,[3] for example, dating from 1982 and 1985 respectively. Previously culture was studied primarily by anthropologists and sociologists at the macro-social level, focusing on the belief systems, values and specific human behaviours that distinguished one society from another. In Chapter 1 we saw how Hofstede[4] sought to compare how work organizations operated in societies across the world, in the process, identifying significant and systematic differences that impacted on the reality of working life and organizational arrangements. It is now generally accepted that societal culture – usually defined as national – culture is an important source of influence on work organizations. However, organizations are one significant subsystem *within* any society and so it can be said that they too can exhibit elements and features that make up their own culture. Thus it is important to have a firm understanding of the elements of organizational culture, what they represent and how some may link to competitive advantage, partly through securing employee commitment and resultant high performance levels.

As indicated earlier, within organizational behaviour, the concept of organizational culture has assumed an increasing importance. It has indeed been suggested that a focus on organizational culture has become *essential* to an understanding of organizations.[5] Many managers believe that a strong and unified organizational culture is the key to competitive advantage within their own sphere of operation. There is evidence that some successful

Organizational culture *is a system of shared beliefs and values that guides behaviour.*

organizations sustain continued growth and development by 'implanting' a strong culture that is shared and acted on by all members of the organization.[6] However, other commentators express concerns about striving for a strong organizational culture, because of the difficulties associated with reconciling strongly integrated belief systems with the need for creative thinking, innovation and the ability to cope with change.[7] Within OB there is also a view (which we will explore later in the chapter) that organizational culture represents an insidious attack on workers' freedoms in its stress on collective values and frequently involves attempts to alter people's identities. In earlier chapters we have alerted readers to important changes in the context facing many organizations, suggesting that old methods of command and control are increasingly being replaced by methods of participation and involvement. Managers in this scenario are becoming facilitators, helpers, guides and coaches. These changes require adjustment of individual, group and overall organizational value systems and affect an organization's culture. In such a setting the so-called 'soft stuff' bound up in the culture concept takes centre stage and assumes an ever greater importance for everyone concerned.

This chapter considers the concept of organizational culture, how it manifests itself within organizations, and its functions. We look at the observable aspects and values of organizational cultures, and common assumptions about organizational culture and discuss the importance of subcultures, countercultures and the increasing diversity of organizational cultures. We will discuss the link between organizational culture and ethical behaviour and, finally, consider links between organizational and national culture.

THE CONCEPT OF ORGANIZATIONAL CULTURE

Just as a person's individual personality is unique, so no two organizational cultures are identical. Most significantly, management scholars and consultants increasingly believe that cultural differences can have a major impact on the performance of organizations and the quality of work–life experienced by their members. However before we analyse this claim in more detail, it is necessary to separate out layers or *levels* of organizational culture. A recognition of the multilayered nature of culture can go a long way towards bringing the topic into focus as it highlights the fact that while some manifestations of culture can be easily observed, others, specifically the deepest aspects of common assumptions, may be difficult to uncover, not least because they are 'taken for granted' by members of that culture.

LEVELS OF CULTURAL ANALYSIS

Figure 8.1 graphically depicts three important levels of cultural analysis in organizations: observable culture, shared values and common assumptions. As noted earlier these are envisaged as layers (other explanatory metaphors include onions, icebergs, the earth's crust and cakes). Importantly, the deeper we get, the more difficult it is to discover the phenomenon from the surface.

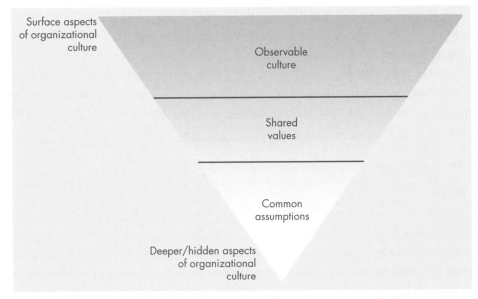

Figure 8.1: Three levels of analysis in studying organizational culture.

The first level relates to observable culture, or 'the way we do things around here'.[8] These are the methods that the group has developed and imparts to new members – either explicitly, for example through induction programmes or more subtly via symbols and identification of heroes and villains. The observable culture includes the unique stories, ceremonies and corporate rituals that make up the history of a successful work group or the organization as a whole. It also includes symbols such as physical design, dress codes, logos and badges. Organizational cultural researchers look for patterns for behaviour or espoused cultural forms when trying to locate and capture this level of culture.

Observable culture *is behavioural patterns that a group displays and teaches to new members.*

OB IN ACTION

In 2005 the Portuguese flag carrier airline TAP launched a new corporate image that the airline intended to reinforce its positioning as a modern global company, while simultaneously highlighting its Portuguese character.[9] Its new look was intended, according to company sources, to translate the airline's prestige, balance and competitiveness, while adding attractiveness, lightness and joy to its corporate identity.

The new-look initiative included a new livery applied to its fleet but also the design and launch of new staff uniforms to be brought into service in 2007.[10]

Corporate uniforms can be one example of a clearly visible manifestation of a company's culture. In this sense organizations may wish their workers to reflect organizational values; when followed to its logical extent, employees could be regarded as brand ambassadors.

In the case of TAP, staff are asked to wear uniforms that embody concepts as diverse as prestige, sophistication, lightness and joy.

Shared values *are the set of coherent values held by members of the organization and that link them together.*

The second level of analysis recognizes that shared values (for example, 'quality in this organization is our cornerstone to success', or 'we value innovative ideas', or 'we will provide the best possible care') can play a critical part in linking people and can provide a powerful motivational mechanism for members of that culture. Organizational values underpin the patterns for behaviour in observable cultural analysis, as in the case of the new TAP staff uniforms. Many consultants suggest that organizations should develop a 'dominant and coherent set of shared values'.[11] The term 'shared' in cultural analysis implies that the group is a whole. Every member may not agree with the shared values but they have all been exposed to them and have often been told they are important. Hence, many managers believe that cultivating a strong organizational culture will have a positive effect in gaining a competitive advantage. Shared values, such as wearing an airline uniform with pride, could have ties to values of the wider society. Unique and shared values can provide a strong identity, enhance collective commitment, provide a stable social system and reduce the need for controls. However, we also need to acknowledge the individual differences within a collective and the value of individuality to the overall organizational culture. Such stress on the positive aspects of shared values has always been common in school systems: from the 1980s onwards, however, writers such as Peters and Waterman extended the scope of the shared values argument to the adult world of work organizations.

Common assumptions *are the collection of truths that an organization's members share as a result of their joint experiences and that guide values and behaviours.*

At the deepest level of cultural analysis are common assumptions, or the taken-for-granted truths that collections of organizational members share as a result of their joint experience. In most organizational cultures there is a series of common assumptions known to everyone in the organization. However these may be implicit and unspoken. A study of farmers in the US,[12] showed how many farmers had work values instilled in them as young children; their parents, grandparents and great-grandparents all farmed. The working culture of farms was thus transmitted from one generation to another with seemingly little change occurring. Farmers continue to 'get up with the chickens' and work until dark. Long hours, self-reliance and the centrality of work in life are still pivotal to farmers' experiences and retirement at the age of 65 is rare. But it is debatable to what extent these deep-rooted common assumptions are frequently discussed or questioned; their very longevity may reinforce their embedded nature. Such common assumptions may plausibly bring us closer to understanding the culture of a farm than either observable artefacts or shared (documented) values.

DOMINANT CULTURE, SUBCULTURES AND COUNTERCULTURES

In Chapter 1 we stressed that organizations do not have goals, only people do. We also referred to the concept of a dominant coalition, namely those individuals and groups who hold power and influence in an organization at any one time. The culture of an organization will also be a reflection of these twin concepts. It is possible that an organization may have a single dominant culture articulated by a dominant individual or group and with a unitary set of shared assumptions, beliefs and actions. Those who view organizational culture as a unified phenomenon in which all cultural elements are consistent with one another, are said to take an integration perspective on the topic. Within this perspective, organizational members, as directed by their leaders, jointly agree on 'the way things are done around here', resulting in cohesiveness, unity and harmony.

Most writers in this field however also draw attention to the existence of subcultures and countercultures and the significant role that they play. Their existence is important if we believe that organizations comprise disparate groups, which may possess their own values and beliefs that can, on occasions, bring them into conflict with other parties. This is termed the pluralist view of organizations – the term is also applied to analysis of the wider society.

> A **dominant coalition** denotes the people who are in a strong position of power and influence within organizations at any one time. Dominant coalitions are shifting and can be replaced by others.
>
> The **integration perspective** views organizational culture as a system of shared meanings, unity and harmony.

SUBCULTURES AND COUNTERCULTURES

Subcultures represent groups of individuals with a unique pattern of values and philosophy that are not necessarily inconsistent with the organization's dominant values and philosophy. Strong subcultures are often found in high-performance task forces, teams and special project groups in organizations. In addition, subculture formation has also been linked to educational background, professional identity and distinctive work paradigms.[13] The culture emerges to bind individuals working intensely together: organizational values and assumptions are shared but actions can be influenced differently by distinct occupational tasks. For example, in a hospital the shared assumption of 'doing things better' could underpin the common value of providing the best possible care for patients. However, the expressed 'care' is performed differently by different occupational groups, each with distinctive interpretations of what 'best care' means. For catering staff this may be providing a meal at the correct temperature; for surgeons it may mean removing the cause of illness and for the occupational therapist it may mean helping patients and their carers to achieve an improved quality of life. Because 'providing the best care' means different things to different individuals and groups, we must expect that conflict arises between occupational subcultures and that this conflict is normal and by no means necessarily dysfunctional.

In contrast, countercultures have a pattern of values and a philosophy that reject the surrounding culture.[14] Within an organization, mergers and acquisitions may produce countercultures. Employers and managers of an acquired organization may hold values and assumptions that are quite inconsistent with those of the acquiring organization. This is often referred to as the 'clash of corporate cultures'.[15]

> **Subcultures** are unique patterns of values and philosophies within a group.
>
> **Countercultures** are the patterns of values and philosophies that outwardly reject those of the larger organization or social system.
>
> The **pluralist** view of organizations views them as being populated by individuals and groups that may have diverse aims and interests and that, as a result, can come into conflict with the dominant coalition and other groups.

Mergers and acquisitions do not inevitably cause cultural clashes, although this may be a matter of opinion among different subcultures within the new organization. Understanding the importance of culture can also help a company to absorb or accommodate the cultures within the organizations that are acquired or merge, or to manage the complex interplays in alliances, company formations and employment relations.[16]

The tone of the preceding section may lead readers to regard countercultures as an intrinsically negative phenomenon. This would ignore the unethical conduct of dominant coalitions in many organizations. Whistleblowers could be regarded as lone members of countercultures, however few would view their role and activities in a pejorative way; on the contrary, many people might accord whistleblowers heroic status. As is often the case in OB, our own reality is filtered by perception, in this instance how we judge the values and actions of the dominant culture.

Whistleblowers *are employees, ex-employees or other people connected to an organization who report perceived misconduct on the part of that organization to a person or body who can take or initiate action.*

OB IN ACTION

The collapse of the Italian dairy company Parmalat in 2003 revealed a culture of corruption amongst several key players in that organization. The founder, finance director, chief financial officer, auditor and legal consultant were among those who subsequently went on trial accused of financial corruption. Specific charges of market rigging, providing false accounting information and misleading the Italian Stock market were brought against these individuals as representatives of the company. This became a corporate scandal. The scale of corruption uncovered in the company was both large and significant. An account supposedly held with the bank of America by Parmalat's Cayman Island subsidiary Bonlat, understood to contain nearly 4 billion euros, did not in fact exist – information that led to the collapse of the company. The fallout from the Parmalat scandal was severe – it was a very

important regional employer and the Italian government intervened to avoid further damage.

This scandal was uncovered through financial scrutiny but what if a whistleblower had emerged from within the company? He or she would have taken on the role of countercultural agent as exposure was always likely to result in the end of the organization in its pre-2003 form. For many, any such whistleblower would have been justified in opposing the culture of the dominant coalition at Parmalat at that time.

CORPORATE OR ORGANIC CULTURES?

The preceding discussion of dominant cultures, subcultures and countercultures opens up a wider debate within this subject area, namely whether an organization's culture can ever be designed or imposed by senior figures. One interesting distinction was put forward by

Smircich,[17] who distinguished between culture as *critical variable* as contrasted with culture as *root metaphor*. Smircich's distinction has practical value for organizational designers as well as utility in expanding academic knowledge of the area. Her conclusion is that culture is often hierarchically defined (most frequently by managers) in an attempt to control aspects of organizational life and improve performance. In this way its status is elevated to that of critical variable, in other words regarded as a key factor in determining an organization's success. If we follow this interpretation of the concept then an organization's culture will be viewed as something that it 'has' and which can be changed through intervention – for example with a managed programme of culture change. This view underlies many attempts to alter a perceived existing culture – it can, for example, be frequently observed when public sector organizations are privatized. In such cases new or existing management teams are often concerned to build and instil a culture of customer service, which may in reality, or in their perception, have been lacking in the past. In contrast, Smircich's location of culture as root metaphor sees it as something 'that is' – in other words it has grown organically (hence the reference to roots) along with an organization's history, employees, technology and strategy. This second approach takes a social constructivist perspective on culture. If we believe that culture is root metaphor then we have to acknowledge that there are multiple rather than single cultures within organizations and that cultures will be very difficult to change.

Needle[18] draws a similar distinction between organizational culture representing the values, beliefs and principles of organizational members, which have grown within the context of a particular setting, and corporate culture, the latter term referring to cultures deliberately created by managers to achieve specified results. Those managers and academics who propound the value of corporate culture claim that strong unified cultures will play a key part in delivering success. We acknowledge the prevalence of the corporate culture view in management literature but lean towards the social constructivist view in this chapter. This regards culture (both at national and company level) as a concept that, in essence, grows organically – it derives, after all, from an agricultural metaphor – and is difficult to change in a top-down manner.

*A **corporate culture** is an attempt by managers to deliberately create and mould organizational culture to achieve specified results.*

LEVELS OF CULTURE IN WORK SETTINGS

Look closely at Figure 8.1 again. We are viewing organizational culture from a social constructivist point of view, so we propose that important aspects of an organization's culture emerge from the collective experience of its members. These emergent aspects of the culture help make it unique and may well help provide a competitive advantage for the organization. Alternatively aspects of its emergent culture can inhibit its performance particularly in a changing environment. Some of these features may be directly observed in day-to-day practices. Others may have to be discovered, for example by asking members to tell stories of important incidents in the history of the organization. We often learn about the unique aspects of organizational cultures through descriptions of very specific events.[19] By observing organizational symbols and rituals, listening to stories and asking organizational members to interpret what is going on, you can begin to understand that organization's culture or subcultures.

STORIES, RITES, RITUALS AND SYMBOLS

Stories indicate the state of an organization's health. Stories offer evidence of unique qualities and characteristics that an organization is proud of. A story may be as simple as telling a new employee about the newly appointed worker who stood up to the CEO of the company and progressed quickly through the company because that CEO admired his or her courage (which may in turn be something that is considered to be an important quality of the company in question).[20] Perhaps one of the most important stories concerns the founding of the organization. The **founding story** often contains the lessons learned from the efforts of an embattled entrepreneur whose vision may still guide the firm. The story of the founding may be so embellished that it becomes a **saga**, a heroic account of accomplishments.[21] Sagas are important because they are used to tell new members the real mission of the organization, how the organization operates (at least in the eyes of managers) and how individuals can fit into the work environment. Rarely is the founding story totally accurate and it often glosses over some of the more negative outcomes along the way. If you have job experience, you may well have heard stories concerning the following questions: How will the boss react to a mistake? Can someone move from the bottom to the top of the company? What will get me dismissed? These are common story topics in many organizations.[22] Often the stories will provide valuable hidden information about who is 'more equal' than others, whether jobs are secure and how things are really controlled. The stories suggest how organizational members view the world and live together.

Among the most obvious aspects of organizational culture are **rites** and **rituals**. Rites are standardized and recurring activities that are used at special times to influence the behaviours and understanding of organizational members. Rituals are systems of rites. Rituals serve to establish boundaries and relationships between the stakeholders of an organization through the repetition of events, such as staff meetings or how long people take for lunch. In Japan, for example, it is common for workers and managers to start their work days together with group exercises and singing the 'company song'. Separately, the exercises and song are rites. Collectively, they form part of a ritual.

Rituals and rites may be unique to particular groups within the organization. Subcultures often arise from the type of technology deployed by the unit, the specific function being performed and the specific collection of specialists in the unit. The boundaries of the subculture may well be maintained by a unique language. Often the language of a subculture, as well as its rituals and rites, emerges from the group as a form of jargon. In some cases, the special language starts to move outside the organization and enter the larger society. For example, the information technology (IT) industry is renowned for its use of technical language and, slowly, terms such as software, download, floppy, desktop, browser, hyperlink, icon, multimedia and online have become part of mainstream language.

*The **founding story** is the tale of the lessons learned and efforts of the founder of the organization.*

*A **saga** is an embellished heroic account of the story of the founding of an organization.*

***Rites** are standardized and recurring activities used at special times to influence the behaviours and understanding of organizational members.*

***Rituals** are systems of rites.*

On the other hand, many of the IT industry's plentiful jargon terms have yet to find wide acceptance. One such term, used by personnel manning an IT help desk to point to a user problem, is 'PEBKAC' – 'Problem Exists Between Keyboard And Chair'.

Language is used to convey the meaning of an organizational culture, with particular words and phrases either being unique to an organization or having a particular meaning in that organization. It has been suggested that many conversations in organizations are making cultural statements when they convey what the company expects and wants to occur;[23] for example, language can convey meaning about daily routines and habits of employees. It can also be a valuable measure in highlighting possible subcultural differences within an organization. Consider again the role of language used in ?What *If!* – our example cited at the start of this chapter. A title like The People Person might be thought to convey a different cultural statement then use of alternative titles such as Welfare Officer or Human Resources Manager.

No discussion of corporate culture would be complete without mentioning the symbols found in organizations. A **cultural symbol** is any object, act or event that serves to transmit cultural meaning. Symbols can include the architecture of a building, the layout of offices and space assigned to employees, the décor of the offices, and the general impression that is communicated to visitors by way of company name and size of the establishment. Although many such symbols are quite visible, their importance and meaning may not be. Other symbols include badges, prizes, organizational branding and stationery.

> A **cultural symbol** *is any object, act or event that serves to transmit cultural meaning.*

The physical layout of the office is an observable symbol of culture. For example, in an organization that values knowledge sharing, an open plan may express that value and encourage collegiality and camaraderie. However, a lack of privacy in the workplace can also affect people adversely and have a subliminal effect on what makes them secure and happy. So a culture may express its respect for employees in such an open-plan office if it makes an effort to provide at least acoustical and visual privacy. In a world in which many businesses are failing, physical space can express culture though the permanency and conservatism of its furnishings and decor. Consider again the attempt at ?What *If!* to use architecture, layout and space to create a 'groovy' workplace, which was a visible expression of the cultural values espoused by managers and, in this case, at least one worker who was a strong advocate of those values.

CULTURAL RULES AND ROLES

Organizational culture often specifies when various types of actions are appropriate and where individual members stand in the social system. These cultural rules and roles are part of the normative controls of the organization and emerge from its daily routines.[24] For instance, the timing, presentation and methods of communicating authoritative directives are often quite specific to each organization. In one organization meetings may be forums for dialogue and discussion, where managers set agendas and then let others offer new ideas, critically examine alternatives and fully participate. In another organization the 'rules' may be quite different. The manager goes into the meeting with fixed expectations. Any new ideas, critical examinations and the like are expected to be worked out in private before the meeting takes place. The meeting is a forum for letting others know what is being done and for passing out instructions on what to do in the future. Cultural rules and roles can become deeply ingrained in organizational behaviour, as they influence 'the way things are done around here', but sometimes, of course, they need to be changed.

OB IN ACTION

Open plan offices are no silver bullet for teamwork

New research shows that it is not the layout and decoration of an office that determines how people cooperate. More important in this regard are the values that they embrace.

Heidi Lund Hansen in research conducted by Consultancy within Engineering, Environmental Science and Economics (COWI) and Copenhagen Business School,[25] questions whether open-plan offices do promote cooperation and learning in workplaces. She found that open-plan office arrangements are managerial tools that will not result in improved communications without deeper analyses of organizational culture. Her research showed that, paradoxically, open plan offices lead to task-related communication being relocated to designated meeting or conference rooms, thereby making them less inclusive to wider groups in the organization.

She also points out that the transparency of open-plan working may lead to a more powerfully controlled hierarchy noting that: 'If the boss says, hmm we have been having a lot of tea breaks, haven't we, you get some indication that you are supposed to be sitting at your desk. And in the process, you foster a culture in which people sit in front of their monitors and quickly bring any dialogue to a conclusion.'

VALUES AND ORGANIZATIONAL CULTURE

Consider Figure 8.1 again. In order to describe the culture of an organization more fully, we have already stated that it is necessary to go deeper than the observable aspects. To many researchers and managers, shared values lie at the heart of organizational culture.

Shared values:

- help turn routine activities into valuable, important actions
- tie the corporation to the important values of society
- may provide a very distinctive source of competitive advantage.

John Weeks, a professor at the French-based INSEAD Business School, spent a year working at and studying the culture of a well-known British High Street bank, known at 'Britarm' in the study, although its identity has since been revealed. He found a ritual of complaint in this bank, described as a culture of shocking negativity characterized by chronic criticism at all levels of the organization.[26] Weeks records that on no occasion did he hear the bank referred to positively by employees. Colleagues would moan to each other continually while managers openly expressed their cynicism regarding the company in front of staff. Britarm's performance in this period was good, however, and it might be thought that this was despite the complaining culture within its branches. Weeks, however, goes further and suggests that the negative culture may, in a roundabout way, link to success. He records his experience of being told that he now knew what it was really like to be a Britarm employee when enduring a stint in the uncomfortable surroundings of its securities centre. Weeks records that: 'if she was right then being a securities clerk at Britarm feels like basking in the warm glow of adversity with sympathizers all around. I felt more like a part of the team than I ever had before ... The ritual of making derogatory remarks about some aspects of the Bank and receiving empathy in return, is a glue that strengthens the bonds between the individual and the group.'

Once more we see the complexity of links between organizational culture, values and performance.[27] It is doubtful whether the paradoxical and convoluted logic of the Britarm example should be taken up as an example of good practice, though, and readers can themselves ponder whether they would wish to be part of such a moaning culture at work and what the long-term effects could be on their mental wellbeing.

Linking actions and values

Individuals collectively learn behaviours and concepts to help them deal with problems. In organizations what works for one person is often taught to new members as the correct way to think and feel. Important values are then attributed to these solutions to everyday problems. By linking values and actions, the organization taps into some of the strongest and deepest realms of the individual. The tasks that a person performs are not only given meaning but value; what one does is not only workable but correct, right and important.

Some successful organizations have been seen to share a number of common cultural characteristics. Figure 8.2 provides a list suggested by two well-known US management consultants, Terrence Deal and Allan Kennedy.[28] As you can see from the figure, organizations with 'strong cultures' possess broadly and deeply shared value systems. Increasingly, organizations are adopting values statements that express their commitment to such areas as customer service, product and service quality, creativity, innovation, and social responsibility.

However, a strong culture can be a double-edged sword. Unique, shared values can:

- provide a strong corporate identity
- enhance collective commitment
- provide a stable social system
- reduce the need for formal and bureaucratic controls.

A widely shared philosophy. This philosophy is not an abstract notion of the future but a real understanding of what the organization stands for, often embodied in slogans.

A concern for individuals. This often places individual concerns over rules, policies, procedures and adherence to job duties.

A recognition of heroes. Heroes are individuals whose actions illustrate the shared philosophy and concerns of the company.

A belief in ritual and ceremony. Management understands that rituals and ceremonies are real and important to members and to building a common identity.

A well-understood sense of informal rules and expectations. Employees understand what is expected of them.

A belief that what employees do is important to others. Networking in order to share information and ideas is encouraged.

Figure 8.2: Elements of strong corporate cultures.

Conversely, a strong culture and value system can reinforce a view of the organization and its environment. If dramatic changes are needed, it may be very difficult to change the organization.

COMMON ASSUMPTIONS AND ORGANIZATIONAL CULTURE

At the deepest level of organizational culture (refer once more to Figure 8.1), there are common understandings known to almost everyone in the corporation: 'we are different', 'we are better at ...' and 'we have unrecognized talents'. These shared truths or common assumptions often lie dormant until actions violate them.

COMMON ASSUMPTIONS AND MANAGEMENT PHILOSOPHY

If culture is considered a variable that can be changed to affect an organization's competitive advantage (we have questioned this assumption to some extent) managers would need to recognize what can and what cannot be changed in the organization's culture. The first step is to recognize the group of managers as a subculture in itself. Senior managers often share common assumptions, such as 'we are good stewards', 'we are competent managers' or 'we are practical innovators'. In many organizations, broadly shared common assumptions of senior management go even further. The organization may have a well-developed management philosophy.

*A **management philosophy** links key goal-related issues with key collaboration issues to come up with general ways by which the organization will manage its affairs.*

A management philosophy links key goal-related issues with key collaboration issues and comes up with a series of general ways in which the organization will manage its affairs. A well developed management philosophy is important because it establishes generally understood boundaries for all members of the organization; it provides a consistent way of approaching novel situations and it helps hold individuals together by assuring them of a known path towards success. In other words, a well developed management philosophy is important because it links strategy with how the organization operates and thus helps an organization adapt to its environment. For example, Cisco Systems's strategy of growth, profitability and customer service is linked to empowering employees to generate best ideas quickly; hiring the best people, with ideas and intellectual assets that drive success; and disseminating information to compete in an 'ideas world'.

Elements of the management philosophy may be formally documented in a corporate plan, a statement of business philosophy or a series of goals. Yet it is the unstated but well understood fundamentals these written documents signify that form the heart of a well-developed management philosophy.

HOW CAN ORGANIZATIONAL CULTURE BE STUDIED?

Organizational culture researchers are interested in researching cultural manifestations while attempting to gather meaning about the patterns that link these manifestations. Studying manifestations includes researching the working environment of a culture; for example, the décor of the office, hierarchical structures and money earned by employees, as well as relationships between organizational members. Joanne Martin identifies four types of cultural manifestations, including cultural forms, formal practices, informal practices and content themes.[29]

Cultural forms are manifestations of organizational culture conveyed to employees. Tools used to convey observable culture include symbols, rituals, stories and language. For example, the 'employee-of-the-month' award or the story of how the company was founded help employees to identify with the organization's culture as these rituals and stories are all part of 'the way things are done here'. Symbols, such as branding (for example, the golden arches of McDonald's) have meaning. What does your company or university brand symbol on the top of any letterhead convey to you? This is a cultural form!

Formal practices are written down and are, on the surface, easily controllable by management. These practices can include structure, task and technology, policies and procedures, and financial controls. The formal practices are all expressions of an organizational culture. Therefore, formal practices need to be observed when studying organizational culture.

Informal practices, by contrast, evolve through interaction, are not written down and take the form of social rules. Informal practices can include the time used for tea breaks throughout the day and the prevalence and acceptability of arriving at work a few minutes late or leaving work a few minutes earlier at the end of the day. Such informal practices serve to highlight possible contradictions within the formal practices that are written down but not always carried out.

Content themes are considered common threads of concern that underlie interpretations of several organizational cultural manifestations. Top companies may try to impress certain images on stakeholders and the general public; for example, by promoting respect for the environment in all business pursuits. Companies that include such values in the mission statement or on company Web sites are attempting to create positive associations with their brands. Often, the way that managers behave in organizations, such as showing a friendly yet competitive nature to the outside world, will communicate to observers the content themes (or the images the organization is attempting to create in an audience's mind) of a company being studied.[30]

The majority of cultural studies within organizations take place via information obtained from the views of those members in management positions. However, it is now widely recognized that organizational culture researchers must also extract information about how the organization works by providing members of the organization who do not hold such posts with a tool through which to express their opinions. This ensures the organizational culture research is conducted from multiple perspectives (see the section on alternative perspectives of culture later in this chapter) and is more complete.

Quantitatively, cultural forms, formal practices and content themes can be measured by asking questions about the organization. This might take the form of an assessment of the general feelings and beliefs participants hold about the organization, their sense of affiliation with the organization and so on.[31] Content themes can be examined by questioning organizational/supervisory characteristics and by ranking the importance of organizational goals, reputation, engagement with the community and service quality. Formal practices are studied by analysing policies and procedures and how these are put into operation. Informal practices are rather more difficult to measure via questionnaire and are best revealed through interview and observation. Quantitative methods can include survey questionnaires.

Qualitatively, manifestations of organizational culture can be observed by participant observers, who may have discussions with organizational members via formal and informal interviews and focus groups, or alternatively may simply observe, with their status as researchers remaining unknown to the group. The researcher who is identified as such tends to examine patterns of behaviour, looks at consistencies and inconsistencies in behaviours, and is particularly interested in patterns of behaviours that are more covert. The interviews can include questions about organizational reputation before and after employment. What has changed? This is important as inconsistencies in what is reported to members outside an organization and what members inside an organization actually experience may reveal important information about the covert behaviours. Furthermore, the way an employee portrays the organization to outsiders may differ depending on the position or the occupational group that the organizational member belongs to. This may reveal patterns of inconsistencies between occupational groups or subcultures. Interview questions can also examine 'accountability' in terms of who sets standards formally and what happens informally. This may highlight the importance of informal practices for the day-to-day functioning of an organization. Observations can reveal a great deal about the organization's reliance on formal and informal practices and organizational content themes. Interpretations help to make sense of interactions between organizational actors and occupational groups and ultimately the relations between organizational culture and overall organizational performance.

Many organizational culture researchers use a mix of quantitative and qualitative methods to obtain a complete picture of 'what is truly going on' in the organization.

In Chapter 1 we drew the distinction between the positivist and interpretative traditions in OB. As can be seen from the preceding paragraphs, although there has been some attempt to capture organizational culture via more scientific (or at least quantitative) research methods, the topic more readily lends itself to interpretive study, relying on more in-depth personal accounts and interpretations of culture and longer-term observation of life in a single case study organization.

 **IN ACTION**

Traders deal in 'babes' and 'dragons'

In 1995, a British academic Belinda Brooks-Gordon, made public the results of her research into the culture present in trading houses in the City of London.[32] Her findings revealed widespread sexist attitudes among male traders at that time. This was reflected in the language used to describe, categorize and indeed stigmatize female colleagues.

Women in this work environment were classified on the basis of perceived attractiveness coupled with imagined sexual availability, age and clothing worn. So-called 'babes' were young and attractive to members of the male workforce. 'Babes' were shown more courtesy than other female workers but had less credibility in career terms. A subgroup of 'babes' were termed 'goers'. These women were perceived to be sexually active, promiscuous and available. Females in the workplace regarded as less attractive were termed 'mums' and, according to the researcher, were mostly ignored by the men. However women perceived as unattractive were labelled 'dragons' and the male workers felt they

were entitled to be ruder to them in their everyday dealings. Any women understood to hold feminist views were termed 'lesbians', regardless of their known sexual orientation. The male traders were seemingly more respectful of women workers who they considered competed with them in terms of aggressive behaviour and also ability. This last group were referred to as 'one of the boys'.

It should be stressed that this to many people doubtless unsavoury picture of a particular work culture is time-framed – in other words it may no longer paint an accurate picture of life in trading houses in the 21st century. It is cited here in part to stress the methods used in the study. Brooks-Gordon worked 'under cover' in the course of her study and was thus able to unravel and put on public display aspects of organizational culture that are likely to remain invisible if other methods, such as questionnaires were used.

TYPES OF ORGANIZATIONAL CULTURE

Although we have indicated that if cultures grow organically out of peoples' specific experiences and situations resulting in cultural *uniqueness*, some commentators have identified commonly found types of culture. Such typologies are useful in crystallizing our thoughts on the topic area and help to bring the subject to life. Nonetheless we should recognize that categorizing culture in this way, although enabling us to locate individual cultures along comparative (sometimes bipolar) frameworks, will not provide us with an in-depth knowledge of the development and workings of any individual culture.

Charles Handy's classification of types of organizational culture, dating from 1989,[33] distinguishes between the following four commonly-found models:

Role culture
is a type of organizational structure in which set rules, task procedures and job descriptions are particularly important.

- Role culture. In this type of culture, set rules, procedures and job descriptions dominate. People's power in such a setting is embedded in the *roles* they occupy. In particular your position within a hierarchy is most likely to underlie your influence. The organization's culture is essentially a depersonalized one; it will continue to operate in a 'machine-like' way even if key staff move or are absent. To many readers this description will be redolent of the concept of bureaucracy set out in Chapter 8 and it is normal for role cultures to be structured in the form of a bureaucracy. It is often felt that public sector organizations, oriented by values of fairness and predictability, provide good examples of the role culture, although commercial organizations in which standardized processes are important – for example in the financial services sector – can also exhibit characteristics of the role culture model.

Power culture
is a type of organizational culture in which a central figure exercises power on a personalized basis, there being relatively few formal rules in place.

- Power culture. It is claimed that this type of culture can be found in small organizations that bear the mark of their founder or owner. This central figure continues to exercise power on a personalized basis, there are as few rules in place as possible and the central figure will attempt to recruit people who 'fit in' or in whom they see echoes of themselves. As organizations grow and become more complex, there is a tendency for this type of culture to evolve into more of a role culture model, although it is possible that it could endure in, for example, family firms even when they expand. More often, however, in a growing company, the central figure becomes more of a figurehead and exerts less day-to-day influence on the culture.

Person culture
is a type of organizational culture in which an organization exists for the benefits of members, particularly star performers. It has been located in barristers' chambers and other professional work settings.

- Person culture. This model of culture is interesting in that it points to organizations that exist for their members benefit. In this sense people use the infrastructure of an organization (space, IT networks and so forth) to help them achieve objectives within a 'pooled' network. This is a more unusual type of culture but one recent contributor to the literature,[34] suggested that it could be characteristic of barristers' chambers, architects' partnerships or could be how hospital consultants view their organizational setting. It might be thought therefore that this type of culture is centred (or revolve around) around 'star performers' who are partly based in that organization.

- Task culture. In this type of culture, people are conceptualized and grouped together in terms of tasks or projects. A task orientation takes priority; people are brought together to work in teams for specific purposes rather than be located in functional or departmental areas as in role cultures. This culture could be found in the case of management consultancies or other client-based agencies.

Another typology of culture was developed by Deal and Kennedy.[35] These authors also identified four archetypal cultures set out below:

- **Process culture.** Organizations with this culture are concerned with ensuring that processes are clear and followed correctly. Highly regulated sectors such as healthcare, waste management and financial services might be driven by a need for precision and uniformity and therefore be associated with formal low-risk hierarchical cultures.

- **Tough-guy culture.** This type of culture is underpinned by a need to take quick decisions leading to a preoccupation with risk taking and a competitive and resilient outlook. The 1987 Hollywood film *Wall Street* painted a picture of just such a workplace culture with the anti-hero lead character played by Michael Douglas, memorably using the catch phrase 'lunch is for wimps' to evoke the mentality required to prosper in this type of setting – which was instilled in younger aspiring employees.

- **Work hard/play hard culture.** As the name indicates organizations identified within this type stress the importance of 'fun' at work. They are also likely to be highly performance-driven. Strong teamwork and a customer-focus are also typically found in this cultural type.

- **Bet-your-company culture.** This type of culture is characterized by a long-term outlook. It was conceived by Deal and Kennedy as appropriate in high-risk but slow feedback situations. Very significant levels of investment may be seen, but it could be many years before the results are apparent. Space technology provides a good example, also highlighting the very high level of technical expertise often associated with the culture. Investment banking has also been included as an example – once again a long-term orientation will be important to success in this field. The cultural features of vision and durability will be exemplified in employees' attitudes in organizations linked to this type.

In Chapter 1 we indicated that many OB topics could be usefully understood with reference to a contingency perspective. The essence of contingency theory is that no one solution, model or perspective will always result in organizational effectiveness. Rather the specific features of the organization, or circumstances faced by it, should be taken into account. The typologies of organizational culture put forward by Handy and by Deal and Kennedy can be seen within the contingencies idea. No one type of culture will be effective in all situations, instead *it all depends,* for example on an organization's size, stated aims, market and technology. It might, for example, be difficult in reality to avoid elements of role or process cultures (Handy and Deal and Kennedy's typologies show similarities) in the health sector, which is highly regulated, driven by a need to treat patients fairly and systematically and where processes, including patients' records need to be carefully documented. However dysfunctions of bureaucracy such as slowness, a departmental outlook and inflexibility may be more damaging in a small company exploring a new market and the founders of a company like this may wish to choose, instil and manage another culture – perhaps the work hard/play hard culture may be more suitable given the situation (contingencies) they face.

Process culture *is a type of organizational culture characterized by clear processes, which need to be followed correctly: it can be found in highly regulated sectors such as healthcare.*

Tough-guy culture *is a type of organizational culture driven by a need to take quick decisions, leading to a preoccupation with risk taking and a competitive ethos.*

Work hard/ play hard culture *is a type of organizational culture that stresses the twin roles of performance and fun at work.*

Bet-your-company culture *refers to a type of organizational culture characterized by a long-term outlook in which significant levels of investment are made, the results of which may take many years to feed through.*

ALTERNATIVE PERSPECTIVES ON ORGANIZATIONAL CULTURE

Many studies of organizational culture adopt only one perspective of culture – the integrationist perspective, which we characterized earlier in this chapter as viewing culture in terms of shared meanings resulting in harmony and a supposed organization-wide consensus.[36] These studies tend either to focus on managers and professionals and/or to present managerial perspectives as representative of organizational culture as a whole. But if a study claims to represent the culture of an entire organization, then employees of diverse levels and functions should also be studied. This gives us an opportunity to include more than one perspective and to be inclusive of views of members throughout the organization, rather than presuming that an occupational group, a profession or a functional level represents all organizational voices. Although the integration perspective is the most commonly researched and published, there are additional perspectives. Two influential approaches are the differentiation and ambiguity perspectives.

Differentiation perspective

In contrast to the integration perspective, which is seen from a managerial functional point of view, the differentiation perspective views organizational culture as a system of shared beliefs in *different* groups (often differentiated by location, function, gender, ethnicity or other demographic variations). These group values are sometimes in tune with the dominant culture and sometimes not. Some researchers believe the differentiation perspective is similar to integration, but is manifested at lower organizational levels. This perspective is not only characterized by harmony but also by diversity and inconsistency.

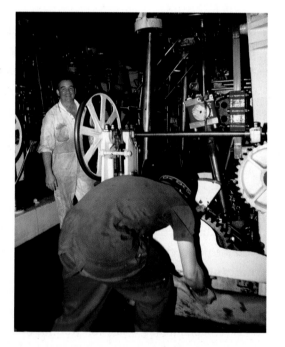

Organizational anthropologists and social researchers believe that organizational cultures, even if they represent a system of shared meaning, are not uniform cultures but rather have sets of subcultures, typically defined by departmental designations and geographical separation. Rather than finding harmony and unity, these researchers see diversity and inconsistency. Subcultures are not necessarily abnormal or deviant; they are natural outcomes of the different groups, departments and occupational cohorts within the organization. Such subcultures can enhance the dominant culture: they accept its core values but bring in other nonconflicting or countercultural values that directly challenge the values of the dominant culture. The tension between subcultures shapes the organizational culture itself. The formation of subcultures is sometimes called 'multiculturalism' in organizations.

Individuals develop differences in perception and opinion because of social bondings. Some of these relationships can span organizations. For example, plumbers in a large engineering factory can develop a shared relationship through their membership of a plumbing staff association.

In contrast to the integration perspective, the differentiation perspective sees organizations as characterized not just by harmony and unity but also by diversity and inconsistency. It accepts the possibility and value of internal conflict and suggests that this normally occurs due to the processes of differentiation and specialization common in modern organizations. As noted earlier, when organizations grow and mature they tend to become more complex, this complexity often taking the form of formal structural arrangements. But the subunits within organizations are very likely to develop their own cultures too.

Ambiguity/fragmentation perspective

The ambiguity or fragmentation perspective does not see clear-cut cultural groupings within organizations as the normal state; rather it views organizations and their members as typically experiencing a high level of ambiguity, as meanings differ both between individuals and within individuals over time. Meanings, values and behavioural norms are diverse because each individual independently assesses his or her environment. If consensus is observed then it is only momentary and such groupings soon dissolve. The ambiguity lies in the formation of associations between identities that are in a constant state of instability, lacking any form or pattern.[37] An ambiguity or fragmentation perspective suggests, therefore, that there are no clearly identified patterns of culture. Instead there is an ever changing flow of consensus, divergent views and confusion. This view rejects the idea of 'shared meanings' in favour of the idea that people attribute meanings to phenomena in organizations. They interpret them in random, ambiguous ways, and sometimes the interpretations are shared or partially shared. This perspective further brings into question whether the attribution of meaning in organizations really falls neatly into categories, as suggested by much 'mainstream' organizational culture theory.

The **fragmentation perspective** *views organizational culture as lacking any form of pattern as a result of differing meanings between individuals and within individuals over time.*

The fragmentation perspective sees attempts at cultural change along normative lines as having no effect, because the impact of any change will be absorbed. You cannot change the culture in any managed way, because change is continual.

CULTURE AS CONTROL

Another alternative to mainstream view of organizational culture stems from the work of Wilmott.[38] This new twist on the concept saw culture as fundamentally an attempt by managers of organizations to control workers by shaping their identities. As such, organizational culture represents one more way of exercising managerial control following on from other control mechanisms such as leadership, motivation or organization structure. Willmott's argument is that this particular form of control is different, however, as it involves an attempt not just to control behaviour but also altering the internal worlds of individuals – their *identities*. Grey,[39] writing in 2005, goes further in linking culture change management programmes with the totalitarian world depicted by George Orwell in his novel *Nineteen Eighty-Four*. For example Orwell showed how a ruling political party attempted to distort meaning by creating a particular mode of language (Newspeak). This resulted in the invention of new terms, such as 'oldspeak', which meant thoughts not consistent with philosophies and policies espoused by the ruling party. At the same time Newspeak was characterized by euphemisms, which often contained meanings exactly opposite to what was denoted, so the Ministry of Truth was, in reality, responsible for issuing propaganda and lies. Grey sees parallels here with what he perceives as counterintuitive language contained in company mission statements and other manifestations of organizational culture change programmes. More seriously, he also questions whether organizational culture places the collective above the individual and whether it involves an insidious attack on freedoms. His thoughtful contribution concludes with self-reflection on how far we can take the *Nineteen Eighty-Four* analogy. If workers cannot, or do not wish to, conform to organizational culture the worst that could happen to them (in most advanced societies) is that they would be dismissed – they wouldn't typically, as employees, be tortured or killed. Nonetheless, being sacked could be a very severe blow to many people depending on their circumstances and future prospects. In one further contribution, Watson[40] brings us back into focus by pointing out that work identities are only one part of our being. We suggest that you will in reality have multiple identities for example as a Czech, female, married Catholic accountant; our work and everything that goes with it is important, but it is only one part of our lives. So if we are controlled through organizational culture then we are only partly controlled.

Hence, understanding multiple perspectives of culture involves us going beyond an understanding of shared values and beliefs in organizational members, as proposed by the integration perspective; it also includes having an in-depth insight into patterns of overt and covert behaviour that link patterns of integration, differentiation and ambiguity. Each of these perspectives can operate at any one time or at the same time.[41] Thus, by adding alternative perspectives, including radical approaches from critical management theory, organizational culture can be more comprehensively defined as 'the socially constructed patterns of behaviours that link expressions of organizational integration, group differentiation and individual ambiguities together. These patterns of behaviour reflect individual, group and organizational values and beliefs.'[42]

▶ COUNTERPOINT

Culture deteriorates in overcrowded prison[43]

An unannounced UK government inspection of Her Majesty's Prison at Leeds in Yorkshire in 2006, noted a deterioration in relationships between staff and prisoners since its last inspection. Specific problem areas highlighted by the visiting inspectors included:

- over a third of prisoners reported feeling unsafe; this figure rising to 43% for black and other minority ethnic prisoners
- there was a high and mechanistic use of force

- the segregation unit ran in a militaristic way, with insufficient support for prisoners at risk and an incident when an alleged assault on a prisoner had not been followed up
- staff were heard referring to prisoners as 'bodies' or 'cons'
- black and ethnic minority prisoners continued to report 'undercover' racism and had no confidence in the race complaints system. Fewer than half of those surveyed believed staff treated them with respect
- there were only spaces for 60% of prisoners and prisoners without work could spend 23 hours in their cells.

Anne Owers, Her Majesty's Chief Inspector of Prisons said:

> This inspection shows how difficult it is to sustain progress in a crowded inner-city local prison, where cultures are hard to change and governors are preoccupied with crisis management. Under such pressure, officers tend to revert to their comfort zone, and governors are preoccupied with crisis management. Managers were aware of the task they faced, and conscious that some fundamental issues remained to be

tackled. However achieving and sustaining lasting change will be difficult with current levels of overcrowding.

Phil Wheatley, Director General of the Prison Service said:

> The Chief Inspector makes it very clear that the main problems faced by HMP Leeds are exacerbated by the serious difficulties which overcrowding presents to busy local prisons. Leeds prison is working hard to address the feelings of insecurity experienced by prisoners and, there is a very active safer prisons agenda currently in operation. The Governor is taking this agenda forward through projects such as the West Yorkshire Community Chaplains, which is working to deliver an inclusive approach to support prisoners and create a positive environment for black and ethnic minority prisoners.

This counterpoint feature shows us that organizational culture is not only to be perceived in positive terms. Note also the impact of resource issues cited as having an impact both on the existing culture and attempts to change it. Consider the steps you would take if you were to embark on a further cultural change programme in this prison.

THE FUNCTIONS OF ORGANIZATIONAL CULTURE FOR MEMBERS

We have now introduced you to some alternative perspectives on this topic, and wish to reinforce the importance of acknowledging multiple perspectives of organizational culture. However returning to mainstream managerial views of the concept, it is undeniable that organizational cultures do have an element of functionality. In other words, organizational culture may be influenced by top management in order to achieve a competitive advantage. For example, ideally in your first managerial job, one of the old hands on the job will sit down with you and explain exactly what is to be done, and how and why it is to be done. Experienced individuals know what to do and are aware of all the informal rules surrounding their roles in the organization.

Through their collective experience, members of an organization resolve two types of extremely important survival issues. The first is the question of external adaptation: what precisely needs to be accomplished and how can it be done? The second survival issue is the question of internal integration: how do members solve the daily problems associated with living and working together?

External adaptation

External adaptation *is the process of reaching goals and dealing with outsiders.*

External adaptation involves reaching goals and dealing with parties external to the organization. These issues involve assessing the tasks to be accomplished, the methods used to achieve the goals, and the ways of coping with success and failure.

Through their shared experiences, members develop common views that help guide their day-to-day activities. Organizational members need to know the real mission of the organization, not just the pronouncements to key constituencies such as shareholders. Members will naturally develop an understanding of how they contribute to the mission via interaction. This view may emphasize the valued importance of human resources, or it may emphasize the role of employees as cogs in a machine or a cost to be reduced.

Closely related to the organization's mission and its view of staff contribution are the questions of responsibility, goals and methods. These need to be translated into specific contributions, identifying clearly what the organization is endeavouring to achieve in its external environment. Organizations often present numerous goals; for example, in relation to strategy or corporate social responsibility and establishing procedures and methods, including the selection of the 'right people' to achieve their aims. They will also define jobs and procedures that reflect their approaches to external adaptation.

In summary, external adaptation involves answering important instrumental or goal-related questions concerning coping with reality, such as:

- What is the real mission?
- How do we contribute?
- What are our goals?
- How do we reach our goals?
- What external forces are important?
- How do we measure results?
- What do we do if specific targets are not met?

Internal integration

Internal integration *is the creation of a collective identity and the means of matching methods of working and living together.*

The external adaptation questions help a collection of individuals cope with a changing environment, the organizational culture also provides answers to the problems of internal integration. Internal integration deals with the creation of a collective identity and with finding ways of matching methods of working and living together.

Through dialogue and interaction, members of an organization begin to characterize their world. They might see it as malleable or fixed, filled with opportunity or threatening. For instance, real progress towards innovation can begin when group members collectively believe that they can change important parts of the world around them and that what appears to be a threat is actually an opportunity for change.

Three important aspects of working together are:

- deciding who is a member and who is not
- developing an informal understanding of acceptable and unacceptable behaviour
- separating friends from enemies.

To work together effectively, individuals need to decide collectively how to allocate power, status and authority and to establish a shared understanding of who will get rewards and sanctions for specific types of actions.

Managers often fail to recognize these important aspects of internal integration. For example, a manager may fail to explain the basis for a promotion and to show why this reward, the status associated with it and the power given to the newly promoted individual are consistent with commonly shared beliefs. For example, at AstraZenica, a pharmaceutical company, the human resource (HR) managers surveyed employees' values in regard to affiliation with the company. They found that employees valued learning and development opportunities, competitive rewards, an energizing work environment and a successful business. So the HR department works in accord with building a capable, talented team with the potential for growth; building credibility by getting the fundamentals right; aligning the HR strategy with the business strategy; and understanding, communicating and measuring the return on investment (ROI) for HR initiatives. HR is committed to constantly reviewing and changing in response to business needs.[44] Although these don't seem to be unusual features, they are applied in the organization in a way that reveals real commitment to the values and principles that underpin them.

We have seen how organizational culture helps members by providing answers to important questions of external adaptation and internal integration. However, there is often an important difference in the answers to these questions between executives towards the top of the organization and members at the bottom. This may be because senior executives may owe their primary allegiance to their position in the organization. They may identify with the organization as a whole and may equate organizational and individual success; and they may want all others in the organization to believe much the same. They also expect to be very handsomely rewarded. On the other hand, less senior employees may see themselves as part of a larger, more varied and complex network of relationships. The job may be just an instrumental mechanism, such as a means of getting the financial rewards necessary to live. The distance between the values and beliefs of employees and those of their managers, expressed in the formation of distinct subcultures, may in itself be a cultural construct of an organization. Some organizations encourage their middle and senior managers to 'stay in touch with their floor workers' by taking on tasks usually done by employees.

This is in an effort to facilitate integration between managers and their employees. However, in practice, employees express a level of discomfort working closely with their managers on their own routine tasks. For example, research found that employees were reluctant to share a task or convey criticism directly to the manager when needed. In addition, managers felt isolated in performing their tasks and expressed discomfort about changing roles. The research concluded that in this organization efforts to facilitate boundary crossing were not very successful and may even reinforce occupational boundaries between managers and their employees.[45]

This finding signifies that, when attempting to initiate organizational culture, different perspectives need to be considered. Approaching organizational culture from a differentiation or fragmentation perspective will be more complex, but that may reflect the findings of organizational cultural research. Nevertheless, we cannot deny that most current management writing echoes (mostly consciously) the integration perspective, giving direction and prescriptions on how to manage an organization's culture.

MANAGERS' ROLE IN REINFORCING AND CHANGING CULTURE

Managers can help foster a culture that provides answers to important questions concerning external adaptation and internal integration. Recent work on the links between corporate culture and financial performance reaffirms the importance of an emphasis on helping employees to adjust to the environment. It also suggests that this emphasis alone is not sufficient. Nor is an emphasis solely on shareholders or customers associated with long-term economic performance. Instead, managers must work to emphasize all three issues simultaneously. Managers are also challenged to consider the challenges of approaching culture change in the same ways for both core and peripheral workforces. Peripheral workers often spend too little time in the company to be socialized into the culture and core workers may resent peripheral workers experiencing the same positive treatments that they receive. But so-called peripheral workers are also important to the organization and it is arguably unethical to treat them in a different way. This is likely to emerge as an increasingly important issue for all concerned: consider for example, the increasing prevalence of 'teleworkers' – employees who spend a considerable amount of time working form home or remotely via telecommunications links. Sometimes managers adopt a two-tier approach to managing culture to deal with these differences.[46] Is this appropriate? It may be tempting for managers to attempt to revitalize an organization by dictating major changes rather than by building on shared values. Things may change a bit on the surface but a deeper look often shows whole departments resisting change and many key people who do 'buy in' for more or less understandable reasons to the new ways. Such responses may indicate that the responsible managers are insensitive to the effects of their proposed changes on shared values. They fail to ask if the changes are:

- contrary to important values held by participants within the organization
- a challenge to historically important organization-wide assumptions
- inconsistent with important common assumptions derived from the national culture(s) outside the organization.

All too often, executives are unable to realize that they too can be captured by the broadly held common assumptions within their organizations (see Effective Manager 8.1).[47] Top management may, for example, take a decision to introduce autonomous working teams to improve productivity and innovation, yet not face the reality that the organizational culture invests all authority in the executive management team. In such circumstances, the introduction of autonomous working teams can be disastrous as decision-making responsibility will not be devolved to the team. Culture influences managerial behaviour as much as that of everyone else in the organization and astute managers who seek to manage culture will seek to understand it first.

EFFECTIVE MANAGER 8.1

Using organizational culture to help an organization compete

As more organizations are moving into volatile industries using advanced technology and confronting international competitors, managers may need to help their organizational culture adjust. Here are some pitfalls to avoid and some factors to emphasize when entering and competing in highly volatile, high-technology markets such as computing and biotechnology:
- when entering the market early, do not allow employees to become disenchanted when facing initial technical barriers and skill development challenges
- when entering slowly, do not give competitors too big a lead; keep stressing to all employees

the necessity of building technical and market skills
- when adding new products to an existing market, take the opportunity to reassess approaches to decision making and management for both new products and old ones; challenge old routines
- when adjusting to new markets with new products, avoid using 'conventional wisdom' and stress the development of new ways to compete
- when entering the market, foster the Internet culture by embracing all forms of open communication in all possible media.

ORGANIZATIONAL AND NATIONAL CULTURE

There is very considerable scope for macro-social factors to affect organizational culture. In this respect national culture is itself a major influence on any organization operating within its boundaries. Societal-level culture can impact on workplaces in the following ways:

• Attitudes towards such things as individual responsibility, group harmony, ambiguity, displaying emotion openly and status will be embodied in the workplace by organizational actors, including those in positions of influence. These attitudes are culturally derived so that an organization will have its organizational culture influenced by wider society through its members' values.

• Institutional factors, for example the relative importance of trade unions in a particular society – itself deriving from a country's economic/political context, will set limits on how an organization operates in important ways, including aspects of its culture. For example a litigious culture such as the US is likely to be manifested at organizational level in cultures that stress the protection of individual rights and formalized health and safety policies.

The links between national and organizational culture are made more complex when you consider the multicultural makeup of workforces within any one society. We are here looking at issues of imported cultures and cultural diversity.

Every large organization imports potentially important subcultural groupings when it recruits employees from the larger society. There is a range of strategies for dealing with this phenomenon. At one extreme, senior managers can merely accept these divisions and work within the confines of the larger culture – in other words informing staff that they will have to fit in to the overriding national culture and do things 'our way'. However, there are three primary difficulties with this approach. First, subordinated groups, such as members of a specific religion or ethnic group, may find it difficult to wholly assimilate in the new culture with a number of potentially deleterious consequences. Academics studying national culture[48] note that individual's core values are formed at an early age, that is within their 'home' culture and will therefore be deeply rooted and potentially difficult to change. Second, the organization may lose valuable knowhow if it discourages diversity amongst its workforce. Third, organizations that accept and build on cultural diversity may find it easier to develop sound international operations. Conversely, for example, many Japanese organizations have had substantial difficulty adjusting to the equal treatment of women in their US and European operations.

A recent study found that people from different ethnic and gender groups filter and process information about organizational culture differently. This means that they may interpret the same cultural messages differently. Thus, attempts by management to manipulate cultural elements may need to take account of the fact that they will not always be universally and consistently understood. Management efforts to homogenize culture will almost inevitably result in subunit variations in interpretation and this is likely to contribute to the development of subcultures.[49]

In Europe multicultural populations are now a reality. In 2004 statistics showed that over 10% of the populations of Austria, Belgium, Germany, the Republic of Ireland, the Netherlands and Sweden were foreign born. The figure was highest in Switzerland with 23.5% of its population originating from outside that country.[50] The clear indication is that cultural change within these societies has occurred within a short period of time. Therefore, it has become important for organizations to manage multiculturalism effectively. Robin Ely and David Thomas[51] discuss three paradigms for assessing an organization's level of openness to multiculturalism. First, the 'discrimination and fairness' paradigm looks at multiculturalism with respect to equal opportunity, fair treatment, recruitment, and compliance with legislation by ensuring certain numbers of staff from ethnically diverse backgrounds are employed. This paradigm insists that individuals assimilate into the existing organizational culture and tends to lead to the development of potentially destructive subcultures (as ethnic differences are ignored or suppressed).

Second, the 'access and legitimacy' paradigm for an organization's level of openness to multiculturalism emphasizes gaining access to new and diverse markets by using cultural diversity within the organization. This may create a feeling of exploitation in staff as they are the 'token representative of their culture'. In addition, this differentiation of individuals from the group can lead to subculture development as differences are highlighted.

Third, the 'learning and effectiveness' paradigm for an organization's level of openness to multiculturalism incorporates elements of the other two paradigms. Additionally, this paradigm firmly connects diverse ethnicity to diverse approaches to work. According to Ely and Thomas, by creating openness, organizations will find that individuals from different national cultures do not feel devalued by assimilation into the existing organizational culture, nor will subcultures along ethnic lines be created.

Managing cultural diversity in organizations is a skill that contemporary managers must acquire. Many organizations run courses on multiculturalism to ensure knowledge and understanding of national and cultural differences. In addition, many organizations have courses for ethnically different groups and individuals, including language tuition related to the workplace. When we talk about cultural differences it is important not to overlook the importance of communication; many intercultural misunderstandings are the result of a lack of facility in a second language.

CONCLUSION

Organizational culture is an important topic within OB. It is concerned with the ways in which its members interpret the everyday realities of organizational life. Such interpretations can be an important influence upon behaviour. Some theorists and managers believe that a strong organizational culture can contribute to high performance and success. Whether or not this is consistently true, the study of organizational culture is key to an understanding of how organizations operate in the real world.

SUMMARY

LEARNING OBJECTIVE 1
What is organizational culture?

Organizational culture is defined as the system of shared values and beliefs that develops within an organization and guides its members' behaviour. It occupies an important role within OB, growing in importance since the 1980s in response to key trends within the business world. It is normally studied by using qualitative or ethnographic research methods in an attempt to capture the meanings that individuals and groups attach to culture.

LEARNING OBJECTIVE 2
Organizational culture and national culture

The concept of organizational culture is as important to the management of an organization as are strategy and structure. As the system of shared beliefs and values that guide and direct the behaviour of members links to macro-level national culture, this level of culture can have a strong influence on day-to-day organizational behaviour and performance. There are connections between organizational culture and national culture but each organizational culture is unique despite being embedded in a national culture.

LEARNING OBJECTIVE 3
Cultural levels, dominant cultures, subcultures and diversity

Culture can be analysed through its three components: observable culture – the behaviours that can be seen within an organization; shared values held by members of an organization and, at the deepest level, common assumptions or truths developed and shared by members through their joint experiences in the organization. Dominant cultures are articulated by dominant individuals or groups. Organizations are also routinely characterized by subcultures among various work units and subsystems, as well as possible countercultures, which can be the source of potentially harmful conflicts.

LEARNING OBJECTIVE 4
Types of organizational culture

Although each organizational culture is necessarily unique, several writers have formulated typologies which establish commonly found forms of culture. In this chapter we have looked at the models put forward by Handy and Deal and Kennedy. Such models enable us to consider organizations we work in or know along a pre-existing continuum framework. This can be useful in crystallizing our thoughts on the topic, although it is rare that real-life organizations fit perfectly into any one category.

LEARNING OBJECTIVE 5
Does culture link to performance?

A well-developed culture can assist in responding to internal and external problems. Through common shared behaviours, values and assumptions, organizational members can clearly understand the organization's mission, strategies and goals in relation to the external environment. Culture also helps to achieve internal adaptation – the ability of members to work together effectively on organizational activities. A third function of culture is to help bring management and employees much closer together in their respective goals.

LEARNING OBJECTIVE 6
Critical perspectives on culture

It may be naïve and misleading to regard organizations as unified entities with one dominant culture to which everyone completely subscribes. The ambiguity and fragmentation perspectives alert us to more pluralist models of culture, which could be more realistic in many instances. If employees hold values that do not mirror those of dominant coalitions within organizations, this may not lead to conflict or confusion and differences in this regard may be a source of creativity and diversity which is otherwise positive, in terms of organizational performance.

CHAPTER 8 STUDY GUIDE

You can also test your understanding and access further resources at **www.wileyeurope. com/college/french**.

REVIEW QUESTIONS

1. What is organizational culture and what are the levels of analysing culture in organizations?
2. What functions do organizational cultures serve and how do subcultures and cultural diversity help in this?
3. What are some alternative perspectives of culture? Why is it important to view organizational culture from more than one perspective?
4. Describe some ethical issues that might be encountered when managing organizational culture.

APPLICATION QUESTIONS

1. You are a manager who wishes to encourage employees to make suggestions and contribute to new ideas. What aspects of culture could be manipulated to try to encourage this?
2. What observable elements of organizational culture can you identify from your own organization or an organization with which you are familiar?
3. Give examples of both formal and informal processes that occur in your organization or at your university. What can you say about the nonobservable culture in your organization?
4. In a small organization with 50 employees, senior management has espoused values of equality, respect and high performance for employees and customers. When the latest performance figures for the company are released, management's response is to call the staff to a general meeting and tell them they all have to 'lift their game' if they expect to retain their jobs. What comments can you make on the cultural features of the organization?

5. Your company has just merged with another that provides a similar service. What issues will emerge in relation to the merging of two organizational cultures and what can managers do to deal with them?

6. Examine the following values and visible elements of culture. What underlying assumptions do you think might exist 'beneath' these aspects of culture?

- Organization A values new ideas and selects its highest-performing employees for special monthly creative workshops. Organization B values new ideas and promises a prize of 4 000 euros to any employee whose idea contributes clearly to increasing profits. Organization C values new ideas and encourages employees, as owners of shares in the company, to contribute ideas in their day-to-day work.

- Organizations D, E and F express the importance of high-performing employees. Organization D conducts annual performance reviews between supervisor and worker and if workers perform according to requirements, they are given an incremental increase in wages. Organization E conducts six-monthly reviews and more regular 'chats' between supervisor and worker. If the workers are not performing according to requirements they are asked to account for their low performance. In Organization F no reviews are conducted but workers and supervisors work closely together. If employees are demonstrating outstanding performance, their work is commended and publicized in the company newsletter. They also receive a bonus.

- In Organizations G and H an employee makes a significant mistake. In Organization G the manager speaks to the employee and tries to analyse the problem and find ways to overcome it. In Organization H the manager discusses the employee's mistake at a team meeting in front of all members of the group and expresses disappointment at his poor behaviour. The incident is also reported to senior management and recorded on the employee's file.

RESEARCH QUESTIONS

1. Search the newspapers and business magazines for news of an impending business merger or takeover. Find out what you can about both organizations' existing cultures.
   (a) From what you have learned about the organizations, what differences do you think there are between the cultures of the two organizations?
   (b) How do you think these differences in culture will affect the merger process and what issues will management have to deal with to develop a new combined culture?

2. Search the Internet for two different organizations in the same industry – for example, two insurance companies, two major retail chains or two universities. It

is especially valuable if you understand the type of activity the organization carries out and/or if you have had some experience with at least one of them as a customer. Set yourself a purpose for your inquiry to give it some focus. For example, look at the Web site and ask questions such as:

(a) As one of your customers, will I expect customer-focused service?

(b) Will your employees be helpful?

(c) Will it be easy for me to do business with your organization?

(d) Will you have up-to-date technological interfaces for customers?

Try to assess the answers to these questions at three levels, in the following order (remember you are looking for information about underlying assumptions, shared values and observable symbols of the culture):

- by looking at the images
- by looking at the structure and layout of the Web site
- by looking at the information available to answer these questions.

The order is important because you will be looking to see how compatible different aspects of the culture are and how they may vary or conflict with each other. An example of conflict might be an organization's claim that 'we put our customers first', while its Web site is very difficult for a customer to navigate. An example of compatibility might be if an organization using the same slogan has a Web site that is extremely easy to navigate, with clear, simple, easy-to-understand navigation tools. Evaluate both Web sites and compare the two in the context of your focus question. What observations can you make from this study of the two organizations about the nature of their particular organizational cultures? Does the exercise give you any insights into how easy or difficult it might be to investigate organizational culture?

RUNNING PROJECT

Complete the following activities for your chosen organization.

1. Outline what you consider the key parts of your organization's observable and nonobservable culture (shared values and common assumptions) and give examples.

2. What does your organization do to manage the organizational culture?

3. To what extent do management's preferred culture and the observable culture correlate? Do any countercultures exist within the organization?

INDIVIDUAL ACTIVITY

Assessing your organization's culture

Choose an organization with which you are familiar. This 15-question survey has been developed to serve as a starting point for the analysis of organizational culture. Answer each true/false question according to what is true most of the time and answer based on how your organization actually acts – not how you would like it to be.

True/false questions

1. I know how my projects contribute to the success or failure of our organization.
2. Management here makes lots of announcements to employees.
3. I have colleagues from a wide variety of professional and personal backgrounds.
4. In this organization people who are not ready to be promoted after a certain length of time at their level are generally encouraged to leave.
5. Departments or teams compete with each other for our organization's resources.
6. When people are not getting along here it is a long time before we directly address the issue.
7. When it is time for me to learn a new skill, training is readily available at no cost to me.
8. When the boss tells us to 'jump!' we ask 'how high?'
9. It takes a long time for this organization to address customer concerns.
10. Many employees expect to work at this organization for their whole careers.
11. Senior management says the door is always open – and they mean it.
12. It is fun to work here.
13. We have three or fewer layers of management.
14. We have performance reviews less often than once a year.
15. Compensation and benefits are relatively low here.

Count your 'true' responses in each third of the quiz (questions 1–5, 6–10, 11–15). The section in which you have answered 'true' the most times corresponds to the culture type your organization most closely matches. If you have the same number of 'true' responses in more than one section, your culture matches this combination of types. Here is a list of primary advantages and potential pitfalls of each one.

For questions 1–5
If you had the most 'true' responses in this set of questions, your company has a deliberative/traditional culture.

Advantages:

- This culture tends to be intellectual and thoughtful.
- People in this type of organization often consider issues carefully prior to making a change.
- The organization probably has many formal systems, yet flexibly forms and reforms teams in accordance with immediate client needs.
- This cultural type regularly hires groups of new employees, generating a valuable flow of diverse talent with fresh perspectives.
- Senior management communicates frequently to employees.

Pitfalls

Although plenty of communication usually flows from the top of this organizational type, management often does not indicate interest in feedback from all levels. Beyond making announcements from management, ask for regular feedback so you don't miss critical information and/or valuable innovations from your staff.

- Be careful that your organization does not discuss change for so long that you miss important opportunities to change for the better.
- Be aware of the cultural implications of fostering competition within a company. Internal competition may create resentment that drives costly turnover.

For questions 6–10

If you had the most 'true' responses in this set of questions, your company has an established/stable culture.

Advantages

- This organization has most likely been around for a long time and/or is a family business. These organizations tend to have solid institutional memories, so they are not likely to waste resources by repeatedly 'reinventing the wheel'.
- This type of company has processes in place to address most situations.
- Organizations of this type tend to cultivate employees by encouraging development through mentoring programmes and/or formal training opportunities.
- This culture type is known for compensating its people relatively well.

Pitfalls

- Typically this type of organization struggles to handle conflict well, often becoming either conflict avoidant or 'command and control'. If your organization tends to be conflict avoidant, it may be time to address those problems that are out of hand, or that have been out of hand in the past.

- 'Command-and-control' style leadership may yield feelings of disconnectedness among employees. Consider assessing employee morale immediately.
- Overall, this culture type tends to be wary of turnover so take a careful look at your organization and consider whether it is holding on to people who might best be let go.
- While established systems can be a positive sign of organizational health, make sure your processes are focused toward addressing customer needs in a timely matter. If your processes impede rapid resolution of customer problems, rework them right away.

For questions 11–15

If you had the most 'true' responses in this set of questions, your company has an urgent/seat-of-the-pants culture.

Advantages

- This culture type features a positive work environment with tight bonds among employees.
- It is likely that an aspect of your organization's mission includes responding to crisis. People care deeply about the organization's mission and work hard to achieve the organization's goals.
- Employees who frequently hurry to beat the clock can create great results in a short time, provided that quality is a strong value in your organization.
- These organizations tend to have a flat structure that fosters communication and collaboration among employees and speeds the decision-making process.

Pitfalls

- Minimum rewards (both tangible and intangible) and minimum feedback are common with this culture type. Rewards and recognition are important not only to generate loyalty but also to foster collaboration.
- The constant rush to get things done quickly can lead to burnout and increase the ever present danger of losing talent.
- Although this type of culture generally features frequent upward communication and grassroots change, top-down communication tends to be inadequate. Beyond staying accessible, take time to share important messages and expectations with your entire staff to keep them motivated and moving in the right direction.
- Making decisions under intense time pressure may lead to a reduction in the quality of your products or services.

Is your type different from what you thought it would be? If so, you might have an unrealistic perception of your organization's character and values.

GROUP ACTIVITY

Your university culture

Preparation
Select a university or college, or a department within this institution, to analyse its culture. Answer the following questions.

1. How many stories do you know about it?
2. How many sagas do you know about it?
3. How many myths do you know about it?
4. Identify as many rites and rituals that are used as you can.
5. Identify as many cultural symbols that are used as you can.
6. Identify as many shared meanings that are used as you can.
7. Identify as many rules and roles that are used as you can.
8. Identify as many shared values that are used as you can. Do these values give the organization or department a competitive advantage?

Objectives
1. To understand the elements of organizational culture
2. To understand how to analyse and manage organizational culture

Total time: 15–45 minutes.

Procedure
1. The lecturer or tutor calls on students to give their answers to the eight preparation questions.
2. The more information you have for each question, the stronger is the culture at your university/college or its department. Based on your answers, do you believe the organization or its unit has a strong or a weak culture?
3. How could the organizational culture be managed to make it stronger?
4. What is the down side of having a strong culture?

Case Study

WE KNOW IT WHEN WE SEE IT

'You can take IKEA out of Smaland, but you can't take Smaland out of IKEA.' This statement is part of the opening section of IKEA's corporate Web site that focuses on the company's shared values, themselves an integral part of the company's culture. Smaland in Sweden where Ingvar Kamprad founded the business that grew into the present-day IKEA, is characterized as a place that embodies the company's values. IKEAs Web site notes that: 'Simplicity, humility, thrift and responsibility are all evident in the lifestyle, attitudes and customs of the place where IKEA began. An example of the Smalanders' way of doing things is not to ask others what you should be doing, but to ask yourself and then get on with it!'[52]

An IKEA executive reinforces the importance of the company culture for employees, stating that successful employees are:

> ...people who accept our values and are willing to act on our ideas. They tend to be straightforward rather than flashy and not too status-conscious. They must be hardworking and comfortable dealing with everyone from the customer to the owner to the cashier. But perhaps the most important quality for an IKEAN is *odmujkhet*, a Swedish word that implies humility, modesty and respect for one's fellow man. It may be hard to translate but we know it when we see it.[53]

Ingvar Kamprad is very clear that maintaining a strong IKEA culture is, in his judgement, one of the most crucial factors explaining IKEA's success. Values of togetherness and enthusiasm are supported by the company through open plan office layouts and by laying out clear goals that co-workers can stand behind. Another espoused value, willpower, is defined as first agreeing on mutual objectives and then not letting anything stand in the way of actually achieving them. It is alternatively stated as involving a sense of knowing exactly what we want and exhibiting an irrepressible desire to achieve it.

IKEA's culture is viewed by the company itself as a strong culture 'living and based on a set of shared values'.[54] The organization claims that its togetherness and enthusiasm makes it unique. Its recruitment section on the IKEA corporate Web site offers potential employees (termed co-workers), the prospect of fun at work and opportunities to contribute to the development of others. IKEA also wishes to build a diverse workforce noting that 'we want to attract people from diverse nationalities, perspectives and approaches because we believe diversity makes IKEA a better place to work and to shop.'[55] The recruitment of suitable co-workers is clearly important to IKEA as it views culture as emerging and being sustained by people enacting values.

Questions

1. To what extent is IKEA's culture as depicted here unique or can it be located within either Handy or Deal and Kennedy's typology of cultures?
2. If you were a manager in IKEA, what would you do to sustain the current culture?

Source: www.ikea-group.ikea.com/corporate/work/why.html

SUGGESTED READING

Fineman, S., Sims, D. & Gabriel, Y. (2005), *Organizing and Organizations*, 3rd edn, Sage: London. In Chapter 2 of this book, 'Entering and leaving', the authors provide some vivid examples of the day-to-day manifestations of organizational culture.

Peters, T. & Waterman, R.H. (1982), *In Search of Excellence*, Warner: New York. This best selling albeit subsequently much-criticized book sets out a clear view of the potential impact of organizational culture on performance.

END NOTES

1. Braham, M. (2005), Cool, cutting-edge offices mean work, rest and some play, see www. timesonline, 19 January 2005, accessed 28 June 2007.

2. Peters, T. & Waterman, R.H. (1982), *In Search of Excellence,* Harper & Row: New York.

3. Schein, E.H. (1985), *Organizational Culture and Leadership,* Jossey-Bass: San Francisco, CA.

4. Hofstede, G. (2001), *Culture's Consequences,* 2nd edition, Sage: Thousand Oaks, CA.

5. Linstead, S. (2004), Managing Culture, in *Management and Organization a Critical Text* (eds S. Linstead, L. Fulop & S. Lilley), Palgrave Macmillan: Basingstoke.

6. Den Hartog, D. & Verburg, R.M. (2004), High performance work systems, organizational culture and firm effectiveness, *Human Resource Management Journal,* **14** (1), 55–78.

7. Ibid.

8. Deal, T. & Kennedy, A. (1982), *Corporate Culture,* Addison-Wesley: Reading, MA.

9. See www.staralliance.com/en/meta/airlines/TP, accessed 30 June 2007.

10. Ibid.

11. Peters, T & Waterman, R.H. (1982), *In Search of Excellence,* Harper & Row: New York.

12. Lueders Bolwerk, C.A. (2002), The culture of farm work and its implications on health, social relationships and leisure in farm women and men in the United States, *Journal of Cultural Diversity,* **9** (4), 102–107.

13. Fitzgerald, J.A. & Teal, A. (2004), Health reform and occupational sub-cultures: the changing roles of professional identities, *Contemporary Nurse,* **16** (1–2), 9–19.

14. Jones, R., Lasky, B., Russell-Gale, H. & Le Fevre, M. (2004), Leadership and the development of dominant and countercultures: a narcissistic perspective, *Leadership and Organization Development Journal,* **25** (1/2), 216.

15. Martin, J. & Siehl, C. (1983) Organization culture and counterculture, *Organizational Dynamics,* 12, 52–64.

16. McColl, G. (2002), Toll's takeover touch, *Business Review Weekly,* (12–18 December), 40–41.

17. Smircich, L. (1983), Concepts of culture and organizational analysis, *Administrative Science Quarterly,* **28** (3), 339–358.

18. Needle, D. (2004), *Business in Context,* 4th edn, Thomson: London.

19. Schein, E.H. (1990), Organizational culture, *American Psychologist,* **45** (2), 109–119.

20. Martin, J. (1992), *Cultures in Organizations,* Oxford University Press: New York.

21. Geertz, C. (1973), *The Interpretation of Culture,* Basic Books: New York.

22. Byer, J.M & Trice, H.M. (1987), How an organization's rites reveal its culture, *Organizational Dynamics,* (Spring edition), 27–41.

23. McManus, K. (2003), The challenge of changing culture, *Industrial Engineer,* **35** (1), 18–19.

24. Den Hartog, D.N. & Verburg, R.M. (2004), High performance work systems, organizational culture and firm effectiveness, *Human Resource Management Journal,* **14** (1), 55–79.

25. See www.cowi.com/en/menu/news/newsarchive/bulidings/openplan, accessed 21 June 2007.

26. Weeks, J. (2003), *Unpopular Culture: the Culture of Complaint in a British Bank,* Chicago University Press: Chicago, IL.

27. Arnold, J. (2003), *Why Clever Companies Have the will to Whinge*, newsvote.bbc.co.uk-BBCNEWS/business, accessed 1 July 2007.

28. Developed from Deal, T. & Kennedy, A. (1982), *Corporate Cultures: The Rites and Rituals of Corporate Life*, Addison-Wesley: Reading, MA.

29. Martin, J. (2002), *Organizational Culture: Mapping the Terrain*, Sage: Thousand Oaks, CA.

30. Ibid.

31. Degeling, P., Kennedy, J., Hill, M., *et al.* (1998), *Professional Sub-cultures and Hospital Reform*, Centre for Hospital Management and Information Systems Research, University of New South Wales: Sydney.

32. Traders deal in 'Babes and 'Dragons' (1995), *Independent*, 21 December.

33. Handy, C. (1989) *Understanding Organizations*, Penguin: Harmondsworth.

34. Brewis, J. (2007), Culture, in *Introducing Organizational Behaviour and Management* (eds K. Knights & H. Willmott), Thomson: London.

35. Deal, T.E & Kennedy, A.A (1982), *Corporate Cultures: The Rites and Rituals of Corporate Life*, Penguin: Harmondsworth.

36. Martin, J. (2002), *Organizational Culture: Mapping the Terrain*, Sage: Thousand Oaks, CA.

37. Ibid.

38. Willmott, H. (1993), Strength is ignorance, slavery is freedom: managing culture in modern organizations, *Journal of Management Studies*, 30 (5), 515–552.

39. Grey, C. (2005), *A Very Short, Fairly Interesting and Reasonably Cheap Book about Studying Organizations*, Sage: London.

40. Watson, T.J. (2006), *Organising and Managing Work*, 2nd edn, FT Prentice Hall: Harlow.

41. Martin, J. (2002), *Organizational Culture: Mapping the Terrain*, Sage: Thousand Oaks, CA.

42. Fitzgerald, J.A. (2002), *Managing Health Reform: a Mixed Method Study into the Construction and Changing of Professional Identities*, unpublished PhD thesis.

43. *HMP Leeds – Culture Deteriorates in Overcrowded Prison*, http://press.homeoffice.gov.uk/press-releases.

44. Donaldson, C. (2002), AstraZenica HR: a study in strategic people management, *Human Resources*, November, 12–14.

45. Fitzgerald, J.A. & Hinings, R. (2004), *Changing Professional Identities: Adjusting Professional Delineations in Health*. Paper presented at the International Federation of Scholarly Associations of Management (IFSAM) VIIth World Congress, Goteburg, Sweden.

46. Ogbonna, E. & Harris, L.C. (2002), Managing organizational culture: insights from the hospitality industry, *Human Resource Management Journal*, 12 (1), 33–53.

47. Cooper, A.C. & Smith, C.G. (1992), How established firms respond to threatening technologies, *Academy of Management Executive*, 6 (2), 56–69.

48. French, R. (2007), *Cross-Cultural Management in Work Organizations*, CIPD: London.

49. Helms, M.M. & Stern, R. (2001), Exploring the factors that influence employees' perceptions of their organization's culture, *Journal of Management in Medicine*, 15 (6), 415–425.

50. OECD *Factbook* (2007), OECD: Paris.

51. Ely, R. & Thomas, D. (2001), Cultural diversity at work: the effects of diversity perspectives on group processes and outcomes, *Administrative Science Quarterly*, 46 (2), 229–274.

52. See www.ikea-group.ikea.com/corporate/work/why.html, accessed 5 July 2007.

53. Konzelmann, S.J. Wilkinson, F. Craypo, C. & Aridi, R. (2005), *The Export of National Varieties of Capitalism; The Cases of Wal-Mart and IKEA*, Working Paper No. 314, Centre for Business Research, University of Cambridge: Cambridge.

54. See www.ikea-group.ikea.com/corporate/work/why.html, accessed 14 August 2007.

55. Ibid.

CHAPTER

9

Leadership

LEARNING OBJECTIVES

After studying this chapter you should be able to:

● explain the difference between leadership and management

● understand and evaluate trait and behavioural theories of leadership

● understand and evaluate situational contingency theories of leadership

● discuss charismatic leadership and transformational leadership

● outline some of the current issues in diversity in leadership.

BEHIND THE BATTLE FOR THE HANDSETS

Ed Zander took over at Motorola after it had slipped behind Nokia in the handset market. The slide had included the failure of a new technology project 'Iridium', which had affected the firm's confidence. One of his first messages was 'Don't be hard on yourself – you took a risk'. Since then, Zander has encouraged risk taking at all levels and the company has produced the remarkably successful RAZR (pronounced 'razor') and KRZR ('crazer') handsets which have a slim design. These innovations are closing the gap for Motorola's market share, and being copied by other manufacturers. How has this terrific success been achieved?

Jim Wicks, a middle manager, credits the change to interteam cooperation so that different departments work with each other to help solve each others' complex problems. In turn this change has several underpinning values. Wicks thinks three have been crucial for them: reforming their culture; changing their management selection, and emphasizing teamwork. The lack of blame for failure has helped people take risks and achieve far more than they might have. Management recruitment generally has placed far more emphasis on managers' people skills rather than just focusing on technical ability and knowhow that dominated previous hiring judgements. Managers have been able to get their teams to work in different ways, and managers have worked together to conquer complex problems at the edge of technical knowledge. So now everyone is talking to each other far more and thinking about the process of working together as well as being able to come up with technical excellence on which their competitiveness relies.

Questions

1. Why do leaders need to sustain employee confidence especially in high-technology organizations?
2. Why do you think Motorola previously failed to emphasize the 'people' skills of their management roles?

Source: Adapted from The cutting edge; Face value, *The Economist*, 7 October, 2006.

INTRODUCTION

As the chapter opening shows, regardless of their rank, most managers are expected to play a leadership role. As leaders, they are expected to foster work environments conducive to self-renewal, thus engaging in change programmes that can be radical. They need to develop a capability to create an appetite and agility amongst employees at all levels for continuous change. They must encourage relationships and be able to build trust across the organization. In fact, for most organizations to prosper and perform nationally and internationally, strong leadership skills are needed. While the importance of leadership is indisputable, there is no singular type or style of leadership that works in all situations.

Yet the kind of leadership that is vital for organizational success is not a phenomenon that develops magically on its own but is a challenge that needs to be tackled in every work environment.[1]

This chapter focuses on the topic of leadership – a form of influence and the subject of enduring interest at every level in the organizational behaviour field. Most attention has been focused on answering the central question – 'what makes a good leader?' Different approaches have been taken, which have included personality and 'personal' traits or characteristics, definitive sets of behaviours, or the ability to adapt leadership style to different followers and situations? How far are we 'born' leaders, and how far do we learn to lead?

When things are going well, we rarely hold back from giving some credit to the leader. But how far should we hold leaders accountable for failures or lack of achievement of their group or organization? Consider a professional sports team that has had a bad season and the likelihood of the senior coach taking the blame for the bad performance. The arguments for and against the coach shouldering the entire responsibility applies to similar situations in all aspects of work.

In this chapter we first examine the traditional approaches to leadership. We will differentiate between notions of leadership and management and summarize and evaluate the major traditional theories of leadership. The essential elements of 'new leadership theory', particularly charismatic and transformational ideas, will then be identified and explored.[2] We will also discuss the issue of diversity as it poses a challenge to leadership.

THE DISTINCTION BETWEEN LEADERSHIP AND MANAGEMENT

In earlier chapters of this book we have often referred to 'managers' and to 'management functions'. A fundamental question is whether leadership and management are (or can be) separated. Is there a clear divide between leadership and management? If so, do all leaders also manage and do all managers also lead? What is the difference between management and leadership?

A simple distinction would be to suggest that management is more concerned with promoting stability and enabling the organization to run smoothly, while the role of leadership is to inspire, promote and oversee initiatives to do with long-term change. We might think of managers as 'minding the shop' whereas leaders are working out where the next shop is going to be and what it will sell. The managerial role sees and solves problems, while the leadership role goes beyond them and works in a broader and longer term way.[3]

The role of leader is distinguishable from that of manager.

- Managers are concerned with problem solving and making things happen within a stable context. They keep work on schedule and have routine interactions to fulfil planned actions.
- Leaders provide inspiration, create opportunities and coach and motivate people to gain (and then use) their support on fundamental long-term choices.

The **management** process involves planning, organizing, leading and controlling the use of organizational resources.

Leadership is a special case of interpersonal influence that gets an individual or group to do what the leader wants done.

We would all agree that the person at the top of an organization is a 'leader'. However, as our understanding of leadership has grown, we have also realized that most people who are 'managers' are expected to play leadership roles as well as their day-to-day management remit. All managers need to be able to influence and inspire the people in their organization to work willingly towards change and improvement, which is at the heart of the leadership role. Many would argue that all 'managers' need to undertake a leadership role, and Adair has recently distinguished three levels of leadership.[4]

- Front-line or team leadership – in which one person (the leader) is responsible for creating specific outcomes usually within a given timescale and with given resources through their own actions and those of their immediate followers.
- Operational leadership – which is to do with day-to-day operations within the organization and is a major determinant of its culture and climate.
- Strategic leadership – about 'big picture' issues such as change, vision, translating that vision into purpose, effective communication, and the behaviour of the CEO and senior management team (also see below).

Potter and Hooper, working with the Chartered Institute of Personnnel and Development[5] show Adair's three facets in Figure 9.1

Figure 9.1: Levels of leadership.

Source: Potter, J. and Hooper, A, (2005), *Developing Strategic Leadership Skills: developing a strategic approach at all levels.* Chartered Institute of Personnel Development, London. Reproduced by permission.

In the main, leadership is a case of interpersonal influence that gets an individual or group to achieve what the leader wants done. Often leadership is about using appropriate interpersonal styles and methods in guiding individuals and groups towards task accomplishment.

OB IN ACTION

Mark Hurd, President, CEO and Chairman of HP comments:

> The definition of managers in my mind is 'I have a hand. I'm going to optimize the hand I've been given.' Leaders actively change the hand to drive the business... Leading is not just about managing people. To lead, you have to help people understand where we're trying to take the company and what their role is in getting there.[6]

This quote helps us see the close link between forward-looking strategy and the leadership role. Leaders at all levels of the hierarchy need to translate the strategic vision for the future and get their staff involved in shaping the reality that will result from strategic action.

Leadership may take two forms:

- **formal leadership** is exerted by those who have positions of formal authority in organizations
- **informal leadership** is exerted by those who become influential because they have special skills or resources that meet the needs of others.

Both types of leadership are important in organizations.

DEVELOPMENT OF THEORIES OF LEADERSHIP

Academic interest in leadership has been going on for many years. The leadership literature is by now vast and consists of numerous approaches.[7] In Figure 9.2 these approaches are shown schematically to help you understand and use them.

We have divided the theories into two categories: traditional leadership and new leadership. The traditional perspectives go back many years and vary in how they approach the role of leadership. The trait and behaviour approaches on the top left of Figure 9.2 conceptualize leadership as central to the achievement of tasks and human resource maintenance outputs emphasized in our individual performance equation (see page 11). Most of the situational contingency approaches consider leadership as central but in combination with various other situational aspects called 'situational contingencies'. The last of these approaches – Kerr and Jermier's substitutes for leadership theory – considers where hierarchical leadership is not needed, suggesting that experienced employees together with well developed organizational policies and procedures may provide so much structure as to act as leadership substitutes. For example, think of how little leadership guidance you need to do something at which you are experienced and where you know the boundaries and limits of your work.

Formal leadership *is the process of exercising influence from a position of formal authority in an organization.*

Informal leadership *is the process of exercising influence through special skills or resources that meet the needs of other people.*

Figure 9.2: Representative traditional and new leadership perspectives.

OB IN ACTION

Midas is a UK construction firm with 500 staff who are based at many construction sites. Often these sites are geographically distant hence local managers and supervisors have to work with their skilled staff to resolve problems quickly and effectively. They have recently released staff for training at a centralized point. Apex is a leadership development programme for future leaders of the business. Chief executive Alan Hope said: 'The construction industry is plagued by recruitment problems and skills shortages, so the purpose of having a clear training strategy is to overcome these issues and help us deliver our business objectives.'[8]

TRADITIONAL LEADERSHIP APPROACHES: TRAIT AND BEHAVIOURAL THEORIES

The trait and behavioural approaches assume that the effectiveness of individuals in their leadership roles depends on their traits, or specific behaviours that have a major impact on leadership outputs – that is, according to these theories, leadership is central and other variables are relatively less important. They differ in how they explain leadership results.

Trait theory

Trait theory is the earliest approach used to study leadership and dates back to the turn of the twentieth century. The early studies attempted to identify those traits that differentiated the 'great person' in history from the masses (for example, how did Napoleon, Margaret Thatcher or Henry Ford differ from their followers?). This approach tried to separate leaders from nonleaders, or more effective leaders from less effective leaders. The argument was that certain traits are related to success and that these traits, once identified, could be used to select leaders. This argument follows that made in Chapter 2 concerning individual attributes. Early research concentrated on leaders who were usually at the top of highly successful organizations or were remarkable in their ability to influence others to make dramatic change. They looked for general traits, cutting across all circumstances and organizations, and considered traits such as height, integrity and intelligence. Proof of this theory lies in predicting and finding a set of traits (charisma, intelligence and so on) that differentiate effective leaders from ineffective ones.[9]

For various reasons, including inadequate theorizing, inadequate measurement of many traits and failure to recognize possible differences in organizations and situations, the studies were not successful enough to provide a general trait theory.[10] But they laid the groundwork for considering certain traits, in combination with other leadership aspects (such as behaviours), that forms the basis for some of the more current theories. In many contemporary biographies of leaders one can still observe writers attempting to emerge the traits of their subject. However as a generalized predictive tool, the theory was not effective. Whatever trait one might take to indicate effectiveness, there are always many 'exceptions to the rule' which then invalidates the value of the 'rule'.

Behavioural theories

By the 1950s attention had turned towards a behavioural position about leadership. In essence, the focus changed from attempting to identify the inner traits of leaders to one of examining their behaviour – what they did.

Like the trait approach, the behavioural theories approach assumes that leadership is central to performance and human resource maintenance. Two classic research programmes at the University of Michigan and Ohio State University provided the groundwork for leadership theory to develop. These were run at similar times and both revealed some key parameters that dominate our understanding of leadership, including whether leaders are focused on the task and/or focused on people.

THE MICHIGAN STUDIES

In the late 1940s researchers at the University of Michigan introduced a programme of research on leadership behaviour. The researchers were concerned with identifying the leadership pattern that results in effective performance. From interviews of high- and low-performing groups in different organizations, the researchers derived two basic forms of leader behaviours: employee centred and production centred. Employee-centred supervisors are those who place strong emphasis on the welfare of their employees. In contrast, production-centred supervisors tend to place a stronger emphasis on getting the work done than on the welfare of the employees. In general, employee-centred supervisors were found to have more productive work groups than those of the production-centred supervisors.[11]

These behaviours may be viewed on a continuum, with employee-centred supervisors at one end and production-centred supervisors at the other. Sometimes, the more general terms 'human-relations oriented' and 'task oriented' are used to describe these alternative leader behaviours.

THE OHIO STATE STUDIES

An important leadership research programme was started at Ohio State University at about the same time as the Michigan studies. A questionnaire was administered in both industrial and military settings to measure subordinates' perceptions of their superiors' leadership behaviour. The researchers identified two dimensions similar to those found in the Michigan studies: consideration and initiating structure.[12] Highly considerate leaders are sensitive to people's feelings and, much like employee-centred leaders, try to make things pleasant for their followers. In contrast, leaders high in initiating structure are more concerned with spelling out task requirements and clarifying other aspects of the work agenda; they may be seen as similar to production-centred supervisors. These dimensions are related to what people sometimes refer to as socio-emotional and task leadership, respectively. They relate to group maintenance and task activities as discussed in Chapter 6.

At first, the Ohio State researchers thought that a leader high on consideration, or socio-emotional warmth, would have more highly satisfied and/or better performing employees. Later results indicated that leaders should be high on both consideration and initiating structure behaviours. This dual emphasis was developed by Blake and Mouton and became the Leadership Grid® approach.

THE LEADERSHIP GRID®

Robert Blake and Jane Mouton developed the Leadership Grid® perspective.[13] It measures a manager's:

- concern for people and
- concern for production.

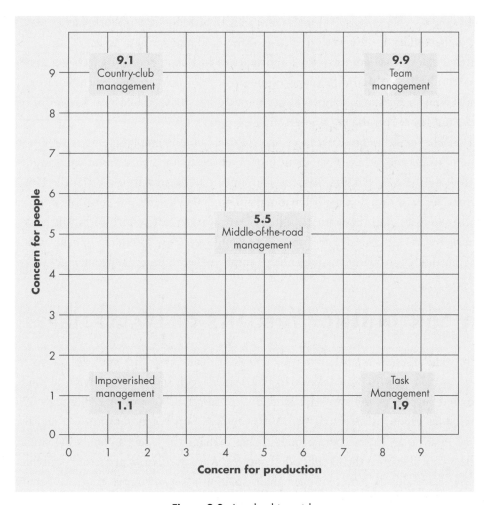

Figure 9.3: Leadership grid.

Source: Blake, R and McCanse, A, (1995), *Leadership Dilemmas - grid solutions*, Gulf Publishing Company, Texas. © Elsevier.

The results are then plotted on a nine-position grid that places these concerns on the vertical axis and horizontal axis, respectively (Figure 9.3). The ideal position is asserted to be a 9/9 position where a leader achieves the task through people. Blake and Mouton did not suggest that behaviours should be done at the same time or interchangeably but rather that every decision a manager/leader makes involves weighing these two facets of people and task and understanding how both demands can be met at the same time. Someone who only thinks of their employees (a 9/1 score) is termed a 'country-club manager' as it is expected that little task achievement can be expected as inferred by the hobbyist title. It is unlikely that in the twenty-first century any country-club managers survive in our highly target-driven and evaluated workplaces. The task management style (scoring 1/9) is more likely to have survived where, although tasks might be achieved, their lack of consideration for people would point to high grievance and turnover rates,[14] which would add to the actual cost of production. Other positions identified are 1/1 – the impoverished management style – where the manager appears to do very little. This has been termed laissez-faire leadership in other work (as will be found later in this chapter) and is reviewed negatively. One suspects that, like the country club style, such leaders are rarely to be found in our workplaces today. A 5/5 style, in the middle of the grid, is a middle-of-the-road management style.

Research evidence points to the importance of task- and people-focus being important. General 'rules' have been difficult to establish in both field studies and laboratory simulations. While a high-task focus will get things done, there are costs in the form of staff leaving and hence recruitment and retraining issues.

The behavioural approaches discussed share a common emphasis on the importance of people-oriented and production- or task-oriented behaviours in determining outputs. But how well do these behaviours transfer internationally? Research in the US, the UK, Hong Kong and Japan shows that the behaviours, although they seem to be generally important in all these countries, must be carried out in different ways in different cultures. UK leaders, for instance, are seen as considerate if they show employees how to use equipment, whereas in Japan the highly considerate manager helps employees with personal problems.[15]

SITUATIONAL CONTINGENCY THEORIES OF LEADERSHIP

Situational control *is the extent to which leaders can determine what their group is going to do and what the outcomes of their actions and decisions are going to be.*

Despite their usefulness, behavioural theories of leadership did not explain success or failure on their own. It was discovered that leaders with the same behavioural tendencies could find success in one situation and not in another. For example although Winston Churchill led the British through World War Two, he was voted out of power shortly after the end of the war. Researchers proposed that perhaps the leader's contextual situation is a critical contributor to the likelihood of success. Adding situational factors underlined the fact that leadership is more complex than isolating a set of unique traits or behaviours. This led to the emergence of the contingency approach to leadership, which encompasses a number of theories.

Some of the main contributions of these theories include the work of Fred Fiedler, Robert House, Paul Hersey and Kenneth Blanchard, and Steven Kerr and John Jermier.

FIEDLER'S LEADERSHIP CONTINGENCY THEORY

Least preferred co-worker *(LPC) scale is a measure of a person's leadership style based on a description of the person with whom respondents have been able to work least well.*

The first situational contingency approach we consider is that of Fred Fiedler. His work essentially started the situational contingency era in the mid-1960s.[16] Fiedler's approach predicts work group effectiveness. His theory holds that group effectiveness depends on an appropriate match between a leader's style and the demands of the situation. Specifically, Fiedler considers the amount of control the situation allows the leader. Situational control is the extent to which leaders can determine what their group is going to do and what will be the outcomes of the group's actions and decisions. Where control is high, leaders can predict with a good deal of certainty what will happen when they want something done.

Fiedler uses an instrument called the least preferred co-worker (LPC) scale to measure a person's leadership style. Respondents are asked to describe the person with whom they are able to work least well (their least preferred co-worker, or LPC), using a series of adjectives such as these:

Unfriendly   ....   Friendly

                    1   2   3   4   5   6   7   8

Pleasant   ....   Unpleasant

                    1   2   3   4   5   6   7   8

Fiedler argues that high LPC leaders (those describing their LPC very positively) have a relationship-motivated style whereas low LPC leaders have a task-oriented style. In other words, relationship-oriented leaders describe more favourably the person with whom they are least able to work than do task-oriented leaders.

Fiedler considers this task or relationship motivation to be a trait that leads to either directive or nondirective behaviour, depending on whether the leader has high, moderate or low situational control (as already described).

Let us now elaborate on Fiedler's situational control concept and its match with task- and relationship-oriented styles. Figure 9.4 shows the task-oriented leader as having greater group effectiveness under high and low situational control, while the relationship-oriented leader has a more effective group under a moderate-control situation.

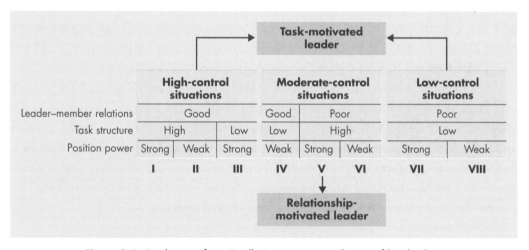

Figure 9.4: Predictions from Fiedler's contingency theory of leadership.

The figure also shows that Fiedler measures high, moderate and low control with the following three variables arranged in the situational combinations indicated:

- leader–member relations (good/poor) – member support for the leader
- task structure (high/low) – spelling out of the leader's task goals, procedures and guidelines in the group
- position power (strong/weak) – the leader's task expertise and reward/punishment authority.

Some examples show how different combinations of these variables provide differing amounts of situational control. First, consider the experienced and well trained manager of a large local supermarket, which is part of a national chain of stores. The local leader is highly supported by his or her department supervisors and can hire/fire and promote and distribute bonuses. This leader would have high situational control and would be operating in situation I in Figure 9.4. Likewise, those leaders operating in situations II and III would have high situational control, although not as high as that of our store manager. In any of these three high-control situations, a task-oriented leader behaving nondirectively would have the most effective group.

Contrast the previous example with the chair of an internal organizational committee, which is tasked with making suggestions for the improvement of the work-life balance of employees. The chair has been 'volunteered' by their own manager, as have other committee members who do not see the chair as necessarily the best person to do the job and are of the same pay grade as the chair. Here we have a low-structured task in a low-control situation (situation VIII). According to the theory the appropriate leadership style would be for a task-motivation and for the leader to behave directively. In other words, Fiedler argues that the leader's decision on how to act is determined by the situation – in this circumstance he or she must act directively to keep the group together and focus on the ambiguous task.

Finally, let us consider a well liked academic department head with a tenured lecturing staff. Fiedler argues that this is a moderate-control situation (IV) with good leader–member relations, low task structure and weak position power, calling for a relationship-motivated leader. The leader should emphasize nondirective and considerate relationships with the lecturing staff. Can you develop one or two moderate-control relationships for situation V?

To summarize, Fiedler's model links effectiveness with the match between the leader's style of interacting with employees and the extent to which the leader has control over the situation. Using Fiedler's developed LPC (least preferred co-worker) questionnaire, it is possible to identify a person's style (person or task oriented) and then assess the situational component through three criteria – leader–member relations, task structure and position power. This work – how and when leaders are effective – continues to be part of the discussion over leadership styles in contemporary texts and research.[17]

FIEDLER'S COGNITIVE RESOURCE THEORY

Fiedler has since moved beyond his contingency theory by developing the cognitive resource theory.[18] Cognitive resources are abilities or competencies. According to this approach, whether a leader should use directive or nondirective behaviour depends on the following situational contingencies:

- the leader's or subordinate group member's ability/competency
- stress

- experience, and
- group support of the leader.

A distinguishing feature of cognitive resource theory is that it incorporates both leader and subordinate group member ability, which other leadership approaches typically do not consider.

The theory views directiveness as most helpful for performance when the leader is competent, relaxed and supported. In this case, the group is ready and directiveness is the clearest means of communication. When the leader feels stressed, they are diverted. In this case, experience is more important than ability. If group support is low, then the group is less receptive and the leader has less impact. Group member ability becomes most important when the leader is nondirective and there is strong support from group members. If group support is weak, then task difficulty or other factors have more impact than do either the leader or the followers.

More recent studies have verified and extended Fiedler's contingency model of leadership effectiveness to followers' behaviour. For instance, a recent study of personnel serving with the US army in Europe re-examined the relationship between followers' motivational disposition, situational favourability and followers' performance. That study found that, in accordance with Fiedler, relations-oriented followers performed better in moderately favourable situations while task-oriented followers performed better in highly unfavourable situations.[19]

Although there are still unanswered questions concerning Fiedler's contingency theory (especially concerning the meaning of LPC), the theory continues to receive relatively strong support both in academia and in practice.[20]

HOUSE'S PATH–GOAL THEORY OF LEADERSHIP

Another well known approach to situational contingencies is one developed by Robert House based on the early traditional studies.[21] This theory has its roots in the expectancy model of motivation (Chapter 4). The term 'path–goal' is used because it emphasizes how a leader influences employees' perceptions of both work goals and personal goals and the links or paths found between these two sets of goals.

The theory assumes that a leader's key function is to adjust his or her behaviours to complement situational contingencies, such as those found in the work setting. House argues that when the leader is able to compensate for things lacking in the setting, employees are likely to be satisfied with the leader. The leader could, for example, help remove job ambiguity or show how good performance could lead to more pay. Performance should improve as leaders clarify the paths by which effort leads to performance (expectancy) and performance leads to valued rewards (instrumentality). Redundant behaviour by the leader will not help and may even hinder performance. People do not need a boss telling them how to do something that they already know how to do!

Directive leadership *is leadership behaviour that spells out the what and how of employees' tasks.*

House's model represents a process approach to leadership that takes into account three interrelated variables. The overall process in sequential order is:

leadership factors → context factors → employee motivation

Taking these three aspects together, they can lead to outputs that enhance the organization, the employee and the leader.

Details of House's approach are summarized in Figure 9.5. The figure shows four types of leader behaviours – directive, supportive, achievement-oriented and participative – and two categories of situational contingency variables – employee attributes and work-setting attributes. The leader behaviours are adjusted to complement the situational contingency variables to influence employee satisfaction, acceptance of the leader and motivation for task performance.

Supportive leadership *is a leadership style that focuses on employee needs and wellbeing, and promotes a friendly work climate; it is similar to consideration.*

- Directive leadership has to do with spelling out the what and how of employees' tasks; it is much like the initiating structure mentioned earlier.
- Supportive leadership focuses on employee needs and wellbeing, and promotes a friendly work climate; it is similar to consideration.
- Achievement-oriented leadership emphasizes setting challenging goals, stressing excellence in performance and showing confidence in the group members' abilities to achieve high standards of performance.
- Participative leadership focuses on consulting with employees and seeking and accounting for their suggestions before making decisions.

Achievement-oriented leadership *is leadership behaviour that emphasizes setting challenging goals, stressing excellence in performance and showing confidence in the group members' abilities to achieve high standards of performance.*

Participative leadership *is a leadership style that focuses on consulting with employees and seeking and accounting for their suggestions before making decisions.*

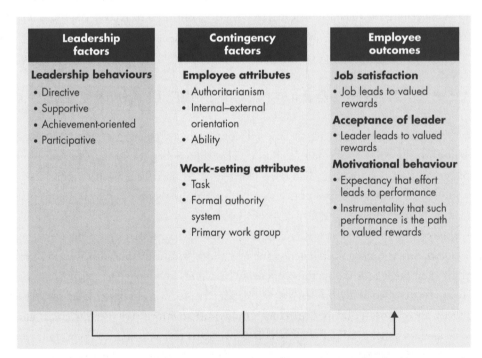

Figure 9.5: Summary of major path–goal relationships in House's leadership approach.

Source: Adapted from Osborn, R.N., Hunt, J.G., and Jauch, L.R., (1980), *Organizational theory: an integrated approach*, John Wiley & Sons, Inc., New York, p. 464. Reproduced by permission of John Wiley & Sons, Inc.

The contingency variables include employee attributes and work-setting or environmental attributes. Important employee characteristics are authoritarianism (closed-mindedness, rigidity), internal–external orientation (locus of control) and ability. The key work-setting factors are the nature of the employees' tasks (task structure), the formal authority system and the primary work group.

House's path–goal approach has attracted considerable research, and there is support for the theory in general as well as for the particular predictions discussed earlier.[22]

Not all aspects shown in Figure 9.5 have been tested and few applications have been reported in the literature. The path–goal approach lends itself to at least a couple of possibilities, however. First, training could be used to change leadership behaviour to fit the situational contingencies. Second, the leader could be taught to diagnose the situation and to learn how to change the contingencies (employee attributes and work-setting attributes).

HERSEY AND BLANCHARD'S SITUATIONAL LEADERSHIP® MODEL

The Situational Leadership® model developed by Paul Hersey and Kenneth Blanchard is similar to the other situational approaches in its view that there is no single best way to lead.[23] Like the approaches discussed earlier, Situational Leadership® emphasizes situational contingencies. Hersey and Blanchard focus on the readiness of followers, in particular. Readiness is the extent to which people have the ability and willingness to accomplish a specific task. Hersey and Blanchard argue that 'situational' leadership requires adjusting the leader's emphasis on task behaviours (for example, giving guidance and direction) and relationship behaviours (for example, providing socioemotional support) according to the readiness of followers to perform their tasks.

The model identifies four leadership styles:

- delegating
- participating
- selling
- telling.

Each emphasizes a different combination of task and relationship behaviours by the leader. The model suggests a particular leadership style for followers at each of four readiness levels.

A telling style is best for low follower readiness. The direction provided by this style defines roles for people who are unable and unwilling to take responsibility themselves; it eliminates any insecurity about the task that must be done.

A selling style is best for low to moderate follower readiness. This style offers both task direction and support for people who are unable but willing to take task responsibility; it involves combining a directive approach with explanation and reinforcement to maintain enthusiasm.

A participating style is best for moderate to high follower readiness. Able but unwilling followers require supportive behaviour to increase their motivation; by allowing followers to share in decision making, this style helps enhance the desire to perform a task.

A delegating style is best for high readiness. This style provides little in terms of direction and support for the task at hand; it allows able and willing followers to take responsibility for what needs to be done.

This Situational Leadership® approach requires the leader to develop the capability to diagnose the demands of situations and then to choose and implement the appropriate leadership response. The theory gives specific attention to followers and their feelings about the task at hand. It also suggests that an effective leader reassess situations over time, giving special attention to emerging changes in the level of readiness of the people involved in the work. Again, Hersey and Blanchard advise that leadership style should be adjusted as necessary to remain consistent with actual levels of follower readiness. They further suggest that effectiveness should improve as a result.[24]

The Situational Leadership® approach has a great deal of intuitive appeal for managers but little systematic research support. What support is available is not very strong and the theory still needs systematic empirical evaluation.[25] It could be argued that Hersey and Blanchard have considered the impact of the role of subordinates to the point where other situational factors are not given sufficient importance.

The approach does include an elaborate training programme that has been developed to train leaders to diagnose and emphasize appropriate behaviours. Internationally, this programme is particularly popular in Europe, where an organization headquartered in Amsterdam provides Situational Leadership® training for leaders in many countries.

SUBSTITUTES FOR LEADERSHIP

Substitutes for leadership *are organization, individual, or task-situational variables that substitute for leadership in causing performance/ human resource maintenance.*

In contrast to the previous approaches listed in Figure 9.2, the 'substitutes for leadership' perspective argues that sometimes hierarchical leadership makes essentially no difference. John Jermier and others contend that certain individual, job and organizational variables can either serve as substitutes for leadership or neutralize a leader's impact on employees.[26] Examples of these variables are shown in Figure 9.6. Experience, ability and training, for example, can serve as individual characteristics; a highly structured or routine job can serve as a job characteristic; and a cohesive work group can serve as an organizational characteristic.

Substitutes for leadership, it is argued, make a leader's influence both impossible and unnecessary. Neutralizers make a leader's influence impossible but not unnecessary; substitutes replace a leader's influence. As you can see in Figure 9.6 it will be difficult, if not impossible, for a leader to provide the kind of task-oriented direction already available to an experienced, talented and well-trained employee. This would apply to, for example the individual managing an actuaries department where all the staff are trained to a

Figure 9.6: Example leadership substitutes and neutralizers.

Source: Based on Kerr, S. and Jermier, J., (1992), Substitutes for leadership: their meaning and measurement, *Organizational Behaviour and Human Performance*, **22**,: 387 and Luthans, F., *Organizational Behaviour*, 6th edn, McGraw Hill, New York.

professional level, keep updated and have discussions about the future of their work and the profession as well as their specific case loads. Further, such direction will be unnecessary, given the employee's characteristics. The figure shows a similar argument for a highly structured task. In this instance one might think of the Macdonald's fast-food approach to defining workers roles where every role and task is minutely specified.

Now let us look at a couple of neutralizing examples. If leaders have low position power or formal authority, their leadership may be negated, even though task structuring and supportiveness are still needed. If leaders are physically separated from employees, their task-oriented and supportive leadership may be negated but still necessary.

The 'substitutes for leadership' perspective is a more generalized version of the situational contingency approaches mentioned earlier, particularly House's path–goal theory. However, the substitutes perspective goes further by assuming that leadership in some cases has no impact on outputs because it is replaced by other factors. The earlier situational approaches argued that both leadership and other factors are needed.

Research on the substitutes theory has shown mixed results. Some work comparing Mexican and US workers suggests both similarities and differences between various substitutes in the two countries.[27] Within the US, some early work appeared to support the theory but two later, comprehensive studies (covering 13 different organizations) provided little support.[28]

Despite this last finding, given the emerging importance and popularity of work teams, leadership substitutes are likely to be important and need to be tailored to the team-oriented workplace. Thus, in place of a leader specifying standards and ways of achieving goals (task-oriented behaviours), the team will set its own standards and substitute these for the leader's. Those occupying formal leadership roles are usually well paid, thus finding circumstances where specific individuals are not required can have an impact on the bottom line. The argument here is not that leadership is not required but rather that the leadership role can be distributed throughout the team (hence substituted).

EMERGING LEADERSHIP PERSPECTIVES

So far, we have taken a well trodden path in presenting theories of leadership from a historical perspective. However, no building-block progression of knowledge is assumed and you should be careful not to jump to the conclusion, for example, that most recent is necessarily best!

More recent ideas are attribution theories of leadership; charismatic leadership, transaction versus transformational leadership and leading through empowerment. The more recent approaches to leadership have tended to move right away from traditional leadership characteristics and endorse charisma, vision and transformation as catalysts to effective leadership.

OB IN ACTION

In his introduction to *Hitler and Churchill: secrets of leadership*,[29] Andrew Roberts suggests Adolf Hitler was a 'charismatic' leader whereas Winston Churchill was an 'inspirational' leader. Hitler rose to power by recognizing and capitalizing on the German resentment towards the Treaty of Versailles. He sustained his power using the convenient scapegoat of the Jewish people. He promoted a vision of a new and glorious German empire. Churchill's vision was to create a powerful alliance to defend freedom. He created a popular mood and sustained it demonstrating his personal courage, publicly valuing it in others and inspiring courage and persistence nationally. In the light of history the inspirational leader prevailed over the charismatic one. Roberts suggests that leaders, be they like Churchill or Hitler, create a common goal with which people can wholeheartedly identify, but that managers lack that guiding vision.[30] One must caution that any leaders' success also depends on issues other than leadership style – in this example military resources would be fundamental. No leader is omnipotent, but has to work within the real world.

The general notion that leadership is largely symbolic or 'in the eye of the beholder' has carried over to a related but diverse set of research directions. Ironically, the first of these argues that leadership makes little or no real difference to organizational effectiveness. The second tends to attribute greatly exaggerated importance to leadership and leads us into charisma and other aspects of the new leadership. Let us briefly examine each of these two directions.

CHARISMATIC APPROACHES[31]

Charismatic leadership uses attribution theory to suggest that we make attributions of heroic leadership competencies or personal characteristics when we see good leaders in action. Conger and Kanungo, for example, thought that charismatic leaders are self-confident, display an articulate vision and have strong conviction of their vision.[32] Robert House and his associates have produced some work based on extensions of an earlier charismatic theory that House developed (not to be confused with House's path–goal theory discussed earlier in the chapter). Especially interesting is the fact that House's theory uses both trait and behaviour combinations.

House sees charismatic leaders as those 'who by force of their personalities are capable of having a profound and extraordinary effect on followers'. Essentially, these leaders are high in need for power and have high feelings of self-efficacy and conviction in the moral rightness of their beliefs; that is, the need for power motivates these people to want to be leaders and this need is then reinforced by their conviction of their moral rightness. The feeling of self-efficacy, in turn, makes people feel that they are capable of being leaders. These traits then influence such charismatic behaviours as role modelling, image building, articulating goals (focusing on simple and dramatic goals), emphasizing high expectations, showing confidence and arousing others' motives to follow them.

Charismatic leaders *are those leaders who by force of their personal characteristics are capable of having a profound and extraordinary effect on followers.*

House and his colleagues also summarize several other studies that support aspects of the theory. Some of the more interesting related work has shown that negative, or 'dark-side', charismatic leaders emphasize personalized power (focus on themselves), whereas positive or 'bright-side' charismatics emphasize socialized power, which tends to empower their followers. This helps explain differences between such dark-side leaders as Adolf Hitler, David Koresh and Reverend Jim Jones and bright-side leaders such as Martin Luther King Junior[33] or Gandhi.

Jay Conger has developed a four-stage charismatic leadership theory based on his work with Rabindra Kanungo.[34] In the first stage, the leader develops a vision of idealized change that moves beyond the status quo; for example, US President John F. Kennedy had a vision of putting a man on the moon by the end of the 1960s. In the second stage, the leader communicates the vision and motivates the followers to go beyond the status quo. In stage three, the leader builds trust by exhibiting qualities such as expertise, success, risk taking and unconventional actions. In the final stage, the leader demonstrates ways to achieve the vision by means of empowerment, behaviour modelling for followers and so forth. Conger and Kanungo have argued that if leaders use behaviours such as vision and articulation, environmental sensitivity and unconventional behaviour, rather than maintaining the status quo, followers will attribute charismatic leadership to them. Such leaders are also seen as behaving quite differently from those labelled 'noncharismatic'.[35]

Research on leadership involving three countries in Asia (Singapore, New Zealand and India) showed that charisma and vision were made up of two charismatic factors (social sensitivity and persuasive personality traits) and two visionary factors ('expert and analytical' and 'visionary and futuristic'). Tests across the three countries showed that the two visionary factors influenced reported performance and the two charismatic factors influenced employee commitment. Only social sensitivity predicted both performance and commitment of employees.[36]

Another important leadership researcher, Gary Yukl, has addressed the issue of whether charismatic and transformational leadership (see the following section) are compatible – can a leader be both highly transformational and highly charismatic at the same time? This issue concerns the role of followers. Transformational leadership usually involves empowering followers and making them partners in the change process, whereas charismatic leadership is more likely to require followers to place their trust in the leader's special expertise to achieve radical change. These leadership approaches are often grouped together but Yukl's work directs us to consider this aspect of leadership behaviour more closely.[37]

TRANSACTIONAL AND TRANSFORMATIONAL APPROACHES

Transactional leadership *involves daily exchanges between leaders and followers and is necessary for achieving routine performance on which leaders and followers agree.*

We made the point earlier that transformational leadership has many similarities to charismatic leadership but involves the followers as partners. Building on notions originated by James MacGregor Burns, as well as ideas from House's work, Bernard Bass has developed an approach that focuses on both transformational and transactional leadership. The high points are summarized in Figure 9.7.

Let us start by discussing Bass's transactional category. Transactional leadership involves daily exchanges between leaders and employees, and is necessary for achieving routine performance on which leaders and employees agree. It is based on transactions that occur between leaders and followers. These transactions may include agreements, contingent rewards, communications or exchanges between leaders and followers. There are many dimensions of transactional leadership.

Contingent rewards *are rewards that are given in exchange for mutually agreed goal accomplishments.*

• Contingent rewards involve providing various kinds of reward in exchange for accomplishing mutually agreed goals (for example, your boss pays you a £500 bonus for completing an acceptable article by a certain date). Conversely, you could be subject to disciplinary action for failing to achieve the goals.

- Active management by exception involves concentrating on occurrences that deviate from expected norms, such as irregularities, mistakes, exceptions and failures to meet standards. This means watching for deviations from rules and standards and taking corrective action (for example, your boss notices that you have a number of defects in a new aspect of your work and helps you adjust by giving you further training).
- Passive management by exception involves intervening only if standards are not met (for example, your boss comes to see you after noticing the high percentage of defects in your work).
- Laissez-faire leadership involves abdicating responsibilities and avoiding decisions (for example, your boss is seldom around and does not follow through on decisions that need action).

Transformational leadership might go beyond this routine accomplishment, as shown in Figure 9.7.

Active management by exception *involves watching for deviations from rules and standards and taking corrective action.*

Passive management by exception *involves intervening with employees only if standards are not met.*

Laissez faire leadership *involves abdicating responsibilities and avoiding decisions.*

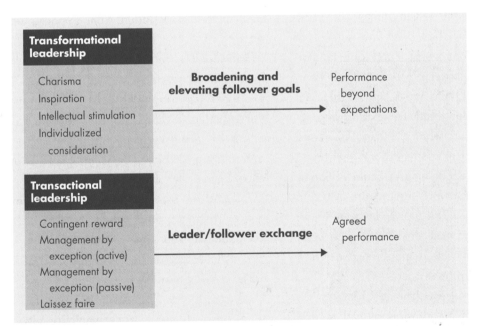

Figure 9.7: High points of Bass's transformational/transactional leadership approach.

For Bass, transformational leadership occurs when leaders broaden and elevate the interests of their followers, when they generate awareness and acceptance of the purposes and mission of the group and when they stir their followers to look beyond their own self-interest for the good of others.

Transformational leadership is a leadership style by which the followers' goals are broadened and elevated, and confidence is gained to go beyond expectations. This

Charisma *is a dimension of leadership, based on personal qualities, which provides vision and a sense of mission and instils pride, respect and trust.*

approach to leadership is based on motivating followers to do more than they originally intended, and often more than they thought possible. It involves guiding, influencing and inspiring people to excel and to contribute towards the achievement of organizational goals.

[handwritten: debate on transformational leadership?]

OB IN ACTION

When Ralph Norris took over as head of Air New Zealand he set out to replace the company's earlier dictatorial leadership model with a model that emphasizes the power of the people working for the company. In his words, 'Companies can no longer get away with telling staff to check in their brain in the morning and then proceed to tell them what to do.'[38]

In recent times, the ethical nature of transformational leadership has been the subject of much debate and controversy. Parry and Proctor-Thomson[39] argued that such debate has been demonstrated through the ways transformational leaders have been described. Labels and descriptors have included 'narcissistic', 'manipulative' and 'self-centred', but also 'ethical', 'just' and 'effective'. Using the Perceived Leader Integrity Scale (PLIS) and the Multi-Factor Leadership Questionnaire (MLQ) in a national sample of 1354 managers, they found a moderate to strong positive relationship between perceived integrity and the demonstration of transformational leadership behaviours.

The more recent research has focused on training requirements for transformational leadership. In particular, Parry and Sinha tested the effectiveness of transformational leadership training, using the Full Range Leadership Development (FRLD) programme. Their research revealed an increase in the display of transformational leadership factors by the participants.[40]

Transformational leadership tends to have four dimensions: charisma, inspiration, intellectual stimulation and individualized consideration.[41]

- **Charisma** provides vision and a sense of mission, and instils pride, along with follower respect and trust (for example, Steve Jobs, head of Apple Computer, showed charisma by emphasizing the importance of creating the Macintosh as a radical new computer and showed it again when he focused on the iMac, another radical departure from computer standards).
- **Inspiration** communicates high expectations, uses symbols to focus efforts, and expresses important purposes in simple ways (for example, Richard Branson, chief executive officer of Virgin Airlines, has been known to personally greet passengers on flights that have experienced difficulties or been delayed).[42]
- **Intellectual stimulation** promotes intelligence, rationality and careful problem solving (for example, your boss challenges you to look at a difficult problem in a new way rather than walking away from it).
- **Individualized consideration** provides personal attention, treats each employee individually, and coaches and advises (for example, your boss drops by and makes remarks reinforcing your worth as a person).

Together, charisma and inspiration transform follower expectations, but intellectual stimulation and individualized consideration are also needed to provide the necessary follow-through.

OB IN ACTION

Nando is a South African-based chicken restaurant chain, which entered the UK market in 1992. By the end of 2001, it had established 40 outlets and planned a major expansion programme to open 20 outlets a year until 2005. However it wanted to keep its values and saw promotion from within as a means of doing so. In 2001 its internal promotion rate was 21%, which was not high enough to sustain this planned growth. How could Nando develop the necessary leadership skills amongst its staff, branch managers and area managers to enable this vision? In 2001 they set up a two-day course on leadership, which was followed up by coaching and a final taught course. Initial takeup was positive but it was an effort to translate the learning from the courses into action. This is where the individual coaching came in.

By 2006 they had doubled the number of branches which an area manager supervises, and grown from 40 to 112 outlets. Management turnover has fallen from 35% to 20%. Crucially 90% of branch managers come from internal promotion and 40% of area managers are appointed from internal candidates.

They have retained their treasured values and culture, and are planning other expansion including into the US.[43]

Bass concludes that transformational leadership is likely to be strongest at the top management level, where there is the greatest opportunity for proposing and communicating a vision. But it is by no means restricted to the top level; it is found throughout the organization. Further, transformational leadership operates in combination with transactional leadership. Transactional leadership is similar to most of the traditional leadership approaches. Proponents of this view suggest that those in a position of power need both transactional and transformational leadership to be successful, just as they need to use both leadership and management.[44]

Inspiration is the communication of high expectations, the use of symbols to focus efforts and the expression of important purposes in simple ways.

EFFECTIVE MANAGER 9.1

The 'four Is' of transformational leadership

The following useful pointers about transformational leadership are given by Bruce Avolio and his associates.[45]

- Individualized consideration – pay attention to individual employees.
- Intellectual stimulation – be concerned with helping people to think through new ways.
- Inspirational motivation – inspire people to give their best.
- Idealized influence – engender respect and trust that gives power and influence over people.

A trend in current business research considers emotional intelligence (EI), and one can easily see how such skills and aptitudes would apply to the 'four Is' to enable someone to become an effective transformational leader. It is always hard for a manager to balance 'task' and 'people' needs – 'the four Is' provide focus points for managers to enable maximum outputs from their staff. But none are easy! Without doubt the field of EI will contribute in future years to our understanding of manager effectiveness.[46]

Intellectual stimulation *promotes intelligence, rationality and careful problem solving.*

Individualized consideration *is a leadership dimension by which the leader provides personal attention, treats each employee individually and coaches and advises employees.*

To summarize, transactional leaders guide employees in their tasks towards the achievement of prestated goals, whereas transformational leaders inspire their employees to challenge and transcend their view of their contribution to the organization.

Bryman has summarized a large number of studies using Bass's approach, ranging from six studies on the extra effort of followers to 16 studies on performance or effectiveness, to nearly a dozen covering various aspects of satisfaction. Still other studies cover such outcomes as burnout and stress and the predisposition to act as innovation champions. The strongest relationships tend to be associated with charisma or inspirational leadership, although in most cases the other dimensions are also important. These findings are impressive and broaden leadership outcomes beyond those used in the traditional leadership studies.[47] Researchers continue to investigate Bass's model and contribute to the generalizability of the model.[48]

Bernard Bass has also recently reviewed the two decades of research into transformational leadership. Recent findings in the field include evidence about why transformational leadership is more effective than transactional leadership and about why female leaders may be more transformational than their male counterparts. Bass concluded, despite an abundance of applied research, that more basic research and theory development is needed. More work needs to be done, for example, on how context affects transactional and transformational leadership and on how transformational leadership moves followers from compliance to the identification and internalization of values and beliefs beyond their own self-interest.[49]

OB *IN ACTION*

Lessons from Jack Welch

Jack Welch's goal was to make General Electric (GE) 'the world's most competitive enterprise'. He knew that it would take nothing less than a 'revolution' to transform that dream into a reality. 'The model of business in corporate America in 1980 had not changed in decades. Workers worked, managers managed, and everyone knew their place. Forms and approvals and bureaucracy ruled the day.' Welch's self-proclaimed revolution meant waging war on GE's old ways of doing things and reinventing the company from top to bottom.

Jack Welch is all about leadership not management. Actually, he wanted to discard the term 'manager' altogether because it had come to mean someone who 'controls rather than facilitates, complicates rather than simplifies, acts more like a governor than an accelerator.' Welch has given a great deal of thought to how to manage employees effectively so that they are as productive as possible. And he has come to a seemingly paradoxical view. The less managing you do, the better off your company. Manage less to manage more.

Welch decided that GE's leaders, who did too much controlling and monitoring, had to change their management styles. Managers slow things down. Leaders spark the business to run smoothly, quickly. Managers talk to one another, write memos to one another. Leaders talk to their employees, talk with their employees, filling them with vision, getting them to perform at levels the employees themselves didn't think possible. Then (and to Welch this is a critical ingredient) they simply get out of the way.[50]

THE NEW LEADERSHIP REVISITED

Thus far we have covered representative approaches to the new leadership, as summarized in Figure 9.2. These approaches have used the concepts of attribution, charisma and transformation. Other related work differs from traditional leadership but does not include charisma and treats transformation differently from Bass's approach. However, all this work includes vision in one way or another. Table 9.1 summarizes the core themes of this work and the charismatic and transformational approaches discussed earlier, in contrast to traditional leadership approaches.

Less emphasis needed on	Greater emphasis needed on
Planning	Having a vision/mission
Allocating responsibility	Infusing vision
Controlling and problem solving	Motivating and inspiring
Creating routine and equilibrium	Creating change and innovation
Retaining power	Empowering others
Creating compliance	Creating commitment
Emphasizing contractual obligations	Stimulating extra effort
Exhibiting leader detachment and rationality	Exhibiting interest in others and intuition
Taking a reactive environmental approach	Taking a proactive environmental approach

Table 9.1: Themes in the new leadership literature.

In addition to contrasting the core themes of traditional and new leadership, it is important to answer questions concerning the role of new leadership in the workplace.

Questions and answers concerning the new leadership

Can people be trained in new leadership? Research in this area argues that training in new leadership is possible. Bass and his colleagues have put a lot of work into such training efforts. They have created one workshop that lasts from three to five days, with later follow-up. Initially, leaders are given feedback on their scores on Bass's measures. Then the leaders devise improvement programmes to strengthen their weaknesses and work with the trainers to develop their leadership skills. Bass and Avolio report findings that demonstrate beneficial effects from this training. They also report on team training and programmes tailored to individual organizations' needs.[51]

Similarly, Conger and Kanungo propose training to develop the kinds of behaviour summarized in their model.[52]

COUNTERPOINT

Roger Eglin, senior columnist for the Sunday Times, has collected an array of evidence that questions whether leadership can be taught in conventional courses. He refers to a review by the firm of business psychologists Kaisen that has revealed many courses are seen as 'value-less'. Their work reflects a similar study by David Feeney at Said Business School in Oxford University. The argument is that in a conventional setting only the theory and cognitive understanding are transmitted. Leaders also need to learn how to implement. Eglin suggests that coaching is a useful tool for such one-to-one attention-giving.[53]

Questions

1. Why do you think coaching is a good tool for helping managers learn?
2. Think of two nonclassroom methods for teaching leadership.

Kouzes and Posner reported the results of a week-long training programme. The programme involved training of leaders on five dimensions oriented around developing, communicating and reinforcing a shared vision. According to Kouzes and Posner, leaders showed an average 15% increase in these visionary behaviours 10 months after participating in the programme. Many of the new leadership training programmes involve a heavy, hands-on workshop emphasis so leaders do more than just read about vision.[54]

- Is charismatic leadership always good? Not necessarily. Khurana suggests that charismatic leaders can destabilize the organization with their radical leadership and lead them to inappropriate paths – consider the leadership that saw the collapse of Enron.[55]
- Is new leadership always needed? No. Sometimes emphasis on a vision diverts energy from more important day-to-day activities. Thus what the vision contains is always fundamental.[56]
- Is new leadership by itself sufficient? No. New leadership needs to be used in conjunction with traditional leadership.
- Is new leadership important only at the top? Probably not. While generally considered most important at the top levels, new leadership is considered by some experts to apply at all organizational levels.

EFFECTIVE MANAGER 9.2

Characteristics of a strong leader:

- a sense of mission that they can communicate to others
- values of decency for everyone so that a perceptibly fair working environment is created
- measurable goals so that everyone knows what they are aiming at and when they have got there
- action orientation whether leading from the front or supporting others from behind – discussion is important but so is action
- courage to push the envelope and ask others to do so too. Also persistency to keep at the job so everyone knows they won't be giving up

- inspiring and motivational through engagement at a personal level. Good leaders can reach in to people and bring them along — requiring visibility to earn the trust and confidence of others
- good at listening to employees, acting on what they hear and letting employees know that
- do not foster a blame culture, so that people can take risks — some won't succeed but this is the only way to real breakthroughs
- take pride in employees and their outputs, demanding high quality performance so that everyone can be proud
- are always consistent in their behaviour and manner — inconsistency undermines trust-building.

Source: Australian Business Limited, *Leadership–do you have what it takes?* http://www.australianbusiness.com.au (accessed 20 December 2005).

COUNTERPOINT

Servant leadership

In recent times, some researchers have attempted to rejuvenate a relatively old concept of leadership: 'servant leadership'. Servant leaders are those who make a deliberate choice to serve others and to put other people's needs, aspirations and interests above their own.[57] The servant leader operates on the assumption that 'I am the leader, therefore I serve' rather than 'I am the leader, therefore I lead', which could be seen as more characteristic of most of the other perspectives on leadership.[58]

People follow servant leaders freely because they trust them. One of the tests of servant leadership is how those served (led) benefit.

Spears[59] identified 10 critical characteristics of the servant leader. Many are similar to the characteristics identified in other models but with a very strong focus on the followers:

- servant leaders must reinforce their communication skills by listening to others
- servant leaders strive to understand and empathize with others
- learning to heal oneself and others is a unique characteristic
- self-awareness strengthens the servant leader – as it does all leaders
- servant leaders rely on persuasion rather than positional authority
- servant leaders are able to conceptualize, to see beyond the day-to-day and to dream great dreams.

- foresight is the characteristic that enables servant leaders to understand the lessons of the past, the realities of the present and the likely consequences of a decision for the future
- in these days of corporate distrust, stewardship is a most attractive element of servant leadership, particularly if it can be combined with foresight.
- servant leaders are committed to the personal, professional and spiritual growth of each individual in the organization

- servant leaders seek to identify means for building community among those who work within any given institution.

Questions
1. Have you experienced servant leadership?
2. What do you think are the strengths and weaknesses of the servant leadership perspective on leadership?

GENDER, AGE AND CULTURAL DIVERSITY – CURRENT ISSUES IN LEADERSHIP

Much leadership theory and research originates from a North American context and has focused primarily on masculine models of leadership. Given the globalization of business, the increasing cultural diversity of domestic societies, the ageing of the workforce and the importance of women in the workforce and the community, this is a significant gap in leadership studies.

Considerable research has been undertaken over many years concerning the 'glass ceiling' and the advancement of women as leaders.[60] It is clear that attitudes vary greatly between cultures such that, in public service for example, many senior leaders in New Zealand and Sweden are women. The issue of women into management and leadership is more prevalent in some cultures than others. In addition as antidiscrimination laws extend into race, religion, age, disability and sexuality as well as gender, patterns for all 'disadvantaged' groups are being explored.[61]

Alice Eagley has recently reviewed the literature connected to women in positions of leadership in the US.[62] She has found that attitudes are changing in a positive way toward women as managers and leaders. She discovered that women continue to do best in female-dominated workplaces. Although there are fewer women in male-gendered occupational areas, when women are leaders in these situations, they tend to out-perform their male counterparts. Eagley's review provides encouraging reading as an example of how attitudes can change for those who can be considered at a disadvantage. Gary Yukl has reviewed the research on leadership and gender differences and argues that it is 'inconclusive', all reviewers pointing out that the differences within men and women on how they behave and perform are far wider than differences between the sexes. Others argue that leadership models need a fundamental re-examination. For example Sinclair argues that we need to review the relationship between heroic masculinity and corporate leadership, and that if this is not done, leadership will remain the privilege of a homogeneous elite. Such homogeneity in leadership, in the face of dramatic changes in workforce and customer diversity, is a potential liability.

The difficulties that disadvantaged demographic groups still face in progressing up the corporate hierarchy lead to diverse paths to leadership positions. Some transfer into leadership positions from other fields (rather than rising within a corporate structure); others become leaders of organizations through succession in family business. Still others start their own small businesses, which may then grow into substantial corporations.

On a wider international scale, a recent study on Arab women's conceptions of leadership compared women's leadership authority values in Oman, the United Arab Emirates and Lebanon. It found evidence of common leadership authority values in the Gulf countries (Oman and the UAE). Lebanon, meanwhile, was distinguished by relatively low levels of 'traditional' authority and very high levels of 'charismatic' authority. The findings demonstrate important regional similarities and difference in leadership authority values in the 'Arab world'.[63]

▶ COUNTERPOINT

Convincing the traditionalists

ComCo is a privately owned software company based in Dublin, Eire. Since its inception in the mid-1970s, ComCo has prided itself on successful staff retention strategies and employee loyalty. Because of this ComCo has been the focus of many business press reports. ComCo's distribution channels are worldwide and the company continues to enjoy growth built on leading-edge development. Frank Barker is the founder and CEO of the company and is highly respected among his peers. A charismatic man, Frank likes to lead from the front in highly visible ways. Frank's senior management team are long-time employees and very experienced in their roles.

Recently Frank has become concerned about the future and succession strategy of ComCo as most of the senior managers are approaching the last years of their working lives. No one has raised retirement and typical of many baby boomers; the senior managers are not thinking about the issue of being replaced or succeeded by someone else. However, Frank is aware of potential health issues

associated with age and the way these might affect ComCo's managers over the next few years.

A senior management team meeting is scheduled for the end of the week. Frank has been surprised at the results of his informal soundings in the firm, hearing enthusiasm from more junior staff for the top team to give way! On the other hand his suggestion of promoting existing deputies into their boss's jobs has been met with less enthusiasm. He thinks the firm needs consistency and all the knowledge the longer tenured staff hold – why would he get new blood in, or try to alter the profile of a well-tested solution for leading a firm in a tough market? His current staff know ComCo's customers, suppliers and other important stakeholders, so any succession planning must be carried out carefully and slowly. Nonetheless Frank knows it is his responsibility as head of the company to develop a new generation of leadership at ComCo but he doesn't want to throw away years of achievement in the process.

Questions

1. How can Frank be enabled to broaden his thinking?
2. There are many 'Franks' in the world – what arguments can be made for taking a fresh look at his plans?

LEADERSHIP AND CULTURE

Using a similar approach to that of Geert Hofstede,[64] Robert House and his colleagues embarked on an ambitious research project involving 62 countries. The GLOBE project investigated how cultural values are related to organizational practices, conceptions of leadership, the economic competitiveness of societies, and the human condition of an organization's members.[65] More than 17 000 managers participated worldwide. Some of the main results of the project indicated that cultural values contributed either positively or negatively to the leadership profiles. For example, power–distance values were found to be a negative predictor of charismatic/value-based and participative leadership, but gender egalitarianism proved to be a positive predictor of the same. One of the key recommendations of the project was that leaders need to be aware of the links between cultural values and leadership practices. Other recent cross-national comparative studies have also reinforced the relevance of culture in leadership.[66] The GLOBE project is ongoing and results from it continue to be published.

CONCLUSION

Leadership can be distinguished from management and all managers have an opportunity to practise leadership. As one progresses up the organizational hierarchy so leadership becomes more important, hence considerable research has been undertaken with top leaders. The development of our understanding of leadership began with somewhat crude trait theories, which, although appealing, failed to stand up to scientific scrutiny. However, studying great leaders has informed our theory development in a positive way. Recent years have seen development towards a far more sophisticated view of leaders and their interface with followers. It has also become apparent that situational and other contingencies are important for effective leadership, hence theory has developed to investigate these aspects to form a broader and more realistic picture.

Training in leadership continues to be a challenge for most organizations. Looking to the future, our appreciation of difference (such as national culture and aspects connected with diversity) and ability to lead within such variations is a challenge as geographic boundaries dissolve. The GLOBE project and other initiatives are broadening our understanding of leadership from its North American theory development roots. This is an engaging area of study, inexorably linked to practice, which no doubt will continue to evolve.

SUMMARY

LEARNING OBJECTIVE 1
Differences between leadership and management

Leadership and management differ in that management is designed to promote stability or to make the organization run smoothly, while the role of leadership is to promote adaptive change. Traditional and new leadership differ. Traditional views of leadership range from trait and behaviour approaches, which give leadership a central role in performance and human resource maintenance outputs, to various approaches that combine leadership with situational contingencies to predict outputs. The new leadership differs from traditional leadership primarily in that it emphasizes vision and change, and focuses on attribution, charisma, transformation and related concepts.

LEARNING OBJECTIVE 2
Trait and behavioural theories of leadership

Trait and behavioural leadership approaches argue that leader traits or behaviours have a major impact on leadership outcomes. Traits are more innate and harder to change than behaviours. They are also often used with behaviours in a situational contingency or new leadership approach.

LEARNING OBJECTIVE 3
Situational contingency theories of leadership

Leader situational contingency approaches argue that leadership, in combination with various situational variables, has a major impact on outcomes. Sometimes, as in the case of the substitutes for leadership approach, the role of the situational variables replaces that of leadership to the point that leadership has little or no impact in itself. Fiedler's contingency theory, House's path–goal theory, and Hersey and Blanchard's Situational Leadership® theory are other approaches that consider the impact not just of leadership but of various situational contingencies.

LEARNING OBJECTIVE 4
Charismatic leadership and transformational leadership

Attribution theory overlaps traditional and new leadership by emphasizing the symbolic aspects of leadership. These aspects are an especially important part of the new leadership, charismatic, transformational and related perspectives, according to which followers tend to attribute heroic or extraordinary leadership abilities to a leader when they observe certain behaviours from that leader. These attributions can then help transform followers to achieve goals that go beyond their own self-interest and, in turn, help transform the organization.

Charismatic leadership approaches emphasize the kind of leader–follower social relationship summarized above. Two of these approaches emphasized earlier are House and associates' approach and the work of Conger and Kanungo.

Transformational leadership approaches are typically broader than charismatic ones. Bass and associates' transformational approach is a particularly well-known theory that includes charisma as one of its dimensions. It separates vision-oriented transformational leadership from day-to-day transactional leadership, and argues that the two work in combination. Transformational and charismatic leadership, and the new leadership in general, are important because they facilitate change in our increasingly fast-moving world.

LEARNING OBJECTIVE 5
Diversity in leadership

Western, masculine models have dominated leadership theory and research. Such a limitation is significant given the increasing diversity of the workforce and society in general. In Australia the progress of women's representation in organizational leadership positions at executive and board level has been slow but recently women have gained a greater presence in leadership roles across many industries, some of which were traditionally male dominated. We are also seeing much younger company leaders, both male and female, who are excelling in their field. Recent research has explored the need to recognize the impact of culture on leadership styles and the appropriateness of approaches across different cultures.

CHAPTER 9 STUDY GUIDE

You can also test your understanding and access further resources at **www.wileyeurope.com/college/french**.

REVIEW QUESTIONS

1. Review and discuss the advantages and disadvantages of the trait and behavioural approaches to leadership.
2. Discuss the reasons for the popularity of the contingency approach to leadership.
3. Explain how leadership and trust may be related.
4. What can managers do to help develop some of the new leadership characteristics?

APPLICATION QUESTIONS

1. You will recall that we discussed that there are two kinds of leadership, formal and informal. Think of a situation in which you have been part of a group or a team, maybe at work or in your recreational time. Reflect on that situation – its actual dynamics and the outcome. Identify the formal and informal leadership roles and how they played out in your example. How did each of the leaders contribute to the outcome? Who was the most effective? What did you learn from that?
2. You have recently formed a new consulting business with three colleagues whom you met while studying at university. Explain the process you will go through to establish the leadership role for the business. For example, would the role of

leader automatically be given to the person who initiated the consulting idea or would you consider another method of selection?

3. Using an example of a situation you are familiar with, ideally in the workplace. Identify and explain the different dynamics between leadership and management.

4. Your company has offered you a promotion as head of a division in a country that has a very different culture from that of your native country. You are excited by the new challenge but you are also aware that you need to consider whether your leadership style will be effective or appropriate for the new location. Using two countries of your choice (your native country and one with a different culture), outline four of the most important factors relating to the style of leadership you should adopt when considering the offer of promotion into the new culture.

5. In this chapter we discussed the concept of new leadership training. Prepare a two-page case either for or against the following statement: 'people can be trained in new leadership'. This exercise could provide an opportunity for an interesting debate among several groups in your organizational behaviour class.

6. Imagine you have been asked to address a class of school students who are in their final year and looking forward to leaving. Their teacher did not provide you with much information other than that she wanted you to deliver a 10-minute speech on how the students can develop their leadership potential. Prepare a list of the things you would include in your speech. Be sure to make the content relevant for the group you are speaking to – that is, young adults who are about to embark on their individual career journeys. Rather than past or current leaders, you may want to consider what the future might demand of leaders and what attributes they will need to cater to that demand. You should consider issues at a macro as well as micro level. This exercise will be interesting as a class discussion, and your lecturer may want to expand the topic into an assignment.

RESEARCH QUESTIONS

1. Some scholars have argued that the new leadership style in its various forms involves mystical qualities that few people possess. Others have argued that it can be readily identified and that people can be trained to display it. You are required to prepare two scripts. The first is a script for the CEO of a major hotel chain to present to a small group of junior managers who show great leadership potential. In this case, the CEO is emphasizing the need for new leadership approaches to be adopted by the junior managers. The second is a script for a leader supporting the case for a more traditional leadership approach to a particular situation. This might be a one-off situation in which a more directive leadership style is appropriate. Several questions now follow that you may want to consider, but you may prepare your own topics if you wish.

(a) How mystical is the new leadership? How desirable is it?

(b) How successful do you think leaders who use your new leadership script might be in convincing followers that they are charismatic or transformational?

(c) Do you think one particular leadership style is more appropriate than another when considering the gender of a particular group – for example, men leading women or women leading men?

(d) Do you think leadership approaches should change depending on the circumstances, the industry or the current environment?

2. Leadership is a topical and controversial subject in the global business arena. Using the Internet, search through leadership sites around the world and find out how different cultures emphasize different aspects of leadership. Compose a list of three common characteristics that successful leaders are currently perceived to display around the world and also find three that are unique in a particular country.

RUNNING PROJECT

Complete the following activities for your chosen organization.

1. Choose a few of the most senior people in the organization and assess whether they are leaders, managers or both, according to the descriptions given in this chapter. Do you think there is a genuine difference?

2. Try to identify the leadership traits of the leaders in the organization. Do the traits vary between the top managers of the organization and lower level managers? Plot each on the Leadership Grid® (Figure 9.2).

3. Choose one of the leadership models discussed in this chapter and use it to analyse the leadership of one of the leaders in your organization.

4. How important is the top manager or other top leader in your organization? Do they individually make a difference? Would you expect the overall performance of the organization to change if a new leader took over? Why or why not?

5. What degree of diversity is there among the leaders in your organization? Explain, specifically for your organization, why the diversity or lack of diversity has occurred.

INDIVIDUAL ACTIVITY

Survey of leadership[67]

Objective

To develop your ability to assess leadership styles. Total time: 15 minutes.

The following 10 questions ask about your supervisor's leadership behaviour and practices. Try to respond on the basis of your actual observations of your supervisor's actions. Choose a response from the following five and place the score alongside it in the box beside each question.

To a great extent	5
To a considerable extent	4
To a moderate extent	3
To a slight extent	2
To almost no extent	1

To what extent:

1. Is your supervisor easy to approach? ☐
2. Does your supervisor encourage people to give their best effort? ☐
3. Does your supervisor show you how to improve your performance? ☐
4. Does your supervisor encourage people to work as a team? ☐
5. Does your supervisor pay attention to what you say? ☐
6. Does your supervisor maintain high standards of performance? ☐
7. Does your supervisor provide the help you need so you can schedule work ahead of time? ☐
8. Does your supervisor encourage people to exchange opinions and ideas? ☐
9. Is your supervisor willing to listen to your problems? ☐
10. Does your supervisor offer new ideas for solving job-related problems? ☐

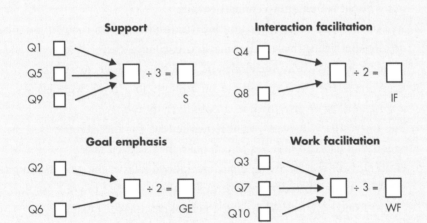

Interpretation

Support (S) and interaction facilitation (IF) are the two dimensions that define inter-personal or relationship-centred leadership behaviours. Support refers to the lead-er's personal concern for employees, while interaction facilitation measures how the leader encourages teamwork among employees. The two scores, S and IF, can be added to yield an overall interpersonal relationship score.

Goal emphasis (GE) and work facilitation (WF) both centre on task-oriented leader behaviour. Goal emphasis simply refers to the degree to which the leader emphasizes the importance of achieving high goals, while work facilitation measures the degree to which the leader engages in behaviour that helps employees to do their jobs effectively. The two scores, GE and WF, can be added to yield an overall task orientation score.

GROUP ACTIVITY

Leadership in action

Objectives

1. To provide an opportunity to observe different types of leadership.
2. To examine the link between leadership and situational contingencies.
3. To develop your understanding of your own leadership behaviour.
4. To develop your ability to analyse leadership in action.

Total time: 90 minutes.

Procedure

1. Form a circle of 8–18 people in a large area of empty space where you can spread out without running into chairs or walls.
2. Ask for a volunteer(s) to be an observer: if your group is small one observer will do; if your group has 18 people you can have three observers. The observers should withdraw from the circle and read the observer instructions.
3. Everyone in the circle should put on a blindfold. (If you wear glasses, place them in your pocket or give them to an observer to hold.)
4. The instructor will read you the instructions for the exercise (see the following page). You have 20 minutes to complete the assigned task.
5. Please answer the following questions individually in the next 10 minutes:
   (a) What types of leadership emerged in this exercise? In your opinion, who were the leaders? Why? What leader behaviours did they exhibit?

(b) What occurred in the group to help you solve the problem?

(c) What occurred in the group that hindered you from solving the problem or from solving it quickly?

(d) What did you learn about leadership from this exercise?

(e) What did you learn about yourself as a leader in this exercise?

6. Discuss the questions in step 5 in smaller groups (four to six people). Ask the observers what they observed. Choose a representative to report a summary of your observations to the entire class.

7. Undertake a plenary debriefing session:

(a) The observer(s) briefly and objectively describe what happened when their group did the blindfold exercise. Next, the group representatives present their report.

(b) Can you see any relationships between this exercise and the 'real world' you experience at work or in other organizational settings?

(c) What are the important contingencies in this particular situation? What type of leadership works best in a situation like this? What leader behaviours are needed?

(d) There are no leaders without followers. In this exercise, what were the characteristics of a good follower?

(e) If you were to repeat this exercise, what would you do differently to be a better leader?

Observer instructions

Do not talk, laugh or make any noises at all during the exercise. Do keep an eye out for the group members' safety; move any items that could trip them and warn them if they are approaching the edge of a cliff (see the following instructions). Otherwise, do not talk to them or to the other observers. Please undertake the following tasks based on your observations:

1. Look for leadership behaviour in the group. Who emerged as leaders? What did they do to become leaders?

2. Please observe and describe the group's communication patterns and nonverbal language.

3. Describe how the group made decisions. Be prepared to share these observations in the group discussion of the exercise.[68]

Instructions for exercise (to be read to the group after they are blindfolded)

You are the last survivors of a secret intelligence unit that has just escaped from an ambush at the local airport. You were on a mission to a small country to rescue a high-ranking official of great strategic importance to your own country, who was being held as a political prisoner. The operation was successful and the official made it onto the last plane, but your unit was left behind; you were all occupied defending the airport against local militia. Unfortunately, you sustained a number of minor casualties and one fatality, your commander. However, there is a backup plan. You know that if your unit does not make the plane you are to assemble at the top of a cliff where military helicopters will ferry you back to a waiting ship. You have made it to the vicinity of the cliff, but it is pitch black. The helicopters will attempt a rescue only if they can identify you as the stranded unit. Before the mission it was agreed that the signal would be established by your unit forming a square on the top of the cliff; if at night, special heat-detecting radar would be used to locate you. Somehow you have to form this square in the dark, on the edge of a cliff with a 50-metre drop to rocks and the ocean. Time is not on your side. Your unit succeeded in destroying five local militia vehicles back at the airport, but this delaying tactic will not hold the enemy for more than 20 minutes.

LEADERSHIP CHALLENGE

ABC Accounting Associates is a small organization with a total of eight employees, including management. The organization has been in operation for 15 years and most of the employees have been there since the beginning. It has a traditional management structure – a managing director, Harry, and two other directors, Stephen and Margaret. The three senior managers – Lou, Mark and Maria – are responsible for most of the clients' basic accounting and bookkeeping needs. Two administration staff – Franco and Betty – are responsible for ABC's day-to-day office duties.

ABC has very few clients; however, they are profitable for the organization and very loyal. Most have been with ABC for more than 10 years and it is highly unlikely that they will move to another accounting firm, as they are completely satisfied.

Internally, however, things are not so good. For many years, ABC functioned well under the leadership of Harry. Harry is now in his late 60s and is getting a little tired and bored with the day-to-day operations. He also suffers from poor health but without ABC his health would probably decline even more. Harry's boredom is reflected in his attitude to work and his motivation to expand the business. Stephen and Margaret are much younger and keen to expand ABC, although Stephen tends to let his outside interests get in the way of work and often disappears for several hours at a time. Over the past 18 months there has been a large inequity of commitment and productivity between the three directors. Harry shows no interest in the business at all. Stephen is keen to build the business but spends only half the amount of time at the office that Margaret spends. Margaret has the most experience and works extremely long hours, so does not have much time to socialize with the other employees.

More than 80% of the clients on ABC's books are there because of Margaret. If Margaret decided to leave ABC, the business would probably not survive, as the clients would no doubt ultimately follow her. The employees at ABC are not aware of this and think that it is Harry's efforts and experience that keep the clients loyal to the organization. Margaret has so far tolerated the situation in the hope that one day she will succeed Harry as managing director – she is, after all, Harry's daughter!

Margaret is getting to the point where her frustrations can no longer be tempered. Although she gets some degree of support from the other employees at ABC, she feels that Stephen and Harry are taking advantage of her. Margaret is a very loyal person, but things are quickly coming to a head.

There is a directors' meeting this afternoon at 4pm, and Margaret has been asked to prepare the agenda – the other two directors are out to lunch. This is the last straw for Margaret so she decides to prepare an agenda but not with the usual topics that Stephen and Harry expect. This time Margaret challenges the leadership issue at ABC.

Source: From Wood *et al.* (2006) *Organizational Behaviour: Core Concepts and Applications.* John Wiley & Sons Australia, Ltd: Milton, Qld.

Questions

1. Briefly explain how Margaret should approach the leadership issue with Harry and Stephen during the meeting.
2. What leadership style do you think would be appropriate for ABC Accounting?
3. Given that the employees are quite satisfied under Harry's directorship, how should they be approached regarding a potential leadership change at ABC?

SUGGESTED READING

Shelton, C.D., McKenna, M.K. & John R Darling (2002), Leading in the age of paradox: optimizing behavioural style, job fit and cultural cohesion, *Leadership and Organization Development Journal*, **23** (7), 372–379. This article is unusual in that it attempts to bridge some of the apparent paradoxes within leadership in a practical manner.

Yukl, G. (2005), *Leadership in Organizations*, Prentice Hall: Thousand Oaks, CA. This is a book that both reviews the literature and provides critical commentary. It is excellent for the student interested in pursuing leadership to a greater depth and provides signposting for specialized work.

END NOTES

1. Kahler, K. (2001), Leadership: different venues, common themes, *Financial Executive International*, (July/August), **www.fei.org/magazine** articles/7-8-2001_CoverStory.cfm.

2. See Bryman, A. (1992), *Charisma and Leadership in Organizations*, Sage: London, Chapter 5.

3. Kotter, J. (1990), *A Force for Change: How Leadership Differs from Management*, Harvard Business School Press: Boston MA.

4. Adair, J. (2006), *Effective Leadership*, Chartered Institute of Personnel and Development: London.

5. Potter, J. & Hooper, A. (2005), *Developing Strategic Leadership Skills: Developing a Strategic Approach at All Levels*, Chartered Institute of Personnel and Development: London.

6. Hurd, M. (2006), Questions and answers with Mark Hurd. *Baylor Business Review*, **25** (1), 26–29, quotation is on p. 26.

7. Yukl, G. (2005), *Leadership in Organizations*, Prentice Hall: Thousand Oaks, CA.

8. *Bristol Evening Post*, 2 April 2007.

9. Stogdill, R.M. (1974), *Handbook of Leadership*, The Free Press: New York.

10. Ibid. Bass, B.M. (1990), *Bass and Stogdill's Handbook of Leadership*, The Free Press: New York.

11. Likert, R. (1961), *New Patterns of Management*, McGraw-Hill: New York.

12. Bass, op. cit., Chapter 24.

13. Blake, R.R. & Mouton, J.S. (1978), *The New Managerial Grid*, Gulf: Houston, TX.

14. For example, Fleishman, E., & Harris, E.F. (1962). Patterns of leadership behaviour related to employee grievances and turnover. *Personnel Psychology*, **15**, 43–56.

15. See Peterson M.F. (1988), PM theory in Japan and China: what's in it for the United States? *Organizational Dynamics* (Spring), pp. 22–39; Misumi, J. & Peterson, M.F. (1985), The performance-maintenance theory of leadership: review of a Japanese research program. *Administrative Science Quarterly*, **30**, 98–223; Smith, P.B., Misumi, J., Tayeb, M. *et al.* (1986), On the generality of leadership style measures across cultures. Paper presented at the International Congress of Applied Psychology, Jerusalem, July.

16. This section is based on Fiedler, F.E. & Chemers, M.M. (1984), The Leader Match Concept, 2nd edn. John Wiley & Sons: New York.

17. For example Vroom, V.H. & Jago, A.G (2007), The role of the situation in leadership. *American Psychologist*, **62** (1),17–24.

18. This section is based on Fiedler, F.E. & Garcia, J.E. (1987), *New Approaches to Effective Leadership*. John Wiley & Sons: New York.

19. Miller, R.L., Butler, J. & Cosentino, C.C. (2004), Followership effectiveness: an extension of Fiedler's contingency model. Leadership and Organization Development Journal, **25** (4), 362–368.

20. For example Hanbury, G.L., Sapat, A. & Washington, C.W. (2004), Know yourself and take charge of your own destiny: The 'fit model' of leadership. *Public Administration Review*, **64** (5), 566–576.

21. This section is based on House, R.J. & Mitchell, T.R. (1977), Path–goal theory of leadership. *Journal of Contemporary Business*, (Autumn): 81–97.

22. House & Mitchell, op. cit.

23. See the discussion of this approach in Hersey, P. & Blanchard, K.H. (1988), *Management of Organizational Behaviour*. Prentice Hall: Englewood Cliffs, NJ.

24. Ibid.

25. For some criticisms see Graeff, C.L. (1983), The situational leadership theory: a critical view. *Academy of Management Review*, **8**, 285–291.

26. The discussion in this section is based on Kerr, S. & Jermier, J. (1978), Substitutes for leadership: their meaning and measurement. *Organizational Behaviour and Human Performance*, **22**, 375–403; Howell, J.P., Bowen, D.E., Dorfman, P.W. *et al.* (1990), Substitutes for leadership: effective alternatives to ineffective leadership. *Organizational Dynamics*, (Summer), 21–38.

27. Posakoff, P.M., Dorfman, P.W., Howell, J.P. & Todor, W.D. (1989) Leader reward and punishment behaviours: a preliminary test of a culture-free style of leadership effectiveness, *Advances in Comparative Management*, **2**, 95–138. Peng, T.K. (1990), *Substitutes for Leadership in an International Setting*, unpublished manuscript, College of Business Administration, Texas Tech University: Lubbock, TX.

28. Based on 'The Columbus effect: unexpected findings and new directions in leadership research', presentation made at annual meeting, Academy of Management, Las Vegas, August 1992.

29. Roberts, A. (2003), *Hitler and Churchill: Secrets of Leadership*, Weidenfeld & Nicolson: London.

30. Why good leaders are hard to find, *The Age*, 2 August 2003, **www.theage.com.au/articles/2003/08/01/1059480538838.html?oneclick=true**.

31. Bass, op. cit., Chapter 12.

32. Conger, J.A. & Kanungo, R.N. (1988), Charismatic leadership, the elusive factor in organizational effectiveness, Jossey-Bass: San Francisco.

33. See Howell, J.M. & Avolio, B.J. (1992), The ethics of charismatic leadership: submission or liberation, *The Academy of Management Executive*, **6** (2) (May), 43–54.

34. Conger & Kanungo, op. cit.

35. Ibid. Halpert, J.A. (1990), The dimensionality of charisma. *Journal of Business and Psychology*, **4** (4).

36. See Hwang, A., Khatri, N. Srinivas, E.S. (2005), Organizational charisma and vision across three countries, *Management Decision*, **43** (7/8), 960–974.

37. Yukl, G. (1999), An evaluation of conceptual weaknesses in transformational and charismatic leadership theories. *Leadership Quarterly*, **10** (2), 285–305.

38. See Huang, M., Cheng, B. & Chou, L. (2005), Fitting in organizational values: the mediating role of person-organization fit between CEO charismatic leadership and employee outcomes. *International Journal of Manpower*, **26** (1), 35–49.

39. Parry, K.W. & Proctor-Thomson, S.B. (2002), Perceived integrity of transformational leaders in organizational settings. *Journal of Business Ethics*, **35** (2), p. 75–96.

40. Parry, K.W. & Sinha, P. (2005), Researching the trainability of transformational organizational leadership. *Human Resource Development International*, **8** (2), p. 165–183.

41. See Bass, M. (1985), *Leadership and Performance beyond Expectations*. The Free

Press: New York. Bryman, A. (1992), *Charisma and Leadership in Organizations*, Sage: London, pp. 98–9.

42. De Vries, K. (1998), Charisma in action: the transformational abilities of Virgin's Richard Branson and AAB's Percy Barnevik. *Organizational Dynamics*, (Winter), 18.

43. Adapted from Blythe, A. (2006), Nando's spices up its leadership style. *Personnel Today*, 50–51.

44. Bass (1985), op. cit.

45. Avolio, B., Waldman, D. & Yammarino, F. (1991), Leading in the 1990s: the four Is of transformational leadership. *Journal of European Industrial Training*, **15** (4), 9–16.

46. See Ashkanasy, N.M. & Dasborough, M.T. (2003), Emotional awareness and emotional intelligence in leadership teaching', *Journal of Education for Business*, **79** (1), p. 18(5)

47. Bryman, op. cit., Chapter 6. Inkson, K. & Moss, A.T. (1993), Transformational leadership – is it universally applicable? *Leadership and Organizational Development*, **14** (4), 1–11.

48. For example Sanders, K. & Schyns, B. (2006), Trust conflict and cooperative behaviour – considering reciprocity within organizations. *Personnel Review*, **35** (5), 538–556.

49. Bass, B.M. (1999), Two decades of research and development in transformational leadership. *European Journal of Work and Organizational Psychology*, **8** (1), 9–32.

50. Kotelnikov, V., 25 lessons from Jack Welch, **www.1000ventures.com/business_guide/mgmt _new-model_25lessons-welch.html**, accessed 24 August 2007.

51. See Bass, B.M. & Avolio, B.J. (1990), The implications of transactional and transformational leadership for individual team, and organizational development, *Research in Organizational Change and Development*, **4**, 231–272.

52. See Conger, J.A. & Kanungo, R.N. 'Training charismatic leadership: a risky and critical task' in Conger and Kanungo, op. cit., Chapter 11.

53. *Sunday Times*, Appointments, 21 January 2007, p. 9.

54. See Kouzes, J.R. & Posner, B.F. (1991), *The Leadership Challenge: How to Get Extraordi-*

nary Things Done in Organizations, Jossey-Bass: San Francisco.

55. Khurana, R. (2002) The curse of the superstar CEO. *Harvard Business Review*, **80** (9), 60–66.

56. For a discussion of this see Spreier, S.W., Fountaine, M.H. & Malloy, R.L. (2006), Leadership run amok. *Harvard Business Review*, **84** (6), 72–82.

57. Greenleaf, R.K. (1977), *Servant Leadership: A Journey into the Nature of Legitimate Power and Greatness*, Paulist Press: New York.

58. Sendjaya, S. & Sarros, J.C. (2002), Servant leadership: its origin, development, and application in organizations. *Journal of Leadership and Organizational Studies*, **9** (2), 57.

59. Spears, L.C. (ed.) (1997), *Reflections on Leadership*, John Wiley & Sons: New York.

60. Ryan, M. and Alexander, S. (2005) The glass cliff: Evidence that woman are over-represented in precarious leadership positions. *British Journal of Management*, **16** (2), 81–90.

61. Sinclair, A. (1998), *Doing Leadership Differently*, Melbourne University Press: Melbourne, p. 13.

62. Eagly, A.H. (2007) Female leadership advantage and disadvantage: resolving the contradictions. *Psychology of Women Quarterly*, **31** (1), 1–12.

63. See Hofstede, G. (1980), *Culture's Consequences: International Differences in Work-related Values*, Sage: Beverly Hills, CA.

64. House, R., Javidan, M., Hanges, P. & Dorfman, P. (2002) Understanding cultures and implicit leadership theories across the globe: an introduction to project GLOBE (global leadership and organizational behaviour effectiveness). *Journal of World Business*, **37** (1), p. 3(8).

65. House, R.J., Hanges, P.J., Javidan, M. *et al.* (eds) (2004), *Culture, Leadership and Organizations: the GLOBE Study of 62 Societies*, Sage: Thousand Oaks, CA.

66. See for example Zagorsek, H., Jaklic, M. & Stough, S.J. (2004), Comparing leadership practices between the United States, Nigeria, and Slovenia: does culture matter? *Cross Cultural Management: An International Journal*, **11** (2), 16–34.

67. Adapted from The survey of organizations, © 1980 by the University of Michigan and Rensis Likert Associates. Reprinted by permission of the Institute for Social Research.

68. Group procedure/process adapted from Kolb, D.A., Osland, J.S., Rubin, I.M. (1995), *Organizational Behaviour: An Experiential Approach*, 6th edn, Prentice Hall: Englewood Cliffs, NJ. Adapted with permission of Prentice Hall, Inc.

CHAPTER
10

Power, politics and decision making in organizations

LEARNING OBJECTIVES

After studying this chapter you should be able to:

- discuss the sources of power for managers and employees
- explain the relationship between power, authority and obedience
- discuss the meaning and importance of empowerment in organizations
- describe various kinds of political behaviours in organizations
- discuss the ethical implications of politics in organizations
- define decision making and contrast the classical and behavioural decision-making models
- summarize the sequential steps in the decision-making process
- evaluate the contributions of intuition, judgement and risk analysis to quality decision making
- state the conditions under which individuals or groups are best placed to make decisions in organizations
- identify contemporary issues affecting the decision-making context.

SIX YEARS OF INDECISION IN THE FAST-PACED MUSIC INDUSTRY

Nick Goodway reported a power struggle between top executives in EMI and Warner Music over who would run a merged business. The two companies have looked at a merger deal at least three times since 2000, and industry analysts believe a marriage is inevitable. Henk Potts of Barclays Stockbrokers said: 'There appears to be a real power battle between the two to determine who exactly is going to be in control . . . It is clear it makes an awful lot of sense for them to combine. It would be good if they could work out a peaceful solution rather than this strange bid and counterbid situation.'

Essentially each firm is trying to take over the other – whoever wins will be in change of the merged group.

The well known music giant, EMI, which includes Coldplay and Joss Stone among its artists, rejected a £2.54 billion takeover bid from its American rival Warner Music. EMI, led by chairman Eric Nicoli, described the 320 p per share offer as 'wholly unacceptable' and said that its own $31 per share offer for Warner 'would be very attractive to both sets of shareholders and would deliver compelling value to EMI's shareholders which is far superior to Warner Music's revised alternative proposal.'

The counterbidding and competition between the two sides suggests that they are far from agreement, with a power struggle causing significant dysfunction and making it difficult for them to combine. Together EMI and Warner Music would rank as the world's second-largest music group with a near-25% market share against Paris-based Universal's 25.5% and Sony BMG's 21.5%. Their combined roster would include Madonna, Eric Clapton, Eminem, the Red Hot Chili Peppers, Green Day and the Scissor Sisters.

Teather & Greenwood's Conor O'Shea said: 'A deal has to be done . . . They both need to do something to compete on the same footing as Sony and Universal.'

Questions
1. What factors are preventing a decision?
2. What needs to occur to enable a decision?
3. Think up two possible solutions – what are the outcomes?

Source: London Evening Standard, Wednesday 28 June 2006. © 2006 Associated Newspapers Ltd.

INTRODUCTION

With fast-paced, complex and rapidly changing business environments, the demands on leaders and managers have multiplied. Decisions need to be made quickly otherwise opportunities are lost. The need for managers to maximize their influence by acquiring and using power effectively is central to effective working, decision making and delegation to enable work to be undertaken efficiently.

As students of organizations, we need to understand that power and politics are very much part of decision making both within and across organizational boundaries.

Most employees find themselves in situations where they need to influence others. This might be at a peer group level, upwards into the management hierarchy or with subordinates. There are many ways to achieve power and influence and, as the EMI Warner case shows, the level of success of any one strategy often depends on their context, which includes the other players and the environmental influences. Money and resources are not the sole vehicles of power. The ability to network, build and retain relationships can also be an important generator of influence in the modern organization. The power of partnerships and alliances is indisputable.

In this chapter we will first examine the issue of power and politics and then progress to apply that knowledge within the area of decision making. Together these topics form key foundations for anyone wishing to enter management grades and progress through an organization, or deal effectively with stakeholders (such as suppliers and clients) over a period of time.

INTRODUCTION TO POWER AND POLITICS

No discussion of organizational behaviour would be complete without a study of power and politics. Every day, in every kind of situation, managers and employees alike use power and politics to do their jobs. A manager hires a personal assistant, a finance manager audits a department, a working group decides the priorities for an improvement programme and a board of directors discusses the strategic plan – all of these are instances of the use of power and they often entail politics. Power and politics may be the source of solutions as well as problems in organizations. They are important but remain quite elusive as academic concepts in organizational behaviour. To be effective, managers need to know how power is acquired and exercised. They also need to know about political behaviour in organizations and about organizational dynamics.

In this chapter we first examine the meaning of power and politics and their effects at the interpersonal and organizational levels. We outline and discuss theories within the field and apply them in practice.

What is affected by organizational power and politics? Is this only relevant to those who are directly involved? Unfortunately not. Allocation of resources such as money, equipment and staff numbers, changes to rules and procedures, reorganization, delegation of authority, personnel changes such as promotions and transfers, recruitment and selection, pay and work appraisals and interdepartmental coordination are most commonly affected by politics, power and influence – and of course these affect everyone.[1]

Power and politics represent the essence of what happens in organizations on a daily basis.[2] This is because organizations are not democracies composed of individuals with equal influence. At the extreme some organizations are more akin to medieval feudal states in which managers believe they can rule through a divine right. In such circumstances any attempt to change can be seen as undermining others' roles and requires immense skill. In such organizations employees are highly political animals. Some organizations have become so political that organizational interests are completely subordinated to individual interests.

Clearly, power and politics are important organizational tools that managers use to get the job done, and their use does not have to be negative. In effective organizations, astute individuals delicately develop, nurture and manage power and politics. In other words, power and politics may be unsavoury notions to some but, when used with care, they can bring together individual desires for joint accomplishment.[3]

POWER AND INFLUENCE

Power *is the ability to get someone else to do something you want done, or the ability to make things happen or get things done in the way you want.*

Influence *is a behavioural response to the exercise of power.*

Power may be defined as the potential ability to influence behaviour. As such it is usually crucial if one wants to change the course of events, overcome resistance, or to convince people to do things.[4] Politics and influence are the processes, actions and behaviours through which this potential power is used and realized.[5] In simpler terms, power may be defined as the ability to get someone to do something you want done or the ability to make things happen in the way you want. The essence of power is control over the behaviour of others.[6] Power is the force that makes things happen in an intended way; influence is a behavioural response to the exercise of power – that is, influence is an outcome achieved through the use of power. Managers use power to achieve influence over subordinates and others in the work setting.

Figure 10.1 summarizes the link between power and influence. It also identifies the key bases of power that managers can use to influence the behaviour of other people at work. Managers derive power from the organization and other individuals. We call these sources position power and personal power, respectively.[7] French and Raven first raised this distinction in their landmark study and it underpins our discussion on the subject. Much of the key research into this area was based in the 1980s, and it is a credit to French and Raven's ideas that they have endured so many decades.

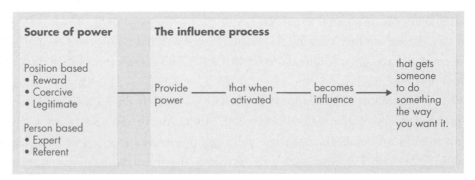

Figure 10.1: Power sources and the influence process.

POSITION POWER

Three bases of position power are available to managers solely as a result of their position in the organization: reward, coercive and legitimate power. These will now be discussed in turn.

Reward power

Reward power is the extent to which a manager can use extrinsic and intrinsic rewards. Managers usually hold power in organizations by virtue of their ability to reward. The strength of the power differs depending on the rewards that the manager controls and the strength of the employee's desire for the rewards.

Examples of such rewards include money, promotions, compliments or enriched jobs. These types of rewards are discussed in detail in Chapter 3. One should not forget that rewards such as praise and positive interaction are some of the 'soft' rewards for which employees will often work very hard. Such types of reward are available to everyone to use.

Reward power is the extent to which a manager can use extrinsic and intrinsic rewards to control other people.

Coercive power

Power can also be founded on punishment as well as reward. Managers can cause others to have unpleasant experiences. In such circumstances coercive power is thought of as a form of punishment for failing to complying with the wishes of the power holder. A manager may withhold a pay rise, allocate least desirable tasks or times of work to a person as a form of punishment or exclude someone from training or crucial information. The strength of coercive power is based on the extent to which a manager can administer punishments to control other people. Naturally there are 'soft' punishments as there are 'soft' rewards. Thus not engaging in positive social interaction with one member of staff can be seen as a coercive and punishing act.

Coercive power is the extent to which a manager can deny desired rewards or administer punishment to control other people.

The availability of formal reward and coercive power varies very much from one organization and manager to another. Given the possible negative effects of this power, they should be used carefully and most organizations devise rules and principles to guide rewards and punishment, formal and informal. Thus employees may be required to treat each other with dignity and respect and this will apply to managers in their handling of subordinates as well as on a peer-to-peer basis. Organizations have complaints systems and a system of 'appeal' to protect employees against coercion and various illegitimate acts, such as harassment in the workplace. Such organizational policies on employee treatment and the presence of unions, for example, can weaken this power base considerably. Unions point out that when unemployment is high and job insecurity is rampant, employees may feel less able to confront coercive power; further, employees may not seek the assistance of unions for fear of further unpleasant consequences such as being labelled a troublemaker, or they might think that any complaint will be career limiting.

Bullying as a coercive power

Workplace bullying is a major source of employee discontent and lost productivity. Around a quarter of people who are bullied leave their jobs, often quietly and without making a complaint. In addition witnesses leave – we presume because they are worried that they will be next in the frame.[8] Cultural differences are apparent with the Scandinavian countries experiencing higher rates of peer-to-peer bullying whereas in the UK, US, Canada and Australia it is managers who are most often identified as the source of bullying.[9]

Regardless of who is the perpetrator of the experience it is very negative for employees who suffer stress[10] and it is thought this issue contributes significantly to absenteeism. Students wishing to explore the estimated costs of workplace bullying should visit their own country's central government Web site to do with safety and health. Both employers and employees are damaged by the presence of workplace bullying and have an equal interest in its eradication.[11]

Legitimate power and formal authority

Legitimate power *is the extent to which a manager can use the internalized belief of an employee that the 'boss' has a 'right of command' to control other people.*

Legitimate power relates to the right (rather than capacity) to command. As the third base of power, legitimate power stems from the extent to which a manager can use the internalized belief of employees that the 'boss' has a 'right of command'. These beliefs are called implicit leadership theories – not an easy phrase – but we each have an internalized idea of what a leader should, should not, can and cannot do.[12]

Legitimate power is based on a mutually accepted perception that the power holder (in this case the manager) has the right to influence the employee. In this context, managers are the bosses, their employees are the subordinates and many routine instructions and requests are accepted simply because everyone agrees that employees should do what managers say.

Legitimate power is often used interchangeably with the term 'formal authority'. It confers a legal authority to use organizational resources to accomplish goals. For example, the organization's board of directors grants the legitimate power of a chief executive officer, which gives him or her authority over all organizational resources. In turn, the chief executive officer has the right to confer legitimate power upon managers lower down in the organization's hierarchy. Supervisors, too, have legitimate power over their employees, which reflects the responsibilities in their job.

Process power *is the control over methods of production and analysis.*

Process power is part of legitimate power and is found in individuals whose positions influence how inputs are transformed into outputs. For instance, an organization may nominate a financial controller to monitor the efficiency of a production process, or an organization may use business process re-engineering systems. Such systems are typically designed to empower workers and supervisory staff by giving them responsibility for specific processes. In such circumstances they can overturn the traditional management hierarchy where processes are managed from the top down. Thus legitimate power does not always follow the direction of the traditional hierarchy.

Information power *is the extent to which individuals have control over information needed by others.*

Information power is the final source of position power. Students reading this text may be seeking to improve their information power base. Managers need access to information and can become dependent on those who hold such information. Hence, when managers exercise their legitimate power, they need to secure information for day-to-day managerial activities. The need for information provides a source of power to those who hold it. If someone withholds the information, this can be termed 'restrictive control'.[13] In the knowledge economy, information power becomes very important. Other sorts of knowledge also fit into this category. Gossip, or being linked into the 'grapevine' of informal information, can be a form of knowledge with which a person may potentially influence the behaviour of others.

PERSONAL POWER

Personal power resides in the individual independent of the position the individual holds. However, the management literature considers that, in essence, the two main bases of personal power are expertise and reference.

Expert power

Very much linked to information power, expert power is the ability to control another person's behaviour through the possession of knowledge, experience or judgement that the other person does not have but needs. Employees would obey someone with expert power because they feel they know more and are making a better decision. Computer specialists can influence nontechnical staff behaviour because they have special knowledge that may be critical to them.

> **Expert power** is the ability to control another's behaviour through the possession of knowledge, experience or judgement that the other person does not have but needs.

Access to key organizational decision makers is another element in expert power. A person's ability to contact key people informally can allow for special participation in the definition of a problem or issue, affect the flow of information to decision makers, and lobbying for use of special criteria in decision making. Managers have to develop good working relationships with employees who hold expert power.

OB IN ACTION

Steve Jobs at Apple uses a rich multipower base

John Plunkett,[14] comments on the extraordinary influence Steve Jobs commands after turning the music retailing industry on its head – what can Jobs do now? 'Steve Jobs transformed the music industry and in the process created a whole new demographic – the iPod generation.' Launched just five years ago, the ubiquitous music players have gone from being the preserve of the early adopter to a part of our everyday language.

Having transformed the way we consume music, Jobs is now doing the same for television with the launch of the video iPod, capable of showing films and TV programmes downloaded from the net. Hit shows such as *Lost*, *Desperate Housewives* and the American version of *The Office* are already available in the iTunes catalogue. A next-generation video iPod and a new iTunes movie service are expected to launch later this year. Broadcasters ignore the new technology at their peril. With around 70% of the market, the one billionth song was downloaded on iTunes this year – Coldplay's 'Speed of Sound', appropriately – prompting some observers to suggest that Apple was on the verge of becoming the most powerful retailer ever.

The phenomenon of podcasting, meanwhile, gave a voice to millions of would-be broadcasters around the globe. It turned newspapers into radio stations, and radio stations into audio and video-on-demand services. Put simply, the old definitions and barriers to entry simply do not apply any more. 'Everyone is trying to second guess what he does next. He is influencing everyone's thinking.' Said a market commentator.

'Apple remains an over-secretive company run by a brilliant if erratic businessman which may well get its comeuppance if its increasingly monopolistic presence is challenged by new-comers,' said a *Guardian* leader in April. It hasn't happened yet.

Referent power

Referent power *is the ability to control another's behaviour because the individual wants to identify with the power source due to his or her perceived attractive characteristics.*

Referent power comes from others wanting to be like you, to be associated with you, or the networks and contacts you have which they also value. Thus you may have chosen a university because it has some high profile academics to whom you can refer at job interviews. A boss who is thought of as a 'good role model' would be a typical way of thinking of referent power. A more subtle approach comes from sociology where the notion of 'prototypes' is useful in this area. A prototype is the 'ideal' – for example what is the ideal police officer? The sociological approach is helpful in that there can be several different prototypes depending on the stakeholder view.[15] For example one person might see the prototypical police officer as someone who uses judgement and will occasionally let someone off speeding. Another person may think that the prototypical police officer will issue a sanction every single time. One person's prototype may not be another's.

Another aspect is working out exactly what one is prototyping. Hence one might be a referent for some aspects of employment and gain power, but not other aspects.[16] For example Richard Branson (founder of the Virgin group) would be acknowledged by most as an excellent publicist and figure-head leader, however some people might find his style of organizing too loose and prefer stronger structures. This would be an example where one might have referent power in some areas perceived by some people, but not others. Referent power can be seen where people are respected as well as liked and admired – for example, the data input clerk who looks after elderly parents but has a spotless attendance record. Admiration and respect for one area of work can infect other areas and lead to an overall good impression, which is called the 'halo effect'.[17]

All individuals have one or more source of power, to varying degrees and in varying combinations. It is important that managers do not rely on a single source of power as this may limit their effectiveness – power is assigned by others and will always change with time. Managers who rely only on legitimate power may have very limited ability to influence the behaviour of others and their efforts may be undermined by the referent power of informal leaders.

POWER, AUTHORITY AND OBEDIENCE

Power is the potential to control the behaviour of others; formal authority is the potential to exert such control through the legitimacy of a managerial position. Yet we also know that people who seem to have power do not always get their way. This leads us to the subject of obedience. Why do some people obey directives while others do not? More specifically, why should employees respond to a manager's authority or 'right to command' in the first place? Further, given that employees are willing to obey, what determines the limits of obedience?

The Milgram experiments

These last questions point to Stanley Milgram's seminal research on obedience.[18] Milgram designed an experiment to determine the extent to which people obey the commands of an authority figure, even if they believe they are endangering the life of another person. The subjects were 40 males, ranging in age from 20 to 50 years and representing a diverse set of occupations (engineers, salespeople, schoolteachers, labourers and others). They were paid a nominal fee for participation in the project, which was conducted in a laboratory in America.

The subjects were told (falsely) that the purpose of the study was to determine the effects of punishment on learning. The subjects were to be the 'teachers'. The 'learner' (an actor), was strapped to a chair in an adjoining room with an electrode attached to his wrist. The 'experimenter' (another actor) was dressed in a grey laboratory coat. Appearing impassive and somewhat stern, the experimenter instructed the learner in a fairly simple task concerning pairs of words.

The teacher was instructed to administer an electric shock to the learner each time a wrong answer was given. The shock was to be increased in intensity each time the learner made a mistake (and the actor delivered many mistakes). The teacher controlled switches that ostensibly administered shocks ranging from 15 to 450 volts (although, of course, in reality there was no electric current). The question was how far the teacher would progress in shocking the learner. A summary of the switch markings and the learner's fake responses to the various levels of shock is shown in Table 10.1.

Switch voltage marking	Switch description	'Learner's' responses
15–60	Slight	No sound
75–120	Moderate	Grunts and moans
135–180	Strong	Asks to leave
195–240	Very strong	Cannot stand the pain
255–300	Intense	Pounds on wall
315–360	Exterme intensity	No sound
375–420	Danger: severe shock	No sound
435–450	XXX	No sound

Table 10.1: Shock levels and set learner responses in the Milgram experiment.

If a teacher proved unwilling to administer a shock, the experimenter would escalate instructions to the teacher up to 'You have no choice, you must go on.' as the fourth level. Only if the teacher refused to go on after the fourth level would the experiment be stopped. In all, 26 subjects (65%) continued to the end of the experiment and shocked the 'learner' to the XXX level! None stopped before 300 V – the point at which the learner pounds on the wall. The remaining 14 subjects refused to obey the experimenter at various intermediate points.

Most people are surprised by these results, as was Milgram. There were many criticisms of Milgram's method, which allowed the 'teachers' to leave thinking that they might have done someone harm. The conduct of this type of experiment would not be permitted under today's more demanding ethical guidelines for research. However a valuable lesson was learned in that many people will obey and comply to a point we all find surprising.

Obedience and the acceptance of authority

Applying Milgram's experiments into the workplace suggests there are strong tendencies among individuals to follow the instructions of the boss. Direct defiance within organizational settings is quite rare. If the tendency to follow instructions is great and defiance is rare then why do so many organizations apparently drift into chaos? The answer to this question lies at the heart of the contribution made by the well-known management writer Chester Barnard.[19] Essentially, Barnard's argument focused on the 'consent of the governed' rather than on the rights derived from ownership. He argued that employees will accept or follow a directive from the boss only under special circumstances and all four must be met:

- the employee can and must understand the directive
- the employee must feel mentally and physically capable of carrying out the directive
- the employee must believe the directive is not inconsistent with the purpose of the organization
- the employee must believe the directive is not inconsistent with his or her personal interests.

These four conditions are carefully stated. To accept and follow an order, employees do not need, for instance, to understand how the proposed action will help the organization; they only need to believe the requested action is not inconsistent with the purpose of the organization. The astute manager will recognize that the acceptance of any request is not assured. If the directive is routine, then it is not surprising that the employee may merely comply without enthusiasm. If the request is unusual, it will be made by a manager giving assurances on the last two rules, which touches on Barnard's valuable concept of the 'zone of indifference'.

The zone of indifference

Most people seek a balance between what they put into an organization (contribution) and what they get from an organization in return (inducement). Within the psychological contract (Chapter 1), employees agree to do many things for the organization because they think they should. That is, in exchange for inducements (such as wages), employees recognize the authority of the organization and its managers to direct their behaviour in certain ways. Based on his acceptance view of authority, Chester Barnard calls this area in which directions are obeyed the zone of indifference.

A zone of indifference is the range of authoritative requests to which employees are willing to respond without subjecting the directives to critical evaluation or judgement – that is, the range in which they are indifferent. Directives falling within the zone are obeyed; other directives may or may not be obeyed. This link between the zone of indifference and the psychological contract is shown in Figure 10.2.

The **zone of indifference** is the range of authoritative requests to which an employee is willing to respond without subjecting the directives to critical evaluation or judgement – that is, the requests to which the employee is indifferent.

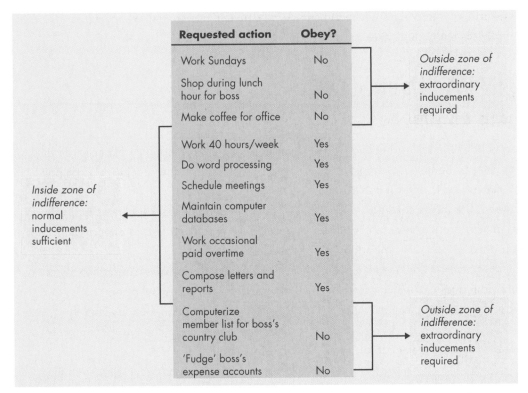

Figure 10.2: Hypothetical psychological contract with a secretary showing zone of indifference.

The secretary whose psychological contract is shown in Figure 10.3 expects to perform a number of activities falling within the zone of indifference (with no questions asked). Examples include scheduling meetings and maintaining computer databases. There may be times when the boss would like the secretary to do things falling outside the zone, such as running personal errands for the boss on the secretary's lunch hour. This requires efforts to enlarge the zone to accommodate additional behaviours. In these attempts, the boss will most likely have to use more incentives than pure position power. In some instances, such as Sunday work and 'fudging' of expense accounts, no legitimate power base may be arguable.

There is another side to power, authority and obedience with which you should be familiar as a manager: your own zone of indifference and tendency to obey. When will you say 'no' to your boss? When should you be willing to say 'no'? At times, work may involve ethical dilemmas, where you may be asked to do things that are illegal, unethical or both. Most of us will face ethical dilemmas during our careers. Saying 'no' or 'refusing to keep quiet' can be difficult and potentially costly, as many whistleblowers discover. Whistleblowing may be the right thing to do but contesting the power of a manager is not easy.

Consider employees in the last days of the Enron collapse when qualified accountants (who were all signed up to professional codes of conduct) spent time shredding documents that would implicate a cover-up.[20] While all those employees had the power and the ethical grounds to refuse to do this, for so many of them to have complied is reminiscent of the pressures of the Milgram experiments – how much power and what 'rights' did those employees really think they had?

EFFECTIVE MANAGER 10.1

Insubordinate employees

All managers need to hone the skill of dealing with insubordinate employees. Sometimes employees are unaware their behaviour is unacceptable and it is important to make sure this is covered.

The guidelines below are useful as a checklist when approaching an interview. It is important to make a note of your discussion in case the employee engages in the behaviour again, at which point you might need to invoke the relevant policies.

1. Explore the reasons for the unacceptable behaviour.
2. Inform the employee that he or she has engaged in unacceptable conduct and that certain conducts are strongly expected of all employees. Refer to the specific rules or policies in that respect.
3. Discuss the negative consequences that will occur if the employee fails to change unacceptable behaviours.
4. Clearly outline the positive consequences of changing the improper behaviour.
5. Develop an action plan that you and the employee agree on to change the unacceptable behaviour.
6. If further transgressions occur, deal with them swiftly, fairly and in line with what you have warned them about in 3.

MANAGING WITH POWER AND INFLUENCE

Managing with power means recognizing that there are varying interests in almost every organization and that different stakeholder groups perceive issues differently. Young managers sometimes find the notion of power distasteful and attempt to manage through consensus and discussion. It is possible to manage in this way but one should never forget that power is sometimes given (such as that which comes with the authority of 'manager') thus, even if as a manager you dislike power, your staff may have already invested it in you!

Power is needed to get things done and anyone who is ambitious will want to get a lot done, hence sources of power must be developed. By learning to manage with power, managers are able to achieve both their own goals and the goals of their organization as well as enhancing others' careers through being associated with success.

Power and influence do not just work within the organization; customers also have the opportunity to exert influence over various processes and decisions in the organization. They do so through increasing consumer demands, creating consumer feedback and responding to the increasing availability of information online. Shareholders, and people in wider society, may also have some potential to influence decisions and behaviours in organizations. Such influence is not necessarily intentional and typically not as strong as

OB IN ACTION

Yukl's review of influence tactics

Gary Yukl has reviewed research around influence tactics for many years. Practically speaking, there are many useful ways of exercising influence.[21] The tactics are:

* rational persuasion – using logical arguments and factual evidence
* consultation – seeking support through asking for suggestions
* collaboration – where each provides different components for the solution
* inspirational appeals – appealing to a person's values, ideals or aspirations
• apprising – explaining why agreement will benefit the collaborator personally
• personal appeals – the request is directed to a person's feelings
• ingratiation – using flattery
• exchange – offering an exchange of favours/benefits

+ pressure – using demands, threats, frequent checking or constant reminders
+ legitimating tactics – shows links with organizational policies, practices etc.
+ coalition tactics – involves others as part of the argument

+ = low effectiveness
• = moderate effectiveness
* high effectiveness

In his overview of research in the area Yukl suggests that consultation, collaboration, inspirational appeals and strong rational persuasion are the most effective tactics. However, variation could be expected based on the context, the direction of the influence attempt and the objectives of the influence attempt. Managers need to diagnose their power relationships carefully in order to be able to use the tactics effectively.

power sources inside the organization. This would be reflected in any external analysis of the forces affecting an organization.

EMPOWERMENT

How far should power be shared, and under what circumstances? It will be seen from Chapter 4 that control over work is a component of motivation and it is also a major factor in reducing stress.[22]

When all goes well, everyone can gain from empowerment. To keep the organization competitive, top management must attend to a variety of challenging and strategic forces in the external environment. While top management tends to concentrate on decisions about strategy and dynamic change, others throughout the organization must be ready and willing to make critical operating decisions. By providing these opportunities, empowerment increases the total power available in an organization. In other words, the top levels do not have to give up power for the lower levels to gain it. The same basic argument holds true in any manager–employee relationship.

EFFECTIVE MANAGER 10.2

Guidelines for implementing empowerment

- Encourage creativity by allowing employees ample flexibility in how they achieve organizational objectives.
- Provide all the necessary information to assist employees to make informed decisions.
- Communicate openly with employees on the organization's activities, performance and long-term goals. Let them know how the organization is doing and how their roles and actions affect the bottom line.
- Train on problem solving, time management and decision making to enhance key skills for increased responsibility.

- Run regular meetings between employees and management.
- Be sure to respond swiftly to input and suggestions from employees because lengthy silence can lead to discouragement and demotivation.
- Allow room for error; encouraging employees to be more creative means some risk taking – errors will occur, and one needs systems to pick these up quickly.

Empowerment *is the process by which managers delegate power to employees who therefore have an enhanced view of their work and role within the organization.*

Empowerment is the process by which managers help others acquire and use the power needed to make decisions affecting themselves and their work. More than ever before, managers in progressive organizations are expected to be good at empowering the people with whom they work. Empowerment is a key foundation of the increasingly popular self-managing work teams and other creative worker involvement groups. Despite this, there are limits to the process of empowerment, which we discuss in some detail on pages 489–490.

Power keys to empowerment

One base for empowerment is a radically different view of power itself. Our discussion so far has focused on power exerted over other individuals. In contrast to this, the concept of empowerment emphasizes the ability to make things happen. Cutting through all the corporate rhetoric on empowerment is difficult because the term has become fashionable in management circles. However, each individual empowerment attempt needs to be examined in the light of how power in the organization will be changed. In this way, Honda has engendered a process of constant improvement by giving teams the power to make decisions for improvement in processes. Naturally this has changed the nature of the power of senior managers. However they have made it a remarkable source of competitive advantage.[23]

Expanding the zone of indifference

When embarking on an empowerment programme, management needs to recognize the current zone of indifference and systematically move to expand it. All too often, management assumes that its directive for empowerment will be followed; however, managers often fail to show precisely how empowerment will benefit the individuals involved.

Power as an expanding pie

Along with empowerment, employees need to be trained to expand their power and their new influence potential. This is the most difficult task for managers and a difficult challenge for employees, because it often changes the dynamic between supervisors and employees. The key is to change the concept of power within the organization – from a view that stresses power over others to one that emphasizes the use of power to get things done. Under the new definition of power, all employees can be more powerful.

In practical terms, empowerment means that all managers will need to emphasize different ways of exercising influence. Appeals to higher authority and sanctions will need to be replaced by appeals to reason, friendliness and bargaining. This will need a manager to draw on sources of power other than legitimate authority and use influence tactics (see above).

 COUNTERPOINT

When an organization attempts to move power down the hierarchy it also needs to alter the existing pattern of position power. Changing this pattern raises important questions. Can 'empowered' individuals give rewards and sanctions? Has their new right to act been legitimized with formal authority? All too often, attempts at empowerment disrupt well-established patterns of position power, and threaten middle and lower level managers.[24]

Empowerment varies in the degree to which it is applied and accepted. It can range from small tasks to full responsibility for important decision making or project completion. Clearly, quantifying the degree of empowerment is a difficult and complex task. In the UK an empowerment audit (EA) was developed to try to measure the degree of empowerment, resulting in a matrix of 15 major indicators, each with a five-point scale of traditional, participative, involved, early self-directed and mature self-directed.[25]

Empowerment involves the development of all employees, including managers. There is a significant risk that trying to introduce the highest degrees of empowerment too quickly will fail to give people time to develop and adjust to new demands. The result may be that they conclude that empowerment can not or did not work, when a slower, steadier programme of introduction may have allowed individuals to adapt to empowerment over time.

The limits of empowering others

Empowerment programmes can transform a stagnant organization into a vital one by creating a shared purpose among employees, encouraging greater cooperation and, most importantly, delivering enhanced value to customers. Despite that potential, empowerment programmes often fall victim to the same structural and cultural problems that made them desirable in the first place. On the one hand, many managers may view empowerment as a threat and may continue to measure their personal status and value in terms of the hierarchical authority they wield. These managers perceive the shift of responsibility for work assignments and output evaluation to employees as a loss of authority and a change to a less satisfying role. As a result, they may resist empowerment efforts.

On the other hand, some employees mistake empowerment for discretionary authority – that is, the power to decide things unilaterally – when a high level of communication and consultation is needed in even the most empowered situation. In addition managers may neglect to train employees in new skills.

ORGANIZATIONAL POLITICS

Any study of power and influence inevitably leads to the subject of 'politics'. Political processes form the dynamic that enables the formal organization to function. In a sense, power and politics act as the lubricant that enables the interdependent parts of the organization to operate smoothly together. Organizations that engage in empowerment open up the area of politics to more employees as they have spread the power base.

The word 'politics' may conjure up thoughts of illicit deals, favours and special personal relationships. This image of organizational politics whereby shrewd, often dishonest, practices are used to obtain influence is reflected in Machiavelli's classic sixteenth-century work, *The Prince*, which outlines how to obtain and hold power via political action. For that reason, political actions are also referred to in terms of 'Machiavellianism'.

Organizational politics may also be described in more positive terms as the art of using influence, authority and power to achieve goals.[26] These goals may be self-interested for an individual, group or department, or have an emphasis geared toward organizational goals. Ideally both are aligned so that personal interests also benefit the organization. Political skills, like technical skills, are a tool for getting things done. Managers should discuss the political ramifications of all decisions confronting a department, frequently and openly. They can use this to illustrate political realities and to explain the many nuances of good political planning.

Political activity is usually stronger where there are no prescribed routine answers or no stated policy. It also centres around the interpretation of existing policies and those situations involving value judgements. Any organization that attempts to reduce these arenas of political activity totally by instituting rules, regulations and policies from the top would quickly strangle in its own red tape.

The two traditions of organizational politics

To survive in a highly political environment requires particular skills, including the ability to recognize those who are working through agendas despite surface appearances of openness and cooperation. It also requires the ability to identify the power sources of the key players and to build your own alliances and connections. There are two quite different traditions in the analysis of organizational politics.

POLITICS AS UNSANCTIONED AND SELF-INTERESTED

This first tradition builds on Machiavelli's philosophy and defines politics in terms of self-interest and the use of unsanctioned means. In this tradition, organizational politics may be formally defined as the management of influence to obtain ends not sanctioned by the organization, or to obtain sanctioned ends through unsanctioned means of influence. Managers are often considered political when they seek their own goals or use means not currently authorized by the organization.[27] It is also important to recognize that where there is uncertainty or ambiguity it is often extremely difficult to tell whether a manager is being political in this self-serving sense.

Organizational politics *is the management of influence to obtain ends not sanctioned by the organization, or to obtain sanctioned ends through nonsanctioned means of influence.*

ORGANIZATIONALLY SANCTIONED POLITICS

The second tradition treats politics as a necessary function resulting from differences in the perceived self-interest of individuals or groups. Sanctioned organizational politics is viewed as the art of compromise among competing interests. In a heterogeneous society, individuals will disagree on whose interest is most valuable and whose concerns should be bounded by collective interests, this applies at the personal level but also at the functional level. For example should a potential customer be put through a credit check before or after a sale is closed? The sales team would suggest after, the finance team before. Politics arise because there is a need to develop compromises, avoid confrontation and live together. Thus organizational politics is about the use of power to develop socially acceptable ends and means that balance individual and collective interests.

THE PERCEPTION OF POLITICAL BEHAVIOUR

The study of power and political behaviour has been described as consistent, logical and finite in many books over many years. However, there are some arguments to suggest that this approach is limiting us in our understanding of how power and politics might actually work in organizations. Power is usually studied in terms of 'sources' of power, as in this chapter. However, there are arguments against a 'sources-of-power' approach, with power being defined instead as a force created by differences. Power can be seen as a far more social and cultural phenomenon where differences are perceived within a socially constructed reality developed through the shared meanings of culture. Thus, you may have power in relation to another person because that person perceives that you have something that he or she does not. This approach is useful in helping to explain not just individual power relations but also power and politics that occurs in groups and organizational structures.[28] These perceived differences emerge, in part, from the wider social distinctions in society such as class, gender, law and education.[29]

The cultural approach to power and politics widens our understanding of political behaviour as being about social change. Different male and female management styles, as well as a range of different ethnic and other aspects of diversity in organizations may increase differences, or perceived differences, in organizations and challenge the existing way that problems are framed there.[30] Earlier we mentioned the idea of 'prototypes' and that prototypes can be the ideal of any group. We used this to think of great managers and leaders. However the cultural approach validates other uses for the prototype, for example – a wonderful woman manager, an excellent black architect. Political behaviour is not necessarily about self-interest, with people stepping outside the accepted rules. Political behaviour does not have to be about advancing self-interest, although it may be about advancing specific interests within organizations. While we understand position power as being linked to authority, rewards and coercion, in this alternative understanding political behaviour provides a wider view of social order.[31]

ORGANIZATIONAL POLITICS IN ACTION

Political action is a part of organizational life; it is best to view organizational politics for its potential to contribute to managerial and organizational effectiveness. It is in this spirit that we now examine political action in organizations from the perspectives of managers, subunits and chief executives. Organizational politics occurs in different ways and across different levels in the organization.

Office politics and the informal network

An organizational chart can show who is the boss and who reports to whom. But this formal chart will not reveal which people confer on technical matters or enter into discussions over lunch, which shape attitudes and beliefs on who has and who has not got power and influence. Much of the real work of an organization is achieved through this informal organization with its complex network of relationships that cross between functions and divisions.

As organizations continue to flatten their structures and rely on teams (see Chapter 6), managers need to understand these informal networks. To thrive in the political landscape of the workplace, it is a good idea to be aware of the 'prototypes' and become allied with these admired people (with referent power) but to focus your concern on your tasks rather than engaging in politics for the sake of it, as unless one is very skilled or powerful, this can backfire.

Political action and the manager

Managers will gain a better understanding of political behaviour by placing themselves in the positions of the other people involved in critical decisions or events. Each action and decision can be seen as having benefits and costs to all parties concerned. Where the costs exceed the benefits, people may act to protect themselves. Being prepared for such reactions can take some time and might also involve some research, especially if you are new to an organization. However it is well worth doing as then you can at least work out some scenarios and think through the various tactics that might be used to influence others, choosing the one most likely to have the desired effect given other's circumstances.

The use of political power requires two sets of attributes: competence and political intelligence. The first (and probably most important) strategy for improving an individual's political intelligence is to be able to read the work climate, preferably before beginning work.

COUNTERPOINT

Consider the Steve Jobs case on page 467.

- If you were his personal assistant for a year, what types of power would you have after this time?
- What potential influence would you have and with whom?

- What might be the ethical dilemmas you would face?
- How *might* you engage in political activity?
- How *would* you engage in political activity?

Political action and subunit power

Political action links managers more formally to one another as representatives of their work units. In Chapter 6 we examined the group dynamics associated with such intergroup relationships. Table 10.1 highlights five typical lateral and intergroup relationships in which managers may engage: work flow, service, advisory, auditing and approval relationships.[32]

Type of relationship	Sample influence requirements
Work flow – contacts with units that precede or follow in a sequential production chain	An assembly-line manager informs another line manager responsible for a later stage in the production process about a delay.
Service – contacts with units established to help with problems	An assembly-line manager asks the maintenance manager to fix an important piece of equipment as a priority.
Advisory – contacts with formal staff units that have special expertise	A marketing manager consults with the personnel manager to obtain special assistance in recruiting a new salesperson.
Auditing – contacts with units that have the right to evaluate the actions of others	A marketing manager tries to get the credit manager to retract a report criticizing marketing's tendency to open bad-credit accounts.
Approval – contacts with units whose approval must be obtained before action may be taken	A marketing manager submits a job description to the company affirmative action officer for approval before recruiting for a new salesperson can begin.

Table 10.2: Relationships of managers and associated influence requirements.

The table also shows how lateral relationships further challenge the political skills of a manager; each example requires the manager to achieve influence through some means other than formal authority.

To be effective in political action, managers should understand the politics of subunit relations. In general, units gain power as more of their relations with others are of the approval and auditing types. Workflow relations are more powerful than advisory associations, and both are more powerful than service relations. Units can increase their power by undertaking new actions that tackle and resolve difficult problems. Certain strategic contingencies can often govern the relative power of subunits. For a subunit to gain power, it must increase its control over:

- *access to scarce resources*. Subunits gain in power when they obtain access to, or control, scarce resources needed by others
- *the ability to cope with uncertainty*. Subunits gain in power when they are able to cope with uncertainty and help solve problems that uncertainty causes for others
- *centrality in the flow of work*. Subunits gain in power when their position in the work flow allows them to influence the work of others
- *substitutability of activities*. Subunits gain in power when they perform tasks or activities that are nonsubstitutable – that is, when they perform essential functions that others cannot complete.[33]

Political action and resource dependencies

Executive behaviour can sometimes be explained in terms of resource dependencies – that is, the organization's need for resources that others control. Essentially, the resource dependence of an organization increases as:

- needed resources become more scarce
- outsiders have more control over needed resources
- there are fewer substitutes for a particular type of resource controlled by a limited number of outsiders.[34]

Thus, one political role of chief executives is to develop workable compromises among the competing resource dependencies facing the organization – compromises that enhance the executive's power. To create such compromises, executives need to diagnose the relative power of outsiders and to craft strategies that respond differently to various external resource suppliers.

ORGANIZATIONAL GOVERNANCE

Organizational governance refers to the pattern of authority, influence and acceptable managerial behaviour established at the top of the organization. This system establishes what is important, how issues will be defined, who should and should not be involved in key choices, and the boundaries for acceptable implementation. Those studying organizational governance suggest that a 'dominant coalition' comprising powerful organizational actors is a key to its understanding.[35]

While you might expect many top officers within the organization to be members of this coalition, the dominant coalition occasionally includes outsiders with access to key resources. Thus, analysis of organizational governance builds on the resource dependence perspective by highlighting the effective control of key resources by members of a dominant coalition. The issue of the governance and accountability of corporations has recently come to the fore following a wave of high-profile corporate scandals and collapses. Undoubtedly the highest profile examples are US companies Enron and WorldCom, where a very large number of employees were left without jobs and pensions, and stakeholders (including stockholders) were taken by surprise when the collapses occurred. These two events made many employees and stockholders revisit their levels of knowledge and their trust in top management teams.[36] In both instances senior executives were allowed to drift into poor practice for some time without being discovered or challenged.

A strong governance system will ensure that the dominant coalition defines a reality which is accurate. The idea of groupthink has already been considered (see Chapter 6) and a recent review in the US suggests that selection onto boards continues to favour prototypical members.[37] Nonexecutive directors are experienced people from outside the organization who have a position on the board and, not being involved with the day-to-day management, can help ensure that the executive directors take an independent view, as far as possible.

In some sectors (such as retail banking) governments impose rules for governance. For example in the UK, finance institutions must submit to being inspected by the Financial Services Authority (FSA). Mutually owned finance organizations (termed 'building societies' in the UK) are one such type of organization. The FSA has recently suggested that nonexecutive directors should only hold position for nine years and that the board should have a majority of nonexecutive directors. In this way the FSA is attempting to ensure that the sheer number of nonexecutives and also their freshness will enhance decisions and prevent any underhand action on the part of the executives.[38] Similar motives to balance opinion are an aspect behind the German work councils and EC directives to ensure workers have a voice within their organizations.

Organizational governance *is the pattern of authority, influence and acceptable managerial behaviour established at the top of the organization.*

THE CONSEQUENCES OF POWER AND POLITICS

Whether or not organizational politics is good or bad may be a matter of perspective and depend on each situation and the outputs. It may be good for an individual but not for the organization, or individuals might suffer but the organization might be better off.

On the positive side it can serve a number of important functions, including helping managers to:

- *overcome personnel inadequacies.* As a manager, you should expect some mismatches between people and positions in organizations. Even in the best managed organizations, some managers will be learning and others burned out or lacking the resources needed to accomplish their assigned duties. Organizational politics provides a mechanism for circumventing these inadequacies and getting the job done
- *cope with change.* Changes in the environment and technology of an organization often come more quickly than an organization can restructure formally. All organizations encounter unanticipated events and to rise to such challenges, people and resources must be moved into place quickly before small headaches become major problems. Organizational politics can help to bring effective decision making to bear and move appropriate, problem-solving managers into the breach
- *substitute for formal authority.* When a person's formal authority breaks down or fails to apply to a particular situation, political actions can be used to prevent a loss of influence. Managers may use political behaviour to maintain operations and to achieve task continuity in circumstances in which the failure of formal authority may otherwise cause problems.

There are negatives, however. Politics can pervade organizations and act against necessary changes. Chapter 12, on change management, emphasizes how important political issues are in achieving successful change. Where a dominant group is against moves that are needed, change initiatives can be stopped in their tracks.

Some individuals view political tactics to be highly counterproductive because they may be used to discredit and disable often more able colleagues.[39]

There may be cases in which politics dominates organizational activity to an extent that the activity is dysfunctional. Alternatively, it is unlikely that political behaviour never occurs, and if such a case existed it might be equally dysfunctional. The following sections on ethics and trust give further insight into political behaviour.

THE ETHICS OF POWER AND POLITICS

All managers use power and politics to get their work done but every employee also bears a responsibility to work in an ethical and socially responsible fashion. By recognizing and confronting ethical considerations, each of us should be better prepared to meet this important challenge. No treatment of power and politics in organizations is complete without considering the related ethical issues. We can begin this task by clarifying the distinction between the nonpolitical and political uses of power.[40]

Power is nonpolitical when it remains within the boundaries of usually formal authority, organizational policies and procedures, and job descriptions, and when it is directed towards ends sanctioned by the organization. When the use of power moves outside the realm of authority, policies, procedures and job descriptions, or when it is directed towards ends not sanctioned by the organization, that use of power is said to be political.

COUNTERPOINT

On 5 February 2007, *PR Week* reported that Todd Thomson, chief of Citigroup's wealth management unit was removed partly for his dealings with CNBC reporter Maria Bartiromo. Maria apparently took trips on the Citigroup jet, actions which were considered improper by Citigroup officials. However, CNBC defended the issue, stating that they have a system whereby such trips were pre-approved within the journalists' ethics code.

It is often the case that reporters buy their interviewees a drink or lunch and vice versa. But where should one draw the line?

Questions

1. If you worked for Citibank, where would you draw the line?

2. If you worked for a newspaper where would you draw the line?

3. If you were a reporter and had accepted a good lunch or a flight on a jet, would you feel obliged to file a positive report on the hosting organization?

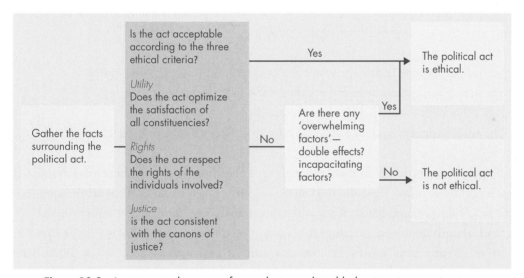

Figure 10.3: An integrated structure for analysing political behaviour in organizations.

Source: Velasquez, M., Moberg, D.J., & Cavanagh, G.F., (1983), Organizational statesmanship and dirty politics: ethical guidelines for the organizational politician, *Organizational Dynamics*, **11**: 73, Elsevier

It is in this context that a manager must stop and consider more than a pure 'ends justify the means' logic. These issues are broader and involve distinctly ethical questions. Work in the area of ethical issues in power and politics suggests the usefulness of the integrated structure for analysing political behaviour depicted in Figure 10.3. This structure suggests that a person's behaviour must satisfy the following criteria to be considered ethical.[41]

- *Utilitarian outcomes.* The behaviour results in optimization of satisfactions of people both inside and outside the organization; that is, it produces the greatest good for the greatest number of people.

- *Individual rights.* The behaviour respects the rights of all affected parties; that is, it respects basic human rights of free consent, free speech, freedom of conscience, privacy and due process.
- *Distributive justice.* The behaviour respects the rules of justice; that is, it treats people equitably and fairly, as opposed to arbitrarily.

The figure also indicates that there may be times when a behaviour is unable to pass these criteria but can still be considered ethical in the given situation. This special case must satisfy the criterion of overwhelming factors, in which the special nature of the situation results in:

- conflicts among criteria (for example, a behaviour results in some good and some bad)
- conflicts within criteria (for example, a behaviour uses questionable means to achieve a positive end)
- an incapacity to employ the criteria (for example, a person's behaviour is based on inaccurate or incomplete information).

Choosing to be ethical often involves considerable personal sacrifice. Four rationalizations are often used to justify unethical choices.

- Individuals feel the behaviour is not really illegal and thus could be moral.
- The action appears to be in the organization's best interests.
- It is unlikely the action will ever be detected.
- The action appears to demonstrate loyalty to the boss or the organization.

While these rationalizations may appear compelling at the moment of action, each deserves close scrutiny. The individual must ask: 'How far is too far?' 'What are the long-term interests of the organization?' 'What will happen when (not if) the action is discovered?' 'Do individuals, groups or organizations that ask for unethical behaviour deserve my loyalty?'[42]

Our chapter now moves its focus to that of decision making. When reading the remainder, remember that ethics need to inform all decisions.

DECISION MAKING

In today's global and highly competitive markets, organizations live and die on the choices made by their members (managers and others) and the extent to which these members can effectively learn to define and make better choices. Decision making really does lie at the heart of successful organizations. Managers need to be aware of all consequences when making decisions, including those beyond their own immediate goals. This section of the chapter evaluates some decision-making models, and processes.

Henry Mintzberg is famous for his work on managerial roles. His research – based on following CEOs around during their working days – suggests that, in performing their tasks, they fulfil 10 distinct roles broadly classified into interpersonal roles, informational roles and decision roles. In the latter category he defined decision making as the process of choosing a course of action for solving a problem or seizing an opportunity.[44] The choice usually involves two or more possible alternatives. Considered diagramatically, it looks like Figure 10.4.

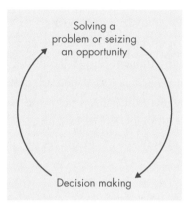

Figure 10.4: Defining decision making – getting things done.

Types of managerial decisions

Two basic types of managerial decisions are distinguished by the presence of routine and nonroutine problems in the work situation. Routine problems are those that arise regularly and can be addressed through standard responses, called programmed decisions. These responses implement solutions that have already been determined by past experience as appropriate for the problem at hand. Examples of programmed decisions are the automatic reordering of inventory when stock falls below a predetermined level and issuing a written reprimand to someone who violates a personnel procedure. The decisions are often the focus of quality improvement initiatives, which seek to find optimal solutions for all situations.

Nonroutine problems are unique and new. When standard responses are not available, creative problem solving is called for. These crafted decisions are specifically tailored to a situation and take more time, sometimes involving many people. Senior managers will spend a greater proportion of their decision-making time on nonroutine problems. An example is the marketing manager who must counter a competitor's introduction of a new product from abroad. Although past experience may help, the immediate decision requires a solution based on the unique characteristics of the present situation.

Decision environments

When making routine or nonroutine decisions, managers do so in environments that can be thought of as certain, uncertain, and risky (which is neither certain nor uncertain). These will now be discussed in turn.

Certain environments exist when information is sufficient to predict the results of each alternative in advance of implementation. When a person invests money in a savings account, for example, absolute certainty exists about the interest that the money will earn in a given period of time. Certainty is an ideal condition for managerial problem decision making

Routine problems are problems that arise routinely and that can be addressed through standard responses.

Nonroutine problems are unique and new problems that call for creative problem solving.

Certain environments are decision environments in which information is sufficient to predict the results of each alternative in advance of implementation.

where one locates the most satisfactory solution and represents areas where empowerment of junior staff can be appropriate. In such circumstances 'management by exception' can be used where the manager only gets involved if something unusual occurs.

Uncertain environments are the most difficult and exist when managers are unable to assign probabilities to the outcomes of various problem-solving alternatives. It requires unique, novel and often totally innovative alternatives to existing patterns of behaviour. Responses to uncertainty are often heavily influenced by intuition, educated guesses and hunches, which in turn are heavily influenced by perception. Some people work in environments that are full of uncertainty, such as those who are developing new products or scientists. Others work in environments which have far more routine and certainty. People in the latter situation often find it difficulty to label their circumstance, as they are so used to routine – as the following OB in action box illustrates.

Uncertain environments
are decision environments in which managers are unable to assign probabilities to the possible outcomes of various courses of action.

OB IN ACTION

The 9/11 Commission report is an extraordinary document.[44] It charts, minute by minute, the events leading up to the hijackings and subsequent chaos. Aircraft controllers know about hijacking although fortunately very few have needed to handle such situations. What had not occurred before was multiple simultaneous hijackings. As such, command systems were in place but the speed of events overtook the decision-making process. Hence military aircraft were scrambled to follow the first plane into New York but were not given coordinates and were absent when the first plane hit the World Trade Centre. The following exchange was recorded after the second plane had hit in New York, and relates to another (United 93) working its way to Washington:

FAA Headquarters: They're pulling Jeff away to go talk about United 93.
Command Centre: Uh, do we want to think, uh, about scrambling aircraft?

FAA Headquarters: Oh, God, I don't know.
Command Centre: Uh, that's a decision somebody's gonna have to make probably in the next ten minutes.
FAA Headquarters: Uh, ya know, everybody just left the room.[45]

This aircraft was subsequently lost from radar but was then spotted by other planes and eventually crashed after passengers counterattacked. No one from the FAA had passed on information about United 93 to the military and no one had requested military assistance. It crashed before any decisions were made.

RISK ANALYSIS

Risk environments involve a lack of complete certainty regarding the outcomes of various courses of action but some awareness of the probabilities associated with their occurrence.

Undertaking risk analysis uses two steps; assigning a probability to the likelihood that an event will occur and then assessing the impact of the event if it did occur. Assessments are usually made with a mixture of evidence and intuition and scores are usually simplified into high/med/low or other short scale. The two scores (probability and likelihood) are then multiplied together. Risk analysis prioritizes risks in terms of importance based on the scores. By articulating the actual risks (to whom and what), enables one to analyse who and what might be affected by the decision and work through who might be involved in the decision-making process.[46]

These risk analyses enable desk-based evaluation to identify areas of high risk. Action can then be taken to eliminate or moderate the risk. Action is guided by examining how to lessen the likelihood of the risk occurring or lessen its impact.

Risk environments *are decision environments that involve a lack of complete certainty but that include an awareness of probabilities associated with the possible outcomes of various courses of action.*

Steps in the decision-making process

Managers make decisions throughout their working day and the four basic steps in systematic decision making are shown in Figure 10.5. The first step is to recognize that a problem or opportunity exists and that something must be done about it. But, more than this, the real nature of the problem or opportunity has to be defined and assessed. A human resource manager investigating the low levels of job satisfaction indicated in an employee survey must first determine the root cause of the problem (low wages, poor physical conditions and so on) before making any attempt to solve the problem. The key is accurate information that is carefully evaluated.

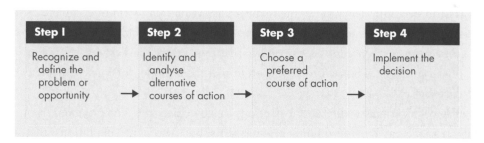

Step 1	Step 2	Step 3	Step 4
Recognize and define the problem or opportunity	Identify and analyse alternative courses of action	Choose a preferred course of action	Implement the decision

Figure 10.5: The decision-making process.

The next step is to pose alternative courses of action to remedy the situation and select the criteria to be used when assessing the relative merits of alternative. Criteria might include ceilings on costs, industry specifications, work experience, ease of use, maintenance requirements and so on. Usually, two or more alternatives are available and they measure up against the assessment criteria in different ways. If poor physical conditions are found to be the root cause of the HR problem just mentioned then the alternative solutions might include moving to a new factory site or refitting the existing facility. Minimizing the cost and production time lost is among the criteria important to management in their search for a solution.

The choice is made during step three, after analysing the various alternatives and implementation of the decision choice occurs during step four.[47]

APPROACHES TO DECISION MAKING

Organizational behaviour theorists maintain that there are two alternative approaches to decision making (Figure 10.6) – classical and behavioural.[48]

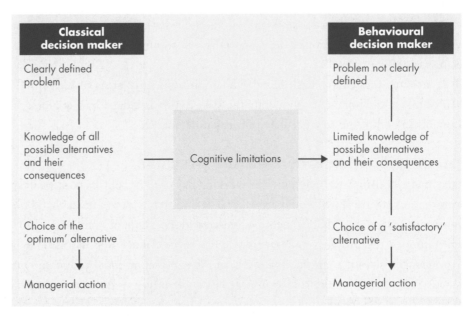

Figure 10.6: Approaches to decision making.

Classical decision theory *views the manager as acting in a world of complete certainty.*

Classical decision theory views the manager as acting in a world of complete certainty. The manager faces a clearly defined problem, knows all possible action alternatives and their consequences, then chooses the alternative that offers the best or 'optimum' resolution of the problem. Classical theory is often used as a model for how managers should make decisions.

Behavioural scientists are more cautious, recognizing the human mind is a wonderful creation, capable of infinite achievements but also with limitations that mean nonoptimal solutions are achieved. Behaviourists suggest the human mind is limited in its information-processing capabilities, which can overload and thus compromise the ability of managers to make decisions according to the classical model. Behavioural decision theory

Behavioural decision theory *refers to the idea that people act only in terms of what they perceive about a given situation.*

states that people act only in terms of what they perceive about a given situation where the decision maker is seen as acting under uncertainty and with limited information.

Managers make decisions about problems that are often ambiguous; they have only a partial knowledge about the available action alternatives and their consequences; they choose the first alternative that appears to give a satisfactory resolution of the problem. This model is referred to by Herbert Simon as a satisficing style of decision making.[49] Simon and his colleagues suggest that in actuality we seek the discovery and selection of *satisfactory* alternatives; only in exceptional cases are we concerned with the discovery and selection of *optimal* decisions.

The key difference between a manager's ability to make an optimum decision in the classical style and the tendency to make a satisficing (or good enough) decision in the behavioural style is the presence of cognitive limitations and their impact on our perceptions. Cognitive limitations impair our abilities to define problems, identify action alternatives and choose alternatives – the key steps in the decision-making process.

IN ACTION

The precautionary principle

The precautionary principle works on the basis that it is better to be safe than sorry. In a way, the principle limits personal perception of scientific data, and directs decision makers to err on the side of caution if the consequences of making the wrong decision are serious or irreversible.[50] For example, what level of scientific certainty on global warming is needed before organizations rethink their policies? According to many scientists, one of the causes of global warming is the destruction of rainforests. In particular, the clearing of South American rainforests is controversial; while governments allow communities to destroy the forests in order to survive, industrialized nations are condemning these practices as being dangerous to the global environment. In response, and based on the precautionary principle, the US pharmaceutical giant Merck & Company Inc has found a creative solution to the commercialization of the rainforest much desired by locals – a solution that does not include the destruction of trees. Merck has an agreement worth US$1 million with the Costa Rican Government for the right to search for usable species within the rainforest. In addition, the company will share 5% of future royalties on any drug it develops from a species obtained in the Costa Rican rainforests. The Merck venture is significantly boosting the Costa Rican national budget of just over US$1 billion. Further, Costa Rica has preserved 25% of its natural environment with the help of Merck and other corporate venturers who have made the areas productive. As any royalties begin to filter into the Costa Rican government they will allow it to preserve even more of the natural environment.[51]

INTUITION AND DECISION MAKING

A key element in successfully making nonroutine decisions is intuition. Intuition is the ability to know or recognize quickly and readily the possibilities of a given situation.[52] Intuition offers the potential for greater creativity and innovation, which are needed in risky and uncertain environments. A debate among scholars regarding how managers really plan highlights the importance of intuition for the practising manager. On one side of the issue are those who believe that planning can be taught and carried out in a systematic step-by-step fashion. On the other side are those who believe that the nature of managerial work is far more 'fuzzy', cannot be taught in this systematic way and that intuition has a fundamental role to play.

Intuition *is the ability to know or recognize quickly and readily the possibilities of a given situation.*

The ideas of Henry Mintzberg illustrate this.[53]

- Managers favour relational or interactive communications. Hence they prefer to obtain others' impressions and feelings about decisions, options and probabilities, rather than just a set of facts, in a way that would be hard to systematize on paper.
- Managers often deal with impressions. They are more likely to synthesize than analyse data as they search for the 'big picture' to make decisions.
- Managers work fast, do a variety of things and are frequently interrupted. Hence they do not have a lot of quiet time alone to think, plan or make decisions systematically.

One might suggest that managers should systematically plan in a step-by-step manner, but the realities of modern working life and its demands generally preclude such opportunities; hence they hone their intuitive skills. However there can be drawbacks. Some commentators think mistakes are often a result of overreliance on intuition rather than objective facts. This can occur because experience combined with intuition can lead to snap judgements that are made before all objective evidence is available for evaluation.[55] In addition, conclusions made by different individuals on the same evidence can vary greatly as decision makers are largely seeking confirmation of their initial hunches or suspicions and do not view information objectively.[55]

On the other hand, it would be naïve to suggest that decisions are best made by ignoring your intuition. In fact there are some individuals who are routinely required to make intuitive decisions, especially those who work in the emergency services (police, paramedics, hospital staff and firefighters). Intuition is said to be an instantaneous, emotional and often irrational reaction to a situation that can be risky. However, it is also said to be a fast analytical reasoning that is clearly based on experience and practice drills, where judgement is simply analysis 'frozen into habit'. Confident decision makers will generally use a combination of logic and intuition to arrive at a sound decision.[56]

THE USE OF JUDGEMENT HEURISTICS

Heuristics
are simplifying strategies or 'rules of thumb' that people use when making decisions.

Judgement, or the use of the intellect, is important in all aspects of decision making. Analysing alternative courses of action and choosing one course (steps 2 and 3 in the decision-making process) involve making judgements.

Research shows that managers and others use heuristics – simplifying strategies or 'rules of thumb' – when making decisions. Heuristics are useful if they deal with uncertainty and limited information, but they can also lead to systematic errors.[57]

MAKING A CHOICE AND IMPLEMENTING A DECISION

Now we turn our attention to steps 3 and 4 in our model. Look back again at Figure 10.6. Once alternative solutions to a problem or opportunity have been developed, a preferred course of action must be chosen and that decision needs to be implemented, because management is about action! The overall aim is to achieve the best result using the least resources, and creating the least amount of risk and uncertainty (if that is possible).

COUNTERPOINT

Setting budgets for expenditure in many organizations, especially those in the public sector, revolves around 'last year and a bit more'. At the end of the financial year while some departments might struggle to contain their expenditure, others spend very freely because otherwise next year they will have their budget cut in a 'use it or lose it' mentality. In such circumstances optimal and logical decision making does not prevail.[58]

Take a few minutes to consider this from the following stakeholder positions:

• the finance director
• the CEO
• the manager of a department and his/her staff.

When it comes to managing the decision-making process, we can say that an effective manager is one who is able to pick precisely which problems are amenable to managerial decision making. Managers are too busy and have too many things to do with their valuable time to respond personally by making decisions on every problem or opportunity that comes their way. The effective manager knows when to delegate decisions to others, how to set priorities and when to empower others.

When confronted with a problem, therefore, managers ask themselves the following questions:[59]

• is the problem easy to deal with? Small and less significant problems should not get as much time and attention as bigger ones. Even if a mistake is made, the cost of decision error is also small

• might the problem resolve itself? Putting problems in rank order leaves the less significant for last. Surprisingly, many of these less important problems will resolve themselves as they will be related to other issues anyway

• is this my decision to make? Routine problems can and should be delegated. Other problems can and should be referred to higher levels. This is especially true for decisions that have consequences for a larger part of the organization – more so than for those under a manager's immediate control.

To these three questions we add one of our own:

• given the power and politics within the organization, who is best suited to be involved with and take this decision?

Strategies for involvement – who decides?

One mistake made by many new managers is to presume that they must solve the problems and make the decisions themselves. In practice, decisions are made in the following ways:

• *individual decisions*. Managers make the final choice alone based on information that they possess and without the participation of others. Sometimes called an authority decision, this approach often reflects the manager's position of formal authority in the organization

- *consultative decisions.* The manager solicits inputs on the problem from other people. Based on this information and its interpretation, the manager then makes a final choice
- *group decisions.* The manager asks others to participate in discussions and in the decision choice. Although sometimes difficult, the group decision is the most participative of the three methods of final choice and the one that seeks true group consensus.

Good decisions can be made by each method – individual, consultative or group – if the method fits the needs of the situation.\

EFFECTIVE MANAGER 10.3

Improving organizational problem-solving skills.

Effective managers often focus on the process of problem solving and pay great attention to who is involved and that the interactions are positive. They:
- believe that most problems can be solved
- ensure there is organizational commitment to solving problems. If top management is committed to continual improvement then a strong message is sent to the rest of the organization
- let people know that solving problems is part of their jobs and that they are

accountable for solving their day-to-day problems
- ensure employees receive training in problem solving
- recognize when problems have been solved and praise successful problem solving
- ensure teams communicate their successful problem solving so other teams benefit from their experience
- work towards problem solving becoming a habit of every employee.[60]

MANAGING PARTICIPATION IN DECISION MAKING

Victor Vroom, Philip Yetton and Arthur Jago have developed a framework for helping managers to choose which of the three decision-making methods is most appropriate for the various problem situations encountered in their daily work efforts.[61] Their framework begins by expanding the three basic decision-making methods just discussed into the following five forms.

- AI (first variant on the authority decision). The manager solves the problem or makes the decision alone, using information available at that time.
- AII (second variant on the authority decision). The manager obtains the necessary information from employees or other group members, then decides on the solution to the problem. The manager may or may not tell employees what the problem is before obtaining the information from them. The employees provide the necessary information but do not generate or evaluate alternatives.

- CI (first variant on the consultative decision). The manager shares the problem with relevant employees or other group members individually, collecting their ideas and suggestions without bringing them together as a group. The manager then makes a decision that may or may not reflect the employees' inputs.
- CII (second variant on the consultative decision). The manager shares the problem with employees or other group members, collectively obtaining their ideas and suggestions. The manager then makes a decision that may or may not reflect the employees' inputs.
- G (the group or consensus decision). The manager shares the problem with the employees as a total group and engages the group in consensus seeking to arrive at a final decision.

The central proposition in this model is that the decision-making method used should always be appropriate to the problem being solved. The challenge is to know when and how to implement each of the possible decision methods as the situation requires.

Vroom and Jago use a flow chart to help managers analyse the unique attributes of a situation and use the most appropriate decision method for the problem at hand. Key issues involve the quality requirements of a decision, the availability and location of the relevant information, the commitments needed for follow-through and the amount of time available.

The Vroom and Jago model at first seems complex and cumbersome yet there is a useful discipline in the model: it helps you recognize how time, quality requirements, information availability and employee acceptance issues can affect decision outcomes. It also helps you to remember that all of the decision methods are important and useful. The key to effectively managing participation in decision making is evident: know how to implement each decision method in situations for which it is most suited and then do it well.

HOW GROUPS MAKE DECISIONS

Edgar Schein, a noted scholar and consultant, has worked extensively with groups to analyse and improve their decision-making processes. He observes that groups may make decisions through any of the following six methods:[62]

- decision by lack of response. A course of action is chosen by default or lack of interest
- decision by authority rule. One person dominates and determines the course of action
- decision by minority rule. A small subgroup dominates and determines the course of action
- decision by majority rule. A vote is taken to choose among alternative courses of action
- decision by consensus. Not everyone wants to pursue the same course of action but everyone agrees to try it
- decision by unanimity. Everyone in the group wants to pursue the same course of action.

Consider the role power and politics might play in Schein's six methods.

Groupthink

Groupthink *is the tendency of members in highly cohesive groups to lose their critical, evaluative capabilities.*

Social psychologist Irving Janis defines groupthink as the tendency of members in highly cohesive groups to lose their critical, evaluative capabilities.[63] Groupthink is a rationalization process that develops when group members begin to think alike. It can be encouraged by leaders who do not tolerate dissent. It can develop when employees underestimate potential problems.

Groupthink is also a mode of thinking that people engage in when they are deeply involved in a cohesive ingroup and when the quest for unanimity overrides their motivation to realistically appraise alternative courses of action.

OB IN ACTION

Seventy-three seconds after its launch on 28 January 1986, the *Challenger* space shuttle exploded, killing the seven astronauts aboard. The cause of the explosion was found to be the failure of the O-ring seals on the solid rocket booster joints on the space shuttle. In the year prior to the *Challenger* launch, test launches and numerous investigations had shown that in low temperatures the O-ring seals failed to seal the joints, leaving them vulnerable to the high temperatures created at launch and thus increasing the possibility of explosion.

The day before the *Challenger* launch, managers were made aware of the low temperature forecast for the launch date and a meeting was called between managers and senior engineers. The engineers presented compelling data that a launch with an outside temperature of –7.8°C was dangerous and strongly recommended against launching *Challenger*. NASA managers, burdened by the economic consequences of the delayed launch, argued for continuation of the mission.

Eventually the engineers' concerns were dismissed as the head of the management team,

Jerry Mason, turned to Bob Lund, vice-president of engineering, and asked him to 'take off his engineering hat and put on his management hat'. After some discussion, it was unanimously recommended that the *Challenger* mission go ahead as scheduled.[64]

Further information and an analysis of groupthink symptoms in this case can be obtained by watching the video *A Major Malfunction*.[65]

During groupthink, small groups develop shared illusions and related norms that interfere with critical thinking and reality testing. Some symptoms of groupthink are arrogance, overcommitment and excessive loyalty to the group. Other symptoms of groupthink are found in Effective Manager 10.4. They can be used to help spot this phenomenon in practice.

EFFECTIVE MANAGER 10.4
Groupthink

Janis suggests the following action guidelines for best dealing with groupthink.[66]

- Assign the role of critical evaluator to each group member; encourage a sharing of objections.
- The leader should avoid seeming partial to one course of action.
- Create subgroups operating under different leaders and working on the same problem.
- Have group members discuss issues with employees and report back on their reactions.
- Invite outside experts to observe group activities and to react to group processes and decisions.
- Assign one member of the group to play a 'devil's advocate' role at each meeting.
- Write alternative scenarios for the intentions of competing groups.
- Hold a 'second-chance' meeting after consensus is apparently achieved on key issues.
- Spot the symptoms of 'groupthink':
  - *Illusions of group invulnerability. Members believe the group is beyond criticism or attack.*
  - *Rationalizing unpleasant data. Members refuse to accept or thoroughly consider contradictory data or new information.*

- *Belief in inherent group morality. Members believe the group is 'right' and above reproach by outsiders.*
- *Negative stereotyping of outsiders. Members refuse to look realistically at other groups; they may view competitors as weak, evil or stupid.*
- *Applying pressure to deviants. Members refuse to tolerate anyone who suggests that the group might be wrong; every attempt is made to obtain conformity to group wishes.*
- *Self-censorship by members. Members are unwilling to communicate personal concerns or alternative points of view to the group as a whole.*
- *Illusions of unanimity. Members are quick to accept consensus; they do so prematurely and without testing its completeness.*
- *Mind guarding. Members of the group keep outsiders away and try to protect the group from hearing disturbing ideas or viewpoints.*

TECHNIQUES FOR IMPROVING DECISION MAKING IN GROUPS

As you can see, the process of making decisions in any group is a complex and delicate one. Group dynamics must be well managed to balance individual contributions and group operations. The following equation helps keep this point in mind:[67]

$$\text{Group decision effectiveness} = \text{individual contributions} + \text{group process gains} - \text{group process losses}$$

When do you back down?

We mentioned at the beginning of this section that effective managers should be making good decisions, and that they should be prepared to override previous commitments and discontinue courses of action that are just not working. Often this means being bold and decisive! However, many managers fall into the trap of escalating commitment. Recognized by social psychologists as common and potentially dysfunctional, it is the tendency to continue with a previously chosen course of action even though feedback indicates that it is not working.

Escalating commitment is encouraged by the popular adage: 'If at first you don't succeed, try, try again.' Current wisdom in organizational behaviour supports an alternative view: good decision makers know when to call it quits. They are willing to reverse previous decisions and commitments, and thereby avoid further investments in unsuccessful courses of action. However, the self-discipline required to admit mistakes and change courses of action is sometimes difficult to achieve. Often the tendency to escalate commitments to previously chosen courses of action outweighs the willingness to disengage from them. This occurs as decision makers:

- rationalize negative feedback as simply a temporary condition
- protect their egos and avoid admitting the original decision was a mistake
- use the decision as a way of managing the impressions of others, such as a boss or peers
- view the negative results as a 'learning experience' that can be overcome with added future effort.

Escalating commitment is a form of decision entrapment that leads people to do things that are not justified by the facts of the situation. Managers should be proactive in spotting 'failures' and open to reversing decisions or dropping plans that do not appear to be working.[68]

CURRENT ISSUES IN ORGANIZATIONAL DECISION MAKING

In today's environments, the problems facing organizational decision makers seem to be harder and more complex. Prominent among the current issues relating to decision making in today's workplace are those dealing with culture technology and the development of risk analysis.

Culture and decision making

The forces of globalization and workforce diversity have brought increased attention to how culture may influence decision making. The cultural dimensions of power-distance and individualism–collectivism have special implications for decision making. Workers from high power-distance cultures may expect their supervisors to make the decisions and may be less inclined than individualists to expect or wish to be involved in decision-making processes.

Values relating to individualism–collectivism also affect cultural tendencies towards participation in decision making. Decision making in collectivist cultures tends to be time consuming, with every effort being made to gain consensus. The results are slower decisions but smooth implementation. Decision making in individualist cultures (such as the Germanic countries), by contrast, is oriented more towards being decisive, saving time and using voting to resolve disagreements. The results are often faster decisions with implementation problems and delays.[69]

Culture may even play a role in determining whether a decision is necessary at all – in other words, whether the situation should be changed. North Americans tend to perceive situations as problems to be solved and want to do something about them. Other cultures, such as Thai and Indonesian societies, are more prone to accept the status quo.[70]

Technology and decision making

There is no doubt that today's organizations are becoming more sophisticated in applying computer technologies to facilitate decision making. Developments in the field of artificial intelligence – the study of how computers can be programmed to think like the human brain – are many and growing.[71] Nobel laureate and decision scientist Herbert Simon is convinced that computers will some day be more intelligent that humans. Already the applications of artificial intelligence to organizational decision making are significant. We have access to decision-making support from expert systems that reason like a human expert and follow 'either/or' rules or heuristics to make deductions; we have fuzzy logic that reasons beyond either/or choices in more imprecise territory and neural networks that reason inductively by simulating the brain's parallel processing capabilities. Uses for such systems may be found everywhere from banks, where they may help screen loan applications, and hospitals, where they check laboratory results and possible drug interactions, to the factory floor, where they schedule machines and people for maximum production efficiencies.

Computer support for group decision making, including developments with the Internet and intranets, breaks the decision-making meeting out of the confines of face-to-face interactions. With the software now available, people working in geographically dispersed locations can define problems and make decisions together and simultaneously. Research confirms that group decision software can be especially useful for generating ideas, as in electronic brainstorming, and improving the time efficiency of decision making.[72] People working under electronically mediated conditions tend to stay focused on tasks and avoid the interpersonal conflicts and other problems common in face-to-face deliberations. On the negative side, decisions made by 'electronic groups' carry some risk of being impersonal and perhaps less compelling in terms of commitment to implementation and follow through, not in keeping with the softer information Mintzberg's original work with CEOs found so essential (see pages 490). There is evidence that the use of computer technology for decision making is better accepted by today's university or college students than by people who are already advanced in their organizational careers.[73]

EFFECTIVE MANAGER 10.5

Ask yourself the following questions to 'road test' your decisions.

- If the decision goes on the public record, how would I feel? If you would not be happy then

that is your inner self telling you that you are about to break your own moral code.

- How would you vindicate the decision to your close family members?

- What will this proposed course of action do to your character or the character of your organization? Reputation is a key business asset; making a decision that will irreparably damage that reputation is not a sound decision.
- Will everyone around you respond to the decision in the same way? If they cannot, then why should you be able to respond in that way?
- How would you like it if someone did this to you? If you would feel bad, then clearly others would probably not like it either.
- Will the proposed course of action bring about a good result for all involved? If the result is not good for all, then why are you doing it?

- Is the proposed course of action consistent with your espoused values and principles? Individuals make up an organization. In business life or personal life, individuals should always be true to their own values.
- Define decision making and the sequential steps in the decision-making process.
- Summarize and contrast the classical and behavioural decision-making models.
- Evaluate the contributions of intuition, judgement and risk analysis to quality decision making.
- State the conditions under which individuals or groups are best placed to make decisions in organizations.

SUMMARY

LEARNING OBJECTIVE 1
Power and its sources

Power is an essential managerial resource. It is demonstrated by the ability to get others to do what you want them to do. Power vested in managerial positions derives from three sources: rewards, punishments and legitimacy. Legitimacy, which is the same as formal authority, is based on managers' position in the hierarchy of authority and the information to which they have access. Personal power is based on a person's expertise and reference; it allows managers to extend their power beyond that which is available in their position alone.

LEARNING OBJECTIVE 2
The relationship between power, authority and obedience

Power, authority and obedience are interrelated. Obedience occurs when one individual responds to the request or directive of another person. In the Milgram experiments, it was shown that people may have a tendency to obey directives coming from others who appear powerful and authoritative, even if these directives seem contrary to what the individual would normally consider to be 'right'. A zone of indifference defines the boundaries within which people in organizations will let others influence their behaviour without questioning it. Ultimately, power and authority work only if the individual 'accepts' them.

LEARNING OBJECTIVE 3
Empowerment

Empowerment is the process through which managers help others acquire and use the power needed to make decisions that affect them and their work. Clear delegation of authority, integrated planning and the involvement of senior management are all important to implementing empowerment. However, the key to success lies in redefining power so everyone can gain. The redefinition emphasizes power as the ability to get things done rather than to get others to do what you want.

LEARNING OBJECTIVE 4
Political behaviour

Organizational politics is use of power to find ways of balancing individual and collective interests in otherwise difficult circumstances. Machiavellian politics involves the use of power to obtain ends not officially sanctioned, or to achieve sanctioned ends through unsanctioned means. Political action in organizations can be examined at the managerial, subunit and chief executive levels. It may also occur formally and informally. For the manager, politics often occur in decision situations in which the interests of another manager or individual must be reconciled with their own. Politics also involve subunits that jockey for power and advantageous positions.

LEARNING OBJECTIVE 5
The ethics of power and politics in an organization

The ethics of power and politics are common to those found in any decision situation. Managers can easily slip into questionable territory unless they keep their behaviour limited to the task in hand. All behaviour can be 'rationalized' as acceptable, however it must meet the personal test of ethical behaviour established in Chapter 1. When political behaviour is ethical, it will satisfy the criteria of utilitarian outcomes, individual rights, distributive justice and/or overwhelming factors.

LEARNING OBJECTIVE 6
Types of decision making and models

Decision making in organizations is a continuing process of identifying problems and opportunities and choosing from alternative options. According to classical decision theory, managers seek 'optimum' solutions, whereas behavioural decision theory recognizes that managers 'satisfice' and accept the first available satisfactory alternative.

Routine problems arise on a regular basis and can be resolved through standard responses called programmed decisions. Nonroutine problems require tailored responses referred to as crafted decisions. Managers make decisions in three different environments: certain, uncertain and risky. Under certainty, everything about the alternative solutions is known and a choice will lead to an outcome that is highly predictable. Under risk, the manager can estimate the likelihood and impact from situations using risk analysis. In uncertain environments the choice is made with little real knowledge of what might happen.

LEARNING OBJECTIVE 7
Steps in the decision-making process

The decision-making process involves four sequential steps: recognize and define a problem; identify and analyse alternative courses of action; choose a preferred course of action and implement the decision.

LEARNING OBJECTIVE 8
Intuition, judgement and risk analysis

Intuition, judgement and risk analysis are all critical in effective managerial decision making. Intuition – the ability to recognize the possibilities of a situation quickly – is increasingly considered an important managerial asset. Judgement is the use of cognitive skills to make choices among alternatives, but heuristics (or simplifying rules of thumb) can potentially bias decision making. Risk analysis is a technique to both evaluate the risk and option outcomes as well as identifying who might be involved in decisions.

LEARNING OBJECTIVE 9
Conditions for decision making

Managers must know how to involve others in decision making and how to choose among individual, consultative and group decision methods. This is often a complex process. The Vroom–Jago model identifies how decision methods can be varied to meet the unique needs of each problem situation, which will also involve the power and political climate. Typically, a group decision is based on more information and results in better member understanding and commitment. The liabilities include greater time requirement and the dangers of groupthink.

LEARNING OBJECTIVE 10
Contemporary issues facing today's managers

Globalization and workforce diversity have brought into play the significance of national culture in managerial decision making. Culture can affect, for example, who should make the decision and the speed of the decision-making process within the organization.

Computers are being used more and more to facilitate decision making, but it is important to recognize both the benefits and the limitations of these sophisticated artificial intelligence initiatives.

Risk analysis is one response to the drive for more decisions to be simulated and thus rehearsed before they are required. In this way the potential for making a poor decision is theoretically reduced through 'uncertain' situations being addressed and hence increasing decision quality overall.

CHAPTER 10 STUDY GUIDE

You can also test your understanding and access further resources at **www.wileyeurope. com/college/french.**

REVIEW QUESTIONS

1. Explain how power is acquired.
2. Explain some of the ethical implications of power and politics.
3. How might personal power differ from authority?
4. How would you know if you were making an ethical decision?
5. Explain the meaning and importance of empowerment in an organizational context.
6. How might risk analysis have improved a difficult decision situation you know about?

APPLICATION QUESTIONS

1. Often students at university are required to work in groups with people they have never met before. When choosing potential group members how do you decide who you are going to work with? In your answer please explain the decision-making environments.
2. A member of your staff has put together a business plan to produce and market a new product. The plan is very comprehensive and conservative figures estimate that the new product would be highly profitable for your organization. However, your previous experience with this particular staff member has caused you to not trust him fully. Despite having no tangible reason for your lack of trust, you decide not to go ahead with the project. Your board of directors now wants an explanation for your decision. How do you justify and explain your behaviour? In your answer comment on rational, intuitive, heuristic and ethical considerations.
3. Why would organizations wish to empower their employees? Describe some of the risks associated with excessive empowerment.
4. Why are organizations unethical? Use the decision sequence to describe the influence of political and organizational power on individuals that might make them behave unethically.
5. Describe some of the political tactics and tricks that an employee may use to gain influence and some power advantage over his or her manager.

6. Identify two situations where you have come across cultural differences in decision-making processes. Undertake an analysis to see if and how these cultural differences affected the power balances within the situation.

RESEARCH QUESTIONS

1. Find out what you can about 'emotional intelligence' and use that information to address the following questions. You may like to add specific examples to support your answers.

   (a) What is emotional intelligence and how might it be used as a source of power for managers in an organization?

   (b) Explain ways in which emotional intelligence might help managers engage in successful political behaviours?

   (c) What are the likely implications for ethics, trust and organizational effectiveness if managers are able to draw upon their emotional intelligence for political behaviours?

2. Search the Internet for information about a major company with which you are familiar. Try to find profiles of the directors either on the company Web site or by conducting name searches. You might find information about their personal lives, their business activities, what other boards they serve on or what other companies they are involved in. Report on the kind(s) of people who hold power on the board of the particular company you are investigating and where else they might have wealth, power and interests. What are the possible implications for the board of your company in terms of power and influence and relationships with other companies?

INDIVIDUAL ACTIVITY

Think about a job you have held:

1. What are the sources of power theoretically available to the post holder?
2. To what extent did you feel able to use the power you could have?
3. Give examples of using your power sources.
4. Why did you choose to use the power sources you did?
5. Why did you choose to not draw on some power sources?
6. To what extent does politics come into play when choosing and using power sources in your examples?
7. Identify two contrasting decision scenarios: one demonstrating optimal decision making; another for satisficing decision making.

INDIVIDUAL ACTIVITY

Influence tactics

Objective
To check your understanding of influence tactics and when they may be most useful

Procedure
Read each of the following 11 statements made by Jackie to Lee and, by applying them to the given scenario:

(a) decide which influence tactic is being used and briefly explain your reasoning

(b) rank each statement from 1 to 11 in terms of how effective it might be in influencing Lee (although you have limited information, consider how you might feel and react if you were Lee)

(c) decide whether and why you think the approach is ethical and briefly explain your reasoning.

Scenario
The senior management of the organization is developing a new proposal to introduce performance pay into the organization. Jackie and Lee are managers at the same level in the organization but in different sections. Jackie is seeking Lee's support to fight the proposal:

1. Come on, Lee. You've got to accept that this is the worst thing the company can do – look at the figures and how they show it won't work.

2. Lee, you've got to join me in fighting this proposal. I have to have your help.

3. I know you've always believed that performance pay will only ever advantage senior management while the rest of us are left carrying the workload. This is the only way our department is going to get ahead, and you're so good at speaking in public.

4. Lee, you need to help me fight this. If you don't, I'll have to reconsider the special arrangements I have for your staff when they want something from my department.

5. We need to get together to fight this proposal before it gets approved and ruins our operations.

6. Come on, Lee. The manager of Finance agrees with me that this proposal won't work.

7. I'd like you to help me fight this proposal. I'd help you out in the same situation, just as I did last year when you needed help with your upgrading application.

8. An intelligent person like you will immediately see that this proposal won't work.

9. Hi, Lee, you're looking great today. That was a great job you did on last month's report.

10. If you support me on fighting this, I'll support you in your promotion application.

11. Lee, would you look at this memo I've prepared to present a counter-argument to the performance pay proposal? I'd value your opinion.

Evaluation

Once you have ranked your responses, compare them to the information in the chapter that explains which influence tactics are likely to be most effective.

GROUP ACTIVITY

Machiavellianism[74]

Objectives

1. To assess individual Machiavellianism (Mach) scores.
2. To explore the dynamics of power in a group environment.
3. To develop an understanding of the rewards and frustrations of held power.
4. To analyse behaviours of various Mach personality types.

Total time: 45–60 minutes.

Procedure

1. Complete the following 10-item Mach assessment instrument.
2. Follow directions for scoring your instrument individually.
3. Form a group of five to seven persons, and designate one individual as the official group 'observer'.
4. The observer will not participate in any of the discussion but will take notes on the activities of the group and later report to the class.
5. Your lecturer will announce the topic to be discussed. The topic should be highly controversial and stimulating, and one that encourages different viewpoints.
6. The observer will begin by handing a specific textbook or magazine to one member of the group. Only that member of the group may speak. The textbook will be held by that person until another member of the group signals, nonverbally, that they wish to have it. The person with the textbook or magazine may refuse to

relinquish it, even when signalled. The group discussion has a time limit of 15 minutes.

7. Following the controversial discussion period, the group observer leads a group discussion on what they observed and learned about power phenomena, frustrations, feedback and so on.

8. Each group observer then presents what the group has learned to the entire class

Mach assessment instrument.

For each of the following statements, circle the number that most closely matches your attitude.

DISAGREE			AGREE	
A lot	A little	Neutral	A little	A lot
1	2	3	4	5

1. The best way to handle people is to tell them what they want to hear.
   1 2 3 4 5

2. When you ask someone to do something for you, it is best to give the real reason for wanting it rather than reasons that may carry more weight. 1 2 3 4 5

3. Anyone who completely trusts someone else is asking for trouble.
   1 2 3 4 5

4. It is hard to get ahead without cutting corners here and there. 1 2 3 4 5

5. It is safest to assume that all people have a vicious streak, and that it will emerge when they are given a chance. 1 2 3 4 5

6. You should take action only when it is morally right. 1 2 3 4 5

7. Most people are basically good and kind. 1 2 3 4 5

8. There is no excuse for lying to someone. 1 2 3 4 5

9. Most people forget more easily the death of their father than the loss of their property. 1 2 3 4 5

10. Generally speaking, people will not work hard unless forced to do so.
    1 2 3 4 5

Scoring key and interpretation

This assessment is designed to compute your Machiavellianism (Mach) score. Mach is a personality characteristic that taps people's power orientation. The high-Mach personality is pragmatic, maintains emotional distance from others, and believes that ends can justify means. To obtain your Mach score, add up the numbers you circled for questions 1, 3, 4, 5, 9 and 10. For the other four questions, reverse the number you have circled, so 5 becomes 1, 4 is 2, and 1 is 5. Then total both sets of numbers to find your score. A random sample of adults found the national average to be 25. Students in business and management typically score higher.

Research using the Mach tests has found the following results:

- men are generally more Machiavellian than women
- older adults tend to have lower Mach scores than those of younger adults
- there is no significant difference between high Machs and low Machs on measures of intelligence or ability
- Machiavellianism is not significantly related to demographic characteristics such as educational level or marital status
- high Machs tend to be in professions that emphasize the control and manipulation of people – for example, managers, lawyers, psychiatrists and behavioural scientists.

TOUGH DECISIONS AT FINANCECO

Case Study

FinanceCo operates in the banking sector providing savings accounts and mortgages to individuals and couples. Not a big player in the market, it avoids direct competition with the large national banks. It has 12 branches in market towns across a geographic territory of 50 km. The small branches have a counter for customers to make payments and withdraw money. All branches have a private room for in-depth discussions such as arranging a mortgage or when someone gets into difficulty repaying their mortgage. FinanceCo competes by treating its customers as individuals. Counter staff often know the people who come into their branches.

A recent change in strategy saw the establishment of a call centre. FinanceCo's sales director made the argument that the branches could not cope with the number of telephone calls coming in from customers, and the poor time-response they had to telephone enquiries was damaging their reputation and otherwise high levels of service. A large room in a building adjacent to Head Office was taken on a short-term rental (one year) to try out the idea. Fitting out the office cost €200 000, took two months and provided seats for 50 staff. It was decided to begin with only 20 staff to enable FinanceCo to understand how to manage the operation. Of this first tranche of staff, six came from the branches. Others were recruited and trained as they had no finance background. The training for new staff took place in parallel to the office refurbishment. All call centre staff arrived on the same morning to start work at the new facility.

The first week had been a nightmare for Georgina and Fred, the two team leaders. The software had worked perfectly, but the staff had ben problematic. The trainers had created two groups from the start, to provide the basis for the two teams Georgina and Fred would manage. On the first day the 'ex-branch' staff were unhappy with the rowdy atmosphere between the two teams of new staff, seeing their banter as unprofessional. Georgina observed that while there was joking around by the new staff, none of this happened while they were talking to customers. She put it down to the ex-branch staff being used to quiet environment. The 'old' staff had been split between the teams equally but by the end of day two, Georgina could see them becoming physically exhausted by the pressure of answering call after call – perhaps FinanceCo had underestimated the nature of this job – it needed more than just knowledge of finance.

At the end of the first week Georgina, Fred and the Sales Director reviewed operations. The Sales Director had received several complaints (via branches) of poor advice given to customers. All complaints were about new staff members, but otherwise there were no patterns. Feed said the he had received a delegation of 'old' staff on Friday lunchtime. They were struggling to cope with the new staff, saying that these employees lacked the correct FinanceCo attitude to customers, but Fred thought there was more to it than that.

At the same time as the management meeting, Mark was on the bus on his way home. He had worked for FinanceCo for many years and was horrified by his first week in the new call centre. The new staff had given all the 'ex-branchers' names, and most were nasty. None of the new staff had asked for his help with queries. He had heard several people give bad advice. When he went to Fred, Fred had said not to worry, it would all work out, but he urged Mark to tell the branches to complain to Head Office if they heard anything bad about the new staff. Mark had sent a quiet message to the branches, away from management 'radar'. Mark had seen Fred telephoning branch managers, but hadn't heard what was going on. His team called Fred 'Boiler', probably because Fred was prone to perspiring. They were making jokes, such as 'Ohh, the Boiler's blowing...' when Fred got upset at lunchtime because half the new staff went for a cafe lunch. Mark had eaten lunch on his own in the local park all week, pleased to get away from the abuse.

The Sales Director was worried by the level of gossip around FinanceCo, which was not used to such disturbances. He wondered if he needed to spend a few days working in the new office himself. He wasn't sure what the problem was and how to solve it. He didn't want to undermine Georgina or Fred, but they were clearly not up to the task of managing this group. Only one week had gone by and the call centre seemed quite out of control. His instinct told him that the problem was wider than the call centre, but where to look for clues?

Questions

1. Use concepts covered in this chapter to identify the problems at FinanceCo and the power dynamics that might be at play.
2. What are the questions the Sales Director needs to be asking, and of whom?
3. What decisions do you think should be given to Georgina and Fred – why do you think this?
4. What ethical issues does the chapter raise?
5. How would you redress the balance of power at the call centre?

SUGGESTED READING

Bazerman, M. (2002), *Judgement in Managerial Decision-making*, 5th edn, John Wiley & Sons, Inc., New York. This text provides a critical view of the realities of management decision making. It strays into the areas of power and politics, in which Bazerman is well versed.

END NOTES

1. Shaw, W.N. (1986), Politics and management services. *Management Services*, 30 (12), 8–12.
2. Buchanan, D. & Badham, R. (1999), *Power, Politics and Organizational Change: Winning the Turf Game*. Sage: London.
3. Kanter, R.M. (1979), Power failure in management circuit. *Harvard Business Review*, (July/August), 65–75.
4. Pfeffer, J. (1992), Understanding power in organizations. *California Management Review*, 34 (2), pp. 29–50.

5. Pfeffer, J. (1994), *Managing with Power: Politics and Influence in Organizations*, Harvard Business School Press: Boston, MA.

6. French, J.R.P. & Raven, B. (1962), *The Bases of Social Power, in Group Dynamics: Research and Theory* (ed. D. Cartwright), Peterson: Evanston, IL, pp. 607–23.

7. Ibid.

8. Rayner, C. (1998). Workplace bullying: do something! *Journal of Occupational Health and Safety – Australia and New Zealand*, **14**(6), 581–585.

9. Rayner, C. & Keashly, L. (2005), *Bullying at work: a perspective from Britain and North America, in Counterproductive Work Behaviour: Investigations of Actors and Targets* (eds S. Fox & P.E. Spector), American Psychological Association Publishers: Washington DC, pp. 271–296.

10. Hoel, H., Faragher, B., & Cooper, C.L. (2004) Bullying is detrimental to health, but all bullying behaviours are not necessarily equally damaging. *British Journal of Guidance and Counselling*, **32** (3), 367–387.

11. Rayner, C., Hoel, H., & Cooper, C. L. (2002). *Bullying at Work: What we Know, Who is to Blame and What Can We Do?* Taylor & Francis: London.

12. Schyns, B. & Sanders, K. (2004) Implicit leadership theories and the perception of leadership in the Netherlands. *International Journal of Psychology*, **39** (5/6), 129–159.

13. Scholl, W. (1999), Restrictive control and information pathologies in organizations. Social influence and social power: using theory for understanding social issues. *Journal of Social Issues*, **55** (1), 118.

14. Adapted from John Plunkett, *Guardian*, 17 July 2006.

15. Turner, J.C. (1987) *Rediscovering the Social Group – Self Categorization Theory*. Basil Blackwell: Oxford.

16. Chattopadhyay, P., Tluchowska, M. & George, E. (2004), Identifying the ingroup: a closer look at the influence of demographic dissimilarity on employee social identity. *Academy of Management Review*, **29** (2), 180–202.

17. O'Donnell, E. & Schultz, J.J. (2005), The Halo effect in business risk audits: can strategic risk assessment bias auditor judgement about accounting details? *Accounting Review*, **80** (3), 921–939.

18. Milgram, S. (1978), Behavioural study of obedience, in *The Applied Psychology of Work Behaviour* (eds Dennis W. Organ), Business Publications: Dallas, TX, pp. 384–398. Also see: Milgram, S. (1963), Behavioural study of obedience. *Journal of Abnormal and Social Psychology*, **67**, 371–8. Milgram, S. (1964), Group pressure and action against a person. *Journal of Abnormal and Social Psychology*, **69**, 137–143. Milgram, S. (1965), Some conditions of obedience and disobedience to authority, Human Relations, **1**, 57–76. Milgram, S. (1974), *Obedience to Authority*. Harper & Row: New York.

19. Barnard, C. (1938), *The Functions of the Executive*, Harvard University Press: Cambridge, MA.

20. Morris, M.G. (2006), The executive role in culturing export control compliance – Michigon Law Review, **104**(7), 1785–2010.

21. Yukl, G. (2005), *Leadership in Organizations*, Prentice Hall: Thousand Oaks, CA.

22. Mackay, R., Cousins, J., Kelly, P. *et al.* (2004), Management standards and work-related stress in the UK: policy and background science. *Work and Stress*, **18** (2), 91–112.

23. Pascale, R.T (1990), *Managing on the Edge*. Penguin: Harmondsworth.

24. Buchanan & Badham, op. cit.

25. Dufficy, M. (1998), The empowerment audit-measured improvement. *Industrial and Commercial Training*, **30** (4), 142–146.

26. Pfeffer, J. (1993), *Managing with Power: Politics and Influence in Organizations*. Harvard Business School Publications: Boston, MA.

27. Ibid.

28. Waters-Marsh, T.F. (2001), Exploiting differences: the exercise of power and politics in organizations, in *Management and Organizational Behaviour* (eds R. Wiesner & B. Millett), John Wiley & Sons: Brisbane, pp. 153–60.

29. Morgan, G. (1986), *Images of Organization*, Sage: London, pp. 141–198.

30. Czechowicz, J. (2001), The winning ways of men and women. *Management Today*, (January/February), pp. 14–19.

31. Morgan, op. cit.

32. Developed from Hall, J.L. & Leldecker, J.L. (1982), A review of vertical and lateral relations: a new perspective for managers, in *Dimensions in Modern Management* (ed. P. Connor), 3rd edn. Houghton Mifflin: Boston, MA, pp. 138–46, which was based in part on Sayles, L. (1964), *Managerial Behaviour*, McGraw-Hill: New York.

33. See Pfeffer, op. cit. and Buchannan & Badham, op. cit.

34. Ibid.

35. Thompson, J.D. (1967), *Organizations in Action,* McGraw-Hill: New York.

36. Satava, D., Caldwell, C. & Richards, L. (2006), Ethics and the auditing culture: rethinking the foundation of accounting and auditing. *Journal of Business Ethics, 64* (3), 271–284.

37. Westphal, J.D. & Stern, I. (2007), Flattery will get you everywhere (especially if you are a male caucasian): how ingratiation, boardroom behaviour, and demographic minority status affect additional board appointments at US companies. *Academy of Management Journal,* **50** (2), 267–288.

38. Edwards, J. & Wolfe, S. (2007), Ethical and compliance-competence evaluation: a key element of sound corporate governance. *Corporate Governance: An International Review,* **15** (2), 359–369.

39. Buchanan, D. & Badham, R. (1999), op cit.

40. Useem, M. (2006), How well-run boards make decisions. *Harvard Business Review,* **84** (11), 130–145.

41. Adapted from G. Cavanagh, D. Moberg & M. Velasquez (1981), The ethics of organizational politics. *Academy of Management Review,* **6**, 363–374.

42. Gellerman, S.W. (1986), Why 'good' managers make bad ethical choices. *Harvard Business Review,* **64** (July/August), 85–97.

43. Mintzberg, H. (1989) Mintzberg on Management: Inside our Strange World of Organizations, Free Press: New York.

44. National Commission on Terrorist Attacks upon the United States (2004), *The 9/11 Commission Report: Final Report of the National Commission on Terrorist Attacks Upon the United States,* WW Norton & Co.: New York.

45. Ibid., p. 31.

46. Borodzicz, E. (2005), *Risk, Crisis and Security Management,* John Wiley & Sons, Ltd: Chichester.

47. Doyle, T.C. & Lang, S. (2005), The leadership issue: managing your way to the top – insights from top executives and experts on management, decision-making and risk-taking, *VARbusiness,* issue 2116, 25 July, p. 30.

48. This discussion is based on March, J.G. & Simon, H.A. (1958), *Organizations,* John Wiley & Sons, New York, pp. 137–142.

49. Ibid.

50. Ashford, N. (2005), Incorporating science, technology, fairness, and accountability in environmental, health, and safety decisions. *Human and Ecological Risk Assessment,* **11** (1), 85–96.

51. De George, R.T. (2006), *Business Ethics,* 6th edn. Prentice Hall: Englewood Cliffs, NJ.

52. Agor, W.H. (1989), *Intuition in Organizations,* Sage: Newbury Park, CA.

53. Mintzberg, H. (2001), Decision making: it's not what you think. *MIT Sloan Management Review,* **42** (3), 89–93.

54. Pipoli, R. (2005), CEOs and mistakes; study, discussion looks at management miscues. *Credit Union Journal,* **9** (7), 1.

55. Pipoli, op. cit., p. 1.

56. Patton, J.R. (2003), Intuition in decisions. *Management Decision,* **41** (10), 989.

57. The classic work in this area is found in a series of articles: Kahneman, D. & Tversky, A. (1972), Subjective probability: a judgement of representativeness. *Cognitive Psychology,* **3**, 430–454. Kahneman, D. & Tversky, A. (1973), On the psychology of prediction. *Psychological Review,* 80, 237–251. Kahneman, D. & Tversky, A. (1979), Prospect theory: an analysis of decision under risk. *Econometrica,* 47, 263–291. Kahneman, D. & Tversky, A. (1982), Psychology of preferences. *Scientific American,* 1, 161–173. Kahneman, D. & Tversky, A. (1984), Choices, values, frames. *American Psychologist,* 39, 341–350.

58. Bazerman, M. (2002), *Judgement in Managerial Decision-making,* 5th edn. Wiley & Sons: New York.

59. Stoner, J.A.F. (1982), *Management,* 2nd edn, Prentice Hall: Englewood Cliffs, NJ, pp. 167–168.

60. Harwood, C.C. (1999), Solving problems. *Executive Excellence*, **16**, 9 September, p. 17.

61. See Vroom, V.H. & Yetton, P.W. (1973), Leadership and Decision Making. University of Pittsburgh Press: Pittsburgh, PA. Vroom, V.H. & Jago, A.G. (1988), *The New Leadership*, Prentice Hall: Englewood Cliffs, NJ.

62. This discussion is developed from Schein, E.H. (1988), *Process Consultation*, Vol. I, 2nd edn. Addison-Wesley: New York, pp. 69–75.

63. Janis, I.L. (1971), Groupthink. *Psychology Today*, (November 1971), 43–46. Janis, I.L. (1982), *Groupthink*, 2nd edn. Houghton Mifflin, Boston, MA. See also Longley, J. & Pruitt, D.G. (1980), Groupthink: a critique of Janis' theory, in *Review of Personality and Social Psychology* (ed. L. Wheeler), Sage: Beverly Hills, CA. Leana, C.R. (1985), A partial test of Janis's groupthink model: the effects of group cohesiveness and leader behaviour on decision processes. *Journal of Management*, 11 (1), 5–18.

64. Boisjoly, R., Curtis, E. & Mellican, E. (1998), Roger Boisjoly and the Challenger disaster: the ethical dimensions, cited in Beauchamp, T. & Bowie, N. (eds) (2004), *Ethical Theory and Business,* 7th edn, Prentice Hall: Englewood Cliffs, NJ, pp. 123–136 quotation at p. 128. *A Major Malfunction*, BBC Education and Training videorecording (1998).

65. *A Major Malfunction*, BBC Education and Training videorecording (1998).

66. Developed from Janis, I. (1972), *Victims of Groupthink*, 2nd edn, Houghton Mifflin: Boston, MA.

67. See Hill, G.W. (1982), Group versus individual performance: are N + 1 heads better than one? *Psychological Bulletin*, **91**, 517–539.

68. Bazerman, op. cit., pp. 79–83.

69. See Trompenaars, F. (1993), *Riding the Waves of Culture*, Nicholas Brealey: London.

70. Adler, N.J. & Gundersen, A. (2007), *International Dimensions of Organizational Behaviour*. Thomson: Mason, OH.

71. See Computers that think are almost here. *Business Week*, 17 July 1995, pp. 68–73.

72. Dinnis, A.R. & Valacich, J.S. (1994), Computer brainstorms: two heads are better than one. *Journal of Applied Psychology*, February, 77–86.

73. Kabanoff, B. & Rossiter, J.R. (1994), Recent developments in applied creativity. *International Review of Industrial and Organizational Psychology*, 9, 283–324.

74. Exercise adapted from Christie, R. & Geis, F.L. (1970), *Studies in Machiavellianism*, Academic Press: New York. Reproduced by permission of Elsevier.

CHAPTER 11

Communication, conflict and negotiation in organizations

LEARNING OBJECTIVES

After studying this chapter you should be able to:

- define communication and discuss its role in organizations
- define conflict and explain how it may affect organizational effectiveness
- explain how managers may deal with conflict effectively
- explain the role of negotiation in organizations
- discuss managerial issues in negotiation.

FIRED BY PHONE!

The UK's largest personal injury claims firm, Accident Group, has sacked 2 400 people – many by text message – after its parent company Amulet Group announced on Friday that it would go into administration.

Staff with company mobile phones received a series of text messages, warning them that salaries would not be paid. The administrators ... blame Accident Group's 'lower than expected claims success rate' for the financial difficulties, which they say 'resulted in increased insurance premiums on new business and retrospective claims from the underwriters.' About 200 Amulet staff are being kept on to process existing claims.

Rumours about the collapse of the Accident Group had been circulating since Thursday evening, when employees with company mobile phones received a series of text messages, warning them they would not receive this month's salary. Workers were first asked to 'check your e-mail for salary news' and then told that 'unfortunately salary is not paid'.

Staff were given the news at Manchester head office at noon on Friday. During the morning, a BBC reporter saw security preventing staff from leaving the building with their personal belongings. One worker, who had just been told she had lost her job, told the BBC: 'They came in and said the administrators have taken over, some of us may have jobs and there are letters going out in the post. It was a bit angry in there. There was a lot of shouting.'

Questions

1. Do you think employees were justified in their angry reaction? What other feelings might they have been experiencing?
2. Although one can be critical of the manner in which this was handled, what are the challenges that a sudden company collapse presents to a manager seeking to inform employees? How would you have handled this situation if you were responsible for getting the message to staff that the firm had failed?

Source: http://news.bbc.co.uk/1/hi/business/2949578.stm, accessed 17 December 2007.

INTRODUCTION

Differences, misunderstandings and disagreements are a part of the daily life of individuals and organizations alike. If not dealt with constructively, such problems can be destructive for both the individual and the organization. Poor communication, or an absence of communication, is often the cause of conflict. Leaving conflict unresolved exposes organizations to greater risk of losing employees: those involved, or those around them who have been drawn in to the conflict, may decide to leave the organization to escape what has become a negative environment. In addition to the loss of knowledge and experience the organization is then faced with the cost of hiring and training a replacement employee.

Communication problems and unresolved conflict cannot be expected simply to disappear of their own accord. While it may seem daunting, it is possible to take constructive steps to improve communication and resolve conflict in organizations. Managers need to strive to improve communication, address conflict and engage in appropriate negotiation processes.

The study of communication uses the topics basic to understanding human behaviour and at the collective level reflects how the organization works. Communication and organizational success are directly related. Good communication can have a positive and mobilizing effect on employees. Poor communication can produce powerful negative consequences, such as distortion of goals and objectives, conflict, misuse of resources and inefficiency in performance of duties.

The ability to manage good communication and handle conflict effectively is a necessary skill in all management roles. In any situation where people interact, there is potential for disagreement, challenge and conflict. No area of an organization is devoid of conflict, and in some cases conflict can be a good and healthy thing. Constructive conflict can promote creativity and make people reassess situations, identify problems and find new solutions. In some instances it can indicate that members of an organization are seeking more effective means of communication that will help resolve the conflict. In other instances, members could be challenging normal processes and procedures in an effort to improve productivity or introduce innovative systems. However, when conflict in the workplace becomes chronic or disproportionate, or leads to lost productivity and stress, then managers must deal with the problem. Hence, in order to resolve conflict, managers are increasingly required to possess negotiating skills. Such skills may also be used as a vehicle to create change or develop new opportunities.

In this chapter we will cover the basic process of communication and related issues in organizations. Also, because the daily work of people in organizations is based on communication and interpersonal relationships, conflict situations often arise and managers need to identify and understand them as well as know how to deal with them. Hence, the chapter will also introduce you to conflict management and negotiation as key processes of organizational behaviour.

COMMUNICATION IN ORGANIZATIONS

Organizational communication *is the process by which entities exchange information and establish a common understanding.*

We can think of interpersonal communication as a process of sending symbols with attached meanings from one person to another. These interpersonal foundations form the basis for discussing the larger issue of communication within the organization.

Organizational communication is the process by which members exchange information and establish a common understanding.

When we communicate with others, we are usually trying to influence other people's understanding, behaviour or attitudes. We are trying to share meaning in some way. As Henry Mintzberg stresses,[1] we are communicating with others to inform, instruct, motivate or seek information. For example, you may wish to inform your chief executive that staff turnover is up 5% this month, or tell your staff about a new policy for sickness absence. Perhaps you want to have an informal chat with Harry to let him 'get things off his chest' in the hope that he will be happier and thus be more motivated to work effectively. Or perhaps you are going to call a staff meeting to gather feedback after hearing 'moans and groans' about the new computer system. Each of these communication tasks will have different aims and involve different skills.

While the function of interpersonal communication is really to share meaning, effective organizational communication can (and should) provide substantial benefits to the organization's members. Four functions are particularly important: achieving coordinated action, developing information, expressing feelings and emotions, and communicating roles.[2]

From a top management perspective, a primary function of organizational communication is to achieve coordinated action. The collection of individuals that make up an organization remains an unfocused group until its members are in effective communication with one another. It is important that managers and individuals are aware of techniques in communication that are appropriate for their organization's structure.

INTERPERSONAL COMMUNICATION

The key elements in the interpersonal communication process are illustrated in Figure 11.1. They include a source (a person who is responsible for encoding an intended meaning into a message) and a receiver (a person who decodes the message into a perceived meaning). The process may appear to be elementary but it is not quite as simple as it looks. Let us examine the model in some detail to identify the main elements in the process, the sequencing of these elements and weaknesses in the process that can lead to communication problems or distortions. The conventional communication process is made up of the following essential components: the information source, the encoding of a message, the selection of a channel, the transmission of the message, the decoding of the message, feedback from the receiver of the message and any 'noise' (or interference) that may have affected accurate decoding (or interpretation of the message).

An **information source** is a person or group of persons with a reason to communicate with some other person(s), the receiver(s).

The **information source** is a person or group of persons with a reason to communicate with some other person(s), the receiver(s). The reasons for the source to communicate can vary enormously and include changing the attitudes, knowledge or behaviour of the receiver. A manager, for example, may want to communicate with the boss to make him or her understand why more time is needed to finish an assigned project. Of course, the manager will want to do so in such a way that indicates respect for the receiver and an understanding that the job is important, among other factors.

Encoding is part of the process of communication and involves translating an idea or thought into meaningful symbols.

The next step in the process is encoding – the process of translating an idea or thought into meaningful symbols. This translation (encoding) process takes into account how the message is to be sent as the medium for transmission affects how the message is framed. For example a personal interaction is a channel that includes verbal, written and/or nonverbal signals and symbols, whereas an email transmission is restricted to written communication.

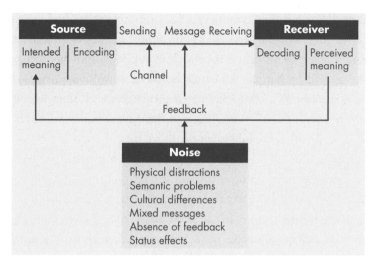

Figure 11.1: The communication process and possible sources of 'noise'.

Channels *are the media through which the message may be delivered.*

The message is what is communicated. A channel is the medium through which the message is delivered. The choice of channels may alter the nature and effectiveness of the intended message. For many people it is easier to communicate face-to-face than in a memo or by email. On the other hand, perhaps our manager would prefer to construct a formal memo carefully to his or her boss to set out the reasons why the work unit needs more time. Our manager should consider whether the boss might interpret the choice of a memo rather than a face-to-face meeting as avoidance. Alternatively, the boss might give the matter more weight if a letter arrives in an envelope in the in-tray than if the issue is briefly mentioned in an email. The manager's message is simple: 'Our work unit needs more time to complete this task' but there are many ways to try to communicate that message.

The receiver *is the individual or group of individuals that hear or read or see the message within the communication process.*

The process of communication does not stop with the sender. The receiver is the individual who hears (or reads or sees) the message. The receiver may or may not attempt to decode the message. Decoding involves interpreting or translating the symbols sent. Deleting emails before you have read them is an example of refusal to decode a message.

Decoding *is the interpretation of the symbols sent from the sender to the receiver.*

This decoding translation may or may not result in the assignment of the meaning intended by the source. Frequently, the intended meaning of the source and the meaning perceived by the receiver differ, or the receiver may have difficulty interpreting the message. Our manager wants the boss to understand that the work unit needs more time to complete a task. Will the boss get the correct message and what interpretation will he or she put on it? Alternative interpretations could be that the work unit is underperforming, that the manager is underperforming, or something about the task has changed beyond the control of the work unit. The sender can influence how a message is interpreted.

Noise *is anything that interferes with the effectiveness of the communication attempt.*

Everyone knows the potential gap between an intended (sent) message and the message that is received. Feedback is the process by which receivers acknowledge the communication and return a message concerning how they feel about the original message. Throughout the process, there may be any number of disturbances. Noise is the term used to indicate any disturbance within the communication process that disrupts the matching process between sender and receiver.

Consider a simple example of noise. A lecturer is delivering a lecture in a lecture theatre filled with attentive students. The students' attention to the lecture means that only the lecturer speaks and there is no interference. The fact that only the professor speaks creates a 'silent' channel that allows the sound of the professor's voice and spoken words to flow freely to the ears of the students. However, if in the midst of an uninteresting lecture topic some students begin to whisper among themselves or giggle, their sounds would creep into the 'silent' channel making the lecture 'noisy' to dedicated students who wish to listen to the lecturer. It is a challenging task to communicate accurately.

OB IN ACTION

Communication failure in New Orleans

The poor response to Hurricane Katrina has been analysed by several authors, most finding that poor communication was one underlying cause. The healthcare agencies (such as the various hospitals in New Orleans) each had individual emergency plans, which had been practised, but there was a lack of coordination between them (for example not all staff knew their 'equivalent' in other facilities in the City) and none of them were in effective contact with the local National Guard who themselves faced confusion.[3] While some IT solutions are being developed, for example a common portal held nationally to enable decision makers access to pollutant information,[4] lack of power to computer and mobile batteries failing would have a paralysing effects in similar circumstances. Here the channels of communication were severely limited, not only by practical issues, but by lack of local knowledge of employees.

EFFECTIVE AND EFFICIENT COMMUNICATION

Effective communication occurs when the intended meaning of the source and the perceived meaning of the receiver are the same. This should be the manager's goal in any communication attempt. However, it is not always achieved. Even now, we worry whether you are interpreting our written words as we intend. Our confidence would be higher if we were face-to-face in class together and you could ask clarifying questions. This opportunity to offer feedback and ask questions is one way of increasing the effectiveness of communication.

Effective communication *is communication in which the intended meaning of the source and the perceived meaning of the receiver are the same.*

Efficient communication occurs at minimum cost in terms of resources expended. Time is an important resource in the communication process. Picture your lecturer taking the time to communicate individually with each student in your class. It would be virtually impossible to do so. And even if it were possible, it would be costly in terms of time. Managers often choose not to visit employees personally to communicate messages. Instead, they rely on the efficiency of telephone conversations, memos, posted bulletins, group meetings, email, teleconferencing or videos.

However, efficient (economical) communications are not always effective. A low-cost communication, such as email, may save time for the sender, but it does not always achieve the desired results in terms of the receiver's perceived meaning. Similarly, an effective communication may not be efficient. For a manager to visit each employee and explain a new change in procedures may guarantee that everyone truly understands the change but it may also be prohibitively expensive in terms of the required time.

Managers are busy people who depend on their communication skills to remain successful in their work. You need to learn how to maximize the effectiveness of your communications with others and to achieve reasonable efficiency in the process. These goals require the ability to overcome a number of communication barriers that commonly operate in the workplace. Such barriers may include cultural differences, defensiveness, misreading of nonverbal communication, and stereotyping.[5]

COMMUNICATION CHANNELS

In a very important sense the organization is a network of information and communication channels. Our opening mini-case makes the news because of the inappropriate channels (mobile phones) used. Traditionally, there were formal and informal channels but the electronic age has added a third category – quasiformal channels. While comparatively few managers are in a position to establish organization-wide communication channels, all managers should understand and be able to use each of the multiple channels for communication within their organization.

Formal communication channels *are communication channels that follow the chain of command established by the organization's hierarchy.*

Formal communication channels follow the chain of command established by an organization's hierarchy of authority. An organization chart, for example, indicates the proper routing for official messages passing from one level or part of the hierarchy to another. As formal communication channels are recognized as official and authoritative, written communication in the form of letters, memos, policy statements and other announcements typically adheres to these channels.

Informal communication *channels are communication channels that do not adhere to the organization's hierarchy.*

Although necessary and important, formal channels constitute only one part of a manager's overall communication responsibilities. Interpersonal networks represent the use of a wide variety of informal communication channels that do not adhere to the organization's hierarchy of authority. These informal channels coexist with the formal channels but frequently diverge from them by skipping levels in the hierarchy and/or cutting across vertical chains of command. 'Water-cooler conversations' are a very good way to pick up 'grapevine' or informal communication. Here one might be including gossip, which is a very important type of informal communication and one which reflects and feeds the types of informal set out in networks (Chapter 10).

There are many instances of chief executive officers of contemporary organizations who go to great lengths to improve communication with the entire staff when communicating organizational messages. In some organizations managers may prefer to walk around to meet with and talk to floor employees as they do their jobs. 'Management by wandering around' (MBWA)[6] can help develop trust in working relationships with employees which in turn can affect commitment and lead to better productivity. Managers who spend time walking around can greatly reduce the perceived 'distance' between themselves and their employees and engage in far more meaningful communication. Management by wandering around can also reduce selective perception biases by reducing the gap between what individuals want to hear and see and what is actually occurring for both the senior executive or manager as well as employees. As a result, more and better information is available for decision making and the relevance of decisions to the needs of lower level personnel increases. Of course, the wandering around must be a genuine attempt to communicate; it should not be perceived as just another way to 'check up' on employees.

Formal channels conform to the organization's chain of command and informal channels emerge from day-to-day activities, but a set of **quasiformal channels** also exists in most organizations today. Quasiformal channels are planned communication connections between holders of various positions within the organization. For example, if the City of New Orleans had held meetings between all people who might be involved in a disaster recovery situation, the response to Hurricane Katrina might have been better.

An organization exists and must be managed as a system of interdependent parts performing distinct but coordinated functions. When workflow interdependence is such that a person or group must rely on task contributions from one or more others to achieve its goals, the circumstances are ripe for developing a quasiformal communication link.

Quasiformal channels *are planned communication connections between holders of the various positions within the organization.*

COUNTERPOINT

Universities have an effect on their local environment. They are large employers and large numbers of students affect the local economy. To bring more people to education, the cost of living for students needs to be reasonable and one often finds a high density of students in poorer sections of university towns and cities. Their impact can be great, and the student presence can lead to areas degenerating as landlords only maintain properties at minimal levels. But it doesn't have to be like this. Where students live near to the university their impact can be great. Perhaps we should be using our university-based skills to help our local communities develop?

Think of a geographical area near your place of study that is known as a trouble spot. Plan a meeting which will be the regeneration of this area. Who might you invite from which agencies to try and work together so that together you could work effectively to improve this area to live and work? Why would you invite these people in particular? How would you expect these quasiformal relationships to benefit the renewal project?

HOW MUCH INFORMATION TO SHARE?

If knowledge is power, it is reasonable to propose that knowledge should be continually channelled to employees to give them the power to develop the organization. In fact, many modern managers no longer believe in the old concept that there is power in senior management holding onto information. Managers need to share information with employees to stimulate feedback from them on what is working, what isn't and why. Information can be an important part of motivation (see Chapter 4) and be an integral part of the leadership process (see Chapter 9). It can, however, be difficult to know how much information and what sort of information to share. For example, employees need to be kept well informed about a company's strategic direction so they are able to make the right decisions in their individual and team capacities, yet there are many cases in which information is considered commercially confidential or private to certain individuals.[7]

Could this lead to an ethical dilemma for senior managers over what information to share and what to protect? The decision often remains at the discretion of the senior manager, who should be well informed on what the organization's leaders consider to be classified information and what information is to be shared with their employees. For example, how the company is performing and what organizational changes are planned are issues that should be discussed openly with everyone who is likely to be involved throughout the process. On the other hand, the early stages of potential takeovers or sensitive issues involving individual staff members are better kept confidential.[8] The increasing tendency for employees to regularly change employers must also be taken into account. Managers should consider the possibility that an employee will be working for a competitor in the future when considering the release of strategic information.

Managers at all levels must impress on their team what is important to employees and what should remain confidential.[9] Depending on the culture of the organization, some managers may encourage open communication and share information that would typically be considered confidential, even to the point of discussing one another's salary levels and other employment incentives.[10]

Those senior managers who do have open, ongoing discussions with their staff may find it easier to gauge how much information to communicate. Regular two-way conversations with employees will not only encourage valuable input from all levels of the organization but also tap into the internal grapevine, which can be a risky form of communication if left unchecked. The internal grapevine will always operate in organizations, so it is important that issues raised on the grapevine are identified and reframed to reflect an accurate picture.

BARRIERS TO INTERPERSONAL COMMUNICATION

Look back now to Figure 11.1. Communication is not always perfect. Interference of some sort in the telecommunication process is called 'noise'. Given the rapid developments in telecommunications over the past 30 years, 'noise' due to technical faults is diminishing. Less tangible barriers to communication relate directly to those people in the communication channel. For example, you will remember that earlier in the chapter we referred to the ever increasing number of incoming and outgoing emails a manager is subjected to each day. Large volumes of emails might mean that they are only part-read, skim-read or posted in folders (without being read) only to be forgotten. While the development of technology can enhance the opportunity to communicate more frequently and faster, it still needs management.

Therefore, managers should select the most appropriate channel of communication to get each message across to the recipient without distortion. For example, a survey found that few managers from the sample researched agreed that email was more persuasive than a face-to-face meeting, yet two-thirds of the same group researched reported that face-to-face communication skills had decreased as a result of email use.[11] Face-to-face communication allows the transmission of body language which can be up to 55% of the message received, with the oral communication (i.e. the words) perhaps as little as 7%. E-conferencing with Web cams is thus a far richer environment than email but it is still very difficult to replace face-to-face interaction, which is favoured by all staff at all levels.[13]

IN ACTION

Mehrabian's rule

Mehrabian studied the relative influence of body language, tone of voice and words in laboratory settings almost 40 years ago (1971). He found the following formula for their influence on the message received:

7% for words
38% for tone of voice
55% for body language.

Known as 'Mehrabian's rule' this formula was of course a very surprising finding. But Mehrabian had never expected it to be generalized to all settings, which is unfortunately what has occurred! Every situation varies and so it is impossible to generalize but the overall findings should not be ignored.

The results help us see how we must pay attention to nonverbal signs such as eye contact and body language. They also help to highlight the huge importance of tone of voice.

None of these are to be found in email contact. This means that care over use of words is crucial in emails. Writing in clear and simple language helps get the message across. Unfortunately you don't know how your email receiver is decoding and so for emails you do not have the ability to obtain feedback and correct the signalled message if it is being understood in the wrong way.

Although retired, Albert Mehrabian continues to research and publish, publishing his most recent book in 2007.[12]

E-conferencing with Web cams is thus a far richer environment than email but it is still very difficult to replace face-to-face interaction, which is favoured by all staff at all levels.[13]

Noise still occurs in interpersonal communication in today's organization; so to improve communications, it is important to understand the sources of noise. The most common sources of noise are physical distractions and cultural differences.[14] Physical distractions include such things as a competing conversation being held in the office while you are trying to concentrate on an important telephone call, or the disturbance caused by someone fixing the road outside when you need to listen to someone who has come to see you. Environmental factors such as too much noise in open-plan offices or uncomfortable temperatures can fall into this category.

Cultural differences can present a number of complications or obstructions to effective communication between individuals. The problems that these blocks pose to managers are usually compounded by managers' deeply rooted orientations to life according to the pattern of their own society. While they may recognize that people from other cultures are different they may find it hard to understand and adjust to the great variety of ways in which this difference manifests itself.[15]

We need to recognize these sources of noise and to subject them to special managerial control. They are included in Figure 11.1 as potential threats to any communication process.

Effective communicators not only understand and deal with communication barriers – they are also exceptionally good at active listening. Effective communicators recognize that being a good receiver is just as important, and often even more important, than being an accurate sender.

The habits of good communicators

For good communication to occur people need to:

- speak clearly
- write clearly
- be aware of cultural differences
- listen attentively
- question precisely
- answer honestly
- pause for feedback signals.

CONFLICT

Conflict is a universal phenomenon. It can facilitate learning, creativity and change but for some people it makes their workday less enjoyable. For others, the frequency and intensity of workplace conflict makes them uncomfortable and impedes their effectiveness. Workplace conflict may reach such levels that people consider leaving the organization. Few people welcome conflict and many managers do not know how to manage it effectively. Yet successful conflict management is at the root of organizational effectiveness. Whether in the boardroom or at the 'coalface', conflict situations, infighting and internal disputes are commonplace. Conflict in the workplace can erupt at any time and at any level of the organization. Much of the focus is on how to resolve conflict among employees at the lower levels of the hierarchy but just as many conflict situations can erupt in the boardroom. It is common to read in mainstream media about disputes and conflict among top managers in major organizations. But not all conflict is negative.[16]

What is conflict?

Conflict occurs whenever disagreements exist in a social situation over issues of substance, or whenever emotional antagonisms create frictions between individuals or groups.[17] Managers are known to spend up to 20% of their time dealing with conflict, including conflicts in which managers are themselves directly involved.[18] In other situations managers may act as mediators, or third parties, whose job is to try to resolve conflicts between other people. In all cases, managers must be skilled participants in the dynamics of interpersonal conflict. They must also be able to recognize situations that have the potential for conflict and deal with these situations to best serve the needs of both the organization and the people involved.

Conflict subscribes to no rules. Petty disputes are common occurrences in all workplaces. Full-scale discord can always occur. Such conflicts cannot be predicted, nor can they be prevented, but they can be managed. Among the common reasons for conflict are differences in personal styles, values and job perspectives. Differing needs for personal success and variations in skill level can also cause conflict.

It is important to listen to individuals in a conflict because their anger or frustration is frequently rooted in a desire to see change effected. A manager needs to know how to resolve such interpersonal conflicts effectively. Where tension develops between individual managers or different management functions, the conflict can have a dramatic impact on organizational performance. Managers who understand the fundamentals of conflict and negotiation will be better prepared to deal with such situations.

If you listen in on some workplace conversations, you might hear the following:

- 'I don't care what you say, I don't have time to do it and that's that!'
- 'I no longer open my emails when I first get to the office. I get so many "fwd", it's an annoying start to the day.'
- 'The lines of communication are pretty bad around here.'

The very words used in these statements are important. They all link to communication and convey a sense of discord in the workplace and 'frame' the thinking of the people making them in a negative or adversarial way. This way of thinking is bound to affect the speaker's working relationships with the other people involved. It is also likely to affect their attitudes and work behaviours. At issue in each case is conflict. The ability to deal with such conflict successfully is a key aspect of a manager's interpersonal skills.

Conflict must be managed effectively for an organization to achieve its goals. Before it can be managed, conflict must be acknowledged and defined by the disputants. However, it may be difficult for the parties involved to agree on what is in dispute in a shared conflict because they may experience, or frame, the same conflict in different ways.[19]

Substantive and emotional conflicts

Conflict in organizations can be as diverse as the people working there. Interpersonal conflict is natural and can actually spur creativity but the objective for managers is to manage it, often by preventing interpersonal differences from culminating in confrontations. As rational adults, we tend to expect that when we present an idea we will achieve consensus. We believe that others will see the logic of our views and support them, even when different cultures and backgrounds are apparent. However, because each of us has a different perspective we tend to support only those ideas and views that align with our own. To deal with conflict effectively, both objective and subjective elements contributing to the conflict need to be examined and addressed.

Two common examples of workplace conflict are a disagreement with your boss over a plan of action to be followed (for example, a marketing strategy for a new product) and a dislike for a co-worker (for example, someone who is always belittling the members of an ethnic or identity group). The first example is a traditional one of **substantive conflict** – that is, a conflict that usually occurs in the form of a fundamental disagreement over ends or goals to be pursued and the means for their accomplishment.[20] When people work together day in and day out, it is only normal that different viewpoints on a variety of substantive workplace issues will arise. It is common for people to disagree at times over such things as group and organizational goals, the allocation of resources, the distribution of rewards, policies and procedures, and task assignments. Dealing successfully with such conflicts is an everyday challenge for most managers. The second example is one of **emotional conflict** – that is, a conflict that involves interpersonal difficulties that arise over feelings of anger, mistrust, dislike, fear, resentment and the like.[21] It is commonly known as a 'clash of personalities'. Emotional conflicts can drain people's energies and distract them from other important work priorities. They can emerge from a wide variety of settings and are common among co-workers as well as in superior–employee relationships. The latter is perhaps the most upsetting emotional conflict for any person to experience. Unfortunately, competitive pressures in today's business environment and the resulting emphasis on downsizing and restructuring have created more situations in which the decisions of a 'tough' boss can create emotional conflict.

Both types of conflict can have a positive influence on management performance. However, substantive (or task-oriented) conflict is likely to have the most positive effect, depending on how it is managed.[22] Performance is what we typically think about when we consider effectiveness; it constitutes the decisions or solutions that affect productive output. Conflict can force managers to address some of their assumptions and override their attempts to achieve premature unanimity, thus leading to better performance. Managers engaged in substantive (task-oriented) conflict tend to direct their actions to their work because the conflict forces them to concern themselves with task functions and related issues. By contrast, emotional conflict, although it affects the organization's development and survival, is inward looking and thus offers a less positive effect on management performance. During such conflict, management actions are directed towards members' relations with each other, rather than with the organization or the team agenda.

Substantive conflict *is conflict that occurs in the form of a fundamental disagreement over ends or goals to be pursued and the means for their accomplishment.*

Emotional conflict *is conflict that involves interpersonal difficulties that arise over feelings of anger, mistrust, dislike, fear, resentment and the like.*

EFFECTIVE MANAGER 11.1

Communication that can lead to conflict

The conflict 911.com 'conflict help centre' warns that there are five types of communication that can lead to conflict. Managers should avoid:

- *negative communication*. We all know a 'negative Nigel/Nancy' in every team – they exist and we find it near impossible to remove them. But constant negativity drains the other team members of enthusiasm, energy and self-esteem
- *blaming communication*. Blamers spray blame around, effectively stopping reflection and scrutiny of their performance and behaviour. However, their impact can be reduced by fostering a learning environment, as well as the use of 'I' messages, peer pressure and individual feedback
- *superior communication*. 'Superiors' frequently order people about, direct, advise and moralize. They are also very skilled at withholding information
- *dishonest communication*. Dishonest communicators frequently fail to practise listening to understand and fail to display empathy. They also display circumlocutory communication – also known as 'talking around the issue, not addressing it'
- *selective communication*. Selective communicators only tell what they think others need to know, hence keeping themselves in a position of power over the other team members. Such behaviour can be effectively addressed through assertive requests for having access to all the information. (*Source:* **http://www.conflict911. com/guestconflict/minimzingconflict.htm** – accessed 16 July 2007.)

Levels of conflict

It is possible to examine conflict from a number of different communication levels. In particular, people at work may encounter conflicts at four levels:

- intrapersonal, or conflict within the individual
- interpersonal, or individual-to-individual conflict
- intergroup conflict
- interorganizational conflict.

When it comes to dealing personally with conflicts in the workplace, how well prepared are you to encounter and deal with various types of conflict?

Intrapersonal conflict

Among the significant conflicts that affect behaviour in organizations are those that involve the individual alone. These intrapersonal conflicts often involve actual or perceived pressures from incompatible goals or expectations of the following types. Approach conflict occurs when a person must choose between two positive and equally attractive alternatives.

An example is having to choose between a valued promotion in the organization or a desirable new job with another organization. Avoidance conflict occurs when a person must choose between two negative and equally unattractive alternatives. An example is being asked either to accept a job transfer to another town in an undesirable location or to have your employment with an organization terminated. Approach-avoidance conflict occurs when a person must decide to do something that has both positive and negative consequences. An example is being offered a higher paying job but one with responsibilities that will make unwanted demands on your time.

Interpersonal conflict

Interpersonal conflict *is conflict that occurs between two or more individuals.*

Interpersonal conflict occurs between two or more individuals who are in opposition to one another; the conflict may be substantive or emotional in nature, or both. Two people debating aggressively over each other's views on the merits of hiring a job applicant is an example of a substantive interpersonal conflict. Two people continually in disagreement over each other's choice of work attire is an example of an emotional interpersonal conflict. Everyone has had experience with interpersonal conflicts of both types. It is a major form of conflict that managers face, given the highly interpersonal nature of the managerial role. We will address this form of conflict in more detail when we discuss conflict management strategies later in the chapter.

Intergroup conflict

Another level of conflict in organizations occurs between groups. Such intergroup conflict can also have substantive and/or emotional underpinnings. Intergroup conflict is quite common in organizations and it can make the coordination and integration of task activities very difficult. Consider a mail-order company where the relationship between the sales department and the stock-ordering inventory department breaks down. Sales staff, often rewarded on the level of sales they are able to invoice, may be greatly affected if there is not enough stock to send once an order has been received. Customers may cancel late orders. These differences are most apparent in terms of how group goals and the handling of information affects decision making in each setting where antagonistic relationships can mean that the whole organization suffers.

Interorganizational conflict

Conflict may also occur between entire organizations or independent units in large organizations.[23] Such interorganizational conflict most commonly reflects the competition and rivalry that characterizes organizations operating in the same markets. However, interorganizational conflict is really a much broader issue than that represented by market competition alone. Consider, for example, disagreements between unions and the organizations employing their members; between government regulatory agencies and the organizations subject to their surveillance; between organizations and those who supply them with raw materials; and between units within an organization competing for organizational resources. If conflict between divisions in a company is ignored, the organization will often be more concerned with internal competition than with external competition.[24]

New organizational structures such as joint ventures, strategic alliances and networks have the potential to release conflicts both between the new partners and also within the participating organizations. These latter conflicts were contained within the old structure or resolved by rules. The changes inherent in restructuring bring them to the surface, and such conflicts within the organization and between organizations may result in the dissolution of partnerships.

When organizations are faced with big decisions such as restructuring or forming strategic alliances, it is the CEO or head of the company who is the focal point of the decision-making process and who is ultimately responsible for the outcome. In difficult, sensitive or hostile environments, when tough decisions are to be made, who does the CEO turn to for advice or to act as a sounding board? His or her immediate staff or a consultant may be obvious choices yet some CEOs are finding the backup support they need in syndicates: formal groups that meet outside the office.

Take, for example, a situation in which a decision will ultimately result in conflict with one or more parties. The CEO is responsible for making the best decision for all parties but in cases such as staff cutbacks or plant relocation the decision is never an easy one to make because people are hurt, so the potential for conflict can be huge. In such delicate situations, discussions with internal staff may not always be appropriate, whereas discussions in confidence with external peers who may have experienced or are likely to experience a similar situation may provide a good source of advice, and even comfort.

Conflict and culture

Most developed countries are by now culturally diverse because of economic migrants and skills shortages. As such our employees come from diverse backgrounds, which are characterized by a wide range of traditions, languages, beliefs, values, ideas and practices.[25] In addition many graduates do not spend the whole of their working lives in the country in which they received their degree. In this world where our borders are becoming more porous for crossnational work, any graduate has good opportunities to work abroad. One of the key reasons for the early return of expatriates is the uncertainty and frustration resulting from poor cross-cultural adaptation. The result of this is an increase in the interpersonal conflict expatriates experience in the workplace abroad, caused by cultural differences.[26] These should not be underestimated by anyone seeking to relocate to another country.

Constructive and destructive conflicts

Conflict in organizations can be dangerous. It is often upsetting both to the individuals directly involved and to others who may observe it or be affected by it. On an emotional level, at least, many of us are more aware of its perils than its possibilities. A common byproduct of conflict is stress. It can be uncomfortable, for example, to work in an environment in which two co-workers are continually hostile towards each other. But conflict is

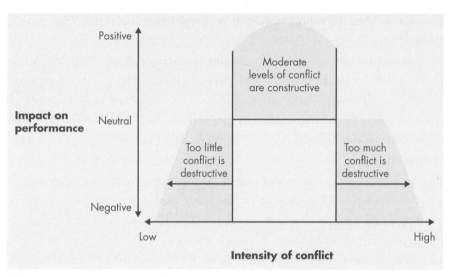

Figure 11.2: The two faces of conflict: functional conflict and dysfunctional conflict.

not always negative. Organizational behaviour recognizes two sides to conflict – the constructive side and the destructive side (Figure 11.2).

Constructive conflict results in benefits to the group or organization. It offers the people involved a chance to identify otherwise neglected problems and opportunities; performance and creativity can improve as a result. Indeed, an effective manager is able to stimulate constructive conflict in situations in which satisfaction with the status quo inhibits necessary change and development. Such a manager is comfortable dealing with both the constructive and the destructive sides of the conflict dynamic. Another value of conflict is that it can prevent stagnation, stimulate interest and curiosity and foster creativity. This is at the heart of the argument to promote diversity in working groups.

When conflict arises, most people's first reaction is to become angry or distressed and to seek to eliminate the problem. However, managers need to realize that if they can understand the issues that are causing the disagreement they will be in a better position to minimize the anger and distress and to use the conflict to the organization's advantage. Conflict presents an opportunity for managers to become aware of substantive issues and to think of ways in which to resolve them. Members of a crossfunctional team may have different information, ideas and perspectives about how the team should proceed, what the important issues are, how to solve problems facing the team and even what role each team member should play. An effective manager will seek to deal with these issues and the conflict will diminish revealing new and innovative ways of approaching business problems.

Innovation can occur when different ideas, perceptions and ways of processing and judging information collide. Positive conflict can help organizations become more innovative. Creative thinking can be a powerful tool in managing conflicts that result from personal disagreements and cognitive differences. Such conflict nurtures creativity. Various organizational members who see the world differently need to cooperate. Even when the parties have different viewpoints, managing those differences can be productive.[27]

Destructive conflict works to the group's or organization's disadvantage. It occurs, for example, when two employees are unable to work together as a result of interpersonal hostility (a destructive emotional conflict), or when the members of a committee fail to act because they cannot agree on group goals (a destructive substantive conflict). Destructive conflict of these types can decrease work productivity and job satisfaction and contribute to absenteeism and job turnover. Managers must be alert to destructive conflicts, quickly acting to prevent or eliminate them, or at least minimize their resulting disadvantages. Effective Manager 11.2 looks at ways to prevent destructive conflict.

EFFECTIVE MANAGER 11.2

How to prevent destructive conflict

- Listen carefully to employees to prevent misunderstanding.
- Monitor employees' work to assist them to understand and coordinate their actions.
- Encourage employees to approach you when they cannot solve difficulties with co-workers on their own.
- Clear the air with regular meetings that give employees a chance to discuss their grievances.

- Provide a suggestion box, check it frequently and personally reply to all signed suggestions.
- Offer as much information as possible about decisions to minimize confusion and resentment.
- Use employee surveys to identify potential conflicts that have not yet surfaced.

Conflict situations faced by managers

The very nature of the manager's position in an organization guarantees that conflict will be a part of his or her work experience. The manager may encounter conflict in supervisor–employee relationships, in peer or intergroup relationships and in relationships with senior management. The manager's ability to deal with such situations may in large part determine whether they have constructive or destructive impacts on the work situation. More specifically, an effective manager is able to recognize and deal with each of the following conflict situations:[28]

- Vertical conflict occurs between hierarchical levels, and commonly involves supervisor–employee disagreements over resources, goals, deadlines or performance results.
- Horizontal conflict occurs between people or groups at the same hierarchical level and commonly involves goal incompatibilities, resource scarcities or purely interpersonal factors.
- Line-staff conflict occurs between line and staff representatives and commonly involves disagreements over who has authority and control over certain matters, such as personnel selection and termination practices.
- Role conflict occurs when the communication of task expectations proves inadequate or upsetting, and commonly involves uncertainties of expectations, overloads or underloads in expectations, and/or incompatibilities among expectations.

Conflict becomes more likely in each of these situations when certain conditions exist. In general, managers should be aware that work situations with one or more of the following characteristics may be predisposed to conflict:[29]

- workflow interdependence
- power and/or value asymmetry
- role ambiguity or domain ambiguity
- resource scarcity (actual or perceived).

As discussed in Chapter 7, the various parts of a complex organization must be well integrated for it to function well. However, interdependencies among components can breed conflicts. When work flow interdependence is high – that is, when a person or group must rely on task contributions from one or more others to achieve its goals – conflicts often occur. You will notice this, for example, in a fast-food restaurant when the people serving the food have to wait too long for it to be delivered from the cooks. Good managers understand that the performance expectations and other aspects of such links must be handled carefully to ensure smooth working relationships. Indeed, one of the central precepts of total quality management is that 'internal customers' – other people or groups inside the organization – should receive the same dedicated attention and service that external customers receive.

Power or value asymmetries in work relationships exist when interdependent people or groups differ substantially from one another in status and influence, or in values. Conflict due to asymmetry is prone to occur, for example, when a low-power person needs the help of a high-power person who will not respond; when people who hold dramatically different values are forced to work together on a task; or when a high-status person is required to interact with – and perhaps depend on – someone of lower status. A common example of the latter case occurs when a manager is forced to deal with another manager through his or her deputy.

When individuals or groups operate with a lack of adequate task direction or clarity of goals, a stressful and conflict-prone situation exists. In Chapter 6 we discussed how role ambiguities might cause problems for people at work. At the group or department level, similar effects in terms of domain ambiguities can occur. These ambiguities involve misunderstandings over such matters as customer jurisdiction or scope of authority. Conflict is likely when individuals and/or groups are placed in situations in which it is difficult for them to understand just who is responsible for what. It may also occur where people resent the fact that their 'territory' is being trespassed upon.

A common managerial responsibility is the allocation of resources among different groups. Actual or perceived resource scarcity is a conflict-prone situation. When people sense the need to compete for scarce resources, working relationships are likely to suffer. This is especially true in organizations experiencing the financial difficulties associated with a period of decline. As cutbacks occur, various individuals or groups will try to position themselves to gain or retain maximum shares of the shrinking resource pool; they are also likely to try to resist or employ countermeasures to defend their resources from redistribution to others.

Most conflicts develop in stages, as shown in Figure 11.3. These stages include antecedent conditions, perceived and felt conflict, manifest conflict, conflict resolution or suppression and conflict aftermath.[30] The conditions that create conflict, as discussed, are examples of conflict antecedents; that is, they establish the conditions from which conflicts are likely to develop. In addition, managers should recognize that unresolved prior conflicts help set the stage for future conflicts of the same or related sort. Rather than try to deny the existence of conflict or settle on a temporary resolution, it is always best to deal with important conflicts so they are completely resolved.

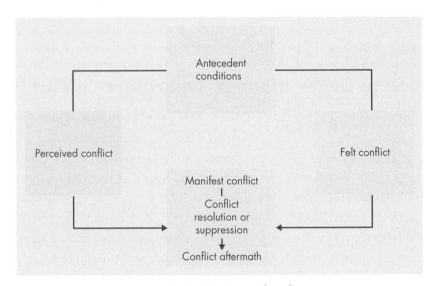

Figure 11.3: The stages of conflict.

When the antecedent conditions actually become the basis for substantive or emotional differences between people and/or groups, such as those situations already described, the stage of perceived conflict exists. Of course, only one of the conflicting parties may hold this perception. There is also a difference between perceived conflict and the stage of felt conflict. When people feel conflict, they experience it as tension that motivates them to take action to reduce feelings of discomfort. For conflict to be resolved, all parties should both perceive it and feel the need to do something about it.

When conflict is openly expressed in behaviour it is said to be manifest. A state of manifest conflict can be resolved by removing or correcting its antecedents. It can also be suppressed by controlling the behaviour (although no change in antecedent conditions occurs); for example, one or both parties may choose to ignore the conflict in their dealings with each other. This is a superficial and often temporary form of conflict resolution. Indeed, we have already noted that unresolved conflicts – and a suppressed conflict falls into this category – may continue to fester and cause future conflicts over similar issues.

Unresolved conflicts of any type can result in sustained emotional discomfort and stress and escalate into dysfunctional relationships between individuals and work units.

Manifest *conflict occurs when conflict is openly expressed in behaviour.*

In contrast, truly resolved conflicts may establish conditions that reduce the potential for future conflicts and/or make it easier to deal with them. Thus, any manager should be sensitive to the influence of conflict aftermath on future conflict episodes.

CONFLICT MANAGEMENT APPROACHES

Conflict in organizations is inevitable. The process of managing conflict to achieve constructive rather than destructive results is clearly essential to organizational success. This process of conflict management can be pursued in a variety of ways. An important goal should always be to achieve or set the stage for true conflict resolution – that is, a situation in which the underlying reasons for a given conflict are eliminated.

EFFECTIVE MANAGER 11.3

What can be done to better manage workplace conflict?[31]

- Reinforce to managers their responsibility for managing conflict.
- Develop conflict management strategies.
- Ensure that employees are familiar with the organization's policy on interpersonal conflict.
- Facilitate discussion sessions to express workplace relationships and interpersonal tensions appropriately.

- Coach employees to effectively communicate to support the resolution of conflict.
- Appoint conflict contact officers to listen to concerns and help staff find ways to resolve them.
- Provide support services such as employee assistance programmes that can be accessed on a confidential, self-referral basis.

CONFLICT RESOLUTION STYLES

Research on the management of conflict shows that it depends to a great extent on the personality characteristics of individual managers. Blake and Mouton were the first to classify personality strategies or styles of conflict resolution into five basic types: forcing, withdrawing, soothing, compromising and problem solving.[32] Afzalur Rahim also points to five different personality styles, or strategies, in conflict resolution, which he analyses according to the orientation towards self or others. His five styles are: integrating, obliging, compromising, dominating and avoiding.[33]

Rahim draws attention to the fact that there is no one best style, because each has its advantages and disadvantages. The effectiveness of applying a particular style depends on the situation. In everyday life people tend to show a preference for a certain conflict-resolution style; for example, a person with high affiliation needs will generally choose an obliging style and avoid a dominating style. It appears that in organizational life, the status of an organizational member could well influence the choice of conflict-resolution style;[34] for example, people may choose different strategies when dealing with a boss, an employee or a peer.

Most researchers share the view that an integrating style is best for managing conflicts in organizations, because this style is aimed at solving the problem, it respects the needs and interests of both sides, and is based on achieving a satisfactory outcome for each side.[35] However, choice of style needs to be contingent on the situation. A manager may choose a dominating style where the goals of the conflicting parties are incompatible, there has been a previous failure to reach agreement and a quick decision needs to be made.[36] In contrast, an integrating style would probably work best in a conflict caused by communication problems or in solving strategic problems linked to goals, policies and long-term planning in organizations. Research shows that managers believe that the frequent use of a compromising style hampers performance and the attainment of goals but that they may endorse such a style in certain situations where mutual concessions are the only possible solution.[37] Research by Krum Krumov showed that the integrating style is used more often by women than men and that its use increases gradually with age. In contrast, the compromising style is used equally by women and men and its use tends to increase with age. However, the use of this style is more typical of employees than managers.[38]

Wayne Pace suggests that preferred ways of handling conflict occur because when two people come together expecting to claim their share of scarce resources, they think somewhat habitually about themselves and the other person. Thus, conflict-resolution styles appear to be a combination of the amount of concern you have about accomplishing your own goals and the amount of concern you have about others accomplishing their goals. These concerns can be portrayed as two axes running from low concern to high concern. This paradigm results in a two-dimensional conceptualization of personal conflict-resolution styles, as depicted in Figure 11.4 and briefly described here. Unfortunately, when conflict occurs people have the tendency to do and say things that perpetuate the conflict.[39]

- Cell 1 – competitor or tough battler. People who employ this style pursue their own concerns somewhat ruthlessly and generally at the expense of other members of the group. The tough battler views losing as an indication of weakness, reduced status and a crumbling self-image. Winning is the only worthwhile goal and results in accomplishment and exhilaration.
- Cell 2 – collaborator or problem solver. People who employ this style seek to create a situation in which the goals of all parties involved can be accomplished. Problem solvers work at finding mutually acceptable solutions. Winning and losing are not part of their way of looking at conflict.
- Cell 3 – compromiser or manoeuvring conciliator. The person who employs this style assumes that everyone involved in a disagreement stands to lose and works to help find a workable position. A pattern of 'giving in' often develops.
- Cell 4 – accommodator or friendly helper. People who employ this style are somewhat nonassertive and quite cooperative, neglecting their own concerns in favour of those of others. The friendly helper feels that harmony should prevail and that anger and confrontation are bad. When a decision is reached, accommodators may go along with it and wish later that they had expressed some reservations.

- Cell 5 – avoider or impersonal complier. The person who employs this style tends to view conflict as unproductive and somewhat punishing. Thus, the avoider sidesteps an uncomfortable situation by refusing to be concerned. The result is usually an impersonal reaction to the decision and little commitment to future actions.

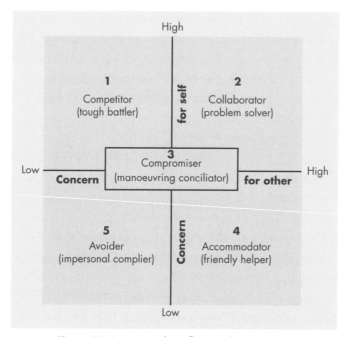

Figure 11.4: Personal conflict-resolution styles.

Source: Wayne, R. and Faules, D.F., (1994), *Organizational Communication*, 3rd edn, Allyn & Bacon, Boston, MA, p. 250

CONFLICT RESOLUTION THROUGH HIERARCHICAL REFERRAL

Hierarchical referral *uses the chain of command for conflict resolution; problems are referred up the hierarchy for more senior managers to reconcile.*

Hierarchical referral makes use of the chain of command for conflict resolution; problems are simply referred up the hierarchy for more senior managers to reconcile. The managers involved will typically be those to whom the conflicting parties mutually report; they will be managers who ultimately have the formal authority to resolve such disputes by directive if necessary.

Hierarchical referral can be definitive in a given case but it also has limitations. If conflict is severe and recurring, the continual use of hierarchical referral may not result in true conflict resolution. For instance, managers may have the tendency to consider most conflicts a result of poor interpersonal relations. They may consequently seek outward signs of harmony as evidence of their conflict management skills, or they may act quickly to replace a person with a perceived 'personality' problem. In so doing, they may actually fail to delve into the real causes of a conflict and conflict resolution may be superficial. Employees may also learn that it is best not to refer any conflict upwards. Future conflicts may be kept from view until they finally erupt into major problems.

CONFLICT RESOLUTION AND ORGANIZATIONAL DESIGN

When the organizational design allows departments to operate in self-contained subunits, conflict between departments tends to be muted. An example would be local councils where refuse and roadwork management are usually handled separately from one another. But when work needs to be coordinated, when resources must be shared and when other workflow interdependencies exist, conflicts often arise. Managers have a number of options available to reduce conflicts by adjusting the organizational design at such friction points. In our example of refuse collection and roadwork management, perhaps vehicles or sign-posts have to be shared – this might be a point of conflict.

One option is decoupling the groups – separating them or reducing contact between them. In our example this might mean setting up a third unit in charge of nonhuman resources such as vehicles, signs and shared resources. In some cases, the tasks of the units can be adjusted to reduce the number of required points of coordination (in our example we could restrict refuse recycling collection days to two per week allowing the shared trucks to be used by roadworkers for three days per week). The conflicting units can then be separated from one another and each can be provided with separate access to valued resources. Decoupling may reduce conflict but it may also result in duplication and a poor allocation of valued resources. Often the question is whether the conflict costs more than do the inefficiencies of resource reallocation.

Conflict management can be facilitated by assigning people to serve as formal linking pins between groups that are prone to conflict. People in linking-pin roles, such as project liaison officers, are expected to understand the operations, members' needs and the norms of their host group. Linking pins are supposed to use this knowledge to help their group work better with other groups to accomplish mutual tasks. In our example we might create the new post of resource manager. Although expensive, this technique is often used when different specialized groups, such as engineering and sales, must closely coordinate their efforts on complex and long-term projects.

A variation of the linking-pin concept is the liaison group. The purpose of such a group, team or department is to coordinate the activities of certain units and to prevent destructive clashes between them. Members of the department may be given formal authority to resolve disputes on everything from technical matters to resource claims or work assignments.

STAKEHOLDER ENGAGEMENT AND CONFLICT RESOLUTION

In order to minimize conflict and community objections to mining projects, some multinational mining corporations involve key external stakeholders. Community involvement means working in conjunction with communities to create acceptable processes for improving communication, managing conflicts and making appropriate decisions.

OB IN ACTION

Newmont Mining Corporation

Newmont aims to engage, as much as possible, with its local communities to ensure that interactions are relevant, that conflicts are resolved quickly and to the mutual benefit of both parties and that they are resolved in such a way that stakeholders feel positive about their involvement with the company.

In Peru, for example, representatives of Yanacocha participate in two dialogue tables – one under the auspices of the Compliance Advisor/Ombudsman for the International Finance Corporation arm of the World Bank and the other through the Office of the President of Peru. These groups include elected officials, community leaders, non-government organizations and representatives from the mine discussing issues and concerns and seeking solutions and greater understanding.

In Ghana, an acquisition in 2002 has been highly successful for the group. Its Web site documents the Ghanaian policies and Newmont's consultation exercise to ensure the local community is respected during the expansion of mining at the sites (see **http://info.icmm.com/ve/6790RQu7531RM9183c/page=6**, accessed 7 December 2007).

NEGOTIATION

Conflict between individuals, groups and organizations is common. When parties are involved in conflict, negotiation is frequently used to resolve differences. This section introduces you to negotiation as an important process in managing people and organizations.

Negotiation
is the process of making joint decisions when the parties involved have different preferences.

Managers need to understand some of the key areas of negotiation in order to improve workplace effectiveness and performance. Negotiation is the process of making joint decisions when the parties involved have different preferences. In other words, negotiation can be considered a way of finding the best solution with others in the process of making decisions.

Negotiation is especially significant in today's work settings, where more people are being offered opportunities to be involved in decisions affecting them and their work. As more people get involved in any decision-making process, so more disagreements are likely to arise over such diverse matters as wage rates, task objectives, performance evaluations, job assignments, work schedules, work locations and special privileges. Given that organizations are becoming increasingly participative, a manager's familiarity with basic negotiation concepts and processes is increasingly important for dealing with such day-to-day affairs.

FOUR TYPES OF NEGOTIATION SITUATION

In the course of their work, managers may be faced with different types of negotiation situations. As shown in Figure 11.5, there are four main types of situations with which managers should be familiar. These are:

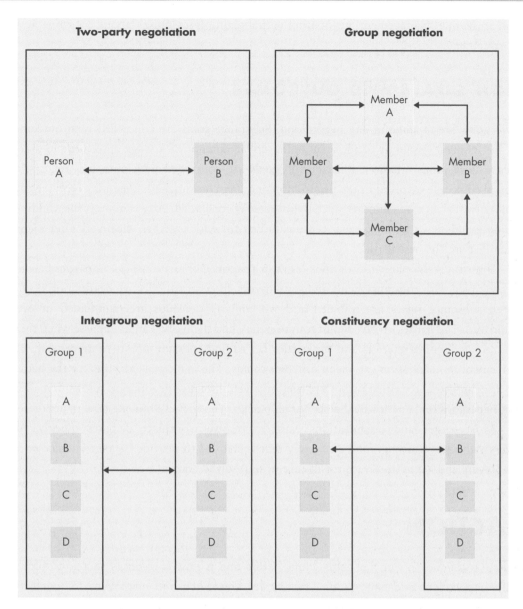

Figure 11.5: Four types of negotiation situation faced by managers.

- *Two-party negotiation.* The manager negotiates directly with one other person, for example a manager and an employee negotiating a salary increase during an annual performance appraisal.
- *Group negotiation.* The manager is part of a team or group whose members are negotiating to arrive at a common decision; for example, a committee that must reach agreement on recommending a new sexual harassment policy.
- *Intergroup negotiation.* The manager is part of a group that is negotiating with another group to arrive at a decision regarding a problem or situation affecting both; for example, negotiation between management groups from two organizations to form a joint venture or strategic alliance.
- *Constituency negotiation.* The manager is involved in negotiation with other people and each individual party represents a broad constituency. A common example is a team

representing 'management' negotiating with a team representing 'labour' to arrive at an agreement.

NEGOTIATION GOALS AND OUTCOMES

Substance goals *are concerned with outcomes tied to the 'content' issues at hand in a negotiation.*

Relationship goals *are concerned with how well people involved in a negotiation, and their constituencies, are able to work with one another once the process is concluded.*

Two goals are at stake in any negotiation. **Substance goals** are concerned with outcomes of the 'content' issues at hand, such as the dollar amount of a wage agreement in a collective bargaining situation. **Relationship goals** are concerned with outcomes relating to how well people involved in the negotiation and any constituencies they may represent are able to work with one another once the process is concluded. An example is the ability of union members and management representatives to work together effectively after a contract dispute has been settled.

Unfortunately, many negotiations result in a sacrifice of relationships, as parties become preoccupied with substance goals and self-interest. In contrast, effective negotiation occurs when substance issues are resolved and working relationships are maintained or even improved. The parties involved in negotiation may find themselves at an impasse when there are no overlapping interests and the parties fail to find common points of agreement. But agreement in negotiation can mean different things. The agreement may be 'for the better' or 'for the worse' for either or both parties involved. Effective negotiation results in making joint decisions that are 'for the better' for all parties. The trick is knowing how to get there.

Most people and organizations want to resolve workplace disputes quickly and fairly. Most governments fund an agency that is enabled to provide balanced advice to all employers and act as an arbitrator in case of unresolved conflict.

OB IN ACTION

Most governments fund a national service that helps employers undertake negotiations and other forms of conflict resolution. In the UK this is called ACAS (Advisory, Conciliation and Arbitration Service). It was originally put into place to help employers cope with the large number of trade union strikes occurring in Britain in the 1970s. Their role was to help all parties on their case (advice), help undertake mediation services so that voluntary agreements could be reached (reconciliation) and, in the final stage decide for the parties as a binding arbitrator.

It has seen a dramatic shift in its activities since the reduction of strike activity during the late 1980s and is now a valuable source of information for employers and employees for conflict avoidance and early conflict resolution. It has local offices and can provide staff who will be available for discussion or to undertake training. It also has a Web site full of helpful guidance and template policies for organizations to download free. It operates a helpline that provides information about terms and conditions of employment and helps to resolve conflicts. It does all of this because it has built a reputation as an 'honest broker' and both employers and employees respect the opinion of their staff and go to them for confidential help in all matters to do with conflict resolution.

DIFFERENT APPROACHES TO NEGOTIATION

Consider the following scenario. It illustrates an important point. Two employees want to book their holidays in the same period (during school holidays). However, the boss can only allow one of them to take holidays in that period. They begin to negotiate over who should take the holiday in that period. For our purposes, the 'holiday' represents a valued outcome for both employees. The approach taken to the negotiation can have a major influence on its outcomes. It is useful to discuss two alternative approaches: distributive negotiation and integrative negotiation.

Distributive negotiation

In distributive negotiation, the focus is on 'positions' that conflicting parties stake out or declare. Each party is trying to 'claim' certain portions of the available 'pie'. Distributive negotiation is sometimes referred to as competitive or positional negotiation. Returning to the holiday scenario, if the two workers adopted distributive bargaining approaches they would each ask the question: 'Who is going to get the holiday at the requested time?' This question and the way in which it frames subsequent behaviour, will have a major impact on the negotiation process and outcomes.

Distributive negotiation *is negotiation in which the focus is on 'positions' staked out or declared by the parties involved, who are each trying to claim certain portions of the available 'pie'.*

A case of distributive negotiation usually unfolds in one of two directions, neither of which yields optimal results. 'Hard' distributive negotiation takes place when each party holds out to get its own way. This leads to competition, whereby each party seeks dominance over the other and tries to maximize self-interests. 'Soft' distributive negotiation takes place when one party is willing to make concessions to the other to get things over with. In this case, one party tries to find ways to meet the other's desires. A soft approach leads to accommodation (one party gives in to the other) or compromise (each party gives up something of value in order to reach agreement).

In the case of the two employees wanting the same holiday period, the hard approach may lead to a win–lose outcome, in which one employee will dominate (perhaps by putting forth a stronger and more convincing case to the boss) and therefore wins the round. Or it may lead to an impasse, in which case neither employee will get the holiday. A soft approach (or compromise) may result in the holiday period being split equally between the two employees, where one employee gets half of the period and the second takes the other half. But here, too, dissatisfaction may exist because both employees are still deprived of what they originally wanted – the entire holiday period at the preferred time.

Integrative negotiation

In integrative negotiation sometimes called principled negotiation, the focus is on the 'merits' of the issues. Everyone involved tries to enlarge the available 'pie' rather than stake claims to certain portions of it. For this reason, integrative negotiation is also sometimes referred to as problem-solving or interest-based negotiation. In the case of the employees, the integrative approach to negotiation would be prompted by asking the question: 'How can the available leave best be used?' Notice that this is a very different question from the

Integrative negotiation *is negotiation in which the focus is on the merits of the issues and the parties involved try to enlarge the available 'pie' rather than stake claims to certain portions of it.*

one described for distributive negotiation. It is much less confrontational and allows for a broader range of alternatives.

The integrative approach to negotiation has much more of a 'win–win' orientation than does the distributive approach; it seeks ways of satisfying the needs and interests of all parties. At one extreme, this might involve selective avoidance, wherein both parties simply realize that there are more important things on which to focus their time and attention. In the holiday scenario, the two workers may mutually decide to forget about the holiday and to attend work. Compromise can also play a role in the integrative approach but it must have an enduring basis. This is most likely to occur when the compromise involves each party giving up something of perceived lesser personal value to gain something of greater value. In the case of the workers, one may get the holiday this time in return for the other getting one during the next school holidays.

Finally, integrative negotiation may involve true cooperation. In this case, the negotiating parties engage in problem solving to arrive at a mutual agreement that truly maximizes benefit to each. In the case of the holidays, this ideal approach could lead to both workers getting half the time off and spending the other half working but from home so they can still attend to their children. As you can see, this solution would be almost impossible to realize using the distributive approach because each worker would be preoccupied with getting the holiday. Only under the direction provided by the integrative approach – 'How can the available leave best be used?' – is such a mutually optimal solution possible. However, it is important to appreciate that the most effective negotiators will have a wide array of negotiation skills and will be able to use both approaches, mixing and matching them, depending on what they think works best for a specific issue or situation.

MANAGERIAL ISSUES IN NEGOTIATION

Given the distinctions between distributive and integrative negotiation, it is appropriate to identify some negotiation issues of special relevance to managers – specifically, the foundations for gaining integrative agreements, classic two-party negotiation and communication problems in negotiation.

Gaining integrative agreements

Underlying the concept of 'principled' negotiation is negotiation based on the 'merits' of the situation. The foundations for gaining truly integrative agreements cover three main areas: attitudes, behaviours and information. To begin with, there are three attitudinal foundations of integrative agreements:

BATNA is the 'best alternative to a negotiated agreement', or each party's position on what they must do if an agreement cannot be reached.

- each party must approach the negotiation with a willingness to trust the other party
- each party must be willing to share information with the other party
- each party must be willing to ask concrete questions of the other party.

As implied, the information foundations of integrative agreements are substantial; they involve each party becoming familiar with the **BATNA**, or 'best alternative to a negotiated agreement'. That is, both parties must know what they will do if an agreement cannot be reached. This requires that both negotiating parties identify and understand their personal interests in the situation. They must know what is really important to them in the case at hand and they must come to understand the relative importance of the other party's interests. As difficult as it may seem, each party must achieve an understanding of what the other party values, even to the point of determining its BATNA.

Reaching this point of understanding is certainly not easy. In the complex social setting of a negotiation things may happen that lead parties astray. An unpleasant comment uttered during a stressful situation, for example, may cause the other party to terminate direct communication for a time. Even when they return, the memory of this comment may overshadow any future overtures made by the offending party. In negotiation, all behaviour is important both for its actual impact and for the impression it leaves. Accordingly, the following behavioural foundations of integrative agreements must be carefully considered and included in any negotiator's repertoire of skills and capabilities:

- the ability to separate the people from the problem and to avoid letting emotional considerations affect the negotiation
- the ability to focus on interests rather than positions
- the ability to avoid making premature judgements
- the ability to judge possible agreements according to an objective set of criteria or standards.

CLASSIC TWO-PARTY NEGOTIATION

Figure 11.6 introduces the case of the new graduate. In this case, a graduate is negotiating a job offer with a corporate recruiter. The example illustrates the basic elements of classic two-party negotiation in many contexts.

To begin with, look at the situation from the graduate's perspective. She has told the recruiter that she would like a salary of €45 000; this is her initial offer. But she also has in mind a minimum reservation point of €35 000 – the lowest salary that she will accept for this job. Thus, she communicates a salary request of €45 000 but is willing to accept one as low as 35 000. The situation is somewhat reversed from the recruiter's perspective. The recruiter's initial offer to the graduate is 30 000 euros and the maximum reservation point is 40 000; this is the most the recruiter is prepared to pay.

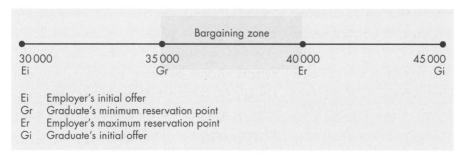

Figure 11.6: An example of the bargaining zone in classic two-party negotiation.

The bargaining zone is defined as the range between one party's minimum reservation point and the other party's maximum reservation point. In Figure 11.6, the bargaining zone is 35 000–40 000; it is a positive bargaining zone because the reservation points of the two parties overlap. Whenever a positive bargaining zone exists, bargaining has room to unfold. Had the graduate's minimum reservation point been greater than the recruiter's maximum reservation point (for example, 42 000), there would have been no room for bargaining. Classic two-party bargaining always involves the delicate tasks of first discovering the respective reservation points (your own and the other's) and then working towards an agreement that lies somewhere within the resulting bargaining zone and that is acceptable to each party.

▶ COUNTERPOINT

Underlying conflict

Olivia is a senior sales manager for VLC Software, a company that customizes telephone answering systems. She has been employed there for five years. VLC Software is a small software development company with 12 employees, but with a share of 25% of the national market. Olivia was initially employed by VLC as a junior IT account support officer and has worked her way through the company hierarchy to the senior position she is in today. Olivia has a very good relationship with all the other employees, horizontal and vertical. Six people – five salespeople and one administration person – report to her as senior manager. All employees at VLC have a lot of respect for Olivia because of her background with the company. They feel she 'knows the ropes' and often consult her about professional and personal problems.

Unfortunately, over the past six months VLC has been losing market share. Industry trends suggest that software sales are consistent, so there do not appear to be any macro issues to account for the downturn in sales. Nelson, the CEO of VLC, is very concerned and feels that if VLC is falling below the industry average then there is a chance the problem could be a human resource issue, either with his own staff or with the distributors. Because of Olivia's strong relationship with the other employees at VLC, and because it is easier to audit VLC than the external distributors, Nelson has asked her to prepare a confidential written report on the entire operation of VLC, identifying any weaknesses in systems and people. Olivia is concerned about the outcome, as over a period of time she has tried to deal with several operational and human resource problems but has ultimately failed. Olivia is aware of an underlying conflict between the five salespeople that is mainly due to the fact that sales territories are not clearly defined and there are no firm incentive or reward schemes in place. As a result of this some of the more experienced salespeople have been quietly operating outside their geographical areas, creating motivation problems among those who are staying within their boundaries.

Olivia is uncomfortable about how to conduct the audit because she is sensing something of an ethical dilemma. On one hand she feels it is her duty as senior manager to improve the operations and sales for VLC; on the other hand she wants to remain loyal to her team. However, to prevent the underlying conflict from erupting, Olivia realizes the time has come to conduct a complete audit and formally report her findings.

Questions

1. Should Olivia make it known to the employees at VLC that she is carrying out an audit? Explain why or why not.

2. If Olivia's findings suggest that the issue of underlying conflict among the salespeople is the reason for the downturn in sales, outline the process she should go through to counter that conflict. Bear in mind that Olivia's loyalty to all of the staff means she may need to draw on her negotiating skills to achieve a win–win outcome among the team.

It is too easy in negotiation to stake out your position based on the assumption that to gain your way something must be 'subtracted' from the other party's way. This myth of the 'fixed pie' is a purely distributive approach to negotiation. The whole concept of integrative negotiation is based on the premise that the 'pie' can sometimes be expanded and/or used to the maximum advantage of all parties, not just one.

Parties to negotiations often begin by stating extreme demands, so the possibility of escalating commitment is high. That is, once 'demands' have been stated people become committed to them and are reluctant to back down. As a result, they may be prone to nonrational escalation of conflict. Concerns for 'protecting your ego' and 'saving face' may enhance these tendencies. It takes self-discipline to spot this tendency in your own behaviour as well as that of others.

It is also common for negotiators to develop the belief that their positions are the only 'correct' ones. This is characterized by overconfidence and ignoring others' needs. In some cases, negotiators completely fail to see merits in the other party's position – merits that an outside observer would be sure to spot. Such overconfidence makes it harder to reach a positive common agreement. It may even set the stage for disappointment if the negotiation is turned over to a neutral third party for resolution.

In arbitration, this third party acts as the 'judge' and issues a binding decision after listening to the positions advanced by the parties involved in a dispute. Sometimes, a manager may be asked to serve as an arbitrator of disputes between employees, from matters as important as the distribution of task assignments to those as seemingly trivial as access to a photocopy machine.

CONCLUSION

Communication is a deceptively easy topic to study but fraught with dangers and challenges, which reflect how hard it is to get a match between the message sent and the message received. Many elements have to be in place, such as effective channels and little noise, as well as senders who are good encoders and receivers who are able and willing to be effective.

It is no coincidence that this chapter is shared by the two topics of communication and conflict. Many conflicts begin with poor communication and are almost certainly exacerbated by weaknesses in communication. All managers need to understand their own communication weaknesses in order to minimize the conflict they cause and to help them mediate and negotiate a solution when conflicts arise form any source. Expertise in conflict negotiation and resolution is a sought-after skill within the workplace and allows for all employees to focus on positive value-creating activities without distraction.

SUMMARY

LEARNING OBJECTIVE 1
Communication and its role in organizations

Communication in an organization is a process by which organizational members share meanings by exchanging information. We communicate to inform, instruct, motivate or seek information, to achieve coordinated action throughout the organization, to develop information for the benefit of the organization, to express our feelings and emotions and to explain respective job responsibilities, roles and expectations. The interpersonal communication process involves an intricate matching of information that is encoded, sent, received and decoded, sometimes with and sometimes without feedback, but always affected by noise. Communication is effective when both sender and receiver interpret a message in the same way. It is efficient when messages are transferred at a low cost.

Communication channels include formal, informal and quasiformal relationships among members of the organization. The organization is a network of information and communication channels. The electronic age has provided organizations with new opportunities to link managers effectively. Barriers to communication include special sources of noise common to most interpersonal exchanges: physical distractions, cultural differences, the absence of feedback and status effects. Each of these sources of noise should be recognized and subjected to special managerial control. Managers can eliminate or reduce barriers through such techniques as wandering around, developing active listening skills, providing effective feedback to the sender of the communication, and articulating job roles and responsibilities.

LEARNING OBJECTIVE 2
Conflict and its effect on organizations

Conflict can be either emotional (based on personal feelings) or substantive (based on work goals). Both forms can be harmful in organizations if, as a result, individuals and/or groups are unable to work constructively with one another. Conflict situations in organizations occur in vertical and lateral working relations and in line-staff relations. Often, they result from workflow interdependencies and resource scarcities. Most typically, conflict develops through a series of stages, beginning with antecedent conditions and progressing into manifest conflict. The conflict may or may not be entirely 'resolved' in the sense that the underlying reasons for the emotional and/or substantive conflict are eliminated. Unresolved conflicts set the stage for future conflicts of a similar nature. When kept within tolerable limits, conflict can be a source of creativity and performance enhancement. Even when managers have different viewpoints, ongoing questioning and discussion about their differences may unleash more creative approaches to a situation as they are further probed. On the other hand, such situations can become destructive when these limits are exceeded and the hostility between individuals or groups continues. In this case, managers must be made aware of such conflicts and take appropriate action to resolve them.

LEARNING OBJECTIVE 3
Managing conflict

Conflict management should always proceed with the goal of true conflict resolution. Indirect forms of conflict management include appeals to common goals, hierarchical referral and organizational redesign. Direct conflict management proceeds with different combinations of assertiveness and cooperativeness on the part of conflicting parties. Win–win outcomes are achieved through cooperation and problem solving most often associated with high assertiveness and high cooperation. Win-lose outcomes usually occur through direct competition or authoritative command. Lose–lose outcomes are typically found as a result of avoidance, smoothing and compromise approaches.

LEARNING OBJECTIVE 4
Negotiation and its role in organizations

Negotiation in organizations occurs whenever two or more people with different preferences must make joint decisions. Managers may find themselves involved in various types of negotiation situations, including two-party, group, intergroup and constituency negotiation. Both substance goals and relationship goals are at stake. Effective negotiation occurs when issues of substance are resolved and human relationships are maintained, or even improved, in the process. To achieve such results, ethical conduct must be carefully maintained even as negotiating parties represent viewpoints and preferences that differ greatly from one another.

LEARNING OBJECTIVE 5
Managers' issues in negotiation

Different approaches to negotiation can have very different results. In distributive negotiation, the focus of each party is on staking out positions in the attempt to claim desired portions of a 'fixed pie'. In integrative negotiation, sometimes called principled negotiation, the focus is on determining the merits of the issues and finding ways to satisfy one another's needs. The distributive approach is often associated with individual styles of competition (the 'hard' approach) or accommodation (the 'soft' approach). The integrative approach ideally leads to some form of cooperation or problem solving to achieve a mutually desirable solution.

CHAPTER 11 STUDY GUIDE

You can also test your understanding and access further resources at **www.wileyeurope .com/college/french**.

REVIEW QUESTIONS

1. Describe the main sources of noise and disturbance in communication. Give examples.
2. Under what circumstances would conflict be accepted and considered to be positive? Give examples.

3. What are some of the most common strategies used in resolving conflict? Briefly explain why conflict in the workplace can be positive.

4. Describe some of the most common managerial issues in negotiations.

APPLICATION QUESTIONS

1. Imagine you are a French national running the European HQ of an American-owned multinational drinks company. Your HQ is based in Paris, and you have just taken over five factories in Spain employing a total of 5000 people. What are some of the ways you would select to communicate your company's vision throughout the new acquisition?

2. If, as a manager, you felt it necessary to criticize the productivity of one of your employees, what would be some of the important factors you would consider before approaching that person?

3. As you read earlier, 'when conflict arises, most people's first reaction is to become angry or distressed, and to seek to eliminate the problem.' Provide an example in which you have been an observer of a conflict situation. The example you describe could be from your workplace or a different environment, such as a bank or an airport. Write down how the reaction of the parties involved in the conflict appeared to an onlooker – in this case, yourself. Then explain how you would have handled the situation if you had been one of the parties in conflict, remembering to take into consideration the emotional aspect that can escalate conflict.

4. Research indicates that managers are known to spend up to 20 per cent of their time dealing with conflict, including conflicts in which managers are themselves directly involved. What implications does this have for business school educators and new managers?

5. Using an example, explain how destructive conflict can have a negative impact on performance. How would you remedy the conflict situation you have discussed?

6. Design a half-day awareness workshop aimed at teaching administrative staff the meaning of conflict and the various approaches to conflict resolution.

RESEARCH QUESTIONS

1. Access the Web site of a large company with which you are familiar. Search the site with a view to identifying how the company:

   (a) Communicates its commitment to new and existing employees and its external customers, such as you.

   (b) Thinks of conflict – does it acknowledge it and manage it or, for example, do you detect an avoidance of conflictual issues?

(c) Select a well-known case of conflict involving multiple parties (including, for example, managers, customers, government and the community).

– Examine the reasons for the conflict.

– Outline how and why the conflict escalated.

– Describe the approach(es) used in attempting to resolve the conflict.

– Critically examine the effectiveness of these approach(es).

INDIVIDUAL ACTIVITY

Disagreeing with your boss

Objective

To develop your understanding and application of different approaches to conflict resolution.

Total time: 45–60 minutes.

Procedure

First think about the following scenario, then provide a solution or approach to the problem. Write down the approach you favour.

Scenario

You work in the sales area of a software distribution company operating in the Scandinavian market. You have been working for the company for seven years and your income depends on the sales figures achieved by the company because you are given a very generous bonus based on these figures.

You and your supervisor, Johansen, have not been getting along well for the past year or so. Johansen is a domineering individual and does not seem to want your input on any major activities being undertaken in your sales unit. However, a major project has been assigned to your unit and Johansen has instructed you to take responsibility for the project. The aim of the project is to develop a strategy for an effective market entry into a new geographical area in the region.

Johansen gives directions for completing the project. You examine the situation and after some thought tell Johansen that you have some ideas about how the project might be undertaken effectively. Johansen responds, 'I am not interested in hearing your ideas. I get paid for having ideas and you get paid for following my directions.'

Against your better judgement you follow Johansen's directions but, as you suspected, Johansen's ideas for the project are not sound and everything goes badly. The organization loses a lot of money on the project and you predict that things are likely to get much worse if the project continues in the way being directed by Johansen.

You are about to go to the regular Monday morning staff meeting, where you will be called on to report on the progress of the project. At this point, no one is aware of how badly the project is going. You have mentioned it several times to Johansen, who does not want to talk about it and says you are making excuses for your own incompetence. You are concerned about disagreeing with Johansen. At the same time you do not want to be embarrassed in front of your colleagues, who are also social acquaintances. Johansen has the ability to greatly influence your career and basically controls your pay, promotional opportunities and other incentive rewards within the company for at least the next three years. Because of family obligations, you do not feel ready to leave the company.

GROUP ACTIVITY 39

Conflict resolution

Preparation

You will be given the opportunity to role play handling a conflict you face or have faced. Select the conflict and write out the information for a class member who will play the role of the person with whom you are in conflict.

1. Define the situation and list pertinent information about the other party (that is, relationship to you, knowledge of the situation, age, background and so on).
2. State what you wish to accomplish during the conflict resolution.
3. Identify the other party's possible reaction to your confrontation (resistance to change).

Plan how you will overcome resistance to change using the problem-solving conflict management style. A good way to open the conflict resolution is to use an X (behaviour), Y (consequences), Z (feelings) statement: for example, 'When you smoke in my room (behaviour), I have trouble breathing and become nauseous (consequences) and feel uncomfortable and irritated (feeling).' Write out an XYZ statement to open your selected conflict resolution. During the role play, open with your XYZ statement, then allow the person to respond as you seek true satisfaction of everyone's concerns by working through differences and finding and solving problems so everyone gains as a result.

Objective
To develop your conflict-resolution skills.

Total time: 30–40 minutes.

Procedure 1
Break into groups of three. If there are any people not in a triad, make one or two groups of two. Each member selects the number 1, 2 or 3. Number 1 will be the first to initiate a conflict role play, then 2, followed by 3.

Procedure 2
1. Initiator number 1 gives his or her information from the preparation to number 2 (the responder) to read. Once number 2 understands, role play (see step 2 below). Number 3 is the observer.
2. Role play the conflict resolution. Number 3, the observer, writes his or her observation. Focus on what was done and how to improve.
3. Integration. When the role play is over, the observer leads a discussion on the effectiveness of the conflict resolution. All three should discuss the effectiveness. Number 3 is not a lecturer. Do not go on until told to do so.

Procedure 3
Same as procedure 2, only number 2 is now the initiator, number 3 is the responder and number 1 is the observer.

Procedure 4
Same as procedure 2, only number 3 is the initiator, number 1 is the responder and number 2 is the observer.

Case Study

CONFLICT OVER NEW BUSINESS STRATEGIES

Carrie recently joined Executive Improvement Strategies (EIS), a small consulting firm specializing in training and development programmes for senior managers. It is based in Prague, with a small client base that takes in several of the foreign multinationals in the city. There are three other consultants working for EIS and one managing partner, John, who started the firm five years ago.

Carrie is highly experienced and well known in the corporate training arena; in fact, her credentials far exceed those of the other consultants, including John, the managing partner. One of Carrie's strengths is successfully targeting new business. Part of this can be attributed to her outgoing, gregarious personality, along with her rather nontraditional, informal approach to obtaining new business; however, it fits Carrie's personality and it works.

As managing partner, John has implemented a very rigid culture at EIS, particularly in relation to seeking new business. Since Carrie has been with EIS, John has not been particularly impressed with her approach to potential clients and on several occasions has had discussions with her about this. These discussions have often resulted in conflict around the need for administration and proper records of conversations as John is worried about what Carrie might be promising to potential clients in terms of fees per day, discounts and products.

Carrie has just learned of an excellent opportunity to move into the public sector in the city. A new government policy has suggested that training for senior public-sector managers should in the future be sourced from the private sector to engender change and the uptake of contemporary management practices. Carrie has heard about this before it is public knowledge through someone she used to train with many years ago and still sees at professional networking events. Of course, Carrie will be following through the public sector lead for EIS, so she is keen to meet with John to brief him on her intentions.

Unfortunately, although the public sector opportunity is a good breakthrough for EIS, Carrie's enthusiasm is dampened knowing that John will have very set ideas about how to approach this market, and that those ideas will be completely contrary to Carrie's strategy. So what should be a positive meeting may ultimately turn into a disaster if it isn't handled correctly.

Questions

1. If you were to advise Carrie about how to approach the meeting with John in order to avoid initial conflict, what would you say?
2. In order to please John, should Carrie attempt to change her approach to potential new clients? Why or why not?
3. Given that Carrie and John have very different approaches to obtaining new business, what processes can they put in place to ensure they can continue in a productive working relationship? Remember that John is head of EIS, yet Carrie has more experience and success.

Source: From Wood *et al.* (2006), *Organizational Behaviour: Core Concepts and Applications.* John Wiley & Sons Australia, Ltd: Milton, Qld.

SUGGESTED READING

Jones, A. (2007), More than 'managing across borders': the complex role of face-to-face interaction in globalizing law firms face-time. *Journal of Economic Geography*, 7 (3), 223–246. This article provides application of theory into real-life multi-site situations that uncover deep preferences for specific types of communication. It raises some interesting questions for the management of globally based organizations.

Mehrabian, A. (2007), *Nonverbal Communication*, Transaction Publishers: Piscataway, NJ. This is an aspect of communication that is extremely important to understand and Mehrabian has been the subject leader since its inception.

END NOTES

1. Mintzberg, H. (1990), *Mintzberg on Management: Inside our Strange World of Organizations*, Free Press, Macmillan: London.
2. Dahle, T. (1954), An objective and comparative study of five methods of transmitting information from management to business and industrial employees. *Speech Monographs*, **21** (March).
3. Kirkpatrick, D.V. & Bryan, M. (2007), Hurricane emergency planning by home health providers serving the poor. *Journal of Health Care for the Poor*, **18** (2), 299–314.
4. Pezzoli, K., Tukey, R., Sarabia, H. *et al.* (2007), The NIEHS environmental health sciences data resource portal: placing advanced technology in service to vulnerable communities. Environmental *Health Perspectives*, **115** (4), 564–571.
5. Wertheim, E.G. (2007), 'The importance of effective communication', Northeastern University College of Business Administration, web. cba.neu.edu/ewertheim/interper/commun.htm (accessed 4 January 2007).
6. Peters, T.J. & Waterman, R.H. (1984), *In Search of Excellence: Lessons from America's Best Run Companies*, Harper & Row: New York.
7. Tarrant, D. (2002), Talking heads. *Australian Financial Review BOSS Magazine* (July 2002), 58.
8. Olson, B.J. (2007), Strategic decision making: the effects of cognitive diversity, conflict, and trust on decision outcomes. *Journal of Management*, 33 (2), 196–222.
9. Tarrant, op. cit.
10. Case, J. (2001), When salaries aren't secret. *Harvard Business Review*, (May), 37–39, 42–49.
11. Tarrant, op. cit.
12. Mehrabian, A. (2007), *Nonverbal Communication*. Transaction Publishers: New Brunswick, NJ.
13. Jones, A. (2007), More than 'managing across borders' the complex role of face-to-face interaction in globalizing law firms face-time. *Journal of Economic Geography*, 7 (3), 223–246.
14. DeChurch, L.A., Hamilton, K.L., Haas, C. (2007), Effects of conflict management strategies on perceptions of intergroup conflict. *Group Dynamics Theory Research and Practice*, 1 1 (1), 66–78.
15. Ibid.
16. Tjosvold, D. (2006), Defining conflict and making choices about its management. Lighting the dark side of organizational life. *International Journal of Conflict Management*, **17** (2), 87–95.
17. Walton, R.E. (1969), *Interpersonal Peacemaking: Confrontations and Third-party Consultation*. Addison-Wesley: Reading, MA.
18. *Managing Conflict at Work: Survey Report* (2004), available from Chartered Institute of Personnel and Development, www.cipd.co.uk.
19. Ayub, N. & Jehn, K. (2006) National Diversity and conflict in multinational workgroups – the moderating effect of nationalism. *International Journal of Conflict Management*, 17 (3), 181–202.
20. Walton, R.E. (1969), *Interpersonal Peacemaking: Confrontations and Third-party Consultation*, Addison-Wesley: Reading, MA.
21. Ibid.

22. Ibid.

23. Crook, T.R. & Combs, J.G. (2007), Sources and consequences of bargaining power in supply chains. *Journal of Operations Management*, **25** (2), 546–555.

24. Ibid.

25. Posthuma, R.A, White, G.O., Dworkin, J.B., Yanez, O. & Swift, M.S. (2006), Conflict resolution styles between coworkers in US and Mexican cultures. *International Journal of Conflict Management*, **17** (3), 242–260.

26. See Jassawalla, A., Truglia, C. & Garvey, J, (2004), Cross-cultural conflict and expatriate manager adjustment: an exploratory study. *Management Decision*, **42** (7), 837–849.

27. Leonard, D. & Straus, S. (1997), Putting your company's whole brain to work. *Harvard Business Review*, **75** (4), 111.

28. Developed from Hellriegel, D., Slocum, J.W. Jr & Woodman, R.W. (1983), *Organizational Behaviour*, 3rd edn. West: St Paul, pp. 471–4.

29. Developed from Johns, G. (1983), Organizational Behaviour, Forsman: Glenview, IL, pp. 415–417. Walton, R.E. & Dutton, J.M. (1969), The management of interdepartmental conflict: a model and review. *Administrative Science Quarterly*, **14**, 73–84.

30. These stages are consistent with the conflict models described by Filley, A.C. (1975), *Interpersonal Conflict Resolution*, Foresman: Glenview, IL. Pondy, L.R. (1967), Organizational conflict: concepts and models. *Administrative Science Quarterly*, **12** (September), 269–320.

31. Adapted from Gaskell, R. (2003), How effectively is your organization managing conflict? *hrconnection*, **8**, www.davidsntrahaire.com.au/upload/HR-Connection-Volume_8.pdf, accessed 15 Febuary 2007.

32. Blake, R.R. & Mouton, J.S. (1964), The *Managerial Grid*, Gulf: Houston, TX.

33. Rahim, M.A. (1985), A strategy for managing conflict in complex organizations. *Human Relations*, **38** (1), 83–85.

34. Jones, R.E. & Melcher, B.H. (1982), Personality and preference for modes of conflict resolution. *Human Relations*, **35** (8), 649–658.

35. Lawrence, P.R. & Lorsch, J.W. (1967), Differentiation and integration in complex organizations. *Administrative Science Quarterly*, **12** (1), 1–47.

36. Robbins, S.P. (1978), 'Conflict management' and 'conflict resolution' are not synonymous terms. *California Management Review*, **21** (2), 67–75.

37. Lawrence, P.R. & Lorsch, J.W. (1967), *Organization and Environment*, Harvard University Press: Cambridge, MA.

38. Krumov, K., Ilieva, S., Karabeliova, S. & Alexieva, L. (2007), Conflict resolution strategies in the transition to market economy. *Annals of the American Academy of Political and Social Science*, **552** (10), 65.

39. Lusseir, R.N., (1993), *Human Relations in Organizations: a skill building approach* (2nd edn), Homewood, IL, Richard D. Irwin. © The McGraw-Hill Companies, Inc. Reproduced by permission.

CHAPTER

12

Organizational change

LEARNING OBJECTIVES

After studying this chapter you should be able to:

- identify the nature and scope of change
- identify who initiates and leads the change
- identify the process of change and change strategies used by managers
- explain why people resist change and describe strategies to overcome resistance
- explain the role of the change agent.

TURNING IT AROUND

St Luke's school has been transformed from an institution labelled as 'failing' into one of the top five most improved schools in the UK. Community engagement and strong leadership have been crucial factors in the change.

Approaching the millennium, St Luke's Church of England secondary in Portsmouth, England could not realistically have viewed the new century with optimism. It was, at that time, a failing 11–16 school on the point of closure. Only 3% of pupils achieved 5 A* to C GCSEs (the UK school-leaving certificate) and rates of exclusion were among the highest in the country. There were also high levels of crime and antisocial behaviour in the surrounding area involving children from the school. The school's Church of England voluntary-aided status saved it from closure and a new head – Krysia Butwilowska – was appointed to turn it around.

Within five terms, St Luke's was out of special measures. A UK Government Ofsted inspection team visiting in May 2003 reported: 'The leadership of the headteacher is excellent and is a significant factor in the climate for improvement in the school. She expects high standards and is very supportive of pupils and staff.' By 2005, some 58% of pupils got 5 A* to C GCSEs and St Luke's was among the top five most improved schools in the country.

At the outset, the headteacher adopted a highly directional style of leadership. She made it clear to staff what the vision was and what needed to be done. She was not collaborative in terms of taking policy and strategy decisions. Once the school was on a path to improvement, the headteacher reinforced the school's senior management, appointing a deputy head, a bursar and six assistant heads. With change embedded, her management style became much more collaborative, although all senior staff were expected to replicate the headteacher's passion and commitment. In addition, she put in place a weekly leadership programme for all staff in the teaching and learning area.

Engagement with the local community was the headteacher's highest priority when she took over. She wanted to tackle crime and antisocial behaviour among pupils and an extensive range of adult learning classes and after-school and holiday activities for pupils grew from this. The school also developed close links with police and other agencies and provided a base for Sure Start (a UK Government initiative focusing on early childhood experience) community wardens. As a result, crime in the area has been dramatically reduced. Her role in these developments has been to seek out the right partners and persuade them to act.

In September, St Luke's became the lead school of a community improvement partnership with Krysia Butwilowska as Chair of the Executive Committee. The partnership – one of five established by Portsmouth

Source: Training and Development Agency for Schools (TDA), **www.tda.gov.uk/case_studies/remodelling/st_lukes. aspx?keywords=st+luke's,** accessed 30 January 2006.

City Council – links 15 schools in the area, three of them secondaries. With the approval of St Luke's governing body, the headteacher has now made partnership working her core business. The partnership plans to put in place in early 2006 a second tier committee representing parents, pupils and community leaders.

The headteacher says that the new structure has taken collaboration between schools and external agencies to a new level. The presence of senior managers of every agency means decisions are taken and acted on much faster than before. She has adopted the same approach to her role as chairperson as she has as headteacher. She says it is not about telling people what to do but asking them what needs to be done.

Questions

1. How would you describe Krysia Butwilowska's approach to change management?
2. What were the critical actions and approaches that Krysia carried out in order to effect successful change?

INTRODUCTION

Change is not a recent phenomenon in organizations but certain aspects of change, for example, technological change, may be more distinguishable since the late 1980s because of the rate of change within that particular area. The rate of change within information technology has been dramatic. In the early 1980s European customers may have been using machines that loaded 56K of data, whereas in the year 2007 customers use 400 GB external devices in addition to machines that contain several hundred GB of memory. This chapter will address the various types of change, as well as provide an understanding of the process of change, and how to address resistance to change.

WHAT IS ORGANIZATIONAL CHANGE?

It could be argued that a common sense definition of change is simply 'making things different'. Two important aspects of organizational change relate to the actual *change itself*, such as changing a manufacturing process in an organization and the *perceived extent* of change in an organization, for example, in an organization that has not experienced much change, any change may be perceived as radical change, and possibly resisted on potential grounds only.

In OB, 'organizational change' refers to organization-wide change rather than to small changes such as adding a new person or making minor modifications to a process. Examples of organization-wide change might include a change of mission, restructuring operations, the adoption of major technologies and mergers.

THE SCALE OF CHANGE

Dunphy and Stace[1] provide a useful framework to analyse the scale of organizational change.

Scale type 1: fine tuning

Organizational change is an ongoing process characterized by fine tuning of the 'fit' or match between the organization's strategy, structure, people and processes, typically manifested at departmental/divisional levels, with one or more of the following:

- refining policies, methods and procedures
- creating specialist units and linking mechanisms to permit increased volume and increased attention to the unit quality and cost
- developing personnel especially suited to the present strategy (improved training and development; tailoring reward systems to match strategic thrusts)
- fostering individual and group commitment to the company mission and the excellence of one's own department.
- promoting confidence in the accepted norms, beliefs and myths.
- clarifying established roles (with their associated authorities and posers) and the mechanisms for allocating resources.

Scale type 2: incremental adjustment

This is organizational change characterized by incremental adjustments to the changing environment. Such change involves distinct modifications (but not radical change) to corporate business strategies, structures, and managerial processes, for example:

- expanding sales territory
- shifting the emphasis among products
- improved production process technology
- articulating a modified statement of mission to employees
- adjustments to organizational structures within and across divisional boundaries to achieve better links in product/service delivery.

Scale type 3: modular transformation

Organizational change characterized by major realignment of one or more departments/divisions. The process of radical change is focused on these subparts rather than the organization as a whole, for example:

- major restructuring of particular department/divisions
- changes in key executives and managerial appointments in these areas
- work and productivity studies resulting in significantly reduced or increased workforce numbers
- reformed departmental/divisional goals
- introduction of significantly new process technologies affecting key departments or divisions.

Scale type 4: corporate transformation

Organizational change that is corporate-wide, characterized by radical shifts in business strategy, and revolutionary change throughout the whole organization involving many of the following features:

- reformed organization mission and core values
- altered power and status affecting the distribution of power in the organization
- reorganization – major changes in structures, systems, and procedures across the organization
- revised interaction patterns – new procedures, work flows, communication networks and decision-making patterns across the organization
- new executives in key managerial positions from outside the organization.

Some experts use organizational transformation to designate a fundamental and radical reorientation of the way the organization operates. Some of this change may be described as radical change.[2] This is change that results in a major makeover of the organization and/ or of its component systems. In today's business environments, radical changes are often initiated by a critical event such as the arrival of a new chief executive officer, a new ownership brought about by a merger or takeover, or a dramatic failure in operating results. Radical change occurs infrequently in the life cycle of an organization. However, when it does occur, this change is intense and all-encompassing. There may be times in an organization's life when its survival depends on an ability to undergo successfully the rigours and demands of radical change. Radical change occurs when an industry's core assets and activities are both threatened with obsolescence, and knowledge and brand capital erode along with the customer and supplier relationships. It is most commonly caused by the introduction of new technologies or regulations, or by changing consumer preferences.

Radical change is change that results in a major makeover of the organization and/ or its component systems.

Another more common form of organizational change is incremental change. This is change that occurs more frequently and less traumatically, as part of an organization's natural evolution. Typical changes of this type include new products, new technologies and new systems. Although the nature of the organization remains relatively unaltered, incremental change builds on the existing ways of operating and seeks to enhance them or extend them in new directions. The ability to improve continually through incremental change is an important asset to organizations in today's demanding environments. Although the nature and size of change is important, the next issue concerns the question of whether change is planned or unplanned.

Incremental change is change that occurs more frequently and less traumatically as part of an organization's natural evolution.

PLANNED AND UNPLANNED CHANGE

Changes in organizations can be planned or unplanned. Planned change occurs when an organization deliberately attempts to make internal changes to meet specified goals or to pursue a set of strategies. For example, organizations often change their structures to meet given objectives or to pursue cost-cutting strategies. An organization might also engage in major updating of its operational systems, which would entail some form of technological change.

Unplanned change is usually prompted by some external driver, such as market forces, economic crises, economic opportunities or social changes. Typically, organizations engage in organization-wide change to respond to these forces and thereby evolve to a different level in their life cycle; for example, going from a highly reactive to a more proactive and planned development. However, not all change in organizations happens as a result of an intended (or change agent's) direction. Unplanned change occurs spontaneously or randomly, and without a change agent's attention. The appropriate goal in managing unplanned change is to act immediately once the change is recognized, to minimize any negative consequences and maximize any possible benefits.

In this chapter we are particularly interested in planned change – that is, change that comes about as a result of specific efforts on the part of a change agent. Planned change is a direct response to someone's perception of a performance gap. This is a discrepancy between the desired and actual state of affairs. Performance gaps may represent problems to be resolved or opportunities to be explored. It is useful to think of most planned changes as efforts initiated by managers to resolve performance gaps to the benefit of the organization and its members.

However, planned change often assumes that the future is predictable and there is an end state to be reached. In other words, managers tend to regard change as a once-only, major alteration to the organization. In reality, in the vast majority of cases change occurs in an incremental way, reflecting the assumption that what worked in the past will also work in the future. However, with contextual dynamism and complexity being the new rule, any linear extrapolation is at best misleading. The line representing the link between past and future is at best dotted and sometimes even discontinuous, with twists and thresholds everywhere.[3]

Unplanned change *is change that occurs at random or spontaneously and without a change agent's direction.*

Planned change *is change that happens as a result of specific efforts on the part of a change agent.*

The performance gap *is the discrepancy between an actual and a desired state of affairs.*

OB IN ACTION

Think about any organization that you have read about or researched. What made the organization change – internal or an external pressure or both? Who started the change agenda? Why was this change agenda initiated? Are there sometimes contradictions between what organizations report their reasons for change are as opposed to the actual reasons for organizational change? If this is the case, then why are organizations dishonest?

The metaphor for change could be described as a series of parallel DVD recordings, rather than a single photograph, as it may be rare for an organization to have a single change process in place running from beginning to end without any other change intervention happening at the same time.

Unplanned change is a change that occurs at random or spontaneously and without a change agent's direction. Planned change is change that happens as a result of specific efforts on the part of a change agent. The performance gap is the discrepancy between an actual and desired state of affairs.

Child[4] discusses the concept of 'emergent change' and links this to the size/range of change. Change may also be defined in terms of the scale of change in relation to the extent to which the change is planned or emergent.

Planned	Emergent
BPR	Organic development
whole org.	
	(e.g. start-up company).
Radical ---	
Merger of departments	Changes to selection of new
	members made by part org. teams
Annual targeted	Organizational Learning
improvements	whole org.
Incremental ---------------------------------------	
Changes agreed in staff	Continuous improvement part org.
performance plans	through project teams

Figure 12.1: Planned and emergent change.

Source: Child, J. (2005) *Organization: Contemporary Principles and Practice*, p. 288. Reproduced by permission of Blackwell Publishing.

LEADING CHANGE

Most change initiatives, especially radical change, require effective leadership, not just on the part of the chief executive and other senior managers but from leaders at all levels in the organization.

So what does the leadership of change involve? It encompasses many dimensions that need to be adapted to each situation. Initially, leadership involves preparing people for the change by challenging the status quo and communicating a vision of what the organization can aspire to become. Next, it involves building the commitment of employees and change agents throughout the organization, and enabling them to act by providing resources and training, delegating power, building change teams and putting appropriate systems and structures in place. Leaders then maintain the momentum of change through symbolic and substantive actions that reward progress and recognize reaching milestones, with the leaders acting as effective role models.[5]

Robert Miles, a successful change management consultant and writer, has summarized the leadership of change in the following terms.[6] First and foremost, according to Miles, radical change is vision led. That is, it involves the creation of goals that stretch the organization beyond its current horizons and capacities. Secondly, it is based on a total-system perspective, wherein all major elements of the organization are carried forward. And thirdly, it requires a sustained process of organizational learning so that people and processes develop synergistically. Figure 12.2 provides a picture of the four essential ingredients of a successful change process.

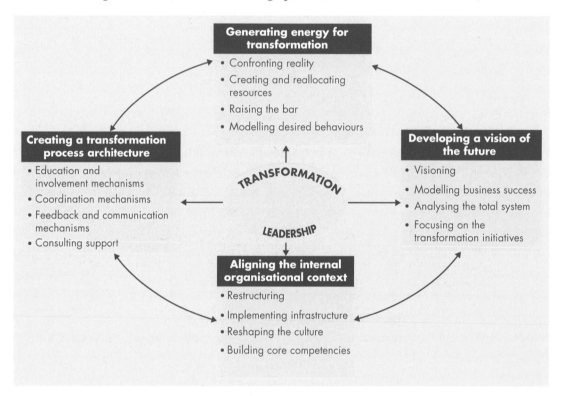

Figure 12.2: A framework for planned organizational change leadership.
Source: Miles, R.H., (1997), *Corporate Comeback: the story of renewal and transformation at National Semiconductor*. San Francisco: Jossey-Bass, p. 6. Reproduced by permission of John Wiley & Sons, Inc.

As Figure 12.2 suggests, the process depends on 'generating energy for transformation'. A key to this is in revealing to employees the shortfalls in current organizational performance – in essence, providing a reality check. One way to do this is by benchmarking the organization against customer expectations, industry leaders or competitors. Another method is to diagnose internal strengths and weaknesses, for example, by conducting a skills profile of employees to gauge their capacity to work cross culturally.

Based on such assessments, resources are released or reallocated to prepare the organization and its staff for the next ingredient – 'developing a vision'. While 'generating energy' puts people into a frame of mind that supports change, the vision provides them with a sense of what the future organization could be like and where they will be heading. A thorough organizational analysis is also needed as a basis for detailed planning of the change, which Miles describes as 'aligning the internal context'. The internal context consists of all the components that make an organization what it is – its structure, culture, technology and so on. Any or all of these components can become targets for change. The final ingredient is 'creating a transformation process architecture'. Key words that express what this is about are education, involvement and communication.

These ideas were specifically developed with radical change in mind but you will see from reading this chapter that they generally apply to incremental change as well. All planned changes require careful preparation to ensure that they achieve the results hoped for and to reduce the likelihood that employees will resist change. You will also learn that there are several stages in the process of planned change, that there are at least four options of change strategy (the employee involvement strategy recommended by Miles is just one of these) and that managers must make careful choices about which aspects of the organization to target for change.[7]

FORCES OF CHANGE

In any change process, certain forces tend to encourage or favour the process whereas others militate against it. Change demands that organization members examine big-picture questions such as 'Who are we?' 'Where are we going?' and 'What do we want?' The major forces favouring organizational change are:

- A sufficient dissatisfaction with the existing situation, or state A.
- A strong attraction to moving towards a more desirable position, or state B. (This position can frequently be described in a vision statement, or in an analysis of the company's goals and performance in comparison to those of competitors.)
- A desire to formulate a well-thought-out strategy that will realize the vision – that is, how the company can move from A to B.[8]

All three of these forces must usually be present for managers to feel compelled to seek change. In the absence of any one of the three, there is little or no motivation to galvanize managers into action. Associated with these factors are other elements such as strong leadership, effective communication, a tight alignment of people and organizational goals, and a clear definition of the compelling reasons to change.

Change may be triggered by internal or external forces. External forces include politics (for example a change in government or government policy), laws (for example antispam legislation), markets (for example competition from foreign companies entering the home market) and technology (for example the convergence of communications devices). Internal triggers include changes of ownership, products, services, process and measures of effectiveness that can happen in an organizational setting. Today's organizations must be able to react quickly and correctly to external change, while managing internal change effectively. External change is usually obvious and has immediate impact. In contrast, the need for internal change is often less obvious.

OB IN ACTION

Marris[9] equates change with bereavement. Organizations that go through change need to allow employees time to 'digest' the changes, as they would if they endured family bereavement. Carrying out continuous changes is stressful and may be harmful to an employees health and well-being, Stuart[10] refers to organizational change as 'trauma'.

If we accept Marris's terminology of loss we might question whether and to what extent organizations have an ethical responsibility to ensure that their employees do not experience high and constant levels of stress during change intervention programmes in organizations.

Consider your own views about whether employers have a duty of care in the way that change is managed.

CULTURAL CHANGE

As we saw in Chapter 8 organizational culture is the pattern of an organization's shared beliefs, values, expectations and assumptions. Culture is a strong influence on people's thoughts and behaviour and affects all aspects of organizational life. It can significantly influence – positively and negatively – the outcomes of change so it cannot be ignored when considering a change initiative. Even the most rigid of organizational cultures can be subject to significant change under the right circumstances.

It is a massive task to achieve a major culture change – one in which new values are antagonistic to the old ones. Successful culture change, in which there is a change in the underlying values that drive behaviour, can take a long time, even years.

In terms of how to effect culture change, Williams, Dobson and Walters[11] suggest that the following should be considered when attempting to change organizational culture:

- changing the people in the organization
- changing people's positions in the organization
- changing beliefs, attitudes and values directly
- changing behaviour
- changing systems and structures
- changing the corporate image.

Organizational growth will engender change and new companies tend to see a rapid evolution of organizational culture as they undergo consistent change. Established companies tend to be more structured and thus slower to undertake change. A long-established company might not seek change until change is forced upon it as the result of a merger or acquisition, adverse media attention or undeniable changes in the environment. When a merger occurs, the question of which partner's organizational culture will become dominant inevitably arises. Both companies may be able to allow a new organizational culture to emerge. Cultural change may also occur internally in an unplanned fashion as the result of a labour dispute, a scandal or an accident.[12]

EFFECTIVE MANAGER 12.1

Pathways to effective cultural change

Gagliardi[13] recommends the following approach to culture change:

- educate stakeholders as to why change is necessary
- communicate the new culture that is desired
- use value statements to embed the new cultural requirements

- give people the skills, knowledge and capabilities they will need to work differently
- create processes, systems and ways of working that enable people to put the new values into practice
- use performance management and rewards to enforce desired behaviours.

▶ COUNTERPOINT

Resistance to change

The idea that people will naturally resist change and that management must plan ways to overcome this is firmly entrenched in the management literature. However, it was not always so. The term was coined by Kurt Lewin as recently as 1948 and its meaning has shifted since then. Dent and Goldberg[14] argue that current conceptualizations present resistance to change as the unproductive or inappropriate actions that people take to thwart the change efforts of management. It suggests an 'us and them' mentality and a tendency to blame employees for the failure of changes that would otherwise have been good for the organization. In combating resistance, the focus is firmly on individuals and groups of employees. Managers are

advised to be proactive in preventing or countering resistance – through education, communication, training and support, negotiation, cooptation and so on. Thus, the suggestion in the contemporary literature is that resistance can be prevented by anticipating employee-related reactions followed by early intervention to deal with them.

So what is the alternative to this conceptualization of resistance? There are two points to consider here. First, people rarely resist change simply for the sake of doing so and few are so entrenched in their habits and certainties that they will not contemplate another way of doing things. On the contrary, we normally resist things that are unpleasant or against our best interests – the possible loss of a job, loss of status, less favourable working conditions, new reporting arrangements or being railroaded into something we don't understand, for example. Even then, we will often accept short-term discomfort for longer term advantages. The second point is that resistance to change is not simply a characteristic of individuals; it can come from any component of an organizational system, of which individuals are only one part. While it is certainly true that planned change is often less than successful, many factors could explain this. It seems unreasonable, therefore, to place undue emphasis on the individual employee.

To better understand this alternative view of resistance to change, we will examine Kurt Lewin's work. For Lewin, nothing much could change in an organization as long as there was an equilibrium between the forces favouring change and the forces against change. To set off an unfreezing effect, the relative strengths of these two sets of opposing forces needed to change, either to weaken the barriers or to strengthen the drivers. Organizations were dynamic entities with many complex interconnections and effects. In short, resistance to change was 'a systems phenomenon, not a psychological one'.[15] If we take Lewin's original conceptualization, the role of employees in moving change forward is through their full collaboration in planning and implementation processes. On the other hand, contemporary conceptualizations of resistance to change often imply that people are 'part of the problem' and that their education and participation is primarily for the purpose of securing cooperation in a process that rests firmly in the hands of management.[16]

Questions

1. How do you normally respond to changes in your life and work? Do you think that resistance to change is a normal response for yourself and others?
2. Explain the two different management rationales for employee participation in the change process that are implied in the last paragraph above.

TECHNOLOGICAL CHANGE

The increased complexity of the business environment and of competition is due to a number of factors but technology is a key driving force for change. Companies are generally receptive to technological change and are ready to accommodate further technological change in the future. Companies use sophisticated networks and information systems that have unprecedented capacity for meeting customer and other business needs. Business transactions take place nearly instantaneously via email and the Internet. These changes have increased the pace of business. This pace is another force of change with which managers must contend.[17]

Technological change that occurred slowly over centuries (such as the invention of the wheel) accelerated to change measured in decades (the impact of the car, for instance), which has now been transformed into continuous and pervasive change brought about by the computer chip and its successors.

OB IN ACTION

All change at CeBIT[18]

How do you maintain interest in an IT trade show over three decades? Sven Pruser, CeBIT's senior vice president believes that a 180-degree shift in focus is needed.

CeBIT, the IT Trade Show Company, first opened its doors in Hanover, Germany 21 years ago. The audience and contextual dynamics have changed from the 1980s to the 1990s and again in the 2000s, from IT directors spending large budgets in the 1980s to 'tyre-kickers' with little buying power in the 1990s to around 85% of visitors who are business or IT decision-makers in the 2000s. However, visitor numbers have halved from a peak of 850 000 in 2001 to about 424 000 in 2006.

Pruser accepts that CeBIT needs to change in line with the fast moving industry to which they cater, so that following intense discussions with exhibitors and the show's professional visitor group, the organizers have decided to change the focus in 2008.

Instead of the emphasis upon the technology, the show will be divided into three halls, reflecting the customer market: professional users, the public sector and retailers and distributors. The intention is for buyers to find things more easily. An example of this would be for Intel not to present its processors but, in cooperation with the gaming industry, it would showcase how its products are being used. Business-oriented presentations by vendors would also be focused on how the technology can help customers. The end result is that everyone benefits.

The example of CeBit draws our attention to some overriding issues set out at the start of this chapter namely: change is focused with specific areas subject to change, specific forces in the organization's environment drive change and the extent and rate of change can be significant and rapid.

THE PROCESS OF CHANGE AND CHANGE STRATEGIES

Phases of planned change

Earlier in the chapter we referred to the work of Kurt Lewin, a famous psychologist who developed a model of the process of change. We will now examine his work in greater detail. Lewin recommended that any change effort should be viewed as a process that includes the phases shown in Figure 12.3. Managers using Lewin's ideas will be sensitive to the need to ensure that any change effort properly addresses each of these three phases of change.[19]

- *Unfreezing* – getting people and things ready for change
- *Changing* – implementing the change
- *Refreezing* – making sure the change 'sticks' as part of new routines.

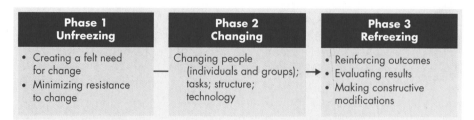

Figure 12.3: Lewin's three phases of planned change.

Source: Adapted from Tichy, N., *Managing Strategic change: technical, political and cultural dynamics*, (1983), John Wiley & Sons, Inc., New York. Reproduced by permission.

Unfreezing *is the first stage of the planned change process in which a situation is prepared to change.*

Unfreezing is the managerial responsibility of preparing a situation for change. It involves disconfirming existing attitudes and behaviours to create a felt need for something new. Unfreezing is facilitated by environmental pressures, declining performance, the recognition of a problem, or awareness that someone else has found a better way, among other factors. Many changes are never tried or fail simply because situations are not properly unfrozen to begin with. As a concept, unfreezing is very similar in meaning to 'generating energy for transformation', which was discussed in relation to Figure 12.1. 'Force-field analysis' is a useful tool for identifying the forces for and against change during the unfreezing stage. Force-field analysis is a management technique to diagnose and encourage change. It is based on the idea that in any situation there are both driving and restraining forces that influence any change that may occur. Driving forces push in a particular direction; they tend to initiate a change and keep it going. In terms of improving productivity in a work group, pressure from a supervisor, incentive earnings and competition may be examples of driving forces. Restraining forces restrain or decrease the driving forces. Apathy, hostility and poor maintenance of equipment may be examples of restraining forces against increased production. Changes occur when the driving and restraining forces are shifted out of equilibrium.[20] The basic steps are to identify the driving forces, identify the restraining forces, identify which forces can be changed, and weight those forces based on the degree to which they can be influenced and the likely effects of that influence.[21] You will find an exercise on force-field analysis in the study guide at the end of this chapter.

Large systems seem particularly susceptible to the so-called boiled frog phenomenon.[22] This refers to a classic physiological proposition that a live frog will immediately jump out when placed in a pan of hot water; but when placed in cold water that is then heated very slowly, the frog will stay in the water until it boils to death. Organizations can fall victim to similar circumstances. When managers fail to monitor their environments, recognize the important trends, or sense the need to change, their organizations may slowly suffer and lose their competitive edge. The best organizations, by contrast, have managers who are always on the alert for 'unfreezing' opportunities.

Changing *involves a managerial responsibility to modify a situation – that is, to change people, tasks, structure and/or technology.*

The changing stage involves a managerial responsibility to modify a situation – that is, to change people, tasks, structure and/or technology. Lewin feels that many change agents enter this stage prematurely or are too quick to change things. As a result, they often end up creating resistance to change in a situation that is not adequately unfrozen. Changing something is hard enough, let alone having to do it without the proper foundations. Successful change requires sustained energy and clear goals to maintain the process.

Successful change also depends on the degree of readiness to change, which suggests that two distinct forces act on people.[23] First, there are the forces within the individual. Second, there are the forces within the system, which (as we have discussed) include the type of leadership, the culture, the climate of the organization and the perceived consequences of success or failure within the organization. The combination of these factors affects the individual's degree of felt security. That is, if the degree of felt security is either high or low, then the efforts to introduce change will most likely be rejected. If people feel secure in their current work situation, then what need is there for them to change? If an individual's degree of felt security is very low, then anything you do to disturb that low state of security will be seen to be highly threatening. Thus, only in the middle ranges of felt security is the response to change most likely to be positive. Such positive response will be expressed through behaviours such as listening, clarifying, negotiating and a willingness to explore alternatives.

Refreezing is the final stage of managerial responsibility in the planned change process. Designed to maintain the momentum of a change, refreezing positively reinforces desired outcomes and provides extra support when difficulties are encountered. Evaluation is a key element in this final step of the change process. It provides data on the costs and benefits of a change and offers opportunities to make constructive modifications in the change over time. Improper refreezing results in changes that are abandoned or incompletely implemented.

> **Refreezing** is the final stage of the planned change process in which changes are positively reinforced.

CHANGE LEVERS AND CHANGE CYCLES

Managers may limit their capacity to manage change by focusing on a restricted set of organizational change levers. In other words, regardless of the nature of the problem that the change is meant to solve, they reach for the same levers every time. This means that the change process is viewed from only one perspective. It may be viewed as a technical problem, a political problem or a cultural problem that needs resolving. Noel Tichy argues that those who design, manage, and change organizations face the following three fundamental sets of problems, and effective change managers can recognize all three.

- *Technical design problem.* The organization faces a production or operational problem. Social and technical resources must be allocated to solve the problem and achieve a desired outcome.
- *Political allocation problem.* The organization faces an allocation of power and resources problem. It must determine how it will use its resources, as well as which parts of the organization will benefit.
- *Culture/ideological mix problem.* An organization is held together by shared beliefs. The organization must determine which values need to be held by which people.[24]

All of these problems tend to occur simultaneously in organizations. They therefore constitute the fundamental levers that prompt managers to contemplate strategic change. They form the basic parts of what could be described as the engine of change, as shown in Figure 12.4. When these areas are considered over time, you can identify cycles in their relative importance. Attempts to resolve each set of problems give rise to new situations and hence new problems which in turn require new solutions.[25]

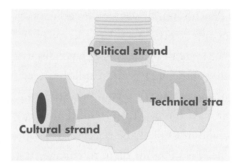

Figure 12.4: The engine of change – a metaphor.
Source: Adapted from Tichy, N., *Managing Strategic change: technical, political and cultural dynamics,* (1983), John Wiley & Sons, Inc., New York. Reproduced by permission.

Seeing the change process as an engine allows us to understand some of the practical aspects of change. Managers may experience all of the problems outlined by Tichy but to a varying degree. At some stage of organizational development, technical problems may be the most pressing. At another stage, cultural problems may need the most urgent attention. As with the oil or water that feeds an engine, none of these issues can be ignored if the engine of change is to run. All components of the engine need attention to ensure high performance. Change agents and participants often fail to understand this. Too often during a change process, one group becomes frustrated because its problems are not seen to be the most pressing. Managers need to understand that the different groups' problems are intertwined and that they must be dealt with simultaneously. In doing so, managers will find themselves addressing strategic change as shown in Figure 12.5.[26]

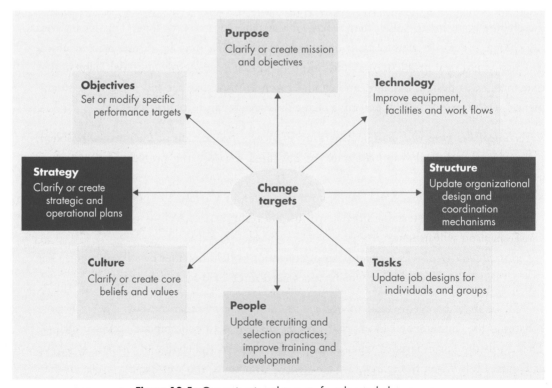

Figure 12.5: Organizational targets for planned change.

ORGANIZATIONAL TARGETS FOR CHANGE

The forces for change are ever present in today's dynamic work settings.[27] They are found in the relationship between an organization and its environment; mergers, strategic alliances and divestitures are examples of organizational attempts to redefine relationships with challenging environments. They are found in the lifecycle of the organization as it passes from birth through growth and towards maturity; changes in culture and structures are examples of organizational attempts to adjust to these patterns of growth. They are found in the political nature of organizational life; changes in internal control structures (including benefits and reward systems) are examples of organizational attempts to deal with shifting political currents. Planned change based on any of these forces can be directed towards a wide variety of organizational components or targets. As shown in Figure 12.5, these targets include organizational purpose, strategy, structure and people, as well as objectives, culture, tasks and technology. Sometimes, these targets for change are addressed mistakenly by management through 'fad' solutions that are offered by consultants and adopted by managers without much thought for the real situation and/or people involved. The logic of truly planned change requires a managerial willingness and ability to address problems concretely and systematically and to avoid tendencies towards an easy but questionable 'quick fix'.[28]

Further, the manager must recognize that the various targets of planned organizational change are highly intertwined. For example, a change in the basic tasks performed by an organization (that is, a modification in what it is the organization does) is almost inevitably accompanied by a change in technology (that is, a modification in the way in which tasks are accomplished). Changes in tasks and technology usually require alterations in the structure of the organization, including changes in the patterns of authority and communication as well as in the roles of members. These technological and structural changes can, in turn, necessitate changes on the part of the organization's members. For example, members may have to acquire additional knowledge and develop new skills to perform their modified roles and work with the new technology.[29]

PLANNED CHANGE STRATEGIES

Often the time frame facing change agents is an unrealistically short one, so that the 'ready, fire, aim' technique is evidenced. Kotter (2007) argues that realizing that change takes time can improve the chances of success.[30]

Managers and other change agents use various means for mobilizing power, exerting influence over others and getting people to support planned change efforts. As described in Figure 12.6, each of these strategies builds from different foundations of social power (as discussed in Chapter 10) and each has somewhat different implications for the planned change process. Among the change strategies commonly used by managers to bring about planned organizational change are:[31]

- *top-down approach to change* – using centralized power to force compliance with change directives
- *force-coercion* – using authority to force compliance with change directives
- *rational persuasion* – using logic and information to persuade people to accept change directives
- *shared power* – involving others in decisions identifying the need for change and desired change directions.

Figure 12.6: Power bases, change strategies, management behaviours and predicted outcomes.

Top-down approach to change

In pursuing the top-down (or directional) approach to change, executives and managers believe that one-way communication backed by the formal authority of their position is enough to implement change. This approach to change is very akin to the military model in its style and assumes that members lower down in the hierarchy will understand what is intended and follow through exactly as requested.

In many situations, this approach is problematic and ineffective, especially when the situation facing the organization is complex and difficult to interpret.[32] With complex problems requiring change, top managers do not have a monopoly on expertise, information and inputs. In such situations, having the additional perspectives of the lower level managers and employees would be an advantage.

Given that members at the lower levels are generally on the firing line (that is, closest to the machinery, the consumer and the community), they are in an excellent position to observe problems and to provide varied and valuable inputs to any required changes. When a directive approach to change pervades the organization, higher level managers are unlikely to listen. Thus, the lower levels become increasingly frustrated and may even refuse to lend their cooperation. Further, the extent to which the change process requires member commitment for successful implementation suggests that the lower level members may not comply automatically.[33] If members do not commit to the change process as intended, what is finally implemented may be a far cry from what top management had in mind.

Many eminent management scholars such as Tom Lupton have also indicated the idiosyncracies of authoritarian change. For instance, Lupton sees that change can be more successfully introduced from the bottom up than from the top down.[34] In general, individuals who are struggling to assert their autonomy tend to resist the efforts of people in authority to exercise control over them. By doing so, individuals do not necessarily reject the legitimacy of the authority but rather seek to extend their own autonomy by working to control their interactions with the authority.

However, the 'bottom-up' (participative) approach to change is often not possible. In the case of public sector organizations, for example, the change process may be imposed on them by drastic changes in government policies and legislation. In this situation, change may be more directive and less participative.

FORCE-COERCION AND PLANNED CHANGE

A force-coercion strategy uses legitimacy, rewards and/or punishments as primary inducements to change. That is, the change agent acts unilaterally to try to 'command' change through the formal authority of their position, to induce change via an offer of special rewards, or to bring about change via threats of punishment. People respond to this strategy mainly out of fear of being punished if they do not comply with a change directive, or out of desire to gain a reward if they do. Compliance is usually temporary and will continue only so long as the change agent remains visible in their legitimate authority, or so long as the opportunity for rewards and punishments remains obvious. If, as a change agent, you were to use the force-coercion strategy for bringing about planned change, the following profile might apply:[35]

> You believe that people who run things are basically motivated by self-interest and by what the situation offers in terms of potential personal gains or losses. As you feel that people change only in response to such motives, you try to find out where their vested interests lie and then put the pressure on. If you have formal authority, you use it. If not, you resort to whatever possible rewards and punishments you have access to and do not hesitate to threaten others with these weapons. Once you find a weakness, you exploit it and are always wise to work 'politically' by building supporting alliances wherever possible.

Force-coercion strategy tries to 'command' change through the formal authority of legitimacy, rewards and punishments.

RATIONAL PERSUASION AND PLANNED CHANGE

Change agents using a rational persuasion strategy attempt to bring about change through the use of special knowledge, empirical support or rational arguments. This strategy assumes that rational people will be guided by reason and self-interest in deciding whether to support a change. Expert power is mobilized to convince others that the cost-benefit value of a proposed change is high; that is, that the change will leave them better off than before. When successful, this strategy results in a longer lasting, more internalized change than does the force-coercion strategy. If you use a rational persuasion strategy, the

Rational persuasion strategy attempts to bring about change through persuasion based on empirical facts, special knowledge and rational argument.

following profile may apply:

> You believe that people are inherently rational and are guided by reason in their actions and decision making. Once a specific course of action is demonstrated to be in a person's self-interest, you assume that reason and rationality will cause the person to adopt it. You approach change with the objective of communicating, through information and facts, the essential 'desirability' of change from the perspective of the person whose behaviour you seek to influence. If this logic is effectively communicated, you are sure that the person(s) will adopt the proposed change.

SHARED POWER AND PLANNED CHANGE

*A **shared power strategy** (or normative re-educative strategy) attempts to bring about change by identifying or establishing values and assumptions so that support for the change emerges naturally.*

In order to minimize the likelihood of resistance, some of the best approaches to change put strong emphasis on involving all parties affected by the change. For example, a leader might meet with all managers and employees to explain reasons for the change and generally how it will be carried out. A plan may be developed and communicated. Staff forums may be organized to give members the opportunity to express their ideas about the proposed change. They are also given the opportunity to express their concerns and frustrations. This approach to change coincides with what is commonly known as a shared power strategy to change. This strategy actively and sincerely involves other people who will be affected by a change in planning and making key decisions in respect to it. Sometimes called a normative-re-educative strategy, this approach seeks to establish directions and social support for change through the empowerment of others. It builds essential foundations, such as personal values, group norms and shared goals, so support for a proposed change emerges naturally. Managers using this approach emphasize personal preference and share power by allowing others to participate in planning and implementing the change. Given this high level of involvement, the strategy is likely to result in a longer-lasting and internalized change. If you use a shared power strategy for bringing about planned change the following profile may apply:

> You believe that people have complex motivations. You feel that people behave as they do as a result of socio-cultural norms and commitments to these norms. You also recognize that changes in these orientations involve changes in attitudes, values, skills and significant relationships, not just changes in knowledge, information or intellectual rationales for action and practice. When seeking to change others you are sensitive to the supporting or inhibiting effects of any group pressures and norms that may be operating. You try to find out their side of things and to identify their feelings and expectations.

RESISTANCE TO CHANGE

Resistance towards change encompasses behaviours that are acted out by change recipients in order to slow down or terminate an intended organizational change.[36] Typically, change initiatives are met by some resistance. This is because employees are often afraid of the unknown. Many of them may think things are already just fine and do not understand the need for change. Many may also be cynical about change. Some may even think that the proposed change goes against the values held by members in the organization. That is why much organizational change is often discussed in conjunction with needed changes in the culture of the organization, including changes in members' values and beliefs. In essence, resistance to

change is often viewed by change agents as something that must be 'overcome' for change to be successful. This is not always the case. It is helpful to view resistance to change as feedback that can be used by the astute change agent to help accomplish his or her change objectives.[37] The essence of this notion is to recognize that when people resist change they are defending something important that appears to be threatened by the change attempt. **Resistance to change** is any attitude or behaviour that reflects a person's unwillingness to make or support a desired change.

Both passive and active resistance work against organizational change. Passive resistance can include the widespread cynicism often found among workers exposed to frequent management change initiatives, where insufficient attention was paid to implementation and the effects on organizational members. Passive resistance can also occur where organizational members feel that the psychological cost of adjusting to new systems and processes is greater than any recommended or perceived benefits. Active resistance occurs where the redistribution of power threatens vested self-interest. This form of resistance can be dangerous for an organization and can undermine even well thought-out change programmes.[38]

Resistance to change is any attitude or behaviour that reflects a person's unwillingness to make or support a desired change.

WHY PEOPLE RESIST CHANGE

There are several reasons for possible resistance to the introduction of a new management practice. People who report directly to a manager, for example, may resist the introduction and use of e-commerce (electronic commerce) in their workplace because:

- they are not familiar with online business and Internet use and wonder whether they could become familiar with it successfully (*fear of the unknown*)
- they may wonder if the manager is introducing e-commerce just to 'get rid' of some of the workers eventually (*need for security*)

- they may feel they are doing their jobs well and do not need the new facility (*no felt need for change*)
- they may sense that the manager is forcing e-commerce on them without first discussing their feelings on the matter (*vested interests threatened*)
- they may have heard from workers in other departments that e-commerce is being introduced to get more work out of people with no increase in pay (*contrasting interpretations*)
- they are really busy at the present time and do not want to try something new until the work slackens a bit (*poor timing*)
- they may believe that they will be left on their own to learn how to operate the new systems (*lack of resources*).

These and other viewpoints often create resistance to even the best and most well intended planned changes. To deal better with these forces, managers often find it useful to separate such responses into resistance to change directed towards the change itself, the change strategy, and the change agent as a person.

Sometimes a manager may experience resistance to the change itself. A good manager understands that people may reject a change because they believe it is not worth their time, effort and/or attention. To minimize resistance in such cases, the change agent should make sure that the people affected by the change know specifically how it satisfies the following criteria:

- *Benefit.* The change should have a clear relative advantage for the individuals being asked to change; that is, it should be perceived as 'a better way'.
- *Compatibility.* The change should be as compatible as possible with the existing values and experiences of the people being asked to change.
- *Complexity.* The change should be no more complex than necessary. It must be as easy as possible to understand and use.
- *Triability.* The change should be something that people can try on a step-by-step basis and make adjustments as things progress.

Managers will always experience some resistance to their change strategy. Someone who attempts to bring about change via force-coercion, for example, may create resistance among individuals who resent management by 'command' or the threatened use of punishment. People may also resist an empirical-rational strategy in which the data are suspect or expertise is not clearly demonstrated, or a normative-re-educative strategy that appears manipulative and insincere.

Finally, managers may experience resistance to the change agent. In this case, resistance is directed at the person implementing the change and may reflect inadequacies in the personality and attributes of the manager as a change agent. Change agents who are isolated from other people in the change situation, who appear self-centred or who have a high emotional involvement in the changes are especially prone to such problems.

Research also indicates that change agents who are different from other key people on such dimensions as age, education and socioeconomic factors are likely to experience greater resistance to change.[39]

RESEARCH IN OB

Look at the article by Kiefer on our Web site **www.wileyeurope.com/college/french.** In her research article Kiefer provides examples of how ongoing organizational change is experienced *emotionally*. Three antecedents of negative emotion are put forward: perceptions of an insecure future, perceptions of inadequate working conditions and perceptions of inadequate treatment by the organization. Two outcomes are also examined namely; variations in trust towards the organization and withdrawal from that organization. The article is useful in highlighting that change – for all the rational models proposed in business and management literature is ultimately *felt* as an emotional response.

HOW TO DEAL WITH RESISTANCE TO CHANGE

An informed change agent can do many things to deal constructively with resistance to change in any of its forms. In general, resistance will be managed best if it is recognized early in the change process. All things considered, the following general approaches for dealing with resistance to change have been identified:[40]

* *education and communication* – using one-on-one discussions, presentations to groups, memos, reports or demonstrations to educate people about a change before it is implemented and to help them see the logic of the change
* *participation and involvement* – allowing others to help design and implement the changes; asking individuals to contribute ideas and advice; forming task forces or committees to work on the change
* *facilitation and support* – providing socio-emotional support for the hardships of change; actively listening to problems and complaints; providing training in the new ways; helping to overcome performance pressures
* *negotiation and agreement* – offering incentives to actual or potential resistors; working out tradeoffs to provide special benefits in exchange for assurance that the change will not be blocked
* *manipulation and cooptation* – using covert attempts to influence others; selectively providing information and consciously structuring events so the desired change receives maximum support; buying off leaders of resistance to gain their support
* *explicit or implicit coercion* – using force to get people to accept change; threatening resistors with a variety of undesirable consequences if they do not go along as planned.

Figure 12.7 summarizes additional insights into how and when each method may be used by managers when dealing with resistance to change. When such resistance seems to be based on a lack of information or the presence of inaccurate information, education and communication are good managerial responses. Once persuaded that the change is for the best, people will often help implement the change. The downside is that the process of education and communication can be time consuming if too many people are involved. Participation and involvement is a good approach when the manager or change agent does not have all the information needed to design the required change. This is especially true if other people have a lot of power to resist. People who are allowed to participate in designing a change tend to be highly committed to its implementation. But, again, this process can be time consuming.

In cases where people are resisting the change because there will be adjustment problems, facilitation and support are recommended responses. In such circumstances, people are probably trying hard to implement a change but they are frustrated by external constraints and difficulties. Here a manager must play the 'supportive' role and try to make it as easy as possible to continue with the planned change. Of course, the manager must be able to invest the time and energy needed to provide this support and to gain needed commitments from the organization. Negotiation and agreement tend to be most useful when a person or group will clearly lose something as a result of the planned change. When the person or group has considerable power, resistance can be particularly costly to the change effort. Direct negotiation can sometimes prove a relatively easy way of avoiding or eliminating this form of resistance. This response requires a foundation of trust and may involve extra 'costs' in terms of any agreements that may be reached.

METHOD	USE WHEN	ADVANTAGES	DISADVANTAGES
Education and communication	People lack information or have inaccurate information	Creates willingness to help with the change	Can be very time consuming
Participation and involvement	Other people have important information and/or power to resist	Adds information to change planning; builds commitment to the change	Can be very time consuming
Facilitation and support	Resistance traces to resource or adjustment problems	Satisfies directly specific resource or adjustment needs	Can be time consuming; can be expensive
Negotiation and agreement	A person or group will 'lose' something due to the change	Helps avoid major resistance	Can be expensive; can cause others to seek similar 'deals'
Manipulation and cooptation	Other methods do not work or are too expensive	Can be quick and inexpensive	Can create future problems if people sense manipulation
Explicit and implicit coercion	Speed is important and change agent has power	Quick; overpowers resistance	Risky if people get angry

Figure 12.7: Methods for dealing with resistance to change.

There is no avoiding the fact that resistance to change can be – and is – managed at times through manipulation and cooptation. These responses may be used when other tactics just do not work or are too expensive. They may also make up a 'style' that a manager or change agent uses on most occasions. In some cases, manipulation and cooptation can provide a relatively quick and inexpensive solution to resistance problems. But a good manager understands that these approaches can also lead to future problems if people feel manipulated. A more extreme approach is explicit or implicit coercion. Coercion is often used when speed is of the essence or when the manager or change agent possesses considerable power. It is a fast response and can overpower resistance. It also runs the risk of offending people, however. People who experience coercion may feel angry at the manager or change agent and be left without any true commitments to ensuring that the change is fully implemented. Coercion may unfreeze and change things but it does not do much to refreeze them.

Regardless of the chosen strategy, managers must understand that resistance to change is something to be recognized and constructively addressed instead of feared. The presence of resistance typically suggests that something can be done to achieve a better 'fit' between the change, the situation and the people affected. A manager should deal with resistance to change by 'listening' to such feedback and acting accordingly.

Whilst recognizing resistance to change is, in itself, important in overcoming the barriers to change, there may be other, more generic issues that need to be addressed. Burnes[41] outlines the top 10 barriers to change:

1. Competition for resources
2. Functional boundaries
3. Lack of management skills
4. Middle management
5. Long IT lead times
6. Poor communication
7. Employee opposition
8. HR issues (such as training)
9. Initiative fatigue
10. Unrealistic timetables.

THE ROLE OF THE CHANGE AGENT

When we consider the complexities involved with change, the range of skills and expertise of the change agent could be considerable. Change agents are more readily associated with planned change but the degree to which planning is reliable and sequential will depend on the context and all the people and processes associated with it. Buchanan and Boddy[42] indicate that the context is vital to the role of the change agent and the extent to which the change agent has support from senior management. It could be argued that the more strategic the change, the more political it will become, and the more 'exposed' the change agent will be.

Buchanan and Boddy argue that there is range of core competences that the change agent needs to exhibit, and these are set into five clusters.

Cluster	Core competence	Description
Goals	1. Sensitivity	to changes in personnel, top management perceptions, and market conditions, and to the way in which these impact upon the project in hand.
	2. Clarity	in specifying goals, in defining the achievable
	3. Flexibility	in responding to changes outside the control of the project manager, perhaps requiring major shifts in project goals and management style, and risk taking.
Roles	4. Teambuilding	bringing together key stakeholders and establish effective working groups, and clearly to define and delegate respective responsibilities.
	5. Networking	skills in establishing and maintaining appropriate contacts within and outside of the organization.
	6. Tolerance of ambiguity	to be able to function comfortably, patiently and effectively in a certain environment.
Communication	7. Communication	transmit effectively to colleagues and subordinates the need for changes in project goals and in individual tasks and responsibilities.
	8. Interpersonal skills	including selection, listening, collecting appropriate information, identifying the concerns of others and managing meetings.
	9. Personal enthusiasm	in expressing plans and ideas.
	10. Stimulating motivation	and commitment in others involved.
Negotiation	11. Selling	plans and ideas to others, by creating a desirable and challenging vision for the future.
	12. Negotiating	with key players for resources, or for changes in procedures, and to resolve conflict.
Managing up	13. Political awareness	in identifying potential coalitions, and in balancing conflicting goals and perceptions.
	14. Influencing	to gain commitment to project plans and ideas from potential sceptics and resistors.
	15. Helicopter perspective	to stand back from the immediate project and take a broader view of priorities.

CONCLUSION

Rieley[43] questions whether organizations change for worthwhile reasons, or is it 'simply rearranging the deck chairs on the *Titanic*'. Change, like any other organizational intervention, must have material benefits, whether it is to the organization's bottom line, employee wellbeing, or simply organizational survival. The ends may justify the means. Taking the counterargument of the means justifying the ends, we have to question and evaluate the process in similar fashion. Some managers may revert to draconian measures like scaring people in order to effect change.[44] The balance of the two arguments may give us an overall idea of the change intervention.

SUMMARY

LEARNING OBJECTIVE 1
Radical versus incremental planned change

Planned change is directed by managers and others acting as change agents. Radical change involves a significant transformation of the organization and/or its objectives, systems and processes. It often occurs in response to a critical event such as the presence of a new chief executive officer, an emerging competitive threat or a merger with another company. Incremental change is more gradual and involves an adjustment to the way things are currently done in one or a limited number of organizational departments. It is less disruptive and generally more frequent than radical change.

LEARNING OBJECTIVE 2
Forces favouring change and the targets of change

Within organizations, change is more likely to take place successfully when there is sufficient dissatisfaction with the way things are currently done, a strong attraction towards a more desirable state and a willingness to work towards a strategic approach to change. External factors in favour of change include increasing complexity in the business environment. Complexity is increased through globalization, technological change competition, and the need to be more efficient, innovative and responsive to customer demands. Organizational targets for planned change include purpose, strategy, culture, structure, people, tasks and technology.

LEARNING OBJECTIVE 3
Change strategies

Planned change strategies are the means used by change agents to implement desired change. Force-coercion strategies of change use aspects of a manager's position power to try to 'command' that the change will take place as directed. Temporary compliance is a common response of people who are 'forced' to change in this manner. Rational persuasion strategies of change use logical arguments and appeal to knowledge and facts to convince people to support change. When successful, this method can lead to more commitment to change. Shared power strategies of change seek to involve other people in planning and implementing change. Of the three strategies, shared power creates the longest lasting and most internalized commitments to the change.

LEARNING OBJECTIVE 4
Resistance to change and what can be done about it

Resistance to change is to be expected. Dealing successfully with resistance begins with awareness that it represents 'feedback' that can be used by a change agent to increase the effectiveness of a change effort. People sometimes resist because they do not find value or believe in the change. They sometimes resist because they find the change strategy offensive or inappropriate. Sometimes they resist because they do not like or identify positively with the change agent as a person. Successful change agents are open to resistance and are capable of responding to it in ways that create a better 'fit' between the change, the situation and all the people involved.

LEARNING OBJECTIVE 5
The role of the change agent

The change agent needs to have a political awareness and a range of skills and abilities in both managing tasks and people. There is no general agreement about a definitive set of competences that a change agent requires but Buchanan and Boddy's 15 core competences provides a useful framework for analysis. No one person can manage all change as change normally happens through people, and therefore need to embody the spirit of change.

CHAPTER 12 STUDY GUIDE

You can also test your understanding and access further resources at **www.wileyeurope. com/college/french.**

REVIEW QUESTIONS

1. Explain the difference between planned and unplanned change. Give examples of situations where these occur.
2. Explain what managers can do to manage change and minimize resistance.

APPLICATION QUESTIONS

1. Design a one-day training course targeting the mid-level managers of a medium-size organization. There would be 20 participants coming from a diverse range of functions in the organization, including production, design, administration, marketing, sales and product development. The aims of the programme are to make participants aware of the meaning of 'cultural change', and also to gauge views on the current culture and potential required changes.
2. As a team leader in an organization facing increasing competition from new entrants to your industry, you have been tasked with implementing changes within

your unit. These changes are likely to disrupt current schedules, rosters and work processes significantly. Prepare a strategy for the unfreezing stage of the change process for your team, with a view to minimizing resistance so that the changes can be implemented as smoothly as possible.

3. The best way to approach change is through the 'shared power' approach. Do you agree?

RESEARCH QUESTIONS

1. Resistance to change is a complex response by employees when confronted with the possibility of unwelcome changes to their working lives. It is based on employee beliefs about the change (for example, there will be job cuts), emotions (such as anxiety, anger) and behaviours (for example, absenteeism, reduced work quality, undermining the changes). Conduct a search of the writing on the topic of resistance, identifying a range of employee response types encompassing beliefs, emotions and behaviours. Where possible, identify organizations and situations in which these various responses occurred. What can you conclude about the way people respond to the possibility of unwelcome changes to their working lives? What can managers do to anticipate and minimize resistance to change?

2. What skills and competencies do good change agents have? Search the Internet to identify people who are presented as successful agents of change. You should find some good examples among the senior managers of large organizations in the business, public or community sectors. What skills and competencies do these people demonstrate? How have they used these skills and competencies to bring about change in their organizations?

RUNNING PROJECT

Complete the following tasks for your chosen organization:

1. Identify factors that are driving change at your organization. Also try to identify factors that are likely to produce a need for change in the near future.

2. (a) Choose one current factor from question 1 and explain the organization's response.

   (b) Choose one future factor from question 1 and suggest an appropriate response. Does the organization need to act now?

INDIVIDUAL ACTIVITY

Innovative attitude scale[45]

Introduction

Change and innovation are important to organizations. The following assessment surveys your readiness to accept and participate in innovation.

Instructions

Indicate the extent to which each of the following statements is true of either your actual behaviour or your intentions at work. That is, describe the way you are, or the way you intend to be, on the job. Use the following scale for your responses.

Almost always true	5
Often true	4
Not applicable	3
Seldom true	2
Almost never true	1

1. I openly discuss with my boss how to get ahead.
2. I try new ideas and approaches to problems.
3. I take things or situations apart to find out how they work.
4. I welcome uncertainty and unusual circumstances related to my tasks.
5. I negotiate my salary openly with my supervisor.
6. I can be counted on to find a new use for existing methods or equipment.
7. Among my colleagues and co-workers, I will be the first or nearly the first to try out a new idea or method.
8. I take the opportunity to translate communications from other departments for my work group.
9. I demonstrate originality.
10. I will work on a problem that has caused others great difficulty.
11. I provide critical input towards a new solution.
12. I provide written evaluations of proposed ideas.
13. I develop contacts with experts outside my firm.
14. I use personal contacts to manoeuvre myself into choice work assignments.
15. I make time to pursue my own pet ideas or projects.
16. I set aside resources for the pursuit of a risky project.
17. I tolerate people who depart from organizational routine.
18. I speak out in staff meetings.

19. I work in teams to try to solve complex problems.
20. If my co-workers are asked, they will say I am a wit.

Interpretation

To determine your score on the 'Innovative attitude scale', simply add the numbers associated with your responses to the 20 statements. The higher your score, the more receptive to innovation you are. You can compare your score with that of others to see if you seem to be more or less receptive to innovation than a comparable group of business students.

Score	Percentile*
39	5
53	16
62	33
71	50
80	68
89	86
97	95

*Percentile indicates the percentage of the people who are expected to score below you.

GROUP ACTIVITY

Force-field analysis

Objectives

1. To improve your analytical skills for addressing complex situations.
2. To show how force-field analysis can aid understanding of change.

Total time: 30–60 minutes

Procedure

1. Choose a situation in which you have high personal stakes (for example, how to get a better grade in a particular course, or how to get a promotion).
2. Using the following force-field analysis form, apply the technique to your situation.
   (a) Describe the situation as it now exists.
   (b) Describe the situation as you would like it to be.

(c) Identify the 'driving forces' – the factors that are presently helping to move things in the desired direction.

(d) Identify the 'restraining forces' – the factors that are presently holding things back from moving in the desired direction.

3. Try to be as specific as possible in these descriptions of your situation. You should attempt to be exhaustive in your listing of these forces. List them all!

4. Now go back and classify the strength of each force as weak, medium or strong. Do this for both the driving and restraining forces.

5. At this point you should rank the forces on their ability to influence or control the situation.

6. Share you analyses in groups of three to four. Discuss the usefulness of and drawbacks to using this method for (a) personal situations and (b) organizations.

7. Be prepared to share the results of your group's discussion with the rest of the class.

Force field analysis form

Current situation	Preferred situation
_____	_____
_____	_____
_____	_____
_____	_____

Driving forces	Restraining forces
_____	_____
_____	_____
_____	_____
_____	_____
_____	_____
_____	_____
_____	_____

OTICON – A DANISH HEARING AID MANUFACTURER – THE TRANSFORMATIONAL ORGANIZATION

Introduction

Oticon, the first hearing aid manufacturing company, was founded in 1904 and specialized in 'behind-the-ear' hearing aids. The situation changed in the 1980s and 1990s and the company suffered both financially and loss of market share. Whilst the likes of companies like 3M, Panasonic Sony, Phillips and Siemens were specializing in digital technology, Oticon was still using analog technology. Oticon was strong in subsidized markets in Scandinavia and northern Europe but it was less strong in buoyant markets in America and the Far East.

The appointment of a new CEO, Lars Kolind, in 1988, was the start of the company transformation. He described the organization as having 'slept for the last 10 years'. Within two years he attempted to transform the organization through cost-cutting measures: paring the company down, cutting staff, increasing efficiency and reducing the price of a hearing aid by 20%. Kolind managed to change the traditional company culture by making it more responsive, speedy and customer focused. By 1990 Oticon made a $16 million profit on a $400 million turnover. However, this was within a market that was growing at 6% per annum. The major difficulty that Kolind now faced was economy of scale – how could a small Danish manufacturer compete with the world's largest electronic companies?

The vision

Kolind came up with a vision by 'thinking the unthinkable'. Technology was not the only factor to consider and Kolind argued that the business that they were in was to 'make people smile'. The new company mission statement embellished this concept – 'to help people with hearing difficulties to live life as they wish, with the hearing they have'. A new holistic approach to customer care was adopted, investigating customer needs, lifestyle and so forth. Married to this was a new mix of expertise in micro-mechanics, microchip design, audiology, psychology, marketing, manufacturing, logistics and all-round service capability. This shift can best be described as moving towards a knowledge-based business, from its previous technology-based business. Kolind saw his role as a naval architect rather than the ship's captain, creating the spaghetti organization – a chaotic tangle of relationships and interactions that would force the abandonment of preconceived ideas and barriers to innovation and competitiveness.

The strategy

The formation of four key principles helped to reinforce the concept of the 'disorganized organization'. The head office was the first line of attack.

- Departments and job titles disappeared, and all activities became project based, pursued informally by groupings of interested people.

Adapted from Burnes, B. (2000), *Managing Change*, FT Prentice Hall: Harlow, pp. 319–327.

- Jobs were redesigned into fluid and unique combinations of functions to suit employees' needs and capabilities.
- The formal office was eradicated and replaced by open space filled with workstations usable by anyone.
- Informal face-to-face dialogue replaced memos as the acceptable mode of communication.

Department, department heads, and other managerial/supervisory roles were eliminated. In liberating staff, the organization nonetheless needed to retain some measure of control and did this through direction and highlighting human values. Direction involved lengthy discussions about where the company was going (strategy) and attempts were also made to establish the fundamental values, summed up in their company statement – 'We build this company on the assumption that we only employ adults, and everything we do will rest on that assumption, so we will not treat our staff as children – we will treat them as responsible adults.'

Implementing the strategy

Kolind's vision relied upon communication. Computers supported employees' work. Oticon attempted to operate a 'paperless office' where any important information was scanned and available to other users. Information access was therefore fluid and available.

Resistance to change

Not all staff welcomed the changes. Some managers' loss of power, information monopoly and status symbols proved problematic. Managers also had to compete with everyone for project leader status and lacked subordinates. The project team role did not suit all staff.

Kolind pre-empted some of these concerns by implementing a range of measures, including providing employees with their own home PC, and encouragement to identify their own training needs. Kolind also offered an ultimatum – 'accept the new arrangements or leave'!

Conclusion

Oticon's market share rose from 8 % in 1990 to 12 % in 1993. By 1994, sales were growing at 10 % per annum, after a period of 10 years without any real growth. Lead time had halved, and 15 new products had been launched.

Burnes identifies seven factors critical to Oticon's success:

- changing the rules of the game
- moving to a project-type structure which fits the strategy and vision of the business
- creating a whole-hearted commitment form everyone to working cooperatively and proactively
- creating a learning organization

- visionary leadership
- consistent vision, with passion
- societal values – industrial and social democracy.

Questions

1. To what extent was Kolind's approach to resistance to change (take it or leave it) a high-risk approach? Could it have turned out to be the wrong approach?
2. What incentives were there for former managers to stay at Oticon?

SUGGESTED READING

Child, J. (2005), *Organization: Contemporary Principles and Practice*, Blackwell: Oxford. This author provides a useful summary of issues related to change within a context of new organizational forms such as strategic alliances and virtual organizations.

END NOTES

1. Dunphy, D. & Stace, D. (1993), The strategic Management of Corporate Change, *Human Relations*, **46** (8), 917–918.

2. For more on the concepts of frame-breaking and frame-bending change see Nadler, D. & Tushman, M. (1988), *Strategic Organizational Design*, Scott, Foresman: Glenview, IL.

3. Tichy, N. M. (1983), *Managing Strategic Change: Technical, Political and Cultural Dynamics*, John Wiley & Sons, Inc. New York.

4. Child, J. (2005), *Organization*, Blackwell Publishing: Oxford.

5. Graetz, F. (2000), Strategic change leadership, *Management Decision*, 38 (8), 550–562.

6. Miles, R. (1997), *Corporate Comeback; the Story of Renewal and Transformation at National Semiconductor*, Jossey-Bass: San Francisco.

7. Graetz, F. op. cit.; Miles, R. op. cit.

8. Deming, W.E. (1986), *Out of the Crisis*, MIT Center for Advanced Engineering Study: Cambridge, MA.

9. Marris, P. (1986), *Loss and Change*, Routledge & Kegan Paul: London.

10. Stuart, R. (1996), The trauma of organizational change. *Journal of European Industrial Training*, **20** (2), 11–16.

11. Williams, A.P.O., Dobson, P. & Walters, M. (1993), *Changing Culture*, 2nd edn, Institute of Personnel Management: London.

12. Silvester, J., Anderson, N.R. & Patterson, F. (1999), Organizational culture change: an intergroup attributional analysis. *Journal of Occupational and Organizational Psychology*, **72** (1), 1.

13. Gagliardi, P. (1986), The creation and change of organizational cultures: a conceptual framework. *Organization Studies*, 7 (2), 117–134, cited in Parker, S. (2004), Tactical change, www2.agsm.edu.au/agsm/web.nsf/Content/AGSMMagazine-Tacticalchange, accessed 5 January 2006.

14. Dent, E. & Goldberg, S. (1999), Challenging 'resistance to change'. *Journal of Applied Behavioural Science*, **35** (1), 25–41.

15. Ibid., p. 31.

16. Ibid., pp. 25–41.

17. Weston, S. & Harper, J. (1998), The challenge of change, *Ivey Business Quarterly*, **63** (2), 78.

18. All change at CeBIT, at http://news.zdnet.co.uk/itmanagement/0,1000000308,39286259-2,00.htm?r=1, accessed 27 August 2007.

19. Lewin, K. (1952), Group decision and social change, in *Readings in Social Psychology* (eds G.E. Swanson, T.M. Newcomb & E.L. Hartley), Holt, Rinehart & Winston: New York, p. 4.

20. Accel Team, Team building, www.accel-team.com/techniques/force_field_analysis.html, accessed 5 January 2006.

21. Charles Sturt University, Managing change, NSW.HSConline, http://hsc.csu.edu.au/business _studies/mgt_changemanaging_change/Manage-change.html#top, accessed 27 September 2005.

22. Tichy and Devanna, Tichy, N.M. & Devanna, M.A. (1986), *The Transformational Leader,* John Wiley & Sons, Inc.: New York, p. 44.

23. Zeffane, R. (1996), Dynamics of strategic change: critical issues in fostering positive organizational change, *Leadership and Organization Development Journal,* **17** (7), 36–43.

24. Tichy, op. cit.

25. See Tichy, N.M. (1983), *Managing Strategic Change: Technical, Political and Cultural Dynamics,* John Wiley & Sons, Ltd: New York.

26. Op. cit.

27. Kanter, R.M., Stein, B.A. & Jick, T.D. (1993), Meeting the challenges of change. *World Executive's Digest,* (May), pp. 22–27.

28. See for example Kilmann, R.H. (1984), *Beyond the Quick Fix,* Jossey-Bass: San Francisco; Tichy, N.M. & Devanna, M.A., op. cit.

29. Cooke, R.A. (1979), Managing change in organizations, in *Management Principles for Nonprofit Organizations* (ed. G. Zaltman) American Management Association: New York. See also Nadler, D.A. (1987), The effective management of organizational change, in *Handbook of Organizational Behaviour* (ed. Jay W Lorsch), Prentice Hall: Englewood Cliffs, NJ, pp. 358–369.

30. Kotter, J. (2007), Leading Change. *Havard Business Review,* 85 (January), 1, 96–103.

31. Chin, R. & Benne, K.D. (1969), General strategies for effecting changes in human systems, in *The Planning of Change,* (eds W.G. Bennis, K.D. Benne, R. Chin & K.E. Corey), 3rd edn. Holt, Rinehart & Winston: New York, pp. 22–45.

32. Zeffane, R.M. (1995), The downsizing paradox: problems in the quest for leaner organizations. *Journal of Industrial Affairs,* **4** (1), 45–48.

33. Zeffane, R.M. (1994), Patterns of organizational commitment and perceived management styles: a comparison of public and private sector employees. *Tavistock Institute Journal of Human Relations,* **47** (8), 13–27; Emery, M. & Emery, M. (1992), Participative design: work and community life, in *Participative Design for Participative Democracy* (ed. M. Emery). Australian National University, Centre for Continuing Education: Canberra.

34. Lupton, T. (1991), Organizational change: 'top-down' or 'bottom-up' management? *Personnel Review,* **20** (3), 4–10.

35. The change strategy examples in this part are developed from an exercise reported in Pfeiffer, J.W. & Jones, J.E. (1973), *A Handbook of Structured Experiences for Human Relations Training,* vol. II, University Associates: La Jolla, CA.

36. Lines, R. (2004), Influence of participation in strategic change: resistance, organizational commitment and change goal achievement. *Journal of Change Management,* 4 (3), 193–215.

37. Donald Klein (1969), Some notes on the dynamics of resistance to change: the defender role in Bennis, Benne, Chin & Corey, op. cit., pp. 117–124.

38. Dervitsiotis, K.N. (1998), The challenge of managing organizational change: exploring the relationship of re-engineering, developing learning organizations and total quality management. *Total Quality Management,* **9** (1), 109.

39. See Rogers, E.M. & Shoemaker, F.F. (1971), *Communication of Innovations,* 2nd edn. The Free Press: New York.

40. Kotter, J.P. & Schlesinger, L.A. (1979), Choosing strategies for change. *Harvard Business Review,* 57 (March/April), 109–112.

41. Burnes, B. (2003), Managing change and changing managers from ABC to XYZ. *Journal of Management Development,* **22** (7), 627–642.

42. Buchanan, D. & Boddy, D. (1992), *The Expertise of the Change Agent: Public Performance and Backstage Activity,* Prentice-Hall: Englewood Cliffs, NJ.

43. Rieley, J. Is it change, or the past preserved? *Telegraph,* 28 January 2005.

44. Diefenbach, T. (2007), The managerialistic ideology of organizational change management. *Journal of Organizational Change Management,* **20** (1), 126–144.

45. Ettlie, J. E. & O'Keefe (1982), Innovative attitudes values and intentions in organizations. *Journal of Management Studies,* **19**, 176.

THE GLASS CLIFF: EVIDENCE THAT WOMEN ARE OVER-REPRESENTED IN PRECARIOUS LEADERSHIP POSITIONS

Michelle K. Ryan and S. Alexander Haslam

There has been much research and conjecture concerning the barriers women face in trying to climb the corporate ladder, with evidence suggesting that they typically confront a 'glass ceiling' while men are more likely to benefit from a 'glass escalator'. But what happens when women do achieve leadership roles? And what sorts of positions are they given? This paper argues that while women are now achieving more high profile positions, they are more likely than men to find themselves on a 'glass cliff', such that their positions are risky or precarious. This hypothesis was investigated in an archival study examining the performance of FTSE 100 companies before and after the appointment of a male or female board member. The study revealed that during a period of overall stock-market decline those companies who appointed women to their boards were more likely to have experienced consistently bad performance in the preceding five months than those who appointed men. These results expose an additional, largely invisible, hurdle that women need to overcome in the workplace. Implications for the evaluation of women leaders are discussed and directions for future research are outlined.

There is little doubt that women continue to be disadvantaged in the workplace and underrepresented in leadership positions (Adler, 2000; Davidson and Burke, 2000; Nieva and Gutek, 1981). Evidence suggests that while women are typically confronted by an invisible barrier preventing their rise into leadership ranks, the 'glass ceiling' (The corporate woman, 1986; Kanter, 1977; Morrison, White and Van Velsor, 1987), men (particularly those in female-dominated professions) are more likely to be conveyed into management positions by means of a 'glass escalator' (Williams, 1992). However, recent reports and research reveal that women are beginning to break through the glass ceiling that has historically prevented them from achieving leadership positions in organizations (e.g. Davidson and Cooper, 1992; Dreher, 2002; Goodman, Fields and Blum, 2003; McRae, 1995; Stroh, Langlands and Simpson, 2004).

However, despite these advances, evidence suggests that, once women attain these leadership roles, their performance is often placed under close scrutiny (e.g. Eagly, Karau and Makhijani, 1995) and their evaluation is not always positive. While research suggests that women tend to receive positive evaluations when their leadership roles are defined in feminine terms, on traditional, masculine measures of leadership women's leadership effectiveness is often perceived to be lower than that of men (Bartol and Butterfield, 1976; Eagly and Karau, 1991, 2002; Eagly et al., 1995; Eagly, Makhijani and Klonsky, 1992). Furthermore, attitudes within the workplace suggest that workers prefer male supervisors to female ones (e.g. Simon and Landis, 1989) and that many men and male managers

Reproduced with permission from the *British Journal of Management*, **16**, 81–90 (2005). © Copyright Blackwell Publishing remain unconvinced about the effectiveness of women leaders (Bowen, Swim, and Jacobs, 2000; Eagly *et al.*, 1992; Sczesny, 2003; Sutton and Moore, 1985). These attitudes derive from, and contribute to, what Schein (2001, p. 675) refers to as a 'think manager—think male' bias.

Are women leaders a hindrance?

A recent example of the scrutiny to which women leaders are exposed is provided by a lead article in *The Times* (Judge, 2003): *Women on the Board: Help or Hindrance?* Noting that more women are securing positions on company boards, Judge goes on to suggest that, although this development is seen as positive within the business and general community, in fact women leaders are having a negative impact on company performance. Thus she argues:

> 'So much for smashing the glass ceiling and using their unique skills to enhance the performance of Britain's biggest companies. The triumphant march of women into the country's boardrooms has instead wreaked havoc on companies' performance and share prices.' (Judge, 2003, p. 21)

To support this argument the article presents data suggesting that companies with women on their boards tend to perform more poorly than those whose boards are wholly male. Using an index compiled by the Cranfield School of Management (Singh and Vinnicombe, 2003) which ranks the FTSE 100 companies in relation to the percentage of women on their boards of directors, Judge (2003) reports that of the top ten companies in the index (i.e. those with the highest percentage of women on their boards), six have underperformed relative to the FTSE 100 throughout 2003. In contrast, Judge reports that the five companies on the bottom of the index – companies that are wholly male – have all outperformed the FTSE 100 in 2003. From this analysis Judge concludes that 'corporate Britain may be better off without women on the board' (p. 21).

Problems with the analysis

However, on their own, these figures are far from conclusive and a number of serious methodological problems can be identified in Judge's (2003) analysis. First, the article reports no statistical analysis, stating simply that six of the top ten companies under-performed. Furthermore, closer examination of the original Cranfield Index (Singh and Vinnicombe, 2003) reveals that, curiously, Judge (2003) failed to report the per-formance of the two companies at the very bottom of the index (i.e. those with the lowest percentage of women on board). Importantly, both of these companies under-performed relative to the FTSE 100 in 2003. Therefore, a more complete picture indicates that six of the ten top companies with women directors (i.e. 60%) underper-formed relative to the FTSE 100, while two of the bottom five companies without women directors (40%) underperformed – a difference that is far from statistically significant ($\chi^2(1) = 0.40$ $p = 0.53$).

In addition, the measures of women in leadership and of company performance used by Judge (2003) are broad and loosely defined. Women in leadership is operationalized simply as the percentage of women on the board of a given company – a measure that takes into account neither (a) changes in the number of women on the board of a given company, nor (b) their date of appointment or length of service. Similarly, the measure of company performance, the average share price over the year relative to the FTSE 100, is crude and does not take account of fluctuations in performance over time. Furthermore, even if the direction of the causal link between women in leadership and company performance is of the form suggested by Judge (2003), the crudeness of variable operationalisation makes it impossible to test this relationship properly. In particular, an appropriate test of the relationship would need to take account of a person's date of appointment. For example, if a poor board member has been *in situ* since 1997 then it is unlikely that the company would only experience a drop in performance in 2003.

An alternative explanation

Taken together – journalistic licence notwithstanding – the evidence garnered by Judge (2003) hardly justifies the conclusion that women are 'wreaking havoc' on the financial success of companies. And yet, having said that, her report raises important issues that demand closer empirical attention. However, a more sophisticated analysis is required to examine the purported link between having women in leadership positions and a company's financial performance. Moreover, if such an association can be identified, the merit of multiple explanations of the relationship needs to be considered.

In particular, if the relationship identified by Judge (2003) holds, one obvious alternative explanation of the association would simply involve reversing its causal sequencing (Haslam and McGarty, 2003). Thus, rather than the appointment of women leaders precipitating a drop in company performance, it is equally plausible that a company's poor performance could be a trigger for the appointment of women to the board. If this is the case, women may be being preferentially placed in leadership roles that are associated with an increased risk of negative consequences. As a result, to the extent that they are achieving leadership roles, these may be more precarious than those occupied by men. Extending the metaphors of the 'glass ceiling' and the 'glass elevator', we propose referring to this predicament as the 'glass cliff'.

There is considerable anecdotal evidence for this phenomenon. For example, recently, within the UK, W.H. Smith has received considerable coverage in the business news both for its 'tumbling share prices', profit falls and proposed job cuts, and for its appointment of a woman, Kate Swann, as its CEO (BBC, 2003a, 2003b, 2004). In her new role, Swann's first, unenviable, task was to turn the company around and restore the retailer's fortunes.

Moreover, within the management literature there is evidence which suggests that women are appointed to management positions under circumstances that differ from those of male managers. For example, women managers tend to occupy particular types of management positions, being more likely to hold support roles in personnel, training, or marketing, rather than performing critical operating or commercial functions (Vinnicombe, 2000). Furthermore, there is a higher proportion of women managers in service sectors (e.g. retailing and banking) than in more industrial sectors (e.g. manufacturing, mining, and information technology; Davidson and Cooper, 1992; Goodman *et al.*, 2003; Singh and Vinnicombe, 2003).

Lastly, there is evidence from the finance literature that has established a link between company performance and managerial turnover. In particular, Kaplan (1995) has shown that when stock performance declines companies are more likely to make changes to their boards of directors than when their performance is stable or improving. There is also evidence of a positive correlation between a company's performance and the number of subsequent directorships held by directors of that company (Fama and Jensen, 1983; Ferris, Jagannathan and Pritchard, 2003). Directors of a company that performs well typically succeed in being appointed to other boards, while those of companies that perform poorly tend to be 'scarred for life'. Both these types of findings serve to underline the point that company performance is not simply the *endpoint* of appointment decisions, but should also be seen as the basis and impetus for *future* decisions of this form.

It is therefore important not only to focus on women leaders themselves, but also to take into account the circumstances surrounding their appointment. However, contemporary analyses of leaders and leadership have tended to neglect these situational variables, placing an emphasis instead largely on personality and individual differences (Cappelli and Sherer, 1991; Meindl, 1993).

The present study

In order to get to the bottom of the phenomenon (potentially) identified by Judge (2003) what is needed is a more nuanced analysis of women in leadership and company performance; one that can take into account situational factors such as the time of appointment and fluctuations in company performance, and can thus shed some light on the causal relationship between the appointment of women leaders and a company's financial performance. To this end, an archival study was conducted which spoke to the same data set that was of interest to Judge (2003). This investigated the share price performance of FTSE 100 companies on the London Stock Exchange both immediately before and after the appointment of a male or female board member. In this way, two alternative accounts can be tested: the one proposed by Judge (2003) – that women leaders produce relatively poor financial outcomes for their companies; and an alternative – that woman are appointed in conditions of relatively poor company performance.

METHOD

Leader appointments

Using the 2003 Cranfield Index (Singh and Vinnicombe, 2003) as a guide, the websites of all FTSE 100 companies were searched in order to identify those companies that had appointed a woman to their board of directors during 2003, and to establish the month in which these appointments were made. Relevant facts were established by accessing annual reports, press releases and director biographies. In total, 19 female board appointments were made in 2003; 17 companies were found to have appointed one woman in 2003, while one company was found to have appointed two women (at different times) in 2003.

In order that relevant gender comparisons could be made, a search was conducted to identify 19 FTSE 100 companies that had appointed a man to their board of directors in 2003. As far as possible, companies were matched for the time of appointment and for business sector (e.g. banking, retail, information technology).

Company performance

Two measures of company performance were computed. The first was a broad measure of annual company performance, similar to that used by Judge (2003). Using the online London Stock Exchange Share Monitoring Service (LSE, n.d.), the performance of each of the companies was calculated as the percentage movement over the 12 months preceding 17 December 2003. A negative value represents a loss in share price over that time, whereas a positive value represents a gain in share price.

In order to investigate fluctuations in company performance a second indicator of company performance was calculated. Using the online monthly trading summaries provided by the London Stock Exchange (n.d.) an average monthly share price was calculated as the total value of shares traded divided by the number of shares traded. The average monthly share price was calculated for the six months before and after the appointment of a board member.

RESULTS

Annual performance

To test for the existence of a relationship between women in leadership and company performance, correlational analysis was performed to assess the strength of the relationship between the percentage of women on the board of a company and its annual performance in 2003. Consistent with Judge's (2003) claims, results revealed that for FTSE 100 companies there was a marginally significant negative correlation between the percentage of women in leadership positions and performance as measured by change in share price, $r(97) = -0.14$, $p = 0.09$ (one-tailed). Thus, the higher the percentage of women on a company's board, the poorer the company's performance.

A t-test was also conducted to see if the annual performance of a company differed depending on whether a male or a female board member had been appointed. Analysis revealed that there was no significant difference in performance in 2003 for those companies that appointed a women ($M = 7.54\%$) compared to those companies that appointed a man ($M = 10.08\%$), $t(36)<1$, ns, although the trend was in the direction suggested by Judge (2003). Further, while neither companies which had appointed a male nor those which had appointed a female performed significantly different from the FTSE 100 (which showed an increase of 10.71% in the 12 months up to December 17, 2003, both $ts < 1$), those companies that appointed men showed a significant increase in share price over that time, $t(18) = 2.81$, $p < 0.02$, while those that appointed a women did not show a significant increase, $t(18) = 1.96$, $p = 0.07$. However, as argued in the Introduction, such analysis does not shed light on the direction of causation, and such broad measures do not take account of the time of appointment or fluctuations in company performance over time.

Fluctuations in monthly performance

In order to investigate fluctuations in the performance of companies immediately before and after the appointment of an individual to their boards of directors, changes in average monthly share prices were calculated. The relative monthly performance was defined as the percentage change in share price from the previous month, with a positive value indicating an increase in average monthly share price and a negative value indicating a decrease in share price. Due to the availability of data, the relative monthly performance was calculated five months prior to the appointment to their boards of directors and three months after the appointment. In total, data were available for 15 companies with female appointments and 16 companies with male appointments.

In order to investigate company performance in the five months prior to the appointment of a board member and three months after the appointment a 2 (gender of appointee: male, female) x 2 (time of appointment: first half of the year, second half of the year) x 8 (relative monthly performance: 5 months prior to 3 months post) mixed-model analysis of variance (ANOVA) was conducted with repeated measures on the last variable. The eight levels of the repeated measures variable allowed for tests of linear, quadratic, cubic, fourth-, fifth-, sixth- and seventh-order trends in relative monthly performance.

The results revealed a main effect for time of appointment, $F(1, 27) = 11.50$, $p < 0.01$. These reflected overall seasonal variations in the stock market such that performance in the months immediately before and after appointments made in the first half of the year ($M = 0.49\%$) was lower than those made in the second half of the year ($M = 2.63\%$). However, this was qualified by a significant two-way interaction between relative monthly performance and time of appointment, $F(7, 189) = 4.20$, $p < 0.001$. Contrasts revealed a significant linear interaction between relative monthly performance and time of appointment, $F_{lin}(7, 27) = 18.73$, $p < 0.001$. For appointments in the first half of the year, relative monthly performance tended to be most negative three to four months prior to appointment, increasing to reveal more positive performance in the months immediately before and after appointment. In other words, for people appointed in the first half of the year, the appointment of new board members was generally associated with improved performance. In contrast, for those appointments made in the second half of the year, relative monthly performance was stable and generally positive.

However, this two-way interaction was qualified by a marginally significant linear three-way interaction between gender, time of appointment, and relative monthly performance, $F_{lin}(7, 27) = 3.17$, $p < 0.09$, and a significant seventh-order three-way interaction,

$F_{7ord}(7, 27) = 7.21$, p < 0.02. In order to decompose these effects, separate analyses were conducted to examine the effect of time of appointment and fluctuations in monthly performance as a function of gender of the appointee (see Figure 1).

Analyses revealed that these three-way interactions arose from variation in the performance of companies that appointed women to their board. As can be seen from Figures 1a and 1b, on average, those companies that appointed a male board member showed a relatively stable performance over time, both for appointments in the first half and the second half of the year, with none of the polynomial contrasts being significant (all ps > 0.05).

However, for those companies that appointed a woman to their board, company performance did vary significantly over time as a function of time of appointment, $F_{lin}(1, 13) = 21.01$, p < 0.01, $F_{cub}(1, 13) = 4.78$, p < 0.05, $F_{7ord}(1, 13) = 3.91$, p < 0.05. As can be seen in Figure 1c, when a woman was appointed in the first half of the year (i.e., when the stock market was down), company performance showed a clear and significant linear increase over time, $F_{lin}(1, 7) = 14.53$, p < 0.01. Between five and two months prior to the appointment of a woman, these companies experienced very low share price. Thereafter, however, company performance increased significantly.

In contrast, for those companies that appointed a woman to their board in the second half of the year (i.e. when the stock market was up), the pattern was more complex (see Figure 1d). Here there was a significant linear decrease in performance, $F_{lin}(1, 6) = 7.51$, p < 0.04, such that performance before the appointment of a woman was generally positive while after the appointment it was relatively stable. However, in addition, this analysis revealed a significant cubic trend, $F_{cub}(1, 6) = 5.70$, p = 0.05. This arose from the fact that performance prior to appointment was not consistently high but fluctuated between being high and being stable.

DISCUSSION

The glass cliff

This archival examination of the performance of FTSE 100 companies questions the rather simplistic assumption that women leaders are responsible for poor company performance. Instead a more complex story is revealed, one that points to the need to take account of situational factors when examining organizational and leadership outcomes (e.g. see Miendl, 1993; Haslam, 2001). First, it is important to note that, contrary to Judge's (2003) intimation, the appointment of a woman to the board of directors was not associated with a subsequent drop in company performance. Indeed, in a time of a general financial downturn in the stock market, companies that appointed a woman actually experienced a marked *increase* in share price after the appointment (Figure 1c), whereas those appointments made in less unsettling times were followed by a period of share price stability (Figure 1d).

However, potentially more interesting findings uncovered by the study related to fluctuations in company performance *leading up* to the appointment of men and women to boards of directors. In particular, it is apparent that for companies which appointed men to

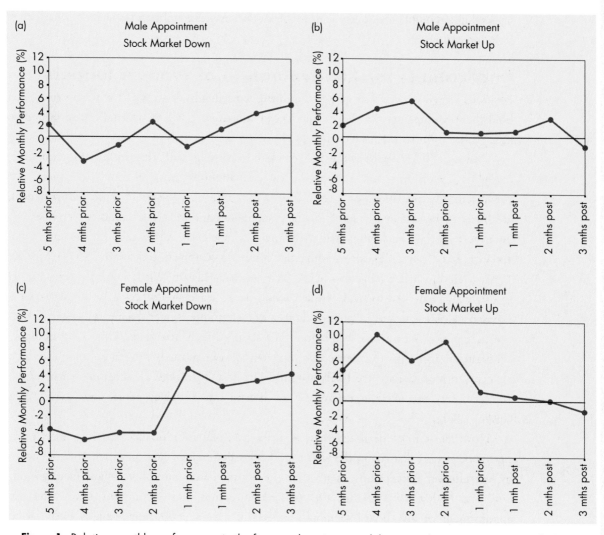

Figure 1: Relative monthly performance in the five months prior to and three months post appointment of a board member as a function of gender of appointee and the time of year of the appointment.

their boards of directors in 2003, company performance was relatively stable, both before and after the appointment. Furthermore, this was true regardless of the time of year that the appointment was made, and hence regardless of the state of the stock market (see Figures 1a and 1b). For companies that appointed women to their boards of directors in 2003 a more interesting pattern of results emerged. *In a time of a general financial downturn in the stock market, companies that appointed a woman had experienced consistently poor performance in the months preceding the appointment* (Figure 1c). In contrast, when the stock market was more stable, companies that appointed a woman had experienced positive (but fluctuating) performance (Figure 1d).

Importantly, then, this archival study has helped to unearth an interesting phenomenon. That is, it appears that women are particularly likely to be placed in positions of leadership in circumstances of general financial downturn and downturn in company performance. In this way, such women can be seen to be placed on top of a 'glass cliff', in the sense that their leadership appointments are made in problematic organizational circumstances and hence are more precarious.

Implications for the evaluation of women leaders

Positions on glass cliffs can be seen as being exceedingly dangerous for the women who hold them. Companies that have experienced consistently bad performance are bound to attract attention to themselves and to those on their boards of directors (as the Swann's experience at W.H. Smith shows). Moreover, consistent with the traditional, 'romantic' model of leadership – and as Judge's, 2003, attributions show all too vividly — in such circumstances explanations of organizational outcomes (e.g. negative share performance), are likely to be couched in terms of the personalities and individual abilities of the leaders involved (e.g. their leadership style or financial competence) rather than on the situational and contextual variables surrounding the company (Cappelli and Sherer, 1991; Meindl, 1993; Meindl, Ehrlich and Dukerich, 1985; see also Haslam, 2001; Haslam *et al.*, 2001). In this way, compared to men, women who assume leadership offices may be differentially exposed to criticism and in greater danger of being apportioned blame for negative outcomes that were set in train well before they assumed their new roles. This is particularly problematic in light of evidence that directors who leave the boards of companies which have performed poorly are likely to suffer from a 'tarnished reputation' (Ferris *et al.*, 2003) and are less likely be offered future directorships (Brickley, Linck and Coles, 1999; Gilson, 1990).

However, it must be noted that, in reality, a company's financial performance, especially one that is floated on the share market, is determined just as much (if not more) by shareholder perceptions as it is by the actual behaviour of its board members (cf. Lord and Maher, 1991). Thus, the financial direction that a company takes after the appointment of any board members, especially over a short time-span, is likely to be more indicative of the confidence that the shareholders have in the appointment than of the actual ability of the appointed board member. Obviously, companies are aware of the importance of shareholder confidence, and therefore the appointment of a woman leader when things are going badly could be seen as a corporate strategy designed to signal to the shareholders that radical change is on the way (Furtado and Rozeff, 1987).

Directions for future research

Although this archival examination of the performance of FTSE 100 companies points to the existence of a glass cliff, it clearly represents only a preliminary investigation of this phenomenon. Further research is therefore required in order to provide more thoroughgoing examination of the psychological processes underlying these findings. One obvious question that needs to be addressed is the nature of the corporate (and general) motivations underlying the appointment of women to precarious positions. Here a variety of motivations could be posited, ranging from confidence in the particular abilities of women leaders (e.g. Eagly, Johannesen-Schmidt and van Engen, 2003) to overt sexism. It is also important to investigate women leaders' sensitivity to, and perceptions of, glass cliff positions (Schmitt,

Ellemers and Branscombe, 2003). Do they see the precariousness as a form of discrimination, or simply as an opportunity to achieve?

As suggested above, another important avenue for research is to examine the way in which women who take on these glass cliff positions are subsequently evaluated by their colleagues, staff and by the public at large. Because women typically constitute a minority on the board of any company (Singh and Vinnicombe, 2003) are they more visible and thus more open to criticism (Miller, Taylor and Buck, 1991)? Are women more likely to be blamed for negative organizational outcomes? Are they equally likely to be praised for any positive outcomes?

Lastly, it is also necessary to establish whether the glass cliff phenomenon extends outside the boardroom and into other leadership arenas. Theoretically, it is also important to see whether the phenomenon is associated with low-status group membership in general and hence is a manifestation of a general social psychological process rather than one specific to gender (e.g. as discussed by Haslam, Postmes and Ellemers, 2003; Ryan and David, 2003; Ryan, David, and Reynolds, 2004). Along these lines, there is some evidence to suggest that, at least in Japan, poor company performance is associated with the appointment of 'outsiders' to boards of directors (Kaplan and Minton, 1994).

In order to explore these possibilities, several experimental and archival investigations are underway and all have revealed patterns commensurate with the above findings (Ryan and Haslam, in prep-a, in prep-b). In particular, there is evidence to suggest that within politics, women who rise to public office often do so under difficult circumstances. Looking, for example, at Margaret Thatcher's political career, a series of glass cliff situations can be identified. Thatcher's first brush with politics was to run as a Conservative candidate (twice) in a strong, safe Labour seat, losing both attempts. She was made Education Minister in the early 1970s when student radicalism was at its peak, facing student riots and strong criticism. Lastly, in 1979 she became Prime Minister at a time when Britain was facing rampant unemployment and economic recession. In Australia too, there have only ever been two women state premiers (Joan Kirner in Victoria and Carmen Lawrence in Western Australia). Both were appointed mid-term and after their party had been exposed to humiliating scandals. As a result, both faced the prospect of unwinnable elections which they duly lost.

CONCLUSION

It is already well established that women face greater challenges than men in their attempts to climb to the top of the corporate ladder. Moreover, it is apparent that even if they arrive there, women are likely to receive greater scrutiny and criticism than men, and to secure less positive evaluations, even when performing exactly the same leadership roles (Eagly *et al.*, 1992). It now seems apparent that in addition to these obstacles, the leadership positions that women occupy are likely to be less promising than those of their male counterparts. So, in addition to confronting a glass ceiling and not having access to a glass elevator, they are also likely to be placed on a glass cliff. Furthermore, as the content of Judge's (2003) article indicates, if, upon finding themselves in a leadership position, they fail (as they are more likely to than men because their positions are more precarious), they may be singled out for blame and humiliation, at the same time that the unpropitious conditions of their appointment are overlooked.

The debate surrounding this process is likely to become more ferocious as women assume more leadership roles in the future (Singh and Vinnicombe, 2003). One important contribution of this paper is to help restore some balance to this debate. It does this by helping to render visible factors that are customarily ignored in the analysis of organizational leadership (Haslam, 2001; Miendl, 1993). Ironically too, it is apparent that, if overlooked, these factors can easily promote the very inequality that women's advancement is intended to redress.

ACKNOWLEDGEMENT

Thanks to Tom Postmes for statistical guidance. This research was funded by a grant from the Leverhulme Trust (Grant F.00144.V).

REFERENCES

The references to go with this article can be found on www.wileyeurope.com/college/french.

QUESTIONS TO CONSIDER

1. Define the terms *glass ceiling, glass elevator* and *glass cliff* used in Ryan and Haslam's study.
2. Why do Ryan and Haslam cast doubt on the validity of previous findings detailing the performance of women in leadership positions? Do you think they are justified in criticising previous research studies in this regard? Give reasons for your conclusions.

PART 5

CASE STUDIES

Case Study 1
Sedlacek Software Spolecnost (SSS):
Applying OB in Practice

Karla Zelenka is General Manager of Sedlacek Software Spolecnost (SSS), a software company, founded in 1983, based in Prague in the Czech Republic. Karla is relatively new to the company – she has only been with it for three months – and she is having a difficult day. On two separate occasions during the morning, two of her senior sales consultants, Ivona and Emil, have approached her asking for more flexible or, if possible, reduced working hours over the next few months. Karla thinks this is not a good time because, although sales have been steady and Ivona and Emil are performing well, she has been getting pressure from the company's directors to win more clients. Competition in the industry is at an all-time high and SSS's market share is constantly under threat.

SSS already has one of its senior sales consultants, Jarmila, working flexible hours. Jarmila has been with the company for two years and has an excellent track record and good client base. She is a single parent with two children aged six and three and last year made an arrangement with Karla's predecessor to work more flexible hours in order to care for her children. While she still completes a full-time working week, Jarmila is able to start later in the morning after taking the children to school, then makes up her time by taking short lunch breaks and working occasional Saturdays.

SSS has always taken pride in being compassionate towards its employees and has adopted the philosophy that all employees should lead a balanced life between work and leisure. Families of employees are encouraged to take part in social activities, and management at SSS has been known to help out those employees who have suffered financial stress or experienced other personal setbacks.

Karla came to SSS after spending three years in the US working for Hardware-Software, a Chicago-based company that had a very different organizational culture to SSS. The software industry in the US is known to be tough and Hardware-Software would expect its employees to work long hours, take work home and be in the office at least one day during the weekend. Trying to take holidays (holiday entitlement in the US is typically less than in European countries) was always an issue, especially as staff were not allowed to accumulate leave entitlement from one year to the next. As a result, staff turnover was quite high and three years at Hardware-Software could be considered a long-term appointment. Karla began work in Chicago as junior sales support and after six months was promoted to senior consultant. A year later she became National Sales Manager. Karla had no problem with the long hours but always planned to move back to Prague, her home city, which she has loved since she was a little girl. It was a difficult decision to make at the time but when the opportunity to be general manager of a software company came up in Prague, how could she refuse? Hardware-Software was Karla's second job after she left university – she had been trained in a Danish software design company after obtaining her bachelors and masters degrees. Other than her jobs in Denmark and the US, her work experience had been limited to short-term casual jobs as a restaurant waitress in Prague during her years of study. Also, Karla was a later entry into university as she chose to travel overseas for 12 months after passing her school leaving certificate.

For Karla, the transition from Hardware-Software to the SSS organization has not been easy and, to some extent, moving across national boundaries has exacerbated her difficulties. She likes to consider herself a relatively easygoing, amiable type of person socially, but her attitude to work is one of strict focus; achieving corporate goals is always her first priority. Karla has been single-minded since adolescence and even while studying at university she was very focused and devoted many long hours working to gain her degrees. After completing her undergraduate studies, Karla stayed on to undertake a masters degree, all the while keeping career prospects in longer term view. Karla's single-minded attitude also resulted in her very quick progress up the corporate ladder at Hardware-Software. For a 28 year old she has certainly achieved a lot and is in a very senior position compared to others of similar age. Possibly because Karla lives alone and has only a small circle of friends and relatives in Prague, she spends much of her supposed leisure time at the office. She does, however, intend joining a social club but hasn't decided exactly what that will be. Whatever interests she had when she was younger have seemed to become completely overtaken by her professional life. When Karla studied at university, she was introduced to the work of Geert Hofstede who categorized cultural differences between nations. When reading his work, Karla was attracted to the values of an individualist type of society and, when in the US, strongly identified with work practices there: in some curious way she felt that deep down she was 'more American than the Americans'.

Karla's appointment at SSS has not been particularly well received by some of its senior staff. Part of that is due to the reputation of Hardware-Software (which is internationally renowned) and the fact that Karla worked there for three years clearly suggests to some people that she is a workaholic with very few other priorities in her life. The senior staff formed this perception soon after Karla's arrival at SSS – very much a first impression – and, as she has only been with the company for a short time there really has not been much opportunity for her to try to change that perception. As we know from our discussion of perception in Chapter 2, first impressions can, in any case, be difficult to change. Karla has been very preoccupied trying to orientate herself into her work role and hierarchical position as general manager and has not really spent much time developing the social aspect of the office environment.

Prior to Karla's appointment, Ivona had applied for the job as general manager with total support from Emil and Jarmila, as well as other members of staff at SSS. In addition to her role as senior sales consultant, Ivona is also supervisor of the entire sales department, which has a total of 14 employees. Ivona has been with SSS for nine years and is an excellent mentor for Emil and Jarmila. Ivona initiated a staff-development programme several years ago and has put many hours of her own time into counselling some of the younger members of the sales team. She is fully aware of the need to develop staff with a view to retaining them in the company, as turnover in the software industry is very high due to the competitive nature of the industry.

When Ivona failed to get the position as general manager and Karla arrived from another country, morale among the senior sales consultants dropped and Ivona in particular began to question her role at SSS, using Emil and Jarmila as 'sounding boards on many occasions. This, of course, did not help the overall acceptance of Karla's appointment and tended to add to the negativity that was already developing. Now, three months later, the hitherto friendly atmosphere at SSS is not what it used to be, even among the senior sales consultants who are seriously considering other options as their loyalty and motivation diminish and priorities are reshuffled.

Since Karla's appointment, and with no other option for promotion in sight, Ivona now wants to work flexible hours as she feels she is suffering burnout and would like to prioritize her domestic life and health as she now plans to have children. She has consulted her doctor who told her that she works too many hours and should cut back. Ivona's boyfriend totally supports this and would really prefer that she gave up work altogether.

Emil has requested a more flexible, reduced workload so he can train for the Czech squash selection game in three months time, as he wants to make the national team. He is a single man who is ranked in the top 10 amateur squash players in the Czech Republic. Emil has been with the company for five years and has an excellent track record and good client base.

Both Emil and Ivona know of Jarmila's flexible working arrangement and, although they appreciate SSS's philosophy towards families, they think this should apply equally to all employees wanting to lead a balanced lifestyle, not just those with children.

Karla has told both Emil and Ivona that she will meet with them tomorrow to discuss their situations. Personally, Karla doesn't think either of them should be given more flexible hours, especially after her time spent with Hardware-Software and the sacrifices she has made in her career. Karla also doesn't think Jarmila should have been given preference merely because she had children but that is something she inherited when she took over as general manager of SSS. Karla is concerned about the pressures placed on staffing issues by the company's directors. All staff issues have to be approved by them and, once they find out that their entire senior sales team now seeks flexible working hours, she knows it will be difficult for them to support, especially as the pressure is on to increase the client base. However, Karla is also vaguely aware that, although there are only three senior sales consultants at SSS, there is a very good pool of second-tier sales people who are currently being developed by Ivona and who could quite possibly be promoted should a vacancy suddenly become available. She makes a mental note to check this out before meeting with Emil and Ivona tomorrow, just in case things get a little heated and she has to offer an ultimatum. Hopefully, it won't come to that. She also realizes that she needs to consult with the company's human resource manager to check out the legal position; as far as she knows, while the right to maternity leave is recognized within national and EU legislation, flexible work arrangements more generally are still within the discretion of individual companies in the Czech Republic.

Karla leaves the office that night knowing she will not sleep well. Tomorrow the situation has to be resolved. Fortunately, the meeting times with Emil and Ivona have yet to be scheduled so Karla decides to meet with them both, separately, in the afternoon so she can spend the entire morning reviewing the staff situation at SSS and developing a sound strategy.

Source: this case is fictional. It has been adapted from 'Solutions Software Company' written by Val Morrison, featured in Wood, J., Zeffane, R. Fromholtz, M & Fitzgerald, J. (2006), *Organizational Behaviour: Core Concepts and Applications,* Wiley: Milton, Queensland.

Questions

1. List and briefly analyse each issue that Karla faces. Consider those things that are directly related to Karla as a manager, linking each of the issues to organizational behaviour theories and concepts.
2. Assuming Karla has no confidante at SSS, if you were a close friend of hers and that evening she called you and asked for advice on how to approach the meetings with Emil and Ivona, what would you say? As a close friend it is expected that you will take into consideration Karla's personal and professional attributes when preparing your answer.
3. Assume that Karla has had harmonious discussions with both Emil and Ivona and they have agreed to consider their existing roles being redesigned to accommodate a flexible work arrangement. Bearing in mind that the outcome of this must be presented, by Karla to SSS directors, how would you structure the redesign in order to benefit SSS corporate goals and to the satisfaction of the employees concerned? Remember to consider all employees at SSS, not just Emil and Ivona.
4. Refer to Hofstede's model of cultural difference as applied to the US and Czech Republic and consider the extent to which it can aid our understanding of the issues and events depicted in this case study.

Case Study 2
Hermitage University: Perceiving Opportunities and Threats

Hermitage University is a large higher education establishment situated in the south of England. It is the thirteenth oldest institute of higher education in the world. It has, in the period since 1950, been recognized as amongst the top 20 universities in the United Kingdom, although its international profile is patchy. It is well known in India, Hong Kong and the West Indies but less so in mainland Europe and North America.

It is a very traditional university and relies largely on its academic reputation and social networking opportunities to attract students, staff and research funding. Its graduates have, for centuries, been successful in forging successful careers, with a particular concentration in the UK public sector and in administrative posts in British Commonwealth countries.

It benefits from substantial endowments from benefactors and, despite the funding and related issues addressed later in this case, it is considered to be financially secure in the foreseeable future. Again, despite the issues addressed later in the case, it benefits from a formidable international reputation, albeit one that is clustered in certain areas of the world.

As with all universities, it prides itself on the range of academic subjects it embraces. Amongst these are Classics, arts, politics philosophy and economics (PPE), law, and pure science. Although its reputation is formidable across the wide range of academic subjects, it has for centuries been seen as one of the market leaders in science and law. Its reputation in other areas, although impressive, is less high profile than other traditional universities in the UK. However, this secondary status is perceived only at the very highest levels of achievement and its reputation in these areas is still world class.

Although the university has a substantial administrative support team, its policies and procedures on teaching, learning and student assessment are limited. Furthermore, although, it has never found a problem with student recruitment, its policies and procedures in this area are somewhat underdeveloped. Its research record and success in attracting research funding is impressive but its actual policies and procedures in terms of sustaining such funding are limited. University academic staff pride themselves in their world-class status and are somewhat resistant to complying with formal procedures, considering administrative functions to be there to support their existence. In some respects the university can accurately be described as exhibiting characteristics of a person culture – see Chapter 8 for a fuller description. Professors and senior lecturers in particular, benefit from a substantial degree of academic independence, which traditionally has been extended into freedom from both managerial and administrative interference.

Over the last few years the world of academia has experienced major change. Some specific initiatives and developments are set out below:

1. Universities are required to operate in a much more public and transparent environment. Government audits of academic procedures at Hermitage University have suggested a number of deficiencies:
   - Academic assessments (although favourably commented upon in the main) have been subject to occasional criticism – assessments have not been subject to peer appraisal (scrutiny by other lecturers); there is a lack of an audit trail in marking; criticisms have been made of the standards of assessments and marking and there is no second marking of any assessments.
   - Quality of teaching – this has been judged to be at best adequate and occasionally poor. The main criticisms have been lack of documentation in syllabus construction, lack of coherent syllabus development, lack of lesson planning and no peer observation of teaching. Students have complained of difficulties in making appointments with tutors in the law and philosophy departments.
   - Lack of a coherent strategy on student recruitment – criticisms have been made particularly of failure to recruit from certain sections of the community, manifested in under-representation of some socio-economic groups, together with imbalances in terms of ethnic groupings, gender and age profiles.

- Limited policies on providing access for the chronically sick and disabled.
- Inadequate liaison with the world of employment.
- Little exposure of students to outside speakers from other business sectors.
- Poor employment advisory services for undergraduate students.

2. Worldwide competition for students.

- Recruitment is still healthy across all academic disciplines but there is some (but limited) evidence which suggests that students who previously entered classics, arts or PPE disciplines, are beginning to seek places elsewhere on more work-related courses.
- There has been a slight but growing difficulty in recruiting the highest calibre teaching staff in classics, arts and PPE. This tendency was first noted in the field of applied science and in 1999 the university took action in this area by establishing 'arm's length' companies where tutoring staff could supplement their income by providing consultancy services to client companies. As will be attested later in this case study, these have been very successful.
- There has been a reduction in applications for some study areas, for example pure science, but this has been matched by a corresponding increase in others such as applied science.

3. The advent of a new student fee regime and, in particular, the introduction of so-called 'top-up' fees in 2006.

- Overall this has not had an adverse reaction on student recruitment but there is some evidence that potential students, other than those in law and applied science, are beginning to look for more job-related courses.
- The reaction of the university is that top-up fees, predicted to rise after 2009, with some suggestion that a free market might be introduced, will place it in an even more favourable position in the student recruitment market. The consensus internally is that students will be more than willing to pay high fees to enter this prestigious institution. However, some academic commentators have suggested that such top-up fees will result in a significant leakage of potential UK students to overseas institutions. A prestigious East Coast American institution has recently established a student recruitment office in London.
- There is some suggestion that students will increasingly regard themselves as customers of higher education resulting in an increasing concern with 'value for money'. This could be manifested in a number of ways. For example, the university has already received unwanted and embarrassing publicity when mobile phone camera footage of Professor Alexander Crustie apparently falling asleep during a seminar was shown on the YouTube Web site and subsequently featured in a British tabloid newspaper. Overall, it is felt that the consequences of an increasing customer orientation amongst students is far reaching, unpredictable and will need managing.

4. Universities being obliged to supplement their government-supported income with self-generated funds.

- The general internal reaction to this change is that Hermitage University will find no difficulty in attracting such funds. Endowments are as healthy as ever, research funding will be secure in an academically prestigious institution, with private sector organizations 'queuing up' to sponsor university activity. Such sponsorship has been evidenced to a massive extent in the applied science area.
- As has been mentioned previously, the applied science part of the university has been complemented with university-owned businesses – undertaking research and consultancy on behalf of private organizations under the knowledge transfer banner. This type of activity has involved Hermitage University entering into partnership with private organizations in developing new applications for scientific knowledge. University-owned establishments in this area have attracted significant levels of sponsorship from private-sector organizations. These ventures have secured substantial and growing funds for the university. There has been disagreement regarding the distribution of surplus funds from these activities. Initially these funds were used to support university-wide initiatives but of late these funds have been used to support applied science activities exclusively. These developments have reversed the leakage of high-quality staff to overseas institutions. In 2005 however, there was extensive tabloid newspaper coverage of financial impropriety in one of the high-profile applied science companies operated by the university.

  In August 2007 Hermitage University created a new staff post of Strategic Developments Director (SDD), reporting directly to the Vice-Chancellor. The first SDD is Dr Christina Raglan appointed in January 2008. Christina has a PhD in earth science, awarded by the University of Edinburgh in the field of environmental sustainability. Prior to her arrival at Hermitage University, she worked at Greenspace a major environmental pressure group, well known throughout Europe, rising to the post of Director of Communications and Fundraising. At the time of her appointment at Hermitage she was 29 years old. In March 2008 she was asked to set up a meeting of the University's Senate; a decision-making body comprising professors from across the university's academic schools. She was asked to make a PowerPoint presentation to the Senate outlining the challenges faced by the university and the opportunities thrown up by the new environment in which it was forced to operate.

Source: case by Tony Dawson, adapted by Ray French. Reproduced by permission of Tony Dawson.

Questions

1. With reference to concepts set out in Chapter 2, advise Christina on how she is likely to be perceived by members of the university senate as she commences her presentation.
2. Suggest three ways in which she could create positive perceptions of her personally and her new role during the upcoming presentation.

Case Study 3
Truly a Great Disappointment: Motivating Employees in a Different Culture

The following case study deals with an Austrian-owned company, Auskunft AG, a business operating in diverse areas of the media industry. With headquarters in Vienna, Auskunft AG has, since 1998, embarked upon a series of cross-border acquisitions. The company's aim has been to strengthen its position among European media conglomerates, taking advantage of the free movement of capital, goods, services and labour between EU member states under the terms of the single European market. In 2004, Auskunft AG took a controlling interest in Chatroux, a long-established French company based in St Etienne. Chatroux was founded in 1886 and grew to specialize in printing high-quality paper-based documents; they had the contract to produce menus and other prestigious materials for many well-known Parisian hotels, clubs and restaurants. Chatroux is headed by M. Jacques Giraud, the President Directeur General (PGD).

Academic models dealing with organization structure, employee attitudes including motivation and leadership styles in different societies, typically characterize French work organizations as being highly centralized, managed through a strict hierarchy (a French word!) with top-down communications and run on functional lines. M.Giraud entered the company as a graduate of a leading *grand école*, after working for 14 years as the public relations director for the Bordeaux wine regional federation. With no previous experience in the printing industry he relied very heavily on his senior managers' experience.

Responsibility for production within Chatroux lay with M. Guy Legris the Production Director who reported directly to the PGD. With 27 years' service at Chatroux, M. Legris had an unparalleled knowledge of the business, which led him to exercise what he perceived as a right to make decisions without consultation. His management style could reasonably be equated to the *patron* model identified by many analysts of French business life. Task-oriented, M. Legris conducted social relations on a paternalistic basis and was greatly respected by the workforce, many of whom were over 45 years old. The organization culture at Chatroux was characterized by a strong sense of duty and compliance, coupled with low employee turnover and a high degree of security.

In recent years M. Legris had suffered several bouts of coronary illness and the PGD had come to believe that it would be prudent to replace him with a younger employee. Close to retirement age, M. Legris agreed with this logic and the company set about recruiting and selecting a successor. However when the decision was communicated to the parent company Auskunft AG, head office in Austria proposed a management exchange and that M. Legris's replacement should be the first appointment under this initiative.

The new Production director at St Etienne was Herr Dr Rudolf Barfuss (all the candidates for the post were male). Dr Barfuss was at that time 32 years old, with a Masters degree in print technology and a PhD in e-business from the Technical University of Bremen in Germany. He spoke fluent English and had, on his own initiative, taken an intensive French language course in Marseilles in which he was awarded a distinction. Overall, head office considered that Dr Barfuss possessed strategic awareness, linguistic facility, academic strength and international experience, all of which, taken together, made him an ideal candidate for the post of Production Director.

Dr Barfuss soon began to introduce a participative style of management to the St Etienne operation. He stressed the importance of delegation of responsibility, teamwork and joint decision making. He introduced a joint consultative committee where employees were encouraged to put forward ideas on improving work procedures. He also began a thorough analysis of employees' training needs and planned to implement a new remuneration scheme, which included elements of performance related pay. He felt confident that he would have the support of the workforce in introducing these changes and saw his initiatives as key to developing the true potential of the company's employees.

For the first three months after his appointment Dr Barfuss was pleased with results at the St Etienne subsidiary. Levels of productivity had remained stable and he was very happy with the conduct of joint consultative committee meetings. Three employees had left the company and after a conscientious evaluation of the reasons he concluded that they had left for reasons unconnected with their work. He was shocked, therefore, when he was called into M. Giraud's office, handed a letter by the PGD and asked for his reactions. The letter had been written by Sacha Aznavour the head of production planning and one of Dr Barfuss's immediate subordinates. Barfuss had a high regard for Aznavour, a highly competent and dedicated employee, 63 years old and with 34 years' experience in the company.

Aznavour had written:

Dear M. Giraud,

I have agonized for several weeks before finally deciding to send this letter. Please do not misconstrue my motives in my criticism of the Production Director. I know that he is technically excellent in his field of work but have to report the unhappiness of my department. I feel that the production operation is not working as well as it could be and foresee even greater difficulties.

When M. Legris dealt with us on a production-related matter he would call us into his office and tell us what the problem was, the solution required and what we had to do by when. We often had arguments with him but we all stood behind him in cases of production difficulties even if we saw him as a dictator. Although he sometimes gave us a brusque response if he thought we should know the answer, we would get a straight yes or no. We always knew what was expected of us. He knew everything there was to know about printing!

With Dr Barfuss things are very different. We have meetings all the time. In April of 140 working hours, 57 were spent in meetings called by him. We have long conversations but he will not come to any decision at the end of them. He constantly says things like, 'the success of the company will depend upon us working together as a team to find a solution we are all committed to.' This may sound great but really we can only be responsible for our own area of work. At the end of meetings we will have talked at length about the advantages and disadvantages of a particular approach, but the last bit of discussion always concerns the date of the next meeting.

Did you know why Jean Le Mesurier the print technician resigned? In his letter he wrote that he was leaving for a new job nearer his home. This was true but it also paid less and he had become worried that he was unable to come up with the new ideas Dr Barfuss had asked for.

Legris was always to be seen in the production area and would joke with us. With the Austrian manager personal contact is rare apart from in meetings. We are unsure of his management style and his personality is alien to us. I am not alone in believing that his ideas will just not work in Chatroux. We are all very worried about the future.

Dr Barfuss put the letter down. This had come as a great shock to him. He knew that he was not good at social conversation but was hurt that his well-intentioned ideas, designed to bring out the best in the workforce had been so negatively received. He turned to M. Giraud and said 'this is truly a great disappointment.'

Source: this case study has been adapted from *My Greatest Failure* by Professor Dr Henner Hentze, originally published in Adam-Smith, D. & Peacock, A. (eds) (1994), *Cases in Organizational Behaviour,* Pitman: Harlow.

Questions

1. With reference to any *two* theories of motivation, suggest why employees at Chatroux have been less than enthused by Dr Barfuss's approach to managing people.
2. How far have Dr Barfuss's problems been caused by differences between the management styles of two distinct national cultures? What other factors could be influencing attitudes displayed in the case study?
3. Use a specific model of cultural difference to explain the events in this case study.
4. If you were in M. Giraud's position what would you do now? Give reasons for your proposed courses of action.

Case Study 4
Teaming in Singapore's Public Service for the Twenty-first Century

The idea of working with groups and teams permeates the public sector in Singapore. The Singapore government's Public Service for the 21st Century (PS21) strategy is built around the ideas of:

- learning
- questioning
- suggesting
- teaming
- sharing.

All the components work together to encourage improvement, responsiveness to citizens' expectations, and a higher quality service. The PS21 strategy also aims to encourage public sector workers to be activists for change who anticipate, welcome and manage it positively. In the PS21 teams, sharing knowledge involves trusting one another and treating people fairly. Team building is an important part of achieving shared knowledge and of achieving all the aims of PS21. The key teams that put PS21 into action across the service are described below.

PS21 teams

Amoebas are groups of junior officers in the service who volunteer to come together to brainstorm issues of interest or to suggest changes. It is thought that these young officers may not be so bound by historical policy interests or entrenched ways of doing things and that they may also be able to bypass supervisors who may not be open to new ideas. The name 'amoeba' draws links with the single-celled organism that has a short lifespan. It implies working as a single unit. These teams have just 90 days to form, discuss their ideas, submit reports and disband. The proposals help the public (or civil) service to look to the future and have, on hand, ideas and solutions that have been previously thought out.

Work Improvement Teams Scheme (WITS) teams have been around for some time in the Singapore public service. Similar to six Sigma teams (invented by Motorola and popularized by General Electric) the WITS teams do not necessarily have the same strict focus on measurement and quantitative data analysis. However, like six Sigma teams, they focus on gaining significant improvements in the organization, are given considerable resources and involve top-down identification of projects and team members. In fact, WITS is aimed at empowerment of officers to come together to create continuous improvement and innovative outcomes. Unlike Amoebas, which use only junior officers, WITS teams can use officers from different grades, from different units within the organizations, and even from different agencies within the public sector as a whole. In some cases, such as that of the Singapore Prison Service (SPS) where there were 274 WITS projects in 2002, they sometimes get the clients (prison inmates) to participate. WITS teams consider questions about problems interfering with work; opportunities for improvement to create better outcomes; doing things differently and creating value in their activities; making the organization ready for changing circumstances and action to make improvements happen. They are free to use whatever tools they wish to deal with the issue but the tools must help them to go through a rigorous thinking process so that they can identify the root cause of the problem or the main factor that will allow capitalization of an opportunity. Project ideas are submitted to supervisors and management prior to being carried out. One of the key problems with WITS teams is that some supervisors lack leadership and interest in the projects and see them as 'just going through the motions' of fulfilling quotas for WITS projects per year. There has also been too much rigidity in adhering to team tools such as 'fishbone diagrams'. Using the quota system for projects works against the aims of the scheme but does add value because it helps to give an overall picture about whether the scheme is making progress. The head of the civil service Mr Lim Siong Guan believes that WITS is about getting good results out of the teamwork that happens when people get together, grow ideas and learn. It operates in conjunction with another programme – the Staff Suggestion Scheme (SSS).

Study teams are another type of PS21 team. These are formed within government agencies (such as ministries and statutory boards) to look into opportunities, or other options, for achieving agency goals. The members of these teams are senior employees with required expertise, not juniors as in the Amoebas. Rather than being restricted to the shorter time frame given to Amoebas, their allocated time is framed around the complexity and nature of the research.

Strategic Issues Group (SIG) teams involve senior officers from different agencies. They come together to examine cross-agency issues at a strategic level, formulating whatever policies or changes to policies are required. They are also expected to question the existing policy approaches during their research process. They report to a steering committee that comprises permanent secretaries (employed heads of the agencies) and ministers (political heads of the agencies).

Zero-In-Process (ZIP) action teams find and resolve (zero-in on) difficult and systemic problems (called 'X-files'). These are problems that involve more than one agency or problems that do not fit clearly into one agency or another. X-files also cover problems that recur excessively or that emerge because rules and regulations have become outdated. The ZIP programme has been described as a programme to smooth out the kinks in projects that straddle different ministries and agencies. In 2003 some 96 X-files had been uncovered and action taken on 68 of them. When such issues emerge, or are found, senior representatives from the relevant agencies are invited, by the ZIP panel, to form a ZIP action team. The ZIP panel is a committee of permanent secretaries. The problems can be found, for example, by an employee such as Nurhana Ismail, who is an executive officer for the Feedback Unit of the Ministry of Community Development and Sports. She reads the content of each mail and email that reaches her department and if it does not apply to any specific agency she channels it through the Zero-In Process.

Zero-In-Process action teams carry out internal reviews of rules and systems, engage with the community and with the relevant agencies to get their views and involve them in developing solutions and recommend changes (within a given time frame) and a plan for executing the changes. The ZIP programme enables the public service to refresh its rules and regulations and its policies and procedures to ensure they are relevant to public needs. The ZIP reforms are not just about continuous improvement in the public sector; they are also aimed at building up the service, managing the flow of talent and strengthening teamwork and team spirit among public servants. The ZIP programme operates in conjunction with the Pro-Enterprise Panel (PEP) – which ensures that government rules and regulations support a pro-business environment – and the POWER (Public Officers Working on Eliminating Red-tape) initiative – which endeavours to give public officers greater flexibility to do their jobs effectively rather than to adhere to rules and procedures.

There are many ZIP team success stories, such as these three:

- The Land Transport Authority (LTA) was mandated by the Street Works Act to repair and upgrade back lanes belonging to the government. Unfortunately, many of these lanes were dumping grounds for unwanted furniture and the LTA was not empowered to remove the furniture when it obstructed its work. The LTA had to seek approval from the Singapore Land Authority before it could take any action. The ZIP team investigations revealed no reason why the LTA should not be able to remove the obstructions and the Act was amended to allow it.
- When household maids had been abused, the police, as the first point of contact, found themselves having to accommodate the maids while they investigated the charges. The ZIP action team made arrangements with employment agencies, voluntary welfare organizations and embassies (as the maids were from other countries) to house the maids and help them to seek alternative work. A time limit of six months was put on each case, encouraging resolution, so the maids could return to their home countries as soon as possible.
- When experiencing noise pollution, citizens not only had to identify the cause of the noise but also decide which agency was responsible (there were three possibilities). Now, as a result of the ZIP action team's intervention, citizens are not put in this situation. If uncertain, they can go to the National Environment Agency (NEA), which will redirect their comments to the relevant agencies.

Other ZIP stories relate to helping people comply with legal requirements when they have a family bereavement, and improving the visitation process at Changi Women's Prison (this involved a six Sigma process that reduced visitor waiting times). These may seem to be necessary improvements but the complexity of public sector agencies and the laws, rules and regulations that govern them can typically slow down action and solutions. The ZIP teams can cross boundaries, focus on particular issues and bring about improvements in creative and prompt ways.

There are other teams and groups associated with PS21 and the public service in general. For example, because employee involvement is so critical in the strategy, there is a Staff Wellbeing Committee (SWC) that is concerned with employee physical, mental and emotional fitness, training and development; and benefits and rewards, including challenge and recognition. There is an excellence through continuous enterprise learning (ExCEL) committee, an organizational review committee (ORC), a functional committee and a quality service subcommittee. Thus, different types of groups and teams are used to facilitate PS21 with the whole strategy managed by the PS21 office and a PS21 central steering committee (comprising permanent secretaries who are the employed heads of agencies). Each ministry, statutory board or department has its own PS21 committee.

Even outside the explicit scope of the teams outlined, it seems that teams and team-work are an essential part of the public service in Singapore. Zaleha bte Ali is a senior officer with the General Investigation Team (GIT) in the Singapore Immigration and Registration's (SIR) Enforcement Division. Zaleha is proud to be part of a team that won the Minister's Award for Operational Efficiency from the Ministry of Home Affairs. The award is given to teams or officers that perform exceedingly well in their cases. Zaleha's team investigates offences relating to illegal immigrants and those who overstay the period specified on their visas. In a different approach, the Economic Development Board (EDB) has shadow CM (corporate management) teams in a bid to involve nonmanagement officers in management-level discussions. This enables fresh perspectives and it is hoped that it results in better decisions, more innovations and better young managers. Those involved in the teams appreciate the learning opportunity it provides. As well as lively discussions on their inputs, their ideas are captured in the EDB's 'ideas portal'. Another interesting EDB development is the establishment of learning clubs (LC) in 2003. These clubs comprise officers who decide what they want to learn, who they want to learn it from and how they want to learn. They can lead their own learning, find an expert, or learn in the community. These clubs emerge from common interests, enabling sharing and learning that enhances the work of the members. In a similar vein, at the Ministry of Manpower, a photography learning circle was formed in 2001 to promote, improve and sustain employees' interest in learning photography. The membership of the learning circle grew after the group held a three-day exhibition of their works. Innovation circles (I-circles) are a development of the Innovation Unit of the Centre for Organizational Excellence. They bring together 'innovation champions' from across the service to encourage learning, knowledge sharing and discussion. At one meeting of the third I-Circle, participants broke into subgroups to consider 'burning questions' about innovation, and expressed their experiences, frustrations and difficulties in getting innovation happening in their agencies.

Sources: PS21, Office of Public Service Division, Prime Minister's Office, 'Public service for the 21st century', 'Sharing', 'PS21 framework', 'Teaming', 'PS network', 'Staff well-being' and 'PS21 office' (August 2005), http://app.ps21.gov.sg/newps21. The following stories and issues of the public sector magazine *Challenge*: 'Organizational review committee' (May 2001), 'ZIP in action: providing peace of mind for bereaved families' (March 2002), 'Keeping illegal immigrants at bay' (October 2002), 'Passionate about photography' (March 2003), 'Speeding up service delivery' (August 2003), 'Tell her what you think' (August 2003), 'Innovators unite!' (January 2004), 'Innovative "Captains of lives"' (July 2004), 'Make a difference – the spirit of ExCEL' (November 2004), 'More EDB officers have a say' (March 2005), 'The hottest club memberships in town!' (May 2005), 'Improving the visitation process at Changi Women's Prison' (July 2005), 'ZIPping up the civil SERVICE' (31 March 2001). Also Teo, L. 'Zip's the way to swifter service at Govt agencies', *Straits Times* (31 March 2001); 'ZIPping through government red tape', *Straits Times* (10 April 2001); Singapore Government, 'About us', Success stories: 'Backlanes'; 'Who takes care of abused maids', 'Zero-in Process (ZIP)' (August 2005), **http://www.zip.gov.sg/success_stories.htm.**

Questions

1. Find two examples in the case study of 'groups' that cannot be identified clearly as 'teams'. Explain your reasons.

2. Consider the types of teams discussed at the end of Chapter 6 (for example, self-managing teams, problem-solving teams, virtual teams). Using these explanations, categorize at least three of the teams outlined in the case study into these types (it is not necessary to find one for each category). Explain why you have categorized each as you have.

3. The duration of some of the teams in the PS21 project varies. How might this affect group (or team) development stages and potential team effectiveness?

4. From the case study, describe at least two of the types of teams and explain why the membership is formulated as it is and how this might relate to the team's purpose and effectiveness, including the team's decision-making processes.

Case Study 5

Transalpine Fitness: Structuring for Success

Background

Transalpine Fitness (TAF) is a community fitness and leisure centre situated just outside Munich in southern Germany. It was officially opened in May 2001 to coincide with the European Athletics Championship being hosted by Munich in August 2002. In the lead-up to its launch, much of Germany and certainly Munich and the wider federal region (Land) of Bavaria was embracing European Athletics Championship fever and, like many other sporting and nonsporting enterprises, TAF used this as a way to gain extra exposure. As part of the grand opening public relations strategy, TAF invited several renowned sporting teams to stay at the facility prior to the commencement of the games.

When the concept of TAF was first proposed, it was eagerly accepted by the *Lander* government, which believed a multi-sport centre would provide a much needed recreational boost to the area. It immediately donated some of the land on which TAF is built. Although no formal agreement was entered into at that time, there was an unwritten understanding that regional government would have a role in overseeing the operation of TAF, in return for its generosity. Nothing was ever clearly documented however.

This state-of-the-art leisure centre comprises a fully equipped gymnasium, two swimming pools, sports fields, a complete health and beauty spa, a sports science institute, three-star apartment-style accommodation for 100 people, a bistro and a snack bar. There are also child-minding facilities operated by qualified staff. Because of the impressive facilities, part of TAF's overall strategy is to attract elite national and international sports teams for off-season training camps, as well as targeting the local community. Teams from first division soccer in Greece, professional basketball in the United States, and the Portuguese national swimming team are just a few of the high profile groups targeted by TAF. To date this has been successful and the business is growing well.

Scenario

It is 07.20 on Monday and Stefan Ritter, General Manager of TAF, is in his office struggling with a presentation in preparation for a meeting with all staff. The meeting is to commence at 08.00. Stefan is feeling uncomfortable about the meeting and is not really sure what the outcome will be. What he does know is that it has to be positive, otherwise TAF might be forced to close its doors by the end of the year.

Assisting Stefan in the meeting will be Gisela Schneider, a consultant in organizational behaviour. Gisela has spent the last month working with Stefan at TAF, trying to resolve some of the issues that have arisen and she is concerned that these have slowly worsened over the past three months. Gisela's report to Stefan is what prompted the meeting. Gisela was initially hired by Stefan to try to find out why there is an obvious division between the departments at TAF. For such a small facility, there is a huge bureaucracy developing and this is having a negative effect on members and potential customers due to the inconsistencies that have arisen across the different services offered by TAF.

Stefan stares out of the window and begins to think about the current situation at TAF.

The current situation

There is a regular team of 44 staff working at TAF. These people are split across five main business units, namely:

- sports science and physiotherapy (four staff)
- residential accommodation, food and beverages (nine staff)
- health spa, fitness and sports centre (14 staff)
- swim centre (seven staff)
- sales, marketing, memberships and administration (10 staff).

Childcare, maintenance and cleaning are run by contractors commissioned by the relevant local government departments. The people in those groups do not report directly to Stefan as they have their own supervisors back at local government headquarters. However, they are required to liaise with Stefan or one of his staff members about any problems they may encounter. Unfortunately this is not always the case; maintenance and cleaning staff in particular work mostly when TAF is either at low occupancy or closed, to enable them to move freely around all facilities without inconveniencing the customers.

When the TAF complex was built, four of the five business units were put out to tender to independent operators and were immediately acquired and run as four separate entities, but still working under the brand of TAF. The fifth unit – sales, marketing, memberships and administration – was maintained by TAF. That is where the problems began. TAF had the responsibility of sales and marketing, managing memberships and the general administration of the centre but had little control over the product delivered by the independent operators in the other four units. As the business developed, so the independent operators have become more isolated, although this may not necessarily have been intentional. Initially, everyone got on well together and although there is now a definite divide among the groups this is something that has evolved because they are entirely separate entities rather than in a situation of conflict.

Stefan's thoughts are interrupted by a knock on the door. It is Gisela.

'Hi Stefan,' says Gisela as she walks into the office. 'How are you? Sorry to get straight to the point but I'd really like to go through some of the topics for discussion at today's meeting. This is a critical time for TAF and if we don't approach the meeting in the correct way, it could be very uncomfortable for everyone concerned.'

Stefan agrees. 'Yes, come in, we've roughly half an hour to talk about the main issues now.'

Gisela sits opposite Stefan and, without even looking at the agenda he was working on, she begins to go through her findings.

'Well Stefan, in a nutshell, as you know there are several areas of concern for TAF and if you don't communicate the potential problem areas to the staff today then things will continue to deteriorate.'

'I know,' says Stefan, 'but please bear in mind that although I'm GM of TAF, my hands are actually tied when trying to coordinate, direct and motivate everyone towards the same goals. The four independent operators have become more and more isolated since we opened. It's got to the point where they are communicating with our members and potential customers directly and, would you believe, are even competing with each other on product offerings. This is very confusing for everyone.'

Stefan continues, 'I know the situation doesn't look great but I'm confident that we can solve the problems because at first everyone shared the same enthusiasm and commitment to TAF. I think it's just that we have all become too involved in our own separate units and have forgotten about teamwork and lost track of the bigger picture.'

Gisela nods in agreement. 'What you have here are four separate, highly experienced teams who believe their way is right. Unfortunately, this is creating a lot of unnecessary bureaucracy and duplication, considering TAF is a relatively small organization. Stefan listen to me, it's time for you to take back control and implement some sound strategies; but you have to do this without seeming too autocratic or overpowering.'

'Yes, but that's easier said than done,' sighs Stefan. 'These people signed a 10-year contract to operate independently. Now I have to try and take back some control. I'm partly to blame for this, trying to be everyone's friend and giving them autonomy, thinking that would create a good working atmosphere when, in fact, it is now becoming quite competitive and sometimes hostile.'

The problems

Leadership

Stefan Ritter has held the role of general manager for 15 years in several different companies. He has been extremely successful and is responsible for the growth of at least two large leisure companies. Prior to coming to TAF he was GM for a five-star resort in Malaysia and before that was with one of Germany's small private aviation companies serving the regional tourism market. TAF was always going to be a challenge for Stefan, given that he has a transformational leadership style and is not particularly directive. However, his likeable manner has usually ensured that people not only sit up and take notice but are also happy to work alongside him.

Communication

Because of the current structure of the business, ongoing and open communication between the separate business units has slowly ceased. When TAF first opened, Stefan held weekly breakfast meetings, which everyone willingly attended and contributed to. However, as the business has grown and everyone has become more involved in their own area of operation, attendance at the meetings is sporadic and many of the staff don't contribute because they want the meeting over quickly so they can get back to their jobs.

Hours of operation

Although TAF is open from 07.00 to 19.00 seven days a week, not all facilities are operating during that time and often no prior notice is given. This is extremely inconvenient and confusing for the members who may want to use two of the four facilities, such as the swim centre and the gym, which are owned and operated by two different companies. This also presents a problem for the maintenance and cleaning contractors, who are never really sure when it is convenient for them to come in and carry out their work. The childcare centre is also affected by the lack of timetabling because it is not easy to roster on the correct number of staff required by government regulations to oversee the children.

Marketing and advertising

Although TAF has an overall branding campaign and marketing communication strategy that incorporates all facilities within the centre, other promotional material is being mailed directly to members and potential customers from each of the independent operators who, not surprisingly, prefer to see their name behind their product, tending to drop the TAF logo in favour of their own. Also, the content of the promotional materials is not shown to Stefan prior to distribution, therefore the administration department at TAF aren't informed about new products when members and customers ask for details.

Increasing memberships

Transalpine Fitness is responsible for attracting new full-time members to the centre as well as short-term visiting groups from domestic and international markets. To date, although this has been relatively successful, coordination between the sales team and the four independent operators ensuring that product offering and pricing strategy fit with TAF's overall plan is becoming more and more difficult to control.

Finding the solution

Gisela looks at her watch. 'Stefan come on, we are due in the conference room in less than half an hour. Let's make the final changes to the agenda then head down there. It might be a good idea to get there before everyone else does so we can welcome them. It will get us off to a positive start.'

Source: this fictional case study is based on Workout World by Val Morrison (2006), in *Organizational Behaviour: Core Concepts and Applications*, Wiley: Milton, Queensland.

Questions

1. Identify at least three problems that you think Stefan is faced with in his role at TAF, then go on to briefly set out some actions he might take to overcome the problems you have identified.

2. It would appear that a conflict situation at TAF is evolving between the five business units. What can Stefan do to try and take control of this before they become even more isolated from each other?

3. Stefan has a very short time before the meeting begins and he is struggling with the agenda. Prepare a brief outline of the agenda and topics he should discuss at the meeting. Be sure to justify your answer and support this with OB theories and concepts.

Case Study 6
Motorola: Seeking Direction

Up until the mid 1990s, Motorola Inc., world famous for its six Sigma quality control programme, was an early success story in the computer/electronics age and viewed on Wall Street as an American Icon. Motorola had moved from being a decentralized but integrated, narrowly focused electronics firm at $3 billion sales in 1980 to being a decentralized and disintegrated broad portfolio firm at $30 billion in sales in 2001. Motorola had been one of the world's leading providers of wireless communications, semiconductors, electronic systems, components, and services. Its cellular phone, analog equipment, and pager products were identified among the very best in the mid 1990s. However, increased competition, the Asian economic crisis, and its short-sighted failure to quickly and fully embrace the digital revolution severely tarnished its operating results and image. In the April, 2004 issue of *Business Week*, Motorola ranked 308 of the top 500 companies of the S&P 500, with 3 F grades and 3 D grades out of 8 categories. The question becomes: what can Motorola do to return to its former high-performance ways and what can new CEO Ed Zander do to change the recent record of failures, intracompany turf battles and oversights?

The making of Motorola

Motorola Inc. was founded by Paul V. Galvin in 1928. Motorola's long history of technological innovation began in the 1930s with the first car radio. In World War II, the Motorola Handle-Walkie Talkie went to war for the U.S. Army. Under the brand name 'Motorola,' suggesting 'sound in motion' the company name was changed to Motorola, Inc. in 1947. It was the goal of Motorola to provide products that would give people the time and freedom to explore new worlds and handle daily tasks in the most efficient manner.

Motorola has accomplished a number of firsts, including the first rectangular television picture tube, the first practical car radio and pagers. In 1988, Motorola won the first Malcom Baldrige National Quality Award in recognition of quality in American business.

Beginning in 1987, Motorola began the design of IRIDIUM. The system was a satellite-based, wireless communications network. It consisted of 66 interconnected, low-orbiting satellites that delivered voice, data, fax, and paging through a hand-held phone. The development of IRIDIUM was intended to provide customers, including business professionals and travellers, with high-quality service at a reasonable rate.

As Motorola continued to expand its worldwide presence in the global marketplace through products and services, the need for talented personnel to uphold these established standards increased. In recognition of this, Motorola demonstrated a high commitment to seeking and developing a broad base of knowledgeable, highly trained employees, as evident through their innovative programs, provided by the establishment of Motorola University, and through the offering of expensive benefit plans to all Motorola associates.

Organizational culture in Motorola

In the early 1990s, Motorola was recognized as a true high-performance organization with its innovations and socially responsible attitude. Its organizational culture was identified as a source of competitive advantage to the firm and one to be copied. Working in quality teams, members sought to provide the highest level of customer satisfaction, measuring defects in incidents per billion. These teams, however, were not always unified with other teams in the company. Motorola also earmarked more than $100 million a year for training, with everyone in the organization spending at least a week each year in the classroom at Motorola University, courtesy of the company.

Motorola listed its fundamental objectives as total customer satisfaction: 'To serve every customer better than our competitors do with products and services of excellent value and quality and thereby earn continued trust and support'. Motorola wishes to accomplish this objective with respect for the individual, a statement it makes clear in its shared beliefs. Somewhere in the 1990s, this philosophy of satisfying customer needs became diluted by organizational egos.

Motorola's people

To treat each employee with dignity, as an individual; to maintain an open atmosphere where direct communication with employees affords the opportunity to contribute to the maximum of their potential and fosters unity of purpose with Motorola; to provide personal opportunities for training and development to ensure the most capable and most effective work force; to respect senior service; to compensate fairly by salary, benefits, and incentives; to promote on the basis of capability; and to practise the commonly accepted policies of equal opportunity and affirmative action.

Integrity and ethics

To maintain the highest standards of honesty, integrity, and ethics in all aspects of our business – with customers, suppliers, employees, governments, and society at large – and to comply with the laws of each country and community in which we operate.

From a proponent of leadership training to a leader in quality control processes, Motorola has created an internal climate that fostered high standards in a high-performance culture. The firm depended on Total Customer Satisfaction (TCS) teams to ensure the firm's commitment to quality products and service. These teams were made up of almost 30 per cent of Motorola's employees, and a goal of 10 times reduction of defects every two years puts pressure on the teams to constantly devise new ways to develop and deliver their products and services.

However, Organizational culture can sometimes be a two-edged sword. Strong and successful organizational cultures, like Motorola, may contribute to high performance for extended periods of time but may actually result in an inability to adjust when conditions change. It is important to foster a balance between stability and flexibility for change; an objective that is difficult to maintain in a global competition that has no respect for previous accomplishments or industrial icons. For the large firms, like Motorola, success in the short term causes problems with inflexibility toward paradigms of changing situations in the long term.

What happened to Motorola on the way to the 21st century?

In early June 1998, then Motorola CEO Chris Galvin announced that the company would take a $1.95 billion charge and lay off 15,000 employees. Currently, Motorola is down to 88,000 employees from a peak of 147,000. Motorola's semiconductor business, which grew 23 per cent in 1995, slowed to a 1 per cent growth rate in 1998. In recent years Motorola stock dropped dramatically, with a 52 week high on July 27, 2004 of $20.89, to a low of $9.03 and its share of the cellular phone market had plummeted as Motorola couldn't produce colour-screen phones in volume. Samsung came from nowhere to become the number two player by revenue after Nokia in the cell phone industry. Motorola's semiconductor unit had a lock on PDAs as recently as three years ago, but lost the lead to Intel. In 2003, the company eked out annual profits of $893 million on sales of $27 billion. This profit would have been even less without the revenues from Motorola's chip business. Critics have come to a simple conclusion: Motorola does too many things—and not enough of them well. The company has earned the unenviable reputation of developing killer technology that got stuck in the labs.

Maggie Wilderotter, a former top executive with AT&T Wireless Services, provided insight into Motorola's problems. In the early 1990s, 85 per cent of the cell phones sold to subscribers were made by Motorola. Their flip phones, the most advanced at the time, were in hot demand. AT&T decided that the future of cellular was digital, and over the next few years Wilderotter met repeatedly with the managers of Motorola at Motorola's Schaumberg, Illinois headquarters, urging them to develop a digital phone. Motorola kept stalling until the beginning of 1996, not long after AT&T had rolled out its digital network. Motorola unveiled its, StarTAC phone: light beautiful—and 'analog'. AT&T had no choice but to turn to cellular phone manufacturers Nokia and Ericsson for 'digital' handsets. By the end of 1997, fewer than 40 per cent of AT&T's wireless cell phones were made by Motorola.

'It was bizarre,' says Wilderotter. 'We were very forthright with what we wanted. I don't know if they didn't listen or they thought it wasn't going to happen. It is absolutely amazing to me that they lost their way.' In 1998, Nokia replaced Motorola as the leading supplier of mobile handsets, a position Motorola had held since the mobile phone industry began.

Much of Nokia's success was based on its digital technology. Motorola remained the world leader in the U.S. market where digital was slower to take off. When Motorola did provide a digital alternative in its popular Strata model, it retailed for $500, compared to Nokia's 6100 model selling at $200 with twice the battery life.

Inspection of the company's IRIDIUM satellite system uncovered other weaknesses. While the system eliminated 'dead cells' by providing complete global coverage, it came with a very expensive price tag. The phones have the look and weight of cell phones years ago along with a thick, ugly, black antenna.

Unfortunately, in order to function, the system needed a completely unobstructed view of the sky, with tall buildings and even thick foliage blocking transmissions.

Some of Motorola's troubles were external, including a drop in semiconductor sales due to the Asian economic crisis, increased competition in cellular products, and a decline in pager sales. Motorola tried to meet these challenges by attempting to restructure its operations in combination with cost-cutting measures. The situation illuminated the need for a culture that was both strong and responsive to such external factors. In the quickly changing high-technology field, companies were being forced to make rapid and costly choices among competing technologies. In facing the challenges of rapid technology, including the staying power of new products, Motorola appears laden with a history of 75 years' worth of stuffiness, obscure acronyms, and lack of a unified team approach.

Another concern for many investors and analysts was the presence and performance of Chris Galvin as chief executive officer (CEO) since 1997. Galvin abruptly left the company in September, 2003. He has since been replaced by new CEO Ed Zander, a loquacious individual of Sun Microsystems fame. Since arriving on the scene, Zander has been travelling worldwide, shaking hands, and getting an 'earful' of adverse opinions of Motorola's lack of, or delays of, new electronic products by unhappy customers.

Even before Zander's arrival, by 2002 Motorola made a plunge into digital technology, introducing a broad range of innovative products using digital technology. Zander has, however, begun to articulate a vision of Motorola in terms of its remaining four big end markets: the individual, the home, the auto, and the big organizations, which includes governments. His focus will include collaboration across the company, targeting the mega-large business customers, potentially merging more units within the company, shedding employees, and developing new ways to combine wireless communications and the Internet.

Since Zander's arrival, Motorola has made impressive performances. On July 20, 2004 the company reported second-quarter sales up a healthy 41% compared to an anaemic 2003. The star of these gains was the mobile-phone division, which has boosted revenues 67% to $3.9 billion dollars. Two-way radios have received a big boost from increased spending by local and national government agencies on homeland-security concerns.

Motorola did decide to drop its boom-or-bust chip division. This leaves Motorola with essentially five businesses: cell phones, infrastructure equipment, two-way radio systems, the cable TV division, and one of Motorola's few recent success stories: electronic equipment for automobiles. Plans may be in the making for further mergers of units.

Source: The OB Skills Workbook in Schermerhorn, J., Hunt, J. & Osborn, R. (2005), *Organizational Behaviour*, 9th edn. John Wiley & Sons: New York.

Questions

1. Discuss Motorola's relative success at the functions of organizational culture presented in the case.
2. How did Motorola lose its leading position in the electronics technology industry?
3. Discuss the various options managers might use in attempting to change the culture at Motorola.
4. How do you think employees at Motorola will react to the efforts of Ed Zander to bring the company back to a leader?

Case Study 7
Channel 6 TV: Power and Politics in Action

Channel 6 was formed in 1998 in Brighton, England as a bidder for a new UK terrestrial television franchise. It was awarded the franchise in 2001. In 2005 the franchise was due for renewal under the terms of the original agreement. The independent regulator and competition authority for the UK communications industry (Ofcom) had already advertised for bids for the franchise.

As a terrestrially available television station – also available via satellite and other digital packages – Channel 6's position is seen as most attractive. A terrestrial television station is regarded as having key advantages in terms of building audience loyalty in the run-up to the switch-off of analogue signals, prior to the advent of an all-digital platform. There is therefore certain to be a number of strong bids for this franchise from other consortia. It has been rumoured that a consortium including two of the largest global media players may be preparing a bid.

Channel 6 has succeeded in attracting its target audience share after a 'shaky' first two years and advertising revenue is strong. However, there have been financial concerns as programmes have regularly run over budget and, furthermore, the station has attracted regular controversy regarding its programme output which has included a large proportion of downmarket late night 'shock shows' or so-called docusoaps such as:

- *I'm a Celebrity: I'm Locked in the Toilet*
- *Britain's Stupidest Bus Drivers*
- *Holiday Reps 'Go Mental'*
- *Footballers' Private Parts*
- *Pregnant Grandmothers*

One programme that has attracted particular scrutiny is *Westminster Sleaze*, screened live late on Friday evenings in which politicians have been doused in porridge and had their clothing removed on air.

The Chair of Channel 6 has, in anticipation of the upcoming franchise renewal, brought in a new Chief Executive, Kamran Malik, who has a successful track record in high street retailing and, specifically, the home improvement or do-it-yourself (DIY) sector, where he was responsible for leading a series of mergers resulting in the creation of Brilliant Homes which is now the second largest DIY chain in the UK. Kamran has been given the remit of giving the company 'more commercial sharpness' and to provide a new public face in dealing with the channel's various stakeholders, including regulatory bodies.

As a condition of his appointment Kamran Malik brought in an old confidante, Claire Holloway, as Human Resources Director. With a history of overseeing substantial staff restructuring in several previous companies while retaining her personal popularity, Claire Holloway's role is seen as crucial in the runup to the franchise renewal in terms of dealing with potentially sensitive staffing and interpersonal issues.

The remaining senior management group members all have a long and successful history in the media area. They include: George Tyson the Finance Director, Ken Redfern as Marketing Director and Liam O'Kane the Director of Programmes. O'Kane is a tall flamboyant individual with over 20 years' experience of first making and later commissioning distinctive television programmes of various types, which have always secured the requisite audience figures. A former Royal Shakespeare Company actor, he has taken on a more populist approach in recent years and has been quoted as saying that 'you should never underestimate the taste of the Neanderthal British public', although he insists this comment was taken out of context. Liam O'Kane has a very considerable reputation as a scheduler and commissioner of programmes. He is also said to be a highly proficient networker within the media world with both formal and informal links to Ofcom. A Labour Party supporter, he is rumoured to cherish friendships with senior government figures.

The problem

Channel 6's turnover, although large by industry standards, formed only a small part of that of the parent company (Stellar Media) who underpin Channel 6's operations. Stellar Media has accrued profits that have been proportionately large. Little has returned to Channel

6 in terms of investment but, on the other hand, not much has been demanded of it in terms of cost control and efficient management. Kamran Malik's appointment is intended to strengthen these areas. His new brief is to control costs and ensure that Channel 6 has an 'appropriate reputation' with its audience, employees, with 'the City' and not least, the regulatory body, Ofcom. However the company is on line to make substantial profits partly as a result of Liam O'Kane's far-sighted selection of admittedly downmarket, not to say outrageous programmes, which have attracted lucrative advertising revenue.

The independent television industry has in the past had a reputation for high spending. Funds are often treated with little genuine concern. This culture is certainly true of Channel 6's Programmes Department, which under Liam O'Kane's leadership regularly runs as much as 300% over budget. This is despite commissioning programmes such as *Cosmetic Surgery Close-ups*, which are cheap to make and do not require extensive creative input. In fact the culture of this department is such that attempts to control costs are resented as interference with 'core business'. A recent argument over the budget of *Pregnant Grand-mothers* proved to be a particularly robust discussion with O'Kane threatening to take his case directly to the Chairman of Ofcom while describing Malik as a 'jumped-up paint salesman'. Kamran Malik regards this approach to expenditure as cavalier and immoral. In the areas that he has been able to control he has succeeded in streamlining operations. Claire Holloway succeeded in introducing a new flexible rewards system for studio staff while averting a threatened strike, which would have shut down the station. Together they have introduced a new Joint Consultative Committee, which, initially, has resulted in improved morale amongst staff.

Perspectives on the situation

The Head of Engineering, Terry Holbrook, recruited two years ago from the BBC, can see the complexity of the issues facing Kamran Malik:

> He is faced with getting things right very fast in order to secure the future. And he doesn't know the industry well. Sometimes he is a stranger to what really goes on here. Liam O'Kane is the best Programmes Director I have ever met. If he feels he must do something he will pursue it and pursue it and pursue it. He definitely does not lack drive or courage. Very much his own man though and if you put him alongside Kamran who has a hell of a track record elsewhere then there is going to be one huge confrontation looming. The tragedy is we need both of them to stay.

Liam O'Kane is also acutely aware of a changing climate at Channel 6. 'I've been told to do a job for this television station and if they don't like the way I operate they can get rid of me. I could walk into a job with the BBC tomorrow and even buy up the Shopping Channel if I want. Don't play daft games with me! What you do running DIY stores has nothing at all to do with television. I will not crawl in and out of Kamran's office telling him every little thing that happens in my department.'

Matters are brought to a head during a senior management meeting when recent newspaper reviews of *Westminster Sleaze* were discussed. Kamran Malik read out part of a review from the *Daily Telegraph* describing the programme as 'mindless putrefying cack: moronic filth of the worst kind.' When he stopped laughing Liam O'Kane retorted by asking why his computer printer had not been fixed for five days; 'the really important issue for me, not your pathetic attempts to go all moralistic on a subject you know **** all about. None of the audience watching it were sober anyway. Why not talk about the ratings? You didn't' mention that the *Daily Sport* thought that the programme was 'a laugh a minute riot' did you? Well next month I plan to do a nude *Songs of Praise* special – are you going to stop me Kamran?'

Source: this case study has been adapted by Dr Ray French from, 'TVN' by Iain Mangham, Chapter 7 in Clegg, C., Kemp, N. & Legge, K (1985), *Case Studies in Organizational Behaviour,* Harper & Row: London. All names and dates contained in this case study are fictional. Channel 6 TV is a fictional organization. Quotations attributed to real-life organizations have been invented.

Questions

Please refer to Chapter 10 on power and politics before attempting the questions.

1. Identify possible sources of power that the following characters may have in Channel 6 TV: Kamran Malik, Liam O'Kane, Claire Holloway.
2. What are the possible options open to Kamran at this stage? What are the likely consequences of each? What would you do now if you were in his position? Explain your answer.
3. To what extent are the issues facing Kamran Malik affected by political behaviour in this particular workplace?

Case Study 8
The Ups and Downs of National Mutual/ AXA: A Case for Change

Introduction

National Mutual was established in Australia and New Zealand more than 100 years ago. Over the years it became a very successful insurance company and by the mid-1980s was pursuing growth so aggressively that it overtook AMP to lead the market in winning new business.

To fund the growth strategy, National Mutual drew heavily on the financial reserves that it had accumulated over a century of successful operations. Specifically:

- National Mutual provided business development loans to its network of agents, many of whom spent the money on personal assets rather than investing it in their business. Therefore, of course, the productivity gains expected to come from this huge expenditure were never realized.
- National Mutual invested significant sums of money overseas in a bid to become a global player in funds management, life insurance and superannuation. However, the company did not have sufficient capital and operational capacity to back up its global ambitions.
- National Mutual offered customers higher returns than competitors. In doing so, though, it had to credit more money to its policyholder returns than it was receiving on its investments.

By the late 1980s, the company had severely undermined its solvency.

Facing up to the realities

The extent of the problem became apparent when it was found that National Mutual would not be able to meet the capital adequacy and solvency standards proposed in the draft 1992 Life Insurance Act. In addition, a proposed merger with ANZ Bank was disallowed, partly due to government concerns about the underlying capital positions of both organizations.

National Mutual had a culture of pride, based on its 120 years of success and its prominent position in the Australian market, but its financial problems could not be denied. The company took several major steps in the 1990s to try to repair its balance sheet. In 1992 it undertook a capital restructuring. The following year it sold off most of its international assets. In 1995, it demutualized (that is, it changed from being owned by its members to being owned by shareholders). French insurance company AXA acquired a 51% shareholding. National Mutual listed on the stock exchange in 1996. In 1999, National Mutual was rebranded AXA.

Despite these significant changes within the company, National Mutual found that the newly deregulated Australasian market was changing even more. New players entered National Mutual's traditional markets, putting substantial pressure on pricing. There was significant growth and innovation in the retail investment and superannuation segments of the industry as competitors responded quickly to changing economic and demographic conditions.

National Mutual's business model was fundamentally unchanged. Its products were not competitive, its costs were 20% above industry standards, and its distribution system was out of touch with the new model of financial advisers offering products tailored to individual needs. As a result, it had lost considerable market share in the profitable and growing retail investment and superannuation markets, but still had a large, unprofitable position in risk insurance. Over the decade of the 1990s it had slipped to become a second-tier player.

Asian markets come to the rescue

While National Mutual had been forced to sell its US and European assets, the Asian interests it had retained had performed surprisingly well. Asia, in fact, would ultimately save National Mutual from financial failure. The international team in Melbourne adapted its low-cost Hong Kong approach to other Asian markets and by 1999, 75% of profit was coming from Asia, compared to 25% from Australia and New Zealand.

Leadership, structure and change

AXA decided the Asia–Pacific operation (now operating as AXA Asia–Pacific) required a major overhaul to improve the performance of the Australian and New Zealand businesses. It appointed a new chief executive officer in 2000, with the specific task of transforming the Australian and New Zealand operations.

Within a few months of arrival the new CEO established an extensive, organization-wide change programme addressing every critical aspect of the business in Australia and New Zealand: distribution, marketing, product, e-commerce, customer service, human relations and others. The former head of the Asian businesses was appointed to oversee the three-year change programme. This ensured the change programme was not complicated by any existing vested interests in the Australian or New Zealand businesses. Most of the senior management team and the team at the next level down were replaced by new teams of internal and external people. This was necessary both to improve the company's management skills and to overcome resistance to change.

Central to the transformation programme – known within AXA as 'K5' (five key strategic objectives) – were five clear targets to be achieved within three years:

- double the value of new business
- enter the top five for net retail funds inflow
- halve the management expense ratio
- obtain a place in the top 25% of ASSIRT/AC Nielsen's service rankings (the ranking is based on aspects of service such as investment capability, investment team quality, investment performance, consistency and investment process quality)
- rank in the top 25% of AXA's global survey of employee satisfaction.

AXA realized that the company culture had to change and that how the business changes were put in place would be as important as the changes themselves. To bring K5 to fruition, AXA engaged in a series of changes at the strategic and structural levels.

The company put a lot of effort into communication. Its communication programme included a 'reality check' designed to create dissatisfaction with the present. This was combined with changes to the management group designed to communicate that the current poor business outcomes would not be accepted in the future. The communications programme was recognized by the Public Relations Community of Australia's awards for employee communications.

A very strong governance and control process was implemented at the executive management level. It was overseen by a steering committee comprising the CEO, programme director, chief financial officer, another executive and a consultant. A number of dedicated centralized project teams led the various facets of the change programme such as project management, and training and development.

The company also looked to better match its capabilities to its needs. The problem of inadequate performance in investment management was solved by entering a joint venture for asset management with Alliance Capital, a company within the AXA Group with a first-class reputation in that field. In areas in which the company did not have the requisite skills internally – such as property management – it outsourced. AXA sold noncore assets such as trustee companies, payroll companies, and mortgage and commercial lending businesses. Core operating processes and systems that had previously been unreliable were stabilized, resulting in better customer service. Key products and key markets were analysed in depth. The analysis then informed significant upgrades and new product launches in retail investment and superannuation, designed to make the company more competitive in the market. The company restructured its relationship with distributors. It terminated unsatisfactory agency arrangements and created new agency terms designed to establish a stronger position, with advisers operating more modern and robust financial planning practices.

By the end of 2000, a new structure backed up by revitalized governance, leadership and management were firmly in place. The company had made a genuine attempt to address many of the problems it had been facing.

Improved outcomes

By mid-2002, results showed the company was clearly headed in the right direction to meet its K5 goals.

In relation to its first goal – to double the value of new business – AXA had achieved growth in new business sales in the sectors most important to its future, including investment, superannuation and master trusts.

In relation to its second goal – to enter the top five for net retail funds inflow – plans to refocus on more profitable retail investment products had caused some increase in outflows. Notwithstanding that, by mid-2000, for the first time in almost five years, the company experienced a net funds inflow. This had grown to almost A\$2 billion for the 12 months to June 2002.

In relation to its third goal – to halve the management expense ratio – the company was doing extremely well. Recurring management expenses had been cut by more than one-third since the start of the programme, against a backdrop of rising sales volumes. Part of the saving has been used to fund reinvestments in the business, with 20% of all costs being business investments.

In relation to its fourth goal – to obtain a place in the top 25% of ASSIRT/AC Nielsen's service rankings – AXA improved relative to its competitors across all the dimensions of service, but was still below the median for the market.

In relation to its fifth goal – to reach the top 25% in AXA's world survey of employee satisfaction – by 2001 employee satisfaction had significantly improved, with the company just outside the top 25%. By the next year, employee satisfaction was the highest of all AXA business worldwide.

Notwithstanding the improvement in all areas, there was a gap between where the company was and where it wanted to be by this stage of the programme, particularly in relation to the second goal of net funds inflow.

Sustaining improvement

By the end of the three-year K5 transformation programme, AXA had made enormous progress. It had achieved four of the K5 goals. The goal it did not achieve was to reduce the management expense ratio by 50%. It had, however, made significant progress in that area too, achieving a 40% reduction.

In April 2004, AXA launched a new set of objectives for Australia and New Zealand in a bid to increase the value of the Australian and New Zealand operations by 65%. The three-year AXA 6 programme included the goals:

1. Double the value of new business.
2. Consistently be in the top five in the market in terms of net retail funds flow.
3. Double the value of funds under advice.
4. Reduce the cost to income ratio by one-third.
5. Consistently be in the top five in the market in terms of service to advisers.
6. Remain in the top 25% of AXA's global survey of employee satisfaction.

By 2005, AXA's Australian operations had A\$45.6 billion of funds under management and total gross inflows of almost A\$10.8 billion. AXA's New Zealand operations had NZ\$6.9 billion of funds under management and total gross inflows of over NZ\$2.1 billion, and were in the top three in the wealth management and financial protection markets.

AXA's progress towards achieving its AXA 6 goals can be found in its annual reports, available from AXA's Web site at **www.axa-asiapacific.com.au**

Source: adapted from Andrew Penn, 'Transformational change: a case study', Mt Eliza Business School, www.mteliza.com.au (accessed 27 October 2005); additional information from: AXA Asia Pacific Holdings Limited, 'Chairman's address', Annual General Meeting, 15 February 2001, www.axa-asiapacific.com.au (accessed 27 October 2005); AXA Asia Pacific Holdings Limited, 'Analyst compendium for the 6 months ending 30 June 2002', **www.axa-asiapacific.com.au** (accessed 27 October 2005), AXA Asia Pacific Holdings Limited, annual reports, **www.axa-asiapacific.com.au** (accessed 28 October 2005).

Questions

1. Explain some of the reasons for the decline of National Mutual from the 1980s to the end of the 1990s.
2. Analyse and describe the change strategy adopted by AXA to redress its problems.
3. What were some of the key ingredients of the resurgence of AXA's fortunes?
4. How would you describe the leadership style of the chief executive?

GLOSSARY

Ability is the capacity to perform the various tasks needed for a given job.

Absenteeism is the failure of people to attend work on a given day.

Achievement-oriented leadership is leadership behaviour that emphasizes setting challenging goals, stressing excellence in performance and showing confidence in the group members' abilities to achieve high standards of performance.

Active management by exception involves watching for deviations from rules and standards and taking corrective action.

An adhocracy is an organizational structure that emphasizes shared, decentralized decision making, extreme horizontal specialization, few levels of management, the virtual absence of formal controls and few rules, policies and procedures.

The adjourning stage is the fifth stage of group development, in which members of the group disband when the job is done.

The affective components of an attitude are the specific feelings regarding the personal impact of the antecedents.

Annualization is a scheme whereby employees' working time and pay is scheduled and calculated over a period of a year.

Anthropology is the comparative study of different societies or tribes.

Aptitude is the capability to learn something.

Arbitration occurs when a neutral third party acts as judge and issues a binding decision affecting parties at a negotiation impasse.

Artificial intelligence, or AI, studies how computers can be made to think like the human brain.

An attitude is a predisposition to respond in a positive or negative way to someone or something in your environment.

Attribution errors occur within the process of perception and relate to the reasons we attribute to events and behaviour. A common attribution error is to overemphasize the contribution of our own efforts and abilities when explaining our successes and to contrastingly, attribute negative occurrences to outside influences such as bad luck.

Authoritarianism is a personality trait that focuses on the rigidity of a person's beliefs.

Automation is a job design that allows machines to do work previously accomplished by human effort.

Autonomous work teams are teams given significant authority and responsibility over their work in contexts of highly related or interdependent jobs.

The bargaining zone is the zone between one party's minimum reservation point and the other party's maximum reservation point in a negotiating situation.

BATNA is the 'best alternative to a negotiated agreement', or each party's position on what they must do if an agreement cannot be reached.

The behavioural components of an attitude are the intentions to behave in a certain way based on a person's specific feelings or attitudes.

Behavioural decision theory refers to the idea that people act only in terms of what they perceive about a given situation.

Behaviourists study observable behaviours and consequences of behaviour and reject subjective human psychological states as topics for study.

Beliefs represent ideas about someone or something and the conclusions people draw about them.

Bet-your-company culture refers to a type of organizational culture characterized by a long-term outlook in which significant levels of investment are made, the results of which may take many years to feed through.

Brain drain refers to a characteristic of today's skilled workforce whose members are now more mobile and prepared to take their knowledge with them to their new workplaces as they pursue opportunities across the globe.

Brainstorming is a technique by which team members generate as many ideas as possible without being inhibited by other team members.

Buffering is a conflict management approach that sets up inventories to reduce conflicts when the inputs of one group are the outputs of another group.

Bullying refers to abusive and intimidating behaviour that leads to the recipient feeling upset, threatened and vulnerable. It is often the result of an abuse of power and can include such behaviours as ignoring employees or excluding people from a meeting.

A bureaucracy is an idealized form of organization whose characteristics include a clear division of labour, hierarchical control, promotion by merit with career opportunities for employees and administration by rule.

Burnout is a negative felt emotion relating to one's work. It is characterized by emotional exhaustion, cynicism and doubts regarding self-efficacy.

Casual work is work where the number and schedule of work hours vary and there is little or no security of ongoing employment.

Centralization is the degree to which the authority to make decisions is restricted to higher levels of management.

Certain environments are decision environments in which information is sufficient to predict the results of each alternative in advance of implementation.

Change agents are individuals or groups that take responsibility for changing the existing pattern of behaviour of a person or social system.

Changing involves a managerial responsibility to modify a situation – that is, to change people, tasks, structure and/or technology.

Channels are the media through which the message may be delivered.

Charisma is a dimension of leadership, based on personal qualities, which provides vision and a sense of mission and instils pride, respect and trust.

Charismatic leaders are those leaders who by force of their personal characteristics are capable of having a profound and extraordinary effect on followers.

Classical conditioning is a form of learning through association that involves the manipulation of stimuli to influence behaviour.

Classical decision theory views the manager as acting in a world of complete certainty.

Coercive power is the extent to which a manager can deny desired rewards or administer punishment to control other people.

Cognitive abilities refer to our mental capacity to process information and solve problems.

The **cognitive components** of an attitude are the beliefs, opinions, knowledge or information that a person possesses.

Cognitive dissonance is a state of perceived inconsistency between a person's expressed attitudes and actual behaviour.

Cognitive learning is a form of learning achieved by thinking about the perceived relationship between events and individual goals and expectations.

Cohesiveness is the degree to which members are attracted to and motivated to remain part of the group.

Common assumptions are the collection of truths that an organization's members share as a result of their joint experiences and that guide values and behaviours.

Commonsense thinking is apparently obvious or assumed analysis of OB topics, without reference to rigorous study or evidence, which can result in false conclusions.

Competency is the umbrella term for any task-related knowledge or skill possessed by an individual. Competencies could be technical or interpersonal.

A **compressed workweek** is any scheduling of work that allows a full-time job to be completed in fewer than the standard five days.

Conflict occurs when two or more people disagree over issues of organizational substance and/or experience some emotional antagonism with one another.

Conflict resolution occurs when the reasons for a conflict are eliminated.

Conglomerates are organizations that own several unrelated businesses.

Constructive conflict is conflict that results in positive benefits to the group.

Consultative decisions are decisions made by an individual after seeking input from, or consulting with, members of a group.

Content theories of motivation offer ways to profile or analyse individuals to identify the needs that are assumed to motivate their behaviours.

A contingency approach in OB identifies how situations can be understood and managed in ways that appropriately respond to their unique characteristics or circumstances.

Contingent rewards are rewards that are given in exchange for mutually agreed goal accomplishments.

Continuous reinforcement is a reinforcement schedule that administers a reward each time a desired behaviour occurs.

Contrast effects occur within the process of perception when an object or person is perceived due to it standing out from its surroundings or group.

Contributions are individual work efforts of value to the organization.

Control is the set of mechanisms used to keep actions and outputs within predetermined limits.

Controlled processing refers, within the topic of perception, to conscious decisions made to pay attention to certain stimuli while ignoring others.

Controlling is the process of monitoring performance, comparing results with objectives and taking corrective action as necessary.

Coordination is the set of mechanisms used in an organization to link the actions of its subunits into a consistent pattern.

A corporate culture is an attempt by managers to deliberately create and mould organizational culture to achieve specified results.

Corporate social responsibility refers to the notion that corporations have a responsibility to the society that sustains them; and the obligation of organizations to behave in ethical and moral ways.

Countercultures are the patterns of values and philosophies that outwardly reject those of the larger organization or social system.

Crafted decisions are decisions created to deal specifically with a situation at hand.

Creativity is the development of unique and novel responses to problems and opportunities.

A cultural symbol is any object, act or event that serves to transmit cultural meaning.

Culture shock describes a series of stages experienced by people when they encounter a new cultural setting. It is normally depicted as a U-curve with initial elation followed by negative feelings, succeeded in turn by recovery and adjustment.

Decentralization is the degree to which the authority to make decisions is given to workers at lower levels in an organization's hierarchy.

Decision making is the process of identifying a problem or opportunity and choosing among alternative courses of action.

Decoding is the interpretation of the symbols sent from the sender to the receiver.

Decoupling involves separating or reducing the contact between two conflicting groups.

Demographic characteristics are background variables (for example, age and gender) that help shape what a person becomes over time.

Departmentalization by customer is the grouping of individuals and resources by client.

Departmentalization by geography is the grouping of individuals and resources by geographical territory.

Deskilling refers to a diminution of the attributes and proficiency required to perform work tasks. In Braverman's view deskilling is a deliberate strategy by owners and managers of organizations in order to reassert control over work.

Destructive conflict is conflict that works to the group's or organization's disadvantage.

The differentiation perspective views an organization's culture as a compilation of diverse and inconsistent beliefs that are shared at group level.

Directive leadership is leadership behaviour that spells out the what and how of employees' tasks.

Disruptive behaviour is any behaviour that harms the group process.

Discourse involves ways of presenting and understanding any facet of the world via ideas, assumptions, vocabulary and actions. In this way reality is *framed*, thereby informing people's understanding and behaviour.

Distributed leadership is the sharing of responsibility for fulfilling group task and maintenance needs.

Distributive justice refers to perceived fairness of how rewards are allocated.

Distributive negotiation is negotiation in which the focus is on 'positions' staked out or declared by the parties involved, who are each trying to claim certain portions of the available 'pie'.

The diversity–consensus dilemma refers to a tendency for diversity in group membership to make it harder for people to work together even though diversity itself expands a group's problem-solving capacity.

Division of labour is the process of breaking the work to be done into specialized tasks that individuals or groups can perform.

Divisional departmentalization is the grouping of individuals and resources by product, service and/or client.

Divisionalized design is an organizational structure that establishes a separate structure for each business or division.

Dogmatism is a personality trait that regards legitimate authority as absolute.

A dominant coalition denotes the people who are in a strong position of power and influence within organizations at any one time. Dominant coalitions are shifting and can be replaced by others.

Effective communication is communication in which the intended meaning of the source and the perceived meaning of the receiver are the same.

Effective groups are groups that achieve high levels of both task performance and human resource performance.

An effective manager is a manager whose work unit achieves high levels of task accomplishment and maintains itself as a capable workforce over time.

Effective negotiation occurs when issues of substance are resolved without any harm to the working relationships among the parties involved.

Efficient communication is communication at minimum cost in terms of resources expended.

Emergent behaviours are those things that group members do in addition to, or in place of, what is formally asked of them by the organization.

Emotion management is exercising emotional self-control and self-regulation influenced by the context in which individuals find themselves.

Emotional conflict is conflict that involves interpersonal difficulties that arise over feelings of anger, mistrust, dislike, fear, resentment and the like.

Emotional intelligence is a form of social intelligence that allows us to monitor and shape our emotions and those of others.

Employee involvement teams are teams of workers who meet regularly outside their normal work units for the purpose of collectively addressing important workplace issues.

Empowerment is the process by which managers delegate power to employees who therefore have an enhanced view of their work and role within the organization.

Encoding is part of the process of communication and involves translating an idea or thought into meaningful symbols.

Environmental complexity is the magnitude of the problems and opportunities in the organization's environment, as evidenced by the degree of richness, interdependence and uncertainty.

Equity theory is based on the phenomenon of social comparison and posits that because people gauge the fairness of their work outcomes compared with others, any perceived inequity will result in an unpleasant feeling that the individual will be driven to remove through a variety of possible actions.

ERG theory categorizes needs into existence, relatedness and growth needs.

Ergonomics involves the application of scientific principles to the interaction between humans and their work environment including task and work areas, including physical layout, work systems and scheduling.

Escalating commitment is the tendency to continue with a previously chosen course of action even when feedback suggests that it is failing.

Ethical behaviour is behaviour that is morally accepted as 'good' and 'right' as opposed to 'bad' and 'wrong' in a particular social context.

The ethical climate is the shared set of understandings in an organization about what is correct behaviour and how ethical issues will be handled.

An ethical dilemma occurs when a person must make a decision that requires a choice among competing sets of principles.

Existence needs arise from desire for physiological and material wellbeing.

Expectancy is the probability that the individual assigns to work effort being followed by a given level of achieved task performance.

Expectancy theory argues that work motivation is determined by individual beliefs about effort–performance relationships and the desirability of various work outcomes from different performance levels.

Expert power is the ability to control another's behaviour through the possession of knowledge, experience or judgement that the other person does not have but needs.

External adaptation is the process of reaching goals and dealing with outsiders.

Externals are persons with an external locus of control who believe that what happens to them is beyond their control.

Extinction is the withdrawal of the reinforcing consequences for a given behaviour.

Extrinsic rewards are positively valued work outcomes that the individual receives from some other person in the work setting.

Feedback is the process of telling someone else how you feel about something the person did or said, or about the situation in general.

Felt negative inequity exists when individuals feel they have received relatively less than others have in proportion to work inputs.

Felt positive inequity exists when individuals feel they have received relatively more than others have.

The five key dimensions of personality are extroversion–introversion; conscientiousness; agreeableness; emotional stability and openness to experience.

Flexible working hours (flexitime) is any work schedule that gives employees daily choice in the timing of work and nonwork activities.

Flexiyear or **annual hours** is a system whereby total agreed annual hours are allocated by workers as they see fit.

Focus groups are a form of qualitative research method in which groups of people are asked about their attitudes towards particular items or issues.

Force-coercion strategy tries to 'command' change through the formal authority of legitimacy, rewards and punishments.

Formal communication channels are communication channels that follow the chain of command established by the organization's hierarchy.

Formal groups are 'official' groups that are designated by formal authority to serve a specific purpose.

Formal leadership is the process of exercising influence from a position of formal authority in an organization.

The **formal structure** is the intended configuration of positions, job duties and lines of authority among the component parts of an organization.

Formalization is the written documentation of work rules, policies and procedures.

The **forming stage** is the first stage of group development in which the primary concern is the initial entry of members to the group.

The **founding story** is the tale of the lessons learned and efforts of the founder of the organization.

The **fragmentation perspective** views organizational culture as lacking any form of pattern as a result of differing meanings between individuals and within individuals over time.

Friendship groups consist of people with natural affinities for one another who may do things together inside or outside the workplace.

Functional departmentalization is the grouping of individuals and resources by skill, knowledge and action.

The **glass ceiling** refers to an invisible barrier that stops women from attaining senior positions within organizations. It can involve unstated or unofficial views of women and their roles at work.

Global management skills and competencies include understanding of international business strategy, cross-cultural management, international marketing, international finance, managing e-business and the Internet, risk management, managing sustainable organizations, re-engineering organizations, managing the virtual workplace, knowledge management, international economics and trade, and Asian languages.

Globalization brings a greater sense of interconnectedness between people from diverse cultures. It has also been defined as the process of becoming more international in scope, influence or application.

Goal setting is the process of developing, negotiating and formalizing an employee's targets and objectives.

A **group** is a collection of two or more people who interact with each other regularly to achieve common goals.

Group decisions are decisions made by all members of the group, ideally with consensus being achieved.

Group dynamics are the forces operating in groups that affect group performance and member satisfaction.

Group inputs are the initial 'givens' in a group situation that set the stage for all group processes.

Group norms are the standards of behaviour that group members are expected to display.

Group outputs are the results of the transformation of group inputs through group processes.

Group roles are the sets of behaviours expected by the managers of the organization and the group members for the holder of a particular position.

Groupthink is the tendency of members in highly cohesive groups to lose their critical, evaluative capabilities.

Growth needs relate to the desire for continued personal growth and development.

The **halo effect** within interpersonal perception occurs when our perception of another person is framed on the basis of a single striking favourable characteristic (the rusty halo phenomenon occurs when the characteristic is perceived negatively).

Heterogeneous groups are groups whose members have diverse backgrounds, interests, values, attitudes and so on.

Heuristics are simplifying strategies or 'rules of thumb' that people use when making decisions.

Hierarchical referral uses the chain of command for conflict resolution; problems are referred up the hierarchy for more senior managers to reconcile.

High-performance teams excel in teamwork while achieving performance advantages.

Higher-order needs are esteem and self-actualization needs in Maslow's hierarchy.

Homogeneous groups are groups whose members have similar backgrounds, interests, values, attitudes and so on.

Horizontal loading involves increasing the breadth of a job by adding to the variety of tasks that the worker performs.

Horizontal specialization is the division of labour through the formation of work units or groups within an organization.

Hot desking occurs where an employer provides a work space or surface that is available to any worker rather than any one worker.

Human resource performance. This must be sustained if it is to have meaning; high performance should be sustainable. High levels of performance are affected by a manager's attention to a range of matters under the people management heading.

Human resources are the individuals and groups whose contributions enable the organization to serve a particular purpose.

Hygienes (hygiene factors) are dissatisfiers that are associated with aspects of a person's work setting.

The **idiographic** approach to understanding personality focuses on individual uniqueness. It regards personality as potentially shifting according to an individual's self-image and experiences.

Incremental change is change that occurs more frequently and less traumatically as part of an organization's natural evolution.

Individual decisions are decisions made by one individual on behalf of the group.

Individualized consideration is a leadership dimension by which the leader provides personal attention, treats each employee individually and coaches and advises employees.

Inducements are what the organization gives to the individual on behalf of the group.

Influence is a behavioural response to the exercise of power.

Informal communication channels are communication channels that do not adhere to the organization's hierarchy.

Informal groups are groups that emerge unofficially and are not formally designated as parts of the organization.

Informal leadership is the process of exercising influence through special skills or resources that meet the needs of other people.

Information power is the extent to which individuals have control over information needed by others.

An **information source** is a person or group of persons with a reason to communicate with some other person(s), the receiver(s).

The **initial integration** stage is the third stage of group development, at which the group begins to come together as a coordinated unit; it is sometimes called the norming stage.

Innovation is the process of creating new ideas and putting them into practice.

Inspiration is the communication of high expectations, the use of symbols to focus efforts and the expression of important purposes in simple ways.

Instinct is made up of inherited patterns of unreasoned and unchangeable responses to particular actions and behaviours.

Instrumentality is the probability that the individual assigns to a level of achieved task performance leading to various work outcomes.

The **integration perspective** views organizational culture as a system of shared meanings, unity and harmony.

Integrative negotiation is negotiation in which the focus is on the merits of the issues and the parties involved try to enlarge the available 'pie' rather than stake claims to certain portions of it.

Intellectual stimulation promotes intelligence, rationality and careful problem solving.

Interest groups consist of people who share common interests, whether those interests are work or nonwork related.

Intergroup conflict is conflict that occurs between groups in an organization.

Intergroup dynamics are the dynamics that take place between groups, as opposed to within groups.

Intermittent reinforcement is a reinforcement schedule that rewards behaviour only periodically.

Internal integration is the creation of a collective identity and the means of matching methods of working and living together.

Internals are persons with an internal locus of control who believe they control their own fate or destiny.

Interorganizational conflict is conflict that occurs between organizations.

Interpersonal conflict is conflict that occurs between two or more individuals.

The **interpretivist** tradition within OB believes that research into human behaviour should incorporate the subject's understanding of their own and other people's behaviour and the meanings attached to actions. Research within this tradition typically uses qualitative methods specific to social sciences.

Intrapersonal conflict is conflict that occurs within the individual as a result of actual or perceived pressures from incompatible goals or expectations.

Intrinsic motivation is a desire to work hard solely for the pleasant experience of task accomplishment.

Intrinsic rewards are positively valued work outcomes that the individual receives directly as a result of task performance.

Intuition is the ability to know or recognize quickly and readily the possibilities of a given situation.

The **job characteristics model** identifies five core characteristics (skill variety, task identity, task significance, autonomy and job feedback) as having special importance to job designs.

Job content refers to what people do in their work.

Job context refers to a person's work setting.

Job design is the planning and specification of job tasks and the work setting in which they are to be accomplished.

A **job diagnostic survey** is a questionnaire used to examine each of the dimensions of the job characteristics model.

Job enlargement involves increasing task variety by combining into one job tasks of similar skill levels that were previously assigned to separate workers.

Job enrichment is the practice of building motivating factors into job content.

Job involvement is the degree to which a person is willing to work hard and apply effort beyond normal job expectations.

Job rotation involves increasing task variety by periodically shifting workers among jobs involving different tasks at similar levels of skill.

Job satisfaction is the degree to which individuals feel positively or negatively about their jobs.

Job sharing is the assignment of one full-time job to two or more persons, who divide the work according to agreements made between themselves and the employer.

Job simplification involves standardizing work procedures and employing people in clearly defined and specialized tasks.

Jobs are one or more tasks that an individual performs in direct support of an organization's production purpose.

Judgement is the use of the intellect in making decisions.

Key performance indicators are standards against which individual and organizational performance can be measured.

A knowledge-based economy is an economy in which the production, distribution and use of knowledge is the main driver of growth, wealth creation and employment across all industries – not only those classified as high-tech or knowledge intensive.

Knowledge management focuses on processes designed to improve an organization's ability to capture, share and diffuse knowledge in a manner that will improve business performance.

Laissez faire leadership involves abdicating responsibilities and avoiding decisions.

The law of contingent reinforcement is the view that for a reward to have maximum reinforcing value it must be delivered only if the desired behaviour is exhibited.

The law of effect refers to Thorndike's observation that behaviour that results in a pleasant outcome is likely to be repeated; behaviour that results in an unpleasant outcome is not likely to be repeated.

The law of immediate reinforcement states that the more immediate the delivery of a reward after the occurrence of a desirable behaviour, the greater the reinforcing effect on behaviour.

Leaders provide inspiration, create opportunities, coach and motivate people to gain their support on fundamental long-term choices.

Leadership is a special case of interpersonal influence that gets an individual or group to do what the leader wants done.

Leading is the process of directing and coordinating the work efforts of other people to help them to accomplish important tasks.

Learning is a relatively permanent change in behaviour that occurs as a result of experience.

Least preferred co-worker (LPC) scale is a measure of a person's leadership style based on a description of the person with whom respondents have been able to work least well.

Legitimate power is the extent to which a manager can use the internalized belief of an employee that the 'boss' has a 'right of command' to control other people.

Liaison groups are groups that coordinate the activities of certain units to prevent destructive conflicts between them.

Line personnel are work groups that are involved with the core business of an organization.

Linking pins are people who are assigned to manage conflict between groups that are prone to conflict.

Locus of control is the internal–external orientation – that is, the extent to which people feel able to affect their lives.

Lower-order needs are physiological, safety and social needs in Maslow's hierarchy.

Machiavellians are people who view and manipulate others purely for personal gain.

Maintenance activities are activities that support the emotional life of the group as an ongoing social system.

A management philosophy links key goal-related issues with key collaboration issues to come up with general ways by which the organization will manage its affairs.

The management process involves planning, organizing, leading and controlling the use of organizational resources.

A manager is responsible for work that is accomplished through the performance contributions of others. A manager is concerned with making things happen and keeping work on schedule, engaging in routine interactions to fulfil planned actions.

Manifest conflict occurs when conflict is openly expressed in behaviour.

Material resources are the technology, information, physical equipment and facilities, raw material and money that are necessary for an organization to produce some product or service.

A matrix structure is a combination of functional and divisional patterns in which an individual is assigned to more than one type of unit.

Mechanistic design emphasizes vertical specialization, hierarchical levels, tight control and coordination through rules, policies and other impersonal methods.

Merit pay is a compensation system that bases an individual's salary or wage increase on a measure of the person's performance accomplishments during a specified time period.

A motivating potential score is a summary of a job's overall potential for motivating those in the workplace.

Motivation to work refers to the forces within an individual that account for the level, direction and persistence of effort expended at work.

The motivator–hygiene theory distinguishes between sources of work dissatisfaction (hygiene factors) and satisfaction (motivators); it is also known as the two-factor theory.

Motivators (motivator factors) are satisfiers that are associated with what people do in their work.

Multiskilling helps employees acquire an array of skills needed to perform the multiple tasks in an organizational production or customer service process.

The nature/nurture controversy is the argument over whether personality is determined by heredity, or genetic endowment, or by one's environment.

The need for achievement (nAch) is the desire to do something better, solve problems or master complex tasks.

The need for affiliation (nAff) is the desire to establish and maintain friendly and warm relations with others.

The need for power (nPower) is the desire to control others, influence their behaviour and be responsible for others.

Negative reinforcement is the withdrawal of negative consequences, which tends to increase the likelihood of the behaviour being repeated in similar settings; it is also known as avoidance.

Negotiation is the process of making joint decisions when the parties involved have different preferences.

A network organization is a delayered organization aligned around the complementary competencies of players in a value chain.

Noise is anything that interferes with the effectiveness of the communication attempt.

Nomothetic approaches to understanding personality locate individuals within types on the basis of their traits. There is also a belief that personality is stable and unchanging, possibly as a result of inherited characteristics.

Nonroutine problems are unique and new problems that call for creative problem solving.

The norming stage in group development refers to the point at which the group forms a coordinated unit. At this stage the group will strive for harmony and balance.

Norms are rules or standards about the behaviour that group members are expected to display.

Observable culture is behavioural patterns that a group displays and teaches to new members.

Open systems transform human and physical resources received from their environment into goods and services that are then returned to the environment.

Operant conditioning is the process of controlling behaviour by manipulating its consequences.

Organic design is an organizational structure that emphasizes horizontal specialization, an extensive use of personal coordination and loose rules, policies and procedures.

Organization charts are diagrams that depict the formal structures of organizations.

Organizational behaviour is the study of individuals and groups in organizations.

Organizational behaviour modification is the systematic reinforcement of desirable work behaviour and the nonreinforcement or punishment of unwanted work behaviour.

Organizational commitment is the degree to which a person strongly identifies with and feels a part of the organization.

Organizational communication is the process by which entities exchange information and establish a common understanding.

Organizational culture is a system of shared beliefs and values that guides behaviour.

Organizational design is the process of choosing and implementing a structural configuration for an organization.

Organizational governance is the pattern of authority, influence and acceptable managerial behaviour established at the top of the organization.

Organizational learning is acquiring or developing new knowledge that modifies or changes behaviour and improves organizational performance.

Organizational politics is the management of influence to obtain ends not sanctioned by the organization, or to obtain sanctioned ends through nonsanctioned means of influence.

Organizational strategy is the process of positioning the organization in the competitive environment and implementing actions to compete successfully.

Organizing is the process of dividing the work to be done and coordinating the results to achieve a desired purpose.

Outsourcing involves organizations obtaining aspects of their work, for example production systems, from external suppliers for reasons of cost and/or quality rather than carrying out the work themselves.

Output controls are controls that focus on desired targets and allow managers to use their own methods for reaching defined targets.

Output goals are the goals that define the organization's type of business.

Participant observation is a method of study that involves researchers becoming members of the groups that they are studying, either overtly or via 'undercover' involvement.

Participative leadership is a leadership style that focuses on consulting with employees and seeking and accounting for their suggestions before making decisions.

Passive management by exception involves intervening with employees only if standards are not met.

Perception is the process through which people receive, organize and interpret information from their environment.

A **perceptual set** comprises those factors that predetermine an individual's ability to perceive particular stimuli and respond in characteristic ways.

Performance is a summary measure of the quantity and quality of task contributions made by an individual or group to the work unit and organization.

Performance equation: job performance = attributes × work effort × organizational support.

The performance gap is the discrepancy between an actual and a desired state of affairs.

The performing stage in group development signifies the emergence of a mature well-functioning group able to deal with complex tasks and handle internal disagreements.

Permanent formal work groups perform a specific function on an ongoing basis.

Person culture is a type of organizational culture in which an organization exists for the benefits of members, particularly star performers. It has been located in barristers' chambers and other professional work settings.

Personality is the overall profile or combination of traits that characterize the unique nature of a person.

Physical abilities refer to our natural and developed motor capacities for speed, strength, flexibility and so on, as well as our use of the five senses.

Planned change is change that happens as a result of specific efforts on the part of a change agent.

Planning is the process of setting performance objectives and identifying the actions needed to accomplish them.

The pluralist view of organizations views them as being populated by individuals and groups that may have diverse aims and interests and that, as a result, can come into conflict with the dominant coalition and other groups.

A policy is a guideline for action that outlines important objectives and indicates how an activity is to be performed.

Positive reinforcement is the administration of positive consequences that tend to increase the likelihood of repeating the behaviour in similar settings.

Positivism is the view that social sciences such as OB can and should be studied in the same way as natural sciences like physics using similar methods with a view to predicting and controlling behaviour and performance.

Power is the ability to get someone else to do something you want done, or the ability to make things happen or get things done in the way you want.

Power culture is a type of organizational culture in which a central figure exercises power on a personalized basis, there being relatively few formal rules in place.

Primary beneficiaries are particular groups expected to benefit from the efforts of specific organizations.

Procedural justice refers to perceived fairness of the process used to determine the distribution of rewards.

A procedure (or rule) is a specific, rigid guideline that describes in detail how a task is to be performed.

Process controls are controls that attempt to specify the manner in which tasks will be accomplished.

Process culture is a type of organizational culture characterized by clear processes, which need to be followed correctly: it can be found in highly regulated sectors such as healthcare.

Process innovation is innovation that results in a better way of doing things.

Process power is the control over methods of production and analysis.

Process re-engineering is the fundamental rethinking and radical redesign of business processes to achieve improvements in performance.

Process theories of motivation seek to understand the thought processes that take place in the minds of people and how these act to motivate their behaviour.

Product innovation is innovation that results in the creation of a new or improved good or service.

Productivity is a summary measure of the quantity and quality of work performance that also accounts for resource use.

Programmed decisions are decisions that implement specific solutions determined by past experience as appropriate for the problems at hand.

Projection involves projecting our own emotions or motives on to another person. It is an example of a perceptual error.

A prototype is a perception of a person based on group characteristics, from which the individual person may diverge.

The psychological contract specifies what an individual expects to give to and receive from an organization.

Psychology is the study of mental life with a particular focus on the individual's thought processes and behaviour.

Psychometric testing involves an attempt to extract an individual's key characteristics via controlled measures such as personality inventories.

Punishment is the administration of negative consequences or the withdrawal of positive consequences, which tends to reduce the likelihood of repeating the behaviour in similar settings.

Quality circles are groups of workers who meet periodically to discuss and develop solutions for problems relating to quality, productivity or cost.

Quality of work life refers to the overall quality of human experience in the workplace.

Quasiformal channels are planned communication connections between holders of the various positions within the organization.

Radical change is change that results in a major makeover of the organization and/or its component systems.

Rational persuasion strategy attempts to bring about change through persuasion based on empirical facts, special knowledge and rational argument.

The receiver is the individual or group of individuals that hear or read or see the message within the communication process.

Referent power is the ability to control another's behaviour because the individual wants to identify with the power source due to his or her perceived attractive characteristics.

Refreezing is the final stage of the planned change process in which changes are positively reinforced.

Reinforcement is the administration of a consequence as a result of behaviour.

Relatedness needs refer to the desire for satisfying interpersonal relationships.

Relationship goals are concerned with how well people involved in a negotiation, and their constituencies, are able to work with one another once the process is concluded.

Required behaviours are those contributions the organization formally requests from group members as a basis for continued affiliation and support.

Resistance to change is any attitude or behaviour that reflects a person's unwillingness to make or support a desired change.

Resource dependencies occur when the organization needs resources that others control.

Reward power is the extent to which a manager can use extrinsic and intrinsic rewards to control other people.

Risk environments are decision environments that involve a lack of complete certainty but that include an awareness of probabilities associated with the possible outcomes of various courses of action.

Rites are standardized and recurring activities used at special times to influence the behaviours and understanding of organizational members.

Rituals are systems of rites.

A role is a set of expectations for the behaviour of a person holding a particular office or position.

Role ambiguity is the uncertainty about what other group members expect of a person.

Role conflict occurs when a person is unable to respond to the expectations of one or more group members.

Role culture is a type of organizational structure in which set rules, task procedures and job descriptions are particularly important.

Role overload occurs when too much is expected of individuals within their role designation.

Routine problems are problems that arise routinely and that can be addressed through standard responses.

A saga is an embellished heroic account of the story of the founding of an organization.

Satisficing means choosing the first satisfactory alternative rather than the optimal decision.

Schemas are cognitive frameworks developed through experience.

Screening is the umbrella term for the ways we selectively perceive objects and people.

Selective perception refers to the ways in which we categorize and organize stimuli leading us to perceive the world in a unique way.

Self-concept is the concept that individuals have of themselves as physical, social and spiritual or moral beings.

Self-efficacy refers to a person's belief that they can perform adequately in a situation.

A **self-fulfilling prophecy** occurs when a prophecy comes true simply because it has been made. For example if we label people in a particular way, they will behave in the expected manner.

Self-managing teams are small groups of people empowered to manage themselves and the work they do on a day-to-day basis.

Shaping is the creation of a new behaviour by the positive reinforcement of successive approximations to the desired behaviour.

A **shared power strategy** (or normative re-educative strategy) attempts to bring about change by identifying or establishing values and assumptions so that support for the change emerges naturally.

Shared values are the set of coherent values held by members of the organization and that link them together.

A **simple design** is a configuration involving one or two ways of specializing individuals and units.

Situational constraints are organizational factors that do not allow workers to perform adequately.

Situational control is the extent to which leaders can determine what their group is going to do and what the outcomes of their actions and decisions are going to be.

The **social information-processing approach** argues that individual needs, task perceptions and reactions are a result of socially constructed realities.

Social learning is learning that is achieved through the reciprocal interaction between people and their environments.

Social loafing is the tendency of people not to work as hard in groups as they would individually.

Sociology is the study of social structures and patterns, both in whole societies and subgroups.

Socio-technical job design is the design of jobs to optimize the relationship between the technology system and the social system.

The **span of control** is the number of individuals reporting to a supervisor.

Staff personnel are groups that assist the line units by performing specialized services for the organization.

Standardization is the degree to which the range of actions in a job or series of jobs is limited.

Status is the indication of a person's relative rank, worth or standing within a group.

Status incongruence occurs when a person's expressed status within a group is inconsistent with his or her standing in another context.

A stereotype is a view of an individual person or group that is derived from assumed wider characteristics, for example the view that Italians are emotional.

Stereotyping describes the process by which we attribute characteristics to an individual based on our understanding of wider groups, e.g. she is Italian therefore she is an emotional person.

Stimulus is something that incites action.

The storming stage is the second stage of group development, which is marked by a period of high emotion and tension among group members. In this stage of group development hostility and infighting may occur while individual members begin to understand each other's interpersonal styles.

Strategic alliances are announced cooperative agreements or joint ventures between two independent organizations.

Stress is a state of tension experienced by individuals facing extraordinary demands, constraints or opportunities.

Stress prevention involves taking action to prevent the emergence of stress that becomes destructive.

Stressors are things that cause stress (for example, work, nonwork and personal factors).

Subcultures are unique patterns of values and philosophies within a group.

Subgoal optimization occurs when a group achieves its goals at the expense of the goals of others.

Substance goals are concerned with outcomes tied to the 'content' issues at hand in a negotiation.

Substantive conflict is conflict that occurs in the form of a fundamental disagreement over ends or goals to be pursued and the means for their accomplishment.

Substitutes for leadership are organization, individual, or task-situational variables that substitute for leadership in causing performance/human resource maintenance.

Supportive leadership is a leadership style that focuses on employee needs and wellbeing, and promotes a friendly work climate; it is similar to consideration.

Synergy is the creation of a whole that is greater than the sum of its parts.

Systems goals are goals concerned with conditions within the organization that are expected to increase its survival potential.

Task activities are the various things members do that directly contribute to the performance of important group tasks.

Task forces are temporary teams created to fulfil a well-defined task within a fairly short period of time.

Task performance is the quality and quantity of work produced.

A teaching organization aims to pass on learning experiences to others, thereby allowing the organization to achieve and maintain success.

Teambuilding is a sequence of planned action steps designed to gather and analyse data on the functioning of a group and to implement changes to increase its operating effectiveness.

A **team** role is a pattern of behaviour characterizing the ways one team member interacts with others.

Teams are small groups of people with complementary skills, who work together as a unit to achieve a common purpose for which they hold themselves collectively accountable.

Teamwork is when members of a team work together in a way that represents certain core values that promote the use of skills to accomplish certain goals.

The **technological imperative** is the idea that if an organization does not adjust its internal structure to the requirements of the technology, it will not be successful.

Technology is the combination of resources, knowledge and techniques that creates a product or service output for an organization.

Telework principles relate to work conducted remotely from the central organization using information technology.

Temporary formal work groups are created for a specific purpose and typically disband once that purpose has been accomplished.

The **total integration stage** is the fourth stage of group development, which sees the emergence of a mature, organized and well-functioning group; it is also referred to as the performing stage.

Tough-guy culture is a type of organizational culture driven by a need to take quick decisions, leading to a preoccupation with risk taking and a competitive ethos.

Transactional leadership involves daily exchanges between leaders and followers and is necessary for achieving routine performance on which leaders and followers agree.

Transformational leadership is a leadership style by which the followers' goals are broadened and elevated, and confidence is gained to go beyond expectations.

Transmission is the communication of a message from one person to another through a chosen channel.

Turnover is the churn of employees into and out of a work organization.

Uncertain environments are decision environments in which managers are unable to assign probabilities to the possible outcomes of various courses of action.

The term '**unconscious**', within Freud's theory of personality, refers to basic desires below the conscious level, which drive our behaviour and potentially conflict with values learned through socialization.

Unfreezing is the first stage of the planned change process in which a situation is prepared for change.

Unity of command is the situation in an organization where each worker has a clear reporting relationship to only one supervisor.

Unplanned change is change that occurs at random or spontaneously and without a change agent's direction.

Valence represents the values that the individual attaches to various work outcomes.

Value congruence occurs when individuals express positive feelings on encountering others who exhibit values similar to their own.

Value-added managers are managers whose efforts clearly enable their work units to achieve high productivity and improve 'bottom-line' performance.

Values are global beliefs that guide actions and judgements across a variety of situations.

Vertical loading involves increasing job depth by adding responsibilities, like planning and controlling, previously held by supervisors.

Vertical specialization is a hierarchical division of labour that distributes formal authority and establishes how critical decisions will be made.

Virtual organizations comprise individuals, groups and businesses that work together across time and space.

A virtual team is one whose members work interdependently towards the achievement of a common goal across space and time.

Voluntary reduced work time (V-time or time–income tradeoffs) is a scheme by which workers trade income for additional leisure time that is packaged to suit their needs.

Whistleblowers are employees, ex-employees or other people connected to an organization who report perceived misconduct on the part of that organization to a person or body who can take or initiate action.

Work flow interdependency is the way work flows in an organization from one group to the next.

Work hard/play hard culture is a type of organizational culture that stresses the twin roles of performance and fun at work.

Work–life balance refers to a concern which people have with balancing work hours with other responsibilities including caring for children or adults. It has become a key issue for employers with the advent of 24/7 societies and customers' expectations of where and when services should be provided for them.

Work teams or units are task-oriented groups that include a manager and his or her direct subordinates.

Workforce diversity means a workforce consisting of a broad mix of workers from different racial and ethnic backgrounds, of different ages and genders and of different domestic and national cultures.

Zero hours contracts are defined as arrangements where work is not guaranteed; rather workers are expected to be available as and when an employer requires them. Workers are paid only for the hours in which they actually perform tasks.

The zone of indifference is the range of authoritative requests to which an employee is willing to respond without subjecting the directives to critical evaluation or judgement – that is, the requests to which the employee is indifferent.

INDEX

PHOTO CREDITS

All effort has been made to trace and acknowledge ownership of copyright. The Publisher would be glad to hear from any copyright holders whom it has not been possible to contact. All images not listed here are provided by www.shutterstock.com.

p3 Used with permission. www.bestcompanies.co.uk

p25 The "Made with Passion" logo is reproduced with the kind permission of The Body Shop International, Plc. www.thebodyshop.com

p73 Reproduced by permission of the BBC Information & Archives services. www.bbc.co.uk/mediabank

p92 © PA Photos

p95 © PA Photos

p132 Reproduced from newsimg.bbc.co.uk

p162 © PA Photos

p219 London Marriott Hotel Lobby, Marble Arch. Reproduced by permission. www.marriott.co.uk

p156 Reproduced by permission of Asda. www.asda-press.co.uk

p231 Reproduced by permission of Thomas-Sanderson Limited. www.thomas-sanderson.co.uk

p233 Reproduced from www.tescocorporate.com

p266 Reproduced by permission of Marks & Spencer. www.mandslibrary.co.uk

p378 Reproduced by permission of ?What If! www.whatifinnovation.com

p381 © TAP Airlines

p494 © PA Photos

p554 Reproduced by permission of Krysia Butwilowska, St Luke's School, Portsmouth.